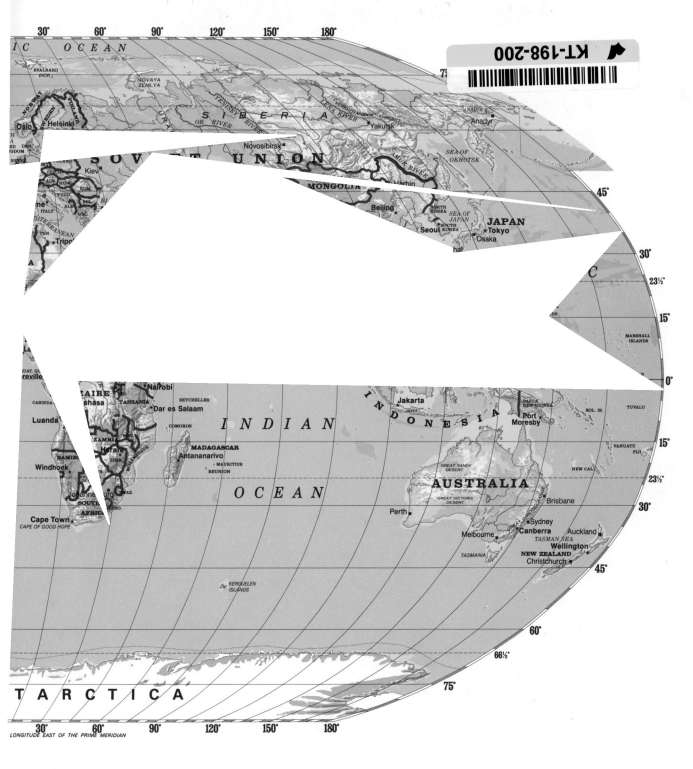

INTERNATIONAL BUSINESS

Theory and Managerial Applications

INTERNATIONAL BUSINESS

Theory and Managerial Applications

Second Edition

Robert Grosse
Duane Kujawa

*Both of the
University of Miami*

Boston, Ma
Homewood, Il

Sponsoring editor: Craig Beytien
Developmental editor: Libby Rubenstein
Project editor: Rebecca Dodson
Production manager: Diane Palmer
Designer: Laurie Entringer
Compositor: Carlisle Communications, Ltd.
Typeface: 10/12 Garamond
Printer: Von Hoffmann Press

Library of Congress Cataloging-in-Publication Data

Grosse, Robert E.
    International business : theory and managerial applications /
Robert Grosse, Duane Kujawa.— 2nd ed.
        p.   cm.
    Includes index.
    ISBN 0-256-08114-X
    1. International business enterprises—Management.   I. Kujawa,
Duane.   II. Title.
HD62.4.G77   1992
658'.049 —dc20

                                                                                        91-26297
                                                                                        CIP

Printed in the United States of America
1 2 3 4 5 6 7 8 9 0 VH 8 7 6 5 4 3 2 1

To Alan, Amanda, David, Laura, and Matthew

Duane Kujawa received his doctorate in Business Administration from the University of Michigan in 1970. Prior to his doctorate, Dr. Kujawa earned an MBA at the University of Santa Clara, where he had a dual major in Management and Economics, and a bachelor's degree in Electrical Engineering from the University of Detroit. He is presently Associate Dean for International Programs at the University of Miami, where he is also a professor in the Department of Management. Dr. Kujawa's teaching interests include Japanese Business, the Management of Multinational Enterprises, and Business Strategy.

Dr. Kujawa's publications have appeared in the *Journal of International Business Studies, Labor and Society,* the *British Journal of Industrial Relations,* and the *Academy of Management Journal.* In addition to this text, he is the author of *Japanese Multinationals in the United States* (Praeger Publishers, 1986).

Professor Kujawa is a fellow and past president of the Academy of International Business and a fellow of the International Academy of Management. He has also served as a consultant to the Academy for Educational Development (Peru Project) and is a member of the Eurobank Board of Directors.

Robert Grosse is Associate Professor and Director of the Center for International Business Education and Research at the University of Miami. He received his Ph.D. in International Economics from the University of North Carolina and his bachelor's degree in Economics and French from Princeton University.

Dr. Grosse has published widely in the academic literature, including articles in the *Journal of International Business Studies,* the *Journal of Banking and Finance, Management International Review, The World Economy,* and the *Journal of Global Marketing.* His recent books include *International Business and Governments* (with Jack N. Behrman, University of South Carolina, 1990), and *Private Sector Solutions to the Latin American Debt Problem* (North/South Center, 1991). He is a member of the editorial review boards of the *Journal of International Business Studies* and the *North American Review of Economics and Finance.*

Professor Grosse is active in international business through work with multinational organizations such as the United Nations Center on Transnational Corporations, the InterAmerican Development Bank, and the Organization of American States. He also consults with many U.S. and Latin American multinational firms and banks, principally in Latin America. He teaches regularly in executive programs in Argentina, Colombia, Chile, Ecuador, Mexico, Peru, Uruguay, and Venezuela.

Preface

International business is the field of study that focuses on business activities that cross national boundaries. It includes exports and imports—the subject of traditional international trade discussions—as well as foreign direct investment, international banking, and international transfer of technology, global business strategy, and many more topics. Our concern is to present a panorama of the most important activities in international business and to offer a framework for thinking about them from the perspective of the company manager.

As countries enter into more highly-linked regional blocs (such as the European Community and the North American Free Trade Area), the analytical techniques and strategies presented here can be applied to inter-regional business. Similarly, as some countries become more decentralized in their power structures (such as Canada with the isolationism of Quebec, or several Eastern European countries with their multi-ethnic divisions—or even in the United States, with its huge Latin American population today), the thinking learned in international business will apply in inter-province or inter-state or inter-cultural business contexts as well.

In fact, what distinguishes international business from its domestic counterparts is not so much the analytical techniques, since most of them can be applied at both domestic and international levels, but rather the context itself. That is, at the international level the key variables that a manager must cope with include different *currencies* whose values change, and different *government policies* (e.g., taxes, antitrust rules, financial controls)—along with the variables that exist in any domestic context, such as competition, cost conditions, and customer characteristics. In addition, different *cultures* exist in different countries, although cultures within individual countries also often differ importantly, as well.

Analysts of international business have developed some perspectives that are uniquely international—such as Vernon's international product cycle (discussed in Chapter 3), Dunning's eclectic theory of international production (discussed in Chapter 4), and all analyses of currency exchange rates (discussed in Chapter 6). Nevertheless, much of what is used in marketing, finance, strategy, and other business functional areas can be applied to international business phenomena. Indeed, the basic analytical perspective used in this book is the competitive advantage view of business strategy, which was developed in the domestic context and can be readily applied to international business as shown throughout the text.

There are many important challenges and problems that face firms that do business outside of their home countries. How can you handle business in different currencies? What are the ways of dealing with governments and operating effectively in diverse legal environments? Is it possible to avoid some of the business problems that arise due to cultural differences among people from different countries? What strategies will enable a firm to compete successfully against rivals from other countries? All of these questions and many other key concerns of decision-makers operating in international business are treated in this book. Conclusive answers are not always possible, but logical methods for dealing with the questions are developed and analyzed.

Many of the concerns of decision-makers in international business have to do with environmental (as opposed to company-specific) factors such as government policies and economic conditions in different countries. Such issues as the oil crisis of the 1970s, the international debt crisis of the 1980s, and the opening of Eastern Europe in the 1990s have forced companies in all industries to come to grips with higher and more volatile inflation and interest rates, greater risks in less developed countries, and possible opportunities or challenges from a much stronger, larger Europe. The evolution of international firms has pushed older, largely ethno-centric, multinationals from North America and Europe to cope with newer rivals from Asia. At the same time, competitive pressures from all sides are pushing firms to become at once global and multi-domestic, that is, to create global strategies to try to maximize efficiency and to be responsive to domestic demand pressures in each major national market served.

These conditions really go to the core of business at the end of the 20th century. Whether a firm is international or not, its competitors may come from different countries, its suppliers likewise may be domestic or foreign, and the environment in which it operates may depend on activities of foreign governments and firms.

It is in this context that the present book has been written. Although its focus is international, the decision-making methods and considerations presented in the book generally apply to domestic firms as well. From another perspective, it is our hope that the content of this book will be developed further in the traditional courses in finance, marketing, strategy, etc. There can be no doubt that business around the world has become open to foreign competitors, foreign markets, and foreign supply sources; so any manager should understand the implications of these phenomena for the firm.

Purpose and Organization

The text was designed for a survey course in international business at the undergraduate or MBA level. It is a comprehensive text, intended to be used in a one-semester course, with the selection of chapters left to the instructor's discretion. It should also prove useful as a reference source both in subsequent courses and in business practice.

The material is organized into five sections. The first section introduces the subject of international business and explores the scope of the field. It also presents the central conceptual base of the text, the theory of competitive advantages. The second section treats the "environment" that faces decision-makers in international business. The basic economic fundamentals that affect trade, investment, and other business activities between countries are presented in this section, along with a description of the institutional structure of the international economy. Part 3 provides in-depth coverage of functional areas of business administration and other broad managerial concerns, at the international level. In addition to chapters on international marketing and international finance, etc., this section examines cultural issues, transfer of technology, and export/import management. Part 4 is a particularly distinctive aspect of the book; it looks at international business activities and government policies in three major kinds of countries: the industrial nations, the less developed countries, and the formerly-communist countries. Finally, the last section presents detailed studies of international business in four industries—oil, banking, autos, and telecommunications. It concludes with some thoughts about where multinational firms—or *international contractors* as we call them—are headed in the 21st century.

This text is distinctive from others in the field because of its unifying theme of "competitive advantages," which gives continuity to what are all too often studied as free-standing topics. Also, throughout the text, real-life business situations are cited to clarify the material being discussed and to make it more exciting and interesting. The cases presented at the end of each chapter give further opportunity for understanding the material in its practical aspects and applications.

New sections called "IB Illustrations" and "Added Dimensions" are used to provide more detailed discussion of some topics and to illustrate the ideas with current examples of international business activities. The "Added Dimensions" are used to cover topics that appear in the text in more depth, when that kind of coverage could detract from the flow of the main text. The "IB Illustrations" are used to separate examples that apply concepts from the text, so that the analytical logic and clarity are maintained, and the examples can be used to reinforce the reasoning in the text.

Based on evaluations from many of the users of the first edition of the book, several structural changes have been made. The chapter on "Developing a Global Strategy" has been moved up to the early part of the book, reflecting instructors' preferences to present the integrative concepts earlier in the course. Chapter 2 on "Competitive Advantages" has been thoroughly revised to present the key analytical tools more clearly. Chapter 12 on the "Cultural Environment" has been completely revised to better deal with this important aspect of international business. And finally, more cases and examples have been added to both illustrate the concepts and update the application of ideas to current international business activity.

Changes in the Second Edition

The world has experienced a huge upheaval since the first edition of this book was published. The fall of the Berlin Wall in 1989 signaled the end of the Cold War, which had been a primary feature of international politics and a limitation on international business since 1945. When the Soviet Union under President Gorbachev chose to open its economy to private-sector business and to pursue a more market-based set of policies, this dramatic change eliminated the communist alternative as a major challenge to the global market system. While the former members of the Soviet bloc are still economically weak, these countries constitute a major new business opportunity for international firms today and a potential source of new challengers to competitors in Europe and elsewhere in the future. The text discusses these major changes in detail in the rewritten Chapter 23, along with the "Skoda" case and text references in other chapters.

Along with the disintegration of the communist bloc has come renewed effort at integration within several regions of the world. The European Community and its "Europe 1992" figure centrally in this picture. The nations of the European Community are dropping literally hundreds of barriers to business among the members—and additional countries are pushing for membership in the group. Similarly, the United States and Canada formed a free trade area in 1988, and Mexico has been negotiating membership in that group. The North American free trade area, even as it is being constituted, is receiving requests from Latin American countries for membership, toward a free trade area of the Americas. These important shifts and other inter-country cooperative efforts are discussed in the rewritten Chapter 10 on "Economic Integration."

The world economy continues to become more dominated by service-sector activities (e.g., financial services, consulting, computer programming, hotels and restaurants, transportation service, telecommunications service, etc.) in the 1990s. This reality is reflected in the greater number of examples and cases related to service industries throughout the text. The increasingly cost-driven competition in manufacturing worldwide is emphasized in the discussion of offshore assembly and foreign sourcing of production in several chapters. And the undiminished centrality of key raw materials industries such as oil is emphasized in Chapter 24, as well as elsewhere through the text.

The increasing use of inter-company alliances (strategic alliances) in domestic and international business is discussed especially in Chapters 5 and 13, but also throughout the book in new examples and new cases. These alliances were first seen extensively in the auto industry, with all of the major multinational manufacturers forming joint ventures and other partnerships with their rivals. The "NUMMI" case in Chapter 12 presents a detailed look at the Toyota-General Motors joint venture plant in California.

As with the first edition, an instructor's guide and a computerized test bank are available to accompany the text. These supplementary materials provide the instructor with suggestions for presentation of the chapters and cases, additional readings, and more than 2,000 test questions based on the text.

ACKNOWLEDGMENTS

We would like to thank the many people who contributed their time, talents, and efforts toward the completion of this book. Most importantly, Diego Aramburu, Nancy Yeldezian, Sivakumar Venkataramany, and Thayer Dolan, graduate students at the University of Miami, all worked diligently and carefully to gather information and check the facts that appear in these pages. In addition, our secretary, Louise Oliver, very capably helped to coordinate the project and keep track of our communications with the publisher and business people who gave inputs into the book.

There are more than 100 business people who provided information and interpretations about their firms' international business activities that are incorporated in the book. Those with whom we worked most closely are the several senior executives in multinational firms and international banks who are also members of our International Business & Banking Institute's Board of Advisors. They are: Pat Oliver, George Barton, Gene Rostov, Gonzalo Valdes-Fauli, Clovis

Estorilio, Tim Reed, Juan Yañes, Derrick Lyth, Burt Landy, Ralph Llop, and Roger Duarte. In addition, we would like to thank Steve Vogel, Jim Widmer, David Friedson, Jerry Brock, John Hume, Ernesto Garuolis, Jose Muzuarieta, and Yves Bobillier. Others assisted in various important ways that we truly appreciate.

Our intellectual debts are to many scholars, but we would like to mention specifically Jack Behrman, whose views and encouragement stimulated this project. Others have also substantially influenced us in our own professional development, and their influences are reflected in this book. These scholars include: Vern Terpstra, Bob Hawkins, Ingo Walter, Gunter Dufey, Steve Robock, Alan Rugman, David Ricks, Jeff Arpan, Bill Ogram, Jim Goodnow, Hans Scholl-hammer, John Daniels, Jose de la Torre, Larry Franko, Raj Aggarwal, Bal Bhatt, Steve Kobrin, Ivan Vernon, Don Pattilo, Riad Ajami, Rosalie Tung, Dick Moxon, Mike Czinkota, Subhash Jain, Arvind Phatak, Phil Grub, Russ Root, Laurent Jacque, John Dunning, Irene Lange, Moises Naim, Jean-Francois Hennert, Ian Giddy, Jerry Watzke, Bob Vichas, John Weber, George Tesar, Jim Sood, Ken Simmonds, Bill Renforth, David Rutenberg, Alex Murray, John Ryans, Attilla Yaprak, and Joe Azel.

Our colleagues who read all or some of the manuscript and offered very valuable comments include: J. Frederick Truitt, David Hopkins, Ellen Cook, Chong S. Lee, Jose Azel, Filemon Campo-Flores, Evangelos S. Djimopoulos, Patricia Tansuhaj, James D. Goodnow, M. Raquib Zaman, and James C. Baker.

While this book reflects valuable inputs and influences from all of these people, we want to note that we alone take responsibility for its contents. In closing, we invite you—professor or student—to share your thoughts on this book with us. A good text is one that lives and that reflects the needs and interests of both professors and students as they and the field evolve over time. We think that this is a good text, and we would value your comments to make it even better.

ROBERT GROSSE
DUANE KUJAWA

Contents
in Brief

Contents

25 Multinational Enterprises and the World Order: A Look to the Future . . . 685

INTERNATIONAL BUSINESS

Theory and Managerial Applications

PART

1

These merchants bartering in the Tunisian marketplace serve
as a reminder of the way business was once conducted.
Gill S. J. Copeland/Journalism Services, Inc.

INTRODUCTION

In today's global business environment, people move easily among many currencies.
Joseph H. Jacobson/Journalism Services, Inc.

Chapter

1

Issues and Concepts

In some ways, international business is an extension of domestic business; in other ways, it is quite different. The purpose of this chapter is to introduce you to the "real world" of international business by discussing actual companies and what they are doing internationally. The effects of international activities on different business functions—as illustrated by these same case examples—are then introduced. The discussion covers the effects of these activities on product definition, marketing research and marketing management, financing, personnel issues, accounting practices, and taxation. A key conclusion to this point is that different firms behave quite differently. But then we must ask what factors in the environment give rise to these behavioral differences and why firms operate differently in the international arena. Implicit in what has been said thus far is the fact that the major focus of this chapter, and of this book, is on multinational corporations. The chapter also discusses importing and exporting and the government activities that relate to them, and it summarizes the general organization of the book. The main goals of the chapter are to:

1. Illustrate important differences between international business and domestic business.

2. Identify the entities involved in international business.

3. Illustrate how important business functions vary firm by firm internationally and question why this occurs.

4. Present the organization of this book.

INTRODUCTION

What is international business? To some people, it means "big business." These people see international business as dominated by giant corporations whose economic power is so great that it may even compromise the political autonomy of nation-states. Other people equate international business with international trade, thinking only in terms of exports and imports. Some of these people may work for firms that sell products to overseas markets; others may work for firms that are battling foreign-made products right here in their home market. For such people, international business can mean either big opportunities or big problems.

A variety of international business examples is shown in Figure 1–1. Let's look briefly at a few of these to get a better idea of what international business is.

Exports—These are products and services a company in one country sells to customers in another country. To illustrate, Canadian Eskimo art may be exported to customers in San Francisco, California.

Direct investment—When the German company Volkswagen, A.G. puts up an assembly plant in Brazil, the investment is termed "direct".

Imports—These are products or services a customer in one country buys from a supplier in another country. A Japanese consumer may, for example, buy Scotch whisky from a distillery in Great Britain.

Licensing—When Germany's Volkswagen transfers robotics technology to its Brazilian plant, it licenses the Brazilian plant (i.e., a subsidiary

FIGURE 1–1

Examples of International Business Activities

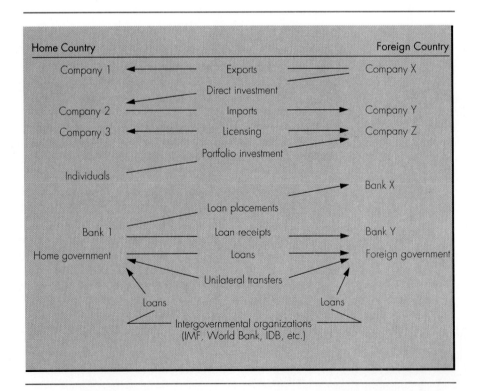

company) to use the robotics technology. It may also license the Brazilian company to use the VW trademark.

Portfolio investment—When Fidelity, the large U.S. mutual fund company, buys stock in British Telecom, a portfolio investment occurs.

Loans—These arise when a borrower in one country becomes indebted to a lender in another country. Chase Manhattan Bank's loan to the government of Hungary is a cross-border loan.

Unilateral transfers—When one receives a gift from someone from another country, a unilateral transfer occurs. The U.S. government's food aid to less developed countries is a type of unilateral transfer.

In addition to the activities shown in Figure 1–1, there are a few others, such as turnkey projects, management contracts, franchising, and so on. An example of a turnkey project occurred when Italy's Fiat built a truck plant for a Russian state-owned enterprise. Management contracts, which are common within multinational companies, involve charging an overseas subsidiary for services provided by the parent company. International franchising, which can be viewed as a licensing and management contract "package," involves a franchisor contracting with franchisees in foreign countries, such as Blockbuster Video contracting with a franchisee in Canada.

What we are really looking at in Figure 1–1 are examples of international business activity. But there are considerably more dynamics to international business than these activities portray—especially for students wanting to learn about business administration. Let's look at a few real-life cases to better appreciate what international business is all about.

INTERNATIONAL BUSINESS HIGH-LIGHTS—COCA-COLA, CITICORP, DOW, AND HONDA[1]

Coca-Cola

The Coca-Cola Company is the world's largest producer and distributor of soft drinks. Its lead brand, Coca-Cola, is undeniably a global product. In 1989 Coca-Cola sold more than 559 million soft drink servings to customers in over 160 countries. Its global revenues totaled more than $9.0 billion. At the close of the 1980s, Coke commanded a 48.5 percent international market share and was outselling its closest competitor by nearly four to one.

Unlike some "high-tech" companies whose products come and go, Coke has been around for over 100 years since its beginnings in Atlanta in 1886. A product that old should be about as mature as a product can be—at least, that's the conventional wisdom. But not so in Coke's case! In the 1980s, the Company introduced several variations of the basic product, especially Diet Coke (a product marketed under the "Coke Lite" brand in Japan where consumers are not so weight-conscious), which have resulted in new growth as new market segments were identified and served. Moreover, its international markets are growing at rates beyond that of its traditional home market, the United States. That's why Coke plans to focus even more on international markets in the future. The situation is really quite simple. Sales of soft drinks are income-driven. As societies' incomes grow, so also will their consumption of soft drinks—and Coke is a big player in the soft-drink market. Why is Coke a big player? The answer is Coke's "secret" formula and its "system," that global production and distribution network kept vibrant by Coke's global expertise in management and marketing.

Coca-Cola concentrate is made in several key countries strategically located around the globe. This concentrate is sold to bottlers and/or distributors in just about every country. Coca-Cola also supplies bottlers with marketing support and production and water purification technologies based on parent-company-provided research and systems designs. Bottlers conduct local market research, provide for sales financing, and handle distribution and promotion. Coke may well be a global product, but it takes a well-organized team effort to deliver it to customers around the world.

Citicorp

One of the world's largest financial services institutions, Citicorp operates in 39 states in the United States and in 89 countries other than the United States. It has a customer relationship with one of every five U.S. households, and its assets totaled $207.7 billion at the end of 1988. Citicorp is headquartered in New York City, but 44 percent of its 89,000 employees and two thirds of its offices were located overseas in 1988. Slightly over half (51 percent) of its net income was generated overseas that year. Citicorp, which calls itself a "global financial services company," is organized at the top into three major business units focusing on individual banking, institutional and investment banking, and information business. It is diversified by customer base, geographic presence, and product line. As might be expected, there is considerable coordination among the different customer and product-oriented operating units both within each country or region and among countries and regions.

The financial services industry is becoming increasingly competitive, and Citicorp's competitive strategy is based on innovation, customer orientation, and management decentralization. Citicorp notes, for example, that a key support element cutting across all three of its major business units is its advanced information processing and transmission capabilities. Citicorp worldwide operates 160 data centers working through 20,000 terminals — 7,000 of which are located in its customers' facilities. In the past few years the company has spent over $500 million in developing and implementing electronic information-handling technologies, and it contends that it is now the world leader in electronic banking for commercial applications. It also contends that these technologies give it special capabilities for generating new products in an industry where old-line, mature products are no longer very profitable. Cases in point here include the establishment of "Citifunds," an Asian-based cash management account marketed to non-U.S. customers with high net worth and the revitalization of its Diners Club and other travel and entertainment-related businesses by enabling more efficient, lower-cost operations. In addition, Citicorp sells its funds transfer service to some 7,000 financial institutions located around the world.

Dow

A globally integrated producer of chemical, health care, and other consumer and industrial products, Dow Chemical Company is headquartered in Michigan and has numerous facilities in the United States, Canada, Europe, the Orient, and Latin America. Dow's foreign operations range from wholly owned subsidiaries, such as those in Canada, the Netherlands, Italy, Greece, Germany, Mexico, Argentina, and Colombia, to joint ventures, such as those in the United Kingdom, Spain, the Netherlands, France, Italy, Germany, Argentina, Ecuador, Colombia, Chile, Mexico, Japan, India, Australia, New Zealand, and Malaysia. In 1988, Dow's sales revenues totaled over $16.7 billion. About 55 percent of Dow's sales are outside the United States—as are about 46 percent of its 55,000 employees. At the end of 1988, The Dow Chemical Company (U.S.) had equity investments in 155 companies located in 32 foreign countries.

Dow's top-level organizational operating structure is geographically defined into five regions: The U.S.A., Canada, Europe, Latin America, and the Pacific. The president of Dow Chemical Europe, for example, has operations responsibility for the entire European region. Management and technical personnel at various organizational levels within the regional divisions coordinate with their counterparts in other divisions on major investment, production allocation, and similar decisions. About one sixth of Dow Chemical U.S.A.'s production is exported to customers in the other four regions.

Dow's mainstream production is in chemical intermediates, and over the years the company has been especially successful in developing families of products around a common product core—as with styrene plastic. Dow is deliberately expanding its presence in specialty chemicals, pharmaceuticals, and other health and consumer products that are less capital intensive and less sensitive to cyclical declines than are chemical intermediates. The company's basic R&D is done in the United States, but applications research, which focuses on adapting products to meet the capabilities and needs of local users, is conducted both in the United States and the foreign divisions. The overseas subsidiaries, whether wholly or partially owned by Dow, produce under licensing agreements with the parent company.

Honda

Honda Motor Company, Ltd. manufactures and sells motorcycles, automobiles, and power products (e.g., portable generators, outboard motors, and lawn mowers). It is headquartered in Tokyo and operates several factories in Japan, as well as at wholly owned subsidiaries in Belgium, Canada, France, Italy, Mexico, New Zealand, the United Kingdom, and the United States. Honda performs additional overseas production at minority-held subsidiaries and 50–50 joint ventures in Indonesia, Iran, Nigeria, Peru, Taiwan, Thailand, and the Philippines. Honda's fiscal year 1989 worldwide sales were 3,489 billion yen (about US $26.4 billion using an exchange rate of approximately 132 yen per dollar, the rate on March 31, 1989). About 56 percent of the company's revenues come from overseas markets. Direct exports from Japan represent approximately one sixth of total Japanese production. (Data on domestic and overseas employment are not routinely made available by the company.)

Honda eschews formal organization structures. Functionally, however, the parent maintains direct responsibility for the manufacture and sale of all products in Japan. Honda Research & Development Company, Ltd. (a Japan-based subsidiary) provides product R&D and product designs and Honda Engineering Company, Ltd. (also a Japan-based subsidiary) performs process-related R&D and manufactures production tooling and equipment for Honda plants worldwide. The situation of the U.S. subsidiary illustrates organizational relationships internationally. The president of Honda of America is also a managing director and member of the board of directors of the parent company. Operational coordination is achieved via varied contacts involving managerial and technical personnel at the parent and subsidiary in the product divisions and specialty areas (e.g., Honda Engineering for use of production technology and equipment).

Honda Motor's growth has traditionally been production driven. It has had to develop markets as outlets for its continuously expanding, low-cost production capabilities. Large markets, which include domestic and foreign segments, enable Honda to take advantage of its large-scale production facilities for certain parts and components, such as motorcycle engines, and to put such low-cost production to its competitive advantage. This was the situation, for example, when Honda first established motorcycle production at its U.S. plant in Ohio (1979). Engines were imported from Japan until sales in the U.S. market became large enough to justify producing engines in Ohio (1984).

Production R&D, conducted at Honda Engineering in Japan, is heavily oriented toward robotics and automated production equipment that have general applicability in Honda plants worldwide. Product R&D, as related, for example, to motorcycle models, is less monolithic. It uses market-generated information from both foreign and domestic operations and technical design expertise housed at Honda Research & Development Company in Japan. Through wholly owned subsidiaries, joint ventures, and licensing arrangements, Honda products are manufactured in 40 countries around the world.

THE CONDUCT OF INTERNATIONAL BUSINESS

Coca-Cola, Citicorp, Dow, and Honda have a lot in common. They export something of value from their home countries and also produce abroad. They implement overseas activities via wholly owned foreign subsidiaries, joint ventures, franchising, and licensing arrangements that display obvious dependence on the parent company. They generally center their R&D at home. But Coca-Cola, Citicorp, Dow, and Honda differ in important ways too. Dow produces abroad to export back to the U.S. market in some cases. At both Dow and Coke, R&D is centered in the home market, while Dow, Citicorp, and Honda conduct product application and consumer research in foreign markets. The four companies exhibit very different organization structures at the top: the divisionalizing of Coca-Cola is on a geographical basis; that of Citicorp and Dow, on a hybrid product, customer, and/or geographic basis; and that of Honda, on a functional basis. What are the implications of these observations for managers? Let's explore them.

Product Impact

Product variations are required to accommodate different technical considerations, such as the electrical characteristics of Citicorp's information-processing equipment, different use conditions, such as with the chemicals used in agricultural applications, and different consumer preferences, such as the infatuation of Americans with powerful, heavy-duty motorcycles (compared, for example, to the smaller, scooter-type motorcycles preferred in some European countries). Product design for different markets also incorporates cost considerations related to scale economies in production, the use of standardized components on a global basis, and the production skills available in the work force at the foreign plant.

For some of the same reasons, the use of certain kinds of production processes, machinery, and equipment may vary between domestic and foreign operations. These are *process* variations. The level of production at a domestic plant may vary with demand conditions in a foreign country or with interruptions of production (caused by a strike, for example) at a foreign plant.

Marketing Impact

Marketing is similarly complicated. Marketing research must now be coordinated among the different countries served—not only to determine product

---

**IB
ILLUSTRATION**

Honda Motor Company

Honda, as the world's leading motorcycle manufacturer for over two decades, is maintaining its commitment to expanding the worldwide market for motorcycles through a steady stream of new products and technologies. For example, in Japan, a rebound in the economy together with Honda's efforts to expand the market via new model offerings, including the U.S.-made Gold Wing touring bike, resulted in a 1988 unit sales increase of 6.3 percent, amounting to 924,000 units. ■

Source: Honda Motor Company, Ltd., 1989 *Annual Report.*

needs but also to arrive at product sales estimates used in setting production and inventory levels and purchasing and staffing needs. Pricing and promotional strategies must be determined for geographically segmented markets with different competitive characteristics. Successful marketing also requires understanding country-specific distribution systems, packaging preferences and standards, and so on.

Financial Impact

Finance is concerned with handling cash flows and funding needs in both domestic and foreign operations, in home-country and foreign-country currencies. Dow Chemical, for example, uses a capital budgeting procedure to evaluate a plant investment proposal in Germany characterized by cash flows denominated in both deutsche marks and U.S. dollars. Moving funds internationally and having the right amount of funds in the right currencies are also major concerns. Coca-Cola needs French francs to pay the wages of its workers at its concentrate plant in Signes; Dow wants to bring home its profits from its Dutch subsidiary; Honda, the licensing fees from its Costa Rican licensee. The currency denomination of assets and of debt funds is also important. What happens, for instance, to Citicorp's loans denominated in Peruvian intis if intis cannot be converted to dollars—or to the U.S. dollar value of Dow's Canadian dollar debt should the relative value of the Canadian dollar climb? Can Citicorp and Dow somehow protect themselves against the risk involved here?

Personnel Impact

Personnel concerns are also different when a company is dealing with foreign operations. Honda uses Japanese nationals in managerial and technical positions at its U.S. subsidiary; Coca-Cola uses some Americans at its German subsidiary. How are these parent-company expatriates in turn managed? What career paths do they tread? Do they mix well with local nationals? Another concern is the management of workers at the foreign plant. The industrial relations environment must be analyzed on several issues—for example, the wage determination process, the implementation of technological change, the propensity for industrial conflict, and the composition, magnitude, and determination of nonwage compensation.

IB
ILLUSTRATIONS

Dow Chemical Company

Behind Dow's international growth is a global network. As early as the mid-1960s, Dow recognized that global success means competing effectively in local markets. So, while it pursues worldwide economies of scale, the company also strives for close ties with customers. Local managers, often working in their native countries, adapt products and strategies to their markets' particular requirements. Yet, whether it's purifying water in Brazil or developing a joint venture in China, Dow answers each market's demands with a worldwide leader's resources. People, plants, and products are linked to combine a local touch with a global perspective. ■

The Coca-Cola Company

On December 31, 1989, The Coca-Cola Company held a Euroyen debt issue with a U.S. dollar equivalent of approximately $213 million, of which approximately $123 million was designated as a hedge against the company's net investment in Coca-Cola (Japan) Company, Ltd. At December 31, 1989, the company held approximately $149 million of Eurobonds denominated in deutsche marks. A portion of such borrowings has been converted into Swiss and Belgian franc-denominated obligations through swap arrangements. The company has designated such borrowings as hedges against its net investments in those respective countries. ■

Citibank

Citibank's foreign-exchange revenues of $616 million in 1988, from both customer transactions and interbank trading, increased by $136 million, or 36 percent, from 1987, a year also noted for its strong performance.... The momentum in foreign exchange revenues continues, due to global volatility of foreign exchange and financial markets, increased customer transactions, and Citibank's success in identifying trends and prices. Foreign exchange revenues include activities in the spot, forward, futures, and options markets. ■

Sources: Dow Chemical Company, 1988 *Annual Report,* The Coca-Cola Company, 1989 *Annual Report* and Citicorp, 1988 *Annual Report.*

Accounting Impact

Financial accounting systems must be developed to reflect operations consolidated on a global basis. Dow Chemical presents a dollar-denominated, consolidated financial report on its worldwide activities—even though its foreign subsidiaries deal in and report their own operations in their own currencies. How is this accomplished? How can managerial accounting systems be designed to convey meaningful information to parent company management when operations cross a variety of national environments?

IB ILLUSTRATIONS

Citicorp

The consolidated financial statements include the accounts of Citicorp and its wholly owned subsidiary, Citibank, N.A., and their majority-owned subsidiaries, after the elimination of all material intercompany transactions.

Affiliates which are 20 percent to 50 percent owned are carried under the equity method of accounting and the pro rata share of their income (loss) is included in other revenue. Income from investments in less than 20 percent-owned companies is recognized when dividends are received.

As a U.S. corporation, Citicorp is subject to domestic taxation currently on all of its foreign pretax earnings if earned by a foreign branch or when earnings are effectively repatriated if earned by a foreign subsidiary or affiliate. In addition, certain of Citicorp's domestic income is subject to foreign income tax where the payor of such income is domiciled overseas. ∎

Honda Motor Company, Ltd.

The consolidated financial statements are expressed in yen. However, solely for the convenience of the reader, the consolidated financial statements of and for the year ended March 31, 1989, have been translated into United States dollars at the rate of Y132 = U.S.$1, the approximate exchange rate prevailing on the Tokyo foreign exchange market on March 31, 1989. This translation should not be construed as a representation that all the amounts shown could be converted into U.S. dollars. ∎

Source: Citicorp, 1988 *Annual Report* and Honda Motor Company, Ltd., 1989 *Annual Report.*

Tax Impact

Coca-Cola, Citicorp, Dow, and Honda operate internationally but within various national tax jurisdictions. Most governments, the United States and Japan included, like to collect taxes. Operating entities, such as parent companies and subsidiaries, generate profits (or losses) and are taxed. Profits can be moved around, however, between parent and subsidiaries depending, for example, on what the latter pay for imported components, management fees, and royalties. Nonetheless, the U.S. Internal Revenue Service reserves the right to determine these charges (for tax purposes) for firms operating in the United States, including foreign-owned subsidiaries such as American Honda Motor Co., Inc.

Certainly, more could be said about the differences between operating just domestically as compared to operating internationally. In fact, that is what this whole book is all about. Table 1–1 presents the differences noted above in summary form. Later in the book, each of these traditional functional areas of management, as put into practice in the international business setting, is discussed in substantial detail.

TABLE 1–1

How the Management Functions Differ in International Business

Management Topics	Selected Highlights of International Business Dimensions of Operations
Product	Adaptive to differences in technical requirements, use conditions, scale economies, consumer preferences, available production skills, and available materials.
Process	Adaptive, as noted above—with emphasis on scale economies and available production skills and materials.
Marketing	Marketing research—decentralized, market specific, yet coordinated across different countries to identify commonalities. Distribution, packaging, promotion, etc., usually market specific. Pricing set via competitive conditions in geographically segmented markets.
Finance	Concerned with cash flows and funding needs in both domestic and foreign currencies, capital budgeting for foreign operations and currency denomination of debt. Focus is on the financial and business risks associated with such activities and on the methods available for reducing or offsetting these risks.
Personnel	Selecting, motivating, and rewarding personnel on foreign assignments. Justification for using expatriate personnel. Managing industrial relations internationally.
Accounting	Accounting for foreign transactions and consolidating financial statements at the multinational level. Developing and implementing informative managerial accounting systems internationally. Minimizing taxes on a global corporate basis.

LEVELS OF ANALYSIS

This text incorporates two levels of analysis. The first level deals with *awareness*, the second with *understanding*.

From a management perspective, the differences between operating domestically and operating internationally are substantial. Just being aware of these differences constitutes the first level of analysis. But what gives rise to these differences? Answering this question gives rise to the second level of analysis. The second level involves understanding and appreciating the environmental and institutional peculiarities that uniquely affect international business and that influence the nature of the management functions.

Included in the second level are knowledge of the pressures resulting in international trade and investment, operation of the foreign exchange markets, cultural environments, and the politically determined presence of trade and investment barriers and incentives. The chapters that follow impart this knowledge.

The second level of analysis, understanding, also involves explanations of the differences in how companies operate internationally. Look at how Coca-Cola, Dow, Citicorp, and Honda differ. Why do these differences exist? The analysis here focuses on how each company operates within a specific competitive and technological setting and within its own corporate culture, and on how this situation may either expand or constrain its options. Honda, for example, may produce components or subassemblies offshore or purchase from offshore manufacturers for consumption in the United States because of labor cost differences; Dow may not. Honda assembles and markets heavy-duty motorcycles in the United States, as does its main competitor, Harley-Davidson. Honda imports lighter-weight vehicles that cater to other market segments where there is no domestic competition. Why? Coca-Cola, with its global product, is not routinely concerned with product modifications; Dow is to some extent. Citicorp has identified global customers with global needs. Honda is very market sensitive with its product planning. Why? All four companies view international operations as important to their success strategies, and yet their strategies vary considerably.

The following text is very much oriented towards this second level of analysis. It deals with environmental differences, the impact of such differences on managerial decisions, and the variations in managerial decisions occasioned by companies' differing approaches to operating internationally.

TOPICS OTHER THAN THE MULTINATIONAL CORPORATION

Thus far, the discussion has focused totally on the multinational corporation. But international business involves a much more diverse set of actors than just multinational corporations.

Governments and International Organizations

As implied earlier, governments are also certainly relevant. They usually implement their policies via specific agencies, and these policies and agencies are certainly proper subjects for this text. In addition, governments often own companies that compete with private-sector firms—so these companies will be discussed. International institutions, typically constituted via government action, help define the environment within which international business functions. The International Monetary Fund, the World Bank, and the International Labor Office are examples of such institutions.

Culture

As noted briefly above, culture is also an important variable in international business where firms operate crossculturally. People are products of specific cultural settings, and international business is conducted through people. Culture affects values, communications, institutions, and so on. Most often it is seen as being national or subnational in character. But there is also the "corporate culture"—people in firms are groups too, and they often share common values, interests, hierarchies, and the like. International business deals with home-country and host-country cultures within a corporate culture. Finding commonalities across cultural groups often facilitates successful operations. The topic of culture is addressed specifically in Chapter 12. The influences of culture, however, will be manifested in various other chapters—especially those dealing with international business operations in the functional areas.

Exporting/Importing Activities

The four companies presented above are all pretty large. International business, however, is also relevant for small and medium-sized firms. Today, many of these firms are involved in exporting and in the foreign sourcing of materials or parts. The example of RECO International, B.V., a Dutch-owned food and beverage processor and distributor, comes to mind. This $12 million (sales) firm operates four factories in Europe and has recently begun exporting processed bananas from an Ecuadoran plant to the United States. The Ecuadoran plant, built with World Bank funds and utilizing automated processing equipment provided by an Australian firm, is government owned. Like the Ecuadoran government, many other governments, including that of the United

States, do much to promote exports—providing tax breaks, special foreign marketing assistance, and so forth. These activities are usually fairly well publicized. Some governments also have special policies that are meant to encourage imports. These often take the form of special tariff reductions on goods imported from selected countries. A case in point here is the duty-free import into the United States of many manufactured goods under the Generalized System of Preferences (GSP) and the Caribbean Basin Initiative (CBI). Export/import management is the subject of Chapter 19. Government activities pertaining to international trade are also discussed in this chapter—and in other chapters as appropriate.

WHY STUDY INTERNATIONAL BUSINESS?

The answer to this question should be fairly obvious by now. We need to study international business because—

1. Almost all of the large enterprises in the United States, Western Europe, and Japan are multinational in character.
2. Many small and medium-sized firms are also involved internationally. This may take the form of export or import operations, support activities directly related to international trade (e.g., freight forwarders, customs brokers), professional services pertaining to international trade or multinational operations (e.g., accounting/auditing, banking, legal counsel), and so on. Some of these firms may also be involved in overseas plant investment or licensing arrangements with foreign firms.

    The Agro-Dominicana case at the end of this chapter illustrates some of the complexities involved when even a small company does business internationally. When you first read the case, try to get a feeling of what is really different because the company is operating internationally. Answering the questions posed at the end of the case should make you appreciate why it is important to study international business. International business is different!
3. Competitive environments are typically industry specific, and industries today are very often competitive internationally. Overseas investment, incidentally, is not a requirement for international competitiveness. International trade, or the potential for such, can also link markets. A popular case in point here would be the U.S. steel industry, which has contracted considerably in the face of expanding imports.
4. Today, more and more personal investments are being placed internationally. The Japanese are often big buyers of U.S. Treasury Bills; Americans are investing more and more funds in European and Pacific-Basin mutuals. International financial markets are increasingly behaving as a single market. Your parents' retirement investments, and maybe even yours, are often buffeted by events in foreign markets. The Tokyo exchange's downfall sours the mood on Wall Street and may cause London's markets to tumble. We all had better understand what is going on in this world of ours!
5. Public policy issues often relate to international trade, investment, and finance. Today, any country's economic policies must consider the foreign sector. These policies are directly concerned with structuring business-to-

government and business-to-business relationships in ways consistent with national interests. Many domestic public issues and policies also have important spillover effects for international business. For example, the British manufacturer of Austin-Healey sports cars abandoned exporting to the United States when it felt that it was in no position to meet U.S. auto safety requirements while remaining competitive. What have air quality standards done to the competitiveness of domestic versus imported steel in the U.S. market? The number of examples here is endless!

Specific data and information on the scope and magnitude of international trade and investment and on the form and extent of multinational corporate activity are presented in the next three chapters. Public policy issues are analyzed in several of the chapters that follow.

Clearly, international business is important to managers. *The Wall Street Journal, Business Week, Forbes,* and other business periodicals typically include articles and commentary on global business activities and on the changing global environment affecting business. Academe also recognizes the importance of international business. To ensure that people study international business, the U.S. business school accrediting agency, the American Assembly of Collegiate Schools of Business (AACSB), now requires that all bachelor's- and master's-level degree programs include a "worldwide business component." From the student's personal perspective, however, the study of international business should also be important. Many business school graduates are or will be employed by firms engaged in international business. Even more business school graduates are or will be employed by firms in industries characterized by, or at least influenced by, international trade or investment. All business school graduates, as business practitioners, will be influenced by public policies pertinent to national interests and the dynamics of a world economy. Business practitioners have a responsibility to operate in a manner consistent with these policies and to work constructively to influence them. "Good citizenship," when viewed in this perspective, means good business too!

COMMENTS ON THE CONTENT AND ORGANIZATION OF MATERIALS PRESENTED IN THIS BOOK

Introduction

As is evident from all of the preceding, the multinational enterprise (MNE) is the key figure in international business—especially for students of business administration. The MNE is also the key figure in this text. The focus is not exclusive, however. Other forms of international business and other issue areas are also discussed. The next chapter presents the operational concepts that affect decision making in the MNE. That chapter and this one constitute the introductory materials.

Manager in the World Economy

The next part, "Manager in the World Economy," provides a thorough discussion of the environments and the institutional and theoretical frameworks within which international business is conducted. The topics covered in this part include international trade and foreign direct investment patterns and theories, with added commentary on their relevance to business decisions; international financial markets and how firms dealing in these markets operate; and the more important business/government issues, such as trade and investment barriers (e.g., tariffs, quotas, exchange restrictions), the partial elimination of these barriers via economic integration, and the methods used by governments in evaluating the potential advantages and disadvantages of investments by foreign firms in manufacturing and other types of operations.

Managing the MNE

Part 3, "Managing the MNE," deals with the challenges and opportunities of multinational operations and with the means by which MNEs develop and sustain a competitive presence. The first chapter focuses on culture. The other nine chapters cover the traditional, and not so traditional, management decision-making areas of organization structure and business strategy, marketing, accounting and taxation, finance and control, industrial relations, personnel, export/import management, and technology transfer.

Doing Business in . . .

Part 4 consists of three chapters focusing on selected, fairly distinctive environments within which international business functions. These are the developed countries, the less developed countries (LDCs), and the emergent Eastern European democracies that once constituted the "communist bloc."

A Look to the Future

The final two chapters take a look at the future. The commentary is structured around analyses of several industries and around political developments affecting the MNE.

CONCLUSIONS

International business is presented in this chapter as being the domain of multinational enterprises and smaller firms that engage in export/import activities or provide related support functions, and of political activities that directly and indirectly influence international trade and finance. International business is implemented via management functions that have to account for different and compelling environmental circumstances—and that are unique unto themselves in some instances, such as those concerned with foreign-exchange markets and host-country assessments of the desirability of foreign direct investment.

Coca-Cola, Citicorp, Dow Chemical, and Honda were cited as examples of international businesses that operated in ways common to all and in ways unique to each. Different aspects of each company's situation were highlighted and subsequently categorized by management function. This procedure resulted in fairly distinctive descriptions of differences in management functions consistent with the international (versus purely domestic) content of the operational environment.

The idea of "level of analysis" was introduced. Two levels were identified: identification of the differences between operating domestically and internationally, i.e., "awareness," and discussion of the environmental circumstances giving rise to these differences, and analysis of the rationales for making management decisions in international business in light of these differences, i.e., "understanding."

The importance of studying international business was discussed. Business today is international! Almost invariably, firms and industries are internationally involved. Business school graduates may find themselves working for an MNE or dealing with management problems occasioned by competition from foreign companies in their industries. Public policy issues, including those often identified with ostensibly domestic problems, strongly influence international business activities.

The general outline of the text was presented. Its five parts were identified: "Introduction" (including the concept of the MNE), "Manager in the World Economy" (analyzing the more significant environmental influences), "Managing the MNE" (focusing on the management functions), "Doing Business in . . ." (covering developed countries, LDCs, and the emergent democracies that once were communist countries), and "A Look to the Future" (examining industry and political trends). The authors believe that this five-dimensional format covers all of the topics necessary for a substantial introduction to international business. For many students, the topics covered in this text will constitute their only academic experience with international business. Other students will use this text as an introduction to courses taken later in international management, marketing, finance, etc. The text has been designed to serve the needs of both groups.

QUESTIONS

1. What is "international business"?
2. What activities of a firm characterize it as being in international business?
3. How important is international business to Coca-Cola? Citicorp? Dow? Honda? Is the domestic competitiveness of these firms in any way affected by their international business success?
4. How might the four firms be different or similar in international business— especially in these areas: product design, marketing, finance, industrial relations, personnel, and accounting and taxation?
5. Why study international business?
6. What are the differences between the two levels of analysis? Is there a logical progression through the levels?
7. Judging from the general knowledge you have, how important is international business to the following firms: IBM, Exxon, Sears, Burger King, Holiday Inns, and General Motors? How do their international business activities differ?
8. How would you differentiate between international business and international trade?
9. Can you identify a current public policy issue that is related to international business? How is that issue important to you as a consumer or citizen? How would it be important to you if you were a business manager? What do you think the government should do in this case? Why?
10. Why do you think a small or new firm would get involved in international business? Would your answer differ if the firm were in, say, Belgium rather than the United States?

REFERENCES

Business Week. Feature articles often refer to international issues or analyze the corporate strategy of an MNE.

Economist. Especially strong on environmental analysis, economic or political, and on non-U.S. MNEs.

Fortune. In-depth analysis and presentation of the Fortune 500 and other companies.

Journal of Commerce. Published daily. Focuses strongly on international trade activities and issues.

The Wall Street Journal. Keep current on daily issues related to international business and the activities of MNEs. Read the International Section, especially. See also, the *Asian Wall Street Journal Weekly*.

Annual reports. Select a company. Study its annual reports for the past five years. Note how "international" fits into its business strategy. Identify the relationships between its domestic business and its international business.

NOTE

[1]The case information presented here is based on company interviews conducted by the authors and/or annual reports published by the companies.

The Agro-Dominicana Group, Inc.*

The Agro-Dominicana Group, Inc. is engaged in the commercial cultivation and wholesale marketing of cantaloupe and honeydew melons for importation to the United States. The Group, through its Dominican project company, maintains controlling interest in its operations from seed to harvest.

Group History and Background

Agro-Dominicana was established in 1983, and is owned and controlled by three private investors. Two of the Group's shareholders are corporations with specialized prior experience in wholesale agribusinesses. Controlling interest of the Group is held by the Ricardo family, which also owns Ricardo Foods, a Group affiliate. Through Ricardo Foods and other related companies, the family has been engaged in the domestic production and wholesale distribution of produce throughout the United States and Canada for 20 years.

The family immigrated from Cuba in the 1950s after a successful export produce and cattle business on the Isle of Pines was confiscated by the Cuban government. The Ricardos subsequently purchased some 1,500 acres of farmland in Orange County, Florida, at an estimated cost of $750,000. Its appraised value is now about $30 million dollars. Cultivation on this land is gradually being phased out. Tree nurseries have been planted, and it is anticipated that the land will eventually be sold and/or developed as commercial property. According to the Group, its primary objective was to reduce the dependence of domestic agrobased production on this increasingly valuable property. The Group identified offshore agricultural production as an alternative given the market opportunities for growth of nontraditional winter crops—especially melons.

The Market for Melons

Prices for melons in the United States are highly volatile and dictated virtually exclusively by supply factors. They typically range from a low of U.S. $8 per 50-pound box, the U.S. standard, to U.S. $25 over the course of a year. The Group looks for an average price range of U.S. $12–14 and peak prices of U.S. $25 during the winter months. Industry sources indicate that in the latter 1980s only 15 to 20 percent of the U.S. winter demand for melons was met. Winter production has increased in the last several years, but it is still a sellers' market.

---

*This case was developed and written by Professor Duane Kujawa with research assistance from MBA students Anthony Abitbol, Guillermo Castro, and Kevin Kendall and from company representatives. Company names and other selected information have been changed to preserve anonymity.

The "winter window" opens between November and April when no melons are produced on the U.S. mainland. Hawaii produces melons, but Hawaiian melons cannot be shipped beyond the Rockies economically. Melons from Mexico and Florida usually come into the market in late February. There is either too much rain or cold for earlier winter production in either area. Production from Mexico or Florida benefits from cheaper transportation costs which, by ship or truck, allow for a 50-pound box of melons to be sold at wholesale for U.S. $7 to U.S. $8. If a box of melons can be brought to market *before* mid-March, however, the seller can command a price of $15 to $25. By targeting delivery of a winter melon harvest, the Agro-Dominicana Group planned to carve itself a niche for a product with a seasonal but virtually unlimited demand and substantial profits often approaching 50 percent of gross sales. Agro-Dominicana estimates it can bring melons to market at an all-inclusive cost of just under $8 per box.

Selecting a Project Site

The Group first embarked on a nine-month mission to find the "ideal farm site." The cultivation of melons requires very specific natural climate and soil conditions. The production cycle for winter consumption is from August to April. A semi-arid climate, hot and without humidity, with no rainfall from October to April is essential. However, sufficient fresh water availability is just as crucial. Several potential sites had to be discarded in coastal Puerto Rico because not enough water for irrigation could be had.

Land tracts of sufficient size for efficient irrigation and cultivation took St. Kitts out of the picture. The country's infrastructure, available refrigeration facilities, and infrequency of refrigerated ship sailings further shortened the prospect list, eliminating sites such as Aruba and Antigua in the eastern Caribbean also.

Two project sites were initially identified. The first was in the Sacapa region of east-northeastern Guatemala and the other in the fertile Azua Valley region in the southwest section of the Dominican Republic. Much development has centered in the Dominican region since 1980. In fact, the Group's decision was "encouraged" by the presence of similar foreign-owned-and-operated projects in the valley. This, together with other shareholder business contacts in the Dominican Republic, led to the selection of the Azua Valley.

Government Incentives

The Dominican Government has targeted the development of export agriculture as a top priority. Agriculture is the most important sector of the Dominican economy in terms of employment and export earnings. It represents 25 percent of gross domestic production and accounts for 70 to 80 percent of export earnings. It employs 45 percent of the labor force. Within the agricultural sector, raw sugar production has traditionally been the most significant industry. In light of the world depression of sugar prices, the government has made a concerted effort to foster an environment for economic development in other areas such as nontraditional crop production. The Group's management viewed this development as critically important in terms of providing a favorable working/investment environment.

In 1982 the government enacted Law 409, the agro-industry law that offers benefits to agribusiness investors consisting primarily of tax remissions. Pursuant to meeting the law's prerequisites, the Group was granted a 15-year federal tax holiday and 100 percent exemption from all import duties on machinery and equipment. (The Caribbean Basin Initiative abolished a 35 percent U.S. import tariff, as well.) In addition, the Group was allowed to repatriate 100 percent of its earnings in dollars (to be converted at the official rate at the time of repatriation.)

Organization and Operating Structure

The Group set up a Dominican corporation, Agro-Azua, S.A., as "the project company." The project company is the company of record and, on behalf of the Group, contracts for the land, hires the farmhands (*campesinos*) to prepare the land, and is responsible for harvesting, processing and packing the crop. The project company is also the exporter of record. It sells the crop to the Group's marketing company, Ricardo Foods. The Group establishes a *transfer price* on the cost-plus basis. The profits of the project company show a 5 to 10 percent profit margin on sales. In addition, Ricardo Foods charges the project company 5 to 10 percent of gross sales for marketing and distribution expenses. These are included in Agro-Azua's cost base.

Most notably, the upside profit potential benefits Ricardo Foods. This is due to the fact that product market prices are variable and are highly influenced by supply factors, while costs of production are invariant. The Agro-Dominicana Group, Inc. is considered "the management company" and 5 to 10 percent of gross sales for export management and technical assistance is billed to the project company. (This, too, is included in Agro-Azua's cost base.) Technical assistance consists primarily of supervision from farmers brought in from Florida and the use of university-trained local agronomists, mostly on a consulting basis. Since 1985, the project company has sold 50 percent of the crop to a Channel Island company—well regarded for its tax haven status. This "paper transaction" involves invoicing the sale to the Channel Island company and consigning the shipment to Ricardo Foods. The physical shipment of the crop is directly to Ricardo in the United States. The Channel Island company in turn invoices Ricardo at a predetermined, marked-up price. In this manner, some of the profits avoid U.S. income taxes. This intricate approach is predicated upon management's strategy to control and protect the flow of funds (profits) by minimizing taxes.

Due to Ricardo's well-established market contacts, the crop is practically presold. Ricardo very seldom takes possession of the crop. Once the shipment leaves the Dominican port, supermarket and wholesale buyers are contacted and arrangement is made with the buyer for pick-up at the port. Ricardo sells to major supermarket chains such as Publix and Winn–Dixie. In addition, the Group sells to food brokers in the Northeast and Canada. According to the Group, the primary concern of the buyers is the grade, quality, and reliability of delivery to market. Usually a supermarket chain like Publix will know its demand estimate for any winter crop by the preceding fall or by late summer, about three months before harvest begins. If the market is "hot" with extra demand, especially towards the end of harvest, melons can be sent up to a week early in what is called "half-slip" condition, a little less ripe than the "full-slip" condition in which the produce is usually sent.

Agro-Dominicana has grossed millions of U.S. dollars each harvest since the project was initiated. Production expanded from an initial 600 acres in 1983–1984 to a 1,000 acre planting farm in 1985–1986. The Group expanded production to 2,000 acres in 1988. (Estimated annual production of melons in the Dominican Republic is 12 million— 90 percent of which are cultivated in the Azua Valley. The Secretary of Agriculture reports that 9,000 acres are now cultivated for melons in the valley by four different concerns.)

The Melon Patch

The minimum size of a commercially tenable melon patch is 200 acres. Though not the case here, much of the land in the Dominican Republic promoted for such production is land once used for sugarcane production, and is cleared and ready to fill. Typically, each acre yields 450 to 500 boxes of melons. The box's weight, depending on the grade of the crop, is 40 to 60 pounds.

Due to the natural climate and soil conditions, the production-cycle time for melons is faster in the tropics than in the United States. In the tropics, the time from seed to harvest is 65 days as compared to 90 days in U.S. subtropic regions. This natural phenomenon facilitates crop turnover and gives the producer enhanced planting flexibility.

A farmer's workday is about 12 hours—from sunrise to sunset. In a highly labor-intensive process such as the cultivation of melons, cheap labor is essential for effective competition. Farm wages in the Dominican Republic are considerably lower than in the United States. There are no labor unions and government interference is minimal. The government prescribes the minimum wage and an additional month's pay at year's end. Due to the seasonal nature of the work, government requirements regarding "lay-off benefits" are not applicable. The minimum wage for the campesino is DR $25.00 per 12-hour day. As is the case with most foreign investors, Agro-Azua generally pays slightly in excess of the daily minimum. It also provides transportation to and from the farm, as well as food and medical services to both field laborers and harvest processors. The variety of export product grown in the valley, and the staggered harvest times for the different crops, ensures that locals will have longer work seasons and steadier incomes than what just one crop will provide. As a result, average campesino income in the valley has risen 300 percent in four years. In addition, four agribusiness firms there have contributed to the building of a hospital and two schools in the area.

Labor is employed in three states of production—land preparation, crop growing, and crop harvesting. Land preparation entails clearing the acreage and leveling the field. Six to seven tractor drivers and their helpers are employed in this process. Land preparation begins early in the year and continues up to seeding time.

The crop-growing stage requires approximately 30 to 40 laborers per acre. It requires irrigation every 7 to 10 days, and periodic planting and fertilizing. The fertilization formula is dependent on soil conditions and a knowledgeable, on-site agronomist is essential. Agro-Azua employs a staggered planting procedure whereby plots are brought to harvest in a time-staggered sequence.

Technical assistance is in the form of U.S.-trained agronomists—one of whom resides at the project site during crop-growing and harvesting. Other agronomists provide assistance on a consulting basis. Three or four local agronomists are employed on a permanent basis. Total employment varies depending on the stage of production and size of the crop. A permanent labor force is composed of eight or nine individuals, mainly the agronomists and a small staff of farm hands. Seasonal farm labor consists of approximately 200 to 250 campesinos from September to April. They are dispatched in teams of various sizes depending on the task—20 to an acre to lay irrigation pipe, 12 to 15 if weeding and cultivating, or doing pest control work, and only 7 or 8 to an acre when planting and fertilizing. The Group estimates labor costs in 1990 reached DR $1,000,000. These costs are representative of a 2,000-acre crop and do not include technological assistance charged to the project company.

Bringing Melons to Market

Once picked, a melon has an average shelf life of 7 to 10 days. State-of-the-art packing processes extend the shelf life to 17 to 21 days. Agro-Azua set itself apart from the other producers in the region by investing in timely process technology. This "hydro-cooling" equipment costs approximately U.S. $250,000. When the harvested melons are brought in from the field, their temperature is the same as the outside air—usually, about 90 degrees Fahrenheit. When the melons are put in refrigerated storage, the fruit does not chill to the center for approximately 36 hours. Just as warmth accelerates its growth, so too does it speed up spoilage. With hydro-cooling, melons are immersed instead in a frigid water bath that reduces the melon's temperature inside and out to 44 degrees in 30 minutes. Once cooled, the melons are stored in a 10,000-sq-ft refrigerated storage facility until shipping. Bringing to market a crop with extended shelf life is a key ingredient to buyer acceptance and satisfaction. Moreover, it affords Agro-Azua longer storage flexibility in the face of production and shipping uncertainties.

At times Ricardo Foods has gone to extra expense to air freight produce by charter when necessary. (It is indicative of the large profit margin that produce can be shipped by air at 11 to 12 cents a pound, instead of by ship at 5 to 6 cents a pound, and a profit can still be made.) Even so, in its first three years, the company reduced its reliance on air freight from 30 percent of the total crop to almost zero.

The hydro-cooler was part of a larger investment made in 1984. A packing plant was built on a 45-acre lot purchased with a U.S. $500,000 OPIC (Overseas Private Investment Corporation) direct loan. OPIC made the loan for a 10-year term, with two years grace on both principal repayment and interest, collateralized by the equipment, land, and building.

The company had been using a government-owned processing facility and worried about the risk of keeping produce there. The U.S. holding company and the individual investors guaranteed the loan. According to the Group, the ability to defer principal payments for two years was helpful, but not critical, in terms of managing the project's cash flow. The Group also purchased an apartment in the capital city of Santo Domingo for prolonged stays of the U.S. staff.

Lack of transportation infrastructure has been a well noted barrier to business in the region. The Azua Valley is surrounded by five active ports. However, the closest ports in Barabona and Haina are 40 and 60 miles respectively from the plant. Local roads and rail methods of transportation have been developed to the point that transportation by truck or rail car is used interchangeably depending on the size of shipments. Local transportation in this regard has not been a problem.

Transportation to the United States is by refrigerated ships to South Florida ports. Presently, three carriers service traffic between these ports twice a week: Seaboard Marine into Palm Beach, CCT into Fort Lauderdale, and Concord/

NOPAL into Miami. By contrast, in the early 1980s, only two shipping lines serviced the Dominican ports twice every two weeks. Transit time is usually four days. Since 1987, the entire crop has been shipped by sea freight.

The Ricardo Family's Present Concerns

At the present time, the Ricardo family has decided to review the activities of the Agro-Dominicana Group, Inc. Agro-Dominicana has proved itself to be reasonably profitable, especially since 1988. But there is always concern that one of the operation's success factors may be eliminated or turn negative. This concern underscores the family's desire to review the entire situation. Stated somewhat differently: What could happen to injure Agro-Dominicana's fundamental business strategy and prevent profitability? What can Ricardo do now to prevent such events, or the negative effects of such events?

Chapter

2

The International Contractor and Competitive Advantages

This chapter introduces the **international contractor** (INC) as the key actor in international business. Under the broad heading of firms that do international business (that is, INCs), one special case is the **multinational enterprise** (MNE). These MNEs have owned operations in at least three countries, and they tend to be very large. The chapter uses examples of both large MNEs and smaller INCs that do not possess foreign affiliates to apply its analysis to small as well as large firms that engage in international business. Also, it recognizes the growing importance of non-ownership forms of international involvement of firms, such as international licensing, international franchising, turnkey contracts, and other strategic alliances. Finally, the chapter presents a conceptual framework that is used throughout the rest of the book: the **theory of competitive advantage.** The main goals of the chapter are to:

1. Define the **international contractor** (INC) and show how the term can be used to describe both large and small firms.

2. Describe the **multinational enterprise** (MNE) and illustrate this concept with a number of firms whose names will recur throughout the book.

3. Explain the theory of **competitive advantage** and show how these advantages can be used by firms to benefit from doing international business.

4. Explain the concept of **internalization,** which can help managers and students alike to understand why MNEs act as they do.

5. Provide examples of how competitive advantages are used in international business (such as in the Caterpillar case), to shed more light on the concepts and on their applications in actual business situations.

INTRODUCTION

The central focus of international business is on the **multinational enterprise (MNE),** or more accurately on the **international contractor (INC).** The multinational enterprise has been defined as a firm with subsidiaries, branches, or other controlled affiliates in three or more countries. The INC is a more broadly defined firm, with business activities that may range from exports to manufacturing in at least two countries. The minimum number of countries involved in international business is two; hence the international contractor is a firm that carries out such business. This definition encompasses firms ranging from small exporters to huge foreign investors such as Exxon and IBM, with affiliates in dozens of countries; all of them are really firms of interest here. The chapter focuses on the international contractor and its relations with customers, suppliers, competitors, and governments in the countries where it does business.

Although **companies** undertake international business, clearly the national **governments** that set the rules of the game in business are important, as are local governments and international organizations that likewise place barriers and incentives in front of international companies. Not to be ignored are the non-international firms that function as competitors, suppliers, and customers of the INCs. Since our interest is to explore the particular problems and opportunities that arise for companies at the international level, we will deal primarily at that level—and with local firms and governments as they relate to the INCs.

Before examining the INC in detail, let us review some of the main activities that constitute international business. Table 2–1 shows that international trade (that is, exports and imports) is the largest category of international business activity, followed by international bank lending, foreign direct investment, and other contractual agreements such as international licensing and franchising. Exports and imports alone accounted for close to $US 3 trillion of business during 1988, while international lending reached about one fourth of that. The values for foreign direct investment and the other contractual forms should be interpreted carefully, since the investment (or the license) implies only the price paid for ownership or control of some business activity; the actual value of sales of a foreign factory or a franchised hotel is generally several times greater. The

ADDED DIMENSION

INCs and MNEs

International contractors are any firms that do international business, ranging from exporters and importers, to franchisers and management contractors, to foreign direct investors. *Multinational enterprises* are firms that have foreign direct investment (that is, affiliates) in at least three countries. Multinational enterprises are one form of INC, but they are not the only one. The distinction is useful because it emphasizes the fact that even small exporters can be involved in strategic alliances and other business that crosses national borders, without being as large as Exxon or as widely spread globally as Procter and Gamble. ■

TABLE 2–1

Some Estimates of the Size of International Business *(in billions of U.S. dollars)*

	World	U.S.
Exports (1988)	2,679.6	322.4
Foreign direct investment (1988)		326.9 Stock
	159.7 Flow	18.9 Flow
Licensing: of affiliates (1988)	N.A.	8.3
Other contractual dealings: with affiliates	N.A.	2.9
International commercial bank lending (1988)	653.8	231.7

Source: *International Financial Statistics*, 1990; *Survey of Current Business*, August 1989; Bank for International Settlements, Semi-Annual International Federal Financial Institutions Examination Council Statistical Release, March 1989.

table does not include intergovernment transactions, which are much smaller in total than the trade or banking values, but which also contribute to the total amount of international business.

The bulk of the **value** of international business transactions comes from activities of large, multinational firms. These firms export and import through their own affiliates and via unrelated firms; they move funds internally through loans, payments for use of technology, overhead, and so on; they borrow from and lend to unrelated parties; they exchange ownership of assets across national borders; and they pass uncountable amounts of information internationally among their affiliates and to and from unrelated parties. By definition, multinational enterprises carry out foreign direct investment, which is used to set up and expand their overseas affiliates. In addition, most international lending (in terms of the value of the loans) is done by large, multinational banks that possess sufficient information about foreign clients to justify the banks' participation in such business. On the other hand, only about one third of the total value of exports and imports is transacted by MNEs, with the rest spread among literally hundreds of thousands of smaller firms that do not operate overseas subsidiaries or branches. In terms of total transactions, non-MNEs constitute the majority of the actors in international business. Together, these various kinds of actors and activities are the essence of international business.

Figure 2–1 presents another view of international business, picturing the INC as the central actor. The INC is a central organizing institution for international transactions involving money, goods, and information. The INC seeks not only to earn profits for its owners, but it also generates income for suppliers in more than one country, provides outputs for customers in more than one country, provides additional competition for firms in each country, and operates under the rules set by governments in each of the jurisdictions involved. This chapter explains what an international contractor is, what kinds of activities it undertakes, and why it undertakes them. The aim of this discussion is to get the reader to think about the kinds of problems and decisions that face an INC manager.

In the next section we define the INC and the MNE in more detail. The following section lists a number of large, visible international firms and discusses some of their attributes. By using the theory of competitive advantage

FIGURE 2-1

The International Contractor
in International Business

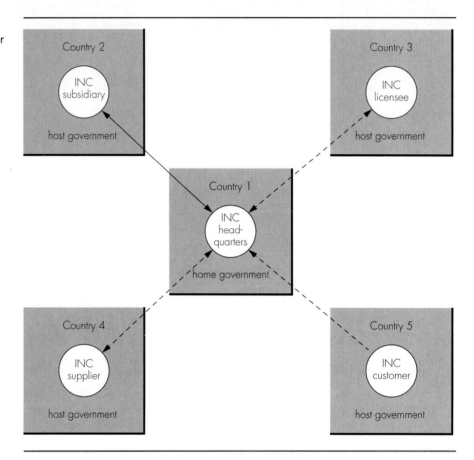

(described in the second half of the chapter), a manager can decide what information to gather and how to use that information to make decisions about INC activities ranging from capital budgeting to market positioning to dealing with governments. Competitive advantage is used throughout the text as a general framework for thinking about the issues facing the INC manager and for defining the basic rationales for key decisions that INC managers must make. The chapter concludes with an extended example of one international contractor—Caterpillar, Inc.—and its competitive situation with respect to key rivals around the world.

CHARACTERISTICS OF THE INTERNATIONAL CONTRACTOR

The term international contractor covers large firms that have been called multinational enterprises and smaller firms with fewer overseas commitments that may be simple exporters or contractors selling some service such as the use of proprietary technology or management skills. During the 1980s the range of contracting activities used by international firms to pursue their competitive objectives grew substantially. It now includes activities such as joint ventures that are used to market products for two otherwise-competing firms, coproduction agreements under which two firms share a factory to produce their separate products, and other so-called "strategic alliances".

Due to the limitations that many countries impose on ownership of local firms by foreigners, firms that carry out substantial international business are finding more and more nonownership forms of activity to undertake (e.g., licensing, franchising, turnkey ventures, and other more complex contracting arrangements, in addition to simple exporting). Also, small firms often discover that international business can be carried out through nonownership forms that do not require the large amounts of resources necessitated by operation of subsidiaries. Thus, for both competitive reasons and regulatory requirements, international firms are finding that contractual agreements help them achieve more and more of their goals. (This issue is discussed again in Chapter 25.)

International contracting has become quite common in raw materials industries and in public utilities such as telephone and electric power companies. Firms such as Exxon, Texaco, ITT, and GTE find themselves entering the 1990s with fewer foreign investments in oil wells or telephone operating companies and more technical consulting agreements with host country firms that monopolize these industries. International banking has traditionally relied on correspondent relationships among banking firms in different countries to provide international services. Even in manufacturing, contracting out to provide managerial or technical services has become very common for large as well as small firms in international business. All of the world's major auto firms contract out extensively to obtain components such as tires, glass, accessories, and other parts, in addition to cooperating with each other in joint ventures in the United States and in other countries.[1]

Strategic alliances other than traditional wholly owned foreign direct investment are becoming very common among the multinational enterprises.[2] This phenomenon demonstrates the MNEs' realization that contractual strategies offer such benefits as pooling scarce resources, sharing risks, and other positive features that cannot be obtained by going it alone. Hence, the concept of the international contractor emphasizes the new perspective of decision makers that a variety of means can be used to serve the end of international competitiveness.

CHARACTERISTICS OF THE MULTINATIONAL ENTERPRISE

No single definition of the MNE has received wide acceptance at this time. Some analysts view large, dominant firms that do at least some international business (such as those appearing in the Fortune 500) as the relevant ones. Others include only firms that have owners from more than one country. Even the label is arguable—the United Nations calls the firms "transnational corporations," and the AFL-CIO calls them "multinational companies." While no definition can be completely objective, Vernon and Wells have offered a view that covers the concept fairly well. Their view is that multinational enterprises are companies

made up of a cluster of affiliated firms [that], although in different countries, nevertheless share distinguishing characteristics as follows:
1. They are linked by ties of common ownership.
2. They draw on a common pool of resources, such as money and credit, information systems, trade names and patents.
3. They respond to some common strategy.[3]

In this view, the MNE may be privately or governmentally owned; it may be very large or relatively small; its ownership may be held by investors from any number of countries; and it may engage in any number of forms of international business—as long as it possesses owned affiliates in more than two countries. This may be called a *functional* definition of the MNE, since it focuses on the functioning of the firm and not on its ownership structure or other characteristics. The one necessary function of an MNE is foreign direct investment, through which the firm obtains or creates affiliates in at least three countries.

Typically, the firms discussed in this book not only have affiliates in three or more countries but also possess the other characteristics of multinational ownership and large size, as shown in the next section. The key point of our definition is that firms need *not* possess these latter characteristics in order to use the strategies and organization structures discussed in later chapters. The ability to utilize more than one country as the firm's market or production site (and to face the concomitant opportunities and constraints) is the distinguishing feature of the MNE. From this arise the competitive advantages peculiar to multinational firms.

EXAMPLES OF MNES

The list of multinational enterprises according to our definition would number in the thousands. Instead of trying to create such a list, we consider a small number of very successful MNEs and a few of their competitive characteristics. Our purpose is to discover not only which companies are multinational but also to see what enables them to operate successfully at the international level. Table 2–2 lists 36 large U.S.-based multinationals that a study by Peters and Waterman (1982) regarded as having been highly successful from 1961 to 1980.

Notice that the vast majority of these firms spend much more on research and development (R&D), and thus are more technology intensive, than the U.S. industry average of 2.1 percent of sales spent on R&D. Also, most of them possess affiliates in far more than the three countries needed to be considered a multinational enterprise. Notice, finally, that the group is spread over a wide variety of industries, despite their similarity of above-average commitments to technology and international diversification.

A similar listing of non-U.S. MNEs cannot be as detailed, because far less information is available on those firms. By ranking firms according to size (defined as annual sales converted into U.S. dollars), however, a listing can be created. Table 2–3 presents a group of the largest non-U.S. MNEs, which appear in the *Fortune* list of the 500 largest non-U.S. industrial companies. These companies are classified by profitability (defined as gross profits divided by total assets), size, country of parent company, industry, and capital intensity (defined as total assets divided by total employees).

Despite the proliferation of countries represented, the industrial concentration of these large, non-U.S. firms is striking: over half are in the petroleum and automotive industries. Most of the firms are in European countries, but Japan has more entries (eight companies) in the list than any other single country.

What can account for the uneven distribution of MNEs across countries and industries? Certainly, no single factor is the key. The next section presents a viewpoint that offers both an understanding of some of the important factors involved and ways for managers to use these factors in operating their own companies.

TABLE 2–2

Characteristics of Top-Performing U.S.-based MNEs (in 1988)

Company	Technology Intensity (R&D/Sales)	Annual Sales ($ millions)	Number of Foreign Countries with Affiliates	Capital per Worker (assets per employee)
Electronics				
Amdahl	12.3	1,802	16	232.6
Data General	12.1	1,365	29	69.9
Digital Equipment	11.4	11,475	27	83.2
Emerson Electric	3.1	6,652	27	71.0
Hewlett-Packard	10.4	9,831	33	86.2
IBM	7.4	59,681	46	188.7
Intel	11.1	2,875	19	170.7
National Semiconductor	11.3	2,470	3	47.1
Raychem	7.7	1,095	6	105.3
Texas Instruments	7.8	6,295	13	58.5
Wang Laboratories	8.7	3,068	20	90.0
Eastman Kodak	6.7	17,034	21	158.0
Cosmetics and health care products				
Avon	0.9	3,063	24	86.7
Johnson & Johnson	7.5	9,000	58	87.6
Bristol-Myers	6.6	5,973	38	147.4
Procter & Gamble	3.4	19,336	27	192.4
Chemicals				
Dow Chemical	4.6	16,682	20	295.2
DuPont	4.0	32,917	28	217.9
Merck	11.3	5,940	35	191.5
Electrical appliances				
Maytag	NA	1,886	2	159.9
Industrial machinery				
Caterpillar	1.7	10,435	16	159.9
Dana	1.1	5,190	3	121.2
3M	6.5	10,581	53	107.7
Oil				
Amoco	1.3	21,150	24	560.0
Project management				
Boeing	4.4	16,962	8	85.6
Fluor	NA	5,132	6	116.0
Services (e.g., hotels, retail sales, restaurants)				
Delta Air Lines	NA	7,323	1	113.4
Walt Disney	NA	3,438	6	131.0
K Mart	NA	27,301	4	34.7
Marriott	NA	7,370	19	26.0
McDonald's	NA	5,566	9	48.3
Wal-Mart	NA	20,649	0	36.7

Sources: Thomas J. Peters and Robert H. Waterman, *In Search of Excellence* (New York: Harper & Row, 1982); *Business Week*, "Innovation in America Supplement" (June 16, 1989); *Forbes* (May 1, 1989); Dun & Bradstreet International, *Who Owns Whom? 1990*. All of these firms passed Peters and Waterman's tests for "excellent" performance during 1961–80. Some companies in our previous edition are omitted here as they have either been acquired by other companies or sufficient details have not been available.

TABLE 2-3

Characteristics of the Largest Non-U.S. Multinationals

S.NO	Name	Profits/ Assets	Annual Sales ($ billions)	Industry	Country	Assets per Employee
1	Royal Dutch Shell	0.061	72.381	Petroleum	Netherlands/U.K	0.64
2	Toyota Motor	0.057	50.790	Motor vehicles	Japan	0.47
3	British Petroleum	0.041	46.174	Petroleum	UK	0.42
4	IRI	NA	45.522	Petroleum	Italy	NA
5	Daimler-Benz	0.033	41.818	Motor vehicles	Germany	0.09
6	Hitachi	0.020	41.331	Electronics	Japan	0.19
7	Siemens	0.024	34.129	Electronics	Germany	0.09
8	Fiat	0.058	34.039	Motor vehicles	Italy	0.15
9	Matsushita Electric Industrial	0.030	33.923	Electrical appliances	Japan	0.29
10	Volkswagen	0.015	33.696	Motor vehicles	Germany	0.11
11	Unilever	0.075	30.488	Food, soaps, cosmetics	UK/Netherlands	0.07
12	Nissan Motor	0.014	29.097	Motor vehicles	Japan	0.31
13	Philips	0.019	28.371	Electronics	Netherlands	0.08
14	Nestlé	0.063	27.803	Food, beverages	Switzerland	0.11
15	Samsung	0.021	27.386	Electronics	South Korea	0.13
16	Renault	0.082	27.110	Motor vehicles	France	0.10
17	Toshiba	0.016	25.441	Electrical appliances	Japan	0.23
18	ENI	0.025	25.227	Petroleum, chemicals	Italy	0.31
19	BASF	0.043	24.961	Chemicals	Germany	0.14
20	Hoechst	0.059	23.308	Chemicals	Germany	0.11
21	Peugeot	0.092	23.250	Motor vehicles	France	0.10
22	Bayer	0.055	23.026	Chemicals	Germany	0.12
23	Honda Motor	0.057	22.237	Motor vehicles	Japan	0.25
24	CGE	0.012	21.488	Electrical appliances	France	0.14
25	Elf Aquitaine	0.043	21.175	Petroleum, chemicals	France	0.38
26	Imperial Chemical Industries	0.088	20.839	Chemicals	UK	0.13
27	NEC	0.008	19.626	Electrical appliances	Japan	0.23
28	Ferruzzi Finanziaria	0.016	18.311	Chemicals	Italy	0.35
29	Asea Brown Boveri	0.020	17.562	Specialty transformers	Switzerland	0.11
30	Daewoo	0.001	17.251	Electrical appliances	South Korea	0.26
31	Nippon Steel	0.010	17.109	Metal manufacturing	Japan	0.42
32	Mitsubishi Electric	0.009	16.857	Electrical appliances	Japan	0.24
33	Thyssen	0.036	16.796	Metal manufacturing, steel	Germany	0.08
34	Volvo	0.056	15.752	Motor vehicles	Sweden	0.18
35	Robert Bosch	0.025	15.747	Motor vehicles	Germany	0.07
36	General Motors of Canada	0.059	15.657	Motor vehicles	Canada	0.11
37	Mazda Motor	0.008	15.151	Motor vehicles	Japan	0.34
38	INI	0.009	14.986	Metal manufacturing	Spain	0.19
39	Petrobras	0.057	14.806	Petroleum	Brazil	0.20
40	Fujitsu	0.016	14.797	Electronic computers	Japan	0.20

Source: "The International 500 Ranked by Sales," *Fortune*, July 31, 1989.

THE THEORY OF COMPETITIVE ADVANTAGE

The theory of **competitive advantage** is a perspective on business strategy that offers the analyst a simple framework for studying a firm's competitive environment. It helps in decision making on key issues such as choosing which markets to serve, selecting sources of supply, and deciding whether to carry out activities within the firm or to contract out for them. The theory is presented here as a sequential process in which the firm must:

1. Define its competitive advantages and disadvantages, as well as analyze the importance of each one in its competition with the relevant rival firms.

2. Choose how to obtain those advantages viewed as crucial in a particular competitive context (and how to minimize the negative impact of competitive *dis*advantages that cannot be eliminated.

3. Decide how to capitalize on the firm's competitive advantages through international business activities such as exports, direct investment, and strategic alliances.[4]

The rest of this section describes the process of strategy formulation using competitive advantages in an international firm.

Defining Competitive Advantages

Studies of successful large firms in industrial countries during the 1970s and 1980s have shown that these firms typically compete in domestic and foreign markets on the basis of competitive advantages that are based on company-specific characteristics. That is, these firms usually possess some **proprietary asset**—a new production process, a superior sales location, facilities that realize economies of scale in production or distribution, and so on (or a combination of such assets)—that allows it to achieve lower costs, higher revenues, or lower risk than its competitors.[5]

For example, Pfizer Corporation has discovered that it can successfully transfer product differentiation strategies developed in one country to other countries in which it does business in pharmaceuticals; the company has managed its internal resources to obtain economies of scale in advertising and physical distribution for its differentiated products. Westinghouse Electric Corporation has demonstrated an ability to negotiate contracts to provide major power generating facilities with governments in less developed countries (LDCs) and Eastern Europe; it now possesses a competitive advantage in government contracting and a protected business position in several national markets. Mobil Oil, Caterpillar, and several other firms have developed internal "codes of conduct" that they publicize widely and use to convince governments and social pressure groups that the company is acting in the interest of the country involved; this is a kind of competitive advantage in social goodwill, since it is expected to result in more favorable treatment of the company by each government or social pressure group. Hewlett-Packard, IBM, and many Japanese companies have corporate philosophies that are passed on to employees and substantially followed by the companies' executives—leading to internal labor and personnel relations superior to those in many other firms. L. M. Ericsson, the Swedish telecommunications manufacturer, has developed small electronic switching systems that suit many customers that need less-extensive, less-costly telephone systems than those produced and sold by its major rivals in international business; Ericsson has developed a market niche advantage. Each of these examples of competitive advantages gives the company the ability to outcompete its rivals in a particular business situation.

Many of these proprietary characteristics are not limited to international firms; in fact, most of them pertain to successful domestic firms as well. Table 2–4 lists a number of commonly cited attributes that create competitive advantages for international firms. Advantages that exist for both domestic and

TABLE 2–4

Competitive Advantages of
Multinational Enterprises

Advantage	Description
General Competitive Advantages	
Proprietary technology	Product, process, or management technology held by a firm, which others can obtain only through R&D or contracting with the possessor
Goodwill based on brand or trade name	Reputation for quality, service, etc., developed through experience
Scale economies in production	Large-scale production facilities that lower unit costs of production
Scale economies in purchasing	Lower costs of inputs through purchasing large quantities
Scale economies in financing	Access to funds at a lower cost for larger firms
Scale economies in distribution	Shipments of large quantities of products/inputs to necessary locations, lowering unit shipping costs
Scale economies in advertising	Sales in several markets, allowing somewhat standardized advertising across markets
Government protection	Free or preferential access to a market limited by government fiat
Human resource management	Skill at fostering teamwork among employees and optimizing productivity
Multinational Competitive Advantages	
Multinational marketing capability	Knowledge of and access to markets in several countries
Multinational sourcing capability	Reliable access to raw materials, intermediate goods, etc., in several countries that reduces single-source costs
Multinational diversification	Operations in several countries so that country risk and business risk are reduced
Managerial experience in several countries	Skill for managing multicountry operations gained through experience in different countries (learning curve gains)

international firms are discussed in this section; specifically international advantages are discussed in the following section.

Historically, 20th-century multinational enterprises began primarily in extractive industries, ranging from oil to bananas to copper.[6] These multinationals competed on the basis of their access to supplies of natural resources and to substantial markets. By the advent of World War II, many of these advantages had been partially or completely competed away, and thus the firms were vulnerable to competition from other firms and to greater regulation by governments.

Analysis of the competitive advantages of large firms in the period after World War II has focused on the idea of *barriers to entry*. Bain (1956) defined these characteristics as arising from **absolute cost advantages** (such as proprietary production techniques and control over limited resources by established firms), from **product differentiation** advantages (such as an established brand name or a patented product), and from **economies of scale** (in areas such as production, advertising, and purchasing).

Studies of multinational enterprises likewise have focused on barriers to entry. The initial investigations (for example, Vernon, 1966, and Kindleberger,

1969) found that **proprietary technology** is a fundamental basis for competitiveness of many such firms. Indeed, many of the most successful U.S.-based MNEs in the 1950s and 1960s produced high-tech products in such industries as pharmaceuticals (e.g., Pfizer, Johnson & Johnson, and Merck), data processing (e.g., IBM, Burroughs, Honeywell), telecommunications (e.g., ITT, GTE) chemicals (e.g., Dow, DuPont, Monsanto), and electronic instruments (e.g., Eastman Kodak, Texas Instruments). The competitive advantage came from some technology created or purchased by the firm that the firm was able to utilize in production to generate better or less-expensive products than those produced by its competitors. For example, DuPont created distinctive products such as nylon, rayon, and more recently Kevlar; IBM was a leader in moving data processing from electromechanical computations to electronic processing; and Eastman Kodak created a higher-quality paper for photographs than its rivals.

Early analyses also focused on the marketing advantages possessed by MNEs (e.g., Vernon 1966 and Caves 1971). Particularly important in this case is the firm's ability to differentiate its product from others. By establishing a **brand or trade name,** the firm may be able to attract additional buyers due to name recognition and trust. Examples of industries in which firms possess this type of advantage include electrical appliances (e.g., General Electric, Maytag, Sunbeam), health care products (e.g., Bristol-Myers, Colgate-Palmolive, Procter & Gamble), foods (e.g., Coca-Cola, Kraft, RJR-Nabisco), and pharmaceuticals. In this case, the advantage arises from the firm's developing a reputation for high-quality products, good service after the product has been purchased, and/or good value relative to competitors' products. These characteristics become identified with the brand or trade name, enabling the firm to sell more output or charge higher prices than competitors.

More recent analysts have looked at multinational firms as holders of a variety of such competitive assets, no one of which is necessary by itself. A fairly extensive list of those advantages appears in Table 2–4. Let us consider the rest of the advantages listed.

Scale economies in production exist when a firm is able to operate a production facility that attains lower costs per unit at large levels of output than the costs incurred by competitors in production facilities that have lower output capacities. That is, as the scale (volume) of production is increased by increasing the size of the production facility, unit costs can be decreased at higher levels of output. (This does *not* mean that companies producing more of a product necessarily have lower costs; such a result may also occur when some producers are producing at quantities below their minimum-cost level of output.) Scale economies in production are important in many industries, especially those that are heavily capital intensive, such as the automotive, airframe manufacturing, industrial chemical, and oil industries. General Motors, for example, is able to achieve substantially lower production costs for its cars than Isuzu or Chrysler, each of which produces in smaller facilities and at lower volumes of output.

Scale economies in purchasing can be attained by firms that are able to buy inputs in large quantities and thus reduce their unit costs. This competitive advantage is usually available to larger firms, which are able to purchase larger quantities than their rivals. It also tends to arise for firms with more standardized production, as the selection of inputs becomes more predictable and larger stocks become justifiable. By contracting to buy literally millions of pounds of beef on a regular basis, such companies as Burger King and McDonald's reduce their hamburger cost far below that of local, single-location restaurants.

Scale economies in financing exist for firms that are able to borrow large sums of funds, and thus can obtain quantity discounts. IBM, because of its very large size (and also because of its extremely good creditworthiness), can borrow at interest rates similar to those paid by the largest commercial banks for their own funds. A small computer manufacturer or component maker will pay far higher rates. By borrowing in the Eurocurrency markets (which are restricted to fairly large-scale transactions, as discussed in Chapter 6), IBM or another large firm may find even lower rates than those available to smaller firms.

Scale economies in distribution arise when the firm is able to contract for shipping to several destinations and for large quantities of products to serve its several markets. The per unit cost of distributing products often falls when the selling firm can contract for multiple shipments and high volumes. (The firm may even purchase its own distribution system, if the cost of so doing is less than the cost of contracting with outside distributors.)

Scale economies in advertising may be attainable when a firm sells products in several countries and can standardize its promotion across countries. In industrial countries, adjusting for language differences, such standardization can often be carried out, and advertising costs can thus be reduced. On the contrary, when products are introduced into very different countries (e.g., less developed nations), the promotion and even the product often need to be adapted to local conditions, and these scale economies cannot be realized. Exxon has used its "Put a tiger in your tank" promotional campaign successfully around the world; in the late 1980s, Beatrice Foods placed the company logo on many of its products around the world (as opposed to previous promotion that downplayed the Beatrice connection among products with different brand names).

Government protection is another source of competitive advantage. This type of advantage is often ignored, since it is based not on the firm's activities in the market, but rather on the legal framework and negotiations with government regulators and government customers. Nevertheless, managers should be aware that in every country temporary or permanent protection from competition may be obtained from the government. Whether it be operation of the national telephone company (which AT&T monopolized in most of the United States until 1984) or establishment of an import-replacing plant that receives tariff protection, the firm may obtain exclusive rights or other protection from competitors by the host government. Such protection precludes other firms from competing, or makes their entry and operations far less profitable than the protected firm's activities. The disadvantage of government protection is that it may be lost when the government decides to alter the protection—for example, to create competition or to assist another company—and the company may not be able to build or obtain another competitive advantage to replace the one lost.

It should be noted that government protection advantages arise from two distinct kinds of relationship. First, the direct protection given to favored firms in the form of tariffs or subsidies clearly can enable a firm to carve out a successful competitive position. In addition, dealing with the government as its supplier of products or services can generate a protected environment for the firm, since governments tend to stay with reliable suppliers without switching frequently. Literally thousands of firms in the United States earn all or most of their income from selling to the U.S. government. Such relationships tend to be fairly stable; and they are common in other countries as well.

Human resource management has proved to be a very important advantage for Japanese firms competing with U.S.-based competitors in recent years. When the firm's managers are able to create a working environment that stimulates employee productivity, the firm can lower its unit costs and improve the quality of the product. Countless stories have been told (e.g., William Ouchi's *Theory Z*) about Japanese firms' greater success at managing people than their U.S. rivals'. Of course, many successful U.S. firms have achieved superior human resource management as well (see the list of firms in Table 2–2).

Multinational Competitive Advantages

All of the advantages already discussed can be used at the international level as well as domestically. Scale economies in purchasing, production, distribution, or financing may be even greater for a firm that is able to spread its sales over several countries rather than just one. A technological lead can be exploited in many countries without necessarily reducing its value. Similarly, the other domestic competitive advantages can be extended to include foreign business. This section examines four competitive advantages that are primarily limited to MNEs, though some of them can be attained by domestic firms that contract with foreign firms.

Perhaps the most important is **multinational marketing** capability, which enables the firm to sell its products in many national markets simultaneously. Compared to competitors that operate in only one national market, the MNE gains a key advantage in being able to sell its excess production in other markets, due to its sales affiliates in those markets. The affiliates function as gatherers of information about market demands, regulatory conditions, and other business intelligence that could benefit the firm, and this enables the firm to quickly take advantage of markets for selling its output. The wider the firm's net of affiliates, the greater is its possibility of maximizing its revenues. From another perspective, shortfalls in demand in one country can be remedied by sending excess output to other countries where the firm encounters an excess demand beyond the ability of the local affiliate to supply.

Another fundamental multinational competitive advantage is **multinational sourcing** of production, which enables the firm to minimize production costs by using facilities in low-cost countries. This advantage enables the MNE to reduce its costs relative to local competitors in any one country. Very frequently in the 1980s, firms set up offshore production facilities in Asian countries (such as Singapore, South Korea, and Taiwan) or Mexico, where labor costs are low, to assemble machinery, clothing, or other products for sale in the United States or Europe. (In some cases, the MNE could realize this advantage through contracting with a local Korean or Mexican firm to do the assembly rather than through investing in local production.)

A third multinational advantage is the risk-reducing benefit of **international diversification.** Many MNEs use facilities in several countries to produce the same products for several markets. That way, if a strike, war, or just a machine breakdown occurs in any one country, markets can be served from the other production sites. Major chemical companies produce the basic petrochemicals, such as ethanol, polyethylene, and butyl rubber, in a "portfolio" of countries, so their supply is assured in the event of a nationalization, a work stoppage, or the

Sources of Competitive Advantages

A basic framework of competitive strategy, used fairly widely by business analysts, views companies as organizations that carry out a set of economic activities. Let us define the economic activity of the firm as essentially production, subdivided into obtaining necessary inputs, actually producing goods or services, distributing to points of sale, and marketing them to customers. Figure 2–2 presents a sketch of the basic aspects of production in which competitive advantages may arise.

At purchasing, the first stage, inputs are assembled for production of the product or service. Then, either in that location or after transferring the inputs elsewhere, basic production is carried out. If additional assembly is needed, it may be done in the same location or at one or more assembly or finishing facilities. Finally, the product or service is marketed to customers in the same location and/or other locations. In some businesses after-sale service adds one more step to the process.

Notice that at each step of the production process the firm must choose combinations of inputs—manpower, physical capital, financial capital, and information—that will generate the output; it must decide how to organize them, and it must decide how to deal with the risks involved. Managers should do this to minimize the cost of completing the economic activity. So, for example, if it is less expensive to buy components than to produce them internally, the firm should contract out for the components. Similarly, if the firm chooses to bear the risk of losses, rather than contract with an outside insurance provider to cover that possibility, it is providing "self-insurance." In all, the firm can be viewed as a value-maximizing organization that decides on optimal combinations of inputs at each stage of the production process to generate its output and thus profit. Two key points here are (1) that the firm must attempt to evaluate the impact on profits, not only of its own activities, but also of the activities of its rivals and of other outside actors (e.g., governments); and (2) that the firm must consider the functioning of its own internal market, including the "people problems" of labor/personnel relations that must be solved to achieve optimal outputs. From this scheme, we can derive the main competitive advantages that have been noted elsewhere (e.g., Porter, 1980, 1990, and Grosse, 1984) and we can see many additional areas in which advantages may arise. ■

like in any one country. Similarly, they try to establish multiple sources of raw materials, such as oil and metals, and even of other inputs, such as labor, in order to avoid dependence on one supplier country. Thus, by operating multiple sourcing and marketing affiliates, the MNE gains this important risk-reducing capability.

Finally, managerial experience in several countries gives the firm the advantage of know-how in dealing with business situations in different countries. This

FIGURE 2–2

Competitive Advantages in the Production Process (or Value-Added Chain)

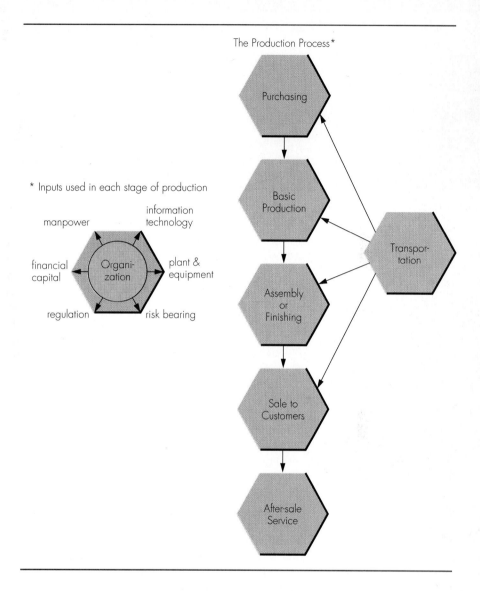

The Production Process*

Purchasing

Basic Production

Assembly or Finishing

Sale to Customers

After-sale Service

Transportation

* Inputs used in each stage of production

manpower

information technology

financial capital

Organization

plant & equipment

regulation

risk bearing

advantage generally helps the MNE possessing experienced managers relative to other MNEs without such people. The managers learn how to cope with business conditions and regulatory environments in different countries, then they can bring that experience to bear on situations in the current country and gain an advantage over rival managers who don't have such experience. By choosing the most capable and experienced local managers, the MNE may even gain an advantage over host country firms. Skill in managing a multicountry operation is itself a scarce factor of production; and firms with managers who possess such skill will presumably obtain better results than firms without them.

Managers of international contractors and potential competitors seek to obtain and benefit from these competitive advantages. While firms can generally either create such advantages from their own activities or buy them from other firms or individuals, we will consider throughout the book many specific ways in which firms can obtain proprietary assets and benefit from them. The key point of this section has been to identify the main sources of competitive advantage. It is up to the manager to then evaluate the importance of each advantage and to decide which ones are needed to compete successfully.

Obtaining Competitive Advantages

The goal of competitive strategy is to obtain, utilize, and sustain competitive advantages to the optimal level. Given the advantages discussed above, and others that may be uncovered, the manager needs to see how the firm can obtain these advantages and when it is desirable to do so. Of course, in simple economic terms, it will be best to obtain each competitive advantage up to the point where the additional economic benefit gained is just equal to the additional cost of obtaining or extending that advantage. (The decision is complicated, however, by uncertainty about future conditions, difficulties in valuing the advantages, and the unclear accessibility of some of them.)

The challenge to managers is to carve out competitive positions based on these advantages; so their potential values must be measured. Perhaps the best way to begin any such evaluation is to consider the possibility of purchasing a competitive advantage from another firm, as opposed to creating it internally within the firm. This "make-versus-buy" decision can be made on the bases of expected revenues, expected costs, and expected risks, just as with the purchase of production inputs. For example, the managerial experience gained from operating in a particular country can either be produced internally through the company's business over time or purchased in the market by hiring a manager from the outside. A distribution system can be constructed by the firm itself or purchased from another firm—as Nestlé did with its purchase of Carnation and as Imperial Chemicals (a British firm) did with its purchase of Atlas Chemicals (a U.S. firm with many affiliates in the United States and Latin America) and as Mitsubishi did with its partial purchase of Chrysler. Technology may be purchased through a licensing agreement or developed within the firm—or even obtained by buying another company, as in the 1983 purchase of Rolm (a telephone switching equipment manufacturer) by IBM and with the purchase of Zenith Data Systems by the French computer firm, Bull. Even a brand name can be obtained without spending many years to develop goodwill in dealings with customers for a particular product; the firm seeking a brand name advantage can simply buy a branded line from another company, or even buy the whole company—an acquisition strategy followed very successfully in food products by Beatrice Foods and Heinz during the past 20 years. (Heinz, for example, bought Weight Watchers.)

In each of the above examples, the firm seeking to obtain a competitive advantage must evaluate the costs and benefits expected from that advantage not only in terms of the firm's own activities but also in terms of the responses that may be expected from its important competitors at home and abroad. The competitive gains from achieving scale economies in production may be zero if all important competitors build large-scale plants too. Thus, while the make-versus-buy view can be applied by the firm to each competitive advantage, the ultimate decision to pursue an advantage depends on the expected reaction of competitors, the firm's own activities, and the amount of time needed by competitors to duplicate the advantage.

The choice even to consider making or buying a particular competitive advantage rests on the assessment of how important that advantage is (or will become) in competition. Economies of scale in distribution, for example, may offer an advantage to firms possessing their own distribution channels, but the advantage may be so slight compared to the costs facing other firms using outside suppliers of distribution that the benefits may not warrant investment in the channels. Instead, the key competitive factor in that industry may be proprietary technology or advertising effectiveness. So rather than focus efforts on accruing as many competitive advantages as possible, the manager should assess the relative importance of each advantage in the industry (and country) and then pursue those that offer the greatest benefits—usually those that create the greatest barriers to entry to and exit from the industry. (Exit barriers are those difficulties facing firms trying to leave a business, such as the problem of selling machinery or other assets specific to that business.)

INTERNALIZATION

Perhaps the most useful concept to employ in studying the strategies (and also the regulation) of INCs is **internalization.** This term, popularized by Buckley and Casson (1976), Rugman (1981) and Casson (1991), refers to the extension of ownership by a firm to cover new markets, new sources of materials, and new stages of the production process.[7] Internalization covers many of the same ideas as horizontal and vertical integration, as discussed in the economics literature related to industrial organization.

Briefly, **horizontal integration** is the expansion of a firm to carry out the same activity in a market other than the one in which it originally operated. Every time Sheraton Hotels builds a new hotel in another city, that company has integrated horizontally. On the other hand, **vertical integration** is the expansion of a firm into a stage of the production process other than that of its original business. A company that manufactures wood furniture can integrate vertically by expanding its activities upstream to include lumber production or downstream to carry out the sale of the furniture through its own stores, rather than through furniture stores belonging to others. (The firm could also do both.)

The key differences between integration and internalization are that (1) *internalization emphasizes the strategic choices* of the firm in deciding whether to buy inputs or to buy suppliers and whether to sell to other firms or to buy those firms and deal with their customers directly and (2) *internalization covers transactions outside the scope of horizontal or vertical integration*, such as the purchase of labor, capital, and technology.

To understand this idea better, consider a company that refines petroleum as its only business. This firm may choose to buy or build another oil refinery located in another market—this would be horizontal integration, that is, entry into a similar business and stage of the production process in a different location. As a second strategy, the oil refining firm may choose to buy a chain of gasoline stations, in order to extend its sales downstream to final customers. Alternatively, the firm may choose to buy into oil exploration and producing (either through acquisition or creation of a new firm), in this case integrating vertically in the upstream direction. Either of these two cases of vertical integration is also a form of internalization, in which additional levels of the production process are brought into the same firm. Finally, the firm may choose to hire a scientist(s) or engineer(s) involved in oil refining research, so that the firm can gain a new low-cost processing technology. By internalizing this research, the firm avoids the need to rely on an outside supplier of the R&D. In all of these examples, the firm is internalizing additional transactions; when a firm does this across national borders, it becomes multinational. Figure 2–3 illustrates this idea.

Hence, just as in the cases of most of the competitive advantages discussed previously, internalization may be either domestic or international; it does not exist solely in the province of MNEs or INCs.

Other classic examples of vertical integration include most mineral and metal industries, in which a few firms have succeeded in creating huge structures that stretch from mining or drilling all the way to sales to final consumers. Exxon, Texaco, Shell, and British Petroleum exemplify international internalization of the oil industry;[8] Kennecott and Anaconda exemplify this structure in the copper industry; Reynolds and Kaiser in the aluminum industry; and so on. In each case, the firm owns some of the natural resource, it explores for and produces some of the metal or mineral, and it then processes and distributes the downstream products, often all the way to final consumers in many national markets.

FIGURE 2–3

Internalization in the Oil Industry

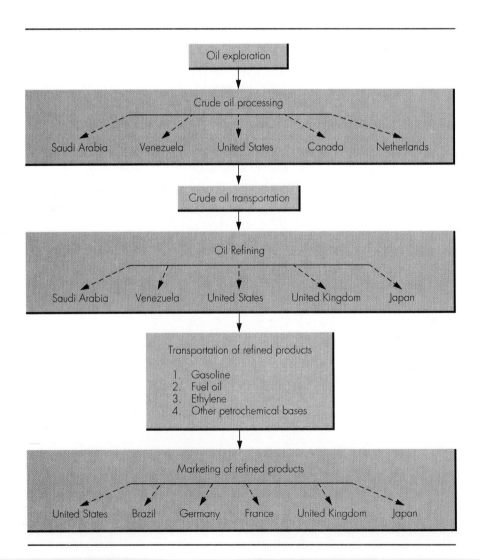

Firms may choose to take advantage of their competitive advantages through internalization when the gains from buying or establishing the new operation outweigh the costs and risks of doing so. For example, it does not necessarily make sense for McDonald's to integrate upstream into cattle raising to service the firm's restaurants, if contracting with cattle ranchers or slaughterhouses proves satisfactory. (Typically, the benefits of internalization are lower when there is a large number of such suppliers than when there are a few, powerful suppliers.) On the other hand, it may make economic sense for a steelmaker to integrate backward into the mining and production of iron ore or for a lumber company to internalize the growing and cutting of timber. In each of these cases, the firm faces a limited number of suppliers that can virtually hold the lumber or steel company hostage for higher prices, unless the firm owns the raw materials supply itself.[9]

Internalization is a powerful concept that instructs the firm's decision makers on how to proceed in maximizing the gains from its competitive advantages.

Internalization applies to domestic or international business, but it is especially vital at the transnational level. In the case of horizontal international integration, the firm gains:

1. A diversified portfolio of markets, including the home country and the countries where affiliates are located.
2. Multiple sources of output, which conceivably can be shipped to any markets that require it.
3. New opportunities to achieve scale economies and to learn about new markets (learning curve effects).

In the case of vertical international integration, the firm gains:

1. New or multiple sources of raw materials, which preclude events in any one country from interrupting the full range of the firm's activities (backward integration).
2. New market outlets, which preclude any one country's economic condition from limiting the firm's sales (forward integration).
3. Experience in new markets (learning curve effects).

Taking Advantage of Competitive Advantages

The final step for the manager in creating a competitive strategy is to determine how to benefit from the firm's accumulated competitive advantages. The solution depends, of course, on the specific set of advantages obtained by the firm and on the competitive conditions in the industries and countries in which it competes. A natural resource company will generally be very limited in its ability to own mines, wells, land, or other sources of raw materials in most countries of the world today. Instead, raw materials must often be purchased through long-term contracts or in spot markets—and a key advantage may accrue to firms that have multiple suppliers. Manufacturers of mature industrial products may need to reduce costs by seeking low-cost assembly locations—perhaps in newly industrializing countries such as Mexico, Taiwan, or Malaysia. Manufacturers of military goods may need to produce some of their components and/or products in foreign countries, to comply with government restrictions in the (foreign) purchasing countries—regardless of cost conditions that favor other sites.

This section considers only *international* business strategies based on the competitive advantages. An array of vehicles for doing business in various national markets is sketched in Table 2–5, which also suggests several criteria for choosing among the alternative methods of exploiting competitive advantages. Notice that the "bottom line" is not a simple cash-flow analysis of market-serving alternatives; rather, it is a strategic evaluation of how the method fits into the firm's full global organization and strategy. For example, a project in Japan whose net present value is lower than that of an alternative project in France may be accepted if the impact of the project in Japan is to reduce the profitability of a competitor in Japan and thus limit the competitor's ability to compete in other markets as well.[10] Similarly, a project with a lower net present value than that of some other alternative should be chosen if the more profitable project demands too much of the firm's scarce management time or if it presents too great an exposure to economic, political, or foreign-exchange risk. All in all, market-serving alternatives should be chosen on the basis of their total impact on the global corporation and not just on the basis of their expected returns as independent activities.

Notice that the *exports* form of foreign involvement may be carried out through several different channels. First, exports may be sold directly to foreign customers, without employing a middleman firm. This alternative often occurs when a firm receives an unsolicited export order from a foreign buyer, specifying the quantity of goods and other particulars for the transaction. A second possibility for exporting is for the initial firm to sell to a distributor that in turn seeks buyers in foreign markets. In this case the distributor may buy the goods from the exporter for delivery overseas, the distributor may arrange to sell on consignment without taking title to the goods, or some other arrangement may be agreed. A third possibility is for the exporter to sell to a trading company that in turn looks for foreign sales opportunities in general, functioning like a distributor but without limiting sales to a single market.

TABLE 2–5

Methods for Exploiting Competitive Advantages through Foreign Involvement

Form of Foreign Involvement	Decision Criteria*						
	Added Income	Capital Commitment	Management Commitment	Technology Commitment	Political Risk	Flexibility	Impact on Rivals
Exports†	?	Low	Low	Low	Low	High	?
Contracting‡	?	Low	Possibly high	Possibly high	Low	?	?
Partially owned direct investment§	?	?	Possibly high	High	Medium	Low	?
Wholly owned direct investment‖	?	High	High	Low	High	?	?

*Each column represents a dimension for decision making that should be considered when choosing a method to use in exploiting a competitive advantage. The rankings will differ from company to company and also across countries.

†Examples: (a) direct, (b) through a distributor, (c) through a trading company.

‡Examples: (a) licensing technology, (b) franchising, (c) management contracting, (d) turnkey venture, (e) joint marketing agreement.

§Examples: (a) joint venture with local company, (b) joint venture with foreign company, (c) joint venture with government.

‖Examples: (a) assembly plant for local sales, (b) basic manufacturing, (c) raw materials extraction, (d) offshore assembly plant.

The *contracting* form of foreign involvement can be used in many, often creative ways. One typical contractual form is **licensing,** under which the initial firm contracts to have a foreign firm produce and sell its product in return for a licensing fee (and according to terms that attempt to assure quality control and protection of the technology involved). This kind of venture is common in high-tech businesses, where the technology is proprietary and the initiating firm chooses to avoid investing overseas because of the expense or other limitations. Another contractual form is **franchising,** under which the initiating firm sells the use of its name to the foreign franchisee, who in turn sells the product or service to customers overseas. This is very common for hotel chains such as Hilton, Marriott, Sheraton, etc., and restaurants such as McDonald's and Burger King.

A third contractual form is the **turnkey venture,** under which the initiating firm agrees to bring into operation a factory, mine, or other capital project, then manage it for a specified time period, and finally "turn over the keys" to a host-country firm or government. Turnkey ventures are common in large electric power plant projects in less developed countries and in Eastern Europe. A company such as General Electric or Westinghouse contracts with the host government to construct the power plant and operate it for three to five years. During that period the company trains local managers, scientists, and workers to operate the plant, so that they can run it independently after the turnkey period ends. (Exxon's coal mine in Colombia, discussed in Chapter 11, is a good example of a turnkey venture.)

The third category of foreign investment is the **joint venture,** which is a form of direct investment in which the initiating firm shares ownership with one or more partners. This partner(s) may be another international contractor, a local firm in the host country, or even the host government. Joint ventures are the most common ownership form for foreign ventures in Eastern Europe, and they are also common in less developed countries where the host government demands local participation in ownership. During the past few years, joint ventures have become a frequent form of strategic alliance (see page 49) between firms in industrial countries, too.

The final form of foreign involvement is **wholly owned direct investment,** in which the initiating firm establishes an affiliate overseas and owns the entire venture. The investment may take place through establishment of a new business in the host country, or it may involve purchase of an existing business there.[11] This topic is the subject of Chapter 4.

The international contractor may exploit its competitive advantages through multiple vehicles in various markets—ownership of a factory or office in each country is unnecessary. Hilton Hotels earns a substantial return on its business activities in different countries, even though most of the hotels in the chain worldwide are franchised out to independent hotel owners. Similarly, pharmaceuticals manufacturers routinely contract with other firms in their industry to produce their drugs under "tolling" agreements, which are essentially licenses to manufacture ethical drugs using the proprietor firm's name. The Dow Chemical pharmaceuticals plant in Argentina formulates drugs for Eli Lilly, Brazil's Astra, and other multinational drug companies; in other countries, Dow contracts out to other firms to produce its products in the same manner. The correct strategy depends on the entire competitive position of the company in all of its markets.

Overall, the firm needs to take stock of its own competitive advantages, plus those of its competitors, and select a strategy that emphasizes its strengths and minimizes the impact of its weaknesses. The multinational firm must consider the strategies of its competitors not only in its home market but also in every relevant foreign market. And finally, managers must realize that no matter how strong the competitive advantage, other firms are likely to chip away at it, so that ultimately the advantage will be gone.[12] For a firm to be competitive in the long run, it must regularly review its competitive position in its various markets and products and then adjust its strategy to take advantage of environmental and internal changes.

An Example: Caterpillar, Inc.

Consider the example of Caterpillar, Inc. (or Cat), the world's leading manufacturer of earthmoving machinery, the second largest producer of diesel engines, and a major competitor in other construction equipment markets. Because of the major decline in growth of its main business segments during the 1980s, the firm's recent performance has been very shaky. Over the period 1982 to 1984, Caterpillar lost almost $US 1 billion, along with a reduction in market share in most key countries to its primary competitor, Komatsu. Cat's $10.4 billion of sales in 1988 still place the firm at the top of its industry, and 1988 profits were a record $US 616 million. However, the competitive challenge of Komatsu, and the stagnant market for construction equipment around the world (due to an estimated 40 percent greater production capacity compared to worldwide demand in 1989), both create conditions that require well-planned corporate strategy for Cat. This section describes how Caterpillar could utilize the competitive strategy approach that was detailed above.

First, Cat needs to take stock of its competitive advantages and those of its major competitors. Table 2–6 shows estimated global market shares of the main earthmoving equipment manufacturers in 1984. Although other firms have significant market shares, Komatsu clearly is the main competitor for Caterpillar, and our discussion focuses only on that rivalry.

From the list of competitive advantages presented in Table 2–4, Caterpillar is generally perceived to possess a highly respected brand name, due to its long history of providing the industry's *highest-quality equipment* and offering the *best after-sale service*.[13] Relative to multinational competitors such as Komatsu, Fiat-Allis, and J. I. Case, it does *not* possess any particular economies of scale in production, financing, or other areas that the other competitors lack. (However, relative to local competitors in many countries, Cat does possess some of these advantages.) Caterpillar's long experience in international business may give its managers an advantage over rivals in dealing with problems in a wide variety of countries.

Technology is considered to be fairly standardized in this industry, as in its sister automotive industry. However, Komatsu and Caterpillar both are investing hundreds of millions of dollars each year in factory automation, flexible production facilities, and new-product generation. Caterpillar calls its efforts to upgrade manufacturing activities the Plant with a Future (PWAF) program. This program seeks not only to achieve just-in-time inventory control and to employ robots where appropriate, but also to provide worldwide information within the company about product and parts availability and feedback from customers.

Strategic Alliances

Strategic alliances have become very popular vehicles for pursuing domestic and international business among large international contractors during the late 1980s and early 1990s. These alliances range from simple licensing agreements to complicated coproduction ventures with management contracts and crosslicensing accords tied together. A strategic alliance is any cooperative agreement between firms that results in some continuing business link between them—for example, a joint venture (such as the NUMMI project owned by General Motors and Toyota described in the case following Chapter 12) or just a joint marketing agreement in which each partner agrees to sell the other firm's products in its own market (as in the discontinued venture between AT&T and Olivetti, in which AT&T agreed to sell Olivetti's personal computers in the North American market and Olivetti agreed to sell AT&T's telephone switching gear in the European market).

Strategic alliances generally are formed when each partner has a weakness in its own ability to carry out a specific business activity, and the partner firm can compensate for that weakness. For example, General Electric Corporation formed a joint venture to produce aircraft engines with the French company, Snecma. This alliance enabled Snecma to obtain state-of-the-art technology and ongoing access to GE innovations, while permitting GE to obtain access to European government-owned airlines (such as Airbus Industrie) that otherwise would have purchased their engines from local suppliers.

Very often the weakness that leads a company to join in a strategic alliance is availability of capital. The fixed costs of undertaking many high-tech industrial projects in the 1990s are so great that individual firms have been seeking partners to share R&D costs as well as operating costs for large production facilities. The European computer consortium, Esprit, was formed so that the eight member companies could pool their financial resources and achieve a level of investment needed to compete with IBM and other non-European giants.

Strategic alliances are not a panacea for international contractors, since such cooperative agreements open the firm's management skills and technology to the partner to some degree—and the partner is generally a competitor in other contexts. Thus, the agreement between AT&T and NEC in 1990, to exchange some of AT&T's computer-assisted design technology for NEC's advanced logic chips, establishes a base of cooperation between these two firms that are and will remain competitors in other key computer and telecommunications products. The agreements between various of the major auto producers around the world do not preclude intense competition among them. Sharing key technology or management skills must be evaluated carefully, or the partner may later outcompete its former ally in another important market. ■

TABLE 2-6

Estimated 1984 Market
Shares for Earthmoving
Machinery (in percent)

	United States	Worldwide
Caterpillar, Inc.	36%	34%
Komatsu Ltd.	4	14
J. I. Case	10	6
Deere & Co.	9	6
Clark-Volvo	4	6
Dresser Industries	4	4
Fiat-Allis	2	3
All others	31	27

Komatsu has moved aggressively into overseas production, including factories in the United States, as well as into industrial partnerships with many foreign firms for the purpose of developing new products via licensing and coproduction. Thus, among the relevant competitors, Cat and Komatsu each have some technological advantages based on their new products and processes that are continuing to evolve.

Given Caterpillar's much greater international business volume, with 30 plants in a dozen countries and sales offices and distributors in most of the rest of the world, the firm undoubtedly has a competitive advantage based on *international distribution.*[14]

Finally, some outside observers (e.g., Peters and Waterman, *In Search of Excellence*) believe that Cat maintains a significantly better internal work environment and a harmony between blue- and white-collar workers that leads to greater productivity than that of other firms. This may be true relative to U.S.-based competitors, but with respect to Komatsu, "people management" probably is not a significant strength for Caterpillar, and it may even be a disadvantage.

The main competitive disadvantages facing Cat may be the firm's large investments in inventory and in plant and equipment, which continue to weigh down its financial position during the protracted slump in the global construction industry. The firm has cut back on physical facilities, eliminating almost a dozen plants during the 1980s, and also on manpower, to a workforce of about 54,000 people in 1989. This is a disadvantage particularly relative to Komatsu, which contracts out for about 70 percent of its parts and components—while Cat makes about two thirds of such inputs within the firm. The slump in worldwide growth does not press Komatsu to cut its own production so much as to cut purchases from outside suppliers.

Having weighed the competitive advantages and disadvantages in this context, Cat next must decide which competitive strengths it wants to obtain. According to company statements in the late 1980s, the desired key advantages are more flexible manufacturing and more offshore production (to reduce exposure to exchange-rate fluctuations and to reduce vulnerability to U.S. conditions in general).

The first goal is being pursued through the PWAF program, in which Cat has invested more than $US 1 billion from 1986 through 1989. The new technology that has been developed is enabling Cat to achieve just-in-time inventory management and to keep worldwide track of parts, inventories, customer demands, and other crucial information. The second goal also is being pursued, with a consistently increasing willingness to contract out for components and to source offshore.

After analyzing competitive advantages and disadvantages and obtaining the additional advantages that appear most crucial to success, Caterpillar must decide how to utilize its advantages in the markets where it competes. Large possibilities still exist to reduce production costs by moving parts of the production process offshore to low-wage countries. The purchase of Solar Turbine Corporation in 1982 enabled Cat to expand into that type of engine; perhaps additional applications of the turbine engine can be developed into new markets or segments.

In each aspect of the new strategy development, Cat needs to judge the likely reactions of its rivals in order to estimate the effectiveness of its own steps. If Komatsu is able to compete with low prices and high-quality products because of the dollar's appreciation relative to the yen, then Cat may choose to compete more strongly in the Japanese market (where Caterpillar already has a large joint venture with Mitsubishi). If American rivals face even greater difficulties than Caterpillar does, then perhaps some of their complementary operations could be acquired at very low prices. If Eastern Europe develops into a major new market, then Cat needs to try to beat Komatsu into that market at the outset.[15]

This sketch (developed by the authors) of possible alternatives facing Caterpillar is intended simply to illustrate the use of the proposed analytical framework. Similar reasoning could be used for any large or small firm competing at the international level; the framework used here provides an approach to strategic decision making.

CONCLUSIONS

The international contractor is unquestionably the central actor in international business today. International firms function as major vehicles for transfer of technology and other knowledge, international financial flows, and exports/imports of goods and services. These firms include huge manufacturers such as IBM and Dow Chemical—but they also include service-sector companies such as Hilton Hotels, Citibank, and Merrill Lynch. In addition, many smaller firms are INCs in the sense that they export, contract with overseas partners, and sometimes even own affiliates in other countries. Much of the strategy designed for the large multinationals is relevant to these smaller firms as well.

The theory of the international contractor is being advanced by analysts along many lines. Competitive advantage and internalization are two concepts that have been widely discussed in the recent literature. Both concepts recognize the highly imperfect competition that characterizes international (and domestic) business throughout the world. Both offer perspectives to the manager for capitalizing on the firm's relative strengths in competition with rival firms. Although this is not the only view of the INC that has merit, it does offer a wide range of applications to decision makers.

Given the perspective outlined in this chapter, we can analyze decisions made in international business as part of the competitive strategy of the firm. In the next few chapters, we will consider some of the environmental conditions facing firms in international business. Then we will look at competitive strategies for decision makers in the various functional areas.

QUESTIONS

1. What are the important differences between a multinational enterprise and a domestic company? Why are these differences important?

2. Explain the competitive advantages of Caterpillar, Inc. What strategy do you think the company should follow during the current severe downturn in farm and construction equipment sales?

3. Why are the largest multinational enterprises concentrated in a few industries such as petroleum and motor vehicles? Why are the most profitable MNEs (measured in terms of, for example, profits per share) *not* concentrated in any one or two industries?

4. How can a company such as Apple Computer Corporation best take advantage of its competitive advantages in foreign markets? Discuss opportunities in both developed countries and LDCs.

5. Should a chemical company such as Dow Chemical Corporation internalize its supply of oil for making petrochemicals by entering the oil business? What other choices does Dow have to ensure competitive access to the raw materials it needs for production around the world?

6. What competitive advantages are possessed by Citibank? How can it use those advantages in international banking competition?

7. Perez Trading Company is a small Los Angeles-based firm that serves as an exporter for several small U.S. manufacturing companies and as an importer for several more U.S. firms. Almost all of the firm's business is done with Latin American customers or suppliers. The only foreign activities that Perez has are sales offices in Mexico and Peru. Is this a multinational company? What do you think are Perez's competitive advantages? Do you regard its 20 years' experience in this business as a competitive advantage?

8. Why are about half of the world's largest multinational enterprises based in the United States? Does this country possess some advantage that its companies obtain automatically? Is that advantage changing over time?

9. What characteristics give companies such as Sheraton Hotels and Holiday Inns the ability to compete in foreign markets? Do you regard these companies as MNEs?

10. Given the nationalizations of foreign oil companies by governments in OPEC (a cartel of Oil Producing and Exporting Countries) during the past two decades, do you expect that Exxon, Texaco, and other companies will no longer be multinational in the future? What are these companies doing to maintain their international operations?

REFERENCES

Alchain, Armen, and Harold Demsetz. "Production, Information Costs, and Economic Organization." *American Economic Review,* December 1972.

Bartlett, Christopher, and Susan Ehrlich. "Caterpillar Inc.: George Schaefer Takes Charge," Harvard Business School case #9-390-036 (April 23, 1990).

Buckley, Peter, and Mark Casson. *The Economic Theory of the Multinational Enterprise.* London: Macmillan, 1985.

Casson, Mark. "Transactions Costs and the Theory of the Multinational Enterprise." In *New Perspectives in International Business,* ed. Alan Rugman. London: Croom Helm, 1982.

———. "Internalization Theory and Beyond," paper presented at Academy of International Business annual meeting, Toronto, October 12, 1990.

Caves, Richard. *Multinational Enterprise and Economic Analysis.* Cambridge, England: Cambridge University Press, 1982.

Davidson, William, and Donald McFetridge. "International Technology Transactions and the Theory of the Firm." *Journal of Industrial Economics,* March 1984.

Davidson, William, and José de la Torre. *Managing the Global Corporation.* New York: McGraw-Hill, 1989.

Dunning, John. "Trade, Location of Economic Activity, and the Multinational Enterprise: A Search for an Eclectic Approach." In *The International Allocation of Economic Activity,* ed. Bertil Ohlin. New York: Holmes & Meier, 1977.

Grosse, Robert. *The Theory of Foreign Direct Investment.* University of South Carolina Essays in International Business, December 1981.

———. *Competitive Advantages and Multinational Enterprises.* University of Miami Discussion Papers in International Business, no. 84-7, November 1984.

———. "An Imperfect Competition Theory of the MNE." *Journal of International Business Studies,* Spring 1985.

Hennart, Jean-François. *The Multinational Enterprise.* Ann Arbor: University of Michigan Press, 1982.

Horst, Thomas. "Firm and Industry Determinants of the Decision to Invest Abroad: An Empirical Study." *Review of Economics and Statistics,* 1972.

Hout, Thomas; Michael Porter; and Eileen Rudder. "How Global Companies Win Out." *Harvard Business Review,* September-October 1982.

Kindleberger, Charles. *Direct Investment Abroad.* New Haven, Conn.: Yale University Press, 1969.

Lall, Sanjaya. "Monopolistic Advantages and Foreign Involvement by U.S. Manufacturing Industry." *Oxford Economic Papers,* March 1980.

Ouchi, William. *Theory Z.* New York: Basic Books, 1979.

Peters, Thomas J., and Robert H. Waterman. *In Search of Excellence.* New York: Harper & Row, 1982.

Porter, Michael. *Competitive Strategy.* New York: Free Press, 1980.

———. *The Competitive Advantage of Nations.* New York: Free Press, 1990.

Rugman, Alan. *Inside the Multinationals.* London: Croom Helm, 1981.

Swedenborg, B. *The Multinational Operations of Swedish Firms: An Analysis of Determinants and Effects.* Stockholm: Industrial Institute for Economic and Social Research, 1979.

Vernon, Raymond. "International Investment and International Trade in the Product Cycle." *Quarterly Journal of Economics,* 1966.

———. *Storm over the Multinationals.* Cambridge, Mass.: Harvard University Press, 1977.

Vernon, Raymond, and Louis T. Wells, Jr. *Manager in the International Economy.* Englewood Cliffs, N.J.: Prentice Hall, 1986. (5th ed.)

Watson, Craig. "Counter-Competition Abroad to Protect Home Markets." *Harvard Business Review,* January-February, 1982.

Williamson, Oliver. *Markets and Hierarchies: Analysis and Antitrust Implications.* New York: Free Press, 1975.

_____. "The Modern Corporation: Origins, Evolution, Attributes." *Journal of Economic Literature,* December 1981.

NOTES

[1]See, for example, U.S. International Trade Commission, *The Internationalization of the Automobile Industry and its Effects on the U.S. Automobile Industry* (Washington, D.C.: USITC, June 1985), p. 5.

[2]Some of these ventures are discussed in Kenichi Ohmae, "The Global Logic of Strategic Alliances," *Harvard Business Review* (March–April 1989); and in Deigan Morris and Michael Hergert, "Trends in International Collaborative Agreements," *Columbia Journal of World Business* (Summer 1987).

[3]Vernon, Raymond, and Louis T. Wells, Jr., *Manager in the International Economy,* 5th ed. (Englewood Cliffs, N.J.: Prentice Hall, 1986), p. 2.

[4]Of course, the firm should periodically review performance and revise its competitive strategy when appropriate. This iterative process of strategy formulation is discussed in Chapter 5.

[5]Some competitive advantages are not *firm specific,* but general to firms of some particular type. For example, MNEs based in the United States had a competitive advantage in the 1960s, when the U.S. dollar was overvalued, because they had access to cheaper financing than foreign firms. Also, firms from Switzerland have been relatively unharmed by world wars, since Switzerland has been consistently neutral in wartime. Along another dimension, many economies of scale are realized by very large firms; such economies are not limited to just one firm in an industry or country.

[6]M. Wilkins, *The Emergence of Multinational Enterprise* (Cambridge, Mass.: Harvard University Press, 1970).

[7]Internalization also refers to bringing an "externality" that markets fail to price from the outside into a firm. For example, governments try to force pollution control costs, previously an externality, onto polluting firms. The firm may use internalization to bring market power within its command by acquiring competitors and then raising prices to monopolized customers. Thus, internalization does not always connote improvement of economic welfare or efficiency.

[8]It is interesting to note that the great vertical integration of the oil industry has been reduced by the participation of OPEC countries at the oil-producing stage; those countries are beginning to integrate downstream into processing, and eventually into the marketing of final products.

[9]Conceivably, the use of long-term contracts, if they are enforced, could offer the firms the same level of assurance of supply and negate the need for ownership of the raw material (i.e., internalization of the source of supply).

[10]Watson (1982) discusses this idea of challenging international competitors in their home markets as a competitive strategy. He concludes that forcing your competitors to compete actively in their home markets will reduce their ability to put resources into competing in your home market.

[11]Generally, direct investment is discussed as meaning investment in production of a product or service in the host country. However, investment in a sales

office in the host country through which products imported from the home country are sold also constitutes direct investment.

[12]Following the international product cycle for any product demonstrates the stages during which proprietary technology, strong advertising and effective distribution channels, and low-cost production are the key competitive advantages. See, for example, Vernon and Wells (1986).

[13]This view appears repeatedly in the literature, e.g., in the two-case sequence by Stephen Allen, "The Construction Machinery Industry," and "Caterpillar and Komatsu in 1987," in Davidson and de la Torre (1989), pp. 69–107.

[14]This argument is made, for example, in Hout et al. (1982).

[15]Caterpillar had beaten its competitors into contracting for construction of the Soviet natural gas pipeline from Siberia to Western Europe in 1981. When the U.S. government revoked Cat's export license, about $200 million of sales were lost directly and an estimated additional $500 million of follow-on sales were lost—all to Komatsu. This "political risk" may continue to haunt Caterpillar in efforts to build business in Eastern Europe.

Mom & Pop's Restaurants, Inc.

Introduction

Sitting at his personal computer one evening in 1990, Pop Westerfield was thinking about the growing food business that he had built up over the past 10 years and that constantly seemed to present him with new, major problems. Just last week, the Burger King restaurant chain had introduced stuffed potatoes and a new salad bar in all of its restaurants throughout his territory of Illinois, Indiana, and southern Michigan. McDonald's was likewise expanding its menu to compete more and more with traditional restaurants such as Mom & Pop's. Pop was beginning to think that he should consider entering some new areas that were not as highly competitive for restaurant business, such as nearby Canada.

The Existing Business

The Westerfields had entered the restaurant business with a small, unassuming operation in Homewood, Illinois, in 1982. Pop, at age 33, had decided that he was unwilling to continue at his job with a large automotive parts firm in Chicago, given the unabated crisis in the industry since 1973. Even while growing up, he had had the desire to open a small business, and restaurants looked like a suitable environment for his easygoing manner and his enjoyment of good food. Every day, while commuting to work in the late 1970s, Pop had passed an attractive family restaurant at the corner of Halsted Avenue and Third Street in Homewood. When a For Sale sign appeared in the window one day in 1980, Pop began to consider the possibility of taking over the business. In early 1981, he finally decided to jump at the opportunity. After a few weeks of fact-finding concerning the owner's asking price, suppliers, the costs of the foods needed to supply his restaurant, taxes, and so forth, Pop made an offer for the building, which was accepted.

The initial "strategy," if it can be called that, was to serve very good meals in traditional American style at reasonable prices. No advertising was undertaken, except for installing the new sign proclaiming "Mom & Pop's Restaurant" (Mrs. Westerfield had agreed to join him in this entrepreneurial venture). Even in the first few months, business picked up enough to pay the bills and generate a small operating profit for the firm. When construction of a new roadway nearby took place in 1982, Mom & Pop's found itself the beneficiary of twice as much traffic on Halsted Avenue and of twice as many customers. By the end of 1984, Mom suggested that they look into the possibility of opening up another res-

---

This case was written by Professor Robert Grosse in 1987 as a basis for class discussion (revised 1990).

taurant to take advantage of their apparently successful formula of simple, home-cooked meals, medium prices, and quiet atmosphere.

After deliberating on this suggestion for a few weeks, Mom and Pop decided to pursue the expansion. Pop hired a realtor friend to check out the availability of corner properties within 10 miles of the initial building, either to buy or rent. Then, armed with a list of four possible locations, the Westerfields chose the one that offered the least commuting problems from their home and from the existing business. The second venture followed the same path as the first, with almost immediate moderate success. By 1987, Mom and Pop had opened three more restaurants—one near their son's college in South Bend, Indiana, and the other two through an arrangement with a trusted friend who lived in Detroit (both of these restaurants were located in the suburbs of Detroit).

In early 1990, the Westerfields owned six restaurants using the Mom & Pop name, all of which were in the three locations noted above. The last one was started in late 1989, located in a new shopping center just off Interstate 94 near Skokie, Illinois. (Another start-up had failed due to last-minute difficulties in agreeing on the rental space in a new building in Chicago.) At this point, the firm employed 9 full-time salaried staff members and about 40 wage-earning waiters, waitresses, cooks, busboys, and other helpers. The firm's financial statements appear below.

Luckily, Pop had found a capable office manager to keep his books and watch over the daily activities of the restaurant chain. He himself, therefore, had more time to think about the future of the business and about the problems and opportunities that arose frequently. The threat of increased competition from the large, well-financed hamburger chains struck him as serious enough to look into alternative markets for long-run survival. The near failure of the second restaurant when road construction almost eliminated customers' access to the building also made him realize the desirability of diversifying into more locations. While neither of the Westerfields was willing to move far from home, they both thought that southern Canada along the border with Michigan would provide a possible starting point for expanding into that country. Pop's main concern was choosing a method of dealing with one or several restaurants that were so distant from the existing businesses and, another nontrivial factor, so expensive to open and operate.

The Canadian Situation

At the time that Mr. Westerfield began to look seriously into a Canadian venture, that country's government had recently reversed its policy toward foreign firms. During the previous decade, Canada had required that all foreign direct investment projects obtain permission from the Foreign Investment Review Agency. This agency was charged with evaluating the impact of proposed investments on Canadian income, employment, and ownership of the Canadian economy. A number of projects were rejected during that period. After several years of serious recession in the early 1980s, Canada's government decided to switch its policy in favor of an open attitude, seeking to attract foreign direct investment and stimulate economic growth. As part of the new strategy, the agency itself had its name changed to Investment Canada. All of this meant that Mr. Westerfield discovered a very responsive Canadian government when he inquired about Canadian laws and rules pertaining to the opening of a new restaurant.

Given the liberal government policies, Mom & Pop's needed primarily to decide on a type of venture to establish and on a location for it. The range of possibilities included a new restaurant, set up in a new location; purchase of an existing restaurant; creation of a joint venture with a local partner who knew the market; franchise of the firm's name and use of proprietary food preparations; and some combination of these choices. A sketch of the costs and benefits of each choice is given below.

A *green field* (or *de novo*) *investment* would require site selection, major financing, legal assistance to comply with local laws, and employment of basically all-new staff. From his previous experiences, Pop knew that the start-up cost of the restaurant would be in the neighborhood of $150,000. The Canadian location might offer somewhat lower costs, but dealing with unknown contingencies arising from the new environment would probably leave the total cost about the same. None of the current employees was willing to move to the Windsor, Canada, area (across the river from Detroit), although the Westerfields' oldest son would be a possibility after his college graduation in another year. There appeared to be no significant limitations on importing any needed equipment or food into Canada, though this point needed to be checked in more detail once the specific location was chosen. The tax situation really confused Mr. Westerfield, but he had heard repeatedly that Canadian taxes were similar to U.S. taxes and that the U.S. government would not double-tax his Canadian earnings.

An *acquisition* of an existing Canadian restaurant would cost somewhat less than the new venture, but it still involved many of the other problems. The lower financial cost and the potential availability of existing staff were very attractive to Pop. However, the purchase of an existing facility would bring with it the problems as well as the benefits of the previous business. Given their experience with acquisitions in the past, neither of the Westerfields was overly concerned with the problems likely to be involved.

A *joint venture* was an approach that they had never tried. By finding a local partner, the Westerfields could reduce all the costs of doing business in Canada. The drawbacks of this strategy are that there is a real risk that the partner may not be a good businessperson or a reliable one and that the earnings from the venture have to be shared with the partner. Management of the joint venture could be a troubling issue, since one of the partners would have to trust the other to run it.

The least costly possibility for entering the Canadian market would be to *franchise* out the name Mom & Pop's, as well as some of the proprietary parts of the business, to a local firm. In this case, Mom & Pop's would allow the franchisee to use the restaurant name and would also help the franchisee to set up and operate the facility. The full set of responsibilities (and sharing of revenues) would be determined in negotiations with the franchisee.

As a last possibility, the Westerfields could try some *combination* of the other strategies. For example, they could set up a joint venture and sell some of the proprietary food preparations to it on a fee basis. Or they could agree on a franchising operation but take some ownership position in that firm. The number of combinations is limited only by the imagination of the Westerfields (and, of course, to some extent by Canadian laws).

Without going into a detailed capital budgeting analysis, Pop felt that it would be best to compare the good and bad points of each alternative and choose the one that seemed best, on balance.

MOM & POP'S RESTAURANTS, INC.
Balance Sheet, Year-End 1989
(in $U.S. 000)

Assets		Liabilities	
Cash	215	Notes payable	643
Marketable securities	68	Accounts payable	274
Accounts receivable	47	Taxes due	59
Inventory	180	Long-term debt	28
Fixed assets	1,302	Retained earnings	217
Total Assets	1,812	Shareholders' equity	591
		Total Liabilities	1,812

MOM & POP'S RESTAURANTS, INC.
Income Statement, 1989
(in $U.S. 000)

Sales		3,152
Cost of goods sold		
Materials	1,051	
Labor	988	
Utilities	213	
Depreciation	130	
Gross profit		770
Selling expense	249	
Overhead	296	
Interest expense	67	
Net income before tax		158
Income taxes	47	
Net income after tax		111

PART

2

From New Jersey to Jakarta, Coca-Cola is truly an
international product.
Arthur Meyerson Photography, Inc./The Coca-Cola Company

MANAGER IN THE WORLD ECONOMY

Busy ports like this one in Seattle, Washington make it increasingly easy for exporters and importers to operate.
Courtesy of the Port of Seattle

3

International Trade

This chapter discusses the economics of international trade. First, patterns of international trade since World War II are described. Then a number of theories are offered to help explain why trade patterns exist and why they differ between countries and products. These theories can also be used to understand why firms export and import as part of their business activities. The main goals of the chapter are to:

1. Demonstrate patterns of trade to give an idea of which countries and which products have been most important during the past half-century.

2. Explain why these patterns exist, based mainly on the theories of comparative cost advantage and the international product cycle.

3. Point out aspects of international trade that do not fit these theories very well and note some new concepts that attempt to deal with these aspects.

4. Show criteria that company managers can use to make international business decisions involving trade—specifically to show how trade fits into the activities of the INC.

INTRODUCTION

The way in which international trade fits within the total range of international business activities has shifted dramatically in the post-World War II period. Early in this century, exports and imports, typically between unrelated firms, constituted the vast majority of intercountry business. At present, however, intra-MNE trade dominates international trade, and foreign-owned production is even larger. This chapter seeks to illuminate the role of trade in the new context.

This first section presents some measures of trade flows and sketches some of the underlying influences that have caused the flows to grow and shift as they do. Then the most fundamental theory of international trade, the comparative cost view is laid out. The third section explains the international product cycle, a more recent view that focuses on the demand side and the technology factor. The fourth section discusses some of the important discrepancies between the theories and actual trade patterns—issues such as the Leontief paradox and the crosshauling of exports of the same type of product in both directions between two countries. The final section reviews the material and relates it specifically to the manager's concerns.

Let us begin with a look at some empirical evidence on trade patterns. Table 3–1a presents a number of comparisons between international trade flows earlier in the post-World War II period and those that have been occurring most recently. Ignoring the cost of insurance and freight, which causes the total figures for exports and imports to be slightly different, some definite trends can be seen. For instance, the industrialized countries maintained a fairly even balance in their aggregate trade flows up until the 1970s. By 1980, these countries showed an annual trade deficit (i.e., imports greater than exports) of about 10 percent with respect to the rest of the world, primarily the oil-exporting countries. The United States in particular maintained a surplus of exports over imports until the recent period, and since 1970 has incurred a substantial deficit in its trade account. Oil-exporting less developed countries (LDCs) have consis-

TABLE 3–1a

World Trade Data (in billions of U.S. dollars)

	1950	1960	1970	1980	1985	1989
World						
Exports*	57.9	115.5	284.7	1868.3	1784.5	2891.7
Imports†	59.3	121.0	298.4	1923.4	1879.3	2974.6
Industrial Countries						
Exports	36.4	83.9	220.3	1239.4	1258.5	2127.3
Imports	39.8	85.5	227.2	1369.6	1361.4	2238.8
Oil-exporting LDCs						
Exports	4.2	7.2	17.1	296.5	143.8	127.6‡
Imports	2.3	5.3	9.6	134.3	110.7	103.8‡
United States						
Exports	10.3	20.6	43.2	220.8	213.1	364.0
Imports	9.6	16.4	42.7	257.0	361.6	492.9
Nonoil LDCs						
Exports	17.6	24.7	46.5	312.0	352.3	621.2
Imports	17.3	30.1	60.5	399.7	387.7	640.5

*Export values are free on board (FOB).
†Import values include cost of insurance and freight (CIF).
‡ 1988 data.
Source: International Monetary Fund, International Financial Statistics, Supplement on Trade Statistics, 1988 and 1990.

tently exported much greater value than they have imported, but of course the situation since the 1973 OPEC oil embargo and price hike is much more striking—exports were 121 percent greater than imports in 1980, for example. Then, with the drastic oil price decline in 1985, oil-exporting LDCs shifted back toward the historical situation, maintaining a 29 percent trade surplus.

Table 3–1b describes the trade flows by region for 1988. Note that the European Community is the largest trading group in the list. The (now formerly) communist countries accounted for only about 2 percent of total exports to the rest of the world.

Table 3–2 presents another look at 20th-century international trade, this time comparing the volume of trade in various highly aggregated industrial sectors.

TABLE 3–1b

World Exports and Imports, 1988 (millions of U.S. dollars)

						Imports into/Exports from				
	U.S.	Japan	EEC	Germany	U.K.	Indust. Countr.	Oil-Exp. Countr.	Non-oil LDCs	Comm.	Total
U.S.	–	42,267	79,582	16,583	19,351	212,490	15,401	110,312	3,377	341,581
Japan	93,168	–	49,869	16,150	11,569	168,183	12,857	90,587	4,237	275,864
EEC	88,714	24,163	625,751	129,774	99,374	851,677	39,189	151,071	20,318	1,062,300
Germany	27,420	8,102	167,936	–	31,389	255,809	9,618	44,108	8,588	318,123
U.K.	18,740	4,190	66,846	17,355	–	106,028	8,876	24,333	1,721	140,957
Indus. Count.	281,325	92,499	866,782	196,893	157,154	1,499,800	75,569	396,215	38,266	2,009,800
Oil-Exporters	23,637	28,472	36,382	6,010	3,285	90,491	4,320	36,155	357	131,324
Non-oil LDCs	154,041	62,984	152,048	41,995	25,750	404,576	26,277	166,319	36,064	633,236
Communist	907	3,526	20,777	5,497	1,941	31,167	1,689	32,234	–	65,090
Total	459,910	187,483	1,084,300	250,554	189,349	2,037,600	108,600	646,164	74,687	–

Note: Data include freight and insurance costs, (c.i.f.).

TABLE 3–2

Development of World Exports between 1960 and 1987

	1960	1968	1970	1973	1975	1980	1985	1987	1988	1989
World Exports (billions of U.S. dollars, FOB)										
Total	129	240	313	575	875	1989	1936	2490	2702	2891
Agricultural products	40	54	64	120	150	299	268	340	357	371
Minerals	22	41	52	96	207	569	425	366	388	405
Manufacturers	65	141	192	348	501	1095	1204	1735	1909	2061
Other	2	4	5	11	17	26	39	49	48	54
Percentage of Total Trade										
Total	100	100	100	100	100	100	100	100	100	100
Agricultural products	31	23	20	21	17	15	14	14	13	13
Minerals	17	17	17	17	24	29	22	15	14	14
Manufacturers	50	59	61	61	57	55	62	70	71	71
Other	2	1	2	2	2	1	2	1	2	2

Source: General Agreement on Tariffs and Trade, 1987/88 (Geneva:1988); and GATT Secretariat Press Release, March 22, 1990.

Notice the huge shift in the composition of trade in the 1960s, toward manufactured goods, and in the 1970s toward minerals (especially oil) and away from other industries. Trade in minerals accounted for about 17 percent of the total in 1970, but for about 30 percent of the total in 1980, after the two major OPEC price hikes. Manufacturing, in comparison, fell from about 61 percent of total exports in 1970 to about 55 percent of the total in 1980. The original relationship was approximately reestablished in 1985, due to the oil price decline.

Both of these tables point up an aspect of international trade that is usually de-emphasized in discussions of the reasons for trading and the distribution of benefits from trade: one fundamental basis for international trade is the **availability of natural resources** in each country. Any nation that possesses known and accessible deposits of oil can export it, while other nations must either import oil or utilize substitute products (such as coal or other energy sources). The fact that a small number of nations possess most of the world's known and accessible oil deposits gives them a near-monopoly position as producers; and in the 1970s they used that position to raise prices and curtail output—leading to the large jump in LDC exports and mineral exports in Tables 3–1 and 3–2. In the 1980s, however, both prices and quantities of oil sold in world markets were declining, due to the demand curtailment and substitution effects encouraged by the increases in oil prices. Chapters 8 and 24 explore some additional aspects of the oil industry and its relations to international business; here, we are mainly concerned with oil's surge to a substantial percentage of total world trade (about 16 percent in 1980). Thus, a very important basis for a country's export/import activities is resource availability.

The next section continues to look at trade from a macroeconomic perspective, focusing on cost conditions that affect trade patterns. Then we present some additional rationales for trade and empirical examples before considering how the decision maker can utilize these perspectives in operating a firm.

THEORIES OF INTERNATIONAL TRADE–COMPARATIVE ADVANTAGE

Among the various views of the underlying *reasons* for trade, the cost-based theory has been developed extensively over more than two centuries, and a number of additional views have been offered to explain much of what it ignores. Anyone trying to understand the full set of reasons for the trade that takes place today should recognize at the outset that no single theory explains it all. Trade in different products occurs for different reasons. Trade in services differs in many ways from trade in tangible products. The theories collectively deal with all types of trade, and individually or collectively they can be used to construct policy, either for government regulators or for company managers.

The **comparative cost theory** of international trade, as developed by Ricardo and refined by Heckscher, Ohlin, and Samuelson,[1] states that *a country will gain from international trade if it specializes in the production and export of products that require relatively more input of its abundant production factors and if it imports products that require relatively more input of its scarce production factors.* If we assume that prices in each country are proportional to costs and that costs are determined by the availability of production factors, then the comparative advantage theory leads to these results.

Before proceeding with this very powerful concept, consider the simple bases that led to the above conclusions. The first step toward today's comparative cost theory was taken by Adam Smith in *The Wealth of Nations,* published in 1776. Smith reasoned that nations would gain from free trade, as long as each partner had an **absolute** cost **advantage** in producing some product. For example, if England and France both produce machinery and wine, the production possibilities, assuming complete specialization in *either* machinery *or* wine, are:

	Machinery		Wine
England	100*	or	40
France	30	or	120

*These quantities are units of output, using the same quantity of factors of production in each country.

This means that each country has an absolute advantage: England in the production of machinery, France in the production of wine. If there are no barriers to trade between these countries, then each can specialize in producing its advantageous product and trade with the other, thus obtaining more of both goods than before trade. (This result is explained in detail below for the case of comparative advantage.)

The second step toward today's comparative cost theory was taken by David Ricardo in *Principles of Political Economy and Taxation,* published in 1817. Ricardo showed that just as there are gains from trade under conditions of absolute advantage for each country, there are also gains from trade when one country has an absolute advantage in producing *both* products (as long as its *relative* superiority differs between products). His example involved England and Portugal producing cloth and wine, as shown in the table below. (The quantities are the outputs produced by the same amount of factor inputs for each product, assuming complete specialization in either cloth or wine.)*

	Wine		Cloth
England	80	or	90
Portugal	120	or	100

England can produce *either* 80 units of wine *or* 90 units of cloth.

Portugal has an *absolute* advantage in producing both products, but it has a relative or *comparative advantage* in producing wine. That is, Portugal's superiority in wine production is 120/80, or 1.5, while Portugal's superiority in cloth production is only 100/90, or 1.1. In the absence of trade barriers and as long as prices are proportional to costs, both England and Portugal can obtain more wine and cloth if Portugal specializes in producing (and exporting) wine and England does likewise with cloth.

Although 20th-century analysts have produced much more detailed assessments of the comparative cost theory, most of the newer work is still based fundamentally on Ricardo's insight.[2]

---

*This presentation reverses Ricardo's original example, in which he discusses work-hours of inputs needed to produce a given level of output. To avoid confusion, we consistently discuss units of output produced by a given amount of factor inputs.

ADDED DIMENSION

Companies and Comparative Advantage

Notice that the theory as presented so far relates to the benefits that a *country* would expect if it allowed international trade to take place. The company manager should view this information as a basis for choosing countries for production and export or countries for import sales. So, if it happens that lower costs of producing product A exist in country 1, then the manager should look at possibilities for producing that product there and for importing it into country 2, based on the theory of comparative advantage. Now let us see why this is true. ■

Comparative Cost Theory

The easiest way to demonstrate the main implications of this theory is with an example involving two countries, two products, and two factors of production. Let us assume that each country's availability of factors of production has already led to a set of domestic costs for producing each product (before trade takes place), and proceed from there.

Just to emphasize that country size is not necessarily important in determining relative costs, consider the United States and Honduras as examples. Let us work with a pair of standardized products that are clearly related to each country's relative endowment of production factors (e.g., agricultural land and physical capital).

For the sake of our discussion, the United States and Honduras are assumed to possess the characteristics depicted in Table 3–3 and Figure 3–1. In this situation, the United States is a substantially larger producer of both good A (*electrical appliances,* such as toasters, blenders, and hair dryers) and good B (*bananas*). Nonetheless, the United States and Honduras may both be able to consume more of each product under free trade than if they use only their domestic capabilities for production to satisfy their own consumption.

These two exhibits demonstrate the capabilities of each country to produce bananas and appliances, assuming that all available productive resources are utilized in these two industries. That is, if all of the people, machinery, and land in Honduras were used to produce bananas, they could produce 80,000 bushels of bananas per month. If all of these same productive resources were used to produce appliances, they could make 60,000 appliances per month. Finally, if some of the people, machinery, and land were used to produce each product, the trade-offs appear as points along the production possibilities curve (or as pairs of output possibilities in Table 3–3). Notice that the P-P curves in Figure 3–1 have been drawn as straight lines, implying that no diminishing returns occur as specialization increases. This also means that, with trade, each country will be induced to specialize completely in the production of one product. If diminishing returns did occur, then trade generally would lead to incomplete specialization in each country.[3] The actual points on the production possibilities curves where consumers in each country choose to purchase appliances and bananas are determined by their preferences, as reflected in indifference curves I_{Hon} and I_{US}.

TABLE 3–3

Production and Consumption Possibilities for the United States and Honduras *(in 000 bushels of bananas/month and 000 appliances/month)*

United States		Honduras	
Appliances	Bananas	Appliances	Bananas
200	0	60	0
160	20	50	15
120*	40*	40*	30*
100	55	30	45
40	80	20	60
0	100	0	80

*Equals initial production and consumption points.

Factors of Production

The theory of comparative advantage states that the production possibilities of each country arise from the productive capabilities of its factors of production. In our example, we can assume that banana production is more land intensive and that appliances production is more machinery intensive. Furthermore, we must assume that, in relative terms, Honduras possesses more fertile land compared to machinery and that the United States possesses more machinery relative to fertile land (or that the **relative productivities** of land and labor give each country the advantage shown).* Stated in measurable terms:

$$\frac{\text{Quantity of fertile land}_{Hon}}{\text{Quantity of available machinery}_{Hon}} > \frac{\text{Quantity of fertile land}_{US}}{\text{Quantity of available machinery}_{US}}$$

If these conditions do hold, then Table 3–1 is a reasonable representation of each country's possibilities. The United States, because of its larger endowments of all production factors, could produce more of either product than Honduras; but the United States is *relatively* more productive in appliances, and Honduras in bananas.

From our initial production/consumption points for each country, we can reason that trade will be beneficial if it leads each country to a final consumption point in which more of either or both goods is consumed, and less of neither. So the final consumption of appliances and bananas must be at least as much as each one of the entries in the table below. Remember that the choice of the initial consumption point is determined by consumers' tastes in each country, limited by the production possibilities. Gains from trade occur only if consumers in each country are able to consume on a higher indifference curve (or at least on the same curve), compared to pretrade conditions.[4]

Initial Consumption (and Production)

	A	B
United States	120	40
Honduras	40	30

Note: Appliances are measured in thousands of appliances per month; bananas are measured in thousands of bushels per month.

---

*Note that the United States can produce more of each good by specializing completely. This is *not* the same as absolute advantage, which occurs if the U.S. (or Honduras) can produce more of each good with the same amount of production inputs.

FIGURE 3–1

Production and Consumption Possibilities for the United States and Honduras

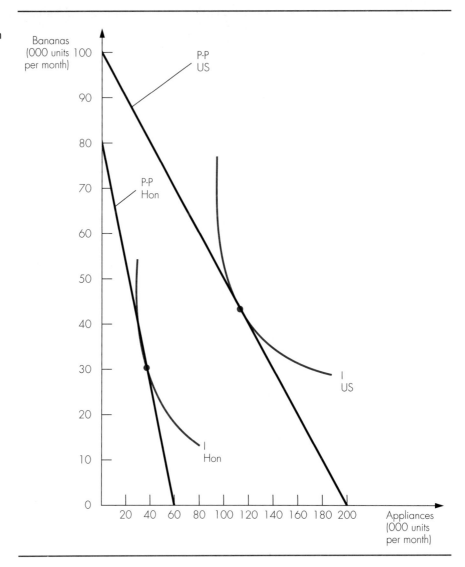

Now consider the relative efficiencies of each country in producing each good. If Honduras were to specialize completely in the production of bananas, the country could produce 80,000 bushels per month (that is, 80 units of 1,000 bushels/month each, and *no* appliances), compared to the U.S. capability to specialize and produce 100,000 bushels per month (i.e., 100 units). Similarly, by specializing in appliance production, Honduras could produce 60,000 appliances per month (and no bananas) and the United States could produce 200,000 appliances per month. Clearly, the United States possesses an *absolute* advantage in the production of both products. However, we can also see that each country has a *relative* (or comparative) advantage in the production of one product.

Assuming complete specialization in the production of *appliances,* the United States has an advantage of $200/60 = 3.33$ over Honduras. If complete specialization in *banana* production were carried out, the United States would maintain

ADDED DIMENSION

Incomplete Specialization

Rather than talk about extremes in which each country uses all of its productive resources in these two industries, one could talk about a given amount of resources (for example, 100 people, 100 acres of land, and 100 tons of machinery) in each country. Then, based on the productivity of these "production units," one can compare the relative efficiency of producing two products such as appliances and bananas in each country. In the case discussed here, the production unit in Honduras could produce either 60 appliances or 80 bushels of bananas during the month; that is, the same resources can produce only three fourths as many appliances as bushels of bananas. In the United States, the production unit could produce either 200 appliances or 100 bushels of bananas; the same amount of resources produces two times as many appliances as bushels of bananas. Clearly (we hope), the U.S. should trade an appliance that is worth only one half of a banana in the domestic market to Honduras, where that appliance is worth four thirds of a bushel of bananas. Analogously, Honduras could trade away a bushel of bananas, which is worth only three fourths of an appliance in the domestic market, in exchange for two appliances in the United States. This discussion, though it may complicate our presentation, paves the way for considering situations where countries do not specialize completely in producing just one product, but rather specialize partially to favor the comparatively efficient product(s)—and they deal in many products rather than just two. ∎

an advantage of $^{100}/_{80} = 1.20$ over Honduras. Thus, the United States has a *comparative advantage* in producing appliances.

On the other side, Honduras would operate at a disadvantage in producing either product. However, the disadvantage in producing bananas is only $^{80}/_{100} = 0.8$, while the disadvantage in producing appliances is $^{60}/_{200} = 0.3$. Honduras possesses a comparative advantage (i.e., less disadvantage) in producing bananas. In other words, Honduras possesses factors of production (i.e., land, labor, and machinery) that are relatively more efficient in producing bananas, and the United States possesses factors of production that are relatively more efficient at producing appliances.

The doctrine of comparative advantage states that when such relative production advantages exist and are reflected in prices, then each country will be better off by specializing and trading, rather than remaining economically independent. These results are more likely to occur (1) the fewer the restrictions that are placed on trade, (2) the lower the transactions costs involved, (3) the wider the gap in production advantages, and (4) the easier it is for productive resources to be shifted into the advantageous industry in each country.

With-trade Production Points

By considering with-trade production points, it can be seen numerically that trade may improve each country's consumption. If each country specializes where it has a comparative advantage, then with-trade production will be as in the table below. Pretrade consumption of each product by *both* countries combined was 160 units per month of appliances and 70 units per month of bananas. Now total production exceeds each of these figures—so it remains only to price the products and distribute the output—unquestionably, each country is *potentially* better off.

With-trade Production *(units/month)*

	A	B
United States	200	0
Honduras	0	80

The final consumption points will depend on consumers' preferences in each country, as reflected in the indifference curves for that country. We do know, however, that the United States will export *at most* 80 units of appliances per month and will demand *at least* 40 units per month of bananas in exchange, in order to remain at least as well off as before trade. Honduras, similarly, will be willing to export *at most* 50 units per month of bananas in exchange for *at least* 40 units of appliances per month, so that consumers there will be no worse off than before trade. Any trade of 40 to 80 units of appliances per month for 40 to 50 units of bananas per month will make each country better off than it was before.[5] We can assume that the final consumption points are as shown in the table below.

With-trade Consumption *(units/month)*

	A	B
United States	150	45
Honduras	50	35

Implicitly, this means that the with-trade relative prices are 45 bushels of bananas/50 appliances = 0.9 bananas/appliances, or 1.11 appliances/bananas. That is, final consumption possibilities (if graphed on Figure 3–1) have a slope of more than the pre-trade U.S. trade-off and less than the Honduran one.

Next, let us consider *prices* explicitly, to show that each country is better off in financial as well as real terms. The adjustment from pre- to with-trade prices can take place through changes in domestic prices in each country or through changes in the exchange rate, or both. To focus our attention on "international prices," let us allow only the exchange rate to change, while domestic prices in each country remain constant.

Assume that the domestic price of bananas in the United States before trade was 200 appliances per 100 bushels of bananas, or 2 to 1. If an appliance cost $10, then one bushel (i.e., one unit) of bananas cost $20, according to Figure 3–1. In Honduras, the pretrade value of a bushel of bananas was three fourths of an appliance. If we assume that an appliance costs 200 lempira, then a bushel of bananas costs 150 lempira.

Pre-trade Prices

	A	B
United States	$10	$20
Honduras	200 lempira	150 lempira

Once international trade is allowed, there must be some rate of exchange between lempira and dollars. Looking at the pretrade domestic prices, appliances were worth 200 lempira or $10, a ratio of 20 lempira/dollar, and bananas were worth 150 lempira or $20, a ratio of 7.5 lempira/dollar. As long as the exchange rate falls somewhere between these ratios, bilateral trade will make each country better off in financial terms. Let us assume, then, that the exchange rate becomes 15 lempira/dollar.

This exchange rate means that U.S. consumers who want to buy Honduran appliances or bananas will face dollar prices of 200 lempira/15 lempira per dollar = $13.33 per appliance and 150 lempira/15 lempira per dollar = $10 per bushel of bananas. On the other hand, Honduran consumers looking at possible purchases of U.S. appliances and bananas will see lempira prices of $10 × 15 lempira per dollar = 150 lempira per appliance and $20 × 15 lempira per dollar = 300 lempira per bushel of bananas. Clearly, U.S. consumers will benefit from importing bananas and Honduran consumers will benefit from importing appliances. Since each country is large enough to satisfy total demand for the product it exports, then complete specialization may occur in each (though not necessarily, due to various market imperfections—tariffs, factor immobility between industries, etc.).

With-trade Prices *(at exchange rate of 15 lempira per US dollar)*

	A	B
United States	$10	$10 (on imports)
Honduras	150 lempira (on imports)	150 lempira

If the exchange rate were to change to a level outside the range of 7.5–20 lempira/dollar, a disequilibrium would exist. At any exchange rate below 7.5 lempira/dollar, both countries would want to buy appliances and bananas from the United States. And at any rate above 20 lempira/dollar, both countries would want to buy both products from Honduras. For example, if the rate is 5 lempira/dollar, then Hondurans can import appliances for 50 lempira/appliance and bananas for 10 lempira/bushel and U.S. consumers have to pay $40 for imported appliances and $30/bushel for imported bananas. In this case, both countries would buy both products from the United States, until the exchange rate moved above 7.5 lempira/dollar or until U.S. prices of appliances and bananas rose enough to accomplish the same result. (Alternatively, Honduran prices could fall to generate this result. The actual adjustment will depend on which prices are more flexible—domestic prices or exchange rates—but the result will be the same.)

ADDED DIMENSION

Comparative vs. Competitive Advantage

Be careful to distinguish between these two concepts! *Comparative advantage* refers to the cost of producing some product or service in one country versus another. It is a concept based on relative cost of production between nations. *Competitive advantage* refers to a skill or capability held by a firm that enables it to outcompete rivals in a given situation. It is a concept used to compare two companies' abilities to compete in the same business. A firm may utilize comparative advantage to further its own strategy, by obtaining inputs and products in locations where they are least expensive. That is, a firm may use imports to obtain low-cost factors of production—or it may set up a sourcing investment in the low-cost country to produce the inputs for itself—or it may move its entire production to a low-cost location. If the location is in another country, then the firm is using **comparative advantage** to improve its competitiveness. Thus, the comparative advantage that exists in any country may be used by companies operating there to create a cost-based competitive advantage. ■

This relatively simple framework is intended to demonstrate the potential real and financial gains available to any pair of countries that begin bilateral trade in two commodities. These results will generally obtain for situations involving many countries and many products, as long as relative production efficiencies differ.[6] The very important problems that arise from market imperfections such as government controls and monopolistic company practices are ignored in this chapter—though they are critical factors for managerial decision making.[7] Our only purpose here has been to present one underlying economic rationale for trade.

THE INTERNATIONAL PRODUCT CYCLE

The **international product cycle** is a concept developed by Raymond Vernon in the mid-1960s, based on the product life cycle in marketing analysis.[8] This concept is far more intuitively appealing than the comparative advantage theory as an explanation of post-World War II trade (and investment), especially regarding manufactured goods (in particular, differentiated products). The product cycle theory explicitly incorporates the multinational enterprise as an actor that undertakes international trade (and also foreign direct investment). It focuses on market expansion and technological innovation, which are relatively de-emphasized in the comparative advantage theory. Finally, it is a dynamic view, exploring the reasons why trade flows shift over time. In all, it puts the phenomenon of international trade in a context that makes business sense in a world of changing technology and multiple markets that face any firm.

The theory of the international product cycle has two fundamental tenets. First, technology is a critical factor in product creation and development, and the existence of proprietary technology gives some firms advantages over others. Second, market size and structure are critical factors in determining trade patterns.

The cycle itself comprises three stages: the new product stage, the maturing product stage, and the standardized product stage. These stages are more or less analogous to the stages of the domestic product life cycle, though the decline and cessation of production of a product are ignored.

New Product Stage

A *new product* is created by some firm or firms and does not exist prior to this. For example, pocket calculators, automobiles, specific drugs, and nuclear power plants were each created by one or a few firms whose scientists and engineers developed each of these products. When such an invention is sold in the market, it is called an **innovation,** or a **new product.** The first step toward a new product, then, is the process of scientific research, which leads to inventions.

The conditions under which an innovation will succeed depend greatly on the type of product and the type of market. If we consider manufactured products and national markets, we would expect a lot of innovations in nations where sufficient scientists and engineers are available and where purchasers have sufficient incomes to buy the products. Vernon, in his reasoning in the mid-1960s, explained that the largest percentage of new products would be introduced in the largest single national market with the highest per capita income—the United States. That is, he believed that innovations had the best chance for success in the United States at that time, because the United States then had more scientists and engineers and a higher per capita income than any other country.

Also important in the new product stage is **flexibility** in production, to suit the needs and desires of new purchasers.[9] Generally, when a new product is introduced, we would expect the demand for it to be relatively price inelastic. Purchasers who have no perfect substitutes available for the new product are likely to be more concerned (initially) with the product's useful characteristics than with its price. As the innovating firm receives feedback from purchasers about performance, reliability, and so on, it can alter the product to suit purchasers' preferences. Close contact with the market is therefore a very important factor in this stage. To achieve flexibility, then, the innovating firm will probably want to locate in or near a major potential market, where good communications are available. Once again, the United States is a very likely candidate for such a firm's location, though of course today Western European countries and Japan serve about equally well as appropriate markets for new products.

As the innovating firm discovers additional customers for sales of the new product, foreign demand may be sought, or it may arise through requests for exports. If the innovating firm is a multinational, it may face the choice between exporting and setting up production in foreign markets. Smaller firms would generally look just at exporting, or perhaps contracting with a foreign firm to produce the product abroad. Thus, the initial entry of the new product into international business will probably occur through exports, and sooner or later that step may be followed by foreign production. Figure 3–2 presents an overview of the international product cycle, assuming that initial production occurs in the United States.

FIGURE 3-2

The International Product
Cycle

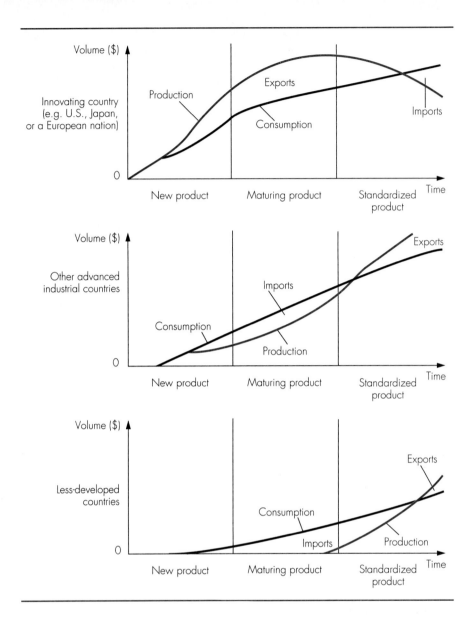

Notice that as the new product stage progresses, exports provide a growing share of total sales. If sale of the new product is truly profitable, the innovating firm is likely to attract competitors both in the United States and abroad. Depending on the firm's success in retaining its proprietary ability to make the product, competition will arise sooner or later. Exports and the start-up of foreign production (in panel 2 of Figure 3–2) may be carried out either by the innovating firm or by competing firms, depending on the ability of these firms to gain information about the product and access to foreign markets.

Two distinct shifts in the nature of the new business mark the transition from the new product stage to the maturing product stage. First, the likelihood that competitors will begin making the product, in the home country or abroad, means that *price* competition is likely to become more important. The innovating firm itself may establish facilities abroad, to achieve lower-cost production as well as to serve foreign markets (especially in Europe, Canada, and Japan) with a product capable of being adapted to local market requirements. Second, the fact that competitors exist at all means that technology is diffusing, so that the original firm does not maintain its monopoly of the product.

Maturing Product Stage

Each of these shifts leads toward the **maturing product** stage, which involves global diffusion of the product through exports and also through foreign production via foreign direct investment. This second stage is characterized by more price-elastic demand for the product, more standardization of the production process, and a change in company strategy away from a focus on production (of this particular product) and toward market protection. Both local and foreign competitors typically challenge the innovating firm in its home market and abroad. In this stage, product differentiation is common, and pursuit of new markets by competing firms becomes active.

Production in the home country typically levels off in this stage, as market growth slows. Lower-cost production methods and locations are often sought as price competition increases. Toward the end of this stage, foreign production may even be exported to the home country. Notice that both competition and production tend to spread from the home country to other industrial countries first, and later to less developed countries.

Standardized Product Stage

Finally, the **standardized product** stage occurs when technology relevant to the product becomes widely available, and price becomes the main basis for competition. In this stage, production of standardized products (or components) is often shifted to low-cost locations, including less developed countries. (see Figure 3–2, bottom panel). Also typical of the standardized product stage is offshore assembly, in which parts of the product are still produced in the home country—but assembly is done in cheap-labor countries, for final sale in many countries. Strategically, firms often try to avoid pure price competition in the standardized product stage by differentiating their products.

An Example: The Pocket Calculator

The standard pocket calculator offers a clear example of a product moving through the international product cycle. This "product" is defined here to be the battery-operated, hand-held computational instrument that adds, subtracts, multiplies, and divides electronically. Scientists at Sunlock Comptometer Corporation invented the product in 1961 and began marketing it soon afterward. At about $1,000 per calculator, the instrument was not cheap. But it performed functions formerly reserved for large computers and mechanical calculators, while offering the user a simple, portable, and independent computational capability. The alternative in terms of portability and independence from electrical outlets was the slide rule, which had far less accuracy than the 6 to 10 digits usually available in a calculator.

Ignoring the refinements that allow pocket calculators to carry out complex calculations, store results, and even act as microcomputers, let us continue to look at the simple, four-function product. (The others can be defined as separate products, to avoid confusion.) Within eight years of the introduction of pocket calculators, several additional firms (including a number of Japanese manufacturers) had entered the market with competing products and the price had dropped to about $400 per calculator. Hewlett-Packard, Texas Instruments, Casio (a Japanese firm), and other electronics manufacturers developed similar models, which forced all manufacturers of pocket calculators to compete on price grounds, in the United States and in several foreign markets. Each of these developments indicates a move into the maturing product stage. (The new product stage lasted for perhaps four to six years.)

In the early 1970s, more firms entered the market, several began to assemble their calculators in offshore locations such as Taiwan and Singapore, and price competition became truly fierce. In 1971, Bowmar Corporation, an American firm, introduced a four-function calculator that retailed for $240. By 1975, these calculators sold routinely for $10 to $15 and sometimes for even less. One could argue that pocket calculators had reached the standardized product stage by 1975, with the production technology widely available, price competition (hence costs) of utmost importance, and product differentiation widely used.

Thus, the international product cycle for simple calculators was completed in less than 15 years. The product itself remains in widespread demand, but producers now compete on the basis of price, other product characteristics, and distribution, rather than on the basis of proprietary technology and new markets.

Another Example: The Polaroid Land Camera

Contrast the case of the pocket calculator with that of the Polaroid Land camera. In 1947, Edwin Land, the founder and manager of Polaroid Corporation, introduced a new photographic process. He had invented an instant-developing film that allowed a photographer to snap a picture and simply wait a few minutes for chemicals on the film to develop the final snapshot. First marketed in 1948, the Polaroid Land camera enjoyed a monopoly position for several *decades*.

Initially, the Polaroid Land camera took only black-and-white photographs and the film processing was done inside the camera. In 1963, Polaroid introduced an improved version that processed the film outside the camera. (Each snapshot was removed from the camera immediately after the picture-taking, in a "sandwich" of developing chemicals, film negative, and print paper. Then the print was pulled away from the other materials, which were discarded.) Later, improved prints of both black-and-white and color pictures were offered. In 1972, Polaroid introduced another modification of the camera, which now gives the final print directly from the camera after each picture. (The print develops in a few seconds, with no materials to be discarded.)

If the instant-developing camera is regarded as one product, ignoring its improvements over the years, then one can conclude that the new product stage in this case lasted approximately 30 years. During that time, Polaroid had a monopoly on the market worldwide, expanding sales through both direct exports and foreign marketing and production affiliates. Today, 42 percent of the firm's sales come from foreign operations located in 22 countries.

It was only in 1976, when Kodak introduced an instant-developing camera using somewhat different technology, that competition began for this product. Then, in 1984, a patent infringement case against Kodak was won by Polaroid, which forced Kodak out of the market for instant-developing cameras. In 1987, the instant-developing camera was still in the late new product or early maturing product stage—a huge contrast with the pocket calculator's cycle. Today, Polaroid's proprietary technology continues to play a major role in competition for instant-developing cameras. Price competition has become more important, though not dominant, in Polaroid's effort to entice photographers away from single-lens reflex and Instamatic cameras. Thus, the international product cycle provides an appealing description of the sequence of events that takes place in the lives of many products—but as we see with the instant-developing camera, it does *not* explain *when* the stages will begin or end.

While the theory of the international product cycle offers us a wealth of insights into international trade and the activities of multinational firms, it leaves some important questions unanswered. This theory does not tell us how long each stage will last, though it does illuminate key competitive aspects of each stage. Nor does it tell us explicitly how or when a firm should choose between exporting and setting up a local plant abroad, though it does mention costs as an important concern. It does not explain which country's firms are most likely to produce in any given market, nor which firms will move first. Lastly, the theory is decidedly vague on the definition of a "product." Despite these limitations, as compared with other theories available today, the theory gives us substantial managerial insights into trade patterns in manufacturing.

An especially fortunate aspect of the theory of the international product cycle is its compatibility with the theory of comparative advantage. If we focus on trade that occurs primarily on the basis of comparative national cost conditions, then the standardized product stage of the international product cycle outlines broad aspects of such trade, and the comparative advantage view lays out a solid theoretical framework for analysis and decision making.

* * * * *

One additional theory of international trade that is based on demand-side considerations deserves comment at this point. Staffan Linder (1961) created a theory based on similarity of **demand patterns** to explain trade patterns in manufactured products. This theory was developed in the early 1960s, at about the same time that the theory of the international product cycle was attempting to move emphasis in trade theory to the demand side. Linder reasoned that a major determinant of trade patterns was the level of a country's economic development. Countries at similar levels of development would have similar demand patterns and would be likely to trade among themselves. Intuitively, this idea is sensible, and one can think of the pharmaceuticals industry, the computer industry, and many others that display large trade volumes among developed countries, and relatively little involving LDCs (with the exception of the offshore assembly done in LDCs for sale in developed countries). Linder's theory offers an underlying reason for expecting so much trade in manufactured goods among developed countries, even when many of their cost conditions are very similar.

EMPIRICAL CONTROVERSIES AND NEW THEORIES

While our discussions of comparative advantage and the international product cycle should offer insights into the patterns of international trade that take place today, there are quite a few phenomena that defy explanation using these tools. The international product cycle itself was developed during a period of controversy about the comparative advantages that are possessed by the United States.

Though this country appears to be quite capital-rich relative to rival nations, Leontief and others found that U.S. exports (compared to U.S. imports) were relatively labor-intensive rather than capital-intensive. The reason for his paradoxical finding may be that the U.S. tends to specialize in more **technology-intensive** products, which utilize skilled labor in their production. (The Leontief paradox is discussed in the Appendix to this chapter.) This rationale is one of the bases used by Vernon in his international product cycle.

U.S. trade can be evaluated along these lines as shown in Figure 3–3. Note that the United States does indeed have a surplus in exports of technology-intensive products relative to imports of those same products. The U.S. also has a trade surplus in services, but a deficit in all of the other categories of products listed. The other industrial countries in the figure, except Canada, also have trade surpluses on high-tech products. These countries broadly show a net deficit in trade of standardized goods, implying that the rest of the world—and particularly the newly industrializing countries (NICs) such as Korea, Taiwan, Hong Kong, and Singapore—are achieving an export surplus on those goods.

FIGURE 3–3

Patterns of comparative advantage: Export/import (X/M) ratios in six leading countries, 1979

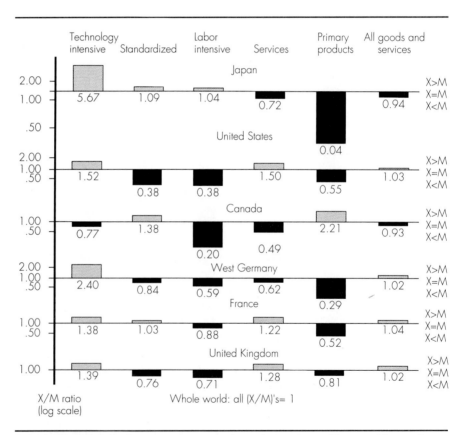

Technology-intensive manufactures = transport equipment (autos, planes, ships, motorbikes, etc.), machinery, chemicals, and professional goods.
Labor-intensive manufactures = textiles, apparel, footwear, and leather goods.
Standardized manufactures = all manufactures − technology-intensive and labor-intensive manufactures.
Sources: Peter Lindert, *International Economics* (Homewood, Ill.: Richard D. Irwin, Inc., 1987); Mutti and Morici (1983. Tables 6 and 10); IMF, *International Financial Statistics*.

This phenomenon is consistent with the comparative advantage concept, since the NICs do indeed possess a *relative* abundance of low-cost labor relative to the industrial countries, and thus the NICs should export labor-intensive, standardized goods.

Similar Demand Conditions

Another phenomenon that has confounded traditional trade theory is the evident concentration of world trade in manufactured goods among the industrial countries. As shown in Figure 3–1, this situation has not changed in any major way in the post-World War II period. Why is manufacturing trade concentrated in this way? Staffan Linder (1961) suggested that similarities in demand patterns would cause countries to trade with others at similar levels of economic development. Since consumers in similar countries are likely to have similar tastes, they would be likely purchasers of products from these same countries. Since most goods that are exported are produced first for domestic consumption, we should find that these kinds of products are the ones most exported and imported for a given country. Linder's idea provides an intuitively sensible rationale for concentration of manufacturing exports among similar countries, but it leaves many issues unanswered.

Another phenomenon that relates to this discussion is the large amount of intra-industry trade. Linder argued that similar demand conditions would lead to trade between similarly developed countries. He did not deal with the fact that a lot of the trade is actually in similar products. If comparative advantage still offers some insight into trade patterns between the industrial countries, how can pairs of countries export cars, chemicals, computers, etc., in both directions? This issue is called intra-industry trade, or crosshauling.

Intra-Industry Trade

Trade statistics are full of examples of two-way trade in apparently the same products between various trading partners. A simple reason for this unexpected phenomenon is that the statistics include many products in one aggregated category, so that what appears to be one product really turns out to be many. Indeed, much of the evidence is of exactly this type. Also, multistage production (including offshore assembly) leads to trade flows of one product both into and out of the same country where processing is done, while the actual items being moved are first inputs and then outputs of the product. However, after misclassified products have been excluded, there still turns out to be a substantial amount of crosshauling in exactly the same products.

Two reasons for intra-industry trade have been developed in recent years. First and more simply, the trade often takes place in *differentiated products.* That is, products such as automobiles that are traded in both directions between the United States and West Germany, or between West Germany and Japan, are highly differentiated. The German cars such as Mercedes and BMW are luxury autos that are sold in Japan and the United States, while those countries export Toyotas and Fords to Germany. This over-simplification of auto trade should not hide the fact that automobiles are highly differentiated, and thus even Toyotas, Volkswagens, and Chevrolets can and do coexist simultaneously in the same market.

A second explanation of intra-industry trade focuses on *economies of scale.* Because such production scale economies limit the range of products that any country can produce (the cost of producing all products is clearly prohibitive for any one country), countries will specialize in a limited range of products. Then, trading partners fill in each other's total product lines through exports. Countries choose which products to import, based on their tastes and based on the demands for different production inputs.*

The Direction of New Trade Theories

Most of the new trade theories to emerge in the 1970s and 1980s have used the base of industrial organization theory to explore the impact of imperfect competition (or monopolistic competition) on trade flows. By allowing for proprietary technology or economies of scale, such theories are able to better explain the trade flows among industrial countries in the past 20 years. (See, for example, Ethier 1983 and Lancaster 1980.) Clearly, these two factors are important determinants of current trade among industrial countries.

Another avenue of investigation that has been very productive is to consider trade as part of multinational business, along with foreign direct investment and other international business activities. Beginning with the general view of the international product cycle, several writers (such as Hirsch 1976 and Grosse 1985) have examined in more detail the relationships between trade and direct investment by multinational firms. First, trade can be seen as a substitute for direct investment when the MNE seeks to supply foreign markets or to obtain inputs for use in the home market. Second, trade can be seen as a complement for direct investment when the MNE seeks to fill out product lines beyond those produced locally in any affiliate.

CONCLUSIONS

Each of the trade theories discussed can be recast in a microeconomic context, focusing on individual firms. The lesson to be learned from the comparative-cost view, for example, is that when costs are very important in competition, it may be best for a firm to produce its products in low-cost countries, rather than try to serve markets from its home country alone. Certainly, this lesson has been learned by the many U.S.-based electronics firms that now manufacture in Singapore, South Korea, or Hong Kong to lower their production costs. Alternatively, a firm may find it best to import some products from low-cost suppliers, rather than try to produce them itself. In fact, many export-import firms make their entire business from finding low-cost suppliers in various countries and sales in others—profiting from the use of comparative cost advantages in each product.

The theory of the international product cycle offers the manager advice about the dynamics of many industries, as competition shifts from being based on proprietary technology, to product differentiation, to price (cost) minimizing. The high-tech firm may choose to leave the markets for its products when they enter the maturing or standardized stage, in order to concentrate its efforts on developing new products and competing on the basis of its technology. The firm with a respected brand name may choose to focus its efforts on finding low-cost production sites and establishing an international distribution network, to minimize delivery costs.

---

*Discussions of intra-industry trade are available in Helpman and Krugman (1989) and Greenaway and Milner (1986).

The other theories can also be used as guides for decision making. In every case, the firm needs to consider other alternatives besides exports (for example, foreign direct investment).

Looking specifically at individual countries, it appears that U.S. companies are competing successfully in export markets with products that are relatively intensive in human capital. This may be restated in terms of companies' competitive advantages: U.S. firms can succeed in export markets where the proprietary skills of these firms (such as technology and management know-how) are relatively important. Foreign firms can export to the United States products whose competitiveness depends more on other factors of production (e.g., low-wage labor, natural resources, different management skills), as well as in some segments of the high-tech markets.

QUESTIONS

1. How can the manager of an international company use the comparative advantage theory in decision making? For example, suppose that the company is Apple Computers and the manager is looking for a site to locate a new plant.

2. Explain the stages of the international product cycle. How can a manager use this theory in decision making? Use the case of the auto industry to help illustrate your answer.

3. What are the main export products/services of the United States today? Why are U.S. exporters able to compete successfully in these markets? (Figure 7–4 in Chapter 7 lists the main merchandise products, and Figure 7–3 shows several key service categories.)

4. Is the exchange rate important in the theory of comparative advantage? Why or why not?

5. Explain Leontief's paradox. Be sure to discuss several reasons why the paradox may be more apparent than real.

6. What competitive advantage do the OPEC countries possess that allows them to compete in export markets? What theory of international trade covers this example?

7. At what stage of the international product cycle are personal computers? Based on that view, what do you expect to happen in this market during the rest of the 1990s?

8. At what stage of the international product cycle is the automobile? What do you expect to happen in this market during the rest of the 1980s?

9. Given the information below, what should each *country* do? Why?

	Computers	Paper
United States	50	40
Canada	100	60

Note: Each cell represents the number of output units produced by one unit of inputs.

10. How does international trade relate to foreign direct investment?

REFERENCES

Baldwin, Robert. "Determinants of the Commodity Structure of U.S. Trade." *American Economic Review,* March 1971.

Blum, Lisa. "Intra-Industry Trade and Market Structure: A Time Trend Analysis." Paper presented at the Academy of International Business annual meeting, 1984.

Buckley, Peter, and Robert D. Pearce. "Exports in the Strategy of Multinational Enterprises." *Journal of Business Research,* 1984.

Ethier, Wilfred. *Modern International Economics.* New York: W. W. Norton, 1983.

Giddy, Ian. "The Demise of the Product Cycle Model in International Business Theory." *Columbia Journal of World Business.* (Spring 1978).

Greenaway, D., and C. R. Milner. *The Economics of Intra-Industry Trade.* Oxford: Basil Blackwell, 1986.

Grosse, Robert. "An Imperfect Competition Theory of the MNE," *Journal of International Business Studies,* Winter 1985.

Gruber, W. H.; Dileep Mehta; and Raymond Vernon. "The R&D Factor in International Investment of U.S. Industries." *Journal of Political Economy,* February 1967.

Haberler, Gottfried. *The Theory of International Trade.* London: William Hodge, 1950.

Helpman, Elhanan, and Paul R. Krugman. *Trade Policy and Market Structure.* Cambridge, Mass.: MIT Press, 1989.

Hirsch, S. "An International Trade and Investment Theory of the Firm." *Oxford Economic Papers,* July 1976.

Hufbauer, Gary. *Synthetic Materials and the Theory of International Trade.* Cambridge, Mass.: Harvard Univ. Press, 1966.

Keesing, Donald. "Labor Skills and Comparative Advantage." *American Economic Review,* May 1966.

Kindleberger, Charles, and Peter Lindert. *International Economics,* 6th ed. Homewood, Ill.: Richard D. Irwin, 1987.

Krugman, Paul. "New Theories of Trade among Industrial Countries." *American Economic Review,* May 1983.

Lancaster, Kelvin. "Intra-Industry Trade under Perfect Monopolistic Competition." *Journal of International Economics,* May 1980.

Linder, Staffan. *An Essay on Trade and Transformation.* New York: John Wiley & Sons, 1961.

Ricardo, David. *Principles of Political Economy and Taxation.* Harmondsworth, Middlesex, England: Penguin Books, 1971. (Originally published in 1817.)

Vernon, Raymond. "International Investment and International Trade in the Product Cycle." *Quarterly Journal of Economics,* May 1966.

3-1

The Leontief Paradox

A large part of the international economic policy of governments worldwide is based on the concept of comparative advantage. That is, national governments tend to view the gains from trade as being quite real and they try to obtain a larger share of the total gains for themselves. The United States has traditionally been the clearest and most consistent advocate and example of free-trade policy. Following the principle of comparative advantage, the United States, then, should specialize in the production and export of products in which the country has an advantage. Which ones are they?

One might expect that if we focus simply on capital-intensive versus labor-intensive goods, the United States would export the former and import the latter. Certainly, with its abundant capital resources, the United States would be expected to behave in this way. A study by (subsequent Nobel Prize-winning economist) Wassily Leontief in 1953 showed that, in fact, export goods from the United States are relatively more labor intensive and import-competing goods are relatively more capital intensive! What happened to the theory of comparative advantage?

A number of explanations have been given for what is now called the **Leontief paradox.** Some authors have attributed the findings to trade barriers that distort trade flows; others have looked at differences in natural resource availability across countries; still others have focused on differences in the characteristics of labor across countries.[10] Most analysts today agree that this last factor plays a large part in determining U.S. trade flows (and also foreign direct investment flows). If we measure the "quality" of labor inputs (i.e., their productivity), rather than just man-hours of work, it turns out that the United States tends to specialize in producing and exporting products that use relatively more "high-quality" labor (e.g., technology-intensive products that require more highly educated labor). Several analysts, including Keesing (1966) and Gruber, Mehta, and Vernon (1967), found empirical evidence supporting this point. This explanation is quite consistent with the international product cycle, which is based on the development of new technology and which sees the United States as the country most likely to be the source of new products.

Both the theory of the international product cycle and the technology-based theory have had to be reevaluated since the early 1970s, to recognize the comparable levels of development and market size in the European Community and Japan relative to the United States. Today, it is possible to argue that both of these theories provide plausible reasons for trade to begin among the industrial countries once an innovation has taken place, but neither of them is able to explain where to look for innovations.[11]

NOTES

[1]The current state of development of this theory is presented in Kindleberger and Lindert (1987).

[2]Ricardo's analysis assumes constant opportunity costs in shifting production from one product to another in a given country. This point has been criticized by Haberler (1950) and others; and current economics texts use the increasing-cost approach. The present text uses Ricardo's model because it allows more clarity in the exposition. See Kindleberger and Lindert (1987), chapters 2–4, for an excellent presentation of the pure theory.

[3]Normally, we would expect diminishing returns to occur as production is specialized more and more in the one product, hence using less and less efficient resources for producing it. And we would therefore expect *incomplete* specialization in each country. Our example simplifies the economics substantially; and any international trade text can be used to explore the added concerns of incomplete specialization. Graphically, the results of trade with incomplete specialization between two equal-sized countries would be:

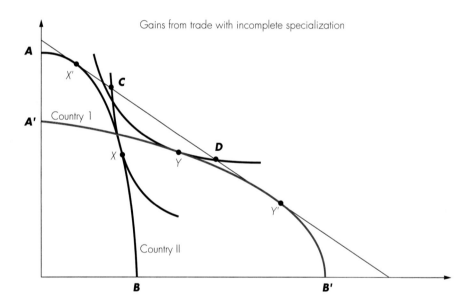

Gains from trade with incomplete specialization

where Country 1 produces and consumes initially at Y, and Country 2 at X. With trade, each country partially specializes its production, at points X' and Y', and each can consume both goods at some point on segment CD, which is above the original indifference curves.

[4]In fact, consumers may choose a little less of one good and a lot more of the other, after trade, as long as they end up consuming on a higher indifference curve. To keep matters simple, we will assume that consumers choose more of both products, when available.

[5]Thus, comparative advantage analysis tells us not only which country will specialize in production of what product; it also tells us what the limits will be on the real rate of exchange.

[6]See Kindleberger and Lindert (1987) for a full and careful treatment of these issues.

[7]Government controls are discussed in Chapter 8; monopolistic practices are treated in the appendix to this chapter as well as elsewhere in the text.

[8]Vernon's theory appeared as "International Investment and International Trade in the Product Cycle," *Quarterly Journal of Economics,* May 1966. The product life cycle in marketing appears, for example, in Chester Wasson, *Dynamic Competitive Strategy and Product Life Cycles* (St. Charles, Ill.: Challenge Books, 1974).

[9]Analogously, the firm may desire the flexibility to test the market using a limited capital commitment, before making expensive, highly illiquid investments in large-scale production runs.

[10]Much of the literature on the Leontief paradox is summarized in Baldwin (1971).

[11]Before the 1980s, several analysts demonstrated some patterns of innovation among industrial countries: for example, U.S. firms tended to be labor-saving in their innovations; European firms were relatively material- and capital-saving; and Japanese firms were relatively material- and space-saving.

EXIM Company (comparative advantage in international trade)

Introduction

A very important factor in determining trade patterns between countries for many products is the cost of production. If this cost is lower in one country than another, then the first country will benefit from producing and exporting the product to the second. For example, if steel costs $300 per ton to make in Japan and $400 per ton to make in the United States, then (all other things being equal) U.S. customers should buy (import) steel from Japanese companies. By the same reasoning, if airplanes cost $4 million to produce in the United States and $5 million in Japan, then Japanese customers should buy (import) airplanes from the U.S. In this example, the U.S. produces and exports airplanes, while Japan produces and exports steel. Each country has a *comparative advantage* in producing one product relative to the other country.

Obviously, countries do not export and import, *companies* do. For any company, the choice of products to export and import depends to some degree on the cost of production in the various countries where the company does business. The company should utilize comparative advantage to decide where (in which country) to produce its products and where to buy its inputs. In the case below, a U.S.-based company sells many products in several different national markets. The problem is to choose whether to obtain computer memory chips in the United States or Japan, and perhaps to consider buying other components and peripheral equipment for resale as well.

The Case

EXIM Company is a Connecticut-based corporation involved in assembling computer circuit boards for use in personal computers manufactured by IBM, Apple, Compaq, NEC, and other original equipment manufacturers. During its six-year history, the company has gone from a two-person operation assembling memory expansion boards to a 30-person manufacturing business, now making a wide variety of multiple-function boards and other peripheral hardware used in the burgeoning personal computer market. The firm's annual sales have grown by about 40 percent per year to just over $8 million in 1985.

EXIM was founded by an electrical engineer (Hans Klauser) and a recent M.B.A. graduate of a local business school (Dwight Sutherland). These two entrepreneurs were able to combine basic knowledge of microcomputer hardware with an aggressive marketing strategy for the circuit boards. After borrow-

---

This case was written by Professor Robert Grosse as a basis for class discussion, 1986.

ing $50,000 from a commercial bank and adding their life savings, EXIM's founders were able to generate enough sales to break even in the second year of operations and to repay their entire loan by the end of the third year. Today EXIM uses 80 percent equity financing (that is, earnings reinvested in the firm by the two owners who continue to own all the stock shares) and 20 percent bank financing, mostly for working capital. The entire operation is housed in a rebuilt factory just outside of West Haven, Connecticut.

Most of EXIM's sales go to the thousands of retail stores that have sprung up in the United States during the 1980s to sell microcomputers and peripheral equipment to businesses, individuals, and other customers. In addition, similar stores in Canada and the United Kingdom have become important customers in the last two years. Export sales to individual customers have been fairly insignificant thus far, but an advertising campaign in two microcomputer magazines has led to sales in Mexico, Ireland, and even in Pakistan.

Recently, competition from lower-priced boards, many of them imported from Asia, has begun to reduce EXIM's rate of growth in sales. Having read about the problems of the automobile industry and others in the United States due to their competition with Japanese and Korean firms, EXIM's general manager, Hans Klauser, was considering the idea of establishing an assembly operation somewhere in Asia. Klauser felt that his products were essentially "commodities," embodying technology that is readily available from several suppliers in the United States, Germany, and Japan. Therefore, his competitiveness would need to be based to some degree on the prices charged to customers. Superior quality and service could be used to improve sales somewhat, but the key factor would be price.

He was particularly concerned about the cost conditions in each country, which were subject to substantial shifts due to differences in national inflation rates and exchange-rate changes. The Japanese yen, for example, had devalued by over 30 percent relative to the dollar in the early 1980s; then it revalued by more than 20 percent in 1985 alone. Japanese inflation, by contrast, had paralleled U.S. inflation during most of the 1980s. Figure 1 depicts the yen/dollar exchange rate during 1973-85 and the inflation rates of each country during the same period.

Labor costs favored the Asian locations, but not necessarily by enough to overcome a severe dollar devaluation that might occur. Total production costs of several relevant components in 1985 appear in Table 1.

Although the table presents only production costs of EXIM's potential suppliers, these are fairly close to the full delivered cost for almost all of the products, since transportation, insurance, and other costs are minimal for such small, lightweight, manufactured goods. Tariffs currently are less than 5 percent *ad valorem* on these electronic products coming into the United States.

FIGURE 1

Yen/Dollar Exchange Rates

Date	U.S. Dollar/Japanese Yen Exchange Rates, 1973–85 (in yen / $)	Inflation Rates in Japan and the United States, 1973–85 (in annual percent rates, ΔCPI)	
		Japan	United States
1973	280.00	11.7%	6.1%
1974	300.95	24.4	10.9
1975	305.15	11.8	9.2
1976	292.80	9.3	5.8
1977	240.00	8.0	6.5
1978	194.60	3.8	7.6
1979	239.70	3.6	11.2
1980	203.00	8.0	13.5
1981	219.90	4.9	10.4
1982	235.00	2.7	6.1
1983	232.20	1.8	3.2
1984	251.10	2.3	4.3
1985	200.50	2.1	3.5

TABLE 1

Production Costs of Computer Components in U.S., Japan, and Korea*

Component	Comparative Costs		
	United States	Japan	Korea
64 K RAM chips (cost per chip)	$ 1.50	$ 1.10	$ 0.90
256 K RAM chips (cost per chip)	$ 7.80	$ 6.60	not available
Internal clock/calendar	$ 9.75	$ 9.70	$ 10.50
Serial port and RS232 cable to attach peripheral equipment	$ 24.00	$ 24.50	$ 23.50
Parallel port and RS232 cable to attach peripheral equipment	$ 23.00	$ 23.50	$ 22.80
Software-in-a-chip to run ramdisk	$325.00	$345.00	not available
Internal modem (300 baud)	$340.00	$335.00	$332.00
Internal modem (1200 baud)	$455.00	$460.00	$470.00

*Data are listed in US dollars at the current exchange rate, December 1985.

Chapter

4

Foreign Direct Investment

This chapter discusses the single phenomenon that most distinguishes the multinational enterprise from other types of firms, namely foreign direct investment (FDI). It explores the reasons why firms undertake FDI and subsequent local production in host countries, and also the effects of FDI on industry structure around the world. Then it shows patterns of FDI, based on countries that are sources and targets of such investment and on companies that engage in FDI. Lastly, it discusses the issue of disinvestment—when a firm sells or closes an FDI project. The main goals of the chapter are to:

1. Define foreign direct investment and show how it fits into the MNE's activities.

2. Explain why firms undertake FDI, especially in comparison with exporting or other kinds of international business ventures.

3. Show patterns of FDI that illustrate the relative size and importance of different countries, industries, and companies—with particular coverage of FDI in the United States.

4. Show how theories of international business, such as the international product cycle and competitive advantage, focus on FDI and discuss additional theories of FDI, such as Dunning's eclectic view.

5. Show how disinvestment fits into company strategy along with foreign direct investment.

INTRODUCTION

Foreign direct investment (FDI) has probably been the most-studied aspect of the activities of multinational enterprises during the last three decades. More accurately, the causes and effects of FDI, and the subsequent operations of foreign affiliates, have been areas of extensive academic and public policy studies, which continue today. Similarly, the strategic fit of FDI and foreign affiliates within a company's global activities has become a central concern of more and more managers, as increasing numbers of firms in many countries have looked abroad for markets and supplies. Both of these aspects of FDI are examined here.

The present chapter, after defining key issues, begins with the manager's view: Why should a firm consider FDI, and how does FDI fit into global strategy? Next, patterns of direct investment since World War II are discussed, with regard to the countries that make and receive the investment and the industries and companies most involved. A section is devoted to examining foreign direct investment coming into the United States, the largest single host country. Fourth, explanations are offered for the observed facts and some conclusions are drawn for company managers and government officials. Finally, the analysis covers *disinvestment,* the sale of an existing affiliate, which is the "final" stage in FDI, though most projects do not reach that stage. Detailed consideration of the operation of a foreign investment project is left for the chapters in Part 3 of this book.

What Is FDI?

Foreign direct investment (FDI) involves ownership and control of a company in a foreign country. In exchange for the ownership, the investing company usually transfers some of its financial, managerial, technical, trademark, and other resources to the foreign country. The foreign company may be created as a new venture by the investor, or it may be acquired from an existing owner. Essentially, a company can view this kind of investment just as it views domestic investment—but in this case the project is located in another country. Just as a firm chooses among projects in capital budgeting domestically, it can add on foreign projects, which constitute FDI. Some investors bring in substantial funding with them, others borrow locally to finance their new affiliates, and yet others do both; some investors transfer many people to work in the new affiliate, while others simply hire locally for staffing needs (or acquire an existing company that already has full staffing). The point is that although no particular type of resource needs to be transferred to carry out FDI, it is usually accompanied by some transfer of money and people.

The main concept behind FDI is the *control* of assets in another country. That is, foreign direct investment is generally undertaken by a firm that seeks to serve a new market for its products or services or that seeks to obtain additional supplies for its existing markets. For example, Du Pont Chemical Corporation has used direct investment in 42 countries to market or produce its various products; Texaco, by contrast, has invested in oil exploration projects in dozens of countries, seeking additional petroleum supplies for its markets in the United States and abroad. In each case, the firm wants *control* over the foreign project in order to utilize its competitive advantages through the new facility.

Notice the contrast between this kind of investment and **portfolio investment,** in which the firm buys stocks, bonds, and other financial assets to hold in its portfolio. Du Pont holds a large and diversified portfolio of financial assets, including shares of other companies. However, its holdings of controlling interest in its own subsidiaries, and now of Conoco (an oil company), are *direct* investments that involve management of the activities involved. In balance sheet terms, portfolio investment relates mainly to the firm's holdings of marketable securities, while direct investment relates to the purchase and management of plant and equipment (plus other assets and liabilities of the direct investment project). The conceptual distinction between direct and portfolio investment is that the former requires control by the investor, whereas the latter is passive and requires no management effort by the investor.[1]

To reiterate: Foreign direct investment involves a controlling interest in a new or existing business enterprise in a foreign country. Such investment may be *financed* in many ways: the parent firm can transfer funds to the new affiliate and issue ownership shares to itself; the parent firm can borrow all of the required funds locally in the new country to pay for ownership; and many combinations of these and other alternatives can be followed. The key point here is that *no* international transfer of funds is necessary; FDI requires only transfer of *ownership* to the investor, which may finance the transaction in innumerable ways.

Who Is Concerned about FDI?

Essentially the same business participants and regulators that appeared in Figure 2–1 as actors in the MNE's global dealings are the ones that are concerned about FDI. The MNE itself must view these actors as key parts of the environment in which it operates. Each home and host country *government* views the MNE and its direct investment projects as generators of income, employment, technology, and so on that must be regulated to obtain the best gains for the government (obviously a contradictory goal, since each actor cannot obtain *all* the benefits of the MNE's activities). *Competitors* in the host country worry about added competition, and competitors in the home country worry about the direct investor's strategic gains from the foreign operations. *Suppliers* and *customers* in each country generally view the direct investment as useful because it brings the MNE closer to host country customers and usually leads to increased need for supplies. Finally, inside the MNE, *managers* and *workers* may have several perspectives on an FDI project, ranging from the expectation of new and interesting assignments to the expectation of job losses due to the foreign project's replacement of domestic output.

Toyota Motors' investment in a joint venture with General Motors in Fremont, California, exemplifies these issues.[2] It is a direct investment because Toyota obtained 50 percent ownership and assumed approximately 50 percent managerial responsibility for the project. The U.S. government views the foreign investment as *desirable* because it has created jobs in California but as *questionable* because it has combined two of the largest auto manufacturers worldwide (which raises antitrust concerns). The Japanese government may view the investment as a necessary step to reduce U.S. protectionist pressures against Japanese exports, but the investment could lead to fewer Toyota exports from Japan and to fewer jobs for Japanese workers, a negative result from their viewpoint. Each of the companies involved views the project as an opportunity to learn from its counterpart: GM is trying to transfer Japanese labor relations and productivity skills to its own people, and Toyota is learning much more about the U.S. auto market and GM's operations. There may be fewer jobs for Toyota workers in Japan if the Fremont plant replaces them—or more jobs if more parts, components, and other Toyota vehicles are sent to the United States as a result of the project. Finally, Toyota's suppliers in Japan may have to follow

Toyota to the United States in order to maintain their sales, and Toyota's customers in the United States may experience a shorter delay before the delivery of new cars (though perhaps a higher price). Unfortunately, there is no simple way to evaluate beforehand all the implications of such a project.

As companies continue to seek better strategies for their businesses in different countries, and as governments change their views on foreign direct investment (through elections and other changes of power), the forces shaping FDI decisions shift over time. Since companies are the central decision makers in FDI, their views of the investment process are considered first.[3]

THE STRATEGY OF FOREIGN DIRECT INVESTMENT

Why does a firm undertake foreign direct investment? A wealth of studies done during the 1960s and 1970s disclosed that the most important reason for entering a foreign market was to sell products that the firm already sold successfully in its home country.[4]* A reason that has grown in importance as international transportation costs have fallen substantially is to lower production costs by producing in a low-cost country for sales in other countries (often called "offshore assembly" or "foreign sourcing"). These and other strategic concerns that may be bases for undertaking FDI appear in Table 4–1.

Notice that the reasons are grouped into supply-side and demand-side categories. While a company may focus on a particular reason as the basis for a given FDI decision, both kinds of factors should be considered when making the decision. Beginning with the supply side, each reason is discussed below.

The Supply Side

Lower Production Costs   On the basis of national comparative advantage, a company may discover that its product can be produced at less cost in the foreign country than at home, because of lower wages, cheaper real estate, or other differences in cost conditions. One strategy is to import the product from the country in which it can be produced more cheaply. Another strategy is to

---

*Since then, other motivations for FDI have been identified.

TABLE 4–1

Reasons for Foreign Direct Investment

Supply Side
1. To lower production costs.
2. To lower delivery costs (costs of transportation, insurance, tariffs, etc.).
3. To acquire a necessary raw material.
4. To do offshore assembly.
5. To establish a "portfolio" of production sources.
6. To obtain technology and skills.

Demand Side
1. To explore new markets, and to serve a "portfolio" of markets.
2. Because an export market was closed by a prohibitive tariff or quota.
3. To establish a local presence with service and product availability.
4. To meet "buy national" rules or preferences in the host country.
5. To gain visibility as a "local" firm, employing local people, paying local taxes, etc.
6. To respond to rivals' threats.

establish operations in the lower-cost country. Such a foreign direct investment may be used to produce and sell in the local, host country market or to export to the home country and elsewhere.

Lower Delivery Costs   The appropriate cost to use in choosing among production locations is **delivered cost**—so the cost of transporting products to the market should be considered along with the production cost. If the distance is long or tariffs are high between the home and host countries, perhaps local production in the host country will minimize the delivered cost, even if the production costs of the home and host countries are equal or somewhat favorable to the home country. Notice that delivery costs are defined to include both the cost of transportation *and* regulatory costs such as tariffs.

Acquisition of a Raw Material   If Japanese manufacturers want to obtain a secure source of oil for their plants, they must look offshore to suppliers, since no oil has been found domestically. Rather than contract with other companies for the purchase of oil, the Japanese firms may decide to invest in oil production abroad, through direct investment. Similarly, U.S. aluminum companies have invested in Jamaica and Brazil to mine bauxite for their manufacturing in the United States. Generally, a firm may look at foreign countries not only as targets for the sale of its products but also as potential sources of needed raw materials.

Offshore Assembly or Foreign Sourcing   This category is really a subhead of the first one, focusing on production for sales outside the host country. Like FDI to obtain raw materials, FDI to do **offshore assembly** is used to gain access to a factor of production, namely labor, that is cheaper or more productive than the home country supply. Many U.S. electronics manufacturers utilize offshore assembly in Taiwan, Singapore, or Hong Kong to assemble their radios, TVs, stereos, calculators, and so on. They produce components in the United States, ship them to the Far East for assembly into final products, and then reexport the products to the United States for sale. Alternatively, a firm may choose to carry out its entire production process in the foreign country, using that site as a source from which to sell to the home country (and elsewhere)—hence the second label, **foreign sourcing.**

Portfolio of Production Sources   Firms that produce any kind of product or service may discover that it is advantageous to have multiple sources of supply. Having several sources of inputs lessens the danger of problems with any one supplier company or type of material. To reduce the risk of bottlenecks in production or distribution caused by problems that may arise in any one country (e.g., strikes, civil unrest, poor quality), it also makes sense to have suppliers in different countries.

Access to Technology and Skills   When proprietary technology and/or management skills are key competitive advantages in an industry, firms may choose to establish operations in markets where those skills are readily available. Thus, direct investment can be expected to flow to locations where high-tech firms are concentrated and where managerial skills are superior.[5] This investment may be in the form of new subsidiaries set up by the foreign investors or joint ventures that tie foreign firms to local firms.

The Demand Side

New Markets   The most common justification for undertaking FDI is to use local production as a means for establishing new national markets for a product. The firm may choose among FDI, export from the home country, or some other strategy of serving the foreign market (e.g., licensing, franchising, a turnkey venture). If the foreign market appears large enough and local production appears feasible, then FDI can be used to enter the market. Even if the firm already sells one product through exports in the host country, direct investment and local production may be used to sell additional products there.

Restriction of Exports   If a national market is closed by a prohibitive tariff or a quota, direct investment may provide an acceptable alternative. Because we are talking about a limitation on the quantity that can be sold in the foreign market, this is a demand-side constraint, not a price or cost constraint. Even if production in and export from the home country are less costly, a quota or total embargo will limit or eliminate sales through exports. In such situations, foreign direct investment and local production can fill the demand of the foreign market. This clearly was a major factor in attracting Japanese auto firms to set up production in the United States.

Local Presence   Many times, a local production presence will enable a firm to sell greater quantities of its products, because customers have confidence that the firm is accessible for service and additional product supply. A firm that sells only through imports may not provide as good after-sale service or as great availability of additional products. Visibility as a local producer may convince buyers that the firm is seriously committed to the host country market and can be counted on to deliver contracted orders. Also, local production permits the firm to adapt products more closely to local demand conditions—a flexibility that does not exist for firms that simply export.

"Buy National" Rules   Under certain conditions, most countries, including the United States, restrict purchases by government agencies to local, home country suppliers. The United States requires government agencies to buy from U.S. suppliers if their product quality is acceptable and if their prices are competitive with those of foreign bidders for the same contract.[6] Many other countries simply close contracts to foreign bidders, regardless of quality or availability. To avoid such restrictions, a firm may choose to establish a local production presence and thus become a local supplier in the eyes of government buyers.

A constraint similar to the "buy national" rules of governments may exist when local customers maintain a preference for buying from local suppliers, again effectively shutting out nonlocal producers from the market. (In the 1960s and early 1970s, may U.S.-based multinationals changed their subsidiaries' names in Latin American countries to local-sounding names, in order to avoid the negative connotation of being North American.) Japanese consumers have long demonstrated this preference; Lee Iacocca has tried to stir up similar nationalism in the United States.

Good Corporate Citizen   Another reason for establishing local manufacture or local provision of services is to gain respectability as a good corporate citizen in the host country by employing local people, paying local taxes, and otherwise participating in the host society. Such respectability may lead to more favorable perception by local buyers, and even to more favorable treatment by the host government.[7] For this reason, sales may be higher through FDI and local production than through exports from the home country. The decisions by Toyota, Nissan, and other Japanese automotive manufacturers to set up plants in the United States in the late 1970s and early 1980s were substantially an effort to present themselves as good corporate citizens in this country (with positive effects, hopefully, on their car sales)—and to avoid having penalizing quotas and other potential barriers placed on their exports from Japan.

Response to Rivals' Threats   If a rival firm enters some national market with local production, a firm may respond by similarly entering that market, to avoid being shut out through tariff or other protection by the host government. A firm would also enter that market to avoid giving its rival an advantage from experience in producing locally. By entering the host market in this way, the firm precludes its rival from building a strong, monopolistic position there, from which the rival could expand into other markets as well.

Each of these bases for deciding to undertake foreign direct investment may be used to justify such a decision, but it should not be the manager's sole justification; in every case, a full analysis is needed to compare direct investment with alternatives for accomplishing the same purpose. (The conditions that justify FDI relative to such alternatives as exporting or licensing are discussed in Chapter 3.) Before we return to the problem of deciding when to invest, we present some empirical evidence on FDI in the next section.

PATTERNS OF FOREIGN DIRECT INVESTMENT

Direct Investment by Country

The vast majority of foreign direct investment that has occurred historically has been made in the period since World War II. This is the result of the growth in national markets, coupled with the continued willingness of developed-country governments to permit foreign ownership of local companies. In addition, such investment (and exports) has been facilitated by the tremendous decline in international transportation costs and improvement in transportation availability that have occurred in the postwar period.

Table 4–2 shows the distribution of worldwide FDI by country of origin—that is, based on the country from which multinational enterprises undertook foreign direct investment projects. Notice that the United States has accounted for about half of the total investment over the whole period, though the U.S. share has been declining fairly steadily, to less than 40 percent by 1983. Also notice that, after rebuilding their economies from war damage, both German and Japanese firms have shown the most rapid growth in FDI during the postwar period. In fact, both of the traditional powers of the early 20th century, the United States and the United Kingdom, have seen a decline in their shares of global FDI, though firms from both countries continue to invest abroad and their FDI shares still lead those of other countries. (The recent trend has simply been for Japanese and German firms to invest abroad at a greater rate of growth.)

FDI undertaken by all less developed countries combined accounted for less than 10 percent of the total reported in Table 4–2.[8]

So far, only the source countries for FDI have been examined. Now consider the target or host countries. (An implicit point of the preceding paragraphs is that virtually all of worldwide FDI comes from developed market economies.

TABLE 4-2

Stock of FDI Abroad by Firms from Developed Market Countries (in billions of U.S. dollars)

Country of Origin	1967	1971	1975	1978	1981	1983	1985	1988
United States	56.6	82.8	124.1	168.1	226.4	226.3	250.7	326.9
United Kingdom	17.5	23.7	30.4	41.1	65.5	73.8	104.7	183.6
Germany, Federal Republic	3.0	7.3	16.0	31.8	45.3	51.8	60.0	62.0
Japan*	1.5	4.4	15.9	26.8	37.1	45.3	83.6	110.8
Switzerland	5.0	9.5	17.6	24.6	36.6	39.9	45.3	n.a.
Netherlands	11.0	13.8	19.0	23.7	32.2	35.7	43.8	64.8
France	6.0	7.3	11.1	14.9	24.6	29.2	21.6	n.a.
Canada	3.7	6.5	10.4	13.6	25.6	30.4	36.5	50.7
Sweden	1.7	2.4	4.4	6.0	n.a.	n.a.	9.0	n.a.
Belgium–Luxembourg	2.0	2.4	3.6	5.4	n.a.	n.a.	4.3	10.4
Italy	2.1	3.0	3.3	3.3	n.a.	n.a.	12.4	39.9
Total above	110.1	163.1	255.8	359.3	493.3	532.4	671.9	849.1
All other†	4.0	5.0	7.2	10.0	52.3	63.1	41.6	n.a.
Grand total	114.1	168.1	263.0	369.3	545.6	595.5	713.5	849.1

*Fiscal year beginning April of the year indicated on the basis of accumulated annual flows of direct investment as reported to the International Monetary Fund.

†Includes Austria, Denmark, Norway, Finland, Portugal, Spain, Australia, New Zealand, and South Africa.

Sources: United Nations, *Transnational Corporations in World Development* (New York: United Nations, 1988); International Monetary Fund, *Balance of Payments Yearbook* (Washington, D.C.: IMF, 1989).

Very little comes from the less developed countries or the formerly-communist countries.) Again, most of the direct investment flows occur between developed countries, and mostly toward Europe, though the United States has been the largest single target country for FDI in the whole period—and in the 1980s the balance of the flow had shifted toward the United States. Table 4–3 shows these flows for selected years.

Direct Investment in Various Industries

The composition of foreign direct investment across industries has favored a few very large industries. In highly aggregated terms, these industries are: manufacturing, raw materials extraction, and trade services. Table 4–4 presents evidence on some more highly aggregated industrial categories of FDI for six of the largest source countries, showing that total manufacturing generally exceeds the other two broad headings of investment. There has been one major shift in FDI among these categories, namely the relative increase in service sector activity, which includes banking, insurance, hotels, and other services. FDI has been growing over time in every sector for each country, with the perhaps anomalous exception of service sector FDI from Italy. The trend in service sector FDI appears to follow the worldwide increase in white-collar, office-type employment, and especially the decreasing growth rate of manufacturing relative to services in the industrial countries.

Direct Investment by Company

Since ultimately we are concerned about the firms that engage in FDI, let us turn finally to a view of the companies most heavily involved in this activity. Studies carried out during the past two decades have regularly found that the most important direct investors are large, technology-intensive firms from the main

TABLE 4–3

Flows* of FDI into and out of Developed Market Countries, 1967–1988 (in millions of U.S. dollars)

Country and Country Group	1967–1972	1973–1978	1979–1984	1985–1988
Outflows of Domestic Capital (annual average)				
United States	6,412	11,641	7,510	22,160
Canada	269	967	3,113	3,852
Western Europe†	4,792	10,495	12,974	46,433
Austria	18	49	117	–
Belgium-Lux	100	308	309	1,667
Denmark	42	68	98	–
Finland	35	36	205	785
France	376	1,051	2,342	6,137
Germany	836	2,137	3,023	7,070
Italy	251	262	1,170	2,489
Netherlands	463	877	543	4,095
Norway	12	123	253	889
Spain	25	81	251	516
Sweden	175	452	659	2,568
Switzerland‡	1,145	3,243	–	3,040
United Kingdom	1,314	3,438	5,422	17,177
Japan	331	1,809	3,587	14,760
Southern Hemisphere§	118	303	1,091	3,206
Australia	95	193	751	3,095
Total†	11,923	25,209	29,774	90,411
Inflows of Foreign Capital (annual average)				
United States	925	4,309	14,903	31,815
Canada	712	704	231	1,407
Western Europe†	4,419	8,241	9,690	25,309
Austria	62	114	212	–
Belgium-Lux	319	959	1,032	1,817
Denmark	101	110	73	–
Finland	21	35	19	141
France	444	1,411	2,006	3,886
Germany	927	1,741	884	1,213
Italy	657	555	771	2,281
Netherlands	454	509	26	2,542
Norway	78	365	246	435
Spain	206	456	1,426	3,402
Sweden	103	59	131	473
Switzerland‡	252	517	–	1,284
United Kingdom	798	1,670	2,906	7,835
Japan	111	89	138	348
Southern Hemisphere§	1,052	1,112	1,683	2,362
Australia	813	860	1,589	2,677
Total†	7,218	14,455	26,694	61,241

*Includes reinvested earnings.

†Including countries not listed separately.

‡Derived from the year-to-year changes of the estimated stock of direct investment assets and liabilities, respectively (estimates of the Union Bank of Switzerland).

§Includes Australia, New Zealand, and South Africa.

Sources: United Nations, *Transnational Corporations in World Development,* (New York: United Nations, 1978), (E/C10/38); International Monetary Fund, *Balance of Payments Yearbook* (Washington, D.C.: IMF, 1984, 1985, 1990); and United Nations, *Trends and Issues in Foreign Direct Investment and Related Flows: A Technical Paper* (New York: UNCTC, 1985), CTC/59, p. 25.

TABLE 4–4

Value of Private Direct Investment Abroad by Industry by Country of Origin

Country and Industry	1971 ($ millions)	Percent	1976 ($ millions)	Percent	1985* ($ millions)	Percent
United States						
Total	101,313†	100	137,244	100	256,536	100
Extractive	30,989	31	36,771	27	57,977	23
Manufacturing	44,370	44	61,062	45	95,175	37
Service, of which	25,954	26	39,411	29	90,301	35
Banking and insurance	9,726	10	16,392	12	–	–
United Kingdom						
Total	23,717	100	31,277‖	100	54,464‡	100
Extractive	8,051	34	8,747	28	4,701	9
Manufacturing	10,043	42	14,131	45	30,846	57
Service, of which	5,633	24	8,399	27	18,916	34
Banking and insurance	1,212	5	1,410	5	–	
Canada						
Total	6,524	100	9,390	100	31,576§	100
Extractive	938	14	1,963	21	7,894	25
Manufacturing	3,437	53	4,729	50	14,525	46
Service, of which	2,149	33	2,698	29	7,926	25
Banking and insurance	405	6	622	7		
Germany, Federal Republic of						
Total	7,277	100	19,915	100	60,050	100
Extractive	350	5	1,419	7	2,342	4
Manufacturing	5,796	80	14,032	71	25,821	43
Service, of which	1,131	16	4,464	22	27,383	46
Banking and insurance	494	7	1,941	10	–	–
Japan						
Total	3,962	100	10,620	100	83,649	100
Extractive	892	23	2,778	26	12,631	15
Manufacturing	1,092	28	3,723	35	24,426	29
Service, of which	1,978	50	4,119	39	43,330	52
Banking and insurance	843	21	2,376	22	–	–

*1985 data do not add to totals, due to unallocated "other" category.
†data for 1973
‡data for 1981
§data for 1984
‖data for 1974
Sources: United Nations, *Transnational Corporations in World Development: A Re-Examination* (New York: UNCTC, 1978); national sources for 1981 data; and United Nations, *Trends and Issues in Foreign Direct Investment and Related Flows: A Technical Paper* (New York: UNCTC, 1985), CTC/59, p. 80; and unpublished UNCTC data.

industrial countries.[9] This means, for example, that an examination of the world's largest firms in major industries is likely to present a clear view of the main MNEs in those industries as well. Appendix 4–1 identifies the largest 5 firms in 18 major industrial categories. In virtually all cases, these firms are also leading direct investors. Exceptions exist in situations where very large economies of scale and/or national defense considerations preclude direct investment—for example, in the production of aircraft, where Boeing is one of the leading firms, yet that firm limits its production to the United States and Canada, while subcontracting out to other firms in several other industrial countries.

It should be noted that Appendix 4–1 groups firms into broad industrial categories. The five firms in each category are not necessarily direct competitors (for example, IBM and Xerox, or Coca-Cola and Anheuser Busch), even though they appear together in the list. Also, the amount of direct investment varies widely among the industrial categories; the aerospace industry and metal manufacturing industries are much less internationalized than the food and beverage industries and consumer product industries in general.

The largest direct investors (in terms of dollar value) tend to be firms that carry out extractive ventures overseas (for example, oil exploration, copper and bauxite mining) and producers of capital-intensive goods (such as automobiles and chemicals). Also, the largest direct investors tend to be large exporters as well. They export machinery, parts, and components to their foreign facilities, as well as filling out product lines with domestically produced and exported products.

FOREIGN DIRECT INVESTMENT IN THE UNITED STATES

The Pattern by Industry

Looking specifically at foreign direct investment coming into the United States, we see a pattern similar to that in the rest of the industrial countries. That is, the dominant industries are petroleum, manufacturing, and services (mainly trade, real estate, banking, and insurance). The growth has been more rapid in services that in the other major sectors. These patterns can be seen in Figure 4–1, which traces FDI into the United States since the early 1970s. In the 1980s, not only had foreign direct investment grown faster than U.S. FDI going abroad, but it had also grown faster than the U.S. economy overall. That is, incoming FDI has provided a substantial boost to U.S. national income (and also forced U.S. firms to compete even harder in their own domestic market).

The Pattern by Country of Origin

The main countries whose firms are undertaking this flow of FDI into the United States are, not surprisingly, the same countries that follow the United States in overall FDI worldwide: Great Britain, Japan, the Netherlands, Canada, Germany, Switzerland, and other European countries. Table 4–5 shows a disaggregation of the recent stock of FDI according to both industry and country of origin.

The British lead in overall FDI in the U.S. market is not surprising, given Britain's number two position in worldwide FDI and its historical, political, cultural, and language ties to this country. Japanese FDI surged in the late 1980s to the second largest group, largely on the impressive strength of Japanese companies in global competition, and particularly in the automobile industry. Dutch direct investment, especially in petroleum (Royal Dutch/Shell) and manufacturing (Philips and Unilever), surprisingly ranks third overall. Canada, with its proximity to this market, ranks among the leading source countries in virtually every category. While source-country rankings give some idea of the nature of FDI in the United States, the real driving force behind successful entry into the U.S. market are the companies that undertake that investment.[10] We focus on these firms next.

FIGURE 4–1

Foreign Direct Investment
into the United States

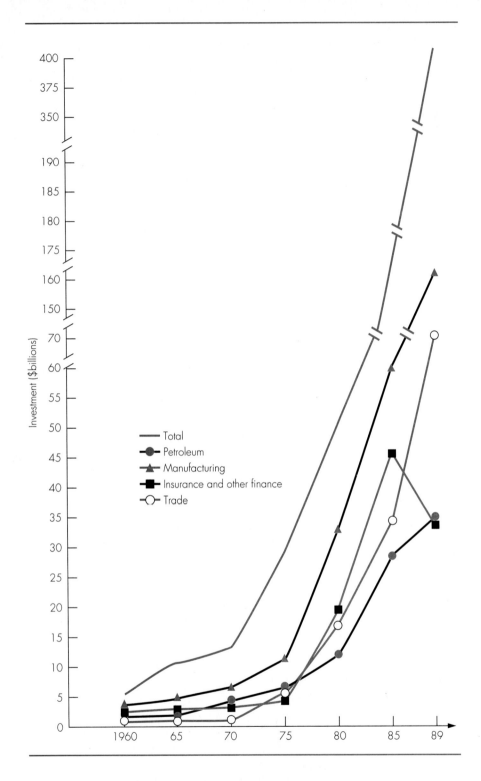

TABLE 4–5

Foreign Direct Investment Position in the United States by Industry and Country (in millions of U.S. dollars)

Industry	United Kingdom	Japan	Netherlands	Canada	Germany	Switzerland	France
Petroleum	16,811	68	10,660	1,679	250	105	n.a.
Manufacturing	50,704	17,255	24,101	11,586	15,232	10,107	13,916
Foods	10,881	397	6,551	895	583	n.a.	780
Chemical	16,248	2,420	6,828	546	9,117	3,169	5,821
Machinery	5,733	4,960	4,751	2,789	2,413	1,516	1,040
Wholesale and retail trade	21,013	21,005	5,549	3,190	7,393	2,083	763
Banking	3,748	4,441	3,148	1,493	699	n.a.	870
Real estate	5,234	14,294	3,410	3,921	1,173	370	73
Total	119,137	60,483	69,699	31,538	28,223	19,329	16,375

Source: U.S. Dept. of Commerce, *Survey of Current Business*, August 1990.

The Major Foreign Investors in the United States

The specific firms that have taken the largest FDI positions in the U.S. economy tend to follow the list of the largest firms in international business throughout the world. Table 4–6 lists the 25 largest foreign direct investors in the United States in 1988, along with some of their characteristics. Note that these firms compete in industries where U.S. competitors are also strong. A fundamental reason for their ability to survive in the U.S. marketplace is simply that demand is large enough to absorb multiple competitors. That is, the foreign firms do not have to outcompete American firms to survive. This is particularly true in the petroleum sector, where 4 of the 25 compete. The competitive advantages that the foreign firms do possess appear to stem largely from proprietary technology, goodwill based on high quality and performance, and lower costs—very similar to those of successful U.S. firms.

Current Trends

FDI in the United States grew tremendously during the 1980s. This phenomenon may be attributed to a variety of causes, including the recovery of the United States from the early-1980s recession before other industrial nations, the devaluation of the dollar relative to other widely traded currencies in the late 1980s, and the faster growth of non-U.S. MNEs in the 1970s and 1980s as they caught up to U.S. firms in size and geographic scope. In the late 1980s, the threat of increased protectionism in the United States encouraged many Japanese firms (such as the auto manufacturers) to set up operations in this country to avoid the possibility of harm due to greater import restrictions.

Because of the very large existing base of U.S. FDI overseas, the *growth rate* of FDI in the United States is likely to exceed that of outgoing FDI into the 1990s. Whether U.S. or non-U.S. firms will be more successful in foreign markets is quite another question—and one that U.S. MNE managers will help resolve in the future. The perhaps even more important question—whether U.S. firms will be able to survive competition *in the United States* from their foreign rivals— also remains to be answered. The grounds on which the competition will take place will almost certainly be the development of sustainable competitive advantages by the successful firms.

TABLE 4–6

The 25 Largest Foreign Investments in the United States

	Foreign Investor	Country	U.S. Company	Percent owned	Industry	Revenue (mil)
1.	Seagram Co Ltd*	Canada	El du Pont de Nemours*	23%	chemicals, energy	$32,657
			Joseph E Seagram & Sons	100	alcoholic beverages	2,540
			Tropicana Products	100	beverages	741
						35,938
2.	Royal Dutch/Shell Group*	Netherlands/UK	Shell Oil	100	energy, chemicals	21,070
3.	British Petroleum Plc*	UK	BP America	100	energy	14,378
4.	B.A.T. Industries Plc*	UK	BATUS	100	multicompany	6,251
	Imasco Ltd*	Canada	Farmers Group	100	insurance	1,191
			Peoples Drug Stores	100	drugstores	1,498
			Imasco USA	100	fast food	1,431
						10,371
5.	Tengelmann Group	Germany	Great A&P Tea*	53	supermarkets	10,068
6.	Grand Metropolitan Plc*	UK	Pillsbury	100	food processors	6,191
			Grand Metropolitan USA	100	beverages, retailing	2,700
						8,891
7.	Campeau	Canada	Federated Dept Stores	100	retailing	6,220
			Allied Stores	100	retailing	1,842
			Ralphs Grocery	100	supermarkets	8,062
8.	Nestlé SA*	Switzerland	Nestlé Enterprises	100	food processing	6,089
			Alcon Laboratories	100	optical products	500E
						6,589
9.	Hanson Plc*	UK	Hanson Industries	100	multicompany	6,030
10.	Pechiney	France	American National Can	100	packaging	4,320
			Pechiney	100	metal castings	1,398
						5,718
11.	Petróleos de Venezuela, SA	Venezuela	Citgo Petroleum	50	refining, marketing	4,110
			Champlin Refining	100	refining, marketing	1,600E
						5,710
12.	Unilever NV*	Netherlands	Unilever United States	100	food processing	5,688
	Unilever Plc*	UK				
13.	Hoechst AG*	Germany	Hoechst Celanese	100	chemicals	5,679
14.	NV Philips*	Netherlands	North American Philips	100	electronics	5,424
15.	BASF AG*	Germany	BASF	100	chemicals	5,000
16.	Bayer AG*	Germany	Mobay	100	chemicals	2,017
			Miles	100	health care	1,706
			Agfa	100	photography	818
			Other companies	100	chemicals	178
						4,719
17.	Groupe Bruxelles Lambert	Belguim	Drexel Burnham Lambert	26	finance	4,660
18.	Brascan Ltd*	Canada	Noranda US	100	minerals, forest prods	2,993
	Noranda	Canada	Johanna Farms	100	dairy, juice products	1,504
	John Labatt Ltd	Canada	other companies	100	package foods, brewing	4,497
19.	Honda Motor Co Ltd*	Japan	Honda of America Mfg	100	automotive	4,400E
20.	BCE*	Canada	BCE Development*(US)	67	real estate	354
	Northern Telecom Ltd*	Canada	Northern Telecom	100	telecommunications	3,480
	Trans Canada Pipeline*	Canada	Great Lakes Gas Trans	50	gas transmission	280
			Northern Border Pipeline	30	gas transmission	210
						4,324

TABLE 4–6

concluded

	Foreign Investor	Country	U.S. Company	Percent owned	Industry	Revenue (mil)
21.	Ferruzzi Group	Italy	Central Soya	100%	food processor	$2,197
	*Montedison Group**	Italy	Himont*	81	chemicals	1,711
			Erbamont	71	pharmaceuticals	211
			Conserv	100	agro-industry	92
			Ausimont USA	88	chemicals	91
						4,302
22.	Bridgestone*	Japan	Firestone Tire & Rubber	100	tire & rubber	3,500E
			Bridgestone USA	100	tire & rubber	584
						4,084
23.	Imperial Chemical Industries Plc*	UK	ICI Americas	100	chemicals, drugs, paint	4,000
24.	Sony Corp*	Japan	CBS Records	100	records	2,577
			Sony (US)	100	consumer electronics	1,300E
						3,877
25.	Delhaize "Le Lion" SA	Belgium	Food Lion*	44	supermarkets	3,815

*Publicly traded in the U.S. in shares or ADRs. E: Estimate. NA: Not available. Note: Some foreign investors on the list own U.S. companies indirectly through companies in italics.
Source: *Forbes*, July 24, 1989, pp. 313–14.

EXPLANATIONS OF THE FOREIGN DIRECT INVESTMENT PROCESS

How can the flows of FDI and the shifts in the company and country composition of FDI be explained? There is no single theory that covers all the characteristics of the foreign investment process. Several views have been presented, however, that offer partial explanations of what is observed. The theory of the international product cycle, discussed in Chapter 3, clarifies several of the reasons for FDI. The theory of competitive advantage, presented in Chapter 2, sheds some light on company characteristics that often lead to FDI. The comparative cost view, presented in Chapter 3, adds some useful points regarding the choice of FDI versus other market-serving alternatives. Dunning's "eclectic view" (below p. 108) focuses attention on three types of variables that play important parts in explaining FDI. Finally, the concept of internalization can be used to tie together several of the other strands of thinking about FDI. This section reviews each of these theories as it relates to foreign direct investment.

International Product Cycle

The theory of the international product cycle hypothesizes that foreign direct investment (*or* host country production by local firms) will take place in countries that originally import a new product from the country where it is developed. That is, once a product has been introduced successfully into one country, subsequent export and foreign manufacture generally follow. If the innovating company chooses to produce overseas, then its establishment of a foreign affiliate is FDI. By the time the product arrives at the standardized stage, cost considerations are foremost and low-cost production locations are sought, perhaps in low-wage areas of developed countries or in less developed countries.

The international product cycle has been discussed in some detail in Chapter 3; here an example may offer additional insights.

Radio Corporation of America (RCA), originally a division of General Electric Company, began producing television sets in the late 1920s. Television had been invented and reinvented in various forms during the previous 30 years by scientists in several countries, but RCA was one of two firms to introduce the product into the market successfully, in the early 1940s. (Du Mont Laboratories was the other firm that began marketing televisions, in 1939, along with RCA.) Initially, TV sets and programming were sold primarily in the United States, though sales occurred in Great Britain as well. The market for television remained very small until after World War II.

Domestic competition in television manufacture arose during the late 1940s, from General Electric itself (which had sold RCA) and from American Telephone & Telegraph. The market for television began to grow rapidly, with about 140,000 sets per month sold by 1948. RCA began exporting into the Canadian and European markets in the late 1940s.

Such U.S. competitors as Westinghouse and Admiral entered the market during the 1950s. The Japanese producers Sony and Panasonic introduced competing products in the early 1960s, and by about 1965 television was in the maturing product stage. At that point (in 1964), RCA decided to use direct investment in Canada to serve that market with locally manufactured picture tubes. At about the same time, it established a manufacturing plant in England to serve the European market.

Ultimately, cost conditions became the overwhelming factor in TV competition, and RCA followed several firms into offshore assembly, choosing Taiwan (in 1970) and Ciudad Juárez in Mexico (in 1969) as its bases. Now the firm produces parts and components in more than a dozen countries, including the offshore assembly sites, and sells them in more than 50 countries. RCA has followed the international product cycle through all three stages, producing first in the United States, then in Canada and Western Europe, and now also in less developed countries.[11]

In an interesting turn of events, General Electric Company repurchased RCA in 1986, returning the firm to its original corporate parent. This merger of the two electronics giants has not altered RCA's direct investment strategy from the path discussed above.

Competitive Advantage

The theory of competitive advantage, presented in Chapter 2, explains foreign direct investment as one of the many ways in which a firm may capitalize on its proprietary assets. RCA was able to use FDI to take advantage of its new technology. Similarly, Texas Instruments and other calculator manufacturers have used FDI to assemble their products in low-cost countries. Of course, not all FDI is based on firms' taking advantage of proprietary technology. Relatively standardized products such as processed foods are produced and sold by foreign direct investors in many countries. Oil companies invest abroad not only to explore for oil but also to operate gas stations and to produce and sell nonproprietary petrochemicals. Producers of farm machinery sell their tractors and other machines through exports to their own sales offices in many countries, and they also assemble many kinds of equipment abroad in direct investment projects.

Walt Disney Company provides a noteworthy example of the use of FDI to benefit from the firm's competitive advantages. After pursuing an essentially domestic strategy for many years, Disney opened a Disneyland theme park in Japan in 1984. The company was trying to profit from its major competitive strengths: the very widely accepted Disney characters, the firm's know-how based on experience in operating theme parks in California and Florida, and the uniqueness of its product.

At that time Disney negotiated an agreement with local investors such that Disney receives royalties and fees from the park but does not own it. The overwhelming success of that venture—and Disney's failure to benefit from any ownership stake in it—convinced Disney's top managers that future ventures should be pursued with some equity interest.

Beginning at about the time of the opening of Tokyo Disneyland, the firm began negotiating to build a EuroDisneyland. This project was very carefully considered, beginning with 200 possible sites in Europe and ending with a choice between Barcelona (with better weather) and Paris (with a more central location in Europe). Disney ultimately invested in Paris and took a 49 percent share in the project, with the remaining shares sold to investors in Europe.[12] Thus, Disney has chosen to use direct investment to benefit from its competitive advantages—after discovering that a contracting agreement (in Japan) was suboptimal.

Comparative Cost

The comparative cost view of FDI follows on the theory of comparative advantage, discussed in Chapter 3. In this case, we look at an individual firm's choice of production locations based on *delivered* cost to its relevant markets. Just as the theory of comparative advantage showed the appropriate *country* to produce and export a given product, based on production costs, the extension to FDI focuses on a *company's* use of this information. If it were really less costly to produce bananas in Honduras and appliances in the United States, then United Fruit Corporation should look at Honduras as a site for FDI to produce bananas, which can then be exported to the U.S. market. (Leave the appliances to another company!) Indeed, this is exactly what United Fruit (whose brand name for bananas is Chiquita) has done—not only in Honduras but also in El Salvador, Costa Rica, Ecuador, and other countries where banana production is very inexpensive, due to climatic conditions and inexpensive labor.

In the final analysis, what counts is *delivered* cost. So United Fruit or any other foreign investor must consider not only the production costs involved in the foreign country but also the transportation costs and tariff or other restrictions that may apply to the product. This differs from traditional comparative advantage theory, which focused only on *production* costs. Even if bananas could be produced more cheaply in Honduras than in Costa Rica, and exported to Costa Rica, firms probably could not take advantage of this condition, because the government of Costa Rica places tariffs and other restrictions on imports. Similar problems often arise as well from high transportation costs: cement can be produced more cheaply in Colombia than in Venezuela, but the cost of delivering it to the Venezuelan market from a Colombian city such as Bogotá or Barranquilla is much higher than the production cost difference. So each country produces cement for domestic consumption and does not export it. The appropriate way for a company to take advantage of this situation would be to invest directly in each country to produce cement for the local market.

Dunning's Eclectic View

John Dunning (1977) has proposed a multifaceted "theory" of FDI that includes emphases on country-specific variables such as production costs and regulatory constraints, company-specific (ownership) variables such as proprietary skills and scale economies, and internalization variables related to the firm's choice to utilize its proprietary capabilities through its own affiliates or through dealings with other firms. Each of these three kinds of variables has been the focus of theories of international trade and investment. Dunning's view is "eclectic" in that it packages a number of competitive advantages together and uses the concept of internalization to provide decision-making rules.

Dunning's view is quite useful in forcing the decision maker to consider not only cost factors or demand forecasts but also other key issues. Thus, the size of the market may well justify entering it, but *location* factors may call for exports rather than FDI. Similarly, local production costs may favor direct investment, but if the company's resources (its *ownership* advantages) are too limited, then FDI may be infeasible and licensing a local firm (that is, *not internalizing*) may offer a viable alternative. By combining three distinct perspectives, Dunning's view enables the decision maker to avoid the trap of narrow-minded focus on only a part of the full picture.

To reiterate, Dunning's **eclectic view** states that the FDI decision should be made on the grounds of these three factors:[13]

1. *Ownership advantages:* the company's competitive advantages, such as proprietary technology, management skills, goodwill, and economies of scale.
2. *Location advantages:* the relevant cost, risk, and regulatory conditions in the countries under consideration. These include national production costs, tariffs, taxes, international transportation costs, and political risks.
3. *Internalization advantages:* the benefits that the firm would realize by itself operating in the host country versus the benefits of operating through a local distributor, licensee, or other contractee. (See the next section.)

Internalization

Chapter 2 presented the idea that vertical or horizontal integration of a firm across national boundaries was a characteristic of the MNE. In fact, that integration is itself foreign direct investment—the firm that buys a metal mine or an oil well abroad is undertaking FDI, just as the firm that sets up a restaurant abroad similar to its domestic restaurants is undertaking FDI.

Internalization is a very useful concept because it focuses attention on the decision to internalize or not to internalize across national borders—that is, the decision to use or not to use FDI. The optimal decision should be based on the product's stage in the product cycle, the competitive advantages of the firm, and the costs of this alternative relative to others that are available. That is, internalization can be used as a broad label to encompass each of the more precisely focused views discussed above. The foreign investment decision then can be stated as follows: The firm should internalize foreign market and supply opportunities up to the point that the additional costs of internalizing outweigh the additional benefits of doing so.

Other Explanations for Foreign Direct Investment

A number of additional explanations for FDI have come from many different social science disciplines.[14] Two of the more important ones are noted here.

Some political scientists writing about the global spread of capitalism have viewed the process of FDI as the natural tendency of capitalist firms, which need to find new markets for their products once existing ones have been saturated. The "exploitation" of foreign markets, then, enmeshes these markets in the international capitalist system.[15] This view of FDI emphasizes its negative aspects, namely control of part of the local economy by foreign owners and transfers of funds to the parent companies. The view is important because it is held by policymakers in some countries and because it always provides a rationale for penalizing foreign firms when a scapegoat is needed for economic or political problems.

Another view, presented by Jean Boddewyn (1983), looks at FDI in three steps: necessary conditions, motivations, and precipitating factors. This view regards virtually all of the reasons for FDI discussed above as *conditions* that may make FDI desirable. Boddewyn points out that all of these conditions are based on the premise or *motivation* that the firm is managed to maximize profits. Each condition offers a way in which the firm can pursue its central goal of profit maximization—for example, reducing costs, enlarging market share, or creating new products. Finally, there must be some *triggering factor* that induces the firm to take advantage of the conditions to seek its central goal. This last point is quite important. Firms have infinite possible strategies at their disposal; but for FDI to result, a clear definition of goals and acceptable alternatives, plus some precipitating event (such as a period of negative earnings or a change in leadership), are required.

In sum, each of the views of FDI presented above offers insights into the managerial and regulatory issues related to such investment. The company manager can benefit from utilizing the various views in considering the firm's choices for doing business in foreign countries, whether it be market-serving or supply-seeking business. The government policymaker can better understand the motivations of company managers by seeing the key factors that affect company investment decisions.

DISINVESTMENT

This chapter has looked mainly at the process of entry into foreign direct investment, without considering in any detail the operation of the foreign affiliate once it has been established.* The termination of a foreign affiliate, that is, **disinvestment** (or divestment), can be seen as almost a mirror image of the entry decision. Using Dunning's three-factor view of FDI, disinvestment can be rationalized when any of the conditions for FDI disappears. If a firm ceases to possess a competitive (or ownership) advantage relative to other firms in the host country, the profitability of operating there may disappear. Or if political or economic changes in the host country make the local project no longer viable, the reason for being there (i.e., locational advantage) may disappear. Finally, the local affiliate may be unjustified if the firm finds it no longer useful to internalize the activity, but may sell or rent it to another firm. In short, disinvestment may be justified once the conditions that originally justified FDI cease to exist.

In Boddewyn's terms, once changes in the conditions make FDI unattractive relative to other alternatives, and profitability would be better served by not operating the affiliate, then all it takes is some precipitating factor to make the disinvestment decision. This precipitating factor may be the assignment of a new

---

*Operation of the foreign affiliate is the subject of much of Part III in this book.

manager to supervise the company division in which the project is based; if the project shows poor results in its sales, profits, or costs, the new manager may look to disinvestment as a method to eliminate the problem. Another factor that may stimulate the firm to consider disinvesting is the threat of host government constraints—ranging from expropriation, to higher taxes, to limits on financial transfers. In any of these cases, the decision to disinvest is usually made at the home office of the firm, by a senior decision maker. This contrasts with the FDI decision, which is often proposed by a middle-level manager or division and simply approved by the home office.[16]

The firm can utilize disinvestment strategically in the context of the international product cycle. A product in the innovation stage is generally produced in one country and sold domestically and through exports. As the product enters the maturing stage, market and cost conditions may justify FDI in host countries for local sales. As the product enters the standardized stage, cost conditions may justify closing high-cost production sites in favor of sites located in low-cost regions or countries. So, especially in the standardized product stage, disinvestment may be part of a planned, strategic process of global production and sales in the MNE.

For example, the Monsanto Corporation, a multinational chemical company, operated synthetic fiber plants for many years in several Western European countries. During the early 1970s, these operations became unprofitable due to price competition from firms that faced lower costs of production. After several years of losses, Monsanto decided to sell all of its synthetic fiber business in Europe, divesting the whole set of subsidiaries.[17] Rather than compete in the standardized stage of the product cycle for these products, Monsanto decided to place its resources into other products in earlier stages of the cycle.

CONCLUSIONS

FDI is a complex form of international business, necessarily involving the transfer of a company's ownership to foreign owners and typically involving transfers of funds, people, products, and other items. During the post-World War II period, the largest sector in which FDI has taken place has been manufacturing, though the single industry with the most foreign investment has been petroleum. The single largest source and target country for FDI is the United States, while German and Japanese FDI has been growing at the fastest rate during the past decade.

Firms undertake FDI to serve new markets, to obtain needed inputs for their domestic businesses, and generally for many of the same reasons that they undertake domestic capital investment. The reasons for going overseas also include international diversification, which allows firms to reduce the variability of their earnings. Foreign disinvestment may be a final step in a firm's strategy in a particular country, though it is by no means the logical end of FDI.

Foreign direct investment is *the* activity that makes a company multinational. It should be viewed, however, as one among several alternatives for serving host country markets (or for obtaining necessary factors of production). How can the manager decide when to utilize this alternative? Based on the criteria laid out above, the company manager needs to consider:

1. Incremental cash flows from the project, as with any other capital investment.
2. The costs of undertaking this alternative relative to the costs of other alternatives available to the firm, such as exports or some other contractual form.

3. The strategic fit of the project within the firm's global activities, taking into account the firm's competitive advantages.

4. Related to 3, the issue of whether this type of internalization is preferable to other strategies, such as contracting with outside firms.

Thus, armed with a pro forma capital budget and a statement of the firm's competitive advantages and strategy, the manager can decide whether or not FDI is the appropriate alternative to serve the company's goals in any given situation.

QUESTIONS

1. What do you think are the reasons that Imperial Chemicals Industries (ICI) decided to invest in the U.S. market? How would these correspond to RCA's reasons for setting up manufacturing in Singapore?

2. In general, why would a company use FDI rather than exports to serve a foreign market?

3. Are direct investment and disinvestment simply mirror images of each other? What are the key differences between the decision process for direct investment and the decision process for divestment?

4. Compare competitive advantage, comparative advantage, and the international product cycle as explanations of FDI. How are the three theories related?

5. How does the concept of internalization relate to FDI?

6. Why did Japanese automobile manufacturers set up operations in the United States in the 1980s? How do your reasons fit with the theories discussed in this chapter?

7. Which countries are the main sources of foreign direct investment in other countries? Why? Which countries are the main recipients of FDI? Why?

8. Which companies have been the main foreign direct investors in the 1970s and 1980s? What enables these companies to compete in the various markets that they serve?

9. Observers note that the United States is becoming a service-based economy. Why has foreign direct investment by service firms not grown dramatically relative to FDI in other sectors?

10. What are the key differences between a domestic direct investment project and a foreign direct investment project? Should both types of project be evaluated similarly?

REFERENCES

Aharoni, Yair. *The Foreign Investment Decision Process.* Boston: Harvard Business School, 1966.

Boddewyn, Jean. "Foreign and Domestic Divestment and Investment Decisions." *Journal of International Business Studies,* December 1983.

Buckley, Peter, and Mark Casson. *The Future of Multinational Enterprise.* New York: Holmes & Meier, 1976.

Calvet, Luis. "A Synthesis of Foreign Direct Investment Theories and Theories of the Multinational Firm." *Journal of International Business Studies,* Spring–Summer 1981.

Casson, Mark. *The Theory of Foreign Direct Investment.* University of Reading Discussion Papers, no. 50, November 1980.

_____ "The Theory of Foreign Direct Investment," in Peter Buckley and Mark Casson, *The Economic Theory of the Multinational Enterprise.* New York: St. Martin's Press, 1985.

Caves, Richard. "International Corporations: The Industrial Economics of Foreign Investment." *Economica,* February 1971.

Dunning, John. "Trade, Location of Economic Activity, and the MNE: A Search for an Eclectic Approach." In *The International Allocation of Economic Activity,* ed. Bertil Ohlin. New York: Holmes & Meier, 1977.

Dunning, John, and Robert Pearce. *The World's Largest Industrial Enterprises.* Westmead, England: Gower Publishing, 1981.

Grosse, Robert. *The Theory of Foreign Direct Investment,* University of South Carolina Essays in International Business, no. 3, December 1981.

Hymer, Stephen. *The International Operations of National Firms: A Study of Direct Foreign Investment.* Cambridge, Mass.: MIT Press, 1976. (Originally published in 1960.)

Itaki, Masahiku. "A Critical Assessment of the Eclectic Theory of the Multinational Enterprise." *Journal of International Business Studies* (1991).

Kindleberger, Charles. *American Business Abroad.* New Haven: Yale University Press, 1969.

Penrose, Edith. "Foreign Investment and the Growth of the Firm." *Economic Journal,* June 1956.

Robinson, Richard (ed.). *Direct Foreign Investment.* New York: Praeger, 1987.

Vernon, Raymond. *Storm over the Multinationals.* Cambridge, Mass.: Harvard University Press, 1977.

4-1 Top Five Firms in 18 Industries (ranked by annual sales in millions of U.S. dollars, 1988)

	Sales 1988	Sales 1977	Growth of Sales, 1977–1988 (in percent)	Rank Position 1977
Aerospace				
United Technologies (U.S.)	18,088	5,551	325.9	2
Boeing (U.S.)	16,962	4,018	422.2	3
McDonnell Douglas	15,072	3,545	425.2	4
Rockwell International (U.S.)	11,946	5,858	203.9	1
Allied Signal (U.S.)	11,909	—	—	—
Office Equipment				
IBM (U.S.)	59,681	18,133	329.1	1
Xerox (U.S.)	16,441	5,077	323.8	3
Fijitsu (Japan)	14,797	—	—	—
Digital Equipment (U.S.)	11,475	7,029	163.3	2
Unisys (U.S.)	9,902	—	—	—
Petroleum				
Exxon (U.S.)	79,557	54,126	147.0	1
Royal Dutch/Shell Group (UK/Netherlands)	78,381	39,680	197.5	2
Mobil (U.S.)	48,198	32,128	150.0	3
British Petroleum (U.K.)	46,174	—	—	—
Texaco (U.S.)	33,544	27,920	120.1	4
Electronics				
General Electric (U.S.)	49,414	17,519	282.1	1
Hitachi (Japan)	41,331	8,222	502.7	4
Siemens (West Germany)	34,129	10,641	320.7	3
Matsushita Electric Ind. (Japan)	33,923	6,888	492.5	5
Philips (Netherlands)	28,371	12,702	223.4	2
Chemicals and Pharmaceuticals				
DuPont (U.S.)	32,514	9,435	344.6	2
BASF (West Germany)	24,961	9,116	273.8	4
Hoechst (West Germany)	23,308	10,042	232.1	1
Bayer (West Germany)	23,026	9,220	249.7	3
Imperial Chemical Ind. (UK)	20,839	8,139	256.0	5

	Sales 1988	Sales 1977	Growth of Sales, 1977–1988 (in percent)	Rank Position 1977
Industrial and Farm Equipment				
Asea Brown Boveri (Switzerland)	17,562	—	—	—
Tenneco (U.S.)	15,707	—	—	—
Mitsubishi Heavy Ind. (Japan)	13,398	8,089	165.6	1
Mernesmenn (West Germany)	11,620	5,049	230.1	3
Caterpillar (U.S.)	10,435	5,849	178.4	2
Rubber				
Goodyear (U.S.)	10,810	6,628	163.1	1
Bridgestone (Japan)	9,296	1,556	597.4	4
Michelin (France)	8,702	3,549	245.2	3
Pirelli (Italy/Switzerland)	7,006	4,233	165.5	2
Continental (W. Germany)	4,498	842	534.2	5
Motor Vehicles				
General Motors (U.S.)	121,085	54,961	220.3	—
Ford Motor (U.S.)	92,446	37,841	244.3	1
Toyota Motor (Japan)	50,790	9,601	529.0	2
Daimler-Benz (W. Germany)	41,818	8,633	484.4	4
Chrysler (U.S.)	35,473	16,708	212.3	5
Metal Manufacture and Production				
IRI (Italy)	45,522	—	—	—
Nippon Steel (Japan)	17,109	8,911	192.0	1
Thyssen (West Germany)	16,796	8,325	201.8	2
INI (Spain)	14,986	—	—	—
Usinor (France)	13,247	—	—	—
Building Materials				
Saint-Gobain (France)	9,887	6,477	152.6	1
BTR (UK)	9,748	—	—	—
Pilkington (UK)	3,973	676	587.7	4
Ube Industries (Japan)	3,848	1,379	279.0	2
Lafarge Coppee (France)	3,809	1,286	296.2	3
Tobacco				
Philip Morris (U.S.)	25,860	3,849	671.9	2
B.A.T. Industries (UK)	14,067	6,616	212.6	1
American Brands (U.S.)	7,477	2,892	258.5	3
Japan Tobacco (Japan)	7,262	—	—	—
Gallaher (UK)	3,240	1,114	290.8	4
Beverages				
Pepsico (U.S.)	13,007	3,546	366.8	2
Grand Metropolitan (UK)	9,025	—	—	—
Anheuser-Busch (U.S.)	8,924	1,838	485.5	3
Coca-Cola (U.S.)	8,338	3,560	234.2	1
Elders IXL (Australia)	7,618	—	—	—
Food				
Unilever (UK/Netherlands)	30,488	15,965	191.0	1
Nestlé (Switzerland)	27,803	8,396	331.1	2

	Sales 1988	Sales 1977	Growth of Sales, 1977–1988 (in percent)	Rank Position 1977
Occidental Petroleum (U.S.)	19,417	6,006	323.3	3
RJR Nabisco (U.S.)	16,956	2,118	800.6	4
Sara Lee	10,424	–	–	–
Paper and Wood Products				
Weyerhauser (U.S.)	10,004	5,206	192.2	1
Canadian Pacific (Canada)	9,743	4,423	220.3	2
International Paper (U.S.)	9,533	3,669	259.8	4
Georgia Pacific (U.S.)	9,509	3,675	258.7	3
Noranda (Canada)	7,040	1,305	539.5	5
Textiles, Apparel, and Leather				
Asahi Chemical Ind. (Japan)	6,882	2,038	337.7	2
Toray Industries (Japan)	5,362	1,709	313.8	4
Haci Omer Sabanci Holding (Turkey)	4,242	2,903	146.1	1
Kenebo (Japan)	4,203	1,807	232.6	3
Hyosung (South Korea)	4,183	–	–	–
Publishing and Printing				
Dai Nippon Printing (Japan)	6,575	1,173	560.5	3
Bertelsmann (West Germany)	6,539	1,173	557.5	2
Toppan Printing (Japan)	6,148	973	631.9	4
Time Inc. (U.S.)	4,507	1,250	360.6	1
News Corporation (Australia)	4,384	–	–	–
Leisure-Time Industries				
Eastman Kodak (U.S.)	17,034	5,967	285.5	1
Minnesota Mining (U.S.)	10,581	3,980	265.9	2
Baxter International (U.S.)	6,861	–	–	–
Fuji Photo Film (Japan)	5,988	1,048	571.4	4
Schulmberger (Neth./Antilles)	4,925	2,160	228.0	3
Other Manufacturing				
Procter & Gamble (U.S.)	19,336	7,284	265.5	1
Ruhrkohle (W. Germany)	11,750	4,730	248.4	2
British Coal (UK)	7,473	–	–	–
RTZ (UK)	6,975	–	–	–
Unilever (U.S.)	6,956	–	–	–

Source: "The Fortune 500," *Fortune*, April 24, 1989; "The International 500," *Fortune*, July 31, 1990.

NOTES

[1]This distinction is often difficult to draw when one firm buys partial ownership of another firm. Such an investment may be direct, even if only 5–10 percent ownership is purchased, if the investor is given management control. It may be a portfolio investment, even if 50 percent or more is purchased, if the investor does not exercise management control. For measurement of FDI, the U.S. Department of Commerce arbitrarily defines ownership of 10 percent or more as direct investment.

[2]"GM–Toyota Accord to Produce Autos Gets Final Approval," *The Wall Street Journal,* April 12, 1984, p. 10.

[3]Governments may also be central decision makers in FDI, because many of the largest LDC multinational corporations are government owned, as are many multinational corporations in Europe (e.g., national oil companies, French banks, and British Steel).

[4]See, for example, Grosse (1981), which cites new evidence and several additional studies.

[5]Ajami and Ricks (1981) found that "obtaining U.S. technology and know-how" was the most useful variable in explaining foreign firms' investment behavior in the United States.

[6]United States Code, Section 10A ff.

[7]The "obsolescing bargain," discussed in Chapter 22, may wipe out expected profitability once the plant has been built. That is, once the firm has committed its funds and built the local facility, the host government gains a better bargaining position, since the physical investment is in place. The host government may then demand a better sharing of the gains from the investment—through higher taxes, greater local management and ownership, and so on.

[8]Some data on FDI from developing countries have been compiled by Louis Wells in *Third World Multinationals* (Cambridge, Mass.: MIT Press, 1982).

[9]See, for example, Caves (1982), Grosse (1981), and Robinson (1987).

[10]The country of origin *does* play an important role in determining FDI patterns to the extent that a strong currency affects all firms in a given source country. A strong currency makes it both less expensive to invest abroad *and* more compelling because exports are more expensive in the target country.

[11]"Television," *Encyclopaedia Britannica,* 1969; Stanley Kemper, *A History of Television* (Atlanta: Television Encyclopedia Press, 1965); and *RCA: An Historical Perspective* (New York: RCA, 1978).

[12]The EuroDisneyland project is described in Robert Wrubel, "Le Defi Mickey Mouse," *Financial World* (October 17, 1989), pp. 18–21.

[13]Dunning's view has been criticized by Itaki (1991), who shows that the firm's ownership advantage is not independent of location. Thus, his model may be collapsed logically to competitive advantages (including location) and the choice of whether to internalize or not.

[14]See Grosse (1981).

[15]Theodore Moran, "Foreign Expansion as an Institutional Necessity for U.S. Corporate Capitalism," *World Politics,* April 1973.

[16]See Boddewyn (1983); and S. C. Gilmour, *The Divestment Decision Process* (Boston: Harvard Business School, 1973).

[17]See "Monsanto to Sell Acrylic Fiber Line in Europe," *The Wall Street Journal,* March 8, 1983.

International Food Corporation – France

Current Difficulties

The situation at International Food Corporation's (IFC) French subsidiary was driving the home office to distraction by the end of 1986. After 10 years of steady growth and profitability during the 1970s, IFC-France began to lose sales in 1980 and actually to lose money beginning in 1983. The problem was initially attributed to the unprecedented rise in the dollar's value relative to the franc during 1981–84, but the subsidiary's performance did not improve in 1985 or 1986, when the dollar dropped precipitously compared to the franc. (See Figure 1, which depicts the franc/dollar exchange rate during 1970–87. Figure 2 then presents financial statements of IFC-France for 1986.)

The home office staff viewed this situation as a cause for real alarm, since the subsidiary had accumulated losses of over $US 160 million by the end of 1986.

FIGURE 1

The Franc/Dollar Exchange Rate, 1970–1986

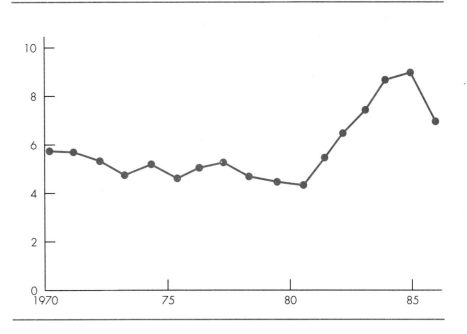

This case was written by Professor Robert Grosse in 1987 as a basis for class discussion.

FIGURE 2

Financial Statements of IFC-France for 1986 (in millions of U.S. dollars)

Income Statement	
Net sales and operating revenues	6,298
Operating expenses	5,974
Gross operating margin	324
Interest expense	345
Earnings before tax	(21)
Income taxes	0
Net income after tax	(21)

Balance Sheet			
Assets		Liabilities	
Cash	163	Short-term debt	660
Short-term investments	411	Accounts payable	410
Accounts receivable	701	Accrued expenses	552
Inventories	709	Long-term debt	1,058
Net property, plant and equipment	1,099	Deferred income taxes	187
		Stockholders' equity	216
Total assets	3,083	Total liabilities	3,083

In contrast, the subsidiary's managers felt that a series of random events had combined to produce the red ink, but that profitability would return even in 1987 and performance would be consistent with that of other IFC units within a few years.

In fact, Jean Bedouin, general manager of the French subsidiary, felt so positive that he sought permission to expand the local operation to manufacture a new line of frozen dessert products that had become very successful in the U.S. market. He proposed that $US 15 million more be invested to build the new assembly line and cold-storage facilities needed for this purpose. Since Bedouin had exceeded company performance goals in the previous divisions that he had run, it was quite difficult for the home office to judge him harshly in this case.

Some Background on International Food Corporation

International Food Corporation was founded in 1949 through a merger of three medium-sized U.S. food processing firms. Each of the three had been feeling severe competitive pressure from such market leaders as Kraft, Borden, and Standard Brands. The managers of the three companies chose a strategy of joining forces to reduce distribution costs and carve out a stronger market position in a greater variety of products than any of the companies had been able to achieve previously.

IFC's main product areas include dairy products such as cheeses, yogurt, and ice cream; canned fruits and vegetables and juices; frozen fruit pies and frozen vegetables; and such specialty products as mineral water, nonalcoholic coolers, and diet fruit-based sodas. Two of the founding companies had produced dairy products, and IFC still viewed dairy products as a core business. Frozen produce and specialty products, however, were the fastest-growing IFC businesses during the 1980s. The firm was committed to expansion in these two areas.

International Foods sells primarily to supermarkets and grocery stores in the United States. In fact, until the early 1960s, the firm's activities were confined almost entirely to North America. The United States and Canada accounted for 97 percent of its sales. The only sales elsewhere were exports on request to a handful of European wholesale customers and some cross-border sales from Texas and California into Mexico.

In 1963, IFC first entered the European market directly through a sales office and warehouse operation in Swindon, England, outside London. Based on the existing level of exports of canned produce to one English grocery chain, IFC's management felt that a local presence would enable the firm to sell to many more British customers. IFC began to process fruits and vegetables in the United Kingdom in 1965, when it became clear that lower costs could be achieved by manufacturing locally. IFC sales in the United Kingdom reached $US 30 million by 1968, and the stage was set for further European expansion.

The IFC French subsidiary was opened in 1969 by a senior manager of the British subsidiary. This was done explicitly to diversify IFC's production base into Europe, since at the time Britain was not a member of the European Common Market. The French plant, near Lille, produced most of the same canned fruits and vegetables as were produced in the English plant. A few products were imported from England to fill out the line.

IFC operations in Italy and Germany were begun in 1975 and 1976, respectively. In each of these cases, IFC chose to license a local food processing firm to manufacture and sell its brand name frozen food products. In return for the use of IFC's processing technology and its brand names, the local firm paid a royalty that amounted to 5 percent of sales. International Foods retained the right to establish quality control standards for these products, but in fact no serious problems arose with either licensee. The home office managers were not sure whether the current arrangements with the Italian and German licensees represented the best strategies for IFC, but since both of them regularly generated profits for the firm, they were left in place.

The Competitive Environment in France

During its entire life, the IFC subsidiary in France never attained a leading market share for any of its products. Although some of the specialty products were relatively novel in the French market when they were introduced, IFC was beaten out by Nestlé in several lines and by a local French producer in others. When price competition became severe at the end of the 1970s, the French subsidiary was unable to match the costs of three of its rivals and began losing market share. A major advertising campaign in 1981 was successful in raising the subsidiary's market share in all of the canned food lines, but recessionary conditions that lasted until 1984 led sales to stagnate all the same.

By the end of 1986, Jean Bedouin felt that the best strategy for escaping the weak market position of IFC-France was to move into local production of frozen fruits and vegetables. He had his corporate treasurer draw up a pro forma capital budget for the expansion needed to enter this segment in a major way. Based on a similar investment in the United Kingdom, he estimated that it would cost $US 15 million to build a modern, highly efficient freezing plant and storage facility. This investment would be repaid within five years. The project would become profitable within two years, assuming no major reaction by rival firms to enter this market segment on a large scale. Bedouin's projections for IFC-France sales and profits, including the new project, appear in Figure 3.

FIGURE 3

Pro Forma Income
Statements for IFC-France
(in millions of U.S. dollars)*

	1987	1988	1989	1990	1991
Sales	379	517	575	652	748
Operating expenses	371	481	532	603	681
Gross operating margin	8	36	43	49	67
Interest expense	4	7	9	9	9
Pretax earnings	4	29	34	40	58
Income taxes	2	13	14	18	26
Net income after tax	2	16	20	22	32

*These data show the *marginal* impact of the frozen food business.

Chapter

5

Developing A Global Strategy

This chapter moves to the highest level of decision making in the firm—the selection of a global business strategy. In fact, two levels of strategy must be distinguished. First, top management must establish overall corporate objectives, such as the kinds of businesses to be in and the ultimate goals of the firm. Second, top management must establish broad strategies for the firm's strategic business units (SBUs)—strategies such as cost leadership, focus on specific market segments and so on. In addition to defining and clarifying the relationships between corporate goal setting and strategy determination, this chapter discusses the means of maintaining control over the firm's effort to pursue its chosen objectives. The main goals of the chapter are to:

1. Define overall corporate objectives.

2. Show how to create strategic business units and use them to pursue corporate goals.

3. Explain four generic SBU strategies that have shown excellent results for companies during the past few decades.

4. Examine the means by which the firm can control its activities to ensure that corporate goals are achieved.

INTRODUCTION

How can the firm's decision makers choose whether or not to enter a new country market or to acquire a new business line? To this point in the discussion, the answer to these questions has been for the firm to carry out a thorough analysis of its competitive advantages and disadvantages relative to rival firms, and to choose alternatives that take best advantage of its strengths and minimize the impact of its weaknesses. This analysis may lead to a decision to invest in overseas production to reduce costs, or to undertake exports to serve untapped foreign markets, etc. How can this reasoning be organized to create a global strategy?

In fact, the basic analysis is useful at each level of decision making in the firm. Competitive strategy is just as important a concern for the individual plant or office of a firm as it is for the entire corporation, which may have dozens of divisions and hundreds of plants and offices. What the firm must do as a whole is decide what kinds of businesses it wants to be in and what kinds of overall goals it has. Divisions and/or individual offices of the firm have more limited (typically *tactical*) choices, since they need to be consistent with the whole corporation's interests. Large corporations have even more levels of decision making, which need to be consistent to achieve the firm's objectives. In sum, while competitive strategy is a valuable concept to apply at each level of company decision making, these levels must be identified carefully and their strategies must be made consistent. This task can be organized into three stages, focusing on three aspects of overall corporate strategy.

First, the firm must have a clear set of *overall objectives.* (For example, is the firm's goal to be in the transportation business; or in information services; or in chemical manufacturing?) These overall objectives then lead to such choices as diversifying into a new industry or serving a major new set of customers (e.g., going out of making trains and into making autos; or going into computers and telephones together instead of either business separately; or concentrating on consumer-oriented pharmaceuticals versus focusing on commodity chemicals). Should a multinational steel producer enter a very different industry such as oil (as U.S. Steel did with its purchase of Marathon Oil in 1982)? Or should a diversified tobacco-producing MNE move heavily into processed foods (as R. J. Reynolds did with its purchase of Nabisco in 1985)? No simple answer can be given to such questions. The fundamental goals of the firm must be clearly established if it is to make decisions of this kind.

Second, the firm must select optimal *operating strategies* for its major business units. That is, it must choose among basic overall competitive strategies, such as Porter's (1980, Chapter 13) four generic strategies: broad-line competition, global focus, national focus, and protected niche. Each of these strategies has proven to be sustainable in competition for major firms, while mixing them has often led to serious difficulties for the firm choosing that approach.

Third, the firm must *maintain control* over its widespread parts. Measurement and evaluation of financial decisions, production strategies, personnel relations, and other key operating activities are fundamental for a successful firm. Methods of achieving the necessary control and key areas that require clear control are discussed below.

Thus, global strategy encompasses overall objectives, specific operating strategies, and efforts to ensure acceptable performance of the firm's units. Figure 5–1 depicts the strategy cycle from the formulation of overall corporate goals,

FIGURE 5–1

Global Business Strategy in Perspective

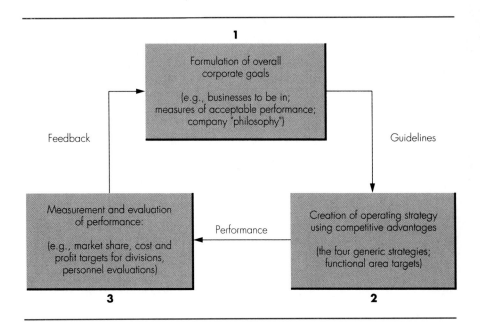

to the creation of operating strategies, to the measurement and evaluation of performance.[1]

We will look at these three levels of strategy sequentially in this chapter. But before examining each of the levels in detail, some additional clarification may be useful.

The formulation of overall corporate objectives requires some judgment as to the appropriate extent of the firm's activities. The question of optimal company size (in terms of sales volume, number of products, etc.) has not been resolved by either theoreticians or company managers.[2] Both diversification into new industries or countries and divestment of existing company activities may yield helpful or harmful results to the firm. (Note that, in terminology used before, this is the decision of whether or not to *internalize* a particular business activity.) Our approach is to point out major considerations that should be weighed in the expansion/contraction decision, rather than to attempt to answer the question conclusively. In this light, some of the major diversifications and divestments of the past few years are examined.

Expansion/contraction decisions need to be made in the broad context of overall corporate policy-making. Although an almost infinite number of strategies have proved successful for firms over the years, in international business since World War II a handful of general or generic strategies have led to success in many industries and countries. These generic strategies, discussed in some detail by Porter (1980), enable firms to maximize the gains from their competitive advantages (such as possession of an international marketing network, proprietary technology, or government protection) and to build defensible positions to ward off rival firms. Each strategy is appropriate not necessarily for an entire widely diversified firm, but rather for each **strategic business unit** (SBU) in a firm. As a firm looks for new business opportunities or seeks to get

IB
ILLUSTRATION:　　　Strategic Business Unit

Strategic business units, which are discussed also in Chapter 13, are groups of products, divisions, or other company activities that have sufficiently similar characteristics to justify their assignment to a single group for strategy development.* Each SBU is an operating unit with profit and loss responsibility for the activities within it. One criterion that may be used to create SBUs is to group product divisions that serve the same end users. Similarly, a second criterion could be products that utilize the same or similar technology, which then should be placed in the same SBU. In contrast, consumer products such as cosmetics should be assigned to a different SBU than bulk petrochemical products in a diversified chemical company. (The criterion is consumer versus industrial products in this case.)

Regardless of the number of industries or countries in which a firm does business, the fundamental strategic business units should be those that have sufficiently *dis*similar characteristics to justify the division of company activities into those units. For example, ITT unquestionably needs separate SBUs (and separate strategies) for its telecommunications division and its Sheraton Hotel division. The production methods of these divisions are very different; their customers are quite divergent groups; and their competition differs greatly. Similarly, no matter how many internal applications General Motors can find for its Electronic Data Systems subsidiary, this computer company needs a separate strategy if it is to continue serving customers outside GM.

A recent organization chart of General Electric Company, the firm that initiated SBUs in the early 1970s, appears as Figure 5–2. Notice that the 30 business units are divided broadly along global product lines, with a handful of matrix-type units such as the international trading company and the corporate marketing division. These divisions have changed over the years, as new businesses have been acquired (e.g., RCA Corporation in 1986) and as changes in the environment have justified different activities in different units.

The four generic strategies apply to strategic business units such as these — and to entire firms that are less diversified (and constitute single SBUs by themselves). ■

---

*One useful discussion of the SBU concept appears in William K. Hall, "SBUs—Hot, New Topic in the Management of Diversification," *Business Horizons*, February 1978. General Electric Company initiated the concept in 1971 and has been a leading proponent of SBUs since then.

out of existing businesses, it must carefully consider the fit of each activity into each SBU.

Finally, regardless of the strategy chosen and the operating policies established, top management at the home office needs some method to evaluate and control performance. Controls may be formulated in financial terms or in many other, often less-quantifiable, ways. For example, one simple means of control is to place highly trusted personnel in charge of foreign (i.e., faraway) affiliates. To guarantee that these managers make decisions as the home office would like to

FIGURE 5-2
General Electric Corporation

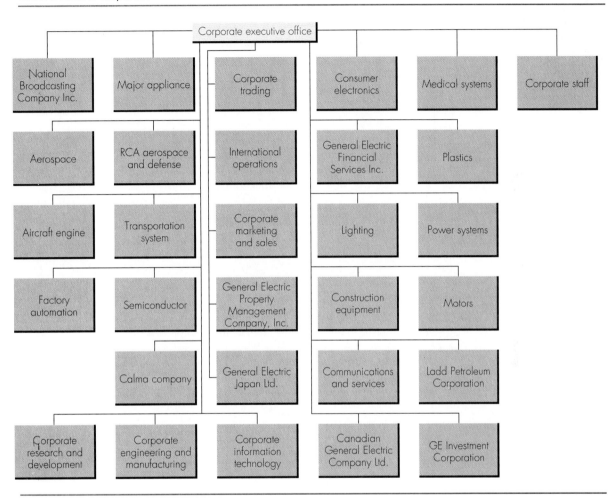

have them made, a period of home office training might be used. Thus, one method of control might be to assign to foreign affiliates only managers with at least 2 (or 5 or 10) years of experience in the home office. Controls are needed to assure that the MNE really does take advantage of its internationally transferable advantages, especially the sharing of *information*.

More common as a control mechanism in MNEs is the use of internal financial and operating reports. Most firms utilize frequent profit and loss reports, foreign exchange exposure statements, plant utilization data, and other information to monitor, evaluate, and direct foreign affiliates. These controls ensure that faraway and often relatively independent subsidiaries and branches are subjected to the same kinds of supervision as more easily accessible domestic affiliates.

The three broad areas of concern—overall objectives, generic strategies, and control—need to be examined in some detail. Let us begin with the formulation of overall corporate objectives.

FORMULATION OF OVERALL CORPORATE OBJECTIVES

Major Considerations

At the highest level of strategy making, the firm must choose the businesses in which to compete and the vehicles through which to operate. In a small, relatively young firm, the strategy may be simple: try to cut costs and raise revenues so that profit is adequate for survival in the given market segment. By contrast, in a large, relatively long-lived MNE, strategy may require decisions to exit from persistently unprofitable businesses or countries and other decisions to enter new types of competition.[3] Whether the firm is large or small, new or old, high- or low-tech, a basic question needs to be addressed periodically: What is the fundamental goal of the firm?

From the theory of finance, we know that the firm's goal should be to maximize shareholders' wealth, and in firms with publicly traded shares, specifically to maximize the share price. The troublesome issue is that a manager must anticipate the reactions of rival firms to business strategies in order to make decisions that will help achieve the goal of maximizing shareholders' wealth. Such reactions are very difficult to forecast, and they create substantial uncertainty about financial plans.[4] Thus, while the goal is easy to define, business strategies to achieve it may be quite difficult to choose.

In nonfinancial terms, the goal of the firm may be to produce high-quality, low-cost products that offer real value to customers. (This type of goal often appears in the statements of company philosophy formulated by major Japanese firms.) While such a broad, imprecise goal does not lead directly to measurable performance criteria, it does focus attention on a central tenet of this chapter, namely, that if the firm does not offer something of value to customers, its position will not be sustainable. A firm whose main product has been electric typewriters or transistor radios or 45-rpm records can maintain its competitiveness only by moving into new products (e.g., electronic typewriters or personal computers, silicon chip-based radios, or compact disks). At the top level of decision makers, the firm must periodically evaluate its products, its industries, and its competitive advantages to see whether redeployment of company assets could yield better results.[5]

An Example: ITT

ITT, originally the International Telephone and Telegraph Corporation, provides an interesting example of asset redeployment under changing conditions. During the 1960s and early 1970s, the firm expanded as a conglomerate (under the leadership of Harold Geneen), with clear financial controls from the home office but with a willingness to enter unrelated businesses that had good financial conditions and growth possibilities. At its peak diversification, in 1970 ITT included such major divisions as the basic telecommunications service (which owned and operated telephone companies around the world), the telecommunications equipment division, Sheraton Hotels, Avis Rent-a-Car, Hartford Life Insurance Company, Continental Baking Company, the Bobbs-Merrill publishing company, Levitt home building, and Rayonier forest products. The U.S. stock market at that time reacted favorably to diversification (which was generally showing positive financial results), so ITT's shares were valued highly.

When the oil crisis struck and two major recessions followed during the 1970s, ITT entered a period of difficulty and transition. Interest rates rose substantially (making the financing of acquisitions much more expensive), the price of the company's stock fell, and the stock market shifted to a negative view toward conglomerates.

Since the early 1980s, ITT has elected to regroup its business activities around three themes: (1) office and defense/space products; (2) insurance, financial, communications, and hotel services; (3) and automotive products, electrical/electronic components, and fluid products. Gone are most of the unrelated divisions, while core, relatively high-tech manufacturing, plus hotels and financial services, remain. Even the original core telecommunications business has been sold (in 1986) to the French firm, CGE.[6] The company has also restructured internationally, with a strong focus on Europe and North America and a substantial retrenchment from the less developed countries. In a changing commercial and financial environment, this ability to reorient its global strategy is necessary for a successful MNE. The results of ITT's strategy for the 1980s will be seen as the firm moves through the 1990s.

Even if a firm has defined its business to be the production and marketing of some specific product (e.g., wood furniture), this fundamental basis of the firm's activity must still be reevaluated from time to time. In an annual plan, or in the context of a three-year or five-year plan, top management must consider the viability of the firm's production and marketing efforts. If competitors are undercutting prices and taking away market share or if other materials are replacing wood for the firm's products, the firm must respond in some way to this change in the competition. It may elect to move production to a lower-cost location or to enter into the manufacture of plastic furniture; it may even elect to operate in a different country with different competitive circumstances. The important point is that top management should face the problem early on and set a strategy to deal with it before the firm is in critical condition. Figure 5–3 sketches the sequential process of definition and redefinition of the firm's businesses as competitive conditions change over time.

This figure shows a hypothetical situation in which the firm discovers that a country SBU (Country 1 for Products A and B) and a product SBU (Product B for Countries 2 and 3) are more suitable to competitive conditions than the original structure. Also, a new product line, C, has been introduced and placed in a separate SBU (Product C, Worldwide). The firm's broad overall objective of providing high-quality, low-cost products—for instance clothing or home electronics—may *not* have changed, but new technologies and shifting cost conditions alter the best way of achieving the objective.

Key International Aspects

Why does it make sense to create a global strategy rather than just a domestic strategy in each country of operation? Obviously, any firm must coordinate its divisions and the MNE must coordinate its affiliates in different countries. But there are substantial advantages to be obtained from the multinationality of the firm itself. (These have been discussed in earlier chapters.) First, each national market is somewhat segmented from other national markets by legal restrictions, currency differences, language differences, and so on—so that a successful strategy in one country can often be passed on to a "new" market in another country. Second, whatever the firm's products or services, some competitive gains arise from being multinational. If nothing more, there are potential benefits from the passage of information among affiliates in different countries as to low-cost suppliers, production methods, market conditions, and risks. Both of these points emphasize the added dimension of strategy making at the international level. The *process* is the same for domestic and international firms.

FIGURE 5–3

The Process of SBU Business Strategy Definition

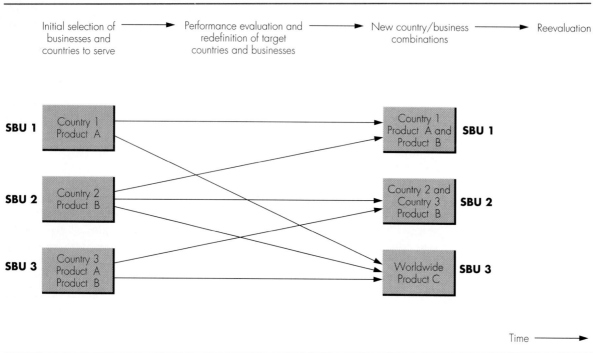

The central distinction of strategy making in international business is that its *alternatives* are far more numerous than those available to domestic firms. While the alternatives of the domestic firm (or the firm with domestic horizons) are limited to those available in the domestic market, the alternatives of the firm with a multinational horizon increase almost exponentially with the increase in the number of its markets. For example, any product that such a firm sells in the home country could conceivably be sold in over 100 other countries; any scale economies that such a firm achieves in one business may become even greater if foreign operations are added; any diversification that such a firm undertakes in the domestic market could conceivably be extended overseas; and so on. Moreover, when competition in one country has reached the maturing or standardized stage of the international product cycle, competition in another country may still be in the new product stage, thus allowing the firm different options there.

This international competitive advantage is nowhere more evident than in the chemical industry. Over the entire 20th century, the major chemical firms have produced some "commodities" such as polyethylene, analine dye, industrial resins, and other basic chemical building blocks that are standardized products in the life cycle and that require large-scale production facilities to achieve low unit production costs. Because demand in any one country is often insufficient to use up the production of such large-scale facilities, the major chemical companies became multinational very early on (several before World War I).

Similarly, because the commodity chemicals do not provide large profit margins, the major competitors have expanded their horizons into production of high-tech specialty chemicals, into products that are related to basic chemicals—such as pharmaceuticals—and into various industry-specific products such as agricultural chemicals. Thus, the major firms tend to be quite diversified both across countries and across product lines. The largest competitors include: DuPont, BASF, Bayer, Hoescht, Dow, ICI, and the chemicals divisions of Exxon and Shell.

Bayer AG provides a good example of the global strategy of a successful competitor in this industry. This German company had operated in the United States since before World War I, but its U.S. assets were expropriated as a result of the war. At that time Bayer lost the right to its well-known Bayer aspirin, which has belonged to Sterling Drug Company ever since. Bayer similarly lost foreign assets as a result of World War II. During the postwar period, Bayer has regained its position as one of the top two chemical companies in the world, along with BASF. (DuPont is larger because of its oil-company subsidiary, Conoco. See Appendix 4–1). Only in 1970 did Bayer regain worldwide exclusive rights to its trademark, except in the United States and Canada. Sterling sold the trademark rights to Bayer for nonpharmaceutical products in North America in 1986.

Bayer's focus has historically been in industrial chemicals, but the firm's goal is to be a worldwide leader in chemical products more broadly. This objective has been served through expansion in agricultural chemicals, pharmaceuticals (Bayer owns Miles Laboratories in the United States), automotive chemicals, plastics, photographic chemicals (Bayer owns Agfa-Gevaert), as well as general industrial chemicals. At the same time the firm has extended its network of affiliates around the world, with main concentrations in Europe and the United States, and growing operations in Japan and Korea, as well as smaller ventures in Latin America, Africa, and Asia.

Bayer's strategy is truly global. In the mid-1980s when the firm wanted to build a pharmaceuticals plant for worldwide sales of a blood-clotting agent, it chose a California location. At the same time it chose to build a polycarbonate (industrial plastic) plant in Belgium for global sales of that product. In both cases, the economics of producing these products called for a central production facility to supply customers in many countries. The company had to operate multinationally in order to achieve competitive costs. And Bayer is fairly typical of the other large chemicals firms mentioned here in terms of its global approach to strategy.

Thus, setting a global strategy for an MNE opens up a huge array of opportunities that simply do not exist for domestic firms in any country and that offer the MNE competitive advantages ranging from cost reductions to added market availability to risk reduction.

The Question of Diversification

Given all that has been said up to now, how can a firm decide on possibilities for **diversification?** The rule of thumb is certainly to enter only those businesses that generate net incremental value to the firm. But how can this be judged a priori? There is no simple answer, but some useful guidelines can be laid out. The discussion below concentrates on diversification possibilities for multinational firms in particular.

Perhaps the best way to evaluate possible new businesses for the firm, whether they be new *countries* to enter or new *products* to sell, is to examine the ways in which the firm's competitive advantages relate to the new business. If there are few or no **spillover benefits** from entering the new market, it is likely that other firms will be better able to compete there. This was what Chrysler experienced after its entry into European auto manufacture in 1964, accounting for its divestment in 1978. If the firm gains substantial cost savings by serving the new market from its existing facilities, then competitiveness is possible.

If the firm is able to enter a business with risk characteristics very different from those of its existing businesses, its overall risk may be reduced. (For example, a new business whose sales patterns are countercyclical to the sales patterns of the existing business, over the year or over the business cycle, will stabilize the firm's sales and subsequent earnings over that period. This was clearly part of U.S. Steel's expectation in acquiring Marathon Oil.) Since the firm's proprietary technology will not be reduced through using it in a new market, that advantage should help carve out a competitive position in any new market where the technology has an application. In short, every competitive advantage discussed in this book may present the firm with capabilities to enter new markets successfully.

Country diversification certainly has worked well for the major Japanese auto companies, which set up U.S. manufacturing plants during the 1980s to preserve their sales in that market, when the U.S. government placed restrictions on their exports from Japan. Honda, Nissan, and Toyota all invested in local manufacturing of their automobiles in the United States, resulting in growing sales and market shares there. (See the discussion of the international auto industry in Chapter 24.) While the decision to invest did not represent first-time entry into the market—that was already being served through exports from Japan—it did signify a major additional commitment to the market, and thus a key strategic decision. The Japanese firms as a group were able to reduce the *risk* of U.S. government restrictions on their imported auto sales, while incurring the risk of losing their production-cost advantage in making the cars. Apparently, after about a decade of experience, the Japanese firms have been able to transfer their management techniques, quality control, and other skills to the U.S. plants sufficiently to maintain their competitive advantages over U.S. rivals.[7]

Product diversification offers analogous benefits if the firm really can find synergies (spillover benefits) between the products involved. These synergies are very common in businesses such as food processing, where customers and technologies are similar among many food products. They also occur frequently in other consumer products businesses, such as home appliances, where brand advertising can cover multiple products, and again customers and technologies are similar.

It appears even today that such benefits should be possible for firms that combine data processing (computer) businesses with telecommunications businesses. Since computer networks imply communication of information among computers, and since remote PCs are often used to communicate data to centrally located computers, the linkage seems obvious. Nevertheless, telecommunications companies such as AT&T have found the going quite rough when seeking to establish a presence in computers (through a joint venture with

Olivetti); and NEC's vaunted "computers and communications" strategy of the 1980s has been revised drastically due to a lack of success in building the computer side of the business. On the other side of the same coin, IBM has not been able to establish a strong presence in telecommunications, despite its widely publicized acquisition of Rolm (telecommunications switch manufacturer) in 1984. Apparently, the logic of diversifying across "related" product lines requires much more careful analysis of the competitive advantages and disadvantages of the situation than a cursory view might suggest.[8]

This point should not be overstated, either. Diversification into related upstream or downstream businesses by oil, chemicals, and food firms has often resulted in stronger, more stable competitive positions for those firms. Virtually all of the leading international oil firms are diversified into gasoline sales, petrochemicals, and other businesses besides crude oil production and refining. Similarly, major international chemicals companies very often produce pharmaceuticals, agricultural chemicals, and industrial chemicals, rather than just one narrow product line.

Timing

The establishment of overall corporate objectives is not a task that can be repeated usefully every month or year in the company's decision making. Unfortunately, there is no frequency for setting objectives that will be appropriate for firms across industries, countries, and times. A task of senior management is to decide when such goal setting should be undertaken and to carry out the process with the participation of people throughout the firm. Generally, the more stable the businesses of the firm and the more stable the countries in which it operates, the less frequently its corporate objectives need to be reevaluated. On the other hand, this task must be much more frequent when technology is changing rapidly, when competition is growing quickly, or when political instability or other severe country-specific risk exists in the countries in which the firm operates.

Having defined the firm's overall objectives, including product lines to sell and markets to enter, top management must select a broad strategic method for pursuing these objectives. Over time and across countries, different strategies will be successful. In current competition in North America, Europe, Japan, and the LDCs, several specific strategy alternatives have proved viable. Four of these strategies are presented here.

THE SBU FRAMEWORK: FOUR STRATEGIC ALTERNATIVES

The business strategy literature is replete with classifications of operating strategies for business units. The approach taken here follows Porter's (1980) analysis of global industries and is consistent with the competitive advantage view developed throughout the text. Based on his work with major MNEs, Porter defined the four generic strategies shown in Table 5–1. Each of these strategies provides a framework both for utilizing the firm's competitive advantages and for choosing additional competitive tools to acquire. The four strategies are presented in increasing order of market focus and adaptation, that is, in decreasing order of product diversity. Broad-line global competition offers the widest variety of products/services to customers in many countries, while the protected niche is generally limited to a single country and a single product.

TABLE 5–1

Strategic Alternatives in Global Industries

Broad-line Global Competition

Uses:	Large firms with substantial resources
	Product lines with sufficiently similar characteristics to enable the firm to benefit from cross-fertilization
Pros:	Allows low-cost production and product differentiation
	Enables spillover of experience-curve benefits across product lines
Cons:	Requires large commitments of capital and management
	Subject to better-focused rivals in specific segments
Examples:	Exxon, IBM, Bayer, Nestlé, Philips

Global Focus

Uses:	Firms that want to specialize in a market segment, based on either cost leadership or differentiation
	Products for which scale economies can be realized by producing or selling in more than one country
	Products that do not require adaptation to local conditions
Pros:	Allows low-cost production or differentiation worldwide
	Allows scale economies in promotion and production across countries
Cons:	Benefits lost if substantial adaptation to local markets in different countries is required
Examples:	Mercedes-Benz, Apple, Polaroid, McDonald's

National Focus

Uses:	Countries in which adaptation to local demand is important
	Firms that have competitive advantage in marketing
Pros:	Targets each national market to outcompete global firms
	May be more responsive to changing environments in each country
Cons:	Does not allow gains from global standardization
Examples:	Johnson & Johnson, Unilever, many consumer-products firms

Protected Niche

Uses:	Countries in which host government is the customer or protector
	Firms that have competitive advantage in government relations
Pros:	May provide sustainable advantage regardless of costs or rivals
	Once established, often easy to maintain
Cons:	Entire advantage subject to shifts in host government policies
Examples:	State-owned enterprises, telecommunications service, defense contractors

Source: Concepts adapted from Michael Porter, *Competitive Strategy* (New York: Free Press, 1980), chap. 13.

Broad-Line Global Competition

This first strategic alternative is perhaps the most difficult to achieve. **Broad-line global competition** requires the production of a wide range of products or services in one or more industries. In computers, IBM competes in the segments for mainframes, minicomputers, personal computers, and software; most of its rivals focus on only one of these segments. (Burroughs is primarily in mainframes; Digital Equipment Corporation, in minis; Apple, in micros; and Microsoft is primarily in software.) In chemicals, Du Pont competes in raw materials (i.e., oil production), industrial chemicals, agricultural chemicals, and pharmaceuticals. Again, its rivals generally focus on only one or a couple of these major industry segments. (Texaco is primarily in oil; BASF, in industrial chemicals; American Cyanamid, in agricultural chemicals; and Merck, in pharmaceuticals.) All in all, very few firms have the resources needed to maintain the strategy of broad-line competition, because of the huge capital costs required and because of the susceptibility to competition from focused companies in individual industry segments. Nonetheless, benefits do accrue to the firms that can achieve this position, so the strategy can be sustainable.

Broad-line competition takes advantage of such major competitive strengths as physical and financial economies of scale, and the possession of a multicountry production and selling network. That is, in order to compete successfully with more focused firms, the broad-line competitor must find spillover benefits from its additional activities. Cost reductions from purchasing inputs that can be used for two or more products (i.e., those not available to single-product firms) are one such benefit. Another is the sales increases that arise from selling complementary products, such as athletic shoes *and* socks, or toothpaste *and* toothbrushes (or even food and beverage service *and* hotel accommodations). Experience curve gains that accrue from the production and sale of one product may be transferable to other products. Finally, even within a product line, a firm that sells products ranging from low-cost to highly specialized items may be able to achieve greater sales and profits than a rival that aims at only one end or segment of the market.

The selection of a broad-line strategy depends, of course, on the benefits that the firm is able to obtain from this strategy in comparison with focused rivals and other broad-line competitors. The strategy should be maintained only as long as its benefits keep the firm ahead of rivals (or in whatever position the firm views as justifying continued participation in the particular business).

Historically, the financial performance of broad-line firms has been better in cases of vertical integration or of diversification into related industries; worse performance has been registered by conglomerated firms—firms that expand into nonrelated businesses and thus find fewer spillover benefits from their other units.

Global Focus

In contrast with broad-line competition, **global focus** targets a particular industry segment for competition worldwide. This strategy fosters the achievement of scale economies by obtaining inputs, distributing inputs and final products, carrying out R&D, producing outputs, and promoting products worldwide. It also achieves cost savings through experience curve advantage; by following the focus strategy, a firm should be able to gain a large market share and thus move rapidly along the experience curve. A strategy of global focus has been followed very successfully by McDonald's in fast-food restaurant service, by Black & Decker in power hand tools, and by Liggett & Myers in generic, unbranded cigarettes, to cite a few examples.

Global focus is *not* limited to a low-cost strategy. Other focal points for competition include specialization in high-quality, expensive products or provision of the best after-sale service. Rolls-Royce, for example, follows a focus strategy in producing automobiles of very high quality, with high costs and high prices. Xerox is known for its rapid and excellent after-sale service of photocopying machines. Maytag is very well known for providing both high-quality electrical appliances and excellent after-sale service. In each case, the focus is on some aspect of competition that enables the firm to show superiority over rivals (i.e., to differentiate its product or service).

Other focus strategies may target any segment of a total market, if the firm can successfully isolate that segment enough to outcompete competitors with broader lines. In the furniture business, for example, focus strategies have succeeded not only in the low-cost end of the market (e.g., Ashley, Dixie, and Singer), and in the high-quality, highly personalized end (e.g., Drexel Heritage, Baker, and Cheryl) but also in plastic furniture, metal furniture, wood-crate furniture, and so on.

At the international level, the focus strategy implies worldwide concentration on one or a few products. While production may be standardized and economies of scale achieved in many activities, marketing may still differ across countries. In particular, successful low-cost producers in Europe, Japan, or the United States may find that their entry into lower-income LDCs places them at the top of the market for their products. Thus, a low-cost U.S. power tool may compete at the expensive end of the power tool market in Latin American countries. Similarly, a low-cost European food processing firm may end up competing at the high-quality, high-price end of an African or Asian market even though it sells the same products both at home and abroad. In every instance, the firm that tries to follow a global focus strategy must evaluate the differences in competition from one market to the next before setting its focus in particular markets.

National Focus

National market characteristics may disallow the firm from pursuing the global focus strategy. If differences from country to country are too extreme, global competitors that standardize their complete strategies may encounter serious problems. For example, sales of the nylon jackets that a clothing firm produces for use in cold weather are likely to be quite low in tropical countries and also in LDCs where nylon is very expensive as compared with such natural materials as wool and leather. Thus, this firm may choose to specialize in outerwear ranging from heavy nylon jackets in most of the industrial countries, to nylon raincoats in tropical countries, to clothing made of natural fibers in LDCs (or high-cost nylon coats for the most expensive segment of the LDC markets). Chapter 14 discusses such issues in more detail.

When important market differences limit the global focus strategy, a **national focus** may be superior. By emphasizing its adaptability to local market conditions, a multinational firm may be able to outcompete its more standardized, less flexible rivals. In the 1980s, as more large MNEs from several countries have arisen in many industries, the ability to offer flexible, individualized products has become increasingly important. The once common form of competition in fairly standardized products (the Model T Ford was said to be available "in any color you like, as long as it is black"[9]) is being replaced by more adaptive styling to serve different customer groups.

Protected Niche

The last of the generic strategies defined by Porter is establishment of a **protected niche.** This strategy aims specifically at obtaining government protection, either through support of the firm against competitors or through government purchase of the firm's product or service. Very often the protected niche is controlled by the government through ownership of the firm in question. For example, in most countries the national telephone company is state owned and is given a monopoly over the provision of domestic telephone service.* The protected niche strategy depends totally on the firm's ability to obtain government protection on a continuing basis.

The first form of protection, government support against competitors, may be obtained through bargaining with the government at the time of an initial investment. When a manufacturing MNE sets up a subsidiary in a developed, less developed, or even communist country, the host government is often willing to negotiate some forms of incentives in exchange for a job-creating, revenue-producing investment. In this negotiation process, especially in LDCs, the MNE may be able to obtain tariff protection against imported goods that would compete with its local production. The MNE may also be able to negotiate a reduced tax burden, especially in industrial countries, which again places it in a preferred position relative to nonsubsidized competitors. These forms of government support need not be obtained at the time of an initial investment, but the firm's bargaining position is usually strongest at that time or at a time when it is deciding whether to close or relocate a facility.

The second form of protection, government purchase of the firm's product or service, may be obtained by negotiating a long-term purchase contract with a government. This gives the firm a guaranteed market, regardless of the activities of competitors during the life of the contract. Since government contracts are subject to nonprice determinants (that is, governments seek to serve goals other than minimizing costs—supporting local firms, rewarding firms that follow government policy prescriptions, etc.), the firm may find that once it has obtained an initial contract, subsequent contracts are highly likely to continue into the future.

Governments often choose to create protected positions for firms that they themselves control, for example through ownership. Thus, in many countries the most significant protected niches are held by state-owned firms that provide electric power, railroad transportation, postal service, and other utilities, as well as minerals and metals such as oil, copper, and bauxite. This limits the ability of a multinational firm to pursue a protected niche strategy in these areas. But plenty of other possibilities exist, and the MNE may even be able to supply products or services to the state-owned firms on a continuing basis.

Obtaining a protected market segment may be much easier than holding onto it. Often, when governments change, so too does the status of favored industries and companies. Unless the firm pursues a policy of keeping the costs of the protected segment low or of carefully differentiating the products of the protected segment, its protected niche may lead to an inefficient position that will be eliminated once protection has been lost. The protected niche strategy is far more subject to political negotiating and positioning than the other three generic strategies, which depend to a greater extent on economic factors (such as cost minimization or tailoring output to satisfy specific market preferences).

---

*This situation is changing, as privatization of state-owned companies becomes common. The national telephone company has been privatized in the UK, Mexico, Argentina, Chile, and several other countries in recent years.

CONTROL IN THE MULTINATIONAL ENTERPRISE

Once a firm's overall strategic objectives have been established and its plans for business units chosen, a final step is needed to ensure that these objectives and plans are implemented. The firm must create a **control** structure. The basic intent of controls is to have managers define goals clearly, to observe whether those goals are achieved, and to reward behavior that works toward achieving the overall corporate objectives. Financial and managerial reporting, personnel evaluation, government relations, and dealing with rival firms are four important areas of management that require corporate-level control within the multinational firm. Highlights pertinent to the present focus are covered below; these areas also are discussed elsewhere in the text.

Financial and Managerial Reporting

Financial reporting is obviously an area that is both appropriate for control and easily measurable for evaluation purposes. Measures of corporate performance include sales, market share, profitability, and return on assets. Each firm may have different goals and capabilities in these areas, but no firm can operate indefinitely without earning positive profits and generating a positive return on assets.

At the international level, financial controls are needed for at least capital budgeting, operating performance evaluation, and exchange risk management. One commonly used form of financial control is the spending limit; foreign subsidiaries often are limited in making financial commitments at some specific dollar ceiling (e.g., $US100,000); expenditures greater than that limit require home-office approval. Another common limitation requires the subsidiary to deal only in host-country currency, except for items approved by the home office such as purchase of intra-company imports and payment of royalties and fees. This limitation avoids the expansion of company-wide exchange risk beyond that generated by the activities of the subsidiary in local currency. These issues are discussed also in Chapter 16.

Managerial reporting refers to periodic information-passing by the subsidiary to the home office on nonfinancial issues. These issues may range from inventory levels to political risk assessments to market analysis. Analysis of market trends in one country may alert the home office to possible shifts in other markets around the world. Analysis of government policies in one national context also may have its application in other countries where the firm operates. This kind of information is just as important to the corporation in making sure that the home office understands the activities of the foreign subsidiary and the environment facing it as is the financial information.

Personnel Evaluation

A second important control area is **personnel evaluation.** Managers must be judged not only on their achievement of financial targets but also on their ability to deal with people and to pursue corporate nonfinancial goals. As noted earlier, one form of control over personnel is to assign managers to affiliates only after they have spent some time at the home office learning the details of the corporate strategy and being indoctrinated in the corporate culture. In addition, the performance of managers and support personnel must be evaluated for the purpose of compensation and career development. Thus, a system of information gathering must be established to obtain data on the administrative, technical, cooperative, and other skills of individuals in the firm.

Internationally, personnel must be chosen to be assigned to different countries and different kinds of operating affiliates. The skills necessary to perform well in foreign environments (e.g., patience, adaptability to cultural differences) add a key dimension to those others that require evaluation. As firms are becoming more and more international over time, it is becoming more and more important to employ managers who can function well with colleagues, superiors, and subordinates from different cultures.

Breaking the ethnocentric base of most firms that have their roots in one culture and one country is often extremely difficult. One of the areas in which Japanese firms may encounter increasing problems is the integration of non-Japanese managers into higher-level corporate positions. Until now almost all general manager positions in Japanese firms' foreign affiliates have been filled by Japanese nationals. As these firms become more global in their activities, more pressure will arise to permit host-country nationals to participate in management of these affiliates—and to be integrated into top management in Japan as well. European and some American multinational firms have been much more successful in creating multicultural environments among senior management at home and in foreign affiliates.

Thus, personnel evaluation really is a strategic imperative in international firms, as their horizons expand beyond ethnocentric, home-country considerations. And control of this function is crucial to ensure that people with the proper skills are assigned to the appropriate positions in the home office and in affiliates around the world.

Government Relations

A third area that requires corporate-level control is **government relations.** In countries or situations in which the firm's activities are subject to a great deal of government intervention, there is undoubtedly a need for careful monitoring and evaluation of relations with the government. Even in relatively free markets, however, the importance of such government policies as taxes, subsidies, and limits on foreign competitors should not be underestimated.

At the international level, government relations become even more crucial to company success, since home and host governments often have different views as to the desirability of specific company activities—for example, foreign direct investment or even exports (imports to the other country). A careful and frequent review of government relations and an exploration of alternatives will help the firm to avoid the hostage problem—the situation in which the firm is at the mercy of shifts in government policy in one country and has no options to ameliorate the impact of those shifts.

This concern has risen to a top priority during the past few years, as the formerly communist countries of Eastern Europe open their economies to western firms. Entering these markets requires a huge commitment of time and effort to build good government relations, as the new governments of these countries decide how to build market-based economies.

Similarly, in the industrial countries of Western Europe, government relations rose to a high priority during the period of negotiations for Europe 1992, the push for creation of a single Europe in terms of business regulation and many other subjects. U.S. firms in particular had to evaluate their regulatory situations in the European countries where they had operations, as well as study the possible impacts of changed regulations that could result from the Common Market's unification effort.

Dealing with Rivals

Finally, dealing with rivals requires corporate-level control. Although the firm cannot determine or control the strategies of its competitors, it can assess those strategies in terms of their impacts on its own activities. In addition, it can influence those strategies by its own actions. Monitoring the activities of competitors and attempting to estimate their reactions to the firm's own activities can enable the firm to develop a better strategy.

Caterpillar, Inc., for example, must assess the strategies of its rival Komatsu in different countries to plan its own global strategy of competing against Komatsu. And in recent years the emergence of strategic alliances such as joint production or marketing agreements and joint R&D ventures requires an international firm to evaluate competitive conditions around the world to see in which cases and places such alliances make sense.

At the international level, the firm must consider rivals such as other multinational firms, local firms in each country of operation, and even firms in other countries that are potential competitors. While the complexity of analyzing international competition is much greater than that of analyzing domestic competition, the stakes are generally also greater. Much of the business strategy literature, and indeed this book, aims at developing sustainable strategies for firms involved in international competition.[10]

STRATEGIC VARIETY

International strategy must be constructed to fit the particular configuration of international activities that the firm possesses. The exporter with only one foreign affiliate that receives its products for sale in the host country will not need the same kind of strategy that is invaluable to a multinational firm such as Royal Dutch Shell or Toyota. Also, a company that uses overseas subsidiaries for offshore production, which ultimately results in products that are sold in the home country, needs a different strategy than the firm that uses foreign production facilities to serve host-country markets.

What really is needed more than any simplistic strategic model, which would not apply in all situations in any event, is a recognition that strategic *flexibility* should be the underlying basis for thinking. That is, the firm should follow careful analytical patterns such as those suggested above, and then forward-looking thinking should be applied to anticipate future conditions and position the firm to take advantage of them. While this point of view does not provide a convenient recipe for managers, it does alert them to the need for anticipating change rather than reacting to it. (Kogut, 1985, and Hamel and Prahalad, 1989, offer some more concrete methods of employing this kind of thinking.)

CONCLUSIONS

The development of a global strategy involves two levels of planning and the process of evaluation and control. First, the firm must establish overall corporate objectives—broad, long-term goals such as businesses to compete in and acceptable kinds of performance (e.g., in the risk/return framework). Second, the firm must develop for its strategic business units goals based on the four generic strategies: broad-line competition, global focus, national focus, and protected niche. Finally, the firm must establish clearly defined targets for performance, must monitor that performance, and must set up a feedback mechanism for realigning itself to meet targets better.

Overall corporate strategy must be to some extent ambiguous or open-ended, since the future business conditions under which the firm will operate cannot be known today and full contingency planning is impossible. However, the firm's top management can define broad corporate goals and acceptable means of pursuing them that will be able to survive changes in the environment. This level of planning needs to be fairly long term, since only over a period of years can the firm's performance and changes in the environment be observed adequately.

SBU strategy can be formulated and changed more frequently, since at this lower level more concrete, measurable goals can be established. Strategic business units can follow any one of the four generic strategies, from broad-line global competition to serving a protected niche, with the additional possibilities of focusing on a market segment worldwide or adapting to national market segments in different countries. Each SBU should be chosen to group activities of the firm that possess similar characteristics, such as technology, customers, location, and inputs.

Performance monitoring, evaluation according to some clear criteria, and reformulation of strategy are also necessary parts of strategy making. The MNE needs to develop methods for monitoring far-flung affiliates on financial conditions, personnel performance, government relations, and the activities of rival firms, as well as other key issues that may arise. More important than specific quantitative goals are targets that are designed to pursue the main strategic objectives of the firm.

QUESTIONS

1. What is a strategic business unit? How should SBUs be selected from among a firm's divisions?

2. Using your knowledge of ITT from the chapter and any other sources, what would be the appropriate SBUs for that firm today? Why?

3. How can you distinguish among corporate strategy, business unit strategy, and operating strategy for a firm? What are the key characteristics of each?

4. Explain the four generic strategies for business units. How does each of these strategies apply in international business?

5. On what grounds can a business unit choose between a global focus and a national focus?

6. Why is control an important aspect of corporate strategy? How can control be achieved in a multinational enterprise?

7. How can a firm decide whether or not to diversify into a new industry in a country where it has not operated before? What criteria can it use to make this decision?

8. What is different about corporate and business unit strategies at the international level as compared with the domestic level? That is, what is different about them for a multinational enterprise as compared with a domestic one?

9. Explain how a firm could establish a protected niche strategy for its business unit in the telecommunications industry. What forms of business activity would be possible, and how could the firm use this strategy in more than one country?

10. Discuss some major spillover benefits from other business activities that could aid the competitiveness of an MNE such as Dow Chemical in the pharmaceuticals industry. That is, what advantages does Dow possess due to its diversified business units (in industrial chemicals, agricultural chemicals, specialty chemicals, cosmetics, consumer products, etc.) that purely pharmaceuticals firms do not have?

REFERENCES

Christensen, Roland; Kenneth Andrews; Joseph Bowers; Richard Hammermesh; and Michael Porter. *Business Policy*. 6th ed. Homewood, Ill.: Richard D. Irwin, 1987.

Davidson, William. *Global Strategic Management*. New York: John Wiley & Sons, 1982.

Donaldson, Gordon, and Jay Lorsch. *Decision Making at the Top*. New York: Basic Books, 1983.

Hall, W. K. "SBUs—Hot New Topic in the Management of Diversification." *Business Horizons*, February 1978.

Hamel, Gary, and C. K. Prahalad. "Strategic Intent," *Harvard Business Review,* May–June 1989.

Kogut, Bruce. "Designing Global Strategies: Profiting from Operational Flexibility," *Sloan Management Review,* Fall 1985.

Ohmae, Kenichi. *The Borderless World*. New York: Harper Business, 1990.

Porter, Michael. *Competitive Advantages*. New York: Free Press, 1985.

Porter, Michael (ed.). *Competition in Global Industries*. Boston: Harvard Business School Press, 1986.

Porter, Michael. "From Competitive Advantage to Corporate Strategy," *Harvard Business Review,* May-June 1987.

NOTES

[1]This scheme generally parallels that of Figure 13–1, with two exceptions. First, we do not cover the level of "implementing the operating plan" in the present chapter, which focuses instead on overall corporate strategy. Second, we do not consider organization structure in any detail in the present chapter.

[2]See, for example, Edith Penrose's classic analysis of this issue in *The Theory of the Growth of the Firm* (Oxford: Oxford Univ. Press, 1951); also see Anthony Sampson, *The Sovereign State of ITT* (New York: Viking Press, 1973), for the real-world case of ITT, a huge conglomerate in the 1960s and 70s and a drastically reduced telecommunications and services firm today.

[3]Some people would argue that small firms are *more* likely to be flexible enough to leave unprofitable market segments, while large MNEs may be relatively inflexible and more likely to remain in weak market segments. This is an empirical question.

[4]This uncertainty cannot be eliminated, but the problem can be managed somewhat by specifying a range of potential rivals' responses and examining the firm's expected performance in each case. Such analysis has been facilitated dramatically by microcomputers and sophisticated financial planning programs.

[5]Gordon Donaldson and Jay Lorsch, *Decision Making at the Top* (New York: Basic Books, 1983), found in a survey of 12 large U.S.-based MNEs that their chief executive officers viewed *company survival,* rather than maximizing shareholders' wealth, as the primary objective of the firm. "They [the CEOs] are committed, first and foremost, to the enhancement of *corporate* wealth, which includes not only the firm's financial assets reflected on the balance sheet but also its important human assets and its competitive position in the various markets in which it competes" (p. 7).

[6]CGE purchased 63 percent of ITT's telecommunications division in 1986, naming the joint venture Alcatel. In 1990, ITT sold an additional 7 percent of the venture to CGE, so that ITT's share is now 30 percent. (*The Wall Street Journal,* June 13, 1990, p. A4.)

[7]The success of the Japanese 'transplant' auto factories has been discussed widely during the 1980s. See, for example, Daniel Jones and Daniel Ross, *The Machine That Changed the World*. New York: Rawson Associates, 1990.

[8]Porter (1987) in fact shows that *most* of the diversification efforts of large U.S. industrial firms during the past decade have led to worse performance by those companies compared to their pre-diversification records. This is a strong argument in favor of 'sticking to your knitting', that is, focusing on the businesses that utilize your firm's distinctive competencies.

[9]Henry Ford, *My Life and Work* (Garden City, N.Y.: Doubleday, 1922), p. 72.

[10]See, for example, Roland Christensen et al., *Business Policy*, 6th ed. (Homewood, Ill.: Richard D. Irwin, Inc., 1987).

The HongKong & Shanghai Banking Corporation

Introduction

HongKong & Shanghai Banking Corporation (HSBC) was the world's 30th-largest bank in 1980. Based in Hong Kong, the bank has carried out most of its business in Hong Kong dollars and U.S. dollars, with substantial amounts of business in European currencies and Japanese yen as well. It has received deposits from local (Chinese) individuals and companies, and has loaned the money to both local borrowers and international banks in the so-called eurocurrency market. HSBC has specialized in financing exports and imports, largely with firms in countries of the British Commonwealth (Great Britain and its former colonies). The vast majority of the bank's business has been done physically in Hong Kong, though it had a large network of branches in Asia, a very large London branch office, and several U.S. branches plus a subsidiary bank in California and a representative office in New York in 1980. (The representative office was not allowed to do business directly; under U.S. law it had to refer all clients to the California subsidiary bank, the London branch, or the Hong Kong headquarters.)

In 1980 the bank was looking to expand in the U.S. market. Its dealings in the eurocurrency market had led to large deposits of U.S. dollars, British pounds, and other currencies, which the bank needed to lend to borrowers somewhere. Rather than continue to accept low profits from lending these funds to other banks, HSBC decided to seek new borrowers in the world's largest market, the United States. Although HSBC had over a century of experience in international banking, it had never considered a major move into the U.S. domestic market. In the late 1970s, at a time when their British pounds, deutsche marks, and Japanese yen could buy far more dollars than in the 1950s and 1960s, many of the bank's clients were establishing offices, factories, and other investments in the United States.

The bank also was interested in moving into the U.S. market as a hedge against the substantial risk of nationalization by the Chinese government. In 1997 the British colony of Hong Kong is scheduled to return to Chinese ownership, which will bring with it the possibility of major legal changes in rules for business. Because the People's Republic of China is a communist country, many observers expect Hong Kong to lose its free market status. As the largest bank in the colony, HSBC very likely faces changes in its business activities. For this reason, the bank's managers and owners have been interested in establishing

This case was written by Professor Robert Grosse as a basis for class discussion. Helpful information was provided by HSBC. Any errors of fact or interpretation are the responsibility of the author. 1986.

domestic activities in the United States, generally viewed as the least politically risky environment in the world.

In addition to having substantial deposits in several currencies and clients of several nationalities, the bank possessed another competitive strength—namely, its large staff of experienced bankers who knew about both lending and borrowing opportunities in Asia that were not well known to potential U.S. clients. By operating directly in the U.S. market, the bank would be able to take advantage of this expertise to earn additional profits.

HSBC has been operating in the United States since 1875, when it opened an agency in San Francisco. A second agency was opened in New York in 1880. The New York agency was converted into a branch in the 1970s, as a result of a change in New York's banking laws. In the 1960s HSBC acquired the Republic Bank of California, which had eleven branches in the state. The bank was renamed the HongKong Bank of California. Other branches were established in Chicago, Seattle, and Portland, and another subsidiary was set up in Houston. Under U.S. banking rules in 1980, if HSBC wanted to open a full-service subsidiary in any other state, then the California branch network and the Houston subsidiary would have to be divested.

The Case

Mr. Michael Sandberg, chairman of HSBC in Hong Kong, was considering the alternatives for expanding in the U.S. market in 1980. The top management of the bank wanted to diversify its assets and activities across the world, placing about one third of the total in Hong Kong, Europe, and the United States. Sandberg felt that it would be possible to set up an agency in New York, where over 90 percent of the international banking in the United States takes place. Similarly, it would be feasible to establish a branch bank, owned completely by HSBC and using a federal U.S. charter, under the existing U.S. laws. Additional representative offices could be placed in cities other than New York, but these facilities would be restricted to providing information to potential clients, who still would need to do business with HSBC in San Francisco, London, or elsewhere outside of the United States. Finally, Sandberg considered the idea of forming a joint venture with an existing U.S. bank, which would give HSBC immediate access to new clients and partial ownership and control of the venture. Each of these alternatives is discussed in more detail below.

Setting up an *agency* would allow HSBC to minimize the capital needed to enter the U.S. market, since foreign bank agencies could use all of the capital of the parent bank as a base for their U.S. lending. The agency would allow HSBC to lend to local clients as well as Chinese or other foreign borrowers. Deposits, on the other hand, were restricted to foreign depositors—U.S. banking law forbids agencies from taking local deposits. Many foreign banks enter the U.S. market through an initial representative office, followed by expansion into an agency. While this alternative had no major financial costs, it would limit HSBC business primarily to dealing with foreign clients.

Note: The largest 50 U.S. banks in 1980 are listed in Table 1 to show the size and other characteristics of relevant competitor banks and banks that could be considered for acquisition or joint venture partnership.

TABLE 1

The 50 Largest U.S. Banks in 1980

	Assets 12/31/79 $ Mil.	Deposits				Loans		
		Total 12/31/79 $ Mil.	Chg. From 1978 %	Time/ Demand %	For- eign %	Total OS 12/31/79 $ Mil.	Chg. From 1978 %	Loan Loss Prov. 1979 $ Mil.
1 BankAmerica (San Francisco)	108,389	84,985	12	75/25	50	58,772	16	226.2
2 Citicorp (New York)	106,371	70,291	13	87/13	75	65,712	21	233.4
3 Chase Manhattan (New York)	64,708	48,456	0	69/31	54	40,364	4	149.0
4 Manufacturers Hanover (New York)	47,675	38,156	18	63/37	46	25,639	14	105.9
5 Morgan (J.P.) (New York)	43,488	30,279	6	67/33	55	22,406	18	29.8
6 Chemical New York	39,375	28,987	16	67/33	43	20,719	14	60.0
7 Continental Illinois (Chicago)	35,790	24,007	13	78/22	48	23,182	26	70.0
8 Bankers Trust New York	30,953	22,437	20	63/37	48	16,228	18	47.5
9 First Chicago	30,182	21,106	21	84/16	57	15,737	14	84.0
10 Western Bancorp (Los Angeles)	29,687	23,631	12	63/37	9	17,353	14	97.3
11 Security Pacific (Los Angeles)	24,923	18,451	9	67/33	24	16,830	15	75.1
12 Wells Fargo (San Francisco)	20,593	15,831	7	73/27	15	15,193	18	62.9
13 Irving Bank (New York)	16,702	13,525	22	53/47	38	7,607(b)	7	34.5
14 Crocker National (San Francisco)	16,139	12,517	12	69/31	20	10,778	18	60.4
15 Marine Midland Banks (Buffalo)	15,728	12,509	11	73/27	39	9,268	12	45.2
16 First National Boston	13,760	8,965	15	74/26	53	7,183	27	49.0
17 Mellon National (Pittsburgh)	13,508	9,503	12	69/31	28	7,046	15	27.3
18 Northwest Bancorp (Minneapolis)	12,416	9,573	13	68/32	7	7,642	16	20.4
19 First Bank System (Minneapolis)	12,119	8,983	13	65/35	4	7,008	14	22.3
20 First International Bancaheres (Dallas)	11,504	8,921	15	67/33	28	6,041	15	24.9
21 Republic of Texas (Dallas)	10,798	7,647	13	68/32	32	5,510	20	16.5
22 National Detroit	9,506	6,896	−4	66/34	16	4,694	12	14.1
23 First City Bancorp of Texas (Houston)	9,505	7,597	16	61/39	12	4,633	18	22.7
24 Texas Commerce Bancaheres (Houston)	9,260	7,226	12	59/41	15	5,026	20	17.7
25 Bank of New York	8,994	6,870	16	67/33	32	4,376	22	24.8
26 First Pennsylvania (Philadelphia)	8,987	5,307	0	76/24	37	4,770	8	46.8
27 Seafirst (Seattle)	8,401	6,652	28	68/32	9	5,419	21	17.8
28 European-American Bancorp (New York)	7,776	6,370	7	55/45	37	4,456	18	19.9
29 Harris Bankcorp (Chicago)	7,108	4,929	9	66/34	24	3,311	22	7.0
30 NCNB (Charlotte, N.C.)	6,365	4,477	24	62/38	22	2,869	12	16.8
31 Philadelphia National	5,916	4,056	12	54/46	21	3,181	7	16.0
32 Pittsburgh National	5,563	3,912	18	69/31	3	2,958	25	11.0
33 AmeriTrust (Cleveland)	5,402	3,763	−6	69/31	5	3,265	13	11.4
34 Michigan National (Bloomfield Hills)	5,399	4,545	7	76/24	0	3,616	11	14.4
35 Northern Trust (Chicago)	5,358	3,912	7	64/36	24	2,405	17	5.0
36 Valley National Bank of Arizona (Phoenix)	5,199	4,331	18	66/35	1	3,386	18	19.0
37 First Wisconsin (Milwaukee)	5,107	3,673	7	56/44	12	2,812	16	5.0
38 Wachovia (Winston-Salem)	5,097	3,825	8	61/39	11	2,771	18	6.7
39 Detroitbank	5,067	3,527	2	73/27	2	2,666	21	5.5
40 Southeast Banking (Miami)	5,028	3,828	24	59/41	2	2,406	15	13.5
41 BancOhio (Columbus)	5,005	3,805	6	68/32	0	2,795	14	11.8
42 National City (Cleveland)	4,972	3,330	19	57/43	5	2,322	29	3.8
43 National Bank of North America (New York)	4,849	3,634	11	70/30	32	3,094	23	14.0
44 Mercantile Texas (Dallas)	4,709	3,332	13	57/43	4	2,678	24	10.5
45 Manufacturers National (Detroit)	4,526	3,608	4	70/30	4	2,808	9	8.0
46 Rainier Bancorp (Seattle)	4,496	3,457	9	67/33	16	3,191	15	13.4
47 U.S. Bancorp (Portland)	4,431	3,512	10	65/35	3	2,963	12	8.0
48 Republic New York	4,408	3,287	36	85/15	41	2,168	32	18.5
49 Girard (Philadelphia)	4,360	3,247	5	57/43	21	2,461	8	11.6
50 Mercantile Bancorp (St. Louis)	4,327	2,941	7	61/39	9	2,177	11	12.2

TABLE 1

Continued

	Loans			Performance							
Chg. From 1978 %	Net Charge-Offs As % of Loans	Fed. Funds Bor-rowed %	Net Oper. Income 1979 $ Mil.	Chg. From 1978 %	Return on Avg. Assets 1979	Lever-age 1979	Return on Com. Equity 1979	Net Int-erest Income 1979	Chg. From 1978 %	Oper. Income As % of Net Int. Income	5-Year Growth EPS %
28	0.3	4(d)	600.2	17	0.64	28.9	18.4	2,770	12	21.7	17.1
−18	0.3	9	544.2	13	0.58	27.9	16.1	2,587	10	21.0	10.8
−12	0.3	11	311.2	58	0.49	31.4	15.3	1,577	18	19.7	8.5
36	0.2(b)	7(b)	211.3	16	0.51	28.0	14.3	1,072	15	19.7	7.9
−11	0.0(b)	10(b)	288.3	8	0.72	21.8	15.6	847	14	34.1	9.0
−34	0.2	19	142.3	15	0.39	32.8	13.0	854	9	16.7	6.7
12	0.2(b)	34(b,d)	194.1	15	0.58	25.7	15.0	677	13	28.7	11.6
−41	0.2	17	114.5	39	0.37	36.8	13.5	608	16	18.8	6.0
−29	0.6	19	115.4	−12	0.45	22.1	10.0	464	−6	24.9	3.7
25	0.3	12(d)	214.9	28	0.77	23.8	18.3	1,184	19	18.1	22.0
2	0.3	11	164.5	24	0.78	24.1	16.8	874	17	18.8	23.3
32	0.3	10	130.2	12	0.68	24.4	16.5	737	16	17.8	20.1
72	0.3(b)	11(b)	69.0	25	0.46	31.1	14.3	399	22	17.3	10.1
22	0.4	5	89.4	19	0.56	28.2	15.8	637	16	14.0	21.2
−5	0.4	12	42.8	74	0.29	32.0	9.2	365	11	11.7	8.9
21	0.4	23	85.0	35	0.66	20.7	13.7	427	25	19.9	9.7
47	0.1	15	101.0	17	0.81	15.6	12.7	366	13	27.6	10.7
2	0.2	11	109.7	17	0.95	17.0	16.1	408	10	26.9	14.2
21	0.2	19	103.3	14	0.95	16.5	15.6	375	12	27.6	12.8
31	0.3	14	100.3	20	0.94	19.1	18.0	345	16	29.1	15.9
12	0.2	19	72.6	21	0.76	20.1	15.3	265	21	27.4	15.0
75	0.2	8	82.0	14	0.91	15.5	14.2	316	19	26.0	11.9
−2	0.3	8(d)	70.0	23	0.86	19.3	16.6	279	15	25.1	16.6
17	0.2	11	82.4	28	1.00	18.0	17.9	289	19	28.5	16.5
255	0.7	11	43.9	12	0.52	24.7	12.9	235	17	18.7	4.6
9	1.0	40	16.5	−47	0.17	28.0	4.7(g)	202	−6	8.2	−8.5
9	0.2	5	65.5	22	0.86	18.8	16.2	311	22	21.1	15.0
32	0.2	14	20.9	48	0.32	28.0	8.9	180	18	11.6	14.7
17	0.2	16(d)	35.5	10	0.55	20.4	11.2	150	11	23.7	0.8
11	0.6	12	44.5	25	0.80	19.8	15.9	193	19	23.0	20.1
3	0.5	7(d)	45.2	35	0.83	18.3	15.2	198	20	22.9	9.4
38	0.3	19	49.0	26	1.04	15.4	16.0	169	18	29.1	10.6
−14	0.2	21(d)	57.4	4	1.12	10.6	11.8	205	8	28.0	8.8
8	0.3	2	44.2	5	0.86	18.4	15.7	231	12	19.2	17.0
400	0.2	24	30.4	5	0.60	19.2	11.4	129	12	23.6	4.1
46	0.1	4	47.5	38	1.03	18.4	19.0	221	30	21.5	20.9
20	0.1	31	23.1	28	0.49	25.1	12.3	120	10	19.3	33.0
60	0.1	10	46.6	21	0.94	15.5	14.7	182	14	25.7	10.0
38	0.2	28	47.0	11	0.99	15.9	15.7	189	12	27.8	13.2
−16	0.6	4	36.9	41	0.86	18.1	15.6	191	18	19.4	14.1
37	0.4	19	32.2	5	0.70	16.1	11.2	183	11	17.6	8.2
21	0.2	29	53.6	10	1.28	12.9	16.5	183	11	32.9	11.7
−7	0.3	18	17.0	−8	0.38	15.6	6.3	143	7	11.9	−3.6
14	0.2	14	40.5	27	0.93	19.3	17.9	151	19	26.7	19.6
3	0.3	13	33.6	9	0.78	18.9	14.7	154	7	21.8	11.7
42	0.4	7	37.2	17	0.87	17.2	14.9	195	16	19.1	17.3
21	0.2	2	52.5	18	1.27	13.6	17.3	201	16	26.1	16.0
16	0.5	4	33.8	20	0.81	23.8	19.2	96	29	35.1	13.0
−9	0.3	22	31.6	32	0.77	19.7	15.3	137	15	23.1	17.2
30	0.4	15	32.7	21	0.88	17.5	15.1	123	14	26.5	7.7

(a) Yearend amounts; (b) Loans include direct lease financing; (c) Data are for banking operations only; (d) Includes other funds purchased and/or other funds sold; (e) Loans are net of unearned income; (f) Total Interest Income is not adjusted for tax equivalents; (g) Includes preferred stock; NA = not available; NM = not meaningful. Data: Standard & Poor's Compustat Services Inc.

The International Banking Act of 1978 allowed foreign banks to establish *Edge Act Corporations,* subsidiaries of banks that are allowed to engage only in international banking. Edge Act Corporations may not take deposits from local residents or make loans to them for domestic business, but they may take deposits from foreign residents and lend to anyone for international business. This alternative was even more restrictive than the use of an agency, so Sandberg quickly rejected it.

A *wholly owned subsidiary,* incorporated as a normal U.S. bank, was another possibility. In this case, HSBC would need to invest enough funds in the subsidiary to start up its local lending business. Once established, the subsidiary could undertake any kind of activity allowed to domestically owned banks. This alternative would allow HSBC access to borrowing from the U.S. central bank (the Federal Reserve). The full range of borrowing and lending possibilities would be open to the new subsidiary. In order to set up a subsidiary in New York, HSBC would need to sell the California and Houston banks, since U.S. banking laws prohibited banks from owning full-service branches or subsidiaries in more than one state.

A subsidiary could be established either by creating a completely new bank with new offices and new employees, or by buying an existing bank with its existing network of offices, people, and accounts. Clearly, the second choice would be preferable, but it would cost much more. Sandberg needed to examine the expected costs of opening new offices, perhaps in New York but also possibly in San Francisco, which is closer to Hong Kong and·more tied to Asian business, and where HSBC already had one subsidiary with several offices.

A *branch* could be established in a state where the bank does not already have an existing affiliate. The branch would be a wholly-owned affiliate of the parent bank not incorporated separately. Establishing a new branch in 1980 would require selling the California and Houston operations, just as would opening a new subsidiary in a different state. The branch could (depending to some extent on differing state rules) take local deposits and make local loans, but it would be greatly restricted in participating in the rest of the U.S. financial market such as in Federal Reserve borrowing. Some states (such as Florida) do not allow foreign bank branches.

The use of additional *representative offices* was rejected immediately, since such offices would not allow HSBC direct participation in the U.S. market. Mr. Sandberg did realize, however, that it might be desirable to have representatives in several cities such as San Francisco, Chicago, Miami, and Los Angeles, in order to seek out additional business for the main office in New York. So representative offices were left as possibilities, to be considered only after the initial investment decision was made.

Finally, a *joint venture* with some other bank could be used. This strategy would enable HSBC to enter the U.S. market with less capital investment than the other alternatives, but it would mean sharing the decision making and the profits of the venture. A joint venture would be formed as a normal U.S. bank, similar to the subsidiary discussed above. The legal restrictions would be relatively unimportant—the key issue would be the management of the joint venture. Historically, very few joint ventures have lasted for more than a few years before the partners decided to stop the project and either operate alone or leave the market. Despite this drawback, Sandberg felt that it would be worthwhile to seek a potential partner and to compare the expected results of a joint venture with those of other alternatives.

Chapter

6

The Foreign Exchange Market

This chapter focuses on the mechanisms through which one country's currency can be exchanged for the currency of another country. The markets in which such transactions take place are called foreign exchange markets, and the purpose of this chapter is to show how these markets work and how firms can use them. The main goals of the chapter are to:

1. Explain how foreign exchange transactions take place.

2. Examine the main foreign exchange markets that operate in the United States.

3. Discuss the full range of participants in foreign exchange markets and their motives for buying and selling.

4. Consider the various types of exchange arbitrage that take place in the inter-bank market and between different foreign exchange markets.

5. Explain the fundamental economic factors that determine the exchange rate in the absence of government intervention in the foreign exchange markets.

6. Show how firms can operate successfully in more than one currency without facing unacceptable levels of exchange risk.

INTRODUCTION

The truly fundamental differences between international and domestic business are that international business extends domestic concerns to include (1) different government-imposed rules and practices for doing business abroad or on a globally integrated scale and (2) the different national currencies that are used in different countries. The focus of this chapter is on these currencies and their interrelations.

This first section discusses the central concern in foreign exchange markets, the exchange rate. The next section examines the major institutions and activities that constitute the foreign exchange market in the United States today. The third section looks at the main categories of participants in foreign exchange markets worldwide. Since the exchange rate is the central variable of interest here, the fourth section introduces the issue of exchange-rate determination. The final section of the chapter explores the problem of exchange risk and methods for protecting the firm against such risk.

Currencies, like any other products, services, or claims, can be traded for each other. The **foreign exchange market** is simply a mechanism through which transactions can be made between one country's currency and another country's currency. Or, more broadly, a foreign exchange market is a market for the exchange of financial instruments denominated in different currencies. The most common location for foreign exchange transactions is a commercial bank, which agrees to "make a market" for the purchase and sale of currencies other than the local one. In the United States, hundreds of banks offer foreign exchange markets in dozens of cities—though over 40 percent of all foreign exchange business is done through the 10 largest banks in New York.[1]

Foreign exchange is not simply currency printed by a foreign country's central bank. Rather, it includes such items as cash, checks (or drafts), wire transfers, telephone transfers, and even contracts to sell or buy currency in the future. Foreign exchange is really any financial instrument that carries out payment from one currency to another. The most common form of foreign exchange in transactions between companies is the draft (denominated in a foreign currency). The most common form of foreign exchange in transactions between banks is the telephone transfer, generally for transactions of $1 million or more. Far down the list of instruments, in terms of the value exchanged, is actual currency, which is often exchanged by tourists and other travelers.

Since no currency is necessarily fixed in value compared to others, there must be some means of determining an acceptable price, or **exchange rate.** How many British pounds (£) should one dollar buy? How many Brazilian cruzeiros should be paid to buy a dollar? Since 1973, most of the industrialized countries of the noncommunist world have allowed their currency values to fluctuate more or less freely (depending on the time and the country), so that simple economics of supply and demand largely determine exchange rates. In graphic form, Figure 6–1 shows that the intersection of the supply curve and the demand curve for German marks (DM) sets the price, or exchange rate, of marks in terms of dollars. A variety of the participants in the foreign exchange market are listed below the graph: their specific activities are discussed in the following section.

FIGURE 6–1

The Foreign Exchange Market at Bankers Trust Company of New York, April 25, 1990

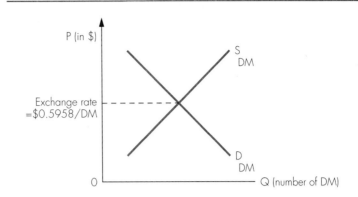

Suppliers of Marks	Demanders for Marks
U.S. exporters	U.S. importers paying in marks
German direct investors	U.S. direct investors in Germany
U.S. foreign investors remitting profits	German foreign investors in the United States remitting their profits
German portfolio investors	U.S. portfolio investors in Germany
Bear speculators	Bull speculators

Arbitrageurs
Government "interveners"

Notice that the exchange rate of $0.5958 per DM is offered by one specific bank. This was the closing exchange rate quoted by Bankers Trust Company of New York for purchases of at least $1 million worth of deutsche marks on April 25, 1990. Another bank in New York may have quoted a slightly higher or a slightly lower rate at the same time; and banks in San Francisco or London or Tokyo probably quoted rates that differed even more. The rates quoted depend on each bank's interest in being involved in foreign exchange transactions and on the varying strategic positions and risks taken by the banks. Thus, the foreign exchange market among banks may be viewed as one large market, or as many small markets with extensive (potential and actual) interrelations. Generally, the interbank market within any country is viewed as one market, and intercountry dealings are somewhat segmented by different rules and risks (though in the United States the San Francisco market often offers quotations from various banks that differ noticeably from rate quotations in New York, due partly to the difference in time zones).

The differences in rate quotations may appear to be very small to an outsider. Deutsche marks may be quoted at $0.5956 at Citibank in New York and at $0.5974 at Bank of America in San Francisco. This difference seems small—but for every DM 1 million sold, the buyer of dollars in San Francisco receives an extra $1,600. Since the transactions are generally rapid and for values of $5-10 million, such differences may add up to a substantial gain (or cost) to the participant in the foreign exchange market.

The various foreign exchange transactions mentioned above involve large commercial banks and large amounts of money. Most of the companies that do international business also utilize foreign exchange markets, but far less frequently than banks and for transactions that involve less money. Consequently, the access of these companies to foreign currencies differs from that of the banks. (Specifically, banks make the market and companies pay for the use of this service.) The next section explains the various parts that constitute the U.S. foreign exchange market.

FOREIGN EXCHANGE MARKETS IN THE UNITED STATES

Figure 6–2 presents an overview of the foreign exchange markets operating today in the United States. In this section, each of these markets is discussed in some detail.

The Interbank Market

Although the foreign exchange dealings of most managers involve a company buying from or selling to a bank, it is important for managers to understand the foreign exchange market between banks. This is because, as noted above, the vast majority of large-scale foreign exchange transactions are interbank, and these transactions tend to determine exchange rates—which occasional market participants such as companies must deal with.

Local and regional commercial banks may offer clients a foreign exchange service, which such banks provide on request by dealing through a larger bank, typically in a large city (such as New York, Los Angeles, or Chicago). If a local bank receives a request to buy Swiss francs (SF) for an importer in New Jersey, it will call its correspondent bank in New York (say, Chemical Bank) and arrange to buy the SF, say for $0.6851/SF. Then the local bank will add on its service charge, so that the importer pays $0.6951/SF. Thus, the local bank earns $0.01 per SF, or about 1.5 percent on the transaction.

Chemical Bank, in turn, will either take the requested Swiss francs from its own holdings of that currency or will enter the **interbank market** to buy them. Assuming that Chemical does *not* have the SF on hand, one of its foreign exchange traders will call several other major banks (or brokerage houses, which are discussed below) and contract to buy Swiss francs from the lowest bidder.

The interbank market generally operates with large transactions only—of about $1 million to $10 million exchanged for the equivalent foreign currency. On a typical day in 1989, the more than 100 members of the main association of commercial banks in foreign exchange dealings (called the Clearinghouse Interbank Payments System, CHIPS) transacted roughly $110 billion of currency trades.[2]

The Brokers' Market

Another facet of large-scale foreign exchange dealing in the United States is the **brokers' market.** About half a dozen foreign exchange brokerage companies make markets for foreign currencies in New York (as well as in London and elsewhere), creating trading in many currencies similar to that in the interbank market. In this case, the key differences are that the brokers seek to match

FIGURE 6–2

U.S. Foreign Exchange
Markets

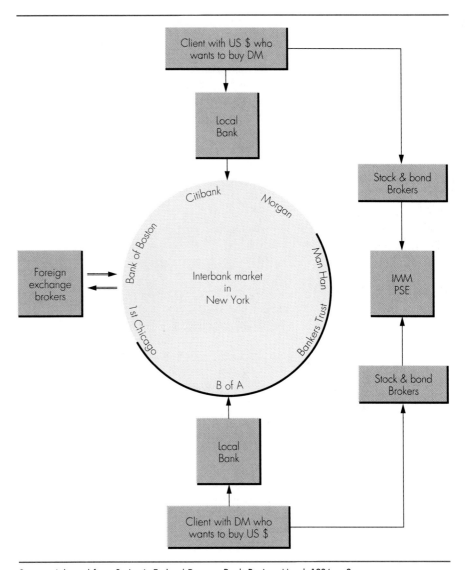

Source: Adapted from St. Louis Federal Reserve Bank *Review*, March 1984, p. 9.

buyers and sellers on any given transaction, without taking a position themselves; that they deal simultaneously with many banks (and other companies);
and that they offer both buy and sell positions to clients (where a bank may wish
to operate on only one side of the market at any particular time).[3] Also, the
brokers deal "blind," offering rate quotations without naming the potential
seller/buyer until a deal has been negotiated. Brokers play a large part in the total
market, arranging about 45 percent of total transactions, as shown in Table 6–1.

Before moving on to other foreign exchange markets, let us consider an
example in which the spot market is used by a tourist planning a trip to Japan.
This person wants to visit Tokyo to see a friend during Christmas vacation and
to do some sight-seeing. She is taking $1,000 with her, having already purchased

the round-trip airline ticket. Since dollars cannot be used for most purchases in Japan, she needs to buy Japanese yen. How should she do it?

Looking at Table 6–2, she sees that Bankers Trust is offering to sell large quantities of yen at the rate of 158.7 yen per dollar. At the "retail" level, that is, for small transactions such as this one, she can expect to receive only about 150 yen per dollar. Indeed, when she called Bank of America and Wells Fargo Bank in San Francisco, rates of 151 yen per dollar were quoted. Instead of carrying the cash with her, she wants to get traveler's checks. Upon calling the office of American Express in San Francisco, she found that yen-denominated traveler's checks were available but that they would cost her $1 for every 145 yen, plus a $5 service charge.

The tourist was willing to pay the extra cost to obtain the protection of traveler's checks, but one final problem arose. A friend who worked in foreign exchange dealing at Crocker National Bank told her that the yen would probably decline in value relative to the dollar in the next few days. Since she would not leave for Tokyo for another week, she wondered whether it was worth waiting for the expected devaluation. The answer to this question is that no one knows! She can hope for a devaluation, and delay purchase of the yen for a week, or ignore the potential gain—or loss!—and buy the yen today. In such a short time period, it is probably best to ignore the few days' variability in the exchange rate—since it could be favorable or unfavorable—and just buy the yen at the most convenient time before departing to Tokyo. (One more point to confuse the matter: she could buy traveler's checks in U.S. dollars and exchange them for yen in Japan when needed. Again, no one can be sure what the yen's value will be during her vacation time in Tokyo!)

TABLE 6–1

Foreign Exchange Turnover in the U.S. Market in April 1989 (in billions of U.S. dollars)

Type of Transaction	Turnover of 127 Banks
Spot	
Direct with banks in United States	382.2
Direct with banks abroad	477.0
Through brokers	859.2
Subtotal	1,718.4
Swaps	
Direct with banks in United States	108.9
Direct with banks abroad	162.8
Through brokers	424.0
Subtotal	695.7
Outright forwards	
Direct with banks in United States	n.a.
Direct with banks abroad	n.a.
Through brokers	n.a.
Subtotal	75.1
Total interbank transactions	
Direct with banks in United States	491.1
Direct with banks abroad	639.8
Through brokers	1,283.2
Unspecified	83.0
Grand total, interbank transactions	2,497.1

Source: Federal Reserve Bank of New York–U.S. Foreign Exchange Market Turnover Survey, April 1989.

While this example does not offer a guaranteed way to make money from foreign exchange dealings, it does illustrate the kinds of problems that beset individuals and companies as they work with foreign currencies. Fortunately, there are some methods to help avoid the uncertainty involved in foreign exchange; they are discussed in the section, "Methods of Protecting against Exchange Risk."

So far, the discussion has focused only on the *spot market,* that is, the market for immediate exchange of one currency for another. An additional, very large part of the U.S. foreign exchange market is the set of instruments that allow contracting today for delivery of currency in the future. The main instruments of this type are forward contracts, foreign exchange futures contracts, and foreign currency options.

The Forward Foreign Exchange Market

The **forward foreign exchange market** at commercial banks in the United States offers banks, companies, and individuals the opportunity to contract *today* for a specific foreign exchange transaction in the *future,* at a fixed price (i.e., exchange rate). Forward contracts are negotiated between the offering bank and the client as to size, maturity, and price. Referring to Table 6–2, we see that Bankers Trust was offering to sell British pounds for $1.5867/£ in 180 days on April 25, 1990 (for quantities of at least $1 million).

TABLE 6–2

Exchange Rates

Wednesday, April 25, 1990

The New York foreign exchange selling rates below apply to trading among banks in amounts of $1 million and more, as quoted at 3 p.m. Eastern time by Bankers Trust Co. Retail transactions provide fewer units of foreign currency per dollar.

Country	U.S. $ equiv.		Currency per U.S. $	
	Wed.	Tues.	Wed.	Tues.
Argentina (Austral)	.0001992	.0001992	5020.08	5020.08
Australia (Dollar)	.7663	c.7667	1.3050	c1.3043
Austria (Schilling)	.08468	.08375	11.81	11.94
Bahrain (Dinar)	2.6522	2.6522	.3771	.3771
Belgium (Franc)				
Commercial rate	.02889	.02852	34.62	35.06
Brazil (Cruzeiro)	.02000	.01997	50.00	50.07
Britain (Pound)	1.6375	1.6340	.6107	.6120
30-Day Forward	1.6284	1.6245	.6141	.6156
90-Day Forward	1.6120	1.6085	.6203	.6217
180-Day Forward	1.5867	1.5840	.6302	.6313
Canada (Dollar)	.8615	.8624	1.1607	1.1595
30-Day Forward	.8578	.8590	1.1658	1.1641
90-Day Forward	.8514	.8521	1.1745	1.1736
180-Day Forward	.8422	.8425	1.1874	1.1870
Chile (Official rate)	.003478	.003478	287.52	287.52
China (Yuan)	.211640	.211640	4.7250	4.7250
Colombia (Peso)	.002128	.002128	470.00	470.00
Denmark (Krone)	.1566	.1549	6.3845	6.4565
Ecuador (Sucre)				
Floating rate	.001266	.001266	790.00	790.00
Finland (Markka)	.25208	.25000	3.9670	4.0000
France (Franc)	.17756	.17556	5.6320	5.6960
30-Day Forward	.17736	.17537	5.6382	5.7022
90-Day Forward	.17703	.17505	5.6487	5.7127
180-Day Forward	.17657	.17460	5.6635	5.7275
Greece (Drachma)	.006098	.006031	164.00	165.80
Hong Kong (Dollar)	.12837	.12837	7.7900	7.7900
India (Rupee)	.05790	c.05790	17.27	c17.27
Indonesia (Rupiah)	.0005464	.0005464	1830.03	1830.03
Ireland (Punt)	1.5925	1.5800	.6279	.6329
Israel (Shekel)	.4949	.4949	2.0207	2.0207
Italy (Lira)	.0008128	.0008034	1230.25	1244.76
Japan (Yen)	.006303	.006292	158.65	158.92
30-Day Forward	.006311	.006299	158.46	158.75
90-Day Forward	.006324	.006311	158.13	158.45
180-Day Forward	.006344	.006331	157.63	157.96
Jordan (Dinar)	1.5076	1.5076	.6633	.6633
Kuwait (Dinar)	3.3939	3.3939	.2947	.2947

The rationale for forward contracts in currencies is analogous to that for futures contracts in commodities; the firm can lock in a price today to eliminate uncertainty about the value of a future receipt or payment of foreign currency. Such a transaction may be undertaken because the firm has made a previous contract, for example, to pay FF 1 million to a supplier in three months for some

TABLE 6–2

Continued

Country	U.S. $ equiv.		Currency per U.S. $	
	Wed.	Tues.	Wed.	Tues.
Lebanon (Pound)	.001682	.001682	594.50	594.50
Malaysia (Ringgit)	.3680	.3678	2.7175	2.7185
Malta (Lira)	3.0166	3.0166	.3315	.3315
Mexico (Peso)				
Floating rate	.0003571	.0003571	2800.01	2800.01
Netherlands (Guilder)	.5295	.5237	1.8885	1.9095
New Zealand (Dollar)	.5815	.5820	1.7197	1.7182
Norway (Krone)	.1537	.1523	6.5050	6.5660
Pakistan (Rupee)	.0472	.0472	21.18	21.18
Peru (Inti)	.00003760	.00003760	26595.04	26595.04
Philippines (Peso)	.04502	.04502	22.21	22.21
Portugal (Escudo)	.006699	.006699	149.28	149.28
Saudi Arabia (Riyal)	.26681	.26681	3.7480	3.7480
Singapore (Dollar)	.5329	.5323	1.8765	1.8785
South Africa (Rand)				
Commercial rate	.3767	.3759	2.6546	2.6603
Financial rate	.2451	.2506	4.0800	3.9904
South Korea (Won)	.0014245	.0014245	702.00	702.00
Spain (Peseta)	.009443	.009328	105.90	107.20
Sweden (Krona)	.1645	.1629	6.0790	6.1390
Switzerland (Franc)	.6847	.6715	1.4605	1.4892
30-Day Forward	.6839	.6707	1.4621	1.4910
90-Day Forward	.6831	.6715	1.4640	1.4892
180-Day Forward	.6825	.6693	1.4651	1.4942
Taiwan (Dollar)	.038022	.038168	26.30	26.20
Thailand (Baht)	.03868	.03868	25.85	25.85
Turkey (Lira)	.0004019	.0004019	2488.00	2488.00
United Arab (Dirham)	.2723	.2723	3.6730	3.6730
Uruguay (New Peso)				
Financial	.001014	.001014	986.00	986.00
Venezuela (Bolivar)				
Floating rate	.02222	.02222	45.00	45.00
W. Germany (Mark)	.5958	.5887	1.6783	1.6987
30-Day Forward	.5960	.5889	1.6778	1.6982
90-Day Forward	.5962	.5890	1.6773	1.6977
180-Day Forward	.5960	.5889	1.6778	1.6982
– – –				
SDR	1.29772	1.29809	.77058	.77036
ECU	1.20896	1.20630	. . . .	. . . .

Source: *The Wall Street Journal,* April 26, 1990, p. C12.
  Special Drawing Rights (SDR) are based on exchange rates for the U.S., West German, British, French, and Japanese currencies. Source: International Monetary Fund.
  European Currency Unit (ECU) is based on a basket of community currencies. Source: European Community Commission.
  c-corrected.

needed inputs to its operations. If the firm wants to eliminate the risk that its payment in three months will change in dollar terms (i.e., that the FF 1 million may cost more dollars then), it can contract with a bank to buy FF 1 million three months forward, at a price established today. (From Table 6–2, we see that that price was $0.17703/FF for a contract with Bankers Trust on April 25, 1990.) Thus,

Rate Quotations

Exchange-rate quotations come as two-digit numbers, bid/asked, with the preceding numbers assumed. A deutsche mark quote of 50/70 on April 26, 1990, will mean an actual price of:

DM 1.67850 bid to buy one U.S. dollar.

DM 1.67870 asked for selling one U.S. dollar.

The bank is offering (bidding) to buy dollars for 1.6785 marks per dollar and also offering (asking) to sell dollars for 1.6787 marks per dollar. Of course, the actual transaction will involve $1 million or more, to be exchanged at those prices.

Rates are typically quoted on the **Continental basis,** as units of foreign exchange per dollar, everywhere. U.S. banks have traditionally used the **American basis,** quoting $U.S. per unit of foreign exchange. Clearly, whether the quote is DM 2.0 per dollar or $0.50/DM, the value is the same. *The Wall Street Journal* offers both types of quotation, as shown in Figure 6–3.

Another means that is used to distinguish the two ways of presenting an exchange rate is to call a quotation of domestic currency/foreign exchange an **indirect quote.** Conversely, a quotation of units of foreign exchange/ domestic currency is called a **direct quote.** This system has more general applicability to any pair of currencies, whereas the American/Continental system relates only to rates involving the U.S. dollar. ∎

firms can use forward contracts to eliminate the risk of variability in future dollar costs or revenues due to exchange-rate changes. This concept, called "hedging," and other motives for using the forward market are discussed below.

Notice that in the above example the forward contract used for hedging does *not* correspond directly to an insurance contract. The forward contract does fix a minimum "loss" for the firm, by setting the guaranteed price of exchange in the future. Even if the dollar devalues to $0.19 per FF in three months, the forward contract holder is still able to buy 1 million FF for $0.17703/FF. However, if the French franc devalues over the next three months to, say, $0.16703/FF, the forward contract holder will have an **opportunity cost** of the difference between the forward rate and the (eventual) future spot rate (a difference of $0.01/FF, or 5.6 percent). Thus, the forward contract insures against potential losses *and* against potential gains in foreign currency value.

Forward markets exist in any currencies and for any maturities that banks are willing to offer. Most of the forward contracts used in the United States involve exchanges of U.S. dollars for German marks, Japanese yen, British pounds, Swiss francs, Canadian dollars, and French francs. Maturities tend to be six months or less, though single-year and multiyear forward contracts are sometimes available.

The Futures Market in Currencies

A very similar type of instrument is available on several securities exchanges in the United States and abroad. The foreign exchange **futures contract** is an agreement to buy or sell a fixed amount of foreign currency for delivery at a fixed future date at a fixed dollar price. The main difference between futures and forward contracts in the United States is that futures contracts have fixed sizes (about $50,000 to $100,000, depending on the currency) and preestablished maturity dates. (All are 3-, 6-, or 12-month contracts maturing on the third Wednesday of March, June, September, or December.) Also, futures contracts are available for only a few currencies (Canadian dollars, German marks, French francs, Swiss francs, British pounds, Japanese yen, European currency units [ECU], and Australian dollars) and only if a buyer and a seller can be found at the time. The futures market at the Chicago Mercantile Exchange is currently very thin (i.e., few contracts are traded) except for the three-month contracts denominated in Canadian dollars, German marks, and Swiss francs.

Futures contracts are more widely accessible to firms and individuals than forward contracts, because of their smaller value and the margin requirements that enable brokers to obtain collateral from market participants. (However, the currently thin nature of this market does not allow participants the wide range of currencies and maturities that are available for large-scale transactions in the forward market.) The standard contracts available at the Chicago Mercantile Exchange are described in Table 6–3.

Foreign currency *options* are an additional instrument of the foreign exchange market in the United States; they are described in the accompanying box.

WHO USES FOREIGN EXCHANGE MARKETS?

Participants in the foreign exchange market range from multinational banks to travelers from Detroit to Windsor, Canada, from multinational companies to foreign central banks. Users of foreign exchange markets fall into five basic classes:

1. Traders/brokers.
2. Speculators.
3. Hedgers.
4. Arbitrageurs.
5. Governments (for intervention; that is, participation in the market to set an exchange rate).

Traders and Brokers

Foreign exchange traders work in commercial banks and may deal in spot market transactions or forward market transactions. Their goal in the market is to match up buyers and sellers of foreign exchange, charging an implicit fee (hidden within the exchange rate quotation itself) for providing this service. Such traders *may* buy or sell foreign exchange for the account of their own bank, thus creating foreign exchange risk for the bank. "Positions" of this kind are generally eliminated during the trading day, so that the trader ends up finding a paired buyer/seller for each maturity and amount of foreign currency. (If the trader *does* accumulate one-sided transactions in one currency, so that the bank finds itself with net foreign exchange due or owed, we call this "speculation.") Among the buyers and sellers of foreign exchange that the traders serve

TABLE 6–3

Currency Futures Contract Specifications[1] at the Chicago Mercantile Exchange

	Australian Dollar (AD)	British Pound (BP)	Canadian Dollar (CD)	Deutsche Mark (DM)	French Franc (FR)	Japanese Yen (JY)	Swiss Franc (SF)	European Currency Unit (ECU)
Trading unit	AD100,000	BP62,500	CD100,000	DM125,000	FR250,000	JY12,500,000	SF125,000	ECU125,000
Quotations	US$ per A$	US$ per pound	US$ per C$	US$ per mark	US$ per franc	US$ per yen	US$ per franc	US$ per ECU
Minimum price change	.0001	.0002	.0001	.0001	.00005	.000001	.0001	.0001
Value of 1 point	$10.00	$6.25	$10.00	$12.50	$2.50	$12.50	$12.50	$12.50
Price limits[2]	150 Points	400 Points	100 Points	150 Points	500 Points	150 Points	150 Points	150 Points
Months traded	March, June, September, December							
Trading hours[3] (Chicago time)	7:20A.M.– 2:00P.M.	7:20A.M.– 2:00P.M.	7:20A.M.– 2:00P.M.	7:20A.M.– 2:00P.M.	7:20A.M.– 2:00P.M.	7:20A.M.– 2:00P.M.	7:20A.M.– 2:00P.M.	7:10A.M.– 2:00P.M.
Last day hours	7:20A.M.– 9:16A.M.	7:20A.M.– 9:16A.M.	7:20A.M.– 9:16A.M.	7:20A.M.– 9:16A.M.	7:20A.M.– 9:16A.M.	7:20A.M.– 9:16A.M.	7:20A.M.– 9:16A.M.	7:10A.M.– 9:00A.M.
Last day of trading	Two business days before the third Wednesday of the delivery month							
Delivery date	Third Wednesday of the delivery month							

[1]Contract specifications are subject to change. All matters pertaining to rules and specifications herein are made subject to and are superseded by official Chicago Mercantile Exchange rules. Current Chicago Mercantile Exchange rules should be consulted in all cases concerning contract specifications. Check with your broker to confirm this information.

[2]Price limits are in effect from 7:20 A.M. to 7:35 A.M. each day, based on change of price from previous day's settlement.

[3]Trading will end at 12:00 noon on the business day before a CME holiday and on any U.S. bank holiday that the CME is open. 10/12/88

are the literally millions of companies and individuals that export, import, or travel internationally, needing foreign currency instruments to make their payments or cancel their receipts.

Foreign exchange brokers work in brokerage firms, which may also deal in spot or forward transactions. As noted earlier, such brokers attempt to match buyer and seller in a single transaction, with the margin between quoted rates plus a fixed fee as their commission. Brokerage firms typically deal only in foreign exchange transactions, not in any other financial instruments.

Both traders and brokers function primarily as *market makers,* profiting from their dealings through fees implicit in their rate quotations. In principle, they do not take one-sided positions in the market, though such speculation does occur and often leads to sizable gains (or losses!) for banks and brokerage houses.

Speculators

Banks, companies, individuals, and governments may all function as speculators in the foreign exchange market at one time or another. A speculator is simply a participant in the foreign exchange market that takes an open position. That is, the speculator buys foreign currency without simultaneously contracting to sell it, or sells foreign exchange without possessing the currency to meet the obligation. Such short (net sale of foreign exchange) or long (net acquisition of

ADDED DIMENSION

Foreign Currency Options

The most recently created type of foreign exchange market offers participants the *right* to buy or sell foreign currency in the future, rather than the obligation to do so. Foreign currency options are similar to foreign currency futures in the United States, in that the contracts are for fixed quantities of currency to be exchanged at a fixed price in the future. The key difference is that the maturity date for an option is only the last day to carry out the currency exchange; the option may be "exercised," that is, presented for currency exchange, at *any* time between its issuance and the maturity date, or not at all.

A **foreign currency option** is a contract offering the holder the right to buy (namely, a **call option**) or sell (namely, a **put option**) a fixed amount of foreign currency for a fixed price during a fixed time period. The buyer of a call option on British pounds obtains the right to buy £50,000 at a fixed dollar price (i.e., the **exercise price**) at any time during the (typically) three-month life of the option. The seller of the same option faces a **contingent liability** in that the seller will have to deliver the British pounds at any time, if the buyer chooses to exercise the option.

The market value (i.e., the price on "premium" that a buyer must pay to purchase the option) of an option depends on its exercise price, the remaining time to its expiration, the exchange rate in the spot market, and expectations about the future exchange rate. An option may sell for a price near zero or for thousands of dollars, or anywhere in between. Notice that the buyer of a call option on British pounds may pay a small price to obtain the option but does *not* have to exercise the option if the actual exchange rate moves favorably. Thus, an option is superior to a forward contract having the same maturity and exercise price because it need *not* be used—and the cost is just its purchase price. However, the price of the option is generally greater than the expected cost of the forward contract; so the user of the option pays for the flexibility of the instrument.

Some recent currency option prices from the Philadelphia Stock Exchange are presented in Table 6–4. ■

foreign exchange) positions subject the speculator to risk that the dollar value of the foreign currency may change before the position is eliminated.

For example, if you feel that the deutsche mark (DM) is going to go up in value relative to the dollar, you may buy 100,000 DM today and deposit them in some interest-earning instrument. You are long in DM. If you don't simultaneously sell 100,000 DM in the spot, forward, futures, or options market, then you have an exposure in DM. If your guess is correct and DM do appreciate relative to dollars, your speculation will be rewarded with a profit when you

TABLE 6-4

Options on the Philadelphia Exchange

Option & Underlying	Strike Price	Calls—Last			Puts—Last		
		May	Jun	Sep	May	Jun	Sep
50,000 Australian Dollars-cents per unit.							
ADollr	...77	r	0.60	r	r	r	r
31,250 British Pounds-cents per unit.							
BPound	155	r	r	8.50	r	r	2.20
163.85	157½	r	r	r	r	1.00	r
163.85	.160	r	r	r	0.30	1.50	r
163.85	162½	1.20	1.94	r	0.93	r	r
163.85	.165	0.64	1.32	r	r	r	r
163.85	.170	r	r	1.20	r	r	11.00
31,250 British Pounds-European Style.							
163.85	.165	r	1.12	r	r	r	r
50,000 Canadian Dollars-cents per unit.							
CDollr	...81	r	r	r	r	r	0.14
86.13	...83	r	r	r	r	0.07	r
86.13	...85	r	r	r	0.08	r	1.27
86.13	.85½	r	r	r	0.20	r	r
86.13	...86	r	r	r	0.37	r	1.95
86.13	.86½	r	0.23	r	r	r	r
62,500 West German Marks-cents per unit.							
DMark	..54	r	r	r	r	0.03	r
59.58	...55	r	4.31	r	r	r	r
59.58	...56	r	r	r	r	0.09	r
59.58	...57	r	r	r	r	0.19	r
59.58	...58	r	r	r	0.09	0.35	r
59.58	.58½	r	r	s	0.19	r	s
59.58	...59	0.64	1.00	r	0.24	0.66	r
59.58	.59½	0.43	r	s	0.58	r	s
59.58	...60	0.31	0.71	1.33	0.82	r	1.96
59.58	...61	r	r	r	r	2.15	r
59.58	...62	r	0.16	r	r	r	r
250,000 French Francs-10ths of a cent per unit.							
FFranc	..18	r	r	r	r	5.30	r

finally sell the marks for dollars. If you are wrong, however, you will receive fewer dollars from your eventual sale of DM than you could have received otherwise.

Hedgers

Many companies and individuals take long or short positions in the foreign exchange market, not to speculate, but to offset an existing foreign currency position in another market. That is, they engage in **foreign exchange hedging.** For example, a chemical company may agree to sell £500,000 of plastic to a buyer in London, payable in 180 days. This company has a de facto foreign exchange exposure, even though it has not entered the foreign exchange market. By contracting with a bank to sell £500,000 forward for dollars in 180 days, the company eliminates its foreign exchange exposure. Thus, one-sided participation in the foreign exchange market may *not* be speculation if the contract offsets an existing exposure of the company in some other transaction.

TABLE 6-4
Continued

Option & Underlying	Strike Price	Calls—Last			Puts—Last		
		May	Jun	Sep	May	Jun	Sep
6,250,000 Japanese Yen-100ths of a cent per unit.							
JYen	...61	r	r	r	0.05	r	r
63.03	...62	r	r	r	0.14	r	r
63.03	.62½	r	r	s	0.30	r	s
63.03	...63	0.44	r	r	0.47	0.79	r
63.03	.63½	0.26	r	s	r	r	s
63.03	...64	0.14	0.52	1.15	r	r	r
63.03	.64½	0.08	r	s	r	r	s
63.03	...65	0.06	0.27	r	r	2.19	r
63.03	...66	r	0.12	r	r	3.06	r
63.03	...67	r	r	r	3.94	r	r
63.03	...68	r	r	r	5.10	5.10	r
63.03	...69	r	r	r	r	5.94	6.10
63.03	...70	r	r	r	r	7.10	6.94
63.03	...71	r	r	r	r	r	8.10
63.03	...72	r	r	r	r	9.10	r
6,250,000 Japanese Yen-European Style.							
63.03	...69	r	r	r	5.90	r	r
62,500 Swiss Francs-cents per unit.							
SFranc	.64	r	3.74	r	r	0.10	r
68.43	...65	r	r	r	r	0.19	r
68.43	.65½	r	2.80	s	r	r	s
68.43	.66½	r	r	s	0.10	r	s
68.43	...67	r	1.74	r	0.18	0.66	r
68.43	.67½	0.71	r	s	0.30	r	s
68.43	...68	0.62	0.89	r	0.48	r	r
68.43	.68½	0.48	r	s	r	r	s
68.43	...69	0.30	0.70	r	r	r	r
68.43	.69½	0.16	0.34	s	r	r	s
68.43	...70	0.04	0.38	r	r	r	r
68.43	...71	r	0.19	r	r	r	r
62,500 Swiss Francs-European Style.							
68.43	...69	r	0.62	r	r	r	r
Total call vol.		13,334			Call open int.	302,528	
Total put vol.		24,141			Put open int.	297,081	

Source: *The Wall Street Journal*, April 26, 1990, p. C12.
r—Not traded. s—No option offered.
Last is premium (purchase price).

Hedging may be carried out in a variety of ways, many of which do not involve the foreign exchange market at all. The general issue of protecting against foreign exchange risk is discussed in a later section of this chapter.

Arbitrageurs

Foreign exchange arbitrage involves simultaneous contracting in two or more foreign exchange markets to buy and sell foreign currency, profiting from exchange rate differences *without* incurring exchange-rate risk. Foreign exchange arbitrage may be two-way, three-way, or intertemporal; and it is generally undertaken by large commercial banks that can exchange large quantities of money to exploit small rate differentials.

Two-Way　The simplest form of exchange arbitrage is two-way, between any two currencies and between two places. Quotations for Swiss francs in the spot market on April 25, 1990, were:

At Bankers Trust in New York: $0.6847/SF.

At Bank of America in San Francisco: $0.6852/SF.

At Lloyds Bank in London: $0.6883/SF.

An arbitrageur can buy SF in New York and simultaneously sell them in London, making a profit of $0.0036/SF, or 0.53 percent per transaction. While the percentage gain is small, it translates to $3,600 for every million SF traded, and it involves no exchange risk. By repeatedly arbitraging this price (exchange-rate) differential, the arbitrageur will make a profit until the exchange-rate differential drops below the transactions cost (i.e., the telephone bill, plus the arbitrageur's salary, plus other relevant costs).

The same two-way arbitrage may also occur in the forward market or between forward and futures markets.[4] From the quotations here, we see that profitable arbitrage opportunities exist between the New York forward market and the Chicago futures market, as well as between New York and San Francisco forward markets:

At Bankers Trust in New York: 157.6 yen/$ for delivery in 180 days.

At Bank of America in San Francisco: 155.4 yen/$ for delivery in 180 days.

At the Chicago Mercantile Exchange: 158.1 yen/$ for delivery on
September 19, 1990.

An arbitrageur can buy yen in New York and sell them in San Francisco, both for exchange in 180 days, and earn 2.2 yen/dollar, or 1.4 percent per transaction. Similarly, an arbitrageur can buy yen in Chicago and sell them in San Francisco, to make 2.7 yen/dollar, or 1.7 percent per transaction. The difficulties with the latter transaction are that contracts may not be available for the desired amount or maturity date and that transactions costs are higher for the intermarket exchanges. Nonetheless, both transactions may be feasible and profitable, even after costs are considered.

Three-Way　When the arbitrageur does not wish to operate directly in a two-way transaction, because of restrictions on the market or for any other reason, profits may still be available through triangular or **three-way arbitrage.** In this case, the arbitrageur moves through three currencies, starting and ending with the same one, and incurring no exchange-rate risk. Quotations from the London *Economist* and *The Wall Street Journal* on April 25, 1990 show the following two-way exchange rates:

$1.6375/£ at Bankers Trust in New York.

$0.1786/FF at Bank of America in San Francisco.

FF 9.350/£ at Lloyds Bank in London.

In this case, two-way exchanges are ignored and the transactions will be to (1) buy FF/sell dollars, (2) buy £/sell FF, and (3) buy $/sell £; *or* (1) buy £/sell dollars, (2) buy FF/sell £, and (3) buy $/sell FF.

The optimal transactions can be illuminated by creating **cross rates** from the quotations. For instance, if the arbitrageur wants to compare the London exchange rate with the other two, a pound/French franc rate can be created as:

$$\frac{\$0.1786/FF}{\$1.6375/\pounds} = \pounds0.1091/FF \text{ in New York and San Francisco (or FF } 9.17\pounds)$$

Similarly the pound/dollar cross rate is:

$$\frac{\pounds1/FF9.350}{\$0.1786/FF} = \pounds0.5988/\$ \text{ in London and San Francisco (or } \$1.670/\pounds)$$

And the franc/dollar cross rate is:

$$\frac{FF\ 9.350/\pounds}{\$1.6375/\pounds} = FF\ 5.7099/\$ \text{ in London and New York (or } \$0.1751/FF)$$

From these comparisons, the arbitrageur can see that the maximum profits from triangular arbitrage come from (1) buying FF for dollars in San Francisco, (2) selling FF for £ in London, and (3) buying $ for £ in New York; *or* (1) buying £ for dollars through the cross rate exchange, (2) selling the £ for FF through the cross rate exchange, and (3) buying $ for FF through the cross rate exchange. Either of the two procedures will yield the same percentage profit, though it must be ascertained that the cross rates are in fact available as calculated. Cross rates available in the New York interbank market on April 25, 1990, are shown in Table 6–5.

Governments

Governments participate in the foreign exchange market as (1) buyers and sellers of foreign exchange and (2) the rulemakers. The reader should not become so engrossed in the economics of the foreign exchange market as to ignore the government's ability to change the exchange rate by fiat or to close trading in foreign exchange at any time. Since the major noncommunist developed countries

TABLE 6–5

Cross Rates in the New York Interbank Market

(Late New York Trading Apr. 25, 1990)									
	Dollar	Pound	SFranc	Guilder	Yen	Lira	D-Mark	FFranc	CdnDlr
Canada	1.1608	1.9041	.79643	.61499	.00731	.00094	.69157	.20602	......
France	5.6345	9.242	3.8659	2.9852	.03549	.00458	3.3569	....	4.8540
Germany	1.6785	2.7532	1.1516	.88927	.01057	.00136	....	.29790	1.4460
Italy	1231.0	2019.2	844.60	652.19	7.754	....	733.39	218.48	1060.5
Japan	158.75	260.40	108.919	84.106	....	.12896	94.578	28.175	136.76
Netherlands	1.8875	3.0961	1.2950	....	.01189	.00153	1.1245	.33499	1.6260
Switzerland	1.4575	2.3907	....	.77219	.00918	.00118	.86833	.25867	1.2556
U.K.	.60964	....	.41828	.32299	.00384	.00050	.36321	.10820	.52519
U.S.	....	1.6403	.68611	.52980	.00630	.00081	.59577	.17748	.86147

Source: *The Wall Street Journal*, April 26, 1990, p. C12.

ADDED
DIMENSION

Intertemporal Arbitrage

Exchange arbitrage across maturities, or **intertemporal arbitrage,** is similar to the previous two forms, in that it requires starting and ending with the same currency and incurring no exchange-rate risk. In this case, profits are made by exploiting *interest-rate differentials,* as well as exchange-rate differentials. Also, the intertemporal exchange arbitrageur (or interest arbitrageur) must utilize funds for the time period between contract maturities, whereas the two- and three-way arbitrageurs only need funds on the delivery date.*

Consider the following information:

At Bankers Trust in New York, the spot exchange rate is: SF 1.4605/$.

At Bankers Trust in New York, the 180-day forward is: SF 1.4651/$.

At Barclays Bank in London, the dollar (eurodollar) deposit rate is: 8.50 percent/year.

At Barclays Bank in London, the SF (eurofranc) deposit rate is: 9.06 percent/year.

The interest arbitrageur who begins with U.S. dollars has two alternatives for using funds in intertemporal arbitrage. First, the funds may simply be invested in a dollar-denominated instrument, such as a eurodollar deposit at Barclays Bank. This investment pays 8.50 percent per year, or 4.25 percent for the six-month investment. Alternatively, the arbitrageur may buy SF, invest in a franc-denominated instrument, and buy dollars forward. These three transactions create a dollar-denominated instrument, which pays 9.06 percent/year, plus the percentage exchange-rate change. The forward premium on Swiss francs (i.e., the implicit exchange-rate change in percentage terms) is:

$$\frac{XRf - XRs}{XRs} = -0.314 \text{ percent/year}$$

agreed to allow floating currency values in early 1973, most of those 10 to 15 countries have largely allowed the market to determine exchange rates. However, the other 150 countries of the world have fixed their currency values to the dollar, pound, or other currency; and/or they have used exchange controls to limit access to foreign exchange; and/or they have not allowed a foreign exchange market to operate. In virtually all of these countries, no forward, futures, or options markets exist. (Mexico, in which a futures market and some forward contracts in pesos are available, is an exception.) The rationales of governments for intervening in the market are discussed below in the context of the balance of payments (see Chapter 8). Here we need to recognize that government intervention is always a potential concern and often an actual one.

As buyers and sellers of foreign exchange, governments act to influence the exchange rate and to reduce or augment holdings of various currencies in the where:

$$XR = \text{Exchange rate} \equiv \$US/\text{foreign currency.}$$
$$f = \text{Forward.}$$
$$s = \text{Spot.}$$

This means that the dollar value of the francs decreases by 0.314 percent/180 days between the purchase and sale of SF. Thus, the full return on this arbitrage is approximately: (9.06 percent -0.628 percent) per year = 8.43 percent per year, or 4.22 percent for six months. This is clearly *less* than the return on a dollar instrument, so interest arbitrage should *not* be undertaken here.[5]

The basic relation between interest arbitrage and domestic investment may be shown as:

$$(1 + i\,\text{domestic}) \overset{e}{=} (1 + i\,\text{foreign})\frac{XRf}{XRs}$$

where i = interest rate. This is called the **interest parity** equation. In equilibrium, both sides are equal. Most of the time, either domestic investment or interest arbitrage will be profitable, and such arbitrage tends to push interest and exchange rates to the point where the equation holds.

Because the interest parity relationship is generally close to equality, the percentage gains available to interest arbitrageurs are low. Large banks, which can commit large amounts of funds to foreign currency investments with low transactions costs (usually in the eurocurrency market), are the main participants in interest arbitrage. (Notice that earnings from interest arbitrage include both interest earnings, which are positive, and exchange rate earnings, which may be positive or negative.) ∎

* The two foreign exchange contracts in intertemporal arbitrage, spot and forward, are a form of *swap* agreement. (That is, dollars are swapped for francs today and francs are swapped back for dollars in the future.) When the swapped foreign currency is invested in a money market instrument, the full set of three transactions constitutes *interest arbitrage.*

central bank. If a country has been running a balance-of-trade deficit, it may be able to reduce the deficit by having the central bank buy foreign currency in the open market. Sufficient purchases will cause the local currency to devalue, making exports cheaper and imports more expensive to buyers. If export and import price elasticities are high enough, this may lead to an improvement in the balance of trade.[6]

DETERMINATION OF THE EXCHANGE RATE

Exchange rates are determined by the activities of the five types of actors described above. If one could calculate the supply and demand curves for each exchange market participant, and anticipate government constraints on the exchange market, then exchange-rate determination would be fairly simple. The composite supply and demand for foreign exchange would be as depicted in Figure 6–1.

Lacking this information, the analyst can still rely on two fundamental economic relationships that underlie exchange-rate determination. Note that this section considers only economic factors; government restrictions on the exchange market are ignored.

The two fundamental economic relationships are *purchasing power parity* and the *international Fisher effect*. The former posits that shifts in exchange rates will occur to offset different rates of inflation in pairs of countries, and the latter posits that exchange rates will shift to offset interest rate differentials between countries.

Purchasing Power Parity (PPP)[7]

If a standard ton of polyurethane plastic costs $200 in the United States and DM 400 in Germany, then **purchasing power parity (PPP)** requires an exchange rate of 2 DM/$. The same reasoning could be used for all products whose production processes are equivalent in two countries and which are traded between these countries. The exchange rate that comes closest to simultaneously satisfying all of these equilibrium conditions is the PPP rate—a rate that equates the internal purchasing power of the two currencies in both countries.

Assuming that we begin from that exchange rate, what will happen if Germany's inflation is 5 percent and U.S. inflation is 10 percent in the following year? Purchasing power parity requires that the exchange rate adjust to eliminate this differential. Specifically, it requires that:

$$\frac{1 + \text{Infl}_{US}}{1 + \text{Infl}_{Ger}} = \frac{XR_{t+1}}{XR_t}$$

where:

Infl = Inflation rate.
t = Time period.

This means that inflation in the United States relative to inflation in Germany should be the same as the future exchange rate compared to the spot exchange rate. The relationship can also be written in a form similar to the interest parity equation, by rearranging terms:

$$(1 + \text{Infl}_{US}) = (1 + \text{Infl}_{Ger})\frac{XR_{t+1}}{XR_t}$$

Purchasing power in each currency will be retained if:

$$XR_{t+1} = \frac{1.10}{1.05}(\$0.50/DM) = \$0.524/DM, \text{ or DM } 1.909/\$$$

International Fisher Effect

The **international Fisher effect** translates Irving Fisher's reasoning about domestic interest rates to the transnational level. Fisher showed that inflation-adjusted (i.e., "real") interest rates tend to stay the same over time; as inflation rises or falls, so do *nominal* (unadjusted) interest rates, such that real interest rates remain unchanged. At the transnational level, nominal national interest rates are expected to differ only by the expected change in the national currency's price (i.e., the exchange rate). The international Fisher effect thus concludes that interest differentials between national markets will be eliminated by adjustments in the exchange rate. In terms similar to PPP, we see that:

$$\frac{1 + i_{US}}{1 + i_{foreign}} = \frac{XR_{t+1}}{XR_t}, \text{ or } (1 + i_{US}) = (1 + i_{foreign})\frac{XR_{t+1}}{XR_t}$$

where i = the interest rate, usually on a eurocurrency deposit denominated in the given country's currency.

If the eurodollar deposit rate is 10 percent/year and the euro-French franc rate is 15 percent/year, the franc will be expected to devalue in the coming year by:

$$\frac{1.10}{1.15} = 0.9565, \text{ or } 4.35 \text{ percent}$$

Notice that the international Fisher effect *will* operate in a free market, because investors will receive a higher return in French francs otherwise. As more and more U.S. investors put their money in eurofrancs, the spot price of FF will rise. Similarly, as U.S. investors return their franc earnings to dollars at the end of the period (year), this increased demand for dollars will cause the franc to devalue (in the future). Thus, dollar and franc earnings will tend to be equalized.

Combined Equilibrium Relationships

The future exchange rate, XR_{t+1}, will be partially determined by both of the above factors (PPP and international Fisher), which can be viewed in a general equilibrium context, as shown in Figure 6–3. This figure also demonstrates the interest parity relationship, which provides another link between current and future currency values. Remember that these relationships are *equilibrium* economic conditions, which hold only approximately since substantial uncertainty exists about future conditions. Also, if a government intervenes to disallow the market from determining exchange rates, the relationships may diverge substantially from the equilibrium conditions. Figure 6–3 shows the main economic influences that—along with government policies and other factors—combine to determine exchange rates.

A final caveat is in order. Despite the strong relationships among interest differentials, inflation differentials, and exchange rates, there are other important *economic* influences operating in international finance. Pure speculation can cause shifts in exchange rates, despite the fundamental economic conditions that have been described above. A country's balance-of-payments position (see Chapter 8) may affect the exchange rate, even though that position also affects interest and inflation rates as well. Since the abandonment of the Bretton Woods system of fixed exchange rates, exchange-rate determination has been extremely uncertain—perhaps similar to the determination of future values of stock exchange indexes.

METHODS OF PROTECTING AGAINST EXCHANGE RISK

Exchange risk is a very real concern for financial managers, whether or not their firms are directly involved in international business. The fact that the prices of imported products and services often vary with the exchange rate means that a local firm's costs may depend on the exchange rate. Similarly, if any of the firm's sales are exported, its earnings may vary as foreign sales change due to exchange-rate changes. Even a purely domestic firm is faced with these problems,

FIGURE 6–3

Exchange-Rate
Determination

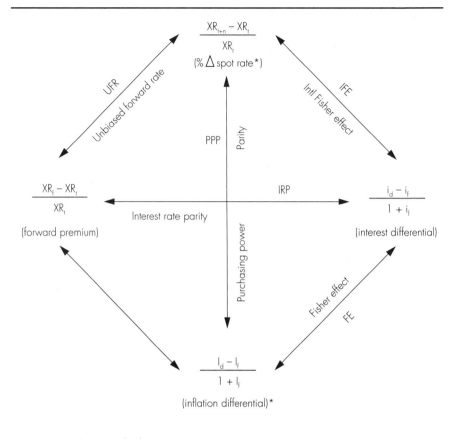

$$\frac{XR_{t+n} - XR_t}{XR_t}$$

(% Δ spot rate*)

UFR
Unbiased forward rate

Intl Fisher effect

IFE

PPP | Parity

$$\frac{XR_f - XR_t}{XR_t}$$

IRP

$$\frac{i_d - i_f}{1 + i_f}$$

Interest rate parity

(forward premium)

(interest differential)

Purchasing power

Fisher effect

FE

$$\frac{I_d - I_f}{1 + I_f}$$

(inflation differential)*

* = Forecasted value
This model ignores government exchange controls and transaction costs.
XR = Domestic currency/foreign currency

since suppliers and competitors that *are* doing international business will adjust to exchange-rate changes—and this will affect the domestic firm.

From this perspective, exchange risk is *not* the risk that a local currency will decrease in value (devalue) relative to the dollar. *Exchange risk **is** the possibility that a firm will be unable to adjust its prices and costs to exactly offset exchange-rate changes.* Thus, if a U.S. importer faces 10 percent higher costs because of a dollar devaluation from DM 1.7/US$ to DM 1.53/US$, he still has no exchange risk as long as he can raise his own prices by 10 percent without lowering total sales. (This result is the microeconomic version of purchasing power parity.) The problem may be viewed as one of "passing through" cost increases to the firm's customers via higher sales prices.

Similarly, the appropriate measure of exchange risk for financial instruments is the firm's possible loss or gain in purchasing power from exchange-rate-adjusted interest rates. Investing in a U.S. dollar account that pays 10 percent per year is better than investing in a French franc account that pays 20 percent per year if during the year the franc devalues by 12 percent.

Alternatives to Minimize Exchange Risk

Exchange risk exists whenever the firm's prices and costs cannot be exactly adjusted to offset changes in the exchange rate. Let us now consider a group of alternatives that will allow a firm to minimize (or at least reduce) its exchange risk. These alternatives fall into four categories:

1. Risk avoidance.
2. Risk adaptation.
3. Risk transfer.
4. Diversification.

The Strategy of Risk Avoidance **Exchange risk avoidance** is the strategy of trying to escape foreign currency transactions. A purely domestic firm can try to make all of its purchases from local suppliers of locally produced goods and to make all of its sales to local buyers in competition only with other domestic firms. Obviously, this strategy is impractical, if only because all firms are affected by goods priced in foreign currency—automobiles, chemicals, steel, and so on. Also, there are very few industries that do not use imported materials, or export some of their output, or compete with imported products.

The Strategy of Risk Adaptation **Exchange risk adaptation** offers a more realistic alternative for protecting the firm against exchange risk. This strategy includes all methods of "hedging" against exchange-rate changes. In the extreme, exchange risk calls for protecting all liabilities denominated in foreign currency with equal-value, equal-maturity assets denominated in that foreign currency. An illustration can best clarify this point.

Assume that a French firm has contracted to buy $100,000 of machinery from a foreign supplier for use in its manufacturing operations. The purchase is payable in six months in U.S. dollars. To eliminate foreign exchange risk completely, the firm may do two things. First, it may raise its own prices to customers once the six months pass, in order to equate franc devaluation to price increase. (Note that this does *not* involve a foreign currency hedge.) If this option is not available, which is often the case, the firm may look to its other option: obtain some equal-value *dollar asset* maturing in 180 days. This may be as simple as depositing funds in a dollar-denominated bank account for six months or as arcane as arranging a swap of the dollar liability for some other firm's franc liability. Fairly standard methods of hedging an exposed dollar liability include:

1. Obtaining a dollar-denominated financial asset (e.g., a time deposit or a CD) that matures when the liability comes due.
2. Finding a buyer for your firm's products and agreeing to receive payment in U.S. dollars for the same value and time as the liability.
3. Finding a bank that will contract to buy francs from you and sell you dollars at a price fixed today for exchange when the liability comes due. (This is called a "forward contract.")
4. Agreeing with another (e.g., North American) firm to exchange your dollar liability for that firm's (i.e., its French subsidiary's) franc liability.
5. Contracting for any other equal-value, equal-maturity dollar-denominated asset that will offset the exposed liability.

The firm's goal in choosing among these methods is to minimize the cost of protection against exchange-rate risk.

The Strategy of Risk Transfer   The third strategy for reducing exchange risk is **exchange risk transfer.** This strategy involves the use of an insurance contract or guarantee, which transfers the exchange risk to the insuror or guarantor. In many countries, the central bank offers exchange risk guarantees to importers and exporters of some products, according to the bank's policies. Technically, though perhaps not realistically, any firm or government agency could issue a guarantee covering exchange rate changes to a local importer—at a price that would presumably reflect the risk.

The Strategy of Diversification   The final strategy for reducing exchange risk is **currency diversification.** That is, a firm can reduce the risk of unexpected local currency devaluations by spreading its assets and liabilities across several currencies (e.g., deutsche marks, Swiss francs, and pounds, in addition to U.S. dollars). This strategy simply means, "Don't put all of your eggs in one basket." Domestically, a firm should deal with several suppliers and a variety of customers in order to reduce risk through diversification. Internationally, a firm should hold assets (and liabilities) in several currencies in order to reduce the impact of unexpected exchange-rate changes.

The strategy that is probably most useful to the majority of firms is risk adaptation, or hedging. A key point of this section is to recognize that other alternatives may be used in many instances when hedging would be more expensive or otherwise less desirable. Nonetheless, the central problem in exchange risk management is hedging, and corporate treasurers should always be on the lookout for new instruments and techniques.

CONCLUSIONS

The foreign exchange market is a central part of international business. That market is really several distinct markets, including spot transactions as well as forward contracts, futures, options, and other instruments that may vary from country to country.

The participants in the foreign exchange market include commercial banks—the most important participants in terms of the value of transactions undertaken—and many other actors in the private and public sectors, such as corporations, individuals, and governments. The main forces determining exchange rates tend to be the large banks that trade billions of dollars worth of currencies daily.

Exchange rates are determined by government choice in each country. When, as in most industrialized countries today, the government allows the free market to operate, such economic factors as inflation differentials and interest-rate differentials tend to determine exchange rates. Even so, forecasting exchange rates is a highly uncertain activity, because of the wealth of factors that influence these rates.

Finally, protection against exchange-rate variations is possible through many kinds of hedging strategies. Generally, companies, banks, and individuals want to find foreign currency liabilities to balance against their existing foreign currency assets, and vice versa. The ultimate decision to hedge or not hedge (i.e., speculate) is a matter of policy for the firm; there is no "right" answer.

QUESTIONS

1. Who are the main participants in the foreign exchange market in the United States? How does each of these participants affect the exchange rate?
2. Based on Figure 6–1, would you expect interest rates in Japan to be higher or lower than those in the United States? Why?
3. Given that France's inflation is about 10 percent per year at present, while U.S. inflation is about 4 percent per year, what do you expect to happen to the franc/dollar exchange rate in the next few months? Why?
4. Explain the business of interest arbitrage. How can a bank profit from it?
5. What is the difference between the forward exchange rate and the future spot exchange rate?
6. How do foreign exchange brokers function in the U.S. foreign exchange market?
7. Explain the influence of the U.S. government in determining the exchange rate between the dollar and the Japanese yen. How does the Japanese government affect this rate?
8. Assume that currently, the interest rate on U.S. dollar deposits in London is 10.375 percent per year and the rate on German mark deposits there is 5.6875 percent per year. The spot exchange rate is U.S. $0.3254/DM. What do you expect the exchange rate to be in one year?
9. How would you hedge the value of your export sale of FF 10 million of computers to a French customer? You will be paid in 180 days in francs. On what basis would you choose among hedging methods?
10. Why do the exchange rates of the forward market and the futures market differ for similar maturities?

REFERENCES

Andrews, Michael. "Recent Trends in the U.S. Foreign Exchange Market," *Quarterly Review*, Federal Reserve Bank of New York, Summer 1984.

Dufey, Gunter. "Foreign Exchange Markets and Currency Risk," in Dennis Logue (ed.) *Handbook of Modern Finance*. 2nd ed. Boston: Warren Gorham and Lamont, 1990. Chapter 41.

Giddy, Ian. "Foreign Exchange Options." *Journal of Futures Markets* 3, no. 2 (1983).

Kubarych, Roger. *Foreign Exchange Markets in the United States*. Federal Reserve Bank of New York, 1981.

Lindert, Peter. *International Economics*. 8th ed. Homewood, Ill.: Richard D. Irwin, 1986.

Pauls, B. Diane. "U.S. Exchange Rate Policy: Bretton Woods to Present," *Federal Reserve Bulletin* (November 1990).

Shapiro, Alan. *Multinational Financial Management*. 3rd ed. Boston: Allyn & Bacon, 1989.

NOTES

1. "Summary of Results of U.S. Foreign Exchange Market Survey Conducted in April 1989," Federal Reserve Bank of New York (xerox), September 13, 1989. p. 12.

2. The clearing member banks of the New York Clearinghouse Association are: Bank of New York, Bankers Trust, Chase Manhattan Bank, Chemical Bank, Citibank, European American Bank, Irving Trust, Manufacturers Hanover Trust, Marine Midland Bank, Morgan Guaranty, National Westminster Bank, and U.S. Trust.

3. "Taking a position" means purchasing an asset (or liability) denominated in a foreign currency without simultaneously matching it with a liability (asset) of the same value and maturity in the same currency. If a U.S. bank buys Swiss francs, it has taken a position in Swiss francs. When the bank sells those Swiss francs to a client, it has eliminated the position.

4. Ian Giddy has shown how similar arbitrage can be used between a forward market and an *options* market, since the combination of a put and a call option on the same currency is analogous to a forward contract. See Giddy (1983).

5. Notice that analogous conditions face Swiss arbitrageurs, who *should* buy dollars, invest in a eurodollar deposit, and buy SF forward under these conditions. (Check the results mathematically.) Thus, interest arbitrage *will* occur in the example, though not by dollar-holding arbitrageurs.

6. The Marshall-Lerner condition requires that the export elasticity of demand plus the import elasticity of demand is less than one in order for a devaluation to improve the balance of trade. See, e.g., Lindert, 8th ed., pp. I–4, I–5.

7. This entire discussion refers to *relative* purchasing power parity (PPP). The stronger, absolute version refers to parity in the values of factor inputs used in the production of products whose prices reflect relative factor productivities. Relative PPP considers only *changes* in the relative price levels between countries, not the initial (absolute) levels.

6-1 Exchange-Rate Arrangements as of March 31, 1989[1]

Pegged					
Single Currency				Currency Composite	
U.S. Dollar		French Franc	Other	SDR	Other
Afghanistan[4]	Liberia	Benin	Bhutan (Indian	Burundi	Algeria
Antigua and	Nicaragua[4]	Burkina Faso	rupee)	Iran, Islamic Rep. of	Austria
Barbuda	Oman	Cameroon	Kiribati (Australian	Libya[6]	Bangladesh[4]
Bahamas, The[4]	Panama	Central African Rep.	dollar)	Myanmar	Botswana
Barbados	Peru[4]	Chad	Lesotho[4] (South	Rwanda	Cape Verde
Belize	St. Kitts and Nevis	Comoros	African rand)	Seychelles	Cyprus
Djibouti	St. Lucia	Congo	Swaziland (South	Zambia	Fiji
Dominica	St. Vincent	Côte d'Ivoire	African rand)		Finland[7]
El Salvador[4]	Sierra Leone	Equatorial Guinea	Tonga (Australian		Hungary
Ethiopia	Sudan[4]	Gabon	dollar)		Iceland[8]
Grenada	Suriname	Mali			Israel[9]
Guatemala	Syrian Arab Rep.[4]	Niger			Jordan
Guyana[4]	Trinidad and	Senegal			Kenya
Haiti	Tobago	Togo			Kuwait
Honduras[4]	Uganda[4]				Malawi
Iraq	Viet Nam[4]				Malaysia[8]
	Yemen Arab Rep.				Malta
	Yemen, People's				Mauritius
	Democratic Rep.				Nepal
					Norway
					Papua New
					Guinea
					Poland[4]
					Romania
					Sao Tome and
					Principe
					Solomon Islands
					Somalia
					Sweden[9]
					Tanzania
					Thailand
					Vanuatu
					Western Samoa
					Zimbabwe

[1]Current information relating to Democratic Kampuchea is unavailable.

[2]In all cases listed in this column, the U.S. dollar was the currency against which exchange rates showed limited flexibility.

[3]This category consists of countries participating in the exchange-rate mechanism of the European Monetary System. In each case, the exchange rate is maintained within a margin of 2.25 percent around the bilateral central rates against other participating currencies, with the exception of Italy, in which case the exchange rate is maintained within a margin of 6 percent.

[4]Member maintains multiple exchange arrangements involving more than one exchange rate. The arrangement shown is that maintained in the major market.

Flexibility Limited vis-à-vis a Single Currency or Group of Currencies			More Flexible	
Single Currency[2]	Cooperative Arrangements[3]	Adjusted According to a Set of Indicators	Other Managed Floating	Independently Floating
Bahrain[5]	Belgium[4]	Brazil	Argentina[4]	Australia
Qatar[5]	Denmark	Chile[4]	China, People's Rep. of[4]	Bolivia
Saudi Arabia[5]	France	Colombia	Costa Rica[4]	Canada
United Arab Emirates[5]	Germany, Fed. Rep. of Ireland	Madagascar	Dominican Republic	Gambia, The
	Italy	Portugal	Ecuador	Ghana[4]
	Luxembourg[4]		Egypt[4]	Japan
	Netherlands		Greece	Lebanon
	Spain		Guinea	Maldives
			Guinea-Bissau	New Zealand
			India[10]	Nigeria
			Indonesia	Paraguay
			Jamaica	Philippines
			Korea	South Africa[4]
			Lao People's Dem. Rep.	Spain
			Mauritania	United Kingdom
			Mexico[4]	United States
			Morocco	Uruguay
			Mozambique	Venezuela
			Pakistan	Zaïre
			Singapore	
			Sri Lanka	
			Tunisia	
			Turkey	
			Yugoslavia	

[5]Exchange rates are determined on the basis of a fixed relationship to the SDR, within margins of up to ±7.25 percent. However, because of the maintenance of a relatively stable relationship with the U.S. dollar, these margins are not always observed.

[6]The exchange rate is maintained within margins of ±7.5 percent.

[7]The exchange rate is maintained within margins of ±2.0 percent.

[8]The exchange rate is maintained within margins of ±2.25 percent.

[9]The exchange rate is maintained within margins of ±3.0 percent.

[10]The exchange rate is maintained within margins of ±5.0 percent on either side of a weighted composite of the currencies of the main trading partners.

Source: International Monetary Fund, "Developments in International Exchange and Trade Systems, September 1989." Washington D.C.: IMF, 1989.

Fred's Furniture, Ltd.

Fred Fox walked out of his Piccadilly Circus store one afternoon in August 1986, shaking his head and wondering whether there was any solution to the foreign currency game. He had just contracted for the third time with his good friend Jean Marnier in Paris for an export shipment of FF 2,000,000 of tables, chairs, and sofas that would be sent in November and paid for in February 1987. The past two times that Fox had dealt with Marnier on similar shipments, he later discovered that devaluations of the franc relative to the pound had left him with virtually no profit on the sales. This time he had been able to get Marnier to accept a 15 percent markup in the price quote (payable in francs) to offset the expected devaluation of the franc between now and next February. Unfortunately, he had been unable to persuade Marnier to pay in British pounds! The exchange-rate risk still existed, and despite the price markup Fox was very unhappy about living with it.

A second, related problem compounded Fox's frustration. He had just agreed to buy a large supply of polyvinyl chloride (PVC) plastic, from which one of his local furniture suppliers would construct the ultramodern tables that currently made up about one fourth of Fox's sales in England. He had already given a price quotation to his manufacturer, so there was no flexibility at that end. The supplier of this PVC was in Germany, and demanded to be paid in German marks (in 120 days). Once again, Fox had tried to anticipate the possible impact of currency changes on this DM 200,000 transaction, but he had been unable to figure out a solution.

Fred sometimes thought that he was blessed with good fortune because he lived within the European Community, since the member countries had eliminated almost all restrictions on exports of furniture among the 12 countries in the Community. His export sales were growing very satisfactorily, except for the foreign currency problem. That problem, however, was a curse to his business, since Fred made no claim to be a "finance man," and he was truly baffled by the fluctuations among pounds, marks, francs, lira, and other currencies.

A trip to the local Barclays Bank office cleared up some of the issues for him. First, he discovered that he could contract for a forward sale or purchase of any of the currencies that he dealt with. By accepting a small premium or discount relative to the current exchange rate, Fox could guarantee a fixed exchange rate

---

This case was written in 1986 by Professor Robert Grosse as a basis for class discussion.

TABLE 1

Interest-Rate and
Exchange-Rate Quotations
Offered to Fred Fox,
August 1, 1986

Spot exchange rates: FF 10.34 per £
DM 3.19 per £
180-day forward rate: FF 10.22 per £
120-day forward rate: DM 3.15 per £
120-day or 180-day British pound deposit interest rate: 9.8125% per year
180-day euro-French francs deposit interest rate: 7.375% per year
120-day euro-German mark deposit interest rate: 4.50% per year
Fred's Furniture would pay the deposit rate plus 2% per year for a loan.
Six-month put options on French francs at FF 10.20 per £ have a premium of £300 per contract; each contract is for FF 100,000.
Six-month call options on German marks at DM 3.20 per £ have a premium of £200 per contract; each contract is for DM 50,000.

Note: Each exchange rate can be used as a bid or offered rate as needed; ignore the difference.

for his future purchases of marks (for pounds) and his future sales of francs (to buy pounds). The rate quotations relevant to the two transactions described above are listed in Table 1.

The Barclays banker also suggested that Fox consider financing his French franc receivable with a loan in francs, rather than using British pound financing during the period from now until payment by Marnier's firm. This would enable Fox to balance out his furniture sale in francs with the loan repayment and also give him funds today that could be used in his ongoing business. Unfortunately for Fox, the young Barclays banker also suggested that he consider taking out an option on future marks in the London International Financial Futures Exchange. Since Fox could not follow the banker's explanation of the way this instrument works he determined to eliminate options as an alternative. All of the rate quotations given by Barclays to Fox are listed in Table 1.

Beyond the short-term problem of dealing with the two transactions described above, Fred wants to establish some kind of system for handling future foreign-currency business. He is highly risk averse when it comes to exchange-rate risk, and his primary objective is to avoid large losses due to currency fluctuations.

Chapter

7

International Financial Markets And Institutions

This chapter considers foreign and international financial markets that allow firms to find sources of funds outside their home countries and to place available funds in portfolio-type investments outside the home country. These markets include national money and capital markets in different countries, plus the euromarkets, both short- and long-term. Since the eurocurrency and eurobond markets are widely used even by purely domestic firms, a knowledge of the instruments and institutions involved will benefit financial decision makers in almost any kind of firm. The main goals of the chapter are to:

1. Review the basic characteristics of all the financial markets that may be available to a firm in international business.

2. Explain how the international monetary (IMF) system functions and how it relates to both private sector firms and governments.

3. Give insights into domestic money and capital markets that exist around the world.

4. Give insights into the functioning of the euromarkets.

5. Show how firms can take advantage of the opportunities available in all of these markets.

INTRODUCTION

Whether or not a company becomes directly involved in international business through exports, direct investment, and the like, there is still an important international market to consider, even for domestic business: the market for borrowing and lending abroad. Many times, companies find that borrowing funds abroad is less expensive than borrowing domestically, in the United States or in any other home country. The relatively unrestricted "euromarkets" generally offer better terms to borrowers (*and lenders*) than do domestic financial markets in any country. This chapter explores the various foreign and international financial markets (except the foreign exchange market, which was discussed in Chapter 6) and examines ways to utilize them for domestic and international business.

Table 7–1 presents an overview of international financial markets. It should be emphasized that the final market to consider in conducting financial transactions in these markets is the market for real goods and services, or consumption. That is, the ultimate use of financial instruments in each of these markets is to claim goods and services, today or in the future. Table 7–1 sketches some of the important characteristics of the six types of international financial markets.

International Financial Markets

The **international monetary system** is a market among the central banks of the countries that belong to the International Monetary Fund (IMF). This organization functions as a kind of central banking system for the national governments of its 151 members. Each member country deposits funds at the IMF, and in return each may borrow funds in the currency of any other member country. This system is *not* open to private sector participants, so it is not directly useful

TABLE 7–1

International Financial Markets

Market	Instruments	Participants	Regulator
International monetary system	Special drawing rights; foreign exchange; position at the IMF	Central banks; International Monetary Fund	International Monetary Fund
Foreign exchange markets	Bank deposits; currency; futures and forward contracts	Commercial and central banks; firms; individuals	Central bank in each country
National money markets (short term)	Bank deposits and loans; short-term government securities; commercial paper	Banks; firms; individuals; government agencies	Central bank; other national government agencies
National capital markets (long term)	Bonds; long-term bank deposits and loans; stocks; long-term government securities	Banks; firms; individuals; government agencies	Central bank; other national government agencies
Eurocurrency market	Bank deposits; bank loans; eurocommercial paper	Commercial banks; firms; government agencies	Substantially unregulated
Eurobond market	Bonds; some equity issues	Banks; firms; individuals; government agencies	Substantially unregulated

to company managers. However, agreements made between member countries and the IMF often lead to major changes in government policies toward companies and banks (such as exchange-rate changes and controls, and trade controls), so an understanding of the international monetary system may be quite important to managers. Regulation in this system comes through rules passed by the IMF's members. The major financial instruments used in the international monetary system are national currencies and a currency issued by the IMF itself, called the SDR (special drawing right). These points are defined more clearly, and the IMF system is discussed in detail, in the next section of this chapter.

A **foreign exchange market,** as seen in the previous chapter, is a market in which financial instruments denominated in one currency can be exchanged for financial instruments denominated in another currency. Typically, most foreign exchange is sold through the commercial banking system of a country, in the form of bank deposits. Cash exchanges by traveling business people and tourists are quite common—but nearly all of the vast quantities of money exchanged goes between banks, as account transfers, and in large amounts. Regulation of foreign exchange markets comes primarily from the national government of the country where the markets are located, through the central bank. The main instruments used in foreign exchange dealings include account transfers by telephone, wire, or otherwise; bank drafts; forward and futures contracts; and currencies.

National money markets and national capital markets are simply the national financial markets of countries other than the home country of the firm. So, for a U.S.-based company, the money and capital markets of France are international (really foreign) financial markets. Access to such markets is often limited to "domestic" firms, which usually include locally incorporated subsidiaries of multinational enterprises. Thus, foreign money and capital markets are additional potential sources and users of funds for the MNE.

Short-term national financial markets, or **national money markets**, generally offer the MNE some opportunities to obtain or place funds. Typically, local bank deposits and short-term investments in Treasury securities give the firm an interest-earning opportunity for its locally available funds. A variety of additional instruments can also be found in many of the developed countries and a number of LDCs. Commercial paper, promissory notes, and short-term government obligations are just a few of them. MNEs can often borrow from local banks or through the issue of some form of promissory notes—or sometimes directly from the government. For short-term funding and investing decisions, the MNE manager needs to be aware of the wide variety of money market instruments that are available in host countries.[1]

Similarly, long-term national financial markets, or **national capital markets,** offer additional opportunities to MNE financial managers. A number of countries have national securities markets in which the MNE can issue its own securities (stocks and bonds) or invest in the securities of other firms. In most countries, long-term bank loans provide a source of funds and national treasury issues provide investment possibilities. Regulation in both of these national financial markets comes from the national government, through such agencies as the central bank, the treasury, and the securities exchange.

The fifth and sixth markets for financial instruments are the **euromarkets**— the short-term eurocurrency market and the long-term eurobond market. Each of these financial markets is characterized by the issuance of instruments (i.e., deposits or bonds) denominated in some currency other than the one of the country where the instruments are issued. The euromarkets are generally unrestricted by governments and establish their own pricing and other conditions.

The **eurocurrency market** is a largely short-term market for bank deposits and loans denominated in any currency except the currency of the country where the market is located. In London, for example, the eurocurrency market is a market for bank deposits (and loans) denominated in dollars, marks, yen, and any other currency except British pounds. In Paris, the eurocurrency market is a market for similar instruments denominated in dollars, marks, yen, pounds, and any other currency except French francs. Most of the transactions in this market have maturities of less than one year, although some deposits and loans are long-term. The main instruments used in the eurocurrency market are certificates of deposit and time deposits, and bank loans. During the past few years, euro-commercial paper has become a significant short-term instrument as well.

The **eurobond market** is a long-term market for bonds denominated in any currency except the currency of the country where the market is located. It is basically the long-term counterpart of the eurocurrency market (though there are also other important differences). The only instruments used in the eurobond market are bonds, denominated in various currencies, typically with a floating interest rate. Since regulation is minimal in the countries that permit eurobond issue, participants in this market depend for protection on the reputations of the other participants rather than on national securities laws.

The euromarkets offer investors and borrowers in one country the opportunity to deal with borrowers and investors from many other countries, purchasing and selling deposits, bonds, and loans denominated in many currencies. Euromarkets may be entered through affiliates of "eurobanks"—banks that participate in the euromarkets—in virtually any country. For instance, a eurodollar loan may be taken by a U.S. company, dealing through the local office of a U.S. bank that legally books the transaction in London. Similarly, a U.S. investor may place a deposit in the eurodollar market simply by instructing a local U.S. bank to create the deposit in its foreign branch in London, Panama, or any one of more than a dozen euromarket centers worldwide. Finally, eurobonds and euro-commercial paper may be issued by investment banking firms on behalf of company or government clients in several national markets simultaneously to many types of investors. In all, the euromarkets offer substantial opportunities to virtually any large or medium-sized firm that deals in financial markets for either borrowing or lending.

The last market of interest here is the **market for goods and services,** which is the ultimate destination of the financial instruments used in the other markets. Either at present or in the future, the various financial instruments will be utilized to purchase real goods or services from suppliers in one country or another. The key *social* benefits of the various international financial markets are that they facilitate the process of matching borrowers and lenders in all parts of the world and that they facilitate payments through widely accepted media of exchange.[2] This chapter does not discuss the market for goods and services, since that is the ultimate target of all activities examined in the book.

Let us begin consideration of international financial markets with a view of the intergovernmental system that provides a framework for the others: the international monetary system.

THE IMF SYSTEM

The first international financial market that we will examine here may be viewed as either the most important of all or as one that is generally irrelevant to private business managers. The international monetary system is a financial market in which only central banks and the **International Monetary Fund** (**IMF,** or the Fund) operate; so private business has no active role in it. On the other hand, rules for international financial dealings among countries are often set at the IMF and substantial international loan decisions are made between governments and the IMF—so that the rules of the game in the other international financial markets are greatly influenced by IMF activities.

The international monetary system determines the exchange-rate regime that prevails among the major developed countries, whose currencies are used for the vast majority of international payments. The IMF negotiates with governments of debtor nations for loans directly from the Fund and for loan conditions that are used subsequently as a basis for lending by private banks to these same borrowers. In addition, the IMF serves as an intermediary for emergency loans between member governments to cope with the capital-flow or exchange-rate crises that occur from time to time due to speculation in foreign exchange markets or other causes. All in all, the international monetary system plays a substantial role in determining the rules of the game for private companies and banks in international business—so its functioning should be understood by managers.

Brief History

The International Monetary Fund was designed in 1944 at a conference of the Allied nations held at Bretton Woods, New Hampshire. Its general purpose was to provide a multilateral framework for avoiding international financial crises by establishing rules for national exchange-rate policies and for adjustment to balance of payments disequilibria (discussed in the following chapter), and it was specifically intended to avoid the disastrous financial contraction that had occurred during the 1930s. As originally negotiated, and as implemented in 1946 when the Articles of Agreement were signed by the initial 46 member countries, the IMF system required *fixed* exchange rates among member countries, with gold as the basis for currency valuation. The U.S. dollar was initially fixed at a value of $35 per ounce of gold, and all other currencies were fixed at values expressed in both dollars and gold.

Fixed exchange rates were a fundamental base of the Bretton Woods system. Under the Articles of Agreement, each country was obligated to maintain its currency value at the initially set value (the "par" value), with a band of ±1 percent of flexibility around the par value. If a foreign central bank demanded to sell a country's currency back to the issuer, that country was required to pay the equivalent amount of gold, U.S. dollars, or some other acceptable currency.

In order to join the IMF, a country was required to make a deposit of gold (25 percent) plus its own currency (75 percent), such that each member country's total deposit relative to the total of IMF deposits was roughly in proportion with its share of world trade. Then each member country received the right to borrow up to 200 percent of its initial deposit at the Fund in any currency to help pay for imbalances such as the one mentioned above. If a country borrowed more than its original deposit, the IMF would stipulate economic policies that the borrower had to follow in order to receive more financial support. (This imposition of policy demands by the IMF is called *conditionality*.)

While the IMF sought to provide assistance for nations facing balance of payments problems, its only resources were the contributions of its member countries: quotas based on each country's part in world trade, which initially constituted about $9 billion. This relatively small amount of liquidity was not sufficient to support the post-World War II economic recovery, or specifically, the payments imbalances, of even the European countries.[3] Ultimately, the U.S. Marshall Plan injected the needed funding into the international financial system, and specifically into Europe, during 1948–52.

In fact, the IMF provided very little funding to its member countries in its early years. During the Suez crisis in 1956, it loaned $1.7 billion to Great Britain, France, and India. Later, during speculative runs on the British pound (i.e., periods when speculators sold large quantities of pounds for other currencies, in expectation of a devaluation of the pound) in 1961 and 1964, it extended loans to Great Britain. By the end of the 1960s, the IMF was regularly providing credit to member countries, though still not at the levels that many analysts believed necessary to stabilize the system. (The alternative view is that the IMF should not provide credit to the member countries at all, but rather that these countries should be forced to adjust their economies to escape balance of payments problems. Balance of payments adjustment is discussed in Chapter 8.)

At the end of the 1960s, the U.S. dollar began to be the object of speculative pressure. The problem was severe, since the dollar constituted the base for the entire system of value (through its formal link to gold at $35 per ounce). The United States was unable to devalue to stop the speculation, and later it was unwilling to continue to sell its gold holdings to foreign central banks that wanted to redeem their dollars. In August 1971 President Nixon announced that the United States would no longer sell gold to foreign central banks in exchange for dollars; and in December 1971 he announced a devaluation of the dollar to $39 per ounce of gold.

These events essentially destroyed the Bretton Woods system of fixed exchange rates. Many initiatives to repair the system were presented during the following two years, but the United States would no longer accept the responsibility of providing the dollar as a fixed base for other currencies. In February 1973 the dollar was again devalued, this time to $42 per ounce of gold. In subsequent months, the IMF system was changed de facto to a floating exchange-rate system that allowed each country to leave the value of its currency free to change with market forces or to fix that value to some other currency. Since that time, the United States has allowed the dollar to float in value relative to all other currencies, with occasional efforts by the Fed (the Federal Reserve System) to influence the dollar's relationship to particular currencies, such as the German mark and the Japanese yen.

The Current IMF System

Under the current IMF system, no limitations are set on each member country's decision either to fix its currency value relative to some other currency or to allow it to fluctuate as supply and demand dictate. (Notice that it is impossible for one country to keep its currency fixed relative to all others, if the others are changing at the same time.) In 1976, an accord called the Jamaica Agreement altered the IMF charter to allow formally for floating exchange rates. Today, the exchange-rate regimes used by each nation are substantially unrestricted, and government strategies to influence exchange rates are altered as desired.[4]

At about the time that the link between the dollar and gold was broken, the IMF's members agreed to create a new currency that the Fund would issue when authorized to do so by a vote of the members. This currency, called the **special drawing right (SDR),** allows its holder to obtain (or draw) other currencies from the IMF (or from other members) when desired. SDRs have been created and issued on seven occasions to date. A total of SDR 21.4 billion existed in 1990; their total value was about $30 billion. In each instance, the SDRs were allocated to Fund members according to their quotas. This new "international money" has served to support a number of countries that encountered financial crises since 1971, allowing these countries to finance their imbalances, but it has not been a solution to imbalances in international financial flows. During the international debt crisis of the early 1980s, SDR use was wholly inadequate to deal with the more than $350 billion of dollar debt owed by Latin American countries to foreign lenders.

Unresolved Problems with the IMF System

The IMF system today differs dramatically from the model established at Bretton Woods in 1944. Flexible exchange rates have been substituted for fixed ones; gold has been greatly reduced as an international monetary asset, and its link to the dollar has been severed; a new reserve currency, the SDR, has been created to increase world liquidity; and perhaps most important, the U.S. dollar is no longer the single base for the IMF system of value. These major changes have come in response to problems and crises that have occurred during the past 45 years—yet the IMF system itself survives. While few people would argue that the IMF has led directly to greater international financial stability over its history, at least the system has been flexible enough to accommodate the various crises that have threatened it.

Several problems that remain in the system deserve note. First, there has always been an uncomfortable tension between the countries that want to utilize the IMF simply as a bank for reducing the negative impacts of balance of payments difficulties and the countries that want to utilize it to subsidize economic development. The "link" between the IMF and development finance was originally delegated to the World Bank (the IMF's sister institution). Traditionally, the IMF has loaned funds only for short-term uses, sometimes extending to two or three years. Many borrowing countries, especially the less developed ones, have repeatedly called for greater use of IMF resources to finance development projects. While there are often no clear differences between financing payments imbalances and financing development projects that may later reduce those imbalances, the IMF has not substantially widened its scope. In the 1980s, under the cloud of multiple international loan renegotiations by Latin American countries, the Fund began to extend longer-term loans and to reconsider its strategy. The ultimate result of this crisis still remains to be seen. It appears in the early 1990s that the Fund will retain its basic form, and the resources of the World Bank will be expanded to assist more in economic development.

A second problem that continues to plague the Fund is the issue of exchange-rate regimes. Even as the flexible rate system moves through its third decade, there are repeated calls for a return to fixed, or more tightly constrained, currency values. The great instability of international financial dealings during the period since the OPEC oil crisis of 1973–74 has led some analysts to argue for a return to fixed rates. The evidence during the entire 20th century tends to

ADDED
DIMENSION

Special Drawing Rights and the Private Sector

During the 1980s, SDRs became fairly widely used as a currency of denomination for private sector financial instruments such as bonds and long-term bank loans. Because the SDR has a value based on five currencies (see Figure 7–1), it is more stable as a borrowing or lending tool than any individual currency.

When the dollar devalues relative to other widely traded currencies, so also does the SDR—but only 36 percent of the SDR's value is affected negatively. The other 64 percent of the SDR's value is based on marks, pounds, yen, and French francs—and these currencies may rise or fall relative to the dollar in such a situation. Overall, the changes must net out over all currencies, and an instrument such as the SDR changes relatively little in value compared to any single currency. The SDR is really a "basket" of currencies whose value is generally more stable than that of any one of its components.

Since the SDR is nothing more than an accounting convention, it cannot be used in final settlement of private sector accounts. That is, no such thing as an SDR bill or coin exists. However, since the SDR does have a value measurable in terms of any other currency, it can always be settled in dollars, marks, or any other currency (e.g., in so many "SDRs worth of dollars.") Financial instruments can be purchased in SDRs worth of different currencies and later paid out in SDRs worth of the same or other currencies at maturity.

Just as the ECU (European Currency Unit) has gained wide acceptance as an instrument for denominating international financial transactions, so too the SDR promises to gain wide acceptance as a risk-reducing instrument. (The SDR has the advantage of including the U.S. dollar in the group of currencies that determine its value, whereas the ECU is based only on European currencies.) At present, however, private sector investors and borrowers are using a much greater volume and value of ECU-denominated instruments than SDR-denominated instruments. ∎

suggest that no matter what exchange-rate regime prevails, if international trade relations are unstable and payments imbalances are substantial, no exchange-rate regime will be able to solve the problem. Thus, this problem most likely cannot be eliminated.

On the whole, the international monetary system plays an extremely important role in all international financial dealings, by being the focal point for establishing rules on exchange rates, exchange controls, intergovernmental loans, and other official transactions.

Since foreign exchange markets already have been examined in detail, the discussion now turns to domestic money and capital markets in foreign countries.

FIGURE 7–1

The Special Drawing Right
(on August 14, 1989)

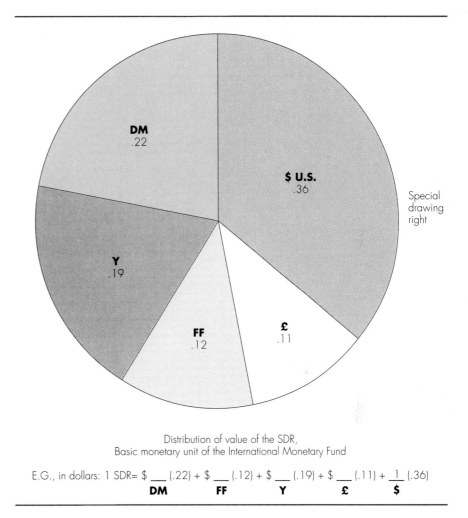

Distribution of value of the SDR,
Basic monetary unit of the International Monetary Fund

E.G., in dollars: 1 SDR= $ ___ (.22) + $ ___ (.12) + $ ___ (.19) + $ ___ (.11) + $ \underline{1} (.36)
 DM   FF   Y   £ $

FOREIGN MONEY AND CAPITAL MARKETS

In each country that the MNE enters, it will be able to obtain some degree of access to local financial markets. The MNE will generally utilize such markets to perform necessary local financial transactions and often to hedge its local asset exposure through local borrowing (or its local liability exposure through local deposits or investments). But the MNE can also utilize local financial markets to obtain additional funding (or place additional funds) for its nonload activities. A Mexican firm, for example, may choose to borrow funds through its Houston affiliate to finance its local needs in Texas *and* to finance some of its needs in Mexico.

Usually national financial markets are not fully accessible to foreign firms; they are reserved for domestic borrowers and lenders to a large degree. In these cases, use of local financial markets must be supplemented by use of the financial markets in the country of the parent company or elsewhere. Typically, such problems arise in countries that impose exchange controls, which limit the MNE's capability to put needed funds in the affiliate. Selected information about national short- and long-term financial markets in a number of countries is

TABLE 7–2

Characteristics of Selected National Money and Capital Market

Issue Country	Limits on Access to Market	Foreign Exchange Market	Borrowing Instruments Available	Size of Stock Market	Size of Bond Market
Argentina	Same treatment as local firms.	Managed floating of austral; official and parallel markets; spot and forward markets.	Short-term bank loans; limited overdrafts; discounted A/R*; limited medium-term bank loans.	Buenos Aires bolsa lists 220 companies, 15 stocks actively traded.	Thin market exists; high cost.
Brazil	FDI limited in certain sectors: informatics, mining, petroleum, and banking.	Managed floating of novo cruzado; active parallel market; no forward market.	Limited overdrafts; short-term bank loans; discounted A/R.	São Paulo bolsa lists over 1,000 firms, fewer than 100 are traded regularly.	Very thin market exists.
Canada	Same treatment as local firms.	Spot, forward, futures, options in Montreal and Toronto.	Short-term bank loans; overdrafts commercial paper;† B/A; long-term bank loans.	Toronto exchange lists 1,154 firms.	In 1988, C$ 16.8 billion issued.
France	Same treatment as local firms.	Spot, forward, and futures markets in Paris.	Overdrafts; discounted A/R; commercial paper; factoring.		In 1987, Ff 294.7 billion.
Germany	Same treatment as local firms.	Spot and forward markets in Frankfurt.	Short-term bank loans; discounted A/R; overdrafts; factoring.		Very deep market for domestic DM and euroDM.
Hong Kong	Same treatment as local firms.	Hong Kong dollar fixed to U.S. dollar; spot, forward and options markets.	Overdrafts; short-term bank loans; discounted A/R; commercial paper.	291 stocks listed; few foreign ones.	None.

presented in Table 7–2. Notice that the developed countries in the table have far fewer restrictions on their money and capital markets and that the United States has the fewest of all. Exchange controls are the rule in LDCs and are fairly common in developed countries as well. During the late 1980s and early 1990s, there has been a clear trend to reduce financial controls in developed, less developed, and formerly communist countries.

MNEs and National Money Markets

The advantages that MNEs obtain from entering national money markets as *borrowers* of funds stem from the portfolio effect of holding liabilities in more than one (fluctuating) currency and from the local risk hedging that occurs as the MNE moves to balance local assets such as plant and equipment with local liabilities, such as local-currency borrowing. Additional benefits may occur if the

TABLE 7–2

Concluded

Issue Country	Limits on Access to Market	Foreign Exchange Market	Borrowing Instruments Available	Size of Stock Market	Size of Bond Market
India	Most FDI limited to maximum of 40% ownership	Rupee pegged to basket of currencies; licensed banks are only dealers; spot and limited forward markets.	Overdrafts; short-term bank loans; discounted A/R.	Over 4,700 companies listed on Indian stock exchanges	Thin market exists.
Japan	Not restricted by law but by discrimination.	Limited to registered banks and brokers; spot and forward markets.	Overdrafts; short-term bank loans; discounted A/R; commercial paper; factoring.	Tokyo exchange is the world's largest stock market.	Very large.
Korea	Not restricted by law but by discrimination.	Managed floating of won; limited spot market.	Overdrafts, short-term bank loans; discounted A/R; commercial paper; factoring.	The Korean Stock Exchange listed 502 companies in 1988.	Strong market developing.
Mexico	FDI not limited, except for financial, petroleum, media, and transportation sectors.	Controlled and free markets; spot and forward markets.	Short-term bank loans; overdrafts, discounted A/R; commercial paper, factoring.	255 firms listed on the Mexican bolsa; 45 are actively traded.	Thin market exists.
U.K.	Same treatment as local firms.	Spot, forward, futures, options in London.	Short-term basic loans; overdrafts discounted A/R; commercial paper, factoring	London Exchange lists 2,660 firms.	Europound common. Very large.
U.S.A.	Same treatment as local firms.	Spot, forward, futures, options in New York and Chicago.	Almost unlimited.	New York Stock Exchange lists 1,822 firms.	Very large and diverse.

*Accounts Receivable.
†Bankers acceptances.
Sources: Business International Corporation, *Financing Foreign Operations* (1990 edition); and various national sources.

local government subsidizes such loans through interest-rate reduction, tax breaks, or otherwise; a policy of this kind may be offered to attract the MNE's investment. This may lower the whole MNE's cost of capital if the subsidy does not disappear and if the interest rate remains below the comparable home currency rate during the borrowing period.

The advantages that MNEs obtain from entering national money markets as *lenders* of funds stem from the portfolio effect of holding financial instruments in more than one currency. There may also be a gain from balancing local-currency assets and liabilities if an excess of local liabilities was held previously.

In addition, local financial investments may be a necessary strategy when exchange controls or profit remittance limits exist—such investments offer the firm an outlet for retained earnings that yields interest. Sometimes an exchange control policy may make the local-currency interest rates higher than those available in other currencies (after adjusting for expected exchange-rate changes). In these cases, higher than normal profits can be earned by investing funds in local instruments, although exchange controls may limit conversion of the profits into the home country currency, or a government-imposed exchange-rate change may wipe out the advantage.

MNEs and National Capital Markets

The advantages that MNEs obtain from entering national capital markets as *borrowers* are similar to those obtained from entering national money markets. However, the opportunities are generally much more limited. Very few countries have substantially developed stock markets, and those that do usually restrict the issuance of shares by foreigners. A few exceptions exist, such as the United States, the United Kingdom, Germany, and France, but even they serve only the largest and most creditworthy MNEs.[5] National bond markets, when they exist, are also very restrictive. Thus far, virtually all of the foreign bond issues have taken place in New York (called "Yankee bonds"), London, Switzerland, Germany, and Japan (called "Samurai bonds"). Table 7–3 gives some idea of the size of the foreign bond market and the eurobond market. Note that the foreign bond market is simply the national bond market of any country as it relates to foreign institutions that seek to issue bonds in that market.

Notice that all of the foreign bond issues combined do not account for nearly as much funding as the eurobond market. Also notice that the eurobond market is dominated by U.S. dollar issues, while the foreign bond market is far less concentrated in any one currency. (Swiss franc foreign bonds dominated such

TABLE 7–3

Foreign Bond and Eurobond Market Characteristics *(in millions of U.S. dollars)*

	1981	1984	1985	1987	1990
Eurobonds					
Total euro	31,616	79,458	136,731	140,535	199,584
U.S. dollar	26,830	63,593	97,782	58,070	70,070
German mark	1,277	4,604	9,491	15,023	21,150
British pound	501	3,997	5,766	15,051	18,030
Japanese yen	368	1,212	6,539	22,563	33,065
European currency units	309	3,032	7,038	7,397	17,526
Other	1,697	3,020	10,114	22,431	12,561
Foreign Bonds					
Total foreign	21,369	27,953	31,025	40,253	30,385
U.S. dollar	7,552	5,487	4,655	7,416	5,940
German mark	1,310	2,243	1,741	n.a.	n.a.
British pound	746	1,292	958	n.a.	n.a.
Swiss franc	8,285	12,626	14,954	24,301	13,741
Japanese yen	2,457	4,628	6,379	4,071	n.a.
Other	538	1,677	2,339	4,465	n.a.
Grand total	52,985	107,411	167,756	180,788	228,904

n.a. = not available.

Source: Morgan Guaranty Trust Company, *World Financial Markets* (various issues); and Salomon Brothers, *Bond Market Research* (July 26, 1991).

issues in the 1980s.) The amount of foreign bonds denominated in currencies other than dollars is more than 80 percent of the total. In contrast, the eurobond market, mostly functioning outside the United States, is dominated by dollar issues, which constitute about half of that total. In all, dollar-denominated issues account for about 40 percent of the two types of international bonds.

Finally, the advantages that MNEs obtain from entering national capital markets as *lenders* come mainly from diversification and from higher returns that may be protected by exchange controls, just as in the short-term market. Since the national capital markets are generally small, opportunities to use them are quite limited for foreigners as well as domestic investors. Of course, since the main currencies of interest to MNEs and other international investors *are* those of the few large industrial countries, opportunities in those national capital markets do exist.

REGIONAL MONEY AND CAPITAL MARKETS

Until recently, the scope of financial markets and instruments was predominantly domestic or fully international, but not regional. In the past two decades, however, the European Community (i.e., the European Common Market, which is discussed in Chapter 10) has designed both a regional monetary system (the **European Monetary System, EMS**) and a regional currency unit (the **European Currency Unit, ECU**) for intergovernmental financial transactions in the Community. While it seems unlikely that either of these institutions will achieve a position of serious rivalry with the private markets and instruments in the United States or the eurocurrency market, they have begun to establish a major presence in Europe. In 1984 a handful of banks began to offer deposits denominated in ECU, and a few years earlier some international lenders offered loans denominated in ECU.[6] Within two years, ECU-denominated eurobond issues became a multibillion-dollar market segment. (See the "tombstone" advertisement of an ECU-denominated bond issue shown in Figure 7–2.) Undoubtedly, this regional financial market will become even more influential in the years ahead as a result of the emphasis on European integration from the "Europe 1992" initiative. Indeed, the ECU may become the official currency in Europe, if monetary integration is achieved.

Historically, financial markets developed among the countries comprised by the colonial empires of England and France. The **sterling area** refers to Great Britain and a group of former British colonies that still deal among themselves in British pounds. Similarly, the **franc area** refers to France and its former colonies, which also continue to denominate a significant amount of business among themselves in French francs. While substantial financial transactions are conducted within the sterling and franc areas, the eurocurrency market now dominates the total volume of financial flows among the countries in these areas.

THE EUROCURRENCY MARKET

Definition

A **eurodollar** *is a dollar-denominated bank deposit located outside the United States.* This simple statement defines the basic instrument called the eurodollar. (Eurodollars are *not* dollars in the pockets of people who live in Europe! They are deposit liabilities of banks.) The widely discussed eurocurrency market is just a set of bank deposits located outside the countries whose currency is used in the deposits. Since almost 70 percent of the deposits are denominated in U.S. dollars, it is reasonably accurate to call this the **eurodollar market.** Notice that the eurodollar market is not limited to Europe; very large eurodollar markets

FIGURE 7–2

Tombstone of a Eurobond
Issue Denominated in ECU

EUROPEAN INVESTMENT BANK

ECU 125,000,000

7³/₄ per cent. Bonds due 1993

Issue Price: 101 per cent.

Bank of Tokyo International Limited

Credit Commercial de France   **EBC Amro Bank Limited**

Merrill Lynch Capital Markets   **Morgan Guaranty Ltd**

Morgan Stanley International   **Orion Royal Bank Limited**

Privatbanken A/S   **Société Générale**

S.G. Warburg Securities

NEW ISSUE   *All these Bonds having been sold, this announcement appears as a matter of record only.*   NOVEMBER 1986

Source: *Europe,* The European Communities, December 1986, p. 22.

exist in Tokyo, Hong Kong, Bahrain, Panama, and other cities throughout the world. For this reason, the eurodollar market is sometimes called the international money market.[7]

This financial market grew from its inception sometime in the late 1950s to a size of about $U.S. 4,509 billion at the end of 1987, as shown in Table 7–4.

TABLE 7–4

Eurocurrency Market Size and Growth (measured by foreign currency liabilities at end of period)*

	1971	1973	1975	1980	1985	1987
Gross market size	150	310	480	1,524	2,846	4,509
Nonbanks	30	55	80	327	585	814
Official monetary institutions	15	40	70	150	112	151
Other banks	105	215	330	1,047	2,149	3,544
Eurodollars as a percentage of total	76	73	78	75	75	66

*In billions of U.S. dollars.
Source: Morgan Guaranty Trust Company, *World Financial Markets* (various issues).

Significance

What is the significance of the international money market? Since the eurocurrency market rivals domestic financial markets as a funding source for corporate borrowing, it plays a key role in the capital investment decisions of many firms. And since this market also rivals domestic financial markets as a deposit alternative, it absorbs important amounts of savings from lenders (i.e., depositors) in many countries. In fact, the eurocurrency market complements the domestic financial markets, giving greater access to borrowing and lending to financial market participants in each of the countries where it is permitted to function. Overall, the eurocurrency market is now the world's single most important market for international financial intermediation.

This market is completely a creation of the regulatory structures placed by national governments on banking, or more precisely, on financial intermediation. If national governments allowed banks to function without reserve requirements, interest-rate restrictions, capital controls, and taxes, then the eurocurrency market would just involve the transnational deposits and loans made in each country's banking system. Instead, national governments heavily regulate national financial markets, in efforts to achieve various monetary policy goals. Thus, the eurocurrency market provides a very important outlet for funds flows that avoid many of the limitations placed on domestic financial markets. Many national governments have found the impact of the eurocurrency market on their firms and banks to be favorable, so they have allowed this market to operate.[8]

Bases

Since the eurocurrency market is a creation of the regulatory structure, it may be helpful to think about the key underpinnings of the system that allow eurodollars. There are essentially three conditions that must be met for a eurocurrency market to exist. First, some national government must allow foreign currency deposits to be made, so that, for example, depositors in London can obtain dollar-denominated time deposits there. Second, the country whose currency is being used—in this example, the United States—must allow foreign entities to own and exchange deposits in that currency. Third, there must be some reason, such as low cost or ease of use, that prompts people to use this market rather than other financial markets, such as the domestic ones. The eurocurrency market has met these conditions for the past three decades, and its phenomenal growth testifies that the demand for such a market has been very large.

A wide range of countries allow foreign-currency deposits to be held in their banking systems. Many of them impose restrictions (interest-rate limits, capital controls, and so on) on these as well as on local-currency deposits, so that a free market does not exist. Other countries, including most of the developed countries and many of the newly industrializing countries, allow foreign-currency deposits that are not subject to the regulations placed on domestic deposits. In such countries, participants find more favorable interest rates, greater availability of funds, and greater ease of moving funds internationally. These countries tend to be the euromarket centers.

Only a few currencies have become popular as eurocurrencies. Generally, these are the ones that are used widely in international trade—the U.S. dollar, the British pound, the French franc, the German mark, and a handful of others. The governments of all the nations whose currency is being used have consented (or, more accurately, have not objected) to allow foreign banks, companies, and individuals to hold and use deposits denominated in that currency. This may appear to be a trivial point, but any limitation on nonresidents' use of dollar (or other eurocurrency) deposits would quickly eliminate that currency from the euromarket. The U.S. government's temporary freeze on Iranian assets held in U.S. banks in 1979 caused a tremendous crisis in the eurodollar market, because other participants saw the possibility of losing use of their eurodollars at the whim of the U.S. government. The potential problem will continue to exist, but on the whole participants in the euromarket expect that full freedom to use the (dollar-denominated) deposits will continue indefinitely.

The third condition that is fundamental to the success of the euromarket is that it must possess advantages that will attract participants to the market. Those advantages include the ability to carry out dollar-denominated transactions outside the United States and the availability of favorable interest rates relative to rates in the domestic market. The first advantage clearly exists, because eurodollar account owners can sell their accounts to pay for other transactions, without any need to deal directly in the United States. The second advantage also exists, primarily because lack of regulation of the euromarket allows banks to reduce their costs and pass on the savings to clients in the form of lower loan rates and higher deposit rates. Figure 7–3, shows that the eurodollar deposit interest rate has a very small spread over the comparable domestic deposit rate. (The difference in lending rates to prime borrowers essentially disappeared during the 1980s.)

Eurocurrency Interest Rates

The base interest rate paid on deposits between banks in the eurocurrency market is called **LIBOR,** the London interbank offered rate. (Outside London, which is the center of the entire euromarket, the base rate on deposits is generally slightly higher.) LIBOR is determined by the supply and demand for funds in the euromarket for each currency. Because participating banks could default (and, infrequently, do default) on their obligations, the rate paid for eurodollar deposits is always somewhat above the domestic Treasury bill rate. Also, because domestic banks must comply with Federal Reserve requirements, they offer slightly lower deposit rates than unregulated eurobanks, as shown in Figure 7–3.

The lending rate has no name comparable to the prime rate, but it is determined as LIBOR plus some margin, or spread, charged to the borrower. Banks generally do not require compensating balances or other implicit charges in

FIGURE 7–3

Interest Rates on Deposits, Domestic and Eurodollar

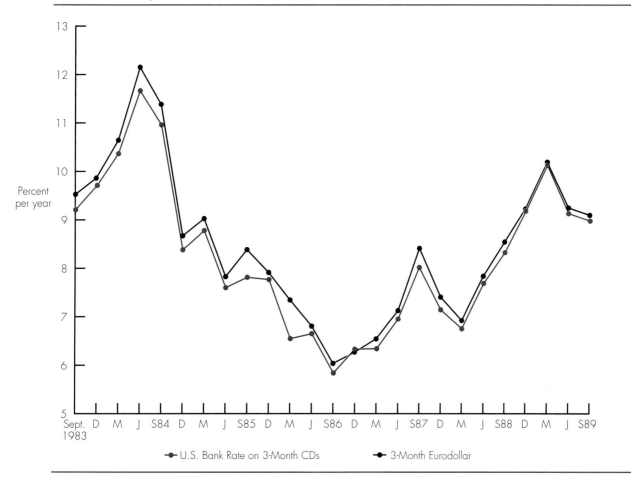

addition to the spread over LIBOR in the euromarket. This also helps reduce the cost of using the euromarket for borrowers. The total cost of borrowing in the euromarket for a prime U.S. corporation historically was marginally below the domestic U.S. prime rate. Because of competition among lenders in both markets, since the early 1980s, prime borrowers have been able to obtain the same rate in both markets.

Interest rates on other eurocurrencies generally follow the same pattern, though when capital controls exist in a particular country (e.g., France), borrowing rates may be higher in the euromarket (which is not restricted) than in the domestic market. Figure 7–4 traces three-month eurocurrency deposit rates during the past two decades. Notice that the countries whose currencies have tended to decline relative to other currencies during this period (such as France and Great Britain) show generally higher eurocurrency deposit rates than the "strong currency" countries (such as Germany and Japan).

FIGURE 7–4

Three-Month Eurocurrency
Deposit Rates *(yearend)*

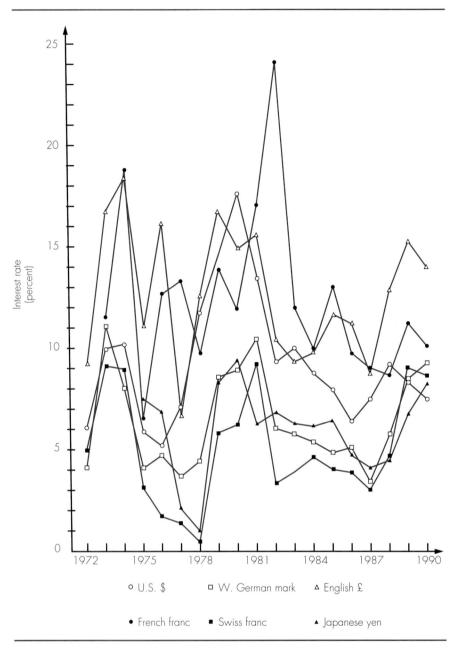

Source: Morgan Guaranty Trust Company, *World Financial Markets* (various issues).

**Other Market
Characteristics**

Transactions in the eurodollar market generally involve $US1 million or more, although in the past several years many deposits of $50,000 to $100,000 have been given at LIBOR, and loans of similar amounts have been offered at the analogous lending rates. The market is directly accessible to banks, which carry out about three fourths of the total volume of transactions among themselves. Companies and individuals participate through their banks, generally at interest rates slightly less favorable than those offered between banks. (Investors may also participate in the euromarket indirectly by purchasing money market funds in the United States, when the funds themselves place large portions of their pooled investments in eurodollar accounts.)

Criticisms of the Euromarkets

The eurodollar market has been criticized over the years as contributing to worldwide inflation and as creating major new risks in the international banking system. While neither of these claims has been proved (or disproved) conclusively, they are worth considering here.

Because the eurodollar market adds to the worldwide volume of dollar-denominated assets, it has been accused of increasing the global money supply beyond the control of the U.S. authorities. This may be true to some extent, but a number of factors mitigate the total impact of eurodollars. First, eurodollars exist only as time deposits and certificates of deposit, never as demand deposits or cash. Hence, in the narrow definition of money that includes only cash and demand deposits, eurodollars do not even appear at all. Second, as already noted, about three fourths of all eurodollars are interbank deposits rather than new credit to companies or individuals that may use it for capital investment and thus economic growth. The interbank transfers (sometimes called "pyramiding") do not create any new credit, however measured. And finally, the eurodollar deposits that are used by companies and individuals for investment and consumption probably replace other (e.g., domestic) bank deposits that would have been used for the same purposes anyhow. That is, because the eurodollar deposits pay interest rates higher than domestic deposits, they often substitute for domestic deposits, and thus they are used for the same purposes that those deposits would have served. All in all, eurodollars probably add slightly to the total volume of economic activity worldwide because they provide a form of financial intermediation between depositors (savers) in many countries and borrowers (investors or spenders) in many countries that is more efficient than that of individual domestic financial markets.

On the issue of increased risk, it has been argued that the eurocurrency market has led to much greater extension of loans to troubled borrowers, such as the governments of less developed countries that were facing virtual impossibility of repayment in the 1980s. Unquestionably, the eurodollar market provided the mechanism through which these governments borrowed most of the money that was loaned to them in the 1970s. It is not clear, however, that any other financial markets would have fared any differently in the absence of eurodollars. Essentially, participation in the euromarket has opened one more type of business to international banks, and these banks must manage this business with the same prudence that they manage the other businesses in which they participate.

EUROBONDS AND EUROEQUITIES

Eurobonds are the long-term analogue of eurocurrencies. They are issued in countries of convenience and denominated in currencies other than the local one. With eurobonds, *taxation* of the interest income received by investors is a key concern, so most of them are issued in tax jurisdictions that do not impose taxes on such interest payments (e.g., Luxembourg). Eurobonds, like domestic U.S. bonds, are issued by corporations and government agencies. They may be convertible into equity, and they may have fixed or floating interest rates.

Borrowers (i.e., issuers of eurobonds) utilize this market for these main reasons: (1) no regulatory agency establishes rules for disclosure by issuers, so that substantial red tape is avoided—though this generally limits participation to blue-chip corporations and governments; (2) the interest rates can be marginally lower than those on domestic issues because investors can usually avoid taxes on their interest income; and (3) the issuer gains access to potential investors in many countries simultaneously because the investment banks that place the issue offer it internationally. From time to time, eurobond issue is stimulated by additional reasons, such as domestic bond market restrictions that lead issuers to seek overseas funding. In 1964, for example, the United States established capital controls that made foreign bonds less attractive to U.S. investors (the Interest Equalization Tax was effectively a tax on interest received by U.S. citizens from foreign bond investments) and that limited lending by U.S. parent companies to their foreign subsidiaries. As a result, both U.S. and foreign issuers that were trying to place dollar-denominated bonds turned to the fledgling eurobond market for their funding.

For the investor, the eurobond market offers these advantages: (1) all issues are structured to allow exemption from interest withholding tax on the income earned; and (2) the terms of eurobond issues are more varied than those of domestic bond issues. For example, eurobonds usually have shorter maturities than domestic bonds (five to eight years), and eurobonds often have floating-rate interest payments.

During the 1970s and early 1980s, the growth of the eurobond market was fairly similar to that of the eurocurrency market. In the 1980s, the vast majority of eurobonds were being issued in U.S. dollars and the market continued to grow in both size and diversity (as shown in Table 7–3).

Euroequities have emerged in the past few years in the London-based International Stock Exchange as another long-term euromarket, analogous to domestic stock markets. As implied in the name, euroequities are shares of publicly-traded stocks traded on an exchange outside of the home country of the firm. They are bought and sold in shares denominated in the firm's home currency, so that both company performance and exchange rate performance affect the returns on investment in euroequities.

In the United States, a market for such issues has operated for many years through an instrument called an **American Depositary Receipt (ADR)**, which is essentially a claim on a share of stock in the foreign stock exchange intermediated by a securities broker who issues the ADR. Euroequities rival the ADRs, and offer the flexibility of being direct share issues by the non-local firms. The market exists primarily in London, and so it encompasses non-British company shares. In fact, even the ADRs of British companies are now traded on the International Stock Exchange, so that full global trading is possible through the exchange.

The International Stock Exchange grew rapidly in the late 1980s. By 1989, 52 brokerage firms were making a market for euroequities issued by 707 firms. The monthly turnover during January of 1989 was 278 million shares. The growing demand for these instruments (based on the firms available for investment and the tax-avoiding structure of the issues), as well as growing supply (by firms that are blue-chip and that want to gain access to investors from many countries through the International Stock Exchange), makes it likely that this market will increase in importance in global equities trading.

CONCLUSIONS

Whether or not a company or bank is involved in international trade, investment, or other international business, it is important for its managers to understand some of the key aspects of international financial markets. The eurocurrency market may offer a low-cost borrowing opportunity; or the eurobond market may provide an outlet for selling new debt to a wider group of investors. The international monetary system establishes a framework within which governments set international financial policies that may affect many firms. The money and capital markets in foreign countries may offer opportunities to multinational firms that operate in those countries. The foreign exchange market determines the cost and availability of foreign currencies, used in business by many firms. Finally, all of these markets influence the functioning of the markets for real goods and services, the ultimate use for all financial claims.

QUESTIONS

1. How can a firm such as Ajax Steel in Peoria, Illinois, utilize the eurodollar market to minimize its financing costs? This firm is a medium-sized manufacturer with no foreign sales.

2. How may the International Monetary Fund affect companies' activities in international business?

3. What is the difference between a eurobond and a domestic bond in the United States? Which one would you prefer to issue as a company manager? Which one would you prefer to buy as an investor? Why?

4. Does the eurodollar market add to world inflation? Explain why or why not using the material in this chapter and your knowledge of macroeconomics.

5. As a French resident, would you prefer to deposit your $1 million inheritance in a U.S. bank or in the eurodollar market? Why?

6. If you were offered the opportunity to establish a deposit in London denominated in ECU, would you choose that rather than a deposit in British pounds or dollars? Why or why not?

7. What are the important differences between the Bretton Woods system and the current IMF system? How do these differences affect the MNE manager?

8. If your firm had a subsidiary in Japan and about 100 million yen in exposed assets (i.e., plant and equipment), how would you protect it against exchange risk?

9. Explain the role that the IMF plays in the international debt crisis. Use outside information as well as that which appears in this book.

10. What are the necessary conditions for existence of a euromarket? Do you expect the eurodollar to exist 10 years from now? Why or why not?

REFERENCES

Business International Corporation. *Financing Foreign Operations.* New York: Business International Corp., various issues.

Dufey, Gunter, and Ian Giddy. *The International Money Market.* Englewood Cliffs, N.J.: Prentice Hall, 1978.

Euromoney. London: Euromoney Publications, Ltd., various issues.

Feiger, George, and Bertrand Jacquillat. *International Finance*. Boston: Allyn & Bacon, 1982.

Grabbe, Orlin. *International Financial Markets*. New York: Elsevier, 1986.

Pennant-Rea, Rupert. "International Monetary Reform: A Survey." *Economist*, October 5, 1985.

Pozo, Susan. "The ECU as International Money." *Journal of International Money and Finance*, no. 6 (1987).

NOTES

[1] A very useful reference for examining the funding instruments in many developed and less developed countries is Business International Corporation's *Financing Foreign Operations*. This publication discusses short- and long-term financial instruments for about 60 countries, and it is updated annually.

[2] Dufey and Mirus (1987), chap. 1, presents this point clearly and discusses its importance.

[3] See the Economic Cooperation Act of 1948 (Public Law 472, 80th Congress), U.S. Code Congressional Service, 1948.

[4] Exchange-rate policies *are* constrained by the IMF if a country seeks to borrow more than its quota from the Fund. Also, a country does operate in violation of IMF rules if it imposes new exchange controls on current transactions without obtaining IMF approval; however sanctions are seldom applied unless the country seeks to borrow as above.

[5] Some information about the rules on access to national stock markets by foreigners appears in Business International Corporation, *Investing, Licensing, and Trading Conditions* (New York: Business International Corporation, 1984).

[6] See *The ECU* (Luxembourg: European Communities, 1984). Also see "European Currency Units," *International Banking Report*, February 17, 1984, published by the London *Financial Times;* and "Edging Closer to a Common Currency," *Euromoney*, September 1985, pp. 19–28.

[7] See, for example, Dufey and Giddy (1978).

[8] Realistically, if any one government disallows the euromarkets, they can still function almost as effectively in other countries and currencies. At present, the U.S. government has the most important role, since about 80 percent of eurodeposits are denominated in U.S. dollars.

7–1 Eurodollar Expansion and Contraction

Eurodollars are *not* money in the same way that checks and cash are. Eurodollars are time deposits or certificates of deposit, some of which have maturities of as little as one day. Hence, eurodollar deposits with very short terms are "quasi money" and can be used by their holders in very much the same way as demand deposits. Other eurodollar deposits can be used in much the same way as domestic time deposits and CDs. This appendix explains the process of eurodollar creation, expansion, and contraction, so that the reader can understand the basic mechanics of the market and of the not-so-arcane transactions that take place.

Let us begin with Metalworks, Inc., a company in Cleveland that produces small metal fittings for auto manufacturers. This company has an interest-earning checking account at Ohio Bank & Trust that regularly contains about $1 million more than the company uses for its operations. Rather than leave the money in a low-interest deposit, the financial manager of Metalworks decides to place the excess $1 million in an alternative, still very liquid, investment. The manager of Ohio B&T suggests a eurodollar negotiable certificate of deposit, placed at the bank's branch in London.

The eurodollar deposit would pay the interest rate, LIBOR, to Metalworks for three months, after which Metalworks could roll over the deposit at the new LIBOR or withdraw the funds and use them otherwise. Metalworks could hold the eurodollar CD for the entire three-month period or sell it at any time in the market for eurodollar CDs at whatever price buyers offered. Ohio B&T guaranteed that it would buy back the CD at a small cost in reduced interest if Metalworks chose to sell it during the three-month period. At this time, LIBOR was at 10.75 percent per year on three-month dollar deposits and Ohio B&T was paying $5\frac{1}{2}$ percent per year on the checking account in Cleveland.

Having made the decision to go ahead, Metalworks deposited $1 million in the eurodollar deposit in London. That is, Ohio B&T created an account on the books of its branch in London payable to Metalworks, even though all of the discussions took place in Cleveland. The three T-accounts below summarize this transaction, which constitutes the creation of 1 million eurodollars. (Note that DD means "demand deposit" and CD means "certificate of deposit.")

Metalworks, Inc.		Ohio B&T, home office		Ohio B&T, London office	
A	L	A	L	A	L
− DD at Ohio B&T + CD at B&T London			− DD owed to Metalworks + DD owed to B&T London	+ DD at home office	+ CD owed to Metalworks

So far, no credit has been extended, even though a million eurodollars have been created. There was simply an exchange of one bank account for another. At this point, Metalworks is satisfied with its position. Ohio B&T, however, has accepted a new deposit that is costing it 10.75 percent per year, so it needs to find a use for the funds that will bring in more than that. Typically, the bank will look to other banks in the London market to purchase the funds. If Ohio B&T can find another bank that offers a slightly higher interest rate, it may lend the funds to that bank. Let us assume that Crédit Suisse needs funds for a loan that it wants to make in Switzerland, so its London branch offers Ohio B&T 10.90 percent per year for $1 million for three months. This second transaction appears as follows in the T-accounts of the participants:

Ohio B&T, home office		Ohio B&T, London office		Crédit Suisse	
A	L	A	L	A	L
	−DD owed to B&T London +DD owed to Crédit Suisse	−DD at B&T home office +CD at Crédit Suisse		+DD at B&T home office	+CD owed to B&T London

In this step, Crédit Suisse has exchanged a CD payable to Ohio B&T, London, for a demand deposit at Ohio B&T, Cleveland, each for $1 million. Now Ohio B&T has solved its problems of finding a borrower for the funds, but Crédit Suisse has taken on the same problem.

Crédit Suisse next uses the funds to make a loan to Nestlé Corporation, at an interest rate of 11.45 percent per year for the three-month period. Thus, Nestlé is paying a spread, or margin, over LIBOR of 0.75 percent per year.) The final transaction in eurodollar expansion looks like this:

Ohio B&T, home office		Crédit Suisse		Nestlé	
A	L	A	L	A	L
	−DD owed to Crédit Suisse +DD owed to Neslté	−DD at B&T home office +Loan to Nestlé		+DD at B&T home office	+Loan due to Crédit Suisse

Now there are $2 million of eurodollars in existence (the CD of Ohio B&T's London office owed to Metalworks and the Crédit Suisse CD owed to B&T London) plus a eurodollar loan of $1 million. Assuming that both deposits and the loan are held to maturity, these eurodollars will have a life of three months. All of the participants are in "equilibrium" in the sense that they are all earning a satisfactory return on their eurodollar dealings (assuming that Nestlé has invested the money in some activity that pays more than 11.45 percent per year).

Eurodollar contraction occurs when the deposits mature and must be paid out. If each depositor simply redeposits the funds in another eurodollar deposit and Nestlé rolls over its loan, then the accounts are rolled over and no change in the total number of eurodollars occurs. However, if any participant does not redeposit the funds in a eurodollar account, then there is a decline in the number of eurodollars (though *not* in the number of dollars in the B&T home office account).

Assume now that Nestlé pays back the loan after three months and that Metalworks shifts its deposit back to a demand deposit in Cleveland. In this case, Nestlé will pay Crédit Suisse $1 million plus interest ($28,625); Crédit Suisse will pay Ohio B&T, London, $1 million plus interest ($27,250); and Ohio B&T, London, will transfer $1 million plus interest ($26,875) to the account of Metalworks in Cleveland. At this point, no eurodollars remain and each euromarket participant is left with a profit (if Nestlé did indeed earn more than 11.45 percent per year on its use of the funds).

Because much of business activity is refinanced repeatedly, the eurodollar market generally does not decline in volume. And because more and more firms and banks are entering the eurodollar market, the volume of eurodollars has tended to grow over the years.

Bell South—Borrowing in International Financial Markets

Introduction

One of the major changes in the business system of the United States in the 20th century occurred on January 1, 1984, when American Telephone & Telegraph (AT&T) was forced to sell its operating telephone subsidiaries. The U.S. Department of Justice decided to deregulate long-distance telephone service by allowing other companies to compete with AT&T. To reduce AT&T's competitive advantage over other companies, the Justice Department required that AT&T sell all of its 22 regional telephone operating companies (i.e., the companies, such as Southern Bell, that actually provided telephone service in 22 regions of the United States). Now AT&T owns only a long-distance operating network of telephone service, its research division (Bell Labs), its manufacturing division (Western Electric), and a new data processing division (AT&T Information Systems).

The "breakup" of AT&T left the operating companies regrouped into seven corporations, with responsibility for providing local telephone service in seven areas of the United States. This change was truly dramatic. AT&T had been the largest private corporation in the world, and before 1984 each operating company had functioned only as a division of the national company and each division had made decisions only about telephone service in its area. Now each operating company had to make *all* decisions as an independent corporation, including decisions on financing, investing, and general business strategy.

The decision of interest in this case is the financing decision. How should a company finance its business activities? More specifically, how should a major capital project be financed? For any large corporation, and for many medium-sized ones as well, the eurocurrency market offers very attractive financing opportunities. Bell South was chosen because its managers do not have experience in dealing with the eurocurrency markets and because it definitely should take advantage of the opportunities available there. Additional financial markets available to corporations in the United States are noted for comparison.

The Case

In the aftermath of the decision by the U.S. Department of Justice to dismantle (organizationally) the national telephone system in 1982, individual operating subsidiaries of AT&T were beginning to face major new decisions as soon-to-be-independent companies. Each of the operating companies was very large by

This case was written by Professor Robert Grosse as a basis for class discussion. The specific borrowing situation is fictitious, and references to Bell South are based on publicly available information, 1986.

current industrial standards—Bell South alone had assets worth more than $21 billion and employed over 100,000 people. None of the operating companies had had experience in large-scale financing, research and development in telecommunications, or the design of a marketing strategy, since all of these functions had previously been performed by AT&T (or Bell Labs) at the national level.

One of the first priorities established by Bell South's senior management in 1983 was to initiate a research program with a laboratory facility in either Raleigh, North Carolina, or Melbourne, Florida (near major concentrations of electronics companies). Since the company would not become independent until January 1, 1984, no actual investment could take place until then. Nonetheless, Bell South's managers wanted to be ready to go with their plans on "independence day."

Among the more difficult problems facing David Green as treasury manager for Bell South was the issue of financing the research lab, which was estimated to cost about $25 million. While this level of funding was not large compared to AT&T's total borrowing, it would present some difficulties for a newly independent Bell South (primarily because of this firm's inexperience in such negotiations). Green was discussing the problem with his recently hired assistant, who had just graduated from a prestigious school of business administration.

The assistant (i.e., you) was proposing to consider the idea of eurocurrency financing, for which lower interest rates were available and fewer restrictions existed on loans. Specifically, the assistant recommended the use of a euro-deutschemark loan, which could be obtained for close to one half of the interest cost that had been offered for a domestic, dollar-denominated loan by NCNB (North Carolina National Bank). Other alternatives should also be considered, of course. Table 1 shows various borrowing options and their costs in August 1983.

The research facility has an expected life of 10 years. It will be financed separately each year, so that every year the lowest-cost source of funds should be chosen. For the first year (effective on January 1, 1984), funding will be available at the interest rates shown in Table 1. Each type of lender also charges fees on

TABLE 1

Possible Sources of $25 Million, One-Year Borrowing for Bell South

Type of Funding	Interest Cost*					Fees (paid up front)
	U.S.$	C$	FF	DM	SF	
Syndicated eurocurrency loan (LIBOR)	11.13	10.31	16.50	6.13	5.00	2.00
Eurobond issue	12.25	12.00	–	8.36	–	1.75
U.S. domestic bank loan (prime rate)	11.50					3.00
U.S. domestic bond issue	12.65					2.25
U.S. domestic equity issue (required rate of return)	18					2.25
Spot exchange rate (fx/$)	1	1.23	8.0	2.6	2.10	
One-year forward XR	1	1.29	9.1	2.3	1.95	

*All interest costs are stated as annual percentage rates. Since one-year loans are being used, the rates must be renegotiated every year during the project. Bell South can be expected to pay a "spread" of ⅜ percent over LIBOR quotes and ¼ percent over prime, plus onetime, up-front fees, based on the value of the loan. Assume for simplicity that all interest is paid at the end of the full loan period.

the loan. The fees are paid one time, at the beginning of the loan period, and they are some percentage of the total loan value (as shown). Right now, the only task is to choose the funding source for the first year; subsequent borrowing decisions will be made at the end of each year.

In addition to a bank loan in the eurodollar market, Bell South can consider using a domestic bank loan. In either case, the company will pay the base interest rate plus some additional margin to the bank lender. If the company issues new bonds, it will have to pay the interest rate shown plus the up-front fee. If it issues new stock, investors would expect a return of about 18 percent per year, much higher than the bank charges. Many other financing sources exist, but the choices shown are very commonly used in the U.S. market.

LIBOR is the London interbank offered rate, the interest rate offered by banks in London for large deposits (eurocurrency deposits) from other banks. The lending rate does not have a name; it is just called "LIBOR plus the spread," and it varies depending on the creditworthiness of the borrower.

QUESTIONS

1. What is the cheapest way to finance the research facility without incurring exchange risk? [*Hint:* To do the calculations, assume that interest rates remain constant during the life of the project.]

2. Should the company use long-term financing, such as a bond issue, so that it would not have to refinance every year?

Chapter

8

The Balance of Payments

This chapter covers the measurement and interpretation of all international transactions between one country and the rest of the world: that is, the balance of payments. Since the system of recording these transactions is fairly complex, a major part of the chapter consists of an explanation of that system. Examples of countries in different balance of payments situations illustrate the use of the system and the implications of deficit and surplus balances. The remainder of the chapter explains what happens when imbalances of payments exist and shows why company managers involved in international business need to understand the balance of payments. The main goals of the chapter are to:

1. Explain how the double-entry bookkeeping system of measuring balances of payments works.

2. Look at recent balances of payments for the United States and discuss their implications.

3. Show how balance of payments adjustment takes place.

4. Discuss the many implications of balance of payments problems from the perspective of private sector managers whose firms do business across national boundaries.

INTRODUCTION

How well do we keep track of the millions of transactions that take place annually between exporters and importers, international banks and multinational companies? The bankers who tabulate the foreign exchange dealings of their own banks are only a part of the picture. How well can we account for the part of direct investment that occurs through overseas borrowing, yet affects the home country's international economic position? Even more simply, how well can we measure "international" transactions that are just transfers of funds from the account of an importer to the account of a foreign exporter in the same bank?

The answer to these questions, realistically, is "not very well." National governments create elaborate accounts for the transactions between their residents and foreigners, but it is often very difficult to obtain full and accurate information. Putting that problem to the side for the moment, let us consider the methods that governments use to record each country's international transactions.

The most widely used measure of international economic transactions for any country is the balance of payments (BOP) statement. This record attempts to measure the full value of the transactions between residents of one country and residents of the rest of the world for some time period, say one year.[1] The balance of payments is a *flow* concept, in that it records flows of goods, services, and claims between countries over a period of time, rather than a stock of accumulated funds or products. It is a *value* concept, in that all the items recorded receive a monetary value, denominated in the given country's currency at the time of the transaction.[2] *The* **balance of payments (BOP)**, then, *is a record of the value of all the economic transactions between residents of one country and residents of all other countries during a given time period.*

Why do we worry about measuring these transactions? Because if a country records a substantial imbalance between inflows and outflows of goods and services for an extended period of time, some means of financing or adjusting away the imbalance must be found. For example, when oil prices rose dramatically in 1973–74 and again in 1979, Brazil continued to import much the same quantity of oil but had to pay a much higher bill (total cost = price times quantity). Given no major change in Brazil's exports, the country ended up spending a lot more foreign currency on imports than it received from exports. This imbalance could have been financed, if Brazil borrowed funds from abroad—with the eventual obligation to repay the loans. The imbalance could also have been adjusted away, if Brazilians bought less of other imported goods or increased their own exports. Finally, the Brazilians could have done nothing and just paid out more cruzeiros, if OPEC countries were willing to accept this currency and hold onto it. (Technically, this would have been borrowing from OPEC, since OPEC would eventually spend the cruzeiros.) Anytime an imbalance occurs between a country's imports and exports of goods and services, it must be covered by an equal and opposite imbalance in flows of claims (e.g., money, bonds, official reserves).

Still, the manager may wonder why he or she should be concerned about this issue. So far, the problem is macroeconomic, referring to a *country's* international transactions. The problem becomes much more important if we realize that national governments are likely to set their regulatory policies to reduce BOP imbalances. Thus, in the above example of Brazil, foreign *firms* may discover themselves faced with new tariffs or quotas; companies operating in Brazil may find that access to foreign exchange for imports or for profit remittance is limited, while subsidies are offered on exports; and foreign *bank* lenders may find new loan requests coming in from Brazil. All in all, the manager should recognize that the balance of payments is an *indicator* of subsequent government policy changes.

In another equally important vein, the manager should be interested in national balances of payments because of their direct importance in determining exchange rates. Since the collapse of the fixed exchange-rate system in 1971, most of the world's developed countries and many of the LDCs have been allowing the values of their currencies to fluctuate in the market (usually with some degree of government intervention). This means that, other things equal, when the supply of a country's currency in foreign exchange markets exceeds the demand, the currency will devalue. Such an excess supply could have occurred in the Brazilian example, unless some demand for cruzeiros arose for another purpose (e.g., for direct investment). Although it is the *total* demand and supply of the currency in foreign exchange markets that leads to exchange-rate determination, many analysts discuss a trade imbalance as being likely to affect the rate, ignoring other sources of currency demand or supply. One must be careful to include all of these sources when attempting to judge exchange-rate changes.

The next section looks at the full set of transactions that constitute the balance of payments and explains the system of BOP accounting that is used to create the records used by governments. The third section presents the various account aggregates that are balances of payments. The BOP of the United States is discussed in some detail in the fourth section. Because the balance of payments is a dynamic concept, changing daily as transactions occur, the adjustment mechanisms leading from surplus and deficit balances toward equilibrium points are then examined. Finally, the last section presents implications of the BOP for managers and shows how managers can use BOP information to make decisions.

BALANCE OF PAYMENTS ACCOUNTING

There is no such thing as "*the* balance of payments," since the accounts are organized in a double-entry bookkeeping system and for every debit entry there is a credit entry of equal value. There are seven or eight BOP measures; these group some international transactions together and leave others in a second, "everything else" category. In each case, the intent is to group the fundamental economic causes of transactions in the first group and the "payments" for them in the second group. Also, the former items are listed "above the line" and the latter are listed "below the line" in the actual accounts.

More specifically, consider the situation in which you (a U.S. resident) go on vacation in Paris, buy some French wine for 35 francs, and bring it back to the United States. Ignoring everything except the wine purchase, we can classify that wine as a U.S. import and list it in a simple balance of payments as follows:

U.S. BOP (in dollars)

	Inflows (−)	Outflows (+)
Products	7 of wine	
Money		7 spent

Note: Assume that the current exchange rate is $.20 = 1FF.

This simple table demonstrates many of the major principles of **balance of payments accounting.** First, all entries in the accounts must be in some currency value (e.g., dollars or dollars' worth, since the example is from a U.S. perspective). Second, inflows of goods, services, and claims are segregated on one side of the ledger and outflows on the other. Third, a set of categories can be created in the vertical direction to separate kinds of flows—in the present example, to separate a product flow from a money flow. Fourth, inflows are recorded with a minus sign (−) and outflows are recorded with a plus sign (+). Fifth, if a horizontal line is drawn anywhere on the ledger, it is possible to add up the entries above the line and, separately, those below the line. (Obviously, a line drawn below all entries will yield a value of zero above the line, and no entries will be below the line. In this sense, there is no "total" balance of payments.) The summation of the entries above the line is called the balance of payments on the particular account (e.g., the trade balance), depending on where the line is drawn.

In our simple example above, if the line is drawn between products and money, we have an above-the-line total of − $7 in value and a below-the-line total of + $7 in value. If this wine is the only item exported or imported in the given time period, then the country has a balance of **trade deficit** of $7. That is, the sum of all the entries above the line, where exports and imports are the *only* items in this category, is − $7, a deficit. The + $7 cash outflow appears below the line and is ignored in measuring the balance of trade; clearly, it *is* the other half of the same transaction.

Notice that this classification system is similar to a company's flow-of-funds statement, or its statement of net change in financial position, in which asset inflows are recorded as debits (−) and liability increases are recorded as credits (+). In the present example, the *country* has gained an asset, namely the bottle of wine, and the country has incurred a new liability, namely the dollars paid out

TABLE 8–1

Balance of Payments for Behrmania, 1991 (*in millions of U.S. dollars*)

	Inflows (debits) −	+ Outflows (credits)
A. Merchandise trade	100 Oil imports 50 Chemical imports	80 Machinery exports 50 Grain exports
B. Trade in services	10 Value of services for foreign shipping	40 Licensing and management contractors
C. Gifts	15 Foreign aid value	5 Gifts from relatives abroad
D. Long-term capital flows	40 Foreign investment undertaken abroad	10 Bonds sold to foreigners 5 Long-term loans issued by foreigners
E. Short-term capital flows	20 Short-term securities bought from ROW	10 Short-term securities sold to foreigners 20 Outflow of funds to ROW
F. Official reserves flows		15 Paid in foreign currency by the central bank to ROW central banks
Total	235	235

to the wine seller. This analogy will be very useful in trying to understand the U.S. BOP, as presented below. At this point, let us continue to develop the various accounts in simple form.

The basic balance of payments table is constructed to present in descending vertical order: flows of goods, services, and gifts (i.e., current items); flows of long-term claims such as stocks and bonds; flows of short-term claims, including money; and finally, flows of official international reserves. At whatever point "the line" is drawn, the items above the line may be viewed as being paid for by those remaining below the line. In our example, the balance of trade shows a bottle of imported French wine paid for by an outflow of $7 in money.

Table 8–1 presents a standard balance of payments table for the country Behrmania in 1991. We will look at each category (or account) individual.

Trade (or Merchandise Trade)

This account includes all inflows and outflows of products, whether they are consumer or industrial goods. It is possible that some of the entries are paid for with funds under heading E, while others are tied to foreign investment projects or gifts. If the oil import transaction takes place simply between a local firm and an OPEC exporter, it may involve just an outflow of cash or checks, with the total transaction appearing as:

	Debits – ($ millions)	+ Credits ($ millions)
A. Products	100 oil imports	
E. Short-term capital flows		100 cash or checks

Similarly, exports of grain to a less developed country may appear as a credit in row A, and cash payment for the grain as a debit (i.e., an inflow) in row E. (The grain shipment appears explicitly in Table 8–1, while the payment has been lumped together with other cash inflows and outflows.)

If a Behrmanian company decided to set up a factory worth $40 million in Germany, then it could send some machinery to Germany, along with some money. Ignoring the purchase of the factory (direct investment) initially, we would record $20 million of machinery exports and $20 million of funds outflow, both credit entries, as constituting half of the transaction. (The other half is foreign direct investment, a $40 million debit entry in row D, as discussed below.) This leaves $60 million more of machinery exports in Table 8–1, which we assume were made to unrelated foreign importers and paid for with checks.

Another Behrmanian company had previously built a plant in France (recorded in last year's BOP) that sells $50 million of chemicals back to the home office for domestic sale. Since the French affiliate is viewed as a foreign resident, this transaction appears as an import (as shown in Table 8–1), though payment for it may be made through an intracompany transfer of funds (i.e., a credit entry in line E) or perhaps through an exchange of technology or other service provided by the home office (i.e., a credit entry in line B). Assume that $10 million of the value was paid for in services and the rest in cash. The full set of entries related to the chemicals and machinery transactions is:

	Debits − ($ millions)	+ Credits ($ millions)
A. Products	50 Chemicals	20 Machinery for FDI 60 Machinery, sold to unrelated importers
B. Services		10 Management services provided to subsidiary in return for chemicals
D. Long-term capital flows	40 Foreign investment in Germany	
E. Short-term capital flows	60 Checks received for machinery from importers	20 Funds for FDI project 40 Payment for chemicals

These two transactions alone begin to give us some idea of the enormous complexity of BOP accounts.

Services

How should we classify an airplane trip to the Bahamas in the BOP? While no physical product is exchanged, the service of airplane passage to Nassau is provided, at some price. We know that souvenirs purchased on this vacation are recorded as Behrmanian imports. In the same sense, the service of an airplane trip, "imported" from Bahamas Air, must be recorded as a debit. (Notice, however, that if Behrmanian Airlines flies to Nassau, tickets purchased by Behrmanians are *not* part of the BOP; they are just a domestic service, which appears in national income accounts.)

A wide variety of services may be supplied—air, land, or sea passenger transport; similar merchandise transport; technology or management assistance; leasing or franchising; and so on. Behrmania has imported $10 million worth of transportation services for shipping merchandise abroad. Once again, this item appears in the BOP only if foreign shipping companies are used; a Behrmanian shipping company's services would not appear. This country has sold licensing and management services abroad—$10 million of which was supplied to the subsidiary in France and the rest to unaffiliated foreign firms. The total impact of service flows on the BOP is:

	Debits − ($ millions)	+ Credits ($ millions)
A. Products	10 Part of chemicals sold to parent firm	
B. Services	10 Shipping	40 Licensing and management contracts
E. Short-term capital flows	30 Cash inflow	10 Cash outflow

Once again, the "payments" associated with service exports and imports need not be money; they may be service-related flows of goods or even other services.

Gifts or Unilateral Transfers

Probably the most difficult aspect of BOP accounting to grasp is the treatment of gifts. Put simply, the problem is that a gift does not create any equal and opposite flow for the double-entry system. When Behrmanians receive checks totaling

$5 million from relatives living abroad, what reverse flow occurs? There is none; so we create a fictitious entry called "unilateral transfers" in which to record the value of gifts given (as a debit) or received (as a credit). Perhaps the easiest way to understand this entry is to view it as a "thank-you note" for the gift. Thus, the Behrmanians record $5 million as a short-term capital inflow and $5 million as a unilateral transfer (or thank-you note) outflow. Behrmania receives the money, and the foreign relatives get only a fictitious thank-you note (plus substantial goodwill).

The government may be involved in making grants to foreign countries, or even in such things as paying pensions to Behrmanians living permanently abroad. Such official (government) gifts, like private gifts, appear as unilateral transfers. In the present year, the Behrmanian government made foreign aid disbursements totaling $15 million, all in the form of checks. Thus, the total gift-related entries are:

	Debits − ($ millions)	+ Credits ($ millions)
C. Gifts	15 Foreign aid value	5 Value of gifts from relatives
E. Short-term capital flows	5 Funds from relatives	15 Funds outflow

Long-Term Capital Flows

We already have seen how one long-term asset, namely a foreign direct investment project, was related to exports of capital goods and a short-term capital flow. Along with FDI in this category of long-term claims are included purchases and sales of stocks[3] and bonds, long-term bank loans, and long-term government claims. The division between long-term and short-term capital flows is the period of one year. That is, short-term claims mature in less than one year, long-term claims in a year or more. Each item is a "claim" in that it provides the owner with future purchasing power over goods and services in the currency of the claim. That is, long-term claims are presumably purchased by individuals or institutions that are willing to hold these stocks, bonds, or notes into the future, when they will be redeemed for cash that can be spent.

In the present year, two separate claims were issued, in addition to the $40 million foreign investment project that Behrmanian investors undertook in Germany. Some local companies issued $10 million in bonds, which were purchased by foreign residents and paid for with checks, and Lloyds Bank in London loaned $5 million to a Behrmanian bank for a period of two years. The loan was disbursed through a wire transfer of funds from Lloyds. The results of these transactions appear in the balance of payments as:

	Debits − ($ millions)	+ Credits ($ millions)
A. Products		20 Machinery for FDI
D. Long-term capital flows	40 FDI in Germany	10 Bonds sold to foreign residents 5 Loan from Lloyds
E. Short-term capital flows	10 Payment for bonds 5 Funds from loan	20 Funds for FDI in Germany

Short-Term Capital Flows   The only remaining items in the balance of payments are short-term claims. These include public and private short-term flows and exchanges of official reserves among central banks. Short-term capital flows include exchanges involving all kinds of money market instruments, such as treasury bills, short-term certificates of deposit, commercial paper, banker's acceptances, and money itself (i.e., M1, currency plus demand deposits). These transactions may involve private firms, individuals, or governments. Much of the activity in this category relates to carrying out payments for exports, imports, and other items in categories A through D. However, a substantial amount of international investment occurs in short-term money market instruments, so this category cannot be viewed as just a set of payments.

In the current year for Behrmania, we have already seen short-term capital inflows worth $50 million and short-term capital outflows worth $85 million. In addition, foreign residents purchased $10 million of Behrmanian money market funds and Behrmanians purchased $20 million of foreign countries' treasury bills, in each case paying with checks. The net effect of these two last transactions is zero:

	Debits − ($ millions)	+ Credits ($ millions)
E. Short-term capital flows	20 T bills bought 10 Payment for money market funds	10 Money market funds sold to foreign residents 20 Payment for T bills

What remains is a net short-term capital outflow of $20 million, as shown in Table 8–1, and an unexplained outflow of $15 million more, which we will now see as a flow of official reserves.

Official Reserves Flows   Official reserves—assets held and traded by central banks and the International Monetary Fund—are the final category of entries in the BOP. Before discussing the types of official reserves that are available, it would be useful to conclude the Behrmania example.

The final $15 million outflow that remains unaccounted for is a buildup of Behrmanian currency in some exporting country's central bank. If we assume that the funds sent to France for FDI were deposited in a bank, then we can also assume that this bank turned $15 million of Behrmanian currency over to the French central bank in exchange for francs. The French central bank then has the right to exchange the Behrmanian currency for French francs or other currency at the Behrmanian central bank. When this occurs, Behrmania's central bank gives up $15 million worth of its foreign exchange holdings. This transaction is entered as an outflow of official reserves. The total set of transactions appears in the BOP as:

	Debits − ($ millions)	+ Credits ($ millions)
A. Products	15* Part of chemicals value	
E. Short-term capital flows	15 Local currency returned by French government	15 Payment for part of chemicals shipment in Behrmanian currency

(continued)

	Debits – ($ millions)	+ Credits ($ millions)

F. Official
   reserves
   flows
		15 French francs given to French
		central bank by Behrmanian
		central bank

*The other $25 million value of chemicals imports is ignored for simplicity here.

Official reserves actually include much more than the foreign exchange held by the central bank of a country. In fact, four kinds of assets are regarded as official reserves:

1. Foreign exchange.
2. Official gold.
3. Special drawing rights (SDRs).
4. Position at the IMF.

Although any country can hold official reserves, discussions of this subject generally refer only to member countries in the IMF, to which items 3 and 4 are available. We will continue on this basis too.

Official reserve assets are either held at the International Monetary Fund or held by a country's central monetary authority and recorded at the IMF. Such assets *must* be owned by the country's central monetary authority, for the simple technical reason that private sector institutions or individuals can hold gold and foreign currencies—and the intent of measuring official reserves is to look *only* at the government's position. Any net outflow of a country's official reserves in some time period means that fewer financial resources are available for the purchase of foreign goods and services (or, in another light, that fewer financial resources are available for intervention in the foreign exchange market to keep the currency from devaluing).

Special drawing rights (SDRs), discussed in Chapter 7, are the basic unit of account at the IMF. All national currencies and official gold holdings are valued in SDRs, which may be transferred among member countries' accounts when requested. SDRs themselves are created by decisions of the IMF, and they are distributed to member countries each time a new supply is created.

A country's position in the IMF is the amount of its net borrowing from the IMF during any period. For the most part, LDCs use such lending opportunities, while the developed countries and OPEC usually do not. When all of the transactions in accounts A–F are summed vertically, the debits and credits each total $235 million. Although this number gives some idea of the approximate size of international transactions, which can be compared across countries, it is used only as a check on the entries in each column. What is much more important is the set of relationships among the accounts in the BOP.

BALANCES OF PAYMENTS

The Behrmanian BOP table can be redrawn in terms of the five most widely used balances, which correspond to the accounts in Table 8–1. Now, in Table 8–2, we need to sum up all of the entries "above the line" drawn below each balance in order to measure that particular balance of payments.

For example, the **trade balance** shows a *deficit* of $20 million, reflecting an excess of debits over credits *above the line* in this amount. This can be

TABLE 8–2

Balances of Payments for Behrmania, 1991 *(in $ millions of U.S. dollars)*

	Inflows (Debits) –	+ Outflows (Credits)	
A. Balance of (merchandise) trade	100 Oil imports 50 Chemicals imports	80 Machinery exports 50 Grain exports	–20
B. Balance on goods and services	10 Value of services for foreign shipping	40 Licensing and management contracts	+10
C. Current account balance	15 Foreign aid value	5 Gifts from relatives abroad	0
D. Basic balance	40 Foreign investment undertaken abroad	10 Bonds sold to foreigners 5 Long-term loans issued to foreigners	–25
E. Official settlements balance*	20 Short-term securities bought from ROW	10 Short-term securities sold to foreigners 20 Outflow of funds to ROW	–15
F. Actual reserve flows		15 French francs sold to French central bank	+15

*Usually the official settlements balance is recorded as those items *below* the line; so in this case the balance should be +15. This means that an *outflow* of official reserves occurred.

contrasted with the balance on goods and services, which shows such a net outflow of services that the balance is a *surplus* of $10 million. That is, merchandise trade plus services trade totals a balance of + $10 million in value. Note that each balance includes the previous balance plus net flows in the next category. Thus, the **current account balance** includes the balance on goods and services plus unilateral transfers (and shows an even balance). Next, the **basic balance** includes the current account plus long-term capital flows and shows a deficit of $25 million. Finally, the **official settlements balance** shows a net outflow of official reserves, which can be viewed as a deficit on the basic balance plus short-term capital flows or as a surplus on official reserves. The latter terminology is generally used, and Behrmania's official settlements surplus means a loss of $15 million in official reserves.

When reading a BOP statement, care should be taken to interpret the official settlements balance properly. A value of + $15 million would normally be given for the Behrmanian example—referring to the net *outflow* of official reserves. All other balances are recorded and interpreted as previously discussed.

THE U.S. BALANCE OF PAYMENTS

U.S. Department of Commerce Accounts

Since 1976, the United States has used a format for presenting its balance of payments that appears very different from the tables shown above. Fortunately, entries in the new format can be interpreted according to the accounting rules already presented here, and indeed the conceptual format can be re-created from it. Table 8–3 presents the U.S. balance of payments statements for selected years of the past decade, as officially registered in the *Survey of Current Business* in the March issue each year.

While this single-column presentation of the U.S. BOP looks substantially different from the format of Table 8–2, that format can be generated by placing

TABLE 8–3

U.S. Balance of Payments *(in millions of U.S. dollars)*

	1980	1986	1987	1988	1989
1. Exports—goods and service	340,887	372,807	424,823	529,806	600,403
2. Merchandise, adjusted, excluding military	221,781	224,361	249,570	319,251	361,872
3. Transfers under U.S. military agency sales contracts	7,470	8,903	11,529	10,050	8,603
4. Travel	9,985	12,913	14,778	29,202	33,855
5. Passenger fares	2,582	3,562	5,398	8,860	9,899
6. Other transportation	11,041	15,190	16,985	18,930	20,355
7. Royalties and license fees	6,993	6,862	9,039	10,735	11,932
8. Other private services	4,645	12,206	13,242	24,331	28,570
9. U.S. gov. misc. services	362	602	526	672	594
10. Receipts of income on U.S. assets abroad	76,029	88,209	103,756	107,776	124,723
11. Direct investment	37,068	36,697	52,308	48,264	51,059
12. Other private receipts	36,436	45,191	46,116	52,840	68,140
13. U.S. gov. receipts	2,525	6,321	5,332	6,672	5,524
14. Transfers of goods and serv. under U.S. mil. grant programs, net	635	101	58	92	47
15. Imports—goods and services	−333,810	−498,501	−565,342	−641,698	−692,005
16. Merchandise, adjusted, excluding military	−249,135	−368,700	−409,850	−446,466	−475,120
17. Direct defense expenditures	−10,779	−12,565	−13,897	−14,656	−14,265
18. Travel	−10,384	−17,627	−20,496	−32,112	−34,229
19. Passenger fares	−3,533	−6,842	−8,785	−7,872	−8,349
20. Other transportation	−10,981	−17,099	−18,161	−19,641	−20,739
21. Royalties and license fee	−757	−1,077	−1,337	−2,048	−1,879
22. Other private services	−2,980	−5,529	−7,540	−11,400	−11,701
23. U.S. gov. misc. serv.	−1,767	−1,696	−1,895	−1,955	−2,029
24. Payments of income on foreign assets in U.S.A.	−43,494	−67,365	−83,381	−105,548	−123,694
25. Direct investment	−8,853	−5,846	−10,504	−16,748	−14,896
26. Other private payments	−22,140	−38,912	−48,825	−59,746	−75,141
27. U.S. gov. payments	−12,501	−22,607	−24,052	−29,054	−33,657
28. U.S. military grants of goods and services, net	−635	−101	−58	−92	−47
29. Unilateral transfers (excl. military), net	−6,959	−15,658	−13,445	−14,656	−14,276
30. U.S. gov. grants (excl. military grants)	−4,506	−11,773	−10,011	−10,377	−10,248
31. U.S. gov. pensions and other transfers	−1,287	−2,231	−2,212	−2,491	−2,439
32. Private remittances and other transfers	−1,165	−1,654	−1,222	−1,788	−1,589
33. U.S. assets abroad, net (incr./cap. outflow < − >)	−84,502	−95,982	−75,987	−82,110	−125,707
34. U.S. official reserve assets, net	−8,155	312	9,149	−3,566	−25,293
35. Special drawing rights	−16	−246	−509	474	−535
36. Reserve position in IMF	−1,667	1,501	2,070	1,025	471
37. Foreign currencies	−6,472	−942	7,588	−5,064	−25,229
38. U.S. gov. assets, other than official reserve assets, net	−5,111	−1,920	1,162	2,999	1,037
39. U.S. credits and other long-term assets	−9,697	−8,915	−6,493	−7,579	−5,478
40. Repayments	4,308	6,075	7,620	10,313	6,540
41. U.S. foreign currency holdings and U.S. short-term assets, net	278	920	35	265	−24
42. U.S. private assets, net	−71,236	−94,374	−86,297	−81,543	−101,451
43. Direct investment	−20,592	−28,047	−44,455	−17,533	−32,264
44. Foreign securities	−3,188	−3,302	−4,456	−7,846	−22,551
45. U.S. claims on unaffil. foreigners reported by U.S. nonbanking concern	n.a.	−3,986	3,145	−1,684	n.a.
46. U.S. claims reported by U.S. banks, not included elsewhere	46,608	−59,039	−40,531	−54,481	−47,244
47. Foreign assets in U.S., net (incr./cap. inflow { + }	47,626	213,386	211,490	219,299	196,671
48. Foreign official assets in the U.S., net	16,179	34,698	44,968	38,882	7,369
49. U.S. gov. securities	11,827	33,301	44,931	42,992	1,706
50. U.S. Treas. securities	9,640	34,515	43,361	41,683	323
51. Other	2,187	−1,214	1,570	1,309	1,383

TABLE 8–3

Concluded

	1980	1986	1987	1988	1989
52. Other U.S. gov. liabil.	1,375	1,723	−2,824	−1,284	55
53. U.S. liabilities report by U.S. banks, not included elsewhere	−84	554	3,901	−331	3,751
54. Other foreign official assets	3,061	−880	−1,040	−2,495	1,857
55. *Other foreign assets in the U.S., net*	31,466	178,689	166,522	180,418	189,303
56. Direct investment	8,204	25,053	41,977	58,436	61,262
57. U.S. Treas. securities	2,693	8,275	−7,596	20,144	29,411
58. U.S. securities, other	7,443	70,802	42,213	26,448	40,334
59. U.S. liabilities to unaffiliated foreigners reported by U.S. nonbanking concern	n.a.	−2,791	2,150	6,558	n.a.
60. U.S. liabilities reported by U.S. banks	10,687	77,350	87,778	68,832	57,983
61. Allocations of SDR	1,152	—	—	—	—
62. Statistical discrepency (sum of above−sign rev.)	35,605	23,947	18,461	−10,641	34,914
63. Seasonal adj. discrep.	—	—	—	—	—
Memoranda					
64. Balance on merchandise trade	−27,354	−144,339	−160,280	−127,215	−113,248
65. Bal. on goods and services	7,077	−125,694	−140,519	−111,892	−91,602
66. Balance on goods, serv. and remittances	4,625	−129,579	−143,953	−116,171	−95,631
67. Bal. on current account	118	−141,352	−153,964	−126,548	−105,878
Transactions in U.S. official reserve assets and in foreign official assets in the U.S.A.					
68. Increase { − } in U.S. official reserve assets, net	−8,155	312	9,149	−3,566	−25,293
69. Increase { + } in foreign official assets in the U.S.	14,804	32,975	47,792	40,166	7,314

Source: *Survey of Current Business* (annual March issue) article entitled "U.S. International Transactions . . . ."

negative entries in a debit (inflow) column and positive entries in a credit (outflow) column. In more specific terms, consider the trade balance. Merchandise imports in line 16 appear as a debit entry, while merchandise exports in line 2 appear as a credit entry. Their sum was − $113,248 million in 1989 — a merchandise trade deficit (which also appears in the memoranda in line 64).

Actually, if lines 2–14 and 16–27 are placed side by side, the entire balance on goods and services has been reconstructed, with lines 1 and 14 as total exports and total imports (and line 65 as the balance itself). Notice that the balance on goods and services consistently shows a lower deficit value than the trade balance. This is because the United States continues to export more services than it imports, partially offsetting the large deficit in merchandise trade. At the beginning of the 1980s, income from U.S. companies' direct investments abroad (line 11) was enough to offset the trade deficit by itself. As the United States ran a larger and larger trade deficit during that decade, the government was forced to borrow increasingly from abroad. By 1989 U.S. government payments to foreign holders of Treasury bills and bonds and other securities (line 27) rose to almost $US34 billion, offsetting the income on U.S. direct investment abroad and requiring ever-increasing borrowing from abroad. Some implications of this situation are discussed in the next section.

In order to understand the main factors contributing to the U.S trade flows, a disaggregation of the accounts would be useful. The same annual article in the

Survey of Current Business presents trade flow data by broad industry categories and regions of the world. Looking at the 1989 balance of trade as shown in Table 8–4, it appears that the main sectors contributing to U.S. merchandise exports were capital goods other than autos ($130 billion), industrial supplies and materials ($98 billion), agricultural products ($41 billion), food products ($36 billion), and automobiles ($35 billion). Before drawing conclusions about the U.S. comparative advantage, imports must be considered too. The second half of the table shows that the largest categories of imports in 1989 were industrial supplies and materials ($134 billion), capital goods other than autos ($113 billion), nonfood consumer goods ($103 billion), autos ($86 billion), and petroleum ($50 billion).

Clearly there is a large overlap of categories that register both imports and exports. To some extent this is attributable to differences in the countries involved. The United States ships lots of autos and parts to Canada, but imports a much greater value in autos from Western Europe and Japan. (Trade in autos is approximately balanced with Canada, under the U.S.–Canada Automotive Agreement.) Similarly, the United States exports capital goods throughout the world, but registered a large deficit in this trade with Japan.

While a careful examination of the underlying reasons for the various flows, and a more detailed look at specific product categories, are beyond the present scope, it can be seen that the United States is clearly a net exporter of agricultural products as well as capital goods (such as electrical and nonelectrical machinery and aircraft). This occurs for two reasons. First, the United States simply produces a surplus quantity of agricultural products that other countries need. Second, the U.S. agricultural industry is technology- and capital-intensive relative to that of the rest of the world. It is likewise clear that the United States is a huge oil importer because of insufficient domestic supply, as well as a net importer of autos and industrial supplies and materials. Notice that the United States has a large trade deficit in each year shown, and that oil, auto, and consumer goods imports have contributed the largest portion of this deficit.

Returning to the summary BOP (Table 8–3) and moving down the column, we find unilateral transfers (gifts) in lines 29–32. In this case, all entries are *net* values—credits minus debits. Since only one column is being used, the total addition to or subtraction from each type of claim is recorded, netting total flows during the given year. Line 29 sums all nonmilitary gifts into and out of the United States for the year, showing a net debit value of $14,276 million for 1989. For most advanced industrial countries, in fact, unilateral transfers are a persistent net debit entry because of foreign aid and private gifts going abroad. Conversely, in many LDCs, with the exception of the OPEC countries, unilateral transfers persistently add up to a net credit entry. The "thank-you notes" pile up in the industrial countries, while the aid itself goes to LDCs. When unilateral transfers are added to trade in goods and services, we obtain the current account balance, which appears in line 67.

The U.S. presentation separates military aid from other gifts, recording the unilateral transfer in line 28 and simultaneously showing the equal value of the goods and services transferred in line 14 (i.e., as exports).

It is the U.S. capital accounts that are extremely different from our conceptual presentation. In the official presentation, assets in foreign countries that are

TABLE 8–4

U.S. Merchandise Trade by Major End-Use Category for Selected Areas and Countries (balance of payments basis, millions of dollars)

	Canada			Western Europe		
	1987	1988	1989*	1987	1988	1989*
Exports	**62,005**	**73,540**	**80,451**	**68,605**	**86,414**	**98,798**
Agricultural products	2,469	2,878	3,244	7,582	8,181	7,527
Nonagricultural products	59,536	70,662	77,207	61,023	78,233	91,271
Food, feeds, and beverages	2,010	2,361	2,801	5,992	6,325	5,816
Industrial supplies and materials	12,268	15,056	16,662	18,402	22,748	25,642
Capital goods, except automotive	14,324	18,232	21,152	30,872	39,734	45,489
Automotive vehicles, parts, and engines	20,554	22,572	23,190	1,705	2,467	3,029
Consumer goods (nonfood), except automotive	3,346	4,190	5,340	5,849	7,885	10,320
Imports	**73,599**	**84,400**	**88,960**	**96,127**	**102,200**	**102,443**
Petroleum and products	5,019	4,958	5,426	4,952	4,676	5,173
Nonpetroleum products	68,580	79,442	83,534	91,175	97,524	97,270
Foods, feeds, and beverages	3,526	3,726	4,066	5,908	5,771	5,691
Industrial supplies and materials	29,714	33,492	34,877	24,345	28,310	27,665
Capital goods, except automotive	7,766	8,927	11,422	26,043	29,848	31,714
Automotive vehicles, parts, and engines	24,531	29,199	29,498	17,466	14,647	13,125
Consumer goods (nonfood), except automotive	3,059	3,392	3,865	18,484	20,127	20,350

	Latin America and Other Western Hemisphere			Mexico		
	1987	1988	1989*	1987	1988	1989*
Exports	**34,971**	**43,624**	**48,748**	**14,558**	**20,573**	**24,676**
Agricultural products	3,725	4,987	5,436	1,218	2,262	2,772
Nonagricultural products	31,246	38,637	43,312	13,340	18,311	21,904
Food, feeds, and beverages	3,109	4,263	4,621	949	1,935	2,334
Industrial supplies and materials	11,182	13,166	14,853	4,420	5,781	6,996
Capital goods, except automotive	12,021	15,128	16,414	5,153	6,956	8,035
Automotive vehicles, parts, and engines	3,178	3,929	4,241	2,126	2,783	3,246
Consumer goods (nonfood), except automotive	2,924	3,909	5,083	850	1,543	2,236
Imports	**47,291**	**51,421**	**57,461**	**20,289**	**23,325**	**27,066**
Petroleum and products	12,832	11,073	14,298	3,872	3,310	4,303
Nonpetroleum products	34,459	40,348	43,163	16,417	20,015	22,763
Foods, feeds, and beverages	8,902	8,659	8,658	2,374	2,232	2,666
Industrial supplies and materials	20,209	20,178	23,247	6,305	6,522	7,525
Capital goods, except automotive	4,724	6,051	6,995	3,722	4,738	5,605
Automotive vehicles, parts, and engines	6,072	7,196	6,438	4,652	5,563	5,114
Consumer goods (nonfood), except automotive	6,341	8,050	10,572	2,529	3,346	5,034

*Preliminary.

Source: Survey of Current Business (March 1990).

brought or sold by U.S. residents are recorded in lines 38–46. This aggregation of all claims in the U.S BOP emphasizes the individuals and institutions that generate these flows, but it obscures the long-term/short-term dichotomy of the conceptual view. Foreigners' assets in the United States appear in lines 48–60 and are summed up in line 47.

TABLE 8–4

Continued

Germany, Federal Republic of			Japan			Australia		
1987	1988	1989*	1987	1988	1989*	1987	1988	1989*
11,533	**14,036**	**16,411**	**27,619**	**37,148**	**43,899**	**5,291**	**6,804**	**8,124**
1,308	1,271	1,026	5,731	7,650	8,202	128	161	158
10,225	12,765	15,385	21,888	29,498	35,697	5,163	6,643	7,966
910	781	604	5,672	8,062	8,501	122	155	155
2,617	3,260	3,497	10,281	12,986	15,529	1,321	1,659	1,994
5,709	6,895	8,815	7,288	10,039	11,370	2,572	3,335	4,038
418	698	748	363	779	1,046	248	343	468
869	1,083	1,344	2,555	3,285	4,893	427	567	800
26,941	**26,295**	**24,688**	**84,578**	**89,760**	**93,621**	**2,965**	**3,516**	**3,892**
46	60	66	104	64	76	354	339	225
26,895	26,235	24,622	84,474	89,696	93,545	2,611	3,177	3,667
580	521	495	465	406	349	965	1,097	958
4,218	4,857	4,988	7,987	8,496	8,573	1,438	1,851	2,174
8,368	9,228	9,122	27,723	32,803	36,935	156	203	267
10,931	8,591	6,949	33,690	32,788	33,741	47	54	63
2,321	2,450	2,415	13,940	14,245	12,983	154	150	196

OPEC (non-Latin America)			Asia (non-OPEC)			Hong Kong, Republic of Korea, Singapore, Taiwan			TOTAL
1987	1988	1989*	1987	1988	1989*	1987	1988	1989*	1989*
6,553	**8,546**	**9,405**	**37,919**	**53,025**	**59,982**	**22,760**	**33,944**	**37,770**	**361,872**
1,638	2,221	2,113	5,743	7,522	8,956	3,758	4,582	5,191	41,433
4,915	6,325	7,292	32,176	45,503	51,026	19,002	29,362	32,579	320,439
1,434	1,889	1,714	3,841	5,645	6,772	2,394	3,026	3,582	35,902
1,225	1,686	2,002	12,239	19,229	19,068	8,503	13,927	12,948	97,849
2,097	2,636	3,060	16,189	20,048	25,066	8,776	12,024	15,014	130,100
762	1,095	1,094	568	1,131	1,369	385	831	1,063	34,625
651	824	1,068	2,143	3,050	4,105	1,480	2,221	2,885	32,118
17,493	**16,609**	**22,290**	**79,703**	**90,740**	**97,729**	**57,545**	**63,191**	**62,756**	**475,120**
15,038	14,199	19,506	1,473	1,272	1,884	250	171	218	50,250
2,455	2,410	2,784	78,230	89,468	95,845	57,295	63,020	62,538	424,870
307	341	399	2,944	3,237	4,128	1,021	927	780	25,102
16,198	15,599	20,836	7,930	8,552	10,388	4,289	4,631	5,203	134,191
352	17	31	18,171	23,666	25,616	14,701	18,930	19,939	113,213
0	4	8	3,270	3,953	3,153	3,142	3,756	2,788	86,118
524	550	885	45,409	48,855	53,088	33,786	34,117	33,100	102,929

It is fairly easy to separate official reserves flows from the other capital accounts. Lines 35–37 list the three categories of official reserves, and line 34 shows the net change in reserves. These entries can be placed at the bottom of the table, after eliminating them from the summary line 33. Thus, in 1989, U.S. asset flows abroad were $125,707 million (i.e., an outflow of assets), but they were only $100,414 million when official reserves are segregated out. The official reserves gain (inflow) was − $25,293 million, which already appears in line 68.

Because the data collection process is so difficult, with literally billions of transactions among millions of entities to record each year, the U.S. BOP (or that of any other country) unquestionably lacks complete coverage. Some international transactions simply do not get recorded, and thus the total volume of transactions is understated. Also, because banks, exporters, and foreign investors, etc., report to different agencies and on different forms, the entities that *are* recorded may not balance overall. Thus, "statistical discrepancy," a special category to account for errors and omissions, is placed in line 62. As the ability to record more and more of the transactions that occur improves, the size of this entry should decline. Considering just the few most recent years, however, the discrepancy is often huge—$34,914 million in 1989 for example.

For additional discussion of the U.S. balance of payments format and specific entries, see *Survey of Current Business,* June 1978, part 2; and Maldonado (1980).

Implications of the U.S. Balance of Payments for International Firms

What do all of these transactions mean to business managers operating in the United States? First of all, the persistent and increasing balance of trade deficits during the 1980s portend increasing government policy restrictions on U.S. imports. These restrictions have included implicit quotas on Japanese auto imports (see Chapter 9 for details) and ever-increasing calls for protectionism to help reduce imports generally. Second, one would expect a tendency for the dollar to devalue relative to the currencies of the major trading partners with which the United States has bilateral deficits, such as Canada, Britain, Japan, and Germany. While protectionism grew somewhat during the period from 1980 to 1987, the value of the dollar shifted wildly from revaluation of about 40 percent in the early 1980s to devaluation of a similar magnitude by early 1987, leaving its value relative to the value of other industrial country currencies about the same in 1987 as it had been in 1980. This is only part of the story, however; capital flows must be considered along with trade flows to get a full understanding of the pressures on the exchange rate.

Initially, the U.S. merchandise trade deficit was financed largely by income on U.S assets abroad, such as remittances from foreign subsidiaries and interest on foreign loans. By 1983 even these flows had become inadequate to balance the excess of imports over exports, and by 1985 the negative balance on goods and services had jumped to over $100 billion per year. This situation would have presented a major crisis for any other country. The United States benefited from the fact that the U.S. dollar was and is the base currency for international business transactions and is viewed as a relatively stable store of value. Thus, the huge deficits have been financed by massive capital inflows—investments by foreign nationals who want to hold U.S securities or invest in U.S. businesses. As a result, by 1986 the United States had become a major net capital importer for the first time since the last century—and this situation continues today.

These circumstances have created major concern among U.S. policymakers, who realize that any important shift in investors' confidence away from the United States could trigger even greater dollar devaluation and serious economic recession. If incoming foreign direct and portfolio investments do not finance the trade deficit, then either official reserves must be used to make payment (i.e., to buy back dollars from foreign central banks) or expenditures on imports must be constrained (and/or exports must be subsidized) by policy to move closer to a balance. Continuing dollar devaluation is expected to improve the trade balance automatically, as exports become cheaper to foreign buyers and imports more expensive to U.S. buyers—but as of 1990 this adjustment has been wholly inadequate to equilibrate exports and imports. Let us consider the adjustment process in more detail.

THE ADJUSTMENT PROCESS

Balance of payments adjustment may occur through any sequence of events that leads from a situation of net positive or negative official reserve flows to a balance, in which no official reserves flow. Such adjustment takes a country from an initial deficit (or surplus) to equilibrium. The means for achieving BOP adjustment are numerous, ranging from trade and capital controls for restricting each of these accounts, to interest-rate policy aimed at influencing capital flows, to exchange-rate change, which affects all accounts. Tracing the intricacies of each policy or event and its impact on a country's internal and external balance goes far beyond the scope of the present text.[4] Let us consider, therefore, the simple adjustment process in the actual world of flexible exchange rates.

The **automatic adjustment mechanism** for a country that allows the value of its currency to fluctuate in the foreign exchange market is based on the exchange rate itself. When a country runs a balance of trade deficit, importing more than it exports, that country's currency will begin to accumulate in the hands of foreign exporters (or their banks). At some point, those foreign firms and banks will view their holdings of this currency as an excess and will begin to sell it off and bid its price down. As in any market under conditions of excess supply, the price of the product (namely, the currency) will fall to eliminate the excess. (This is exactly the same mechanism that was discussed in Chapter 6 as the adjustment process for the foreign exchange market.) When the price of the home currency falls, exports become cheaper to foreign purchasers and imports become more expensive to domestic consumers, leading to a tendency toward trade equilibrium as exports increase and imports decline.[5]

The automatic adjustment mechanism also responds to imbalances in the capital accounts; however, such interactions are substantially more complex. In the 1990s the capital accounts have greatly overshadowed the value of trade flows among the industrial countries, so it is all the more important to examine adjustment of capital flows to BOP imbalances. As noted earlier, interest arbitrageurs will operate to equate interest differentials and forward premiums (or discounts) among major convertible currencies. Since the forward exchange rate is a good estimator for the future spot rate between any two countries' currencies, we can see that any change in either country's interest rate or the spot exchange rate will have an impact on the forward rate (and hence the future spot rate). Now if for some reason our domestic interest rates rise, foreign arbitrageurs and investors will purchase our assets now and sign forward contracts to convert back to their own currencies in the future. The net result will be that the initial outflow of claims (i.e., ownership of home country assets) causes the spot exchange rate to revalue (home currency/foreign currency ↓) and the forward rate to devalue (home currency/foreign currency ↑). Foreign interest rates may also rise as other countries try to lure back investors. In addition, the initial inflow of investment may cause home country interest rates to fall as demand for home country assets rises. Initially, the home country will export additional financial claims, pushing the official reserves BOP toward surplus; once the exchange rate changes (and interest rates adjust), there will be a reserve flow of claims.

A clearer and no less important phenomenon relates to the long-term capital account. If home country investors and banks invest/lend more abroad than foreigners lend to the home country, we will face a deficit on long-term capital. Other things equal, this will lead to a devaluation of the home currency, because there is an excess demand for foreign exchange to buy foreign long-term assets. The devaluation will make foreign assets more expensive, thus enticing both foreign and home country investors to buy home country assets. The final tendency is toward equilibrium in capital flows, with the final exchange rate being an equilibrium rate.

All of the above description of the adjustment process is intended to demonstrate the *automatic* steps that would occur without government intervention. Once a deficit or surplus occurs, the government may impose controls on various BOP accounts—or it may "finance" the deficit by borrowing from foreign banks and other foreign lenders. For example, when copper prices fall and Chile faces a BOP deficit on the current account, Chile's government may borrow from the IMF or from a private bank. By borrowing foreign currency in exchange for a loan commitment, Chile obtains an inflow of official reserves (the foreign exchange) that may exactly offset the outflow needed to pay for the trade deficit. Chile's BOP returns to equilibrium, with the commitment to repay the loan eventually (and lose official reserves in the future).

Chile could avoid the need for future repayment of the loan by aiming instead to control specific balance of payments accounts. For example, Chile could place restrictions on imports and offer incentives to exports, thus pushing the trade balance in a favorable direction. Similarly, Chile could offer incentives to foreign direct investment, in this case improving the long-term capital account and leading toward a basic balance surplus. These policies can be used separately or together by a country to avoid letting the automatic adjustment mechanism function, with the problem that ending the policies may lead to the automatic adjustment anyway. At any given time, however, a country may prefer to utilize these policies rather than accept a currency devaluation or a need to borrow more from international lenders.

Even from this brief view, it can be seen that BOP adjustment may be a very complex process—though one that has important implications for a company or bank dealing with any given country. The main concern of this chapter has been to sketch the components and determinants of the BOP itself, not to investigate the adjustment process in detail. The conclusions then relate to the *pressures* on a country to adjust—which may be alleviated by automatic adjustment or by government policies on foreign exchange, trade, and investment (or by both).

EVALUATING THE BALANCE OF PAYMENTS

How can one interpret a deficit (or surplus) on any given balance of payments? That is, what should one expect, in terms of exchange-rate changes or government policies, when a particular balance of payments is not balanced?

Consider the situation of the United Kingdom during the past two decades, as presented in Table 8–5. The United Kingdom ran a fairly persistent trade deficit during this time (line 77ac*d*), with surpluses only during the global recession of 1980–82. This deficit was frequently compensated for by exports of services (such as interest on foreign loans), which resulted in current account surpluses except in the early 1970s and late 1980s.

As a result of the current account balance of payments, a fairly stable British pound would be expected. Line ag in the table shows that the dollar/pound exchange rate declined (the pound devalued) steadily until the discovery of large North Sea oil deposits in U.K. territory in 1976, after which the pound moved up in value until the global recession beginning in 1980. During the 1980s the pound generally devalued for the first half of the decade and revalued during the second half, finishing at $US1.81 per pound at yearend 1988. There appears to be a rather weak relationship between trade flows and the exchange rate in this situation—which has been true for the largest industrial countries for most of the period since the change from fixed to floating exchange rates in 1971–73.

Looking further down in the balance of payments, capital flows can be seen to play an important role in the overall picture. Since only net flows are shown here, it is not obvious that the inflows and outflows of both short-term and long-term investments are much greater than the value of export and import trade. Given that the euromarkets are centered in London, the huge value of euromarket activity discussed in Chapter 7 indicates this point more clearly. The capital-flow picture itself is fairly mixed over the period, with generally large net long-term capital inflows (increased ownership of British direct and portfolio investment abroad) and mostly short-term outflows. In fact, the official reserves balance is needed to draw some conclusions.

The official reserves BOP demonstrates a much closer link to the exchange-rate changes than previous balances. Line 79c.*d* lists official reserve inflows (with a − sign) and outflows (+). In almost every year that official reserves increase, e.g., up to 1975 and after 1984, the pound increases in value. In almost every year that official reserves decline, e.g., the first half of the 1980s, the pound declines as well. This outcome is broadly in line with balance-of-payments economics as outlined earlier in the chapter.

It should be recognized that the industrial (OECD) countries tend to be the ones whose economic conditions are reflected in the BOP most directly, since these countries impose few barriers to trade and investment. The United Kingdom, for example, despite the swings in trade and investment flows, only proceeded to open its economy even further during the past two decades, regardless of "problems" in the BOP.

Less developed countries, with typically much smaller amounts of capital flows relative to trade flows, tend to have a greater correspondence between the trade balance and the exchange rate—but their governments also intervene much more in the foreign exchange market and in import and export trade. In Latin America, for example, most countries have intervened to push their exchange rates (relative to the U.S. dollar) toward maintaining purchasing power parity between domestic and U.S. goods. The balance of payments indicates pressures for exchange-rate change and for government policy intervention, but there are many additional factors that determine whether or not the anticipated results actually take place.

TABLE 8–5

The U.K. Balance of Payments Position (1970–1988)

	1970	1971	1972	1973	1974	1975	1976	1977	1978	1979	1980
SDRs per Pound: End of Period (ac) Period Average (rd)											
	2.3937	2.3510	2.1627	1.9258	1.9182	1.7285	1.4653	1.5691	1.5616	1.6883	1.8700
	2.4000	2.4272	2.3043	2.0570	1.9449	1.8299	1.5645	1.4951	1.5331	1.6421	1.7873
US Dollars per Pound: End of Period (ag and dg) Period Average (ah and rh)											
	2.3937	2.5525	2.3481	2.3232	2.3485	2.0235	1.7024	1.9060	2.0345	2.2240	2.3850
	2.3960	2.4441	2.5018	2.4522	2.3390	2.2218	1.8062	1.7455	1.9195	2.1216	2.3263
	2.4000	2.6057	2.6057	2.3232	2.3485	2.0235	1.7024	1.9060	2.0345	2.2240	2.3850
	2.4000	2.4344	2.5018	2.4522	2.3390	2.2218	1.8062	1.7455	1.9195	2.1216	2.3263
	37.37	43.63	64.90	112.25	186.50	140.25	134.75	164.95	226.00	512.00	589.50
Millions of Pounds											
	8,096	9,070	9,602	12,087	16,309	19,607	25,277	31,990	35,380	40,637	47,365
	9,113	9,799	11,073	15,723	23,139	24,046	31,084	36,219	39,533	46,925	49,773
	925	1,185	1,166	1,678	4,537	4,167	5,486	5,030	4,454	5,136	5,880
	687	930	914	1,296	3,725	3,369	4,445	3,966	3,528	3,671	4,180
	8,142	8,820	10,154	14,448	21,513	22,440	29,041	34,006	36,574	43,868	45,794
1985 = 100											
	53.6	57.4	58.1	65.6	69.1	67.5	73.4	79.5	81.7	84.8	85.5
	56.3	58.4	64.2	73.0	73.2	66.9	71.3	72.6	77.4	84.0	80.7
	18.0	19.1	20.2	22.8	29.0	35.6	42.6	50.4	55.2	61.2	69.9
	17.7	18.6	19.4	24.7	35.7	40.6	49.6	57.3	58.9	62.8	69.3
Millions of US Dollars: Minus Sign Indicates Debit											
	1,985	2,719	508	−2,419	−7,481	−3,417	−1,683	−209	1,858	−875	7,520
	19,507	21,994	23,510	29,106	38,105	42,475	45,033	55,317	67,121	86,018	109,615
	−19,512	−21,462	−25,364	−35,359	−50,345	−49,747	−52,103	−59,323	−70,185	−93,105	−106,272
	−5	533	−1,854	−6,253	−12,239	−7,272	−7,070	−4,006	−3,064	−7,087	3,343
	11,695	13,200	19,008	24,774	29,956	31,530	33,037	35,693	45,483	67,999	91,848
	−9,266	−10,533	−15,965	−19,848	−24,209	−26,617	−26,219	−29,927	−37,115	−57,109	−83,078
	−31	−3	−129	−244	−280	−307	−29	−81	−244	−413	−473
	−408	−477	−552	−849	−709	−751	−1,403	−1,888	−3,202	−4,265	−4,121
	−190	−217	−809	−2,259	−2	318	−1,332	253	−3,028	−6,070	−1,104
	−118	581	−786	1,620	2,444	−137	877	2,492	−2,404	271	−6,636
	−758	−1,079	−671	−155	−942	−1,435	−1,325	524	−787	−1,381	−1,400
	919	2,005	−1,759	−3,213	−5,982	−4,671	−3,462	3,061	−4,360	−8,054	−1,620
	1,886	1,186	2,128	767	−1,354	2,642	−1,918	2,066	−1,769	−12,558	−184
	−171	652	−1,902	319	358	−41	1,045	7,004	3,737	1,984	1,115
	2,635	3,843	−1,532	−2,127	−6,978	−2,070	−4,335	12,130	−2,392	−18,628	−689
	−	−	−	−	−	−	−	−	−	−	−
	410	300	322	−	−	−	−	−	−	393	402
	−8	2,050	−2,306	149	196	−22	191	26	113	222	699
	3,037	6,193	−3,516	−1,978	−6,782	−2,092	−4,144	12,157	−2,279	−18,013	412
	−	197	−	2,479	4,113	1,946	3,402	1,999	233	888	−749
	−2,333	764	853	225	3,122	−1,294	−2,455	674	−198	20,770	1,989
	−704	−7,153	2,663	−726	−452	1,440	3,197	−14,830	2,244	−3,645	−1,652
Billions of Pounds											
	11.51	12.92	13.62	17.07	22.87	26.86	35.10	43.31	47.48	54.90	62.93
	9.04	10.31	11.75	13.40	16.72	23.12	27.04	29.47	33.41	38.89	49.02
	9.74	10.89	11.94	14.73	17.50	21.04	24.50	27.04	31.06	36.93	41.56
	.38	.11	.03	1.53	1.05	−1.35	.90	1.82	1.80	2.16	−2.57
	32.03	35.88	40.55	46.15	53.20	65.47	75.98	86.89	100.22	118.65	137.90
	−11.11	−12.16	−13.74	−18.95	−27.16	−28.78	−36.82	−42.59	−45.53	−54.40	−57.62
	51.59	57.95	64.14	73.92	84.17	106.35	126.71	145.93	168.44	197.14	231.21
	.60	.55	.59	1.33	1.51	.89	1.56	.27	.81	1.21	−.20
	52.19	58.50	64.73	75.25	85.68	107.24	128.27	146.19	169.24	198.34	231.01
	265.06	271.93	278.03	300.67	297.30	295.36	306.32	309.46	321.73	328.93	322.54
	19.5	21.3	23.1	24.6	28.3	36.0	41.4	47.2	52.4	59.9	71.7
Millions: Mid-Year Estimates											
	55.42	55.61	55.78	55.91	55.92	55.90	55.89	55.85	55.84	55.88	55.95

Source: IMF, *International Financial Statistics Yearbook, 1989*, Washington, D.C.: IMF, 1989, pp. 718, 719.

TABLE 8–5

Continued

1981	1982	1983	1984	1985	1986	1987	1988		
								Exchange Rates: Preference indicated	
1.6392	1.4636	1.3855	1.1798	1.3151	1.2055	1.3192	1.3447	Market Rate/Par or Central Rate	ac
1.7198	1.5856	1.4191	1.3037	1.2767	1.2505	1.2675	i.3255	Par Rate/Market Rate	rd
1.9080	1.6145	1.4506	1.1565	1.4445	1.4745	1.8715	1.8095	Market Rate/Par or Central Rate	ag
2.0279	1.7505	1.5170	1.3363	1.2963	1.4670	1.6389	1.7814	Market Rate/Par or Central Rate	ah
1.9080	1.6145	1.4506	1.1565	1.4445	1.4745	1.8715	1.8095	Par or Central Rate/Market Rate	dg
2.0279	1.7505	1.5170	1.3363	1.2963	1.4670	1.6389	1.7814	Par Rate/Market Rate	rh
397.50	456.90	381.50	308.30	327.00	390.90	484.10	410.25	London Gold Price (US $ per ounce)	c
								International Transactions	
50,700	55,558	60,590	70,373	78,263	72,812	79,849	81,476	Exports	70
51,170	56,978	65,993	78,967	84,790	86,067	94,026	106,413	Imports, cif	71
6,136	6,088	6,213	7,226	8,057	....	....	....	Petroleum	71a
4,112	3,873	3,818	3,715	4,235	....	....	....	Crude Petroleum	71aa
47,318	53,112	61,773	74,843	80,334	81,356	89,594	100,714	Imports, fob(on a b.o.p. basis)	71.v
84.5	86.9	87.2	95.0	100.0	103.0	109.0	110.0	Volume of Exports	72
77.6	80.8	87.2	97.0	100.0	107.0	114.0	129.0	Volume of Imports	73
76.1	81.5	88.1	95.0	100.0	92.0	96.0	97.0	Unit Value of Exports	74
74.8	80.8	87.8	96.0	100.0	96.0	98.0	98.0	Unit Value of Imports	75
								Balance of Payments	
14,500	8,041	5,831	2,608	4,765	158	−4,913	−26,089	Current Account, nie	77a.d
102,160	96,660	91,960	93,484	100,858	106,472	130,285	142,745	Merchandise: Exports fob	77aad
−95,005	−92,950	−93,636	−99,593	−103,511	−119,272	−147,008	−179,259	Merchandise: Imports fob	77abd
7,155	3,710	−1,676	−6,109	−2,653	−12,801	−16,723	−36,514	Trade Bal., 77aad+77abd	77acd
109,048	108,479	94,472	98,005	99,456	107,962	125,471	147,324	Other Goods, Serv.&Income: Cre	77add
−98,624	−101,130	−84,524	−86,923	−88,208	−91,858	−108,028	−130,448	Other Goods,Serv.&Income: Deb	77aed
115	82	500	510	415	143	−273	−556	Private Unrequited Transfers	77afd
−3,194	−3,100	−2,940	−2,875	−4,244	−3,287	−5,359	−5,894	Official Unrequited Trans., nie	77agd
−6,274	−1,750	−3,005	−8,276	−6,470	−9,390	−17,279	−13,949	Direct Investment	77bad
−9,120	−12,431	−8,487	−11,265	−18,301	−27,846	17,241	−13,424	Portfolio Investment, nie	77bbd
−2,365	−2,206	−4,519	−3,387	1,208	5,355	1,031	2,813	Other Long-Term Capital, nie	77bcd
−3,259	−8,345	−10,180	−20,320	−18,798	−31,723	−3,919	−50,649	Total, lines 77a.d+77bad−77bcd	77c.d
2,395	17,630	7,379	496	6,557	15,002	−22,736	29,321	Other Short-Term Capital, nie	77d.d
1,271	−4,133	684	7,484	6,929	20,086	20,209	27,128	Net Errors and Omissions	77e.d
407	5,153	−2,117	−12,339	−5,311	3,365	−6,447	5,800	Total, lines 77c.d−77e.d	77f.d
−	−	−	−	−	−	−	−	C'part to Mon./Demon. of Gold	78a.d
378								Counterpart to SDR Allocation	78b.d
−622	−414	−145	−591	2,868	4,124	3,107	−2,498	C'part to Valuation Changes	78c.d
163	4,738	−2,262	−12,930	−2,443	7,490	−3,340	3,302	Total, lines 77f.d−78c.d	78d.d
−1,135	521	910	1,608	2,186	2,760	1,153	−143	Exceptional Financing	79a.d
−4,002	−7,803	353	9,429	3,676	−4,695	25,481	−772	Liab.Const.Fgn. Author. Reserves	79b.d
4,974	2,544	999	1,893	−3,419	−5,555	−23,293	−2,387	Total Change in Reserves	79c.d
								National Accounts	
67.69	73.02	80.54	92.35	102.78	98.48	107.24	107.65	Exports	90c.c
55.46	60.45	65.87	69.87	73.96	79.61	85.55	91.67	Government Consumption	91f.c
41.30	44.82	48.62	55.03	60.28	64.24	73.11	86.53	Gross Fixed Capital Formation	93e.c
−2.77	−1.19	1.47	1.27	.57	.70	1.04	2.36	Increase in Stocks	93i.c
153.57	168.55	184.62	197.49	215.54	237.64	259.97	290.71	Private Consumption	96f.c
−60.42	−68.04	−77.90	−92.99	−99.17	−101.54	−112.08	−124.78	Less: Imports	98c.c
254.83	277.61	303.22	323.02	353.96	378.85	414.18	453.28	Gross Domestic Product	99b.c
1.21	1.45	2.85	4.43	2.80	5.08	5.39	5.77	Net Factor Income from Abroad	90e.c
256.04	279.05	306.07	327.46	356.76	383.93	419.57	459.05	Gross Nat'l Expenditure = GNP	99a.c
318.86	322.88	335.36	341.31	353.96	366.21	381.97	391.99	Gross Dom. Prod. 1985 Prices	99b.r
79.9	86.0	90.4	94.6	100.0	103.5	108.4	115.6	GDP Deflator (1985=100)	99bir
56.35	56.34	56.38	56.49	56.62	56.76	56.93	57.08	**Population**	99z

225

CONCLUSIONS

The balance of payments is a very complex subject for nonspecialists. Managers should understand BOP accounting, so that they can use BOP data in company strategy formulation. Generally speaking, BOP data for several years are needed in order to draw useful conclusions. Because automatic adjustment to BOP imbalances is limited by governments, no simple management decision rules can be derived from BOP data alone. Also, because governments intervene in different ways and at different times to alter exchange rates and exchange policies, BOP analysis can only enable a company manager to understand the key influences involved—the timing of government policies remains fairly unpredictable. Understanding these influences can help the manager to create a business plan that minimizes the risks associated with likely BOP conditions in a given country.

Balance of payments accounting is similar to financial accounting for a company, especially to the financial statement called "statement of net change in financial position." It is a flow concept, measured over a period of time. It includes all transactions between residents of a country and residents of all foreign countries during a given period.

There is no such thing as *the* balance of payments. The debits and credits in the total set of entries in a BOP account must add up to the same amount. If only certain entries are included, the BOP may not balance—for example, if the BOP is confined to exports and imports of merchandise, the trade balance. The official reserves balance is the final balance in a BOP account, and even it may not provide a clear picture of a country's position. Borrowing of official reserves that must be paid back later adds to the official reserves balance surplus, and the country may use such a loan to try to hide its BOP problems.

BALANCE OF PAYMENTS PROBLEMS

Instructions:

1. Make the proper entries for the following transactions on the accompanying worksheet.
2. Calculate the current account balance of payments surplus or deficit.
   ROW = Rest of the world. You may assume that all values are in thousands of U.S. dollars, if you wish.

1. Residents of the United States exported $5,000 of merchandise to residents of ROW, who paid by drawing on their accounts with the Chase Manhattan Bank.
2. U.S. tourists spent $120 for goods and services while traveling in ROW. They paid in ROW currency, which they obtained by cashing American Express traveler's checks at ROW banks.
3. Diplomatic missions of foreign governments spent $150 in the United States, drawing on their deposits in U.S. banks.
4. The U.S. government made cash grants of $1,000 in economic aid to less developed countries. The governments of these countries utilized $300 of the grants to buy machinery in the United States. They held the remainder on deposit in a U.S. bank.
5. Residents of the United States imported $7,200 of merchandise from ROW residents, of which $4,000 was paid by drafts drawn on deposits of U.S. banks

in ROW banks and $3,200 was paid through an increase in the deposits of ROW banks in U.S. banks.

6. The ROW central bank bought $200 of gold from the U.S. government, paying for it by check drawn on its deposit with the Federal Reserve Bank of New York.

7. U.S. ships carried goods for ROW merchants. The shipping charges of $300 were paid through a draft drawn on the ROW merchants. (ROW merchants paid their bank, the ROW bank increased the deposits of U.S. banks, and U.S. banks paid the shipping companies.)

8. Private citizens in the United States received merchandise gifts from foreigners valued at $60.

9. U.S. residents bought $400 of bonds issued by a Japanese utility and paid for the bonds with checks drawn on their accounts in U.S. banks. The Japanese utility held the proceeds in U.S. banks.

10. U.S. residents sent $250 of U.S. currency through the mail as gifts to persons in ROW.

11. The U.S. government donated $1,000 of surplus wheat to needy countries in ROW.

12. A U.S. multinational firm set up a factory in ROW, sending $5,000 in cash and $10,000 in machinery to the ROW location.

13. Bank of America made a $7,500 loan, payable in one year, to an ROW businessman (who had a deposit of $2,500 at Bank of America).

14. The U.S. Fed floated a $100,000 bond, denominated in SDRs and payable in two years. The bond was purchased by the ROW central bank and paid for in SDRs.

Worksheet

	Debit	Credit
A. Goods and services		
1. Merchandise		
2. Transportation		
3. Travel		
4. Miscellaneous, government		
B. Unilateral transfers		
1. Private		
2. Government		
C. Long-term capital		
1. Foreign direct investment		
2. Private portfolio investment		
3. Government investment		
D. Short-term capital		
1. Private		
2. Government		
E. Official reserves		
1. SDRs		
2. Foreign exchange		
3. Position in the IMF		
4. Gold		

QUESTIONS

1. What, exactly, is measured in a balance of payments? In a double-entry BOP accounting system, how can the accounts fail to balance?

2. Explain how the trade account in a country's BOP may be related to the short-term capital account.

3. Of what importance is the BOP of a host country (such as Great Britain in the text example) to the MNE manager? Of what importance is the home country's BOP?

4. How can a country's balance of trade be in a deficit while its current account is in a surplus?

5. Explain why the balance of payments is organized into trade, gifts, long-term capital, short-term capital, and official reserve accounts. Why is it useful to draw these distinctions?

6. As a company manager in Great Britain in 1983, when oil prices have fallen 25 percent compared to 1981 prices, what would you expect the trade balance to show? What government policies would you expect? What automatic adjustment would you expect to occur, other things being equal?

7. If interest rates are higher in the United States than in Japan, what would you expect the capital accounts to show? (*Note:* What if the interest rates in both countries have not changed from last year?) Does the exchange rate make any difference?

8. What impact does the IMF have on balances of payments when it creates new SDRs and distributes them to member countries? (The Chapter 7 discussion of SDRs may help you in answering this question. SDRs are the liabilities of the IMF itself, and they are reserve assets to the countries that receive them.)

9. Looking at the U.S. BOP in Tables 8–3 and 8–4, what automatic adjustments and policy changes do you anticipate for the next year?

10. How can a country such as Brazil finance its foreign debt, which was about $100 billion in 1991? Specifically, use balance of payments categories to show what kinds of transactions would generate foreign currency for Brazil.

REFERENCES

International Monetary Fund. *Balance of Payments Manual.* 4th ed. Washington, D.C.: IMF, 1977.

Maldonado, Rita. "Recording and Classifying Transactions in the Balance of Payments." *International Journal of Accounting,* 1980.

Stern, Robert. *The Balance of Payments.* Chicago: Aldine Publishing Co., 1973.

"U.S. International Transactions." *Survey of Current Business,* various issues.

NOTES

[1] A "resident" for balance of payments purposes is generally defined as an entity or person residing in the country for one year or more.

[2] This valuation scheme then leads to a summary BOP that includes home-currency values of transactions from different dates, when exchange rates may have been different. Because the BOP is a flow measure, no end-of-period adjustment is made for asset/liability valuation changes.

[3]The distinction between stock ownership as portfolio investment and stock ownership as direct investment is not easy to draw. The U.S. Department of Commerce defines FDI as 10 percent or more ownership of a firm (see Chapter 4) for most purposes. Other governments often use 25 percent ownership as the dividing line.

[4]The various views of BOP adjustment are presented very clearly in Stern (1973).

[5]This result will occur only if the devaluation causes export quantity to rise enough so that export *value* (price × quantity) increases, and vice versa for imports. The mathematical condition that underlies this reasoning is the Marshall-Lerner condition.

The Debt Equity Swap—American Express Bank in Mexico

Introduction

During the entire decade of the 1980s, borrowers in Latin American countries faced a continuing crisis of debt servicing to foreign creditors. Conversely, the foreign lenders saw their Latin American loans shift from fairly ordinary risks to nonperforming, rescheduled, and otherwise impaired assets. The Latin American countries encountered major difficulties in obtaining sufficient foreign currency (mainly U.S. dollars) to meet their needs for interest and principal payments to foreign banks and other lenders, in addition to suffering through the global recession of 1981–83. While the problem originated with government-sector borrowers, nonetheless by 1982 it had spread to creditworthy private-sector borrowers as well, since they were unable to obtain foreign exchange except at staggering cost and often with substantial delay.[1]

The fundamental reason for the crisis throughout Latin America is the period of overborrowing from foreign lenders during the 1970s, immediately after both oil shocks (1973–74 and 1979–80). The OPEC cartel's successful effort to raise oil prices caused a massive transfer of purchasing power to the oil-exporting countries. They in turn spent some of the new income on increased imports, and invested most of the rest in the international banking system. The commercial banks were left with huge amounts of new deposits (although most of the money was just taken from accounts of industrial-country depositors and moved to accounts of OPEC depositors), but, more importantly, a need to lend them out. Because the oil crisis caused large transfers of purchasing power from industrial, oil-importing countries, those nations experienced economic downturns in the aftermath. The recessionary conditions (especially in 1975–76 and 1981–82) meant that the banks encountered a reduced demand for borrowing among their traditional clients and a need to seek out new ones. In addition to new clients in the industrial world and in the communist countries, the banks extended much more credit to less developed country borrowers, especially in Latin America. International indebtedness increased by over 20 percent per year in all four of the largest countries in the region (viz., Argentina, Brazil, Mexico, and Venezuela) during 1973–82, while national income and exports grew by less than half that rate.

This case was written by Prof. Robert Grosse as a basis for group discussion. The detailed information provided by American Express Bank, Ltd. is gratefully acknowledged. Any errors of fact or interpretation are the responsibility of the author. The continued help of Mr. Jose Muzaurieta is gratefully acknowledged. Revised April 1989.

During the time since the Latin American debt crisis "officially" began with the declaration of Mexico's government that it could not meet foreign debt payments on August 20, 1982, dozens of government policies and corporate strategies have been suggested and tried as solutions to the problem. One of the most successful of these ideas is the debt/equity swap—that is, the exchange of an existing, typically value-impaired bank loan for an equity investment in the borrower country. This case explores the structure and functioning of such a swap in Mexico that involves the central participation of American Express Bank.

A Debt/Equity Swap	The basic concept of a debt/equity swap is to transform a problem loan into another form of credit to the borrowing country, namely, an equity investment. Typically, the loan is a problem because the debtor fails to make the interest and principal payments on time, often because of unavailability of the foreign currency in which payment must be made. This situation, in turn, occurs due to balance of payments problems in the given country.[2] The debt/equity swap then calls for exchange of foreign loans for equity investments in local businesses. This type of transaction bolsters capital investment in the local economy and does not lead directly to severe pressures to exchange the local currency for dollars.

The debt/equity swap involves at least four key parties in the total group of transactions. First, there is a foreign bank that wants to dispose of a loan to the government or a private-sector borrower in the country in question. Second, there is another foreign firm that wants to invest in a capital project in that same country. Third, there is the monetary authority (and perhaps other government agencies) of the given country that must agree to permit exchange of the loan contract for local currency that will be used in the investment. Finally, there is an investment banking intermediary that looks for buyers and sellers of the loans and negotiates with the monetary authorities for permissions that are required. A simple debt/equity swap is depicted in Figure 1, which also shows the specific process involved in the American Express project.

Since the loan is nonperforming or otherwise impaired in its servicing, the originating bank may be willing to sell it at a discount just to dispose of it. As shown in Table 1, the discounts at which foreign commercial banks have been willing to sell their Latin American loans have grown to over 50 percent for most countries in the region. Typically, the potential loan seller is contacted by an intermediary, such as an investment banking firm, that is seeking sources of funds for clients who want to invest in Latin American countries, and vice versa. The most active brokers in these swaps have been NMB Bank (of the Netherlands), Morgan Guaranty, Shearson Lehman Hutton, Bankers Trust, and Merrill Lynch. These intermediaries seek out both loan sellers and buyers, trying to profit by putting them together and arranging the deals.

Once a loan seller and buyer have been found, the intermediary must negotiate with the Latin American government involved to obtain whatever permissions may be necessary to redeem the dollar loan for some value in local currency. The value received by the loan buyer typically is some percentage below the direct face value of the loan translated from dollars into local currency. This amount is still substantially higher than the dollar value that the buyer paid to obtain the loan. Once permissions have been arranged, the loan

FIGURE 1

A Swap of Sovereign Debt for Equity in a New Capital Project

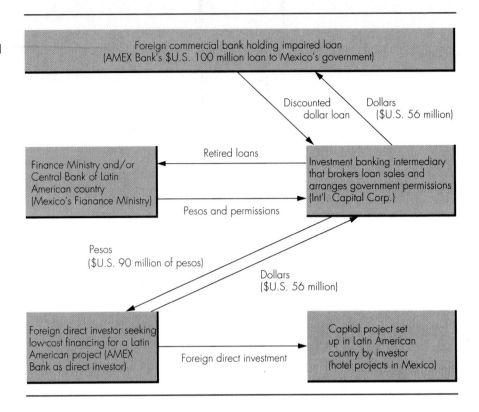

TABLE 1

Prices of Latin American Loans

	Loan Sale Price Relative to Face Value (in percent)				
Country	July 1985	July 1986	July 1987	July 1988	May 1989
Argentina	60–65%	63–57%	46–49%	24–26%	15–16%
Brazil	75–81%	73–76%	58–61%	51–52%	36–37%
Chile	65–69%	64–67%	68–70%	60–61%	58–60%
Colombia	81–83%	80–82%	81–83%	65–67%	55–58%
Ecuador	65–70%	63–66%	45–47%	25–27%	10–12%
Mexico	80–82%	56–59%	55–57%	51–52%	41–42%
Peru	45–50%	18–23%	10–12%	05–06%	04–06%
Venezuela	81–83%	75–78%	70–72%	54–55%	37–38%

Source: Shearson Lehman Brothers International, Inc.

buyer takes the local currency, e.g., pesos, and invests them in a capital project that was proposed in the permission request to the government in that country.

This transaction is viewed favorably by each of the participants. First, the original lending bank is able to sell its problem loan, taking the discount as a real loss in value of the original loan as the price of this sale. (The bank usually is able to lower its tax liability as a result of the loan loss, so all of the discount is not really "lost".) The new investor is able to obtain local currency at a substantial discount relative to ordinary financing costs. The host government is able to eliminate some of its foreign dollar debt and related servicing problems by replacing it with new direct investment. And finally, the investment bank earns fees by bringing the various parties together.

The debt/equity swap should still be seen as an imperfect solution by the original lender and the borrowing country. The original lender takes a real loss on its loan rather than continue to hope for improved loan servicing in the future. The borrowing country eliminates a foreign debt that was not being serviced as contracted, but the country replaces this obligation with an increase in foreign equity investment, which itself implies costs (e.g., dividend remittances and other funds flows from subsidiary to parent).

The Mexican Government's View of $US100 Billion of Foreign Debt

The Mexican government had participated actively in the exorbitant expansion of foreign indebtedness during the 1970s. Although not an OPEC member, Mexico nonetheless is a major oil exporter. When extensive new petroleum reserves were discovered in 1976, foreign lenders flocked to Mexico City to extend new credit to the government and other borrowers. (The national oil company, PEMEX, controls all petroleum producing and refining in the country. PEMEX is one of the most important international borrowers in Mexico.) As shown in Table 2, Mexico's foreign debt skyrocketed to over $U.S.100 billion by 1986, growing at an annual rate of about 29 percent during the 1973–81 period.

Most of the growth in foreign credit to Mexican borrowers during this period went to the government sector, and much of it was invested in projects that did not lead to generation of dollars for repayment. The foreign lenders did not have a full grasp of the extent of credit being extended, since no formal information channels existed for aggregating total dollar loans to public or private Mexican borrowers. By 1982 the Mexican government found that it could not meet interest obligations on its part of the total foreign debt, since insufficient dollars were available at the Central Bank. The first step taken, in August of that year, was to declare a moratorium on debt servicing. Subsequently, the government has repeatedly renegotiated maturities, interest rates, fees, and other loan conditions with its foreign creditors. No single solution has appeared to limit the process of renegotiations, but a number of suggestions were made by the Mexican government.

One proposal was to convert some of the loans into long-term obligations such as bonds. As a result of negotiations with the U.S. Treasury and Morgan Guaranty Bank, in 1988 Mexico was able to issue about 1.1 billion dollars of 20-year, zero-coupon bonds backed by the U.S. Treasury in exchange for $3.7 billion of existing (discounted) loans.[3] Another proposal was to reduce debt-servicing payments and/or the debt itself via renegotiations of the loan terms. This proposal was used in the Brady Plan begun by the U.S. government in 1989, and it has led to both loan principal reductions and lower interest rates on the outstanding debt. A third proposal was to convert some of the debt into capital investment in Mexico. This proposal has resulted in a formal program of debt/equity conversion, which was used in the present case.

The program began haltingly in 1986 with a small number of transactions, including the American Express agreement discussed below. Despite the uncertainties involved, over $US2 billion of swaps were authorized in the first two years of the program.

TABLE 2

Indicators of Mexico's International Financial Position

	1970	1971	1972	1973	1974	1975	1976	1977	1978	1979	1980
Pesos per SDR: End of Period (aa) Period Average (rb)											
	12.5	13.6	13.6	15.1	15.3	14.6	23.2	27.6	29.6	30.0	29.7
	12.5	12.5	13.6	14.9	15.0	15.2	17.8	26.4	28.5	29.5	29.9
Pesos per US Dollar: End of Period (ae) Period Average (af and rf)											
	12.5	12.5	12.5	12.5	12.5	12.5	20.0	22.7	22.7	22.8	23.3
	12.5	12.5	12.5	12.5	12.5	12.5	15.4	22.6	22.8	22.8	23.0
	12.5	12.5	12.5	12.5	12.5	12.5	15.4	22.6	22.8	22.8	23.0
Billions of Pesos											
	17.5	18.8	21.2	28.3	37.3	36.3	53.5	102.0	135.6	204.9	357.5
	.5	.4	.3	.3	1.5	5.8	8.4	23.2	41.4	89.3	225.7
	—	—	—	—	.5	5.4	8.4	22.3	40.7	86.4	214.4
	1.1	1.0	1.1	2.0	1.9	2.3	5.2	10.3	8.8	12.4	10.2
	....	....	....	....	....	....	2.5	4.2	3.4	8.2	8.0
	30.8	30.1	34.0	47.7	75.7	82.1	90.9	133.0	184.2	275.6	447.0
	29.3	28.7	32.4	45.4	72.1	78.3	86.4	117.8	175.5	262.5	425.7
Millions of US Dollars: Minus Sign Indicates Debit											
	-1,068	-835	-916	-1,415	-2,876	-4,042	-3,409	-1,854	-3,171	-5,459	-10,750
	1,348	1,409	1,717	2,141	2,999	3,007	3,475	4,604	6,246	9,301	15,511
	-2,236	-2,158	-2,610	-3,656	-5,791	-6,278	-5,771	-5,625	-7,992	-12,131	-18,896
	-888	-749	-894	-1,515	-2,791	-3,272	-2,295	-1,021	-1,745	-2,830	-3,385
	1,587	1,762	2,100	2,699	3,369	3,352	3,728	3,608	5,178	6,702	6,483
	-1,822	-1,906	-2,187	-2,673	-3,574	-4,263	-4,996	-4,610	-6,797	-9,556	-14,132
	25	26	25	41	57	59	73	88	104	131	245
	30	31	39	33	65	81	83	82	88	94	39
	323	307	301	457	678	609	628	556	824	1,332	2,156
	-19	23	50	64	-82	156	430	1,345	737	-393	42
	322	436	477	1,298	2,450	3,902	3,936	2,710	3,560	4,239	8,332
	-442	-69	-89	404	171	625	1,585	2,757	1,949	-281	-220
	219	125	13	185	381	782	551	-2,138	-1,420	-58	1,042
	252	74	254	-431	-479	-1,203	-2,996	3	-143	654	-4
	29	130	178	157	74	204	-860	622	386	315	818
	8	7	-11	-13	-41	—	-87	7	6	3	195
	45	40	43	—	—	—	—	—	—	72	73
	—	15	2	27	4	-58	-3	—	17	6	-8
	83	192	212	171	37	146	-950	629	409	396	1,079
	—	—	—	—	—	—	—	—	—	—	—
	—	—	—	—	—	—	300	-300	—	—	—
	-83	-192	-212	-171	-37	-146	649	-328	-409	-396	-1,079
				8.6	12.8	16.9	21.8	27.1	33.6	40.8	53.8

Sources: IMF, *International Financial Statistics Yearbook, 1989*, Washington, D.C.: IMF, 1989; and World Bank, *World Debt Tables, 1989–90*. Washington, D.C.: World Bank, 1990.

The government's view of debt/equity swaps is decidedly ambivalent.[4] Foreign debt reduction is carried out by allowing greater foreign direct investment (i.e., greater foreign ownership in the economy) and printing new pesos to finance it. This technique has inflationary implications, though not excessive ones if the amount of debt swapped is small relative to the domestic money supply. Also, the borrowing country may find that new investment is not generated by the swap program; rather, investors who would have invested anyway just use the swap mechanism to reduce their financing costs. (This possibility apparently has not been borne out in Mexico, where swap-financed investments led to a doubling of foreign investment from 1986 to 1987, and then a large decline in 1988 when the swap program was suspended.)

TABLE 2

Continued

1981	1982	1983	1984	1985	1986	1987	1988	
								Exchange Rates: Preference indicated
30.5	106.4	150.7	188.7	408.3	1,129.6	3,134.8	3,069.5	Market Rate/Par or Central Rate .... aa
28.9	62.3	128.4	172.0	260.8	717.7	1,782.1	3,054.9	Par Rate/Market Rate .... rb
26.2	96.5	143.9	192.6	371.7	923.5	2,209.7	2,281.0	Market Rate/Par or Central Rate .... ae
24.5	56.4	120.1	167.8	256.9	611.8	1,378.2	2,273.1	Market Rate/Par or Central Rate .... af
24.5	56.4	120.1	167.8	256.9	611.8	1,378.2	2,273.1	Par Rate/Market Rate .... rf
								International Transactions
480.9	1,231.8	2,632.0	4,082.4	5,705.1	10,083.5	28,939.2	47,208.0	Exports 70
338.3	941.9	1,822.0	2,754.3	3,799.9	3,896.2	11,788.7	15,075.0	Petroleum 70a
325.5	912.5	1,780.5	2,507.7	3,438.2	3,426.2	10,751.3	13,215.0	Crude Petroleum 70aa
8.2	19.0	61.6	79.5	139.6	519.0	680.6	1,082.4	Coffee 70e
5.5	27.4	46.8	68.1	92.0	98.5	658.6	832.3	Shrimp 70bl
590.1	774.7	972.4	2,010.8	3,597.5	7,229.7	17,951.0	44,577.5	Imports, cif 71
563.7	742.8	923.4	1,920.2	3,456.0	6,905.2	17,145.1	42,573.0	Imports, fob 71.v
								Balance of Payments
−16,061	−6,307	5,403	4,194	1,130	−1,673	3,968	−2,905	Current Account, nie 77a.d
20,102	21,230	22,312	24,196	21,663	16,031	20,655	20,657	Merchandise: Exports fob 77aad
−23,948	−14,435	−8,550	−11,255	−13,212	−11,432	−12,222	−18,905	Merchandise: Imports fob 77abd
−3,846	6,795	13,762	12,941	8,451	4,599	8,433	1,752	Trade Bal., 77aad + 77abd 77acd
7,535	6,290	6,266	8,182	7,881	7,653	9,244	11,172	Other Goods,Serv.&Income: Cre ...77add
−20,053	−19,695	−14,927	−17,339	−16,202	−14,389	−14,357	−16,444	Other Goods,Serv.&Income: Deb ..77aed
246	232	255	325	327	345	384	452	Private Unrequited Transfers 77afd
57	71	47	85	673	119	264	163	Official Unrequited Trans., nie 77agd
2,835	1,655	461	390	491	1,523	3,246	2,594	Direct Investment 77bad
1,160	921	−653	−756	−984	−816	−397	−627	Portfolio Investment, nie 77bbd
14,943	5,773	−67	42	−796	−274	1,195	−2,464	Other Long-Term Capital, nie 77bcd
2,877	2,042	5,144	3,870	−159	−1,240	8,012	−3,402	Total, 77a.d + 77bad− 77bcd 77c.d
7,414	−6,886	−8,527	−3,574	1,782	694	−5,047	−2,770	Other Short-Term Capital,nie 77d.d
−9,016	−6,791	−925	−973	−1,765	458	2,605	−467	Net Errors and Omissions 77e.d
1,275	−11,635	−4,308	−677	−3,706	−88	5,570	−6,639	Total, lines 77c.d− 77e.d 77f.d
19	42	120	65	72	46	74	21	C'part to Mon./Demon. of Gold 78a.d
69	−	−	−	−	−	−	−	Counterpart to SDR Allocation 78b.d
−30	−12	30	139	−313	−190	39	−171	C'part to Valuation Changes 78c.d
1,333	−11,605	−4,158	−472	−3,947	−232	5,684	−6,789	Total, lines 77f.d−78c.d 78d.d
−	6,846	7,558	2,827	975	−	−	−	Exceptional Financing 79a.d
−	1,217	−1,217	−	−	−	−	−	Liab.Const.Fgn Author. Reserves 79b.d
−1,333	3,542	−2,183	−2,355	2,972	232	−5,684	6,789	Total Change in Reserves 79c.d
67.0	82.0	89.3	97.5	98.1	103.9	104.8	−	Total Foreign Debt Outstanding (in billions of U.S. dollars at yearend)

Furthermore, for the borrowing country, the swap may be viewed as a subsidy for foreign investors to the detriment of domestic investors. This eventuality has been seen by the Chilean government (and others) as a reason to open the swap program to *domestic* as well as foreign investors who seek to undertake capital projects. Finally, the borrowing government needs to recognize that the swap does not eliminate foreign indebtedness; it just alters the form. Direct investment projects generate dividends, royalties, and often other income to the foreign investors. These flows replace the interest payments on foreign debt. Although the net effect on funds flows is difficult to measure a priori, it can be argued that, whereas the principal of a foreign loan is ultimately repaid along with the periodic interest payments, foreign direct investment projects are generally not divested, so the initial capital infusion is not usually returned to the foreign firm.

The AMEX Bank Swap

In 1985 the American Express Bank (hereafter AMEX Bank or the Bank) had loans outstanding to Mexican borrowers worth about $US650 million. About 80 percent of these loans were to official Mexican government agencies such as the Central Bank and the Ministry of Economy. The Bank was looking for methods of restructuring its Mexican portfolio such that the total amount of funds committed could be reduced and/or the loans could be shifted onto some basis that would permit debt servicing to resume more or less normally. One of the options that had surfaced in the previous year was the idea of swapping dollar loans for pesos that would then be invested in Mexican businesses. Since American Express Company has a clear, long-term commitment to operating in Mexico, the idea of buying into a Mexican company or financial institution instead of continuing the interminable struggle for servicing the dollar loans was appealing. While the Bank was prohibited from entering into commercial, nonbanking ventures in the United States, this restriction did not apply to overseas activities.[5] Accordingly, AMEX Bank began to investigate possible investments in the Mexican market.

The Bank considered the purchase of an existing Mexican banking company, or a new investment in a financial services company, but these choices were eliminated because Mexico forbids foreign purchases of financial institutions. Given the American Express Company's overall goals of providing travel-related services as well as regular commercial and investment banking services, the Bank also considered possible investments in the tourism industry. After substantial internal discussions within American Express and talks with Mexican government officials, it was agreed the first step into debt/equity ventures would be the purchase of pesos to invest in a series of new hotels to be constructed in various sites in Mexico.

Discussions with the Mexican government began with the Ministry of Finance, which is the agency responsible for representing the government in negotiations with participants in debt/equity swaps. Simultaneously, the firm undertook discussions with officials in the Ministry of Tourism, which is also centrally involved in the industry affected by the project. Senior officers of the Bank traveled to Mexico to meet with the Finance Minister and other officials who needed to give approvals for redeeming the initial loans, disbursing the pesos, incorporating the hotels, and various other key aspects of the total arrangement. These discussions took place over a period of about six months, when a basic agreement was reached to permit American Express Bank to sell approximately $US100 million of its own sovereign loans (i.e., AMEX Bank's loans to the Mexican government and its agencies). When the final agreement was reached, the chairman of American Express Company, James Robinson, flew to Mexico, where the contract was signed by him and Mexican President Miguel de la Madrid.

The sale of the loans was agreed to be paid in pesos at the current market exchange rate, with disbursement over time as the funds would be used in hotel construction and operation. At the time of this deal, when the Mexican government was just beginning its swap program, the discount offered to AMEX Bank was about 10 percent below the face value of the loans translated into pesos. In 1988, this discount was about 20 percent. (Note that this percentage is *not* the swap discount rate for sale of dollar loans. It is the final discount for acquisition of pesos that is received by the foreign investor. Since American Express Bank sold its own loans, it did not enter into the dollar swap with another intermediary.) That meant that the Bank received $US90 million worth of Mexican pesos. Subsequently, these pesos were disbursed to pay bills involved in the hotel business, when invoices were presented by AMEX Bank to the Finance Ministry. Thus, the swap itself involved immediate cancellation of the original bank debt, but only periodic disbursement of pesos for specific expenses (e.g., *not* for working capital or for imported products) incurred in creation of the hotel businesses. The key transactions involved in the entire swap process are sketched in Figure 1.

The original agreement called for construction of five hotels in three cities around the country, namely Cancun, Acapulco, and Puerto Vallarta. Each hotel project had to receive approval when the specific details of construction, additional financing, partnerships with Mexican investors, etc., were decided. That is, the original swap agreement called for using the pesos to finance construction and operation of five hotels, but the detailed hotel projects each required subsequent specific approval before funds would be authorized.

The disbursements of funds are *not* made to AMEX Bank; rather, they go directly to the suppliers and contractors involved in the hotel projects. Since the payout is not immediate, the funds in the swap account earn interest, in this case at a rate in dollars that is slightly above the original loan interest rate.[6] Payout is in pesos, but they are drawn out of the dollar-denominated swap account at the market exchange rate prevailing at the time of the disbursement.

AMEX Bank has entered into joint ventures with Mexican partners in all seven of the hotels that have been constructed under the agreement, retaining majority ownership in three of them. While Mexico's Foreign Investment Law of 1973 requires at least 51 percent Mexican ownership of new ventures established after that date, exceptions are made when the government deems the projects to be important to national development interests. Apparently, the hotel investments do meet these criteria, and AMEX Bank has decided to remain majority owner in three of the projects. In addition, AMEX has a strong minority position in the other hotels. The partners are all large Mexican construction firms that the Bank brought into the discussions early on, and which are doing the hotel construction in each location.

As far as actual management of the hotels is concerned, the Bank does not possess the expertise needed in such ventures. Thus, contracts with Sheraton (three cases), Radisson, Hilton, Club Med, and Marriott have been concluded in each of the hotel projects for one of those firms to operate and manage the facilities. The fees paid by AMEX Bank for this service are similar to those paid by other hotel owners who obtain franchises from the major hotel chains.

Since the original swap agreement was signed in 1986, the number of hotels permitted has been extended from five to seven. Four of them were operating in mid-1989, and the other three under construction. Additional projects are possible.

For a variety of reasons, not the least of which is the distinctly different nature of the swap business compared to traditional commercial banking, American Express decided to create a new division for dealing in these activities. Accordingly, AMEX Bank formed a wholly owned subsidiary called International Capital Corporation as its own intermediary in the Latin American debt swap business. The managers of this subsidiary had the responsibility for negotiating with the Mexican government, the various contractors and subcontractors in Mexico, and with any other participants in the swap process just described. The subsidiary also seeks other opportunities for AMEX Bank to swap its Latin American debts elsewhere in the region, and opportunities to serve as intermediary for other banks and investors who can use its expertise in debt/equity swaps.

CASE APPENDIX: BACKGROUND ON THE AMERICAN EXPRESS COMPANY

American Express Company (AMEX) was one of the three or four leading financial institutions in the United States in 1986. Its major competitors include CitiCorp, Merrill Lynch, and credit card associations such as VISA and MasterCard that are controlled by banks, as well as other major firms in the various market segments served by AMEX subsidiaries.

American Express began as a credit card and tourist service firm in the early 1900s. By the time of the case, AMEX had grown into a gigantic provider of financial services, with annual sales of over $US10 billion. Even so, the basic business of providing credit and access to funds for business and pleasure travelers continued to play a major role in the company's activites. The Travel Related Services division accounted for about 42 percent of the entire firm's sales in 1986.

The strategic goals of American Express include positioning the firm as one of the top three providers of financial services in the United States. Similar positions are sought in other countries in those segments of the financial markets that are open to foreign competitors. Since U.S. banking laws still prohibit full-scale national commercial banking, as well as direct participation by AMEX in commercial banking due to its other activities, the firm has positioned itself in the 'non-bank' area through acquisitions of Shearson Lehman Brothers (a major investment banking firm), Investors Diversified Services (a large investment advisory service), and expansion into the insurance business.

In the United States, American Express does *not* function as a commercial bank, due to the banking laws which prohibit deposit-taking and some other functions from companies that are involved in investment banking, insurance, or any commercial or industrial activity. However, due to a historical quirk, AMEX Bank Ltd. does operate in New York as a provider of international banking services such as trade financing, eurocurrency transactions, syndicated lending, and other generally wholesale-type services to domestic and foreign clients. The bank also has branches throughout the world, including Latin America, where it provides a broad range of banking services.

American Express views Latin America as a highly desirable market for its various services and has been expanding there for the past decade. Most of the firm's business is in the larger countries such as Brazil, Mexico, Venezuela, and Argentina. Due to its proximity to the United States and its many tourist attractions, Mexico always has been the leading Latin American market for AMEX. Brazil ranks second among AMEX's Latin markets, followed by Argentina and Venezuela.

NOTES

[1]Most private-sector debt was and still is in the form of short-term trade financing and working capital loans. The medium-term portion of private foreign borrowing in many cases has been assumed by Latin American governments, which then collect local currency from the private-sector borrowers and 'consolidate' the foreign-currency liabilities with their other official foreign debt.

[2]The logic can be taken further. The balance of payments crisis is often due to reduced demand for (or prices of) exports and/or government policies that stimulate excessive domestic demand.

[3]Mexico's government "auctioned" the bonds to interested banks, accepting 55 percent of the offers from 139 banks from 18 countries. The resultant bond sales were discounted at an average of 70 percent of loans face values, reducing Mexican official debt by $2.6 billion. The bonds mature in the year 2008, they pay LIBOR $+ 1\frac{5}{8}$ percent interest, and they are collateralized by U.S. Treasury zero-coupon bonds. See Morgan Guaranty Bank, *Press Release,* March 1988.

[4]In fact, the formal debt/equity swap program outlined here has been held in abeyance since the end of 1987, pending the Salinas government's decision on whether or not to restart it.

[5]See, for example, *The Wall Street Journal,* August 13, 1987, p. 3, for discussion of the Federal Reserve ruling that permits U.S. banks to be exempted from Regulation K limits for the purpose of acquiring non-financial companies in Latin America and other heavily-indebted less developed countries.

[6]This was viewed as a major positive feature of the agreement by AMEX Bank. In 1988 the Mexican government chose to fix the exchange rate (during the period before national elections, such that Mexicans' purchasing power rose as local prices rose). Thus, the dollar interest gain of something around 7 percent was swamped by Mexican inflation of about 60 percent during the year, making the funds in the swap account lose approximately half of their value during 1988.

Chapter

9 Barriers to International Trade and Investment

This chapter begins the direct consideration of government policies that affect international business transactions. In particular, it analyzes the rules on imports and exports that restrict trade flows. In addition, it discusses rules on investment flows. The implications of government trade and investment policies for national welfare, and for company managers, are presented in some detail. The main goals of the chapter are to:

1. Examine six major types of trade and investment barriers and note why they exist.

2. Explain the reasons that governments use barriers to imports and to capital outflows.

3. Show the economic impacts of three specific trade barriers—tariffs, subsidies, and quotas.

4. Discuss current U.S. trade policies.

5. Note some of the current government policies that limit international capital flows.

6. Suggest some strategies for company managers to deal with barriers to trade and investment.

INTRODUCTION

Thus far, our attention has focused primarily on the activities of companies and on the functioning of the markets they compete in. Little emphasis has been placed on the regulatory restrictions that companies face. Direct investment (plus local production) and exports have been seen as substitutes when barriers disallow or restrict one or the other—but the barriers themselves have not been discussed in any detail. This chapter covers some of the major types of restrictions that exist on company exports (on *imports*, from the view of the receiving country's policymakers) and international capital flows.

In the next section, some of the most common forms of restrictions are discussed and analyzed. Then we consider the host government's point of view on trade and investment policies. The economic impacts of three major types of trade barriers are laid out in the fourth section. With these basics in place, we then discuss actual policies, looking specifically at U.S. commercial policy. Home and host country *investment* controls are discussed in the sixth section. Finally, suggestions for corporate strategy in light of the barriers are offered, followed by conclusions.

COMMON FORMS OF BARRIERS

Barriers to international flows of goods and services can be grouped into six broad categories for convenience of discussion:

1. Price-based constraints (e.g., tariffs, subsidies).
2. Quantity limits (e.g., quotas, embargoes).
3. Buyers' or sellers' cartels (e.g., OPEC, the International Sugar Agreement, the Multifiber Arrangement).
4. Other *NTBs* (nontariff barriers) on trade.
5. Financial limits (e.g., exchange controls, profit remittance limits).
6. Limits on FDI entry and operations.

Each of these categories is described in this section and discussed in more detail in subsequent sections.

Tariffs and Subsidies

All countries use price-based constraints, i.e., **tariffs**, on their imports. In fact, tariffs are a form of tax, paid on goods shipped internationally. Tariffs are generally charged on imports, as a tax that raises the cost of importing goods. They are usually charged as a percentage of the value of the goods shipped, that is, on an *ad valorem* basis. The United States, for example, has a long list of tariff rates charged on imports, ranging from zero to 117 percent (on tobacco), with an average of about 3.7 percent *ad valorem*.[1] Clearly, tariffs are intended to raise the cost of importing into a country. This accomplishes three goals: (1) it makes local production more competitive; (2) it generates revenue for the government; and (3) it reduces the quantity of imports. Tariffs present a cost to consumers, who must pay a higher price for protected goods than they would have paid if there were no tariffs.

Following similar reasoning, most countries also offer **subsidies** to some domestic companies, so that their products can compete better with imports. In this case, domestic producers are aided directly, typically through low-cost loans or tax breaks that lower their cost of doing business, while imports are not aided and may still be faced with additional tariffs. The federal government of the United States does not offer much of this type of support, though some individual states and local governments offer incentives that constitute subsidies for local producers.[2] The main cost of a subsidy is that someone must pay for it—generally the taxpayers of the subsidizing country.

A second form of subsidy is the export subsidy, which a government may offer to stimulate the exports of domestic firms. In this case, the government provides financial aid to exporting firms through, for example, tax breaks or low-interest loans. These firms in turn export more and stimulate national income. This form of protectionism also has a cost: the country receiving the exports will face unfair competition from the subsidized firms.

Quotas and Embargoes

Quantity limits, such as **quotas**, are also used to restrict international trade. Here the limitation is on the number of units of a product that may be imported or on the market share allowed to imports. Quotas are sometimes imposed on exports as well. For example, a "voluntary" quota on Japanese auto exports to the United States allowed the Japanese automobile producers to export 2.3 million cars to the United States from April 1990 through March 1991, leaving the rest of the market to domestic producers (*and* to imports from other countries). In a slightly different policy, Canada allows foreign banks to hold a total of not more than 16 percent of bank deposits in the country—a limit on market share rather than a limit on the amount of deposits. A quota can be established at any level of import quantity. The particular type of quota that sets the limit at zero imports is called an **embargo**. Often an embargo is placed on imports for clearly political reasons (e.g., to penalize an adversary during a war) rather than to stimulate domestic production or serve any strictly economic goal. For example, the United States has had an embargo on imports from Cuba since 1961. The main economic costs of quotas are that they limit access by consumers to otherwise available products and that they tend to raise the prices of the protected products.

Cartels

Cartels operate in international trade to fix prices or quantities sold in various markets. The restrictions function in much the same ways as the controls of individual governments that were noted above, however they are imposed, not by individual governments, but by a group of producers or consumers of a particular product. Virtually all of the cartels in operation today are associations of countries, because most countries have outlawed company cartels through their antitrust policies. The OPEC cartel is a group of oil-producing countries that restrict both the quantity and the price of the oil that its members sell. (See Chapter 24 for a detailed look at the international oil industry.) The International Sugar Agreement establishes a base price for exports of sugar and market shares for the exporting countries that participate in the agreement. Cartels constrain the market for international trade in individual products in many of the same ways as the controls imposed by individual governments.

Nontariff Barriers

Other **nontariff barriers (NTBs)** to international trade appear in national regulations and practices. These include a wide variety of barriers, ranging from bureaucratic delays in processing requests for import permits, to quality standards that preclude foreign-produced goods, to buy-national programs that require governments to purchase from domestic suppliers. In each case, the NTBs

The Multifibre Arrangement—An Attempt to Manage Textile Trade

The **Multifibre Arrangement (MFA)** is an especially interesting commodity cartel, which groups 42 producing and consuming countries. It is an umbrella agreement that establishes basic principles for negotiating bilateral textile trade arrangements between participating countries. This market-sharing agreement was originally begun in 1957 as a temporary restriction of Japanese cotton textile exports to the United States. In 1961 this was expanded to cover several cotton exporting countries. Subsequently the agreement was reformulated in 1974 into the first Multifibre Arrangement, covering multiple producer and consumer nations. This Arrangement was renewed for the fourth time in 1986, with another new accord to be negotiated in 1991.

The MFA basically permits consuming countries to establish import quotas for their trading partners. It is diametrically opposed to the GATT principles, and it was implemented and has been renewed primarily due to the strong U.S. textile lobby of several southeastern states, whose production competes with these imports. The Arrangement is particularly thorny for the United States in its dealings with Latin American and Caribbean countries, because it limits those countries' key textile exports at the same time that the U.S. is demanding that those countries open up their economies to U.S. exports. The United States currently operates bilateral quotas with 41 countries (many LDCs plus Japan) on cotton; wool; synthetic; and silk, linen, and ramie textiles. The estimated cost to U.S. consumers of this protectionism was about $US52,000 per job saved in the U.S. industry in 1986 (Cline, 1987, chap. 8). ■

raise the cost of importing and thus tend to reduce the country's total imports. Consumers in the protected country generally find that NTBs lead to lower availability and higher prices of protected products.

A second set of restrictions that relate to the trade controls discussed above are capital controls. These government policies are used to limit flows of funds or other financial instruments across national borders. Capital controls can also restrict trade as well, by limiting exporters' and importers' access to foreign exchange.

Exchange Controls

Financial limits, such as **exchange controls**, are generally used to limit out-flows of foreign exchange. A country may choose this policy in order to avoid devaluation of its currency, which would otherwise take place through the free market for exchange-rate determination, because of an excess supply of the currency in the foreign exchange market. A country may also limit access to foreign exchange in order to curb importers' ability to pay their suppliers—thus restricting imports. Another purpose of exchange controls is to stimulate exports, by simply offering exporters a more favorable rate of exchange (so that they can sell their foreign-currency receipts for more local currency). For example, several Latin American countries allow exporters to exchange their dollars at the unrestricted exchange rate, which gives more local currency for each dollar sold. Brazil, among other countries, then restricts importers' access to dollars by requiring a large deposit of funds several months before an import shipment has been received—a very costly process. Brazil and other countries have also frequently limited the number of dollars that domestic travelers are allowed to purchase for trips abroad.

Exchange controls may be used specifically to regulate capital markets, rather than aiming at exports or imports. Many times, a country has discovered that speculators have begun to push down the value of its currency; and to stop this activity, the country may limit access to foreign exchange or otherwise restrict financial transactions that tend to devalue the currency. Such controls undoubtedly have an impact on exports and imports as well.

The main forms of exchange controls in use today include fixed exchange rates, with limited access to foreign exchange; different exchange rates for different categories of market participants; and bureaucratic controls, such as "red tape," that require the expenditure of substantial time and effort to get access to foreign exchange. Each of these forms of exchange controls can be used both to restrict imports and to control capital flows. The main costs of exchange controls are the loss of trade and investment that would have taken place in their absence.

Foreign Investment Controls

Foreign investment controls range from the rejection of all foreign direct investment, as formerly existed in several communist countries, to limits on the activities of foreign-owned firms, such as limits on profit remittances and other financial transfers. Controls of this kind include both price-based policies, such as taxes or price controls, and quantity restrictions, such as limits on the entry of foreign investment. Mexico, for example, requires that foreign investors sell 51 percent ownership to local investors when an investment is made; it taxes profit remittances to parent firms; and restricts various other activities of foreign investors. Until the end of 1984, Canada limited the quantity of foreign direct investment through a screening of potential investors carried out by the Foreign Investment Review Agency.[3]

Foreign investment controls generally create competitive conditions that favor local firms competing with foreign-owned firms within the country. The costs of foreign investment controls are the lost FDI that they deter; these costs are difficult to measure, though Chapter 11 looks carefully at this issue.

Altogether, the barriers to international trade and investment examined above create tremendous limitations on the ability of market participants to determine the prices and quantities of products sold in international business. The purpose of this chapter is not to criticize the barriers but to understand them and to see how to deal with them. Let us look next at governments' reasons for utilizing the various barriers.

REASONS FOR BARRIERS: THE HOST GOVERNMENT'S VIEW

Tariff, subsidy, quota, and other policy constraints on trade vary, literally from month to month, not only between countries but also within individual countries, as economic and political conditions, and even governments, change. While there is no single main reason for imposing these barriers, it is possible to construct an overview of the government concerns that lead to them. Table 9–1 presents the reasons that underlie much of the trade and investment policy in use today.

The principal goals of controls on trade or direct investment flows are to promote national economic growth (usually the primary objective of less developed countries) and to forego balance of payments adjustment (and save jobs—usually the primary objective of industrial countries). These goals can be approached in many ways. For example, the classic strategy of CEPAL (the United Nations Economic Commission for Latin America) during the 1960s and 1970s was to replace imports with local production; this called for raising tariffs to cut imports. In contrast, the strategy of Japan and ASEAN (the Association of South East Asian Nations) has been not to restrict imports, but to subsidize exports and thus help them compete in world markets. Altogether, the reasons for imposing trade controls that appear in Table 9–1 can be traced to the goals of stimulating or preserving national economic output or improving the balance of payments. (An additional goal that should be noted is protection to achieve political ends, such as penalizing unfriendly countries.)

Improving the balance of payments may mean eliminating a deficit or reducing a surplus. For the most part, countries facing a balance of trade surplus simply acquire financial claims on deficit countries, without encountering any pressure to "improve" the situation toward a balance. Countries with a trade deficit, on the other hand, spend their available foreign exchange to pay for imports, and ultimately they must either eliminate the deficit or run out of foreign currency with which to finance it (unless recurring loans can be used to finance the deficit indefinitely). Thus, for balance of payments purposes, governments use trade controls most often in efforts to eliminate trade deficits. Consider separately each of the reasons for controls listed in Table 9–1.

Protecting Import-Competing Domestic Firms

This rationale is used virtually everywhere. The United States imposes tariffs on imported steel, uses "voluntary" quotas on imported autos, and subsidizes domestic exporters to improve their ability to compete with foreign producers. Such measures are used widely because, among other reasons, the companies and people hurt by the foreign competition make strenuous efforts to convince the government that restrictions would be beneficial to them. For example, the United Auto Workers and the Big Three auto manufacturers (GM, Ford, and Chrysler) in the United States are highly visible groups that can lobby relatively

TABLE 9–1

Reasons for Trade and Investment Controls

1. To protect import-competing domestic firms (includes saving jobs).
2. To promote import substitution.
3. To reduce reliance on foreign suppliers.
4. To encourage local and foreign direct investment.
5. To reduce balance of payments problems.
6. To promote export-based growth.
7. To promote infant industries.
8. To achieve health and safety standards.
9. To restrain foreign firms from dumping.
10. To serve political goals.

effectively for protection against foreign competition. Similar conditions exist in every country for some industries, and various forms of protection exist everywhere to protect import-competing firms.

Promoting Import Substitution

Using this justification, many less developed countries have established very high tariffs on selected products. In this way they hope to encourage local or foreign investors to inaugurate local production of formerly imported products. This would both reduce a trade balance deficit and provide additional jobs for local workers. Import substitution policy has not proved effective for any country trying to achieve an "economic miracle," such as occurred in Japan in the 1950s and 60s or Singapore and Hong Kong in the 1970s, but it can be part of a development strategy aimed at fostering new capital investment in specific industries. In this sense, the import substitution argument can be compared to the infant industry argument that is presented below.

Reducing Reliance on Foreign Suppliers

Most national governments prefer to obtain domestically whatever goods and services may be needed for protection against a foreign political/military power. With few exceptions, most countries supply their own armed forces, their own defense systems (though equipment may be imported) and their own supplies of many critical materials, such as food. The types of controls usually imposed to achieve this objective are not tariffs but government contracting agreements, under which the government buys the required products or services only from domestic suppliers or produces them through government agencies. The U.S. government, for example, must buy its supplies from domestic suppliers, unless foreign competitors offer substantially lower prices and acceptable quality.[4] It purchases some products, especially defense-related ones, *only* from domestic suppliers.

Encouraging Local and Foreign Direct Investment

Tariffs and NTBs are sometimes used to encourage the replacement of imported goods with locally produced goods. Often Latin American governments raise tariffs on specific goods that they want to see produced locally, as part of a development strategy. Many governments raise barriers on imports of specific products in order to foster local production of those products—regardless of the nationality of the companies that produce them. In an often cited case, the Mexican government negotiated with John Deere Company and several other tractor manufacturers to allow four of them to produce their products locally, while denying other tractor manufacturers access to the Mexican market.[5]

Reducing Balance of Payments Problems

All of the points made up to now have related directly or indirectly to the attempts of governments to increase domestic economic activity. These attempts *also* affect the balance of payments. Some restrictions on trade and investment, however, are imposed specifically to improve the BOP. These restrictions are generally not product or industry specific; rather, they limit broad classes of imports or all imports or they support exports or local production generally. Moreover, restrictions aimed at improving the BOP may be placed on capital flows as well as imports and exports. This type of government policy generally is imposed during balance of payments crises, when official reserves are flowing out of the country.

Promoting Export-Based Growth

The strategy of export-led growth is based on a combination of the two basic economic reasons for trade and investment barriers. By encouraging exports through subsidies of some type, a government can foster greater production (and employment) at the same time that it reduces a balance of payments deficit, *without* limiting other countries' access to the national market. During the period since World War II, this strategy has vied for acceptability among less developed countries with the CEPAL strategy of import substitution (though there is no conceptual reason why both strategies cannot be followed simultaneously).[6]

Promoting Infant Industries

Virtually every developed country raised tariffs and NTBs during its period of development, to enable new industries to start up without overwhelming competition from established firms abroad. Wide acceptance has been given to a policy of imposing a tariff or other barriers for a limited period of time to enable an infant industry to begin operation. Unfortunately, there is no clear measure of the appropriate time period for infant industry protection, so that such policies often tend to continue indefinitely. Brazil, for example, has established an embargo on imports of microcomputers. All microcomputers must be produced by Brazilian firms. This policy excludes IBM, Burroughs, Apple, and other companies from the Brazilian market for these products during an indefinite period of time, since it is not clear when Brazil's infant industry will be mature enough to allow elimination of the protection. The infant industry argument for protection rests completely on the premise that the protection will be eliminated when the new industry has achieved competitive status, which is often difficult to define.

Achieving Health and Safety Standards

National health and safety requirements for products and services are generally applied to imports *and* locally made goods or services. The process of verifying that imported items meet these standards may be used as a barrier to entry. Imports may be discouraged by simple red tape that forces the potential importer to expend much time and money to obtain proof of qualification. Or rules may be set that require expensive alterations of foreign-made goods to meet domestic product norms. The U.S. requirement that imported cars be modified from their home country configurations to meet the pollution control standards of the Environmental Protection Agency are a barrier that substantially raises the prices of these cars. Similarly, the U.S. Food and Drug Administration uses a lengthy and expensive process of testing pharmaceutical products before they are allowed to be sold in the domestic market. The result of these standards may be simply to ensure the safety of consumers—or it may in fact be to keep out competition.

Restraining Foreign Firms from Dumping

A monopolistic practice often seen in business is the attempt by one firm to cut prices temporarily in order to take sales away from competing firms. When the competing firms leave the market or go bankrupt, that firm controls the market and is free to raise its prices. In international trade, the practice of selling into a foreign market at a price below the firm's cost is called **dumping**. Because dumping tends to harm local firms and strengthen foreign competitors, it is restricted in most countries. While dumping is widely agreed to be "unfair" trade, it is quite difficult to measure a firm's actual costs or arrive at some "fair" market price. Very little consensus exists on any measure of dumping that would be appropriate for use as a standard for limiting the practice; and "dumping" is often used unjustifiably to criticize the practices of foreign low-cost producers that enter a home market. (The steel imports case in this chapter provides a useful example of the problems in defining and coping with dumping.)

Serving Political Goals

This last rationale may in fact be a part of the basis for many protective policies that are ostensibly pursued for other reasons, but here we focus on restraints that are imposed for specifically political reasons. For example, the motives for the U.S. embargo on exports to the Soviet Union after the Soviet invasion of Afghanistan were essentially political. Similarly, political motives have given rise to the various limitations on trade that the U.S. government has imposed on communist countries and on South Africa from time to time. The policies adopted to pursue a noneconomic goal may actually cause some degree of economic hardship.

Evaluation of Barriers

The reasons for restricting international trade that are presented here generally are not justifiable on economic grounds. That is, typically, the functioning of comparative advantage is hindered by the barriers, and so world welfare is reduced by them. (The next section of the chapter shows how the costs arise from these restrictions. The following section presents measures of the economic impact of U.S. trade barriers, which consistently demonstrate a significant cost to U.S. consumers due to the tariffs, quotas, etc.)

When a country imposes tariffs or nontariff barriers to limit imports, the resulting decline in imports raises consumers' costs and/or reduces availability of the product relative to free-trade conditions. If the foreign country retaliates against the initiator of such restrictions, the initiator may lose exports as well. Overall, consumers will suffer because of the barriers, total jobs may actually decline in the country (though jobs in the protected industry may not fall), and the country may not even improve the trade balance due to retaliation by the foreign country. This fundamental problem serves to reject the first six reasons for trade barriers listed in Table 9–1.[7]

Not all trade barriers can be rejected so easily. For example, the infant industry argument is a *dynamic* rationale for temporary support of industries that will become freely competitive after a period of protected incubation. Similarly, the argument for encouraging local investment can be a rationale for *temporary* protection to support creation of an infant industry.

The use of trade barriers to preclude dumping by foreign competitors is certainly appropriate on economic grounds, since it eliminates a monopolistic practice by the foreign firms. Also, the imposition of health and safety standards that apply to *all* firms, domestic and foreign, can restrict imports—but such standards presumably serve the public interest by protecting consumers from unwanted health and safety risks. Other logical, economically defensible rationales for trade barriers that protect the public interest may be found as well; the fundamentally flawed rationales are mainly those that invoke barriers for the sake of protecting domestic jobs or improving the balance of trade.

Finally, it should be recognized that trade policy, as other government policy, is not driven solely by economic reasoning. Political, social, and other types of concerns may justify barriers to imports or funds flows even though economic costs arise. It may well be in the U.S. interest to disallow trade with Cuba and North Korea for political reasons, despite the (fairly minor) economic costs involved. Similarly, it may be rational for Israel to restrict trade with Arab countries and vice versa, for religious and cultural rather than economic reasons. These noneconomic criteria should not be ignored.

The foregoing discussion has simply explained some of the reasoning behind trade and investment barriers. Next, let us consider some of the economic problems raised by the use of three trade barriers.

AN ECONOMIC COMPARISON OF THREE TRADE BARRIERS

A Simple Graphic Analysis

Typically, when a government seeks to protect a domestic industry, it implements a tariff on imports, or a quota on imports, or a subsidy of domestic producers. Let us consider the economic implications of each of these policies in a hypothetical situation. Figure 9–1 compares the three policy choices for Bhagwatia, a country that wants to protect its steel industry.

DS_s and DD_s are the domestic supply and demand for steel, respectively. WS_s is the production of steel available from all other countries combined—the world supply of steel. If the home country's supply of and demand for this product are relatively small compared to the world supply, then the world price is essentially a "given" to Bhagwatia and the world supply curve is perfectly elastic, a horizontal line across the figure. The price charged by foreign suppliers is WP_s, the world price of steel. Under conditions of free trade, producers in the home country will supply OA of steel and importers will sell AB of steel, so that total sales equal OB of steel. Notice that the figure is drawn so that domestic consumers would gain by importing, because they could consume more steel at a lower price than if the country simply produced all steel locally (and consumed at point X on the figure).

If the government wants to raise domestic output of steel to OA', then it could use a *tariff* of size CE (which is an *ad valorem* percentage of $CE/A'E$), as shown in panel 1 of Figure 9–1. This raises the import price for domestic consumers to OT. Domestic producers of steel will sell OA' of output at the new, higher price, while foreign suppliers sell only $A'B'$. The initial effects of this policy are:

1. Increased domestic production and employment, assuming no retaliation by foreign governments (domestic producers sell AA' more *and* charge CE more).

2. Decreased domestic consumption of steel at the new, higher price (from OB to OB').

FIGURE 9–1

The Bhagwatia Steel Industry

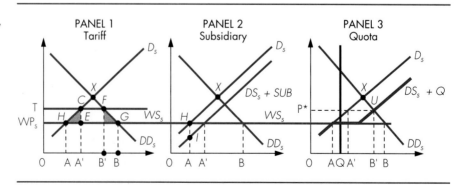

3. Improved balance of trade, because of reduced imports (from *AB* to *A'B'*).
4. Increased government revenue from the tariff receipts (*CE* times *A'B'*).
5. Loss of Bhagwatia welfare (equal to the two shaded areas in panel 1).

The tariff alters consumers' marginal allocations of income, since it raises the price of steel relative to the prices of other goods and services sold in the country. If the country began in free-market equilibrium, then this represents a misallocation of income. A tariff may be easy to impose politically, since it appears to penalize "foreigners" relative to domestic producers, and the true costs are not readily apparent.

If the government wants to raise domestic output to *OA'* using a *subsidy*, then the subsidy must push domestic supply out to *A'* at price WP_S. This is shown by the new supply curve, $DS_S + SUB$, in panel 2. In this case, the domestic price stays at WP_S, and imports are reduced by only AA'. (To cut imports by as much as the tariff did, the government would need a subsidy large enough to shift out the supply curve by *AA'* + *BB'*.) The subsidy shown in the graph has the following initial effects:

1. Increased domestic production and employment, assuming no retaliation (from *OA* to *OA'*).
2. No change in total domestic consumption of this product; no change in price.
3. Improved balance of trade, because of reduced imports (from *AB* to *A'B'*).
4. New government revenue needed to pay for the subsidy (value equal to HI times OA').

Subsidies do not alter consumers' marginal allocations of income, because they leave prices unchanged. When a government chooses a revenue-generating policy (such as raising taxes) to pay for a subsidy, taxpayers can see clearly the impact of the policy; thus, a subsidy is more visible than a tariff to consumers and taxpayers. In conceptual terms, a subsidy is generally preferable to a tariff, because although they both have economic costs, the subsidy does not affect relative prices. In pragmatic political terms, and in the United States in particular, subsidies are viewed as "handouts," not to be distributed freely to companies without clear and substantial justification; so tariffs tend to be more readily acceptable.

If the government of Bhagwatia wants to raise domestic output to *OA'* using a *quota*, then the quota must be set such that domestic output is pushed up to *OA'* from panel 1, as shown in panel 3. The quota will delegate *OQ* to imports, leaving the rest of the market at any given price to domestic producers. Essentially, this can be viewed as a case with a supply curve shaped as shown in heavy lines in panel 3. The imports take *A'B'* at price *P**, and domestic producers sell *OA* plus *AA'*. This quota has the following initial effects:

1. Increased domestic production and employment, assuming no retaliation (from *OA* to *OA'*).
2. Decreased domestic consumption of steel at the new, higher price.
3. Improved balance of trade, because of reduced imports.
4. No change in government revenues or expenditures.
5. Loss of consumer welfare, because consumption is reduced by *BB'*.

The initial impact of a quota is as obvious as that of a tariff. Like a tariff, a quota misallocates income by altering the relative price of the product being protected. A quota does not generate revenue for the government—a tariff does—or require government expenditure to pay for it.

All of these results will be somewhat different if domestic demand is very price elastic, or if domestic supply is very price elastic, or if the world price is not perfectly price elastic. The results will also be different if the country began in an already biased position—that is, with some trade barriers already being used. In that case, the value of the new barrier must be compared with the situation under the previous conditions—a kind of second-best problem.

Empirical Estimates of the Costs of Protectionism

A number of estimates have been made of the impact of trade restrictions on the U.S. economy in recent years. Table 9–2 presents a summary of findings from several studies concerning the economic impact of U.S. tariffs on U.S. consumers; and Table 9–3 presents findings from several studies on quantitative restrictions used by the United States to limit imports. Each of these estimates is intended to measure the net cost to consumers in terms of higher prices, reduced availability of imports, and spillovers into other parts of the economy. Notice that virtually every protectionist policy has a very large cost associated with it, in terms of losses incurred by consumers. For instance, quotas on textile imports under the Multifibre Arrangement cost U.S. consumers over $3 billion per year; tariffs on imported iron and steel cost U.S. consumers over $4 billion per year. Estimates from the same sources showed that the average cost of protection *per U.S. job saved* in the steel and auto industries was about $100,000 per year!

U.S. COMMERCIAL POLICY

The basic tariff structure of the United States remains as outlined by the Smoot-Hawley Act (the Tariff Act of 1930) and amended from time to time. In 1934, for example, the Reciprocal Trade Agreements Acts amended Smoot-Hawley, allowing the president to negotiate tariff changes. More recently, the Trade Reform Act of 1974 spelled out detailed provisions for aiding U.S. industries harmed by imports, ranging from additional protection to financial assistance for the injured firms and employees.

The attempts to lower trade barriers since World War II have been largely *multilateral* rather than bilateral. That is, the objective has often been to set tariff treatment that applies to many trading partners rather than only two. In 1946, the General Agreement on Tariffs and Trade (GATT) was formed by 22 countries as a forum for negotiating multilateral tariff reductions. (GATT is discussed in more detail in Chapter 10.) The United States has participated in seven rounds of negotiations since that time, with the result that U.S. tariffs today average only about 4 percent *ad valorem* to most countries of the world.

Additional U.S. commercial policy has taken a wide variety of forms in recent years, such as:

1. Trigger-price penalties on steel imports.
2. An orderly marketing agreement for color TV imports.
3. A "voluntary" quota on imports of Japanese automobiles.
4. A Caribbean Basin Initiative that eliminates tariffs on a wide variety of goods imported from Caribbean countries.

TABLE 9–2

Costs of Tariffs, by Product Category

Product	Annual Cost to U.S. Consumers (in millions of 1980 U.S. dollars)	Source	Year of Estimate
Selected agricultural	317	a	1980
Aluminum	286	b	1980
Chemicals	829	b	1980
Copper	1,589	c	1979
Flatware (stainless steel)	31	c	1979
Footwear	1,037	b	1980
(Footwear, nonrubber)	(14)	d	(1977)
Furniture and fixtures	926	b	1980
Glass and glass products	906	b	1980
Jewelry	83	a	1980
Leather products	183	b	1980
Iron and steel	4,047	b	1980
Machinery (electric)	5,646	b	1980
Machinery (nonelectric)	5,324	b	1980
Metal products	386	b	1980
Miscellaneous manufacturing	1,005	b	1980
Paper, paper products	129	b	1980
Printing and publishing	466	b	1980
CB transceivers	57	d	1977
Sugar	1,742	d	1977
Textiles	3,160	b	1980
Transport equipment	4,955	b	1980
Wearing apparel	11,795	b	1980
Wood, wood products	710	b	1980
Zinc	175	c	1979
Total cost of tariffs listed	45,784		

[a] International Trade Commission, statistical services.

[b] Authors' estimate.

[c] Charles Pearson, "Adjusting to Imports of Manufacturers from Developing Countries," in *The International Economy: U.S. Role in a World Market*, prepared for the Joint Economic Committee of Congress, December 1980.

[d] Morris E. Morkre and David G. Tarr, *Effects of Restrictions on United States Imports: Five Case Studies and Theory* (Washington, D.C.: Federal Trade Commission, Bureau of Economics, June 1980). Source: Michael Munger, "The Costs of Protectionism," *Challenge* (January–February 1984), p. 55.

5. A Trading-with-the-Enemy Act that forbids trade with a small number of communist countries (e.g., Cuba and North Korea).

6. An Export Sales Company Act that subsidizes U.S. exports.

7. "Buy American" requirements for some government purchases.

8. Trade adjustment assistance, which compensates firms and workers whose income has been harmed by imports.

Each of these policies serves to "distort" the free-market process of international trade. However, since the initial situation was *not* one of free trade, each of the policies should be evaluated as a second-best alternative, compared with other choices.

The **trigger-price mechanism** on steel imports from 1978–82 (see the case on the steel imports problem at the end of this chapter) required the U.S. International Trade Commission to judge whether the pricing of imported steel

TABLE 9–3

Costs of Quantitative Restrictions to U.S. Consumers

Product	Restriction	Annual Cost to U.S. Consumers (in millions of 1980 U.S. dollars)	Source	Year
Apparel, textiles	Quotas	3,416	a	1982
Ball bearings	OMA	N.E.		
Batteries	OMA	N.E.		
Coffee	OMA	720	b	1975
Footwear	OMA	1,634	c	1977
Footwear	OMA	681	d	1979
Footwear (plastic)	OMA	197	d	1977
Meat	Quota	816	e	1977
Meat	OMA	1,362	e	1977
Mushrooms	OMA	N.E.		
Steel (carbon)	OMA	1,706	f	1977
Steel, alloy tool	OMA	N.E.		
Steel, stainless	OMA	N.E.		
Sugar	Quota	1,000	g	*1980
Televisions	OMA	600	h	1977
Televisions	OMA	251	i	1980
Televisions	OMA	0	d	1979
Televisions	OMA	0	j	1980
Tin	OMA	N.E.		
Total costs of quantitative restrictions listed*		11,532		

N.E. = Not estimated. OMA = orderly marketing agreement.

* Assuming television OMA cost is zero.

a "Talking Business: With (Martin) Wolf of the Trade Policy Research Center," *New York Times*, January 1, 1982.

b General Accounting Office, "International Commodity Agreements."

c International Trade Commission, in CWPS-217.

d Morris E. Morkre and David G. Tarr, *Effects of Restrictions on United States Imports: Five Case Studies and Theory* (Washington, D.C.: Federal Trade Commission, Bureau of Economics, June 1980).

e Council on Wage and Price Stability, TA-201-25.

f Robert W. Crandall, "Federal Government Initiatives to Reduce the Price Level," in *Brookings Papers on Economic Activity*, 1978.

g Consumers for World Trade, Newsletter, "Special Issue Trade Roundup," Fall 1982.

h International Trade Commission, in CWPS-227.

i Charles Pearson, "Adjusting to Imports of Manufacturers from Developing Countries," in *The International Economy: U.S. Role in a World Market*, prepared for the Joint Economic Committee of Congress, December 1980; and International Trade Commission statistical services.

j Victor Canto and Arthur Laffer, "The Effectiveness of Orderly Marketing Agreements: The Color TV Case," *Business Economics*, January 1983.

Source: Michael Munger, "The Costs of Protectionism," *Challenge* (January–February 1984), p. 56.

was "fair" (i.e., whether it reflected cost conditions in the exporting country) and not just **dumping** (i.e., selling at a low price to get rid of excess steel output). The trigger-price mechanism was used to place penalties on steel imports from Japan, European countries, and even newly industrializing countries such as Korea and Brazil. The objective of this program was to protect U.S. steel manufacturers against unfair foreign competition, which may be either steel production subsidized by the foreign government or steel sold below a fair price to help the foreign producer use up excess inventory. The trigger prices actually used in this instance were all based on *Japanese* production costs.

The **orderly marketing agreement** for color TV imports followed reasoning similar to that of the trigger-price mechanism. In 1977, the U.S. government negotiated an orderly marketing agreement with the government of Japan that established a quota on TV imports from Japanese companies and an additional quota on imported unassembled TVs from Japanese companies. Much of the TV imports then began to come from Korea and Taiwan. So in 1980, the orderly marketing agreement with Japan was extended to TV imports from those two countries as well. By the end of 1981, color TV imports had leveled off and U.S. domestic production had increased substantially—though much of the additional U.S. production was just assembly of unfinished TVs from the restricted countries.[8] This program was discontinued in the mid-1980s.

The **voluntary quota** on Japanese auto imports can be viewed as a form of orderly marketing agreement. It established annual limits on total Japanese auto exports to the United States. If these "voluntary" limits are not followed, then the U.S. government is expected to impose mandatory constraints on auto imports. Thus, the implication is that the limits are actually mandatory. As of 1990, a maximum of 2.3 million cars per year were permitted to be imported from Japan.[9]

The **Caribbean Basin Initiative** simply eliminates tariffs on most imports from countries in the Caribbean region (including Central America). This policy was proposed in 1982 as a measure to improve the economic conditions of U.S. allies in the region, and thus to help ensure their support for U.S. political policies. The tariff part of the initiative was implemented in January 1984. While some major exports from the region are excepted (e.g., sugar, coffee, tin, textiles), thousands of manufactured products and other goods are covered. Obviously, this is a free-trade policy, not a restriction on trade.[10]

The **Trading-with-the-Enemy Act** disallows exports to and imports from countries that have been determined to be enemies of the United States by the U.S. government. North Korea has been included among such countries since 1950; Cuba, since 1961; and Vietnam, since 1975. Depending on the particular year and circumstances, other communist countries have also been included. Immediately after the Soviet invasion of Afghanistan in 1979, for example, U.S.-Soviet trade was severely limited. Most of the restrictions imposed at that time were terminated in 1980.[11]

In 1984, the U.S. policy of encouraging exports through income tax deferral (the DISC legislation) was replaced by the **Foreign Sales Corporation Act.** This act allows U.S. exporters to establish overseas affiliates to manage their export sales, and these affiliates are legally exempt from current U.S. taxation on the income from such sales until the earnings have been remitted to the parent firm in the United States.[12] This policy offers a direct subsidy to U.S. exports, by reducing the taxes paid by exporters.

For some purchases, when bids from domestic suppliers are competitive with bids from foreign suppliers, the federal government of the United States is required to **buy American.** This policy has not been clearly implemented, and individual government agencies appear to be following it in a relatively uncoordinated way.[13] As previously noted, however, purchases of defense-related materials by the U.S. government are carefully restricted to reliable, U.S.-based suppliers.

Finally, **trade adjustment assistance (TAA)** is offered to aid U.S. firms and individuals that have been harmed by competition from imports. This assistance takes such forms as loans to help companies retool so that they can compete with imports; direct unemployment compensation to individuals, who are expected to seek new jobs in other industries during the period of compensation; and counseling to help individuals find alternative employment.[14]

In 1988 the U.S. Congress passed the Omnibus Trade and Competitiveness Act, which reaffirmed the country's position in favor of free trade but established new means for dealing with unfair trade practices by foreign exporters. This legislation gave the U.S. Trade Representative authority to impose penalties on foreign exporters when they can be shown to be dumping products in the U.S. market or when their products are subsidized by a foreign government. It also called for new penalties in the area of intellectual property rights, disallowing imports when the foreign firm(s) are shown to infringe on patents of U.S. firms. More broadly, the Act allowed the U.S. government to impose penalties on imports from countries that restrict U.S. exports through nontariff barriers, thus trying to generate more "fair" trade.

The 1988 Act also expanded the coverage of Trade Adjustment Assistance, adding more benefits (namely unemployment compensation and retraining subsidies) for employees laid off due to competition from imports and offering incentives to firms hurt by imports if they either retool to become more competitive or shift their activities to other kinds of business. In addition, a 12-member Competitiveness Policy Board was established to examine the ability of U.S. firms to compete in domestic and foreign markets and to recommend policy to assist firms toward that end.

In sum, U.S. commercial policy is a patchwork of regulations, most of which are intended to promote free trade and economic growth, but a small number of which are highly visible programs to aid specific (politically powerful) industry sectors. The trade adjustment assistance program is intended to help companies and workers shift to more competitive activities, thus allowing comparative advantage to work, yet not ignoring the burden of adjustment felt by the less-competitive parts of the economy.

EXCHANGE CONTROLS AND CAPITAL CONTROLS

Though often not as clearly linked to international trade as trade barriers, *exchange and capital controls* do play a part in restricting trade flows. In this case, the controls are placed on the movement of money or other financial instruments between countries. A simple control such as limited access to foreign exchange can cut imports just as effectively as a tariff, if it disallows importers from obtaining the needed means of payment for their purchases. Such **exchange controls** are used widely throughout the world, though in recent years the industrial countries have largely eliminated them.

In addition, **capital controls** generally intend to help a country's balance of payments deficit, by limiting capital outflows. This policy goes beyond improving the trade balance and includes the possibility of improving the basic balance (which includes direct investment and long-term loans), or even the official reserves balance (which includes short-term capital flows). Capital controls focus on limiting investment activity, where exchange controls generally focus on limiting trade flows.

For example, from 1982 to 1989 Venezuela used a system of multiple exchange rates both to reduce imports and to encourage capital inflows. Importers, in most cases, were required to buy foreign exchange at the market rate, which in mid-1988 was about 30 bolivars per U.S. dollar. Most new and existing loans from abroad, on the other hand, could be repaid at a rate of 15 bolivars per dollar—a much more manageable cost for the local borrowers. (Exporters could sell their foreign exchange receipts at the market rate, thus receiving more bolivars for their domestic needs than what the official rate would give.) In early 1989, Venezuela's government unified the exchange rate and now allows the market to determine the rate.

The United States has not used exchange controls, though it has imposed some financial controls. The most widely discussed U.S. controls were the capital controls imposed on U.S.-based multinational firms in the mid-1960s. Initially (in 1965), these controls were voluntary, requesting that MNEs finance their foreign subsidiaries through foreign borrowing, rather than through financial transfers from the United States. In 1968 the controls were made mandatory, requiring that affiliates in Europe and a few non-European countries not receive additional financing from the U.S. parent firms, while allowing limited funds transfers to affiliates in less developed countries. The MNEs found so many ways to circumvent the controls (not the least of which was a tremendous expansion of borrowing in the eurodollar market) that the ultimate effect on the U.S. balance of payments was probably minimal. The controls were dismantled in 1974.[15]

Investment controls may be defined to include limits on foreign *direct* investment. This type of control is the rule rather than the exception today. Almost every country restricts foreign direct investors of some kind from doing business in the domestic market. The limits range from total disallowance (in Cuba and Albania, for example) to selective permission of investors (in many less developed countries and formerly communist countries). Direct investment controls generally do *not* seek to improve the balance of payments; their purpose is to maintain domestic ownership and control over key segments of the economy. These controls are discussed in detail for selected countries in Chapters 21–23.

COMPANY STRATEGIES FOR DEALING WITH THE BARRIERS

The fundamental strategy for coping with trade and investment barriers is to utilize the firm's competitive advantages to best function under them. Since methods for using trade and investment to overcome constraints on either were presented in Chapter 2, there is no need to discuss them again here. However, a few specific strategies that may be appropriate when additional barriers to imports are imposed are worth considering.

Each time the cost of importing a product is raised, the relative advantage of producing it locally increases. This points toward the alternatives of direct investment, licensing of a local firm, use of a turnkey venture, or some other organizational strategy that employs local production. The multiproduct firm may consider negotiation with the government to produce or just assemble a small number of products locally in return for permission to import other products without prohibitive tariff barriers. The increase in import cost due to the new barrier may force the firm to consider the other alternatives for the first time—and it may actually have been less costly (i.e., more profitable) to produce locally even before the new barrier was in place.

Another strategy that the firm should consider is the establishment of production in more than one country, to remove the "hostage" problem, in which the firm is dependent on supply from one national source for sales in perhaps several countries. By using a portfolio of production sources, the firm can reduce the bargaining power of any one national government over its multi-country operations. Even though costs would probably be minimized by producing in just one country, the risk of regulatory change or other problems may make using a portfolio of production sources a better solution. The trade barriers discussed in this chapter should remind the manager that each national operation of the firm is subject to the national rules of that country—rules that can be altered at any time.

Many countries allow relatively unrestricted importation of intermediate goods (e.g., unassembled TVs or autos) but impose substantial tariffs and NTBs on final products. Such a regulatory environment may favor local assembly of a product, while the vast majority of the product's value is produced elsewhere. This strategy is widely used in Latin America, where most countries want to encourage the growth of domestic manufacturing and to reduce dependence on imports. Pharmaceutical firms, auto companies, and other manufacturers have found that local assembly (formulation in the case of drugs) enables them to avoid very high tariffs and NTBs without committing a large capital investment to a small or politically unstable country.

The major Japanese producers of cars and trucks have already chosen to set up local production in the United States to reduce the expected impact of increasingly restrictive U.S. policy on auto imports. Nissan manufactures both cars and trucks in South Carolina; in 1984, in a joint venture with General Motors, Toyota began producing a compact car in California; Honda produces cars and motorcycles in Ohio and lawn mowers in South Carolina; and other Japanese firms are following close behind. This strategy is clearly political, since the costs of delivering a car to the U.S. market are far lower for Japanese producers than for U.S. producers. (See the auto industry analysis in Chapter 24.)

The appropriate strategy in any situation, of course, will depend on the specific conditions involved. However, it is possible to conclude that, as suggested in Chapter 2, the approach to thinking about alternative strategies is to evaluate the firm's competitive advantages and to compare the ownership strategies on that basis.

CONCLUSIONS

This chapter has covered a wide range of aspects of barriers to international trade and investment. We defined the most common forms of barriers first, and then looked at the reasons that governments utilize them. Economic analysis of the barriers showed that they generally harm an economy more than they help it, but strong conclusions in any case depend on the situation faced by the country. An economic loss may well be justified in the face of political gain. Most of the evidence regarding U.S. barriers appears to show that they have not benefited the U.S. economy as a whole, though they may have helped firms protected by them. The policy of trade adjustment assistance attempts to reduce the burden of adjustment borne by workers and companies that become non-competitive vis-a-vis imported products.

Company strategies for dealing with protectionist policies follow the same criteria noted previously. Firms can shift between such alternatives as foreign direct investment and imports when barriers make one alternative preferable to the other. They can diversify their international operations to avoid the hostage problem that occurs when they are dependent on one national market or supply source, and thus one national government has sovereignty over their activities. And, of course, they can try to pass on the costs of trade and investment controls to their customers.

QUESTIONS

1. How can a French clothing manufacturer cope with a new increase in the tariff on its shipments of garments to the United States, its biggest export market? Present your answer in terms of cost conditions, competitive market conditions, and strategic goals.

2. What are the basic principles of U.S. trade policy today? Explain how specific policies follow these principles.

3. What is the difference between a tariff, a quota, and a subsidy, in terms of their economic impact. (Assume that all three limit imports to achieve a given increase in domestic production and sales.)

4. Assume that South Korea's government offers low-cost loans to exporters as a way to stimulate the economy. How would you, as a company manager of a U.S. firm competing with Korean firms, react in your activities? That is, how would you alter your present business, which is 100 percent domestic production and sales? Also, would you try to influence the U.S. government or to utilize its programs in this situation? How and why?

5. What is a solution to the steel imports problem in the United States, viewed from the perspective of a U.S. steel company? (Use the case at the end of this chapter for additional information.)

6. What should the U.S. government do to deal with the current problems of the steel industry? Why?

7. What is the probable impact of direct investment controls on the flow of FDI into a country? Does the United States use any such controls? Which countries do?

8. Is there any industry in which the United States could justify using an infant industry tariff? What justifications are used for U.S. tariff policy?

9. Explain the idea of dumping. What is an appropriate policy that a national government might adopt to deal with the dumping of foreign products?

10. What would you do, as manager of Toyota Motors Company in Japan, when faced with a "voluntary" limit on the number of cars you can export to the United States? Give details.

REFERENCES

Bhagwati, Jagdish. *Protectionism*. Cambridge, Mass.: MIT Press, 1988.

Canto, V., and A. Laffer. "The Effectiveness of Orderly Marketing Agreements: The Color TV Case." *Business Economics*, January 1983.

Cline, William. *The Future of World Trade in Textiles and Apparel*. Washington, D.C.: Institute for International Economics, 1987.

Coughlin, Cletus, and Geoffrey Wood. "An Introduction to Non-tariff Barriers to Trade." Federal Reserve Bank of St. Louis *Review* (January–February 1989).

Hufbauer, Gary, and Howard Rosen. *Trade Policy for Troubled Industries*. Washington, D.C.: Institute for International Economics, 1986.

Khanna, Ram. "Market Sharing under the Multifibre Arrangement: Consequences of Non-tariff Barriers in the Textile Trade." *Journal of World Trade Law* (1990).

Lindert, P. *International Economics*. 8th ed. Homewood, Ill.: Richard D. Irwin, 1988.

Munger, M. "The Costs of Protectionism." *Challenge,* January–February 1984.

NOTES

[1]According to the U.S. International Trade Commission, U.S. tariffs in 1990 averaged 6 percent on *dutiable* items. Many items enter the United States with no tariff at all—including thousands of goods imported from less developed countries under the generalized system of preferences (GSP). Overall, the average U.S. tariff in 1990 was about 4 percent *ad valorem*.

[2]The program of trade adjustment assistance (TAA) does support U.S. firms hurt by import competition, but this support is paid mainly as unemployment compensation to laid-off workers. See *United States Code Annotated*, Title 19, Custom Duties, Sections 2271–2298. The compensation arrangement lapsed in December 1985 and was passed into the general federal program of unemployment compensation. In March 1986, the compensation arrangement was reinstated for six years, retroactive to December 1985.

[3]In 1984, Canada switched from a policy of using the Foreign Investment Review Agency to limit FDI coming into the country, to a policy of promoting inward FDI to stimulate economic growth, with a change in the agency's name to Investment Canada.

[4]The requirements for U.S. government purchases from domestic suppliers appear in the *United States Code Annotated*, Title 41, Public Contracts, Sections 10a–10d.

[5]John Deere de Mexico, S.A. de C.V., Harvard Business School case 9-313-239.

[6]Of course, promotion of exports is a means of subsidizing one country's products at the expense of import-competing products in other countries. The OECD (industrial) countries generally disallow export subsidies by their trading partners, since these subsidies offer unfair competitive advantage to the recipient firms. On the other hand, less developed countries are usually permitted to use such subsidies to increase their firms' abilities to compete internationally. (That is, the industrial countries usually do not retaliate against such subsidies by LDCs.)

[7]It should be recognized that the reasoning presented here compares free trade with restricted trade using the stated barriers. If the country begins with some existing situation of trade restrictions, one cannot simply conclude that reducing one trade barrier will unequivocally improve the country's welfare.

The argument in favor of reducing reliance on foreign suppliers *may* have a justifiable political/strategic basis. That is, if the foreign country at some time chooses to restrict its supply of the product due to a political decision, the importing country may indeed suffer a loss of critical goods. On economic grounds, this problem should be factored into the calculus as a risk of buying from the foreign supplier, which may or may not be cause for replacing the imports.

[8]Canto and Laffer (1983).

[9]*Automotive News*, February 16, 1986, and March 10, 1986.

[10]The Caribbean Basin Initiative was passed into law in 1983. In January 1985, the tariff provisions of the initiative were finally enacted.

[11]The Trading-with-the-Enemy legislation appears in the *United States Code Annotated*, Title 50, War and National Defense Appendix, Emergency and Post-war Legislation, Sections 1–43.

[12]The Foreign Sales Corporation was established as part of the Trade and Tariff Act of 1984.

[13]See note 4 above.

[14] See note 2 above. See also Hufbauer and Rosen (1986).

[15]A very useful discussion of the U.S. capital control program appears in Gunter Dufey and Rolf Mirus, *International Finance* (New York: McGraw-Hill, 1987), chap. 10.

The Steel Imports Problem

Competitive Conditions in the Industry

"The U.S. steel industry was hard hit by the deep recession of 1974–75 and the sluggish recovery of world steel demand that followed. . . . Current capacity utilization rates in the industry are near 80 percent compared to a peak of 97 percent in 1973. Profit rates are less than half of 1974 peak levels." In addition. "the U.S. balance of trade in steel has shifted. In 1955, the U.S. exported more steel than it imported; today, imports are supplying nearly 18 percent of domestic requirements, and our exports of steel are negligible." (1977)[1]

"The large U.S. steel producers are running out of time . . . . If we have no desire as a government to have a viable, strong steel industry . . . then we will not have one. . . . From 1978 to 1981 the real cash flow of six major U.S. steelmakers fell to minus $7.4 billion. . . . Last year (1982) when only 48 percent of the nation's steel capacity was operating, imports accounted for 22 percent of the U.S. market. If current trends continue, they could grow to 40 percent within the next decade." (1983)[2]

Both of the statements above reflect the continuing crisis in the United States steel industry in the 1980s. Many of the major firms have gone into bankruptcy or have been acquired by remaining firms in the industry, so that in 1987 only half a dozen major steelmakers remain. Average return on equity in the industry has been negative for the past decade. Even the leading firm, U.S. Steel, has diversified such that about half of its business is now in the oil industry (from the acquisition of Marathon Oil Company). This case presents a perspective of the industry that focuses on the possible strategies domestic steelmakers and the U.S. government can take to deal with the crisis.

The difficulties encountered by U.S. steel producers in the 1970s arose because of (1) increases in the cost of producing steel products, and (2) increases in steel imports, especially from Japan. The cost increases from 1972 to 1977 occurred mainly because (a) coal prices rose 138 percent, (b) iron ore prices rose 76 percent, and (c) steel scrap prices rose 133 percent. Additionally, from 1973 to 1977 hourly employment costs rose 66 percent while productivity rose at only 1.9 percent per year.[3] Profitability in the steel industry was 3.5 percent in 1976, well below the average for all manufacturing.

The difficulties that continue into the early 1990s include relatively high wage costs; relatively low productivity, a strong dollar until 1985, which led to higher

---

A teaching note by Professor Robert Grosse, October 1978 (revised 1991).

U.S. prices compared to major trading partners such as Japan and Germany; increasing competition from such newly industrializing countries as Brazil and South Korea; and finally, worldwide overcapacity in the industry, which is leading to widespread losses and government subsidies to local steel industries in many countries. Profitability for the U.S. industry has been negative in almost every year during this decade. Table 1 compares some of the industry conditions in the United States with major trading partners such as Japan, West Germany, and the United Kingdom.

The Perspective of the U.S. Government

The U.S. government's policies will reflect basic views of international economics. Since World War II, the United States had been the champion of free trade. This position has clear theoretical implications—that free trade leads to increased world output and employment and increased economic interdependence. Empirical studies tend to support the view that output, employment, and interdependence all increase with freer trade. Free trade, however, requires free competition in the markets for production factors in each country, and adoption of a laissez-faire policy by each national government, in order to satisfy the theoretical assumptions and generate the expected benefits. If a government subsidizes exports, then retaliation by the government of the importing country may be justified, since such subsidies interfere with free-market operations, thus altering the distribution of benefits from trade. The facts of the present case need to be clarified on three counts:

1. What are the costs of production in each country?
2. What subsidies are offered by Japanese and European governments?
3. What existing U.S. policies are available?

See Table 1 on the first point. Since we lack the time and resources to do further analysis, let us accept the U.S. government conclusions on the second point: "Recent evidence suggests that the value of the various subsidies offered by governments to their steel producers does not represent a significant share of total production costs. Unpublished FTC figures place the value of these subsidies at less than 1 percent of total cost for Japan, West Germany, and Italy." With respect to the third point, the U.S. government has used tariffs, voluntary restraints, trigger prices and subsequent fines, and trade adjustment assistance to remedy the problems created by imports.

If we wish to pursue the free-trade ideal, and disallow "cheating" that may occur through government subsidies, we need to evaluate the Japanese steel prices versus Japanese steel production costs, adjusted to exclude subsidies. Graphically, we need to see whether the Japanese price is less than the average total cost (of production *plus* delivery).

As long as the Japanese sell steel in Japan at prices high enough to pay for total fixed costs plus variable costs, they can sell any excess abroad at prices that cover only the variable costs and still remain profitable. As far as our data are concerned, it does *not* appear that the Japanese are dumping the steel products shown.

The "trigger price" system, which allowed the United States to penalize Japanese (or other) importers if dumping occurred, offered a highly visible means of protection for U.S. steel producers. Unfortunately, this system did not improve the efficiency of these manufacturers.

TABLE 1

Steel Industry Operating Conditions in Four Industrial Countries, 1976, 1986, and 1990 *(US$/metric ton)*

	United States	Japan	West Germany	United Kingdom	Korea
1976					
Labor costs					
Manhours per ton shipped	11.12	9.47	9.53	18.27	
Employment cost per hour	12.18	5.62	8.17	4.44	
Employment cost per ton	135.37	53.09	77.90	81.03	
Materials costs					
Iron ore per ton	48.78	32.77	38.29	38.30	
Coal cost per ton	44.54	57.39	62.18	58.95	
Total materials cost	190.26	159.42	203.21	188.91	
Total cost/ton*	350.61	262.50	308.22	306.38	
Total revenue/ton	352.52	280.59	333.97	301.67	
1986					
Labor costs					
Manhours per ton shipped	6.41	6.05	7.21	6.49	
Employment cost per hour	24.14	14.16	15.96	12.12	
Employment cost per ton	154.64	85.73	115.06	78.69	
Materials costs					
Iron ore per ton	69.35	42.18	61.98	60.24	
Coal cost per tone	51.63	64.79	73.31	60.22	
Total materials cost	289.82	251.14	269.48	264.75	
Total cost/ton*	481.71	426.47	428.97	366.67	
Total revenue/ton	603.89	553.55	508.38	470.74	
1990					
Labor costs					
Manhours per ton	5.3	5.6	5.7	5.7	7.1
Employment cost per hour	26.5	24	31	22	8
Employment cost per ton	141	142	178	128	57
Materials costs	64	79	80	74	76
Iron ore per ton					
Coal cost per ton	39	48	49	44	49
Total materials cost	144	144	160	146	159
Total cost/ton*	459	470	510	446	384
Total revenue/ton	517	620	592	625	n.a.

*Does not include financing costs.

n.a. = Not available.

Source: Paine Webber, Inc., *World Steel Dynamics*, "Cost Monitor #9," 1987 and "Cost Monitor #13," 1991, New York: Paine Webber, Inc.

Any real solution to this problem will require the U.S. steel producers to become cost competitive. Perhaps this competitiveness could occur if U.S. producers specialized in some steel products and left others to be sold by importers. Trade adjustment assistance, which is consistent with the goal of free trade, will allow workers to be retrained and factories retooled so that U.S. employment is not seriously harmed. Consumers will benefit, of course, from the lower prices of steel imports.

This brief commentary certainly does not "solve" the steel imports problem. It does provide, however, some factual information necessary for taking an informed position and carrying out an analysis of many of the major issues involved in the controversy. There are two key questions: (1) What are the potential strategies for U.S. steelmakers; and (2) What is an optimal policy for the U.S. government?

CASE NOTES

[1]Taken from the Council on Wage and Price Stability (COWPS) report to President Carter, October 5, 1977.

[2]Taken from the article, "Time Runs out for Steel," *Business Week*, June 13, 1983.

[3]All data from the report to the president from the Council on Wage and Price Stability.

10 Economic Integration and International Business

This chapter continues the discussion of government policies that affect international business, focusing on multinational agreements among governments to reduce business barriers among member countries. The European Community is the most important regional example of such an agreement. In addition, the worldwide General Agreement on Tariffs and Trade (GATT) is discussed. This chapter is institutional in nature; it describes the rules and institutions in the various integration groups and notes implications for company managers operating in these groups. The main goals of the chapter are to:

1. Note the basic costs and benefits of economic integration (such as trade creation and trade diversion).

2. Explain the structure and functioning of GATT.

3. Present a panorama of types of economic integration and discuss country groups that illustrate each type.

4. Explain the structure and functioning of the European Community.

5. Explain the structure and functioning of the Andean Pact and other integration efforts of less developed countries.

6. Explore company strategies for dealing with integration rules.

INTRODUCTION

Economic integration involves the establishment of transnational rules on economic activity that lead to greater trade and economic cooperation between countries. That is, a group of nations can (often painstakingly) negotiate a set of commonly accepted rules on intragroup trade and other economic relations that lead to increased (more beneficial) commercial dealings among them. By creating a multicountry market, the group encourages larger-scale (lower-cost) production and greater competition among firms in the group, promoting efficiency in each of the national economies involved. Generally, economic integration efforts have been made at the regional level, encompassing 5–10 countries in close geographic proximity—though one of the most important transnational agreements is the General Agreement on Tariffs and Trade (GATT), which now involves 96 nations throughout the world.

The most visible result of regional economic integration at present is the European Community. This group was formed after World War II, when it sought to pool resources to promote reconstruction and generate rapid economic growth after the destruction caused by the war. The European Community (often called the Common Market) is discussed below in some detail, as are Comecon (among Eastern European countries), the Andean Pact (among five Latin American countries), ASEAN (among five Asian countries), and Caricom (among more than a dozen Caribbean islands).

Economic integration efforts among less developed countries (LDCs) tend to pursue the goals of increased economic ties and growth, plus a goal of increased political power in dealing with the developed countries. Countries within Latin America, the Caribbean, Africa, and Asia have joined together in almost a dozen regional integration agreements. Each of these agreements has sought to raise the level of economic development of the member countries and to create a better bargaining position with the developed countries. Thus far, the accomplishments of the LDC integration efforts have been small, but the goals remain important, and such efforts are likely to continue.

Economic integration involves a sharing of the costs and benefits that result from reducing barriers to commerce and financial dealings among member countries. Each member of an integration group must agree to give up some national policy prerogatives to a transnational (regional) authority, typically on such issues as tariffs and movements of labor and capital among the countries in the group. Each of these countries expects this to generate gains from increased trade and other business activity, such as foreign direct investment, that will exceed the costs of adjusting to the new rules.

The groups that have implemented regional economic integration affect company activities in a number of ways, but primarily by altering the rules on exports and imports among members of the group. Additional effects include changes in tax rates and policies, removal of restrictions on movements of money and people among member countries, and other regulatory changes. These effects are discussed below in the context of specific economic integration efforts.

The basic economics of regional integration concern the shifts in business activity that occur as a result of the integration process. Two fundamental principles relate to the trade effects of integration. First, if the integration group causes member countries to alter their production toward greater efficiency (i.e., toward their comparative advantages) and to trade more extensively with one another, then **trade creation** occurs. Trade creation is the result of reducing trade barriers among member countries, whose firms subsequently compete more freely with one another. More efficient, lower-cost producers in member countries will gain markets from less-efficient producers, thus creating more exports among the countries in the group. The creation of new trade is demonstrated in Figure 10–1.

S_1S_1 and DD are the supply and demand curves for any good that may be traded between countries 1 and 2. The graph assumes that country 2 is the more efficient producer of the product, as shown by its supply curve S_2S_2. The trade barriers before economic integration are depicted by the vertical distance between country 2's supply curve and the supply-plus-tariff curve labeled TT. When countries 1 and 2 agree to eliminate tariffs between themselves, then country 1's consumption of the product increases from B to B'. Consequently, country 1's firms supply only OA' (instead of OA) amount of the product, and the rest, $A'B'$, is imported from country 2. This trade creation benefits country 1 by lowering the price of the product to consumers and by forcing productive resources to be shifted to other, more efficient uses.

Second, if the integration group causes member countries to decrease their trade with nonmember countries, then **trade diversion** occurs. Trade diversion would occur in the above example if the tariff reduction caused imports from country 2 to replace other imports from the rest of the world, which is more efficient but which still faces the unreduced tariff of country 1. Thus, trade diversion is the loss of production and exports from more efficient nonmember countries to less efficient member countries that are protected by tariffs or other barriers against nonmembers.

Empirical studies of these effects in regional integration groups have tended to demonstrate substantial trade creation and little trade diversion within developed-country groups, but less impressive results among less developed countries. Table 10–1 presents measures of the trade creation effects of regional economic integration in both industrial and developing-country groups. Notice

FIGURE 10–1

Trade Creation in Product X between Countries 1 and 2

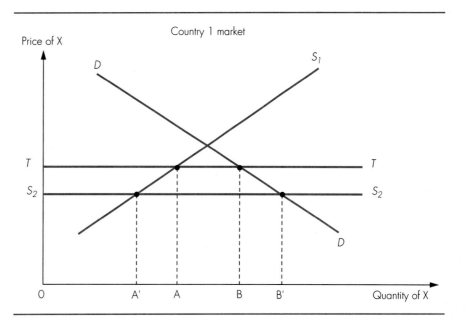

TABLE 10–1

Trade Creation Effects of Regional Integration

A. Intra-trade of Developed Countries by Region

Economic Groupings (regions)	Value of Intra-trade[a] (US $ billions)					Share of Intra-trade in:									
						World Exports (%)					Total Group Exports (%)				
	1960	1970	1975	1980	1982	1960	1970	1975	1980	1982	1960	1970	1975	1980	1982
EEC (6)	10.3	43.4				8.0	13.9				34.6	48.9			
EFTA[b]	2.9	9.4				2.3	3.0				15.7	21.8			
EEC (expanded)[c]			145.9	347.0	303.0			16.7	17.3	16.4			49.4	52.8	51.9
Trade in manufacturers between expanded EEC and residual EFTA member countries			45.1	105.9	85.1			5.2	5.3	4.6			12.9	13.7	12.4
Intra-trade in manufacturers of residual EFTA member countries			8.5	14.8	12.4			1.0	0.7	0.7			16.1	12.8	12.0
USA–CANADA[d] (preferential)	—	5.1	11.1	15.7	19.6	—	1.6	1.3	0.8	1.1	—	8.7	8.0	5.7	7.2
CMEA[e]	8.1	18.4	44.4	79.0	82.3	6.3	5.9	5.1	4.0	4.5	62.3	59.4	57.4	51.0	49.8
Total	21.2	76.1	225.0	562.4	502.4	16.6	24.4	29.2	28.1	27.2	34.6	34.5	45.2	46.7	44.7

[a]Based on exports (f.o.b.) data.
[b]Excluding goods shown in annex D of the Stockholm Convention.
[c]The expanded nine-country EEC.
[d]Trade under the U.S.–Canada Automotive Products Agreement negotiated in 1965.
[e]Council for Mutual Economic Assistance.
Source: UNCTAD (1984), p. 38.

that among the LDC blocs, only the Central American Common Market demonstrated a large percentage of intra-group trade (over 20% of total trade)—and that group virtually ceased to operate after the fall of the Somoza regime in Nicaragua in 1979. The European Community countries have moved from about one third intra-group trade to over 50 percent, though membership has increased importantly as well.

From a conceptual point of view, the total economic gains generated by the formation of an integration group tend to be larger when (1) the member countries initially have very high trade barriers among themselves, so that more trade creation occurs; (2) the member countries possess relatively similar comparative advantages, so that less trade diversion occurs; (3) the number of member countries is larger, so that more comparative advantages can be exploited; and (4) the tariffs imposed on nonmember countries are lower, so that less trade diversion occurs.[1]

Before turning to *regional* integration examples, we discuss the most important *global* agreement on the reduction of trade barriers.

TABLE 10–1

Concluded

B. Intra-trade of Developing Countries and Territories by Region															
Economic Groupings (regions)	Value of Intra-trade (US $ millions)					Exports to Developing Countries as Percent of Total Group Exports					Intra-trade of Group as a Percent of Total Exports of Each Group				
	1960	1970	1976	1979	1982	1960	1970	1976	1979	1982	1960	1970	1976	1979	1982
ASEAN[a,b]	839	860	3,619	8,658	16,109	32.8	31.7	30.3	33.6	36.5	21.7	14.7	13.9	17.0	23.3
Bangkok Agreement[c]	—	47	142	444	688	—	20.4	25.7	27.5	31.8	—	1.5	1.0	1.8	2.1
CACEU[d]	3	33	75	132	150	8.3	11.9	15.0	23.7	14.5	1.6	3.4	3.9	4.0	3.6
CACM[e]	33	299	653	896	820	10.0	29.6	29.2	27.6	30.3	7.5	26.8	21.6	19.3	21.8
CARICOM[f]	27	73	212	256	414	12.2	16.6	17.6	19.9	23.2	4.5	7.3	6.7	6.6	9.0
ALADI[g]	564	1,290	4,434	8,289	10,400	19.4	21.2	26.9	29.6	30.3	7.7	10.2	12.8	13.7	13.2
Of which: Andean Group[h]	25	109	594	770	1,167	28.8	29.3	36.2	31.2	39.2	0.7	2.3	4.2	3.3	4.5
WAEC[i]	6	73	117	247	374	14.8	15.1	13.6	17.2	21.0	2.0	9.1	6.7	6.7	10.7
Total Excluding ASEAN and Bangkok Agreement	633	1,768	5,551	9,820	13,325	18.1	21.0	25.2	28.1	28.9	7.2	10.8	12.3	12.9	14.1
Total	—	2,675	9,313	18,922	30,122	—	19.8	26.8	29.8	32.1	—	8.8	11.0	12.5	15.4

[a]Association of Southeast Asian Nations, 1967.
[b]Figures adjusted to exclude entrepot trade. Figures for Singapore exports to Malaysia and Thailand are derived from import statistics of these two trading partners.
[c]Bangkok Agreement.
[d]Central African Customs and Economic Union, 1964.
[e]Central American Common Market, 1960.
[f]Caribbean Community, 1968; Eastern Caribbean Common Market is not included.
[g]Asociacion Latino Americana de Integracion, formerly LAFTA, 1960.
[h]Andean Group, 1969.
[i]West African Economic Community, 1959 (initially West Africa Customs Union).
Source: UNCTAD (1984), pp. 39, 40.

THE GENERAL AGREEMENT ON TARIFFS AND TRADE (GATT)

GATT is an institutional structure that the industrialized countries established just after World War II to promote expanded trade among its members and to avoid the protectionism practiced during the prewar depression years. Initially, in 1948, GATT had 23 member countries. In 1990 there were 96 members, including industrialized, less developed, and formerly communist nations. Clearly, GATT is more than a regional effort to share trade benefits among a small group of countries; it is a global effort at economic integration to enhance the gains generated by trade.

GATT maintains a permanent secretariat of about 300 people located in Geneva, Switzerland. The main functions of the secretariat are to collect information and to carry out studies of trade issues that are relevant to the governmental negotiations held under GATT's auspices. Decision making is reserved for the representatives of the member countries, who approve exceptions to the basic rules that favor global free trade (e.g., permission for the European Community to extend tariff reductions only to its members).

GATT has been used as a forum to negotiate multilateral reductions in trade barriers. Since 1948, there have been eight "rounds" of negotiations, ending with the Uruguay Round, which was under way in 1990. In each round, tariff levels among GATT's members have been reduced, and other trade-liberalizing steps have been taken. The Tokyo Round, in the 1970s, was the first to focus specifically on reducing nontariff barriers, namely customs valuation (which can be used to overassess imports), government procurement, import licensing, subsidies, antidumping measures, and technical barriers to trade. By the end of the Tokyo Round, tariffs among GATT member countries averaged less than 10 percent *ad valorem* on all products, though greater tariffs and other restrictions still exist in some countries, and on agricultural products more than on manufactured goods.

GATT was formed as a multilateral institution for improving trade relations among its members, specifically seeking to avoid bilateralism, in which pairs of countries negotiate trade agreements that exclude other countries. A fundamental concept in GATT negotiations is the **most-favored-nation** (MFN) principle, which requires that any tariff reduction negotiated between any two members of GATT be extended to all members of GATT. Thus, if the United States and Japan agree to reduce tariffs on their trade in electrical appliances, the same reduction must be passed on to the other members of GATT. Most-favored-nation treatment has ensured the continued multilateralism of a large part of international trade negotiations since World War II.

Many exceptions have been made to GATT's basic rules. Since sovereignty ultimately rests with national governments, any transnational agreements such as GATT are of course subject to the continued willingness of countries to participate and accept the rules. The main exceptions to adherence to GATT's rules have been allowed to countries facing a balance of payments crisis. Such countries are generally permitted to erect temporary restrictions on imports until the balance of payments crisis ends. In addition, countries that form a regional bloc for economic integration are allowed to create trade policies that are more favorable to members of the bloc than to outsiders, as long as the bloc does not raise new trade barriers against other members of GATT. Each of the regional blocs discussed below has tried to eliminate trade barriers among its members and to leave in place barriers to the imports of other countries.

In 1986, a conference was held in Punta del Este, Uruguay, to discuss the formal opening of a new round of GATT. The Uruguay Round began in 1987, but it is not expected to conclude until the early 1990s. This round of negotiations focuses on four previously neglected areas: trade in agricultural products; trade in services, such as banking and data processing; constraints on foreign direct investment that limit trade; and protection of intellectual property, such as patents, copyrights, and trademarks.[2]

REGIONAL ECONOMIC INTEGRATION—THE BASIC TYPOLOGY

Economic integration in its broadest sense signifies the expansion of commercial and financial ties among the nations of the world. This process has been going on for centuries, making rapid advances as transportation and communication among nations become easier and less costly. Various political empires of the past pursued economic integration as a policy for economic development, seeking in this way to realize gains from trade and specialization. Since World

War II, economic integration has been pursued by small groups of countries that wanted to expand their national markets, increase their economic and political power, and realize the economic gains of greater intra-group trade. Half a dozen regional blocs were established in the 1950s, and several more have been established since then. To understand the rationales behind these blocs and to see their impacts on business activities, it will be useful to present a typology of integration forms.

Though no regional bloc fits perfectly into any of the following categories, each can be placed reasonably accurately in one or another, and the categories are quite distinct. Five increasing levels of **regional economic integration** can be distinguished:

1. Free-trade area.
2. Customs union.
3. Common market.
4. Economic union.
5. Political union.

Each succeeding level of integration involves greater cooperation among the bloc's member countries, and at the ultimate level the bloc members become unified into a single political entity, a new country. Countries need to follow the steps sequentially until political union has been achieved—most regional blocs remain at some level of integration without seeking to attain closer ties. Some analysts do argue, however, that the greatest integration yields the greatest gains from integration—so underlying pressures toward greater ties may exist.[3] These pressures were certainly seen as Great Britain debated entry into the European Common Market from its inception and in 1973 eventually joined that regional group. Pressures to dissolve or limit political union while retaining economic integration have become quite visible in Canada (with the Quebec separatist movement) and in the Soviet Union (with several states seeking political independence).

Free-Trade Area

The first level of economic integration, the **free-trade area,** involves the elimination of tariffs on trade among the countries in the regional group. Most of the integration efforts in the post-World War II period have begun from this base. Following the reasoning of Chapter 3 concerning the benefits of free trade, each participant in the free-trade area expects to gain by specializing in the production of goods and services in which it possesses comparative advantages and by importing from other countries in the group products and services in which it faces comparative disadvantages. Thus, trade should be *created* among member countries, giving them less-expensive access to more goods. (Note that this trade may take place between unrelated firms or within MNEs that operate in more than one member country.)

A cost of free-trade areas to member countries is trade diversion from outside countries. Since tariffs remain on imports from nonmember countries, some trade may be diverted from the most efficient producers outside the area to less-efficient producers inside the area, who are still protected by tariffs. In the extreme, if every country belonged to one free-trade area, then the gains to all would be maximized. Given the numerous and complex reasons for trade barriers that exist today, regional blocs have formed free-trade areas to obtain a kind of second-best gain, since full free trade appears unattainable.

Among the free-trade areas is the European Free Trade Area (EFTA), formed at about the same time as the Common Market (in 1960) and comprising those Western European countries that did not become Common Market members. Today, the members of the EFTA are Austria, Norway, Sweden, and Switzerland. (The United Kingdom and Denmark left EFTA to join the Common Market in 1973, as did Portugal in 1985.) The Latin American Free Trade Association (LAFTA), originally composed of the Spanish-speaking countries in South America plus Brazil and Mexico, has evolved into a group called ALADI (Asociación Latino Americana de Integración), which includes the same countries. Even after 30 years of existence, this group has *not* been able to eliminate tariffs or other trade barriers among its members. It has, however, led to some reduction of trade barriers and an increase in economic cooperation.[4]

A final free-trade area that was negotiated fairly recently illustrates a possible trend in international economic agreements for the 1990s. The United States and Canada in 1988 signed the U.S.–Canada Free Trade Agreement, effectively creating a free-trade area in North America. The remaining country in North America, namely Mexico, has subsequently entered into discussions with the United States and Canada to explore possible membership or other links to the free-trade area. This movement parallels the highly publicized effort of the European Community countries to expand their integration and the various efforts in Asia to create a regional trading bloc there. The U.S.–Canada agreement provides for elimination of tariffs and NTBs to virtually all trade between the countries (with exceptions such as auto trade, that is governed by a previous bilateral agreement).

Customs Union

The second level of regional economic integration, the **customs union,** involves the elimination of tariffs among member countries *plus* the establishment of a common external tariff structure toward nonmember countries. As with each succeeding form of integration, member countries are required to give up control over more economic policies to the group than they gave up at the previous level—in this case the regulation of imports from outside countries. The additional benefit form this policy is intended to be the avoidance of bias in attracting imports to the group; if external tariffs differ from country to country, then outsiders will favor importing into the lowest-tariff member country in order to sell in the whole group. In this way, the lowest-tariff member of the group would benefit at the expense of the other members. The common external tariff takes away that possibility.

None of the regional integration groups in existence today has been formed specifically to achieve a customs union. Most of these groups aim for even greater economic ties among their members—that is, a common market or even economic union. In fact, because of slow progress in attaining further levels of integration, several of the regional integration groups can be categorized as customs unions. The Caribbean Common Market is one such group, and the Andean Pact is another. The former group includes 12 of the English-speaking islands of the Caribbean (all former British colonies), and the latter includes

Bolivia, Colombia, Ecuador, Peru, and Venezuela. In both of these groups, efforts are under way to reduce trade barriers and increase intra-group business, but thus far neither has achieved the regulatory harmonization of a common market.

Common Market

The third level of economic integration, the **common market**, is characterized by the same tariff policy as the customs union *plus* freedom of movement for factors of production (i.e., labor and capital) among member countries. A common market is perhaps the ultimate feasible step in multi-country associations for permitting individuals and firms to carry out their transnational business activities in member countries without facing barriers to movements of products, people, or money. This level of integration avoids the intercountry regulatory bias on trade and direct investment, both of which are thus left to determination by market factors.

The best example of a regional group that constitutes a common market is the European Common Market, also known as the European Community. This bloc of 12 countries includes Belgium, Denmark, France, Germany, Greece, Ireland, Italy, Luxembourg, the Netherlands, Portugal, Spain, and the United Kingdom. It is discussed in some detail below.

A regional group that possessed some of the characteristics of a common market was the Council for Mutual Economic Assistance, or COMECON, which included the Soviet Union and most of its allies (Bulgaria, Cuba, Czechoslovakia, the German Democratic Republic, Hungary, Mongolia, Poland, Romania, and Vietnam). These countries were all communistic, so their economic systems did not permit free trade in the first place. However, they did utilize agreements to stimulate reciprocal exchanges of materials, technical assistance, and specialization of production, while limiting participation by outsiders in the members' economies.[5] As a result of the opening of Eastern Europe that began in 1989, COMECON has lost its importance; many of the members are seeking to join the European Community in the early 1990s.

Economic Union

An **economic union** is characterized by harmonization of economic policy beyond that of a common market. Specifically, an economic union seeks to unify monetary and fiscal policy among its member countries. A common currency, or a permanently fixed exchange rate, is one aspect of an economic union. Harmonized tax rates and tax-rate structures are other aspects. To a large degree, national governments participating in an economic union relinquish control over much of national economic policy to the group.

As one might expect, due to these major policy constraints, there are not many economic unions in existence. At present, only the Belgium–Luxembourg Economic Union (BLEU) fits into this category. Belgium and Luxembourg maintain a fixed exchange rate (1 Belgian franc = 1 Luxembourg franc) and a highly coordinated set of monetary policies. Their tax rates and structures are virtually identical. They reach their other political decisions on a largely separate basis, and they each maintain a quite distinct political existence. These two countries are the smallest in the Common Market, and they have allied themselves with each other primarily to gain a larger voice in European affairs.

The European Community, via its "Europe 1992" initiative, has defined its objectives broadly to achieve the status of an economic union. That is, the community seeks to establish a monetary harmonization that would lead to a common currency, plus much greater harmonization of fiscal policies. These goals are accompanied by a long list of other steps that are leading to reduced restrictions on business and on individuals as they move between member countries of the EC. It is conceivable, as the European countries continue to pursue competitiveness with North America and Japan, that the EC may indeed achieve most of the characteristics of an economic union during the 1990s.

Political Union

The highest level of regional economic integration is **political union,** under which all economic policies are unified. Countries that unite under a common government lose their national identities and become parts of a single state. Important examples of political unions are Canada, the Soviet Union, and the United States, each of which combined independent states into a single country. In fact, since the members of a political union cease to be separate countries, perhaps political union should not be considered a part of economic integration at all. Political union, however, does form the logical end point of increased economic cooperation among a group of nations.

The issue of political union has become especially significant in the early 1990s, as the Soviet Union grapples with its opening to a pluralistic political system and simultaneously the acceptance of a market economy. This overwhelming shift in direction has lead some of the states within the Soviet Union (such as Lithuania) to seek political independence and to redefine economic interdependence. And among the former members of the Soviet-led bloc of communist countries, new economic linkages are rapidly evolving. East Germany has joined West Germany in forming a political union, i.e., a single country. Several other Soviet allies are pursuing membership in the European Community, which may imply economic (though not political) union. It remains to be seen just how much economic union can be achieved without a single political power.

The fall of the Berlin Wall and the opening of the Eastern bloc is by far the most significant international political and economic event of the second half of this century. Nonetheless, major changes in direction are occurring in other parts of the world as well. Political union in Canada, for example, has been challenged once again by the Province of Quebec, that seeks to protect its unique (French-based) culture and society through greater independence. It appears that this independence will occur through greater political freedom within the sovereign state—but the results may very well include increased ability for the provincial government to tax its residents and spend revenues according to its own decisions. Other Canadian provinces are examining their own options in light of the Quebec strategy, so that we may see a much weaker federation of provinces in Canada by the end of the decade.

One conclusion to be drawn from this discussion is that the forms of economic integration themselves are evolving during the 1990s. Most countries view freer trade as desirable and are promoting this goal through membership in GATT and through development of regional economic blocs. Full fiscal and monetary unification have historically been achieved only within nation states. The events of recent years show that some regional blocs are pursuing greater unification at the same time as some nations are permitting states or provinces greater autonomy in their fiscal and monetary affairs. The definitions of political and economic union may need to be redefined by the year 2000.

TABLE 10–2

Levels of Economic Integration

Level	Examples	Members
1. Free-trade area	European Free Trade Area	Austria, Norway, Sweden, Switzerland
	Latin American Free Trade Area (ALADI)	Argentina, Bolivia, Brazil, Chile, Colombia, Costa Rica, Ecuador, El Salvador, Guatemala, Honduras, Mexico, Panama, Paraguay, Uruguay, Venezuela
	U.S.–Canada Free Trade Agreement	United States, Canada
2. Customs union	Andean Pact	Bolivia, Colombia, Ecuador, Peru, Venezuela
	Caricom	Antigua and Barbuda, Bahamas, Barbados, Belize, Dominica, Grenada, Guyana, Jamaica, Montserrat, St. Kitts-Nevis, St. Lucia, St. Vincent, Trinidad and Tobago
3. Common market	European Community	Belgium, Denmark, France, Germany, Greece, Ireland, Italy, Luxembourg, Netherlands, Portugal, Spain, United Kingdom
4. Economic union	Belgium–Luxembourg Economic Union	Belgium, Luxembourg
5. Political union	United States, Soviet Union, Canada	

In sum, the five levels of economic integration do not necessarily represent a sequence of steps toward political and economic union. But they do present strategic alternatives for groups of countries that seek to increase their international (intragroup) trade and thus to benefit from the larger market created by the integration group. Examples of integration groups are shown in Table 10–2.

THE EUROPEAN COMMUNITY

History

Soon after the end of World War II, various policymakers and analysts began promoting the idea of a Western European union of some sort.[6] One goal of the union was to assure the cooperation of the countries in the region and thus avoid another cataclysmic war. A second goal was to create another economic and political force to deal with the Soviet Union and the United States, which arose from World War II as the leading world powers. U.S. policy has broadly supported these goals from the beginning, and through the Marshall Plan it provided substantial funding for European reconstruction (about $200 billion) from 1948 to 1952. Several regional organizations were formed in the early postwar years, including the Organization of European Economic Cooperation (OEEC), in 1948, which later became the Organization for Economic Cooperation and Development (OECD), and the Council of Europe, in 1949, which focused more on political issues than on economic ones.

The European Coal and Steel Community, a cooperative venture among Belgium, France, Germany, Italy, Luxembourg, and the Netherlands, began operating in 1952. This organization removed barriers on intra-group shipments of coal, iron, steel, and scrap. In 1957, the same six countries established Euratom to regulate and monitor the production of nuclear energy. Finally, also in 1957, they formed the European Economic Community (EEC). The combination of these three integration efforts has become known as the **European Community (EC).**

The Treaty of Rome, which established the European Economic Community, laid out a schedule for the elimination of intra-group tariffs, the creation of a common external tariff, and guidelines for additional harmonization of such economic policies as tax structures, exchange rates and controls, immigration among member countries, and agricultural support programs. Although the objectives of the integration process were not achieved exactly as scheduled, all of them have been realized—even with the expansion of the EC to include Denmark, Ireland, and the United Kingdom in 1973. (Greece entered the EC in 1981; Portugal and Spain, in 1985.) Thus, the European Community is truly a common market, and its members are continuing to pursue harmonized and joint economic policies that could lead to the further level of economic union.

Institutions

The European Community operates through four main institutions:

1. The Council of Ministers, which has one plenipotentiary representative from each member country.
2. The Commission, which has 17 members chosen by the member governments. (The 5 largest countries each choose 2 commissioners.)
3. The European Parliament, which has 518 members who are elected directly by the voters in each member country.
4. The Court of Justice, which has one judge from each member country, plus one additional judge chosen from France, Germany, Italy, or the United Kingdom on a rotating basis.

The *Council of Ministers* is the ultimate decision-making body of the European Community. Its 12 members are the foreign ministers of each country, though other representatives are often used when specific issues are under discussion—for example, the agriculture ministers when agricultural policy is being debated. With the exception of the budget, which is handled primarily by the Commission and the Parliament, the Council makes all the final decisions of the EC. It meets and has staff in Brussels, Belgium.

The Council of Ministers makes decisions only on proposals presented to it by the Commission. The main technical analysis and consensus building take place in the Commission, which is generally viewed as being relatively Europe-oriented and not biased toward the national interests of any individual country.

The *Commission* functions mainly as the executive branch of the European Community, drafting legislation for proposal to the Council, overseeing the implementation of Community policies, and carrying out studies of key policy issues. Although the Council retains the ultimate authority to adopt Community legislation and policies, the Commission prepares the decisions and regulations and does most of the technical work. The approximately 10,000 members of its staff form the main body of EC employees. The Commission's staff, like that of the Council, is located in Brussels.

The *European Parliament,* consisting of 518 members who are elected directly by voters in the 12 member countries, has been developing its range of functions only in the past few years. Although established by the Treaty of Rome in 1957, the Parliament did not become a directly elected body until 1979. At present, the Parliament serves mainly as the watchdog on Community expenditures, though it also evaluates other decisions of the Council. It meets in Strasbourg, France, but its secretariat of over 2,000 people is located in Luxembourg.

Finally, the *Court of Justice* serves as the official interpreter of European Community law. Most of its cases have related to interpretation or application of the Treaty of Rome, based on actions by member countries, individuals, and companies. As EC rules have become more closely interwoven with national laws in the member countries, the Court has been serving increasingly as a court of appeals for national courts when EC issues are concerned. The Court's 460 staff members and 11 judges have offices in Luxembourg.

Impact on Business

The European Community's impact on business activity in and among the member countries has been widely debated over the years. Most of the empirical studies on that impact have shown that on balance the EC has created much more trade than it has diverted from the rest of the world. Table 10–3 summarizes a number of such studies that appeared in the 1960s and 1970s. Similar conclusions have been drawn concerning the effects of the accession of Denmark, Great Britain, and Ireland to the EC.

TABLE 10–3

Estimates of Trade Creation and Diversion in the EEC

Author	Period Studied	Trade Created				Trade Diverted†			
		All Goods ($ billions)	(%)*	Manufactures ($ billions)	(%)*	All Goods ($ billion)	(%)*	Manufactures ($ billions)	(%)*
Prewo	1970	19.8	23	18.0	34	−2.5	6	−3.1	15
Truman	1968								
Unadjusted		–	–	9.2	26	–	–	−1.0	7
Adjusted		–	–	2.5	7	–	–	0.5	4
Balassa	1970	11.3	13	11.4	21	0.3	1	0.1	0
Kreinin (unweighted average of three estimates)	1969–70	–	–	8.4	–	–	–	1.1	–
Williamson and Bottrill	1969	–	–	11.2‡	25	–	–	0	0
Aitken	1967	9.2	14	–	–	0.6	2	–	–

*Percentages relate to total and extra-area imports of all goods and of manufactured products.
†Numbers with negative signs represent external trade creation.
‡Unweighted average of alternative estimates.
Source: Robson (1980), p. 177.

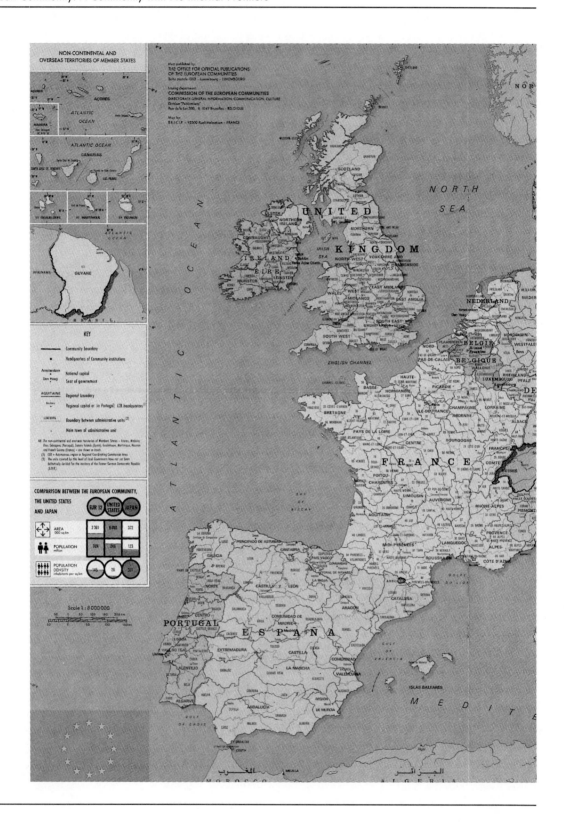

As far as foreign direct investment is concerned, the conclusions are somewhat different. Studies have shown that the EC played an insignificant role in the growth of FDI in its region; what mattered most appears to be the size of the individual national markets (Scaperlanda and Mauer 1969). A 1986 study of both trade and direct investment impacts on national incomes in each EC member country showed across-the-board favorable effects. Denmark is the only country to show a negative net impact of integration during 1974–1981, mainly because of very little trade creation (Marques Mendez, 1986).

The effects of the EC on other business activities have not been studied in as much detail as its impact on trade and direct investment. Most likely, some additional transnational business activity in Europe has resulted from the establishment of the European Community, given the Community's focus on creating a regional market. For example, efforts to create regional MNEs to compete with U.S.-based firms have led to the formation of Airbus Industries, which currently competes actively with such firms as McDonnell Douglas and Boeing. An intra-EC effort to create a globally competitive semiconductor and electronics consortium recently produced a pooling of resources by several European electronics companies (although IBM is seeking to be included in the group). The regional MNEs are expected to gain economies of scale and access to additional technology (and perhaps other competitive advantages) that would not be available to any one firm. Overall, Community-wide initiatives to stimulate additional business activities appear to have generated more than just trade and direct investment in the EC.

These initiatives have included efforts to facilitate the movement of working people among member countries. As a result, in the late 1960s the labor markets of each member country were opened up to the residents of other member countries, but additional policies were needed to harmonize health and pension benefits for workers who moved between member nations (and also to harmonize licensing requirements for various professions, which are somewhat different in each member country). Another initiative is the European Monetary System (discussed in Chapter 7), which is part of the EC's attempt to facilitate capital movement among its members. Although this system has not eliminated the problems of exchange-rate fluctuations and speculative capital flows, it has improved the ability of EC member countries to deal with intraregional financial problems.

EC 1992

The Commission of the European Community issued a white paper, called *Completing the Internal Market,* in 1985. This paper outlined the steps needed for the EC to achieve a single market for products, services, people, and financial dealings by yearend 1992. It essentially calls for the EC to finish the process of becoming a full common market—with free movement of labor, capital, and goods—by the end of 1992.

This process was formally reinforced by the Single European Act, that was ratified by the governments of all 12 members of the Community and went into effect in 1987. The Act commits each member country to eliminate restrictions on trade and financial flows by the end of 1992. A list of 300 key barriers to a single market was compiled, for systematic elimination during the period up to December 1992. (By mid-1990, agreement had been reached to eliminate over 100 of these barriers.)

**IB
ILLUSTRATION**

Airbus Industrie

One of the major consequences of forming a single European market is to enable European firms to achieve scale economies large enough to be competitive on a global scale with U.S.-based and Japanese competitors. One very interesting partnership was founded as a consortium of European aircraft manufacturers to produce commercial aircraft. In 1966 four European firms formed a joint venture called Airbus Industrie to begin design and production of a passenger aircraft capable of competing with Boeing, Lockheed, and McDonnell Douglas in the international market. The four European firms—Aerospatialle (France), Messerschmitt (Germany), British Aerospace, and Construcciones Aeronauticas (Spain)—individually did not have the capital base needed to design, test, produce, and sell large passenger aircraft in competition with the U.S. giants.

By pooling the partners' financial and technological resources, as well as by obtaining guaranteed orders from government-owned airlines in Europe, Airbus Industrie was able to begin selling wide-bodied jets in the early 1970s. Although the consortium has not yet reached profitability (losses are estimated at about $US10 billion through 1987), by 1989 the firm had taken almost one-third of the wide-bodied segment of the market with its A300, A310, and A320 planes. Because the Airbus planes served a market segment that had not been met by the large U.S. manufacturers at the time (viz., wide-bodied planes for 250–300 passengers on short and medium hauls), the firm carved out a short-term competitive advantage. The advantage has been eroded with the development of the Boeing 767, but Airbus had captured several major sales commitments of more than $US1 billion in the late 1980s, so it appears that the consortium may become a viable competitor against the U.S. producers.

The governments of each of the European partners in Airbus Industrie have judged that the technological, political, and other benefits of a locally owned and managed aircraft manufacturer outweigh the continued financial burden that the firm has placed on them since the early 1970s. They have each been satisfied to have a *piece* of the total, since each realized that its own economy was not large enough to sustain commercial aircraft production.[7] ∎

The impact of the expected policy changes for foreign businesses may very well be quite significant. For large multinational firms that already have extensive operations in European countries, the creation of a single market will enable them to rationalize their production and distribution systems, as barriers to crossnational shipments are fully dropped. In fact, these firms will be pressured to become truly European, as their competitors feel the same pressures and move to achieve economies of scale in both production and distribution. Companies such as Nestlé and Philips, along with Ford of Europe and IBM will challenge their rivals to become equally European in order to achieve the same low costs and high efficiency as these leaders in regional integration are attaining.

For non-European firms that do not have active operations in the region, EC 1992 will provide the challenge to enter the world's largest single market. Obviously, the EC's policy changes will *not* eliminate cultural differences that lead to different tastes and preferences, most importantly for consumer goods. It still will be necessary to advertise in different languages across the Community, and to provide different clothing styles, food tastes, etc., where preferences differ. However, for industrial-goods producers, the single Europe will truly be attractive, with its market of over 320 million people whose incomes rival those of U.S. consumers, and its geographic concentration.

As the reductions in barriers take place, more and more companies will create European strategies and presences. Their size will encourage such firms to pursue additional industrial-country markets—such as those in Japan and North America. For this additional reason, companies from North America or Japan need to consider EC 1992 as a challenge, since future competitors in their home markets are increasingly likely to come from Europe.

Because the EC 1992 initiative has a deadline of December 1992, it is very likely to stimulate many forms of strategic alliance between firms in the different European countries and with firms from outside countries as well. That is, since the single market will exist in formal terms starting in 1993, many firms want to have an established, ongoing business in place by then. New investment is not likely to achieve such an ambitious schedule—but acquisition of an existing firm in one EC country, or a joint venture, a joint production agreement, etc., with such a firm can enable the Europe-minded company to be fully operational by that time.

One of the fears of non-European firms is that the EC may create a "Fortress Europe" that is hostile to business from nonmember countries. This concern is probably overstated, since any outside firm still will be able to establish a subsidiary within the EC. One serious concern, however, is the Community's position of requiring "reciprocity" in the home country for EC firms if companies from that country want access to the EC. If a country such as Brazil does not allow foreign microcomputer firms to operate there, or Canada (and many other countries) does not allow foreign banks to open operations there, then firms in those industries from those countries will very likely encounter restrictions in the EC. This is a possible problem for U.S. firms in industries such as textiles (where the U.S. has quotas on foreign textile imports), banking (where the U.S. does not permit nationwide banking), and agriculture (where the U.S. has quotas and other restrictions on various products such as sugar and coffee).

To balance the optimistic tenor of the preceding discussion, it should be noted that many difficulties continue to hinder the EC's functioning. Primary among these difficulties is the Common Agricultural Policy, a system of subsidies and other support for EC farmers, which currently uses up over half of the EC budget. As new members join the EC, the problems presented by agricultural policy become even greater.

THE ANDEAN PACT

This section focuses on the **Andean Pact,** an economic integration effort among LDCs in Latin America. The institutional structure and goals of this group are largely based on those of the EC, but its impact on international business has been vastly different. The experience of the Andean countries is instructive with respect to the results of transnational LDC integration in general and with respect to policies toward foreign direct investment in particular.

History

The Andean Pact (or Ancom) was formed in 1969, when Bolivia, Chile, Colombia, Ecuador, and Peru signed the Cartagena Agreement. This group of countries actually constitutes a subgroup of the Latin American Free Trade Area (now called ALADI), comprising the smaller members of that association. In fact, the Andean Pact grew out of ALADI, when the six Andean countries (including Venezuela) decided that they were not satisfied with ALADI's sharing of benefits or its rate of progress. In 1966, the subgroup members signed the Declaration of Bogota, underlining their intent to create a new integration scheme. The Cartagena Agreement then spelled out integration steps, which included a tariff reduction program, the creation of a common external tariff, a transportation policy, industrial (sectoral) programming, and special concessions for the smallest members, Bolivia and Ecuador.

While progress since 1969 has been quite slow in virtually every area of integration, in 1971 Ancom did establish a highly visible economic policy that has been the focal point of much discussion about its effectiveness. That policy was the Common Regime on Foreign Investment, Licensing, and Patents—or *Decision 24*. Decision 24 disallowed foreign direct investment in some sectors (e.g., banking, telecommunications, and retail sales) and required foreign investors in all other sectors to sell at least 51 percent ownership to local investors over a 15-year period. It also disallowed payment of royalties for technology transfer within a multinational enterprise, limited annual profit remittance to 20 percent of the firm's registered capital in the given Andean country, and restricted reinvestment in registered capital (until the firm became a mixed enterprise, with at least 51 percent local ownership). Although Decision 24 was not implemented uniformly by Ancom member countries, most of its rules were followed by most of the member countries, with various exceptions allowed.

The industry *sectoral programs* are another policy area that has attracted attention to the Andean integration process. Under these schemes, a number of industries have been selected for "rationalized" development in the Ancom market. Each of these industries has been "programmed" to produce certain products in one Andean country and other products in the others. In the Automotive Sectoral Program, for example, cars with engines smaller than 1,050 cc are assigned to Colombia, while those with engine sizes between 1,500 and 2,000 cc are assigned to Peru and Venezuela. Assignment of a product entitles the receiving country to tariff-free access to the other Andean countries for 20 years, while nonassigned countries must pay normal tariffs on their exports of that product. So far, none of the sectoral programs has progressed very far; the entrance of Venezuela into Ancom in 1973 and the exit of Chile in 1976 required complete overhauls of product assignments. At present, only the metalworking, petrochemical, and automotive sectoral programs are in place.

By 1990 the Andean Pact had not achieved tariff-free trade among its members, or a common external tariff, or substantial harmonization of other economic policies. As with all other integration schemes among LDCs to date, the problems of economic development have tended to limit the ability of member countries to achieve group-wide goals when domestic difficulties such as unemployment, social and political unrest, and (for the past decade) the debt crisis are so pressing. Thus far, Decision 24 has been the most visible common policy of the Andean Pact, and even that policy was under attack since its adoption. Chile left the Andean Pact in 1976 explicitly because it wanted to attract FDI and could not accept the restrictive nature of the Decision 24 investment rules. By 1987, at the height of the Latin American debt crisis, the ANCOM members replaced the restrictive Decision 24 with a much more open Decision 220, permitting most FDI and reducing barriers to remittances.

Institutions

The Andean Pact is structured fairly similarly to the European Community. The *Junta* or Secretariat serves as the executive arm of the Pact, analogous to the European Commission. Its three members are supported by a staff of over 1,000 people. The *Commission* is the decision-making body of the Andean Pact. It is composed of one plenipotentiary representative from each member country—analogous to the European Council of Ministers. The Commission votes on the policies proposed by the Junta, a situation similar to the one that exists in the EC.

The Andean Pact does not have a parliament at present; this lack of an EC counterpart is probably due to the fact that until 1980 three of the six Andean Pact member countries were ruled by military governments. By now all of the members have elected regimes; but the political will for an ANCOM-wide parliament still does not exist.

The Andean *Court of Justice* serves as the official interpreter of the Treaty of Cartagena, hearing disputes brought by any party from a member state concerning the treaty itself or subsequent decisions of the Commission—analogous to the functioning of the EC's Court. Thus far, the five-member court has heard few cases, so its importance remains to be developed.

On the whole, the institutions of the Andean Pact have been patterned on the European model, adjusted to suit the very different economic and political conditions in its Latin American member countries.

Impact on Business

Because the Andean Pact has made little progress on tariff policy and harmonization of monetary and fiscal policies, its main effect on business came from Decision 24.

Decision 24 of the Andean Pact Commission in 1971 reflected the growing dissatisfaction of less developed countries in their dealings with multinational enterprises. The surge of Latin American nationalism that led populist or socialist governments to power in Colombia, Chile, Bolivia, and Argentina at the end of the 1960s was embodied in policies adopted by those governments during the early 1970s. Decision 24 presented a hard line to foreign companies, seeking to force them to leave more of the economic gains from FDI with the host countries. Financial limitations were used to try to bolster host country balances of payments; ownership requirements were used to try to force more local sharing in company earnings; and sectoral limitations on foreign entry were used to reserve some economic activities to local companies. While implementation of Decision 24 varied across countries and over time, this one rule had a greater effect on foreign company managers' views about Andean Pact business than any other of the group's policies.

One would expect such a restrictive approach toward foreign business to discourage FDI from the region. In fact, during the first few years of its existence, Decision 24 appears to have contributed to a decline in FDI growth in the Andean Pact countries. After about 1975, however, Decision 24 appears to have had no significant impact on incoming FDI; apparently, companies found the rules to be manageable (or avoidable, because of the many exceptions granted) and resumed the flow of investment into these countries, as elsewhere in Latin America.[8] Nevertheless, as the ANCOM countries desperately sought new capital inflows during the 1980s, the group chose to reverse Decision 24 (with Decision 220 in 1987) and actively seek to attract FDI.

One would also expect the sectoral programs for industrial development to have some impact on business in the region. However, since MNEs find so many barriers to intra-ANCOM trade, geographic as well as regulatory, they are relatively uninterested in taking advantage of the tariff reductions available under the programs. Also, since so few programs are in place and since product assignments often go to two or more countries, the programs have not played much of a role in regional development. In fact, the *regional market* appears to be a very small factor in the decision making of MNEs, since they still regard the area as essentially five separate countries.

OTHER INTEGRATION EFFORTS

Caricom

Since the mid-1960s, the British colonies in the Caribbean have moved through several regional alliances, beginning with the West Indies Federation, passing through the Caribbean Free Trade Area, and ending with the current **Caribbean Common Market (Caricom).** Since its establishment in 1973, Caricom has created a common external tariff (which completed the customs union) and pursued several additional steps toward becoming a full common market. A regional market standards council now attempts to unify product standards, thus avoiding that nontariff barrier; a Caribbean Enterprise form of incorporation allows regional companies to move money and people freely among the member countries; a regional air transport policy ensures full air service to the member countries on a regionally owned airline (LIAT); and several financial agreements have been made, including the creation of a regional development bank and a balance of payments stabilization fund. Mainly because of the small size of the entire market, the fact that the countries are not industrialized, and the difficulties of transportation among members, Caricom has not become a major economic policy tool.

ASEAN

The **Association of Southeast Asian Nations (ASEAN),** founded in 1967, includes six less developed countries of Asia: Brunei, Indonesia, Malaysia, the Philippines, Singapore, and Thailand. These countries are characterized by an abundance of natural resources (except Singapore), very large international trade sectors, and an emphasis on liberal (free-market) economic development. Singapore is already the site of substantial offshore assembly of manufactured goods, while the others still rely heavily on exports of raw materials. ASEAN has reduced intra-group tariffs and eliminated some nontariff barriers to trade. It has undertaken industry sectoral programming somewhat similar to that of the Andean Pact, and thus far with similarly unspectacular results. Overall, the ASEAN group is different from other LDC blocs in its orientation favoring private enterprise, though, as with other LDC blocs, its efforts to promote intra-group trade and investment have been only somewhat successful. The most noted impact of ASEAN has resulted from its strategy of bargaining collectively with the European Community, Japan, and international organizations to obtain better market access for ASEAN exports.[9]

Comecon

The **Council for Mutual Economic Assistance (Comecon)** was founded in 1949 by the Soviet Union and its satellite communist countries. The charter of the group called for "extension and improvement of cooperation and the development of socialist economic integration."[10] Cooperative activities that Comecon has undertaken include reciprocal deliveries of raw materials, foodstuffs, machinery, and equipment and the exchange of scientific and technological advances. Comecon gives special assistance to its three least-developed members: Cuba, Mongolia, and Vietnam. In addition, many intra-group agreements have been made to undertake joint production, joint research, and other shared tasks. Ultimately, of course, Comecon has become virtually inoperative due to the opening of Eastern Europe. (This issue is pursued further in Chapter 23.)

THE U.S.–CANADA FREE-TRADE AGREEMENT

This Agreement created a free-trade area in North America, beginning to function on January 1, 1989. The two countries agreed to eliminate all tariffs on products traded in either direction by the end of 1998, except for those few cases where previous treaties exist (namely the bilateral Auto Agreement and the international Multifibre Arrangement). Periodic tariff reductions are underway, with the 10-year goal of complete free trade. To keep a perspective on the significance of this step, note that Canada previously had an average tariff of about 9 percent on goods from the United States, and the United States placed an average tariff of about 4 percent on Canadian goods before the agreement.

The Agreement also calls for reduced restrictions on crossborder investment flows and on trade in services. It guarantees U.S. companies access to Canadian oil, natural gas, and uranium. It does *not* cover the use of government subsidies or protection of intellectual property rights. A key consideration from the Canadian side was that the Agreement calls for disputes over subsidies and other nontariff barriers to be resolved by a new U.S.–Canada Panel, that will make binding decisions on such disputes.

The U.S.–Canada Free Trade Agreement reflects integration movements in Europe and Asia in recent years. It has led to initiation of discussions between the United States and Mexico for a free-trade pact that could include Canada, thus encompassing all of North America. It seems that the impact on international firms of this type of agreement is to open up opportunities in larger, regional market areas—when global initiatives such as GATT are unable to produce such sweeping coverage of industries and other specific issues.

STRATEGIES FOR DEALING WITH ECONOMIC BLOCS

There are as many strategies for dealing with integration groups as there are groups, since each set of countries offers different opportunities and risks to firms. Because a central aim of every economic bloc is to create a multicountry market with few restrictions on business among member countries, international firms should consider establishing operations within each bloc as the market there justifies. For example, if the combined market of Caricom countries is large enough to justify local production, then such production should be considered. If the bloc has not achieved free trade internally or if barriers to the outside firm are not too difficult to overcome, then local operations may not be justified. In the case of Caricom, most foreign firms set up operations in the country or countries that offer adequate market size or access to some desired raw material (e.g., Jamaica or Trinidad) and regard other members of the bloc as marginal additional markets. Because few of Caricom's policies affect foreign firms significantly, Caricom as a bloc is unimportant in most company decisions. Similar conclusions generally apply to the other LDC groups, since all of them have either failed to carry out their intended integration policies or have established rules that do not play a key role in company decisions.

The European Community is a different story. This bloc of developed countries offers the foreign investor an opportunity to set up a facility in one or more of the 12 countries to serve, tariff-free, a combined market of over 320 million people with very high average per capita incomes. Many companies have set up one or a few facilities to serve the 12 countries. Several major U.S. pharmaceuticals manufacturers have set up plants in Ireland (which offered key tax incentives) to produce basic chemical entities for use throughout the EC. Ford has plants in France, Germany, Belgium, and England that supply autos for sale throughout the Community. The list of U.S. firms that use a regional strategy in the EC is very long indeed. In this case, low barriers to international business and a very large regional market have attracted firms that view the EC as one market, just as the EC members intended. The Europe 1992 initiative only serves to focus more attention on this already-attractive market.

Regardless of the size of the integration group, or the level of development of its member countries, there is still some risk facing the firm that designs a regional strategy. It arises from the fact that the member countries remain separate political entities, free to undo group policies or to raise new barriers to intra-regional business. Thus, an investment in one member country that has been set up to serve the entire integration group may be greatly affected by a shift in that country's willingness to continue participating in the integration group on the same basis. At this time, such risk appears to be fairly small in the EC, whose member countries are committed enough to justify regional companies' strategies. However, in virtually every other example of free-trade areas, customs unions, or common markets (especially among LDCs), the regional market shows signs of breaking down or failing completely.

CONCLUSIONS

Economic integration efforts play an important role in international business primarily because they signal groups of countries that are trying to create regional markets, which may be attractive to firms. Probably the most important integration project in existence today is GATT, which is not regional at all. GATT has led to reductions in tariff barriers to trade among 90 countries, such that firms operating in any one of these countries usually face relatively low tariff costs when they ship internationally. Other integration schemes have also created new opportunities for firms to take advantage of low intragroup barriers to trade and other business activities. The European Community is clearly the most important of the regional blocs, because its large market and high degree of success in eliminating barriers offer substantial gains to firms that pursue a regional strategy.

The competitive advantages that firms may realize from participation in a regional integration scheme generally relate to the economies of scale—particularly in production and distribution—that are possible from operating in a larger (regional) market in comparison with a smaller (national) one. For most regional blocs thus far, the multicountry market has *not* become a full reality, so firms have not been able to benefit as much as expected. The EC, on the other hand, has stimulated a large amount of regional business, since markets of its member countries have become linked sufficiently for firms to operate relatively freely throughout the region.[11]

Economic integration has not proved to be a solution to the problems of economic development, which are far more than a simple tariff-reducing or investment-stimulating program could resolve. However, it may have demonstrated that specific regional cooperation efforts can lead to successful projects, such as regional development banks, technical cooperation, and political power—not to mention increased intra-regional trade.

QUESTIONS

1. What are the main benefits to a *country* from joining an economic integration group?

2. What are the main benefits to a *company* from entering an economic integration group (through foreign direct investment)?

3. How does GATT affect the pattern and trends of international business?

4. How would you expect a GATT on foreign direct investment to affect international business? (Assume that it would try to accomplish goals analogous to those pursued by the existing GATT on international trade.)

5. Define the five levels of regional economic integration. Where do the European Community and the Andean Pact fall within this range?

6. How would a common market among the United States, Canada, and Mexico affect business in those countries? Who would receive benefits, and who would pay costs?

7. What are the major differences in approach between ASEAN and other LDC integraton schemes? Do you expect ASEAN to be successful over the next five or six years? Why or why not?

8. Compare the institutions and policies of the European Community with those of the Andean Pact. Will the Andean Pact approach the EC in importance as its member countries develop more and more?

9. What is Comecon, and how does it function? What kind of strategy could a firm follow to operate in this group?

10. Explain how a company such as Beatrice Foods could establish a strategy for operating in the European Community. How would a strategy for Lockheed Aircraft need to differ from that of Beatrice?

REFERENCES

Arndt, H. W., and Ross Garnaut. "ASEAN and the Industrialization of East Asia." *Journal of Common Market Studies*, March 1979.

Chernick, Sidney. *The Commonwealth Caribbean.* Baltimore: The Johns Hopkins Press, 1978.

CMEA Secretariat. *The Council for Mutual Economic Assistance: 30 Years.* Moscow: CMEA, 1979.

Behrman, Jack N. "The Halting March to International Economic Integration." *Business in the Contemporary World,* Autumn 1989.

Grosse, Robert. *Foreign Investment Codes and the Location of Direct Investment.* New York: Praeger Publishers, 1980.

Magee, John. "1992: Moves Americans Must Make." *Harvard Business Review,* May–June 1989.

Morawetz, David. *The Andean Group.* Cambridge, Mass.: MIT Press, 1974.

Robson, Peter. *The Economics of International Integration.* London: Allen & Unwin, 1980.

Scaperlanda, Anthony, and Laurence Mauer. "The Determinants of U.S. Direct Investment in the E.E.C." *American Economic Review,* September 1969.

Swann, Dennis. *The Economics of the Common Market.* 5th ed. Harmondsworth, Middlesex, England: Penguin Books, 1984.

United Nations Conference on Trade and Development. *Handbook of International Trade and Development Statistics.* Geneva: UNCTAD, 1984.

NOTES

[1] See Jacob Viner, *The Customs Union Issue* (New York: Carnegie Endowment for International Peace, 1950).

[2] On the Uruguay Round, see "Launching of Global Trade Talks Could Reshape International Rules," *The Wall Street Journal,* September 22, 1986, p. 31; and S. J. Anjaria, "A New Round of Global Trade Negotiations," *Finance & Development,* June 1986, pp. 2–6.

[3] See, for example, Peter Robson, *The Economics of International Integration* (London: Allen & Unwin, 1980), chaps. 1, 2.

[4] See, for example, "A Long Road Ahead for ALADI," *Latin American Weekly Report,* September 24, 1982, p. 9.

[5] CMEA Secretariat, *The Council for Mutual Economic Assistance: 30 Years* (Moscow: CMEA, 1979), pp. 5, 7.

[6] See, for example, Carl Friedrich, *Europe: An Emergent Nation?* (New York: Harper & Row, 1969), chap. 1.

[7] See Badiul Majumdar, "Upstart or Flying Start? The Rise of Airbus Industrie," *The World Economy* (September 1987).

[8] See Robert Grosse, "The Andean Foreign Investment Code's Impact on Foreign Investment," *Journal of International Business Studies,* Fall 1983.

[9] See H. W. Arndt and Ross Garnaut, "ASEAN and the Industrialization of East Asia," *Journal of Common Market Studies,* March 1979.

[10] CMEA Secretariat, *Council for Mutual Economic Assistance,* p. 5.

[11] Many limits to intra-European business, even in manufactured goods, still exist. An interesting example of problems encountered by Philips, the Dutch electrical equipment firm, appears in *The Wall Street Journal,* August 7, 1985, pp. 1 ff.

11

Costs and Benefits of Multinational Enterprises

This chapter offers a social cost/benefit view of multinational enterprises and of international business activities. This means that the perspective of the home or host country government is taken, and the "goal" is to maximize the benefits received from operations of the MNEs. The discussion begins by examining the efficiency and monopoly aspects of MNEs. The bulk of the chapter presents and explains the full range of economic impacts that MNE activities generate. The main goals of the chapter are to:

1. Explain the efficiency and monopoly effects of MNEs.

2. Distinguish among the economic impacts of different kinds of business, such as extractive, manufacturing, and service activities.

3. Encompass the full range of the economic impacts that occur and show how they may be evaluated.

4. Consider *home* country concerns.

5. Demonstrate some widely used evaluation schemes.

6. Show some implications of social evaluation of MNEs for company managers.

INTRODUCTION

MNEs have encountered hostility and resentment in all countries that host substantial foreign investment, but nowhere more than in the LDCs, where they get blamed for the national economy's manifest shortcomings, not to mention the historical sins of colonial domination.[1]

This point made by Professor Caves in 1983 is a clear reminder that MNE affiliates are visible extensions of home country business and will therefore be subject to scrutiny by the government and other concerned observers in host countries, especially LDCs. Whether one approves or disapproves of multinational enterprises, it is important to understand the impacts of their sales, production, and other operations on the countries involved. For company managers in particular, it is crucial to understand the viewpoints of government regulators, host and home country competitors, and the various pressure groups that concern themselves with MNEs. This chapter presents an overview of the most important economic costs and benefits of MNEs on countries and offers some ideas about how to evaluate these costs and benefits. Ultimately, if the government of a country judges that an MNE creates a net economic (or political) cost for the country, then the MNE is likely to lose its acceptability there. Understanding this point and demonstrating how MNEs can avoid arriving at such a position are the goals of this chapter.

The perspective here is primarily economic; that is, the discussion focuses on important economic impacts. Political and social factors also play an extremely important part in the overall evaluation of MNE activities, so they are discussed along with the economic factors. Since all three types of factors are highly interrelated, it is useful to examine them together.

Efficiency versus Monopoly Power

Consider the fact that the multinational enterprise in itself is a method of organizing economic activity. If one country wants to obtain products from another, it can do so through trade between government agencies, trade between private enterprises, or business done within multinational enterprises (e.g., FDI, intra-firm exports). By allowing an MNE to operate, the government of that country may find that **transaction efficiencies** occur, if the MNE has access to low-cost factors of production, an international distribution network, and/or current technology. That is, the MNE may be able to produce lower-cost and higher-quality products for consumers than local firms can. On the other hand, the government will also find that the MNE possesses some degree of **monopoly power** because of its competitive advantages. This power enables the MNE to earn profits that may be taken out of the country, or to force local competitors out of the market, or to otherwise take advantage of its position to the country's disadvantage. Thus, two fundamental considerations must be kept in mind when judging the economic impact of an MNE on a country: (1) the benefits of transaction efficiencies; and (2) the costs of monopoly power. The problem is to try to decide through quantitative or judgmental measures whether the net benefits of the MNE in terms of transaction efficiencies outweigh the costs that result from the MNE's exercise of its monopolistic power. In fact, an appropriate measure would compare the benefits to the country from allowing the MNE to operate versus the benefits of available alternatives.

Of the competitive advantages discussed in Chapter 2, all of the cost-reducing ones provide benefits that may be shared with the host country. For example, economies of scale in production that may be realized through foreign direct investment lead to lower unit costs, which result in higher profits for the firm. These efficiency gains can be shared with the host country through lower prices to consumers, incomes of local employees, spillover to other industries, and tax payments to the government. Similarly, sound management practices may be implemented by a foreign investor to raise local productivity and resource utilization; these efficiency gains can also be shared with the host country in various forms, including human resource development and taxation.

On the other hand, any use of competitive advantages that enables the MNE to outcompete other firms may lead to the elimination of some competitors and thus to market domination by the MNE. The MNE's ability to shift its resources to other countries when problems arise in the given host country also presents a risk to the host country without offering it any clear benefit. In sum, most of the competitive advantages realized by MNEs in their foreign investment projects have a potential for being harnessed for benefits by the host country; but such sharing of benefits is not automatic. Therefore, the government of the host country needs to devise careful regulatory policies to assure the distribution of benefits that is best for the country.

Home versus Host Government View

Since the governments, plus companies and consumers, of more than one country are affected by MNE activities, it is necessary to ask whose view will be taken to evaluate the MNE. For our purposes, two views warrant consideration: that of the country from which the MNE originates (the **home country**) and that of the country in which particular MNE activities are undertaken (the **host country**). While both parties to the MNE's activities may gain from them, the benefits received will necessarily be different for each of them. For example, exports of chemicals from a French MNE's subsidiary in Germany to the same MNE's subsidiary in Belgium will improve Germany's balance of trade and cause that of Belgium to deteriorate. The MNE may earn more profits in either or both countries—and possibly remit them to the home office in France. Overall, the impacts of the MNE's activities on each country are different, and they may lead to different policies toward the firm.

The *host* country generally looks to the MNE to provide products and services that would otherwise not have been available at the same cost in the country (because of the MNE's efficiency). At the same time, the host country wants to protect itself against the MNE's exercise of monopoly power, perhaps by charging high prices, forcing local companies out of the market, or shifting investable funds to other countries. Since World War II, most of the developed, noncommunist countries have encouraged MNEs to enter their markets, in the expectation that competition from other firms and antitrust rules would limit the monopoly power of MNEs. The LDCs, which generally possess smaller, more monopoly-prone markets, have variously encouraged and restricted MNE activities in efforts to gain more benefits from them. Our discussion in the next section, which focuses on the costs and benefits of foreign direct investment, will look most closely at the host country's concerns.

The *home* country often views favorably the MNEs' extension of business abroad, because this leads to greater exports and remittances of earnings. At the same time, it may view FDI as an "export of jobs," replacing operations that were formerly carried out in the home country. This certainly holds true for the U.S. auto industry, which has lost several hundred thousand jobs in the past two decades as U.S. firms have set up overseas plants in Mexico, Korea, and elsewhere. (See Chapter 24 for a closer examination of the auto industry.) All in all, no clear conclusion has been drawn about the net benefit or cost of MNEs for their home countries. Most home countries seek to judge the impacts of specific MNE activities abroad and to construct policies that improve the home country's share in the benefits. (Recall the U.S. capital controls from 1968 to 1974, discussed in Chapter 8, which tried to limit MNEs' transfers of funds abroad.) Some measures of these impacts appear in the next section.

Specific MNE Activities

No conclusions can be drawn about MNE impacts without looking specifically at the kinds of dealings that the MNEs undertake. Exporting is easy to *measure,* because prices and quantities are reported to the government in each country. However, even exports are difficult to *evaluate* because they may replace foreign direct investment or they may complement it; and they may have additional ramifications. For example, Rawlings Company exports baseballs from its foreign factories in Haiti to the United States.[2] These exports appear to bolster Haiti's balance of payments, but the situation is really much more complex than that. First, Rawlings exports the baseball's rubber core and cover from the United States to Haiti; so the net of exports and imports related to its Haitian assembly plant must be measured. Second, the full balance of payments effect must include the financial flows involved—such as capital investment, profit remittances, and fees charged to the Haitian factory by the parent company. A full measure of the BOP impact of this factory on either Haiti or the United States needs to include all of these factors, as well as other factors that may be relevant, such as employment effects and worker skill development. Table 11–1 lists the relevant flows of funds, products, and so on between Haiti and the United States in this example.

One way to categorize MNE dealings that allows for some generalization is to consider separately three types of FDI: (1) **extractive FDI**—for obtaining raw materials; (2) **market-serving FDI**—for serving the local market; and (3) **sourcing FDI**—for sourcing production locally to take advantage of local

TABLE 11–1

Funds, Goods, Technology, and People Flows in the Haiti Baseball Assembly Example

To Haiti from United States	To United States from Haiti
Initial FDI, including money and machinery to set up assembly plant	Assembled baseballs
Baseball components (e.g., core windings, cover)	Remittances of profit obtained from sales of baseballs
Managerial and technical staff	Managerial and technical fees charged to subsidiary
Payment for baseballs received in the United States	Payment for components shipped to Haiti for assembly
Skills gained by Haitians trained in the United States and in Haiti by Rawlings	Haitian employees sent to United States for training programs

production conditions in order to serve foreign markets.[3] Generally, extractive operations such as oil drilling, metal mining, farming, and animal raising lead to greater exports than imports in the host country. Market-serving investment tends to result in more imports (of machinery and other products) than exports. Local sourcing of production often involves some importing of parts and machinery but usually results in exports of much greater value than these imports. Thus, two of the three kinds of FDI mentioned lead to an expected favorable BOP impact on the host country, a priori. This conclusion should not be over-extended, however, since most FDI today is market-serving.

Impact on Whom?

Focusing our attention on home and host governments as judges of the costs and benefits of MNE activities on each country misses an important underlying point. Ultimately, it is the *people* of each country whose well-being is affected by MNEs. Thus, even if a host government is satisfied with the performance of an MNE, important pressure groups such as labor unions or the opposition party may be highly dissatisfied. Many U.S. firms in Iran met the shah's criteria for acceptable behavior. However, when Khomeini and his religious followers overthrew the shah, some of these same firms were forced out of business or penalized in other ways. In the present context, the specific lesson to be learned from this experience is that MNEs need to be concerned about their impacts on the entire host country, not just on those things of interest to the host government. In addition, it should be recognized that in some situations, conflict is inevitable. For example, no matter what kind of business foreign firms carry out in South Africa, they are subject to criticism by anti-apartheid activists, by foreign governments, by the South African government, and/or others.

In countries such as the United States, Canada, and Japan and in Western Europe, the consumer is often used as the base for evaluating business dealings. If a company's business has no adverse effect on consumers and if the company meets the government's rules, then the company will generally be judged to be providing adequate net benefits to the country. But if consumers are adversely affected by such externalities as air or water pollution, or excessive noise, then the company, whether multinational or not, may expect government intervention to demand that it pay the cost involved. In less developed countries, however, "consumer sovereignty" often does not hold; instead, business dealings are evaluated on the basis of their impact on the economy or on the basis of their impact on domestic firms or other local groups.

Company managers must also consider the impact of their firms' activities on the stockholders, the ultimate owners whose interests must be served if management is to be allowed to remain in power. So while cost/benefit analysis focuses on the country's position, the manager must remember that any activity undertaken must also serve the interests of the firm's owners.

ECONOMIC COSTS AND BENEFITS OF FDI

So far, we have looked at points of view about the impact of MNEs, but we have not focused directly on the costs and benefits that should be evaluated. This section explores the main kinds of economic impact of MNEs on *host* countries. Most of the empirical evidence relates to FDI, rather than the total of MNE business, so our discussion will emphasize FDI. Also, while all of the costs and benefits can be evaluated for any host country, somewhat greater emphasis is placed here on MNEs operating in less developed countries. This is because the industrialized countries tend to be characterized by developed market economies that cause MNE advantages to be shared more fully with host countries. Competition among firms in these developed economies tends to dissipate the monopoly power of the MNEs and to distribute their benefits to the public. (Nonetheless, the discussion below pertains to both developed and less developed countries.) More detailed discussion of both LDCs and developed countries in their relations with MNEs appears in Chapters 21 and 22.

The table below lists a set of the key economic concerns in which MNEs play a part. Each of these concerns is reviewed below, without coming to a general conclusion, because the impact of MNEs depends on the company, on the country, and on a number of other variables. The empirical evidence offers at least some idea of the economic effects of some firms in some countries during the post-World War II period.

Economic Costs and Benefits of FDI

Income/employment effects

Price effects

Balance of payments effects

Distribution effects

Technology transfer

Ownership and control of the economy

Income/Employment Effects

Income and employment effects are considered together since, generally speaking, any increase (decrease) in aggregate income is accompanied by a fairly proportional increase (decrease) in employment, and vice versa. The income effects of a foreign investment project include the *direct* effect of the construction and operation of the new facilities. This project may replace one owned by the same company that already exists in the home country or elsewhere, and/or it may replace previous local production by another firm, or it may be an entirely new operation creating entirely new employment and output. *Indirect* effects, such as the provision of goods and services to the project by local suppliers, also add to local income. Finally, national income may be raised less by the foreign project than it would have been raised if local investment had occurred, since typically some portion of the earnings of the FDI project is remitted to the parent company and not reinvested in the host country.[4]

An *extractive* FDI project generally creates very large opportunities for local employment, since the mine, farm, or other type of project must be staffed by laborers and managers, most of whom are hired locally. Since natural resources are the target of this kind of investment, it is not likely that such a project will *replace* another supplier of the same product; natural resources are often exhaustible, and new supplies *add* to total output worldwide. National income generally rises by a multiple of the investment, as secondary effects occur and as taxes and payments to workers and suppliers are spent locally. Since the prices of natural resources are usually set in world markets (in U.S. dollars), ordinarily the MNE does not have much leeway to charge nonmarket prices for its exports. One criticism often levied at MNEs is that they carry out less processing of raw materials in the host country than would be desirable, so that the value added locally in production of the final products is less than it should be (from the host country's viewpoint).

A *sourcing* investment project generally creates new local employment for manufacturing workers. Such a project usually does not replace the same firm's local facility, although its output could replace the output of local competitors. Sourcing is based on the concept of cost minimization, so if some inputs are most efficiently supplied by imports to the facility, then the MNE may use such imports rather than additional local production. The MNE often has substantial leeway to price the output of sourcing facilities, to reduce its tax burden world-wide; so the host government must be aware of this potential strategy. Intel Corporation's decision to source its computer chips in Taiwan rather than the United States created a new manufacturing facility in Taiwan that employs several hundred workers and exports the chips back to the United States (and else-where) for use in electronic equipment.[5] Similarly, Brunswick Corporation has chosen to manufacture its billiard tables in Brazil for sales worldwide, thus benefiting from lower production costs and large-scale, centralized production.

A *market-serving* investment project may involve very little local production, if most or all of the products sold locally are imported from the MNE's facilities elsewhere in the world. If a market-serving facility is built locally, it may compete with other local suppliers in the host country market; this competition may lower prices and expand choices to the consumer, or it may tend to force previous competitors out of the market. A market-serving facility can be ex-pected to buy some inputs from local suppliers and to add to local tax revenues. Pharmaceuticals companies typically produce basic chemicals in a few locations and then ship them to manufacturing (formulation) plants in dozens of coun-tries. The formulation facilities in the host countries mainly assemble pills, syrups, and other final products with large amounts of imported ingredients and fairly small local manufacturing facilities.

Price Effects

Economic theory asserts that additional suppliers of a product, for example through foreign investment, will compete with existing suppliers, tending to reduce the prices charged and benefiting consumers. If the FDI project supplies a new product, or at least one not available locally, it may not be faced with price competition of this type. Generally, the effect of FDI on the price of the product or service generated is to lower it. FDI is expected to raise the prices paid to the factors of production, as MNEs compete with local firms for these factors. The price of labor does tend to be driven up by FDI. Studies by several analysts have shown that foreign-owned businesses tend to pay higher wages than their local competitors.[6]

An *extractive* venture would most likely not affect the world price of a raw material such as copper or wheat, though it might lower the price by adding a large amount of additional supply to the market. Either result assumes that the price of the raw material is established by international supply and demand, denominated in some base currency, usually U.S. dollars. The price of bulk supplies of coffee is set in the New York coffee market, for example; and the spot price of oil is set in the London market.

A *sourcing* venture would probably tend to reduce the price of the product in the various national markets served. Since the goal of sourcing is usually to

Exxon Coal Venture in Colombia

In 1976, the Exxon Corporation, the world's largest industrial company at the time, completed negotiations with the government of Colombia to undertake a joint venture that would extract coal from a massive deposit located in the northeastern coastal region of Colombia called El Cerrejon. The initial projections called for a $3 billion investment over 10 years, leading to the production of 15 million tons of coal output per year by 1983. Each partner owns a 50 percent share in the project, and each contributes half of the costs and receives half of the coal produced. The agreement is for 30 years, after which 100 percent ownership passes to the Colombian government. Today, El Cerrejon is the largest coal mine in Latin America. This direct investment project offers an interesting model for the 1990s-style business of extractive MNEs in less developed countries.

In the late 1970s, Exxon was actively pursuing a strategy of diversifying its industrial base away from almost total dependence on the oil industry. After having had its operations nationalized in the Middle East, Peru, and Venezuela in the 1970s, Exxon was quite wary of committing funds and manpower to oil investments in LDCs. (Exxon entered the Colombian market in 1917, operating an oil field and later building two refineries. All of these oil businesses had been sold to the Colombian government by 1974, although Exxon still operates a technical service subsidiary in the country.) One direction of the diversification was entry into new businesses, and particularly businesses that had something in common with oil. Coal has many similarities with oil as a mineral energy source, and it fits fairly readily into the global portfolio of Exxon products. In addition to purchasing major coal deposits in the western United States, Exxon decided to obtain an interest in the rich ore deposits at El Cerrejon.

The project operates as a 50–50 joint venture between the Colombian government's coal company, Carbocol, and Intercor, an Exxon subsidiary. While responsibilities are shared, Exxon provides mainly the technical and managerial skills, including operation of the mine and support facilities, as well as the training of Colombian nationals to take eventual full responsibility over the operation. Colombia provides the coal, the workers (the continuing work force numbers about 4,000 employees), and domestic services such as transportation and communications. Exxon then sells its 50 percent of the mine's output on world markets, while Carbocol disposes of its 50 percent both at home and abroad.

By 1987, the project was fully under way but was providing revenues somewhat below the original projections, because of a worldwide decline in the prices of raw materials such as coal. The start-up costs overran the original estimates, and as a result the profitability of the project has been less than was expected initially. Relations between Exxon managers and their Colombian counterparts sometimes prove difficult, due to differences in the perspectives and skills of the two partners. Despite these problems, both Exxon and the Colombian government view El Cerrejon as a successful venture and as a model for future cooperation. ∎

Source: Based on *The Cerrejon Project* (Bogota, Colombia: Exxon [Intercor], 1982) and on discussions with Exxon executives responsible for the project.

reduce costs and to compete through low prices, such a venture should lead to lower prices of the product being produced. Whether or not lower costs are passed on to consumers as lower prices depends on the degree of competition in the business. The widespread sourcing of computer components in LDCs clearly has led to lower prices of these components in world markets.

A *market-serving* venture could lower the local price for the product by increasing competition, if additional suppliers are in the given market. If the product is new to that market, then no comparison can be made.

Balance of Payments Effects

Balance of payments effects and income effects are probably the most difficult ones to measure, and they are surely the most controversial to host governments and pressure groups. Balance of payments effects to the host country include the capital inflow that often accompanies the establishment of the project. They also include the funds outflows (profit remittance and capital repatriation), which will ultimately be greater than the original investment if the project is profitable. Third, they include exports generated by the local facility for sales elsewhere and imports used to supply the local facility. Any other financial flows between the parent and the subsidiary must also be included (e.g., intracompany loans, royalty payments). All of the above BOP effects should be relatively easy to measure.

A fifth category of BOP effects may be called "replacement effects." If the local production replaces formerly imported products, then there is an improvement of the host country's trade balance. If the local production replaces other locally produced products, then there is no additional BOP effect of this kind. If the local production is used for export to replace products formerly made elsewhere, then there is a positive trade effect on the host country. Figure 11–1 represents the full set of potential balance of payments effects of an FDI project.

FIGURE 11–1

Balance of Payments Impacts of a Foreign Investment Project

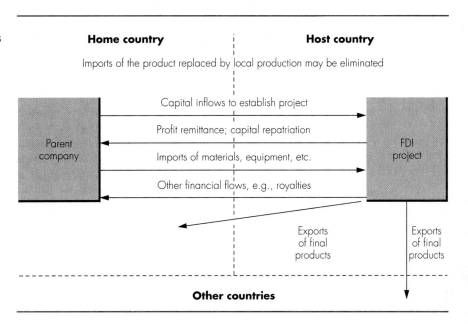

Extractive (including agricultural) investments virtually always have positive effects on the trade balance of the host country. Bauxite, oil, fruit, or vegetable exports generally far outweigh imports of machinery and other inputs. Even with profit remittances and other financial outflows, these types of investments tend to improve all of the host country's balances of payments, from the trade balance to the official reserves balance. Exxon's coal venture in Colombia clearly falls into this category of highly positive BOP impacts.

Sourcing investments tend to produce a slighter trade surplus for the host country, since often some or much of the inputs used are imported from the parent company or elsewhere. For example, the Rawlings baseball factory in Haiti mentioned previously adds to Haiti's exports, but it also adds substantially to Haiti's imports—the net result still being a surplus of exports over imports. Because sourcing investments, like extractive investments, are aimed at export markets, their overall BOP effects tend to be favorable to the host country.

Finally, *market-serving* investments tend to have negative BOP impacts on host countries. Some inputs are imported in most cases, and often additional product lines are imported for local sale. By definition, such investments are aimed at the host country's market—though very often some exporting does take place and local production does replace imports. Thus, the final judgment depends on the specific case. Japanese auto company investments in the United States could reduce imports of those cars; however, because of the de facto quota on such imports, the FDI may hurt the U.S. BOP due to imports of parts and machinery plus remittances to Japan. The net result here is ambiguous, unfortunately.

Distribution Effects

Because MNEs tend to come from the most developed countries and because their operations tend to add to host country production, MNEs presumably improve the distribution of income between richer and poorer countries. Within the host country, however, it is quite difficult to judge whether a direct investment project improves or aggravates income distribution. The literature critical of MNEs demonstrates that FDI often helps the economic elites of host countries to improve their well-being, while benefiting lower-income people very little if at all.[7] Perhaps the tax revenues that the host government receives from the foreign investor offer the main possibility for an impact on income redistribution. These revenues may or may not improve income distribution, but the firm generally has no influence on their use.

In principle, FDI is expected to improve for labor the distribution of income between capital and labor, since it is expected to lower the local return to capital (by providing more competition) and to raise the local return to labor (by paying higher wages). Very little evidence exists regarding the impact on returns to capital, but as already noted, the returns to labor tend to improve as a result of FDI.[8]

An *extractive* investment project should improve the incomes of local participants in the project: laborers, managers, and investors. It may have very little direct impact on the rest of the economy, especially if the raw material is simply exported. Extractive projects can generally be expected to offer large numbers of jobs for relatively low-skilled employees, thus improving their incomes. Some managerial and technical jobs usually exist for locals, but such jobs tend to be far fewer in number. Exxon, for example, employs about 4,000 workers in its joint-venture coal project in Colombia, almost all of whom are locals. Only a few expatriate managers and technical personnel have been employed there. Overall, extractive investment appears likely to have a favorable impact on host country income distribution.

A *sourcing* facility can also be expected to employ local laborers at the low end of the income scale, to take advantage of the low production costs that such employment implies. Therefore, its distributional impact should be very similar to that of an extractive project.

A *market-serving* project has less of a focus on obtaining local, low-cost labor, since its main task is to *sell* in the host country market. Since the market segments served by MNEs tend to be consumers with relatively high incomes, there may be a tendency for market-serving projects to reinforce the existing income pattern in the host country. However, since manufacturing investors will try to utilize low-cost local inputs such as workers and materials in order to reduce their expenses, the distributional effects of these projects may still be similar to those of the other types of FDI.

Technology Transfer

Possibly the main benefit associated with the global expansion of MNEs is the transfer of information, specifically product, process, and managerial technology, that they carry out. By making additional products available in host countries, MNEs expand consumers' choices. By bringing in new technologies and training local people to use them, MNEs improve each host country's knowledge base. Simply by operating in a host country, a multinational firm transfers many kinds of knowledge about products, living conditions, business strategies, and other matters.

A main criticism made by LDCs is that the technology transferred by MNEs is often "inappropriate"; that is, it does not take the best advantage of host country factors of production. Specifically, it is argued that the technology used in relatively poor LDCs should employ more labor relative to capital than the technology used in developed countries, since unemployment is generally so high in LDCs. The economics of the situation (i.e., local labor and capital costs) may reinforce this contention. MNEs prefer to use the same technology wherever possible, however, to avoid the costs (and risks) of adapting machinery and procedures to local operations. While some adaptation of production to meet local conditions usually does take place in FDI projects, the fundamental argument is that LDCs would like to see more adaptation, whereas the MNEs would like to reduce their costs by not altering their already proven techniques. This issue is very difficult to measure, and disagreements are likely to continue—our purpose here is just to raise the issue for consideration.

Extractive activities often transfer knowledge about the process of mining, farming, or animal raising to local managers and technicians. This knowledge has apparently been sufficient to enable many countries to nationalize minerals and metals production, as was seen in the 1970s, when oil and copper companies were nationalized in most of the third world. Since access to foreign markets for sale of these products was *not* transferred, most of the MNEs involved still function in these countries as purchasers of the minerals or metals for sale in other countries. Many host countries are seeking to entice MNEs to carry out local downstream production (e.g., refining or smelting), which would allow even more inward transfer of technology.

Firms that *source* production in host countries transfer production technology—(knowledge and skills)—to the local workers and managers employed by the facilities. Such knowledge and skills may have applicability in other firms or businesses in the host country, so the impact tends to be favorable. Because the firms seek to minimize production costs, there is often little incentive to adapt technology to local conditions, so that the issue of appropriate technology becomes an important one in government/business relations.

Market-serving investments also transfer production technology and information about business practices that may benefit the host country. A key criticism of such investments is that through advertising they may create new demand for products that are "inappropriate" in some sense. That is, the advertising may be viewed as creating "false" demand for branded products or luxury goods that the host government sees as wasteful consumption. Although a marketing manager may refute this argument, it is still used and it should be taken into account by foreign investors in market-serving businesses.

Ownership and Control of the Economy

This final concern is as much political as economic. Host countries find that FDI by powerful, efficient foreign firms may lead to foreign ownership of large parts of important industries, such as computers, chemicals, pharmaceuticals, and telecommunications. While such ownership may not be inherently bad, the xenophobia that exists in every country may lead to the view that it should be avoided if possible, or at least closely controlled. Both less developed and industrialized countries have taken this position during the last two decades. From Jean-Jacques Servan-Schreiber's warning about the "American challenge" (the control by U.S. firms of much of Europe's economy) to Canada's Foreign Investment Review Agency, which sought to limit foreign direct investment in the early 1980s, to the fear of Japanese control of key parts of the U.S. economy in the early 1990s, developed nations have demonstrated concern about foreign ownership. From the expropriations and nationalizations of foreign oil and copper companies in the late 1960s and early 1970s to the restrictions that continue today on foreign ownership in Latin American, African, and Asian countries, LDCs have demonstrated the same concern. Table 11–2 demonstrates the degree of foreign MNE participation in several sectors of Canada's economy, implying why host countries may be concerned about this issue. Note that about one third of Canadian business is owned by foreign firms and that such industries as transportation equipment, rubber, chemicals, and tobacco are more than three fourths foreign owned.

Host countries are as concerned about foreign *control* as they are about foreign ownership. In fact, much of the criticism of foreign ownership focuses on the exercise of control over host country industry by foreign decision makers. The control issue is thus central. Since control may be obtained through a management contract, or through minority ownership of a company, or through other contractual means (such as long-term purchase or supply contracts), it is not necessarily synonymous with ownership. Nonetheless, ownership and control are clearly related, since they usually do go together in the form of majority-owned or wholly owned foreign direct investment.

Extractive ventures have tended to be the focal point of host country concerns about foreign control of the economy. Most petroleum production and marketing in most less developed countries have been nationalized wholly or partially, so in these areas the foreign challenge has been met through forced divestment. Other extractive ventures have met with similar fates, especially in

TABLE 11–2

Foreign Ownership of
Canadian Industry (ranking
of 33 major industries,
measured by 1983 sales)

	Percentage of Foreign Controlled			
	Sales		Assets	
	1982	1983	1982	1983
1. Tobacco products	100	100	100	100
2. Storage	1	1	5	6
3. Communications	12	12	13	13
4. Transportation equipment	84	88	70	73
5. Petroleum and coal products	78	72	60	61
6. Primary metals	17	17	14	15
7. Rubber products	88	90	92	92
8. Public utilities	4	3	—	—
9. Transportation	7	6	6	4
10. Metal mining	30	28	23	23
11. Beverages	34	37	26	28
12. Textile mills	51	52	51	51
13. Paper and allied industries	28	27	26	26
14. Electrical products	63	63	53	51
15. Mineral fuels	59	62	38	39
16. Nonmetallic products	56	53	73	71
17. Printing, publishing, and allied industries	11	13	13	12
18. Chemicals and chemical products	77	76	73	71
19. Leather products	24	20	26	21
20. Wood industries	13	14	15	13
21. Miscellaneous manufacturing	42	44	39	39
22. Food	26	26	32	30
23. Other mining	34	34	34	38
24. Knitting mills	15	16	17	21
25. Machinery	52	52	48	48
26. Metal fabricating	33	32	33	31
27. Retail trade	13	12	13	13
28. Wholesale trade	26	25	22	22
29. Furniture industries	17	15	17	17
30. Services	16	17	15	15
31. Clothing industries	11	10	14	12
32. Agriculture, forestry, and fishing	4	3	4	4
33. Construction	11	9	11	10

Source: Statistics Canada, *Corporations and Labour Unions Returns Act* (Ottawa: Statistics Canada, 1986), p. 48.

less developed countries. Because the MNEs involved in such ventures have weak bargaining capabilities relative to those of the host governments, which control their national territories and resources, these MNEs have been forced to accept the pressure to give up ownership of the ventures. Even in the oil industry, however, MNEs have retained control over international distribution and marketing of the product—so the host governments have not pushed them completely out of the industry.

Sourcing investments present an almost inverse situation. MNEs choose countries for sourcing based on production costs, distribution costs, and the risks involved. If a country does not favor the particular investment project, then the MNE will usually look elsewhere for a more favorable environment. In the case of sourcing, the competitive advantages tend to favor the MNE, which is

**IB
ILLUSTRATION**

IBM Microcomputer Negotiations with the Government of Mexico

From the start-up of Apple Computer in 1978 to the end of that decade, personal computers took off in popularity and sales in the industrial countries. Apple alone sold over 5 million PCs in 1982. In 1981 IBM, the world's largest computer manufacturer, finally entered the microcomputer market with the opening of its Boca Raton (Florida) PC plant. Starting with sales in the United States, almost immediately IBM began exporting and looking for overseas sites to produce more PCs.

Mexico was a particularly attractive location for IBM's consideration, since that country is the second largest in Latin America, its wage costs are less than 10 percent of those in the United States, and production facilities could be located very near the United States border to allow easy access to transport of parts, machinery, and computers. In addition, many of the larger less developed countries such as Mexico were instituting policies to force computer makers to produce increasing percentages of their machines locally and to accept local ownership of their operations. In early 1984, IBM began negotiating with the Mexican government to expand its existing Guadalajara minicomputer plant to produce PCs.

The positions of IBM and the Mexican government can usefully be viewed as a bargaining relationship (see Chapters 21 and 22 for more details on this issue) in which each side wanted to achieve a successful negotiation with the other. Mexico had to evaluate the costs and benefits of IBM's proposal on that country, while IBM had to evaluate the potential impact of the proposal on the company.

Mexico was facing very difficult economic conditions, with the price of its main export commodity, oil, quite depressed, and a huge burden of foreign debt that left the government in default on its obligations to foreign banks. The IBM proposal offered to improve the balance of trade by generating exports of computers to other Latin American countries, as well as directly creating jobs for several hundred Mexicans, transferring computer skills to these people, and reducing the large volume of imported microcomputers.

relatively "footloose" in its choice of a national location, because the local market is *not* the target of the firm, and scarce natural resources are not at issue.

Market-serving investments fall somewhere in between extractive ventures and sourcing investments. They depend on the host country for their sales, so the host government has substantial ability to control their activities. They typically do not rely on the natural resources over which countries want to retain sovereignty, so this confrontation does not occur. The MNE often brings with it some proprietary technology or other knowledge that the host government views as beneficial; this raises the firm's bargaining strength relative to that of the host government. However, if foreign firms dominate the industry that they operate in, the host government may view the situation as undesirable and search for some limitations on their activities. Market-serving investments have historically been allowed by host countries, with restrictions, to try to improve the distribution of benefits toward the host country.

However, Mexico had recently (1983) seen Apple Computer begin production of PCs in a minority-owned joint venture, and two other majority-Mexican-owned plants already were in operation. Mexican law since 1973 called for majority Mexican ownership of businesses in all industries, and a computer decree in 1983 reaffirmed this policy for the computer industry in particular. All of this means that Mexico did *not* rely on IBM for PCs, and that other firms had been attracted to the market without the conditions requested by IBM.

IBM's initial proposal called for new investment of about $US7 million to expand the factory for production of 200,000 computers per year within six years. The firm would export 75 percent of the PCs from Mexico and would import necessary production machinery. An additional 80 production workers would be hired at Guadalajara, and about 800 ancillary jobs would be created. Annual income from the PCs made in Mexico would be about $US600 million per year. IBM wanted to maintain 100 percent ownership of the project, seeking an exception from the Mexican rules.

The negotiations took almost two years to complete, and on two occasions the IBM proposals were rejected by the Mexican government. Each time the company increased its offer of specific benefits to Mexico, while holding fast on its request for 100 percent ownership. Despite opposition from the local computer manufacturers and from groups that oppose foreign direct investment, a successful agreement was finally reached. IBM agreed to invest $US91 million (of which about $US20 million went into the plant and most of the rest went into a variety of ventures for transferring computer technology to Mexico, such as a semiconductor research center and a grant to several academic institutions) in Mexico. The plant was projected to employ 240 additional workers (instead of 80) and to export 91 percent of its output (instead of 75 percent). The amount of local content to be used in PC production was raised from 51 percent to 71 percent. In all, Mexico received very large concessions in almost every area—in exchange for allowing IBM to maintain 100 percent ownership of the facility. Thus, Mexico traded off (accepted) additional foreign ownership and control in the economy for additional exports, jobs and income, and technology transfer.* ∎

---

*A more detailed look at these negotiations appears in Steven Weiss, "The Long Path to the IBM–Mexico Agreement: An Analysis of the Microcomputer Investment Negotiations, 1983–86," *Journal of International Business Studies* (1990).

SOME CONCERNS OF THE HOME COUNTRY

Essentially, the concerns of a home country are the same as the concerns of a host country. Income effects, balance of payments effects, and so forth all occur for the home country too. In some cases, MNE activities may have opposite effects in the home country and the host country. Exports from the parent company to the foreign subsidiary are imports for the host country and exports for the home country. Production set up in a host country through FDI may replace production formerly done in the home country. In most cases, however, the home and host country do *not* end up on opposite sides of the benefit distribution. Extractive investment adds national income to the host country, while supplying needed natural resources to the home country. Production set up in the host country may have no effect on home country output—or it may lead to more home country production to supply input materials for the foreign subsidiary. The transfer of technology does not reduce the availability of that technology in the home country. In fact, adaptations that the firm makes in the host country may lead to useful changes in its home country business. As in the case of trade according to comparative advantage, foreign direct investment may be a positive-sum game, leading to higher incomes in both home and host country.

Studies of the impact of MNE activities on home countries have not led to simple conclusions. Depending on the assumptions made, FDI may improve or harm the domestic economy. An analysis of the U.S. economy by Hufbauer and Adler (1968) estimated that income and balance of payments effects would be negative if FDI replaced investment in the United States and that they would be positive if the investment abroad had no impact on investment in the United States. An analysis of the U.S. economy by the U.S. Tariff Commission (1973) led to similarly varied results with regard to impacts on U.S. employment, prices, and other economic variables. More recent studies have likewise failed to draw clear conclusions.

To this point, we have not made any effort to define an evaluation scheme for judging the net impact of MNE activities on home or host countries. Let us turn now to that task.

EVALUATION SCHEMES
Social Benefits

One commonly used framework for evaluating privately owned and managed projects is to create a measurement of each expected cash inflow and outflow of the project, discounted to present values and adjusted to account for "social" values. This kind of social valuation looks only at the income (as opposed to price and other) effects of the project. Similar analysis is typically done by the MNE in deciding whether or not to invest. The difference between the MNE's valuation and the host government's lies in the assignment of "social" values. For example, the company will view profit remittance to the parent firm as a cash *inflow* from the project. The host government will value it as an *outflow* from the country, since it is taken out of the country. Similarly, taxes paid by the company to the host government are a cash outflow for the firm but a cash inflow for the country. The total set of discounted cash flows to the country can then be considered the net social benefit to the country. Table 11–3 shows an example of an FDI project as viewed by the company and by the host government.

Notice that the automobiles sold by International Auto Company in Wellsonia have a value of $5,000 per car in developed-country markets, but IAC will sell them for $6,000 per car in this country, because the small market size necessitates small-scale production and higher costs. (Imports will be restricted through tariff policy, to protect the new investment project.) Although Wellsonia could import the cars at the lower cost, local production was judged desirable and IAC was allowed to charge the higher price in return for investing. The country values the car at $5,000, since this is the cost to it of importing a car.

Local materials cost is judged to be of equal value by the company and the country, since the prices paid for materials represent an expense to the firm and an equivalent **opportunity cost** to the country. That is, the country gives up potential alternative uses of the materials when the company uses them up in production.

TABLE 11–3

International Auto Company in Wellsonia (*in thousands of U.S. dollars*)

	Company Income Statement		"Social" Income Statement	
Revenues			Benefits	
Sales (1,000 cars)		6,000		5,000
Expenses			Costs	
Local materials cost		1,200		1,200
Imported materials cost		900		900
Labor cost		2,000		700
Administrative overhead		400		400
Interest (funds borrowed locally)		500		500
Taxes paid (40%)		400		0
Net income after tax (assume remitted)		600		600
Net Social Benefit				700

Imported materials are valued equally in both measures, although the host government may question the value of inputs imported from the parent company, since the company can charge a high or low transfer price to its subsidiary for these inputs. (The problem of transfer pricing is discussed in some detail in Chapter 16.)

Local salary and wage (labor) costs are valued by the company at the price it pays, but often at a lower value by the host country. If substantial unemployment exists in the host country and the employment of people by the foreign investor reduces the number of unemployed overall, then the economic cost to the host country is less than the wages and salaries paid. That is, as long as the project generates new employment and does not just shift people from one company to another, then a social benefit occurs from the reduced unemployment. This benefit offsets to some degree the hiring of people away from other firms, and it can generally be judged to lead to a lower social than private cost of labor.

Overhead may involve some administrative charges by the parent firm that are not easily valued by the host government, but it is difficult to generalize about the appropriate social valuation. Let us just assume that social and private valuations are equal in this example.

Interest expense is valued similarly by the company and the government, unless the government judges that the MNE's local borrowing drains the economy of scarce financial resources and thus has a higher opportunity cost than the interest paid. If the MNE borrows abroad, this could add financial resources to the country, and/or it could create an exchange risk that causes a high opportunity cost to be incurred. Let us assume that the borrowing is done locally and that the opportunity cost is equal to the interest payments.

Taxes paid to the host government reduce the private benefits of the project, but they remain as social benefits in the host country.

Profit remitted to the parent firm is a cash inflow for the parent firm but a cash outflow for the host country. Profit reinvested in the host country is a benefit to the host country, and it is usually valued as a benefit by the company as well. However, if the reinvestment occurs because the host country does not allow profit remittance, then the value to the company may be zero or at least somewhat less than the amount of the funds involved.

Consequently, the valuations of the same IAC investment project differ from the social and the private perspectives. The company must, of course, achieve an acceptable rate of return on its investment in order to justify the investment to stockholders. The country must achieve acceptable social benefits to justify the project relative to alternative uses of national resources. The Wellsonia project has a positive rate of return to both the investor and the host country, but we need to know their costs of capital and value of the investment to judge if the project is acceptable or not.

Other Financial Measures of Social Benefit

The social income statement shown in Table 11–3 is not the only financial measure of a project's social value. Additional measures include the social benefit/cost ratio, and others.

The **social benefit/cost ratio** is simply the ratio of the positive entries in the social income statement to the negative entries. If the ratio is greater than one, then the project has a positive social value; if the ratio is less than one, the project is undesirable from a social standpoint. (The Wellsonia project has a social benefit/cost ratio of 1.16, or 5000/4300.)

The Best-Alternative Basis

Measures of the entire spectrum of economic impacts of MNE projects are seldom made by host governments or by the companies themselves. There are simply too many factors to include, many of which are quite difficult to measure. One possibility that makes sense conceptually is to compare an MNE activity with the **best alternative** available for accomplishing the same thing. For example, what would Wellsonia's alternative be in order to obtain the 1,000 automobiles it needs? Imports from another multinational auto manufacturer are one possibility; FDI by another MNE is another; local production by a Wellsonian firm is a third. The investment project discussed above should be judged in comparison with the best alternative source of the autos. The alternative that offers the highest net social benefit to the host country is the one that the host country should choose.

National governments often use one or more of the above evaluation schemes to judge whether or not to permit a proposed foreign investment project. International organizations such as the United Nations have developed detailed measurement techniques to aid governments in carrying out such analyses.[9]

IMPLICATIONS FOR MANAGERS

There are several important lessons that MNE managers can draw from the discussion above. First, the MNE manager should be aware that governments and pressure groups in the countries where the firm does business will be concerned about the costs and benefits of the firm's local activities. While the particular measurement schemes discussed here may not be used in a given instance, the idea of measuring such costs and benefits is well accepted worldwide. In order to present the best corporate face to the host country, the MNE manager should be able to justify the firm's activities in terms of social benefits. Generally, the task is easier for extractive and sourcing investments, whose income and balance of payments effects are often better from the host country's view than those of market-serving investments.

Second, knowing that host governments are going to evaluate the MNE's activities, the MNE manager may want to choose a *hedging* strategy to reduce the risk of adverse government policies. For example, if local borrowing costs are higher than the costs of borrowing from abroad, the firm may still choose to borrow locally, to hedge its exposed assets with a local-currency liability (the loan). Borrowing locally also allows interest to accrue to a local financial institution, which adds to national income in the host country.

Third, the manager may find from examination of a social benefit analysis that the firm is close to the social "break-even" point. In this case, the firm may want to embark on an active program of demonstrating good corporate social responsibility (e.g., through sponsoring cultural events; supporting schools, hospitals, and other social institutions; or even helping to clean up some kind of host country pollution). In addition, the firm may alter its activities to improve the social benefit measure itself.

CONCLUSIONS

Multinational enterprises are destined to face criticism from the national governments of the countries they enter, if only because these companies are able to make decisions and control resources in more than one country, while the governments are limited to their internal, domestic sovereignty.[10] The criticism is often based on political or social issues that are not easily dealt with on a rational, objective basis. Even in such cases, and in all disputes on economic grounds, managers of MNEs can establish measures of company impacts on the country involved and can seek rational negotiations on benefit/cost issues with government regulators.

It should be noted that there have been many (some highly visible) examples of MNEs acting against local governments in host countries—such as ITT's effort to bring down the Allende government in Chile in the early 1970s and the efforts of United Fruit Company to influence government policy in Guatemala during the same period.[11] Such efforts of MNEs to influence the political environment in host countries must generally be denounced; in our context, they must also be recognized as one of the reasons for widespread criticism of MNEs in many less developed countries.

Returning to cost/benefit evaluations, income and balance of payments effects are the major types of economic effects that are usually judged; but several other types are very important as well, including price and distribution effects, technology transfer, and control of the economy. Empirical evidence shows that the total impact of an MNE on a host country depends substantially on the circumstances, that is, on the company and country involved. Generally, the income and balance of payments effects of extractive and sourcing direct investments on a host country can be expected to be positive, while market-serving investment may have a negative BOP effect and a positive income effect.

The single most important point to keep in mind regarding costs and benefits is that MNEs should be evaluated, not in comparison with an ideal situation, but rather in comparison with available alternatives. That is, an MNE may not offer the total set of benefits that any home or host country would prefer, but in many cases the MNE offers the best available alternative. In order to make policy in a government or to set strategy as a company manager, it is fundamental to recognize this point.

QUESTIONS

1. What important balance of payments effects does a foreign direct investment project have on the host country?

2. Why would a sourcing investment probably have a better BOP impact on the host country than a market-serving investment?

3. Is the balance of payments impact of a foreign investment project on the home country exactly opposite to its impact on the host country? Explain.

4. Give a plausible explanation of the costs and benefits to the United States of the Toyota–General Motors joint venture in Fremont, California, that began production in 1984. Is the net social benefit likely to be positive or negative to the United States? To Japan?

5. What is the correct way (conceptually) for a host government to evaluate the desirability or undesirability of a proposed foreign direct investment project? What criteria can generally be used in making such a judgment?

6. Assume that you work for the Nigerian Foreign Investment Review Board. Hoffmann-La Roche & Cie. is a Swiss pharmaceuticals company that manufactures or sells drugs in almost every nation of the world. How would you evaluate the company's proposal for a formulating (final processing) plant in Nigeria, in which 5 percent of the value of the pharmaceuticals sold locally would come from the local plant and the rest would be imported? The plant would sell only in Nigeria. Make your assumptions explicit, and compare this project with any alternative that you think is relevant.

7. If the plant is established by Hoffmann-La Roche, how can the company protect its position in Nigeria? Discuss strategic as well as financial methods of protection.

8. Several years ago, Stephen Hymer wrote that there were "efficiency contradictions" in the activities of the MNE. That is, these firms can create substantial efficiencies in the organization of economic activity worldwide, but there are some contradictory aspects of MNEs for the host (and home) countries. What are some of these contradictions? (*Hint:* Look back at the introduction of this chapter.)

9. We have discussed costs and benefits of MNEs to host countries. How may *governments* and *consumers* differ in their views of these costs and benefits?

10. How do ownership and control differ, with respect to foreign activities of MNEs? What is the concern of host countries on this issue?

REFERENCES

Bergsten, C. F., T. Horst, and T. Moran. *American Multinationals and American Interests.* Washington, D.C.: Brookings Institution, 1978.

Caves, Richard. *Economic Analysis and Multinational Enterprises.* Cambridge: Cambridge University Press, 1983.

Dixon, C. J., D. Drakakis-Smith, and H. D. Watts (eds.). *Multinational Corporations and the Third World.* Boulder, Colorado: Westview Press, 1986.

Grosse, Robert. "The Economic Impact of Foreign Direct Investment in Venezuela." *Management International Review,* January 1986.

Hawkins, Robert, ed. *The Economic Effects of Multinational Corporations.* Greenwich, Conn.: JAI Press, 1979.

Hufbauer, Gary, and M. Adler. *Overseas Manufacturing Investment and the Balance of Payments.* Washington, D.C.: U.S. Treasury Department, 1968.

Hymer, Stephen. "The Efficiency (Contradictions) of Multinational Corporations." *American Economic Review,* May 1970.

Johnson, Harry. "The Efficiency and Welfare Implications of the International Corporation." In *The International Corporation,* ed. C. Kindleberger. Cambridge, Mass.: MIT Press, 1970.

Lall, Sanjaya, and Paul Streeten. *Foreign Investment, Transnationals, and Developing Countries.* London: Macmillan, 1977.

Lecraw, Donald. "Performance of Transnational Corporations in Less Developed Countries." *Journal of International Business Studies,* Spring–Summer 1983.

Moran, Theodore (ed.). *Multinational Corporations: The Political Economy of Foreign Direct Investment.* Lexington, Mass.: Lexington Books, 1985.

Robinson, Richard (ed.). *Direct Foreign Investment: Costs and Benefits.* New York: Praeger, 1987.

United Nations. *Transnational Corporations in World Development: Third Survey.* New York: UN, 1983.

NOTES

[1] Richard Caves, *Economic Analysis and Multinational Enterprise* (Cambridge: Cambridge University Press, 1983), p. 252.

[2] This investment by Rawlings is discussed in Thomas Ricks, "It's Sure a Long Hop from Asia to Haiti to a Pitcher's Hand," *The Wall Street Journal,* April 7, 1983, pp. 1 ff.; and Allan Ebert-Miner, "Haitians Slave to Hatch Our Baseballs," *Business and Society Review,* Spring 1983, pp. 12–13.

[3] Caves, *op. cit.,* chap. 9.

[4] If local investment had occurred, it would have been financed through local or foreign borrowing. Foreign borrowing would have yielded cash outflows similar to those resulting from FDI, without bringing in the knowledge that is transferred through the MNE.

[5] Some computer chip manufacture has returned to the United States (or has never left), due to the need for high-tech, nonstandardized modifications. Intel now produces its capital-intensive specialty chips in California. Note that this outcome is quite consistent with the international product cycle.

[6] Grant Reuber et al., *Private Foreign Investment in Development* (London: Oxford University Press, 1973), p. 175; and Robert Grosse, "Economic Impact of Foreign Investment in Venezuela," *Management Int'l Review,* January 1986.

[7] See, for example, Robert Ledogar, *Hungry for Profits: U.S. Food and Drug Multinationals in Latin America* (New York: IDOC, 1975).

[8] This entire discussion ignores the people in LDCs who are peripheral to the market economy. That is, there are many, many people who live away from cities and other sites of MNE business. These people are essentially not affected by the MNEs' activity, because they live and work outside of the scope of business that relates to MNEs.

[9] See, for example, I. M. D. Little and J. A. Mirlees, *Project Appraisal and Planning for Developing Countries* (New York: Basic Books, 1974); and Colin Bruce, *Social Cost-Benefit Analysis,* World Bank Working Paper no. 239, August 1976.

[10]Governments have collaborated to set multilateral rules on MNEs, such as the United Nations Code of Conduct, which has yet to be adopted after more than a decade of debate. On the other hand, individual countries have sometimes extended their jurisdiction to other countries—the United States often tries to regulate the activities of foreign affiliates of U.S.-based firms.

[11]See, for example, Ledogar, *Hungry for Profits;* and Prakash Sethi, "ITT in Chile," in *Up against the Corporate Wall,* ed. Prakash Sethi (Pacific Palisades, Calif.: Goodyear Publishing, 1976).

Case

Masasi Corporation

The Masasi Corporation is a British multinational chemical company with operations in eight countries and annual sales over $500 million in 1988. Most of the firm's business until now has been oriented toward Europe and North America. Because of the slow growth rates of sales in those markets, and the economic crisis in Latin America, Masasi's managers have decided to consider expansion into Asian countries. The first step was to consider entering the largest market, Japan. Assessment of competitive conditions there showed a very dynamic market with strong price competition. Subsequent looks at Hong Kong, Singapore, Taiwan, and other Asian countries showed greater possibilities of profitable expansion there, but no one country appeared large enough to absorb the output of a local plant for the polyethylene that Masasi wants to produce.

Three of the company's top managers flew from London to several cities in the region in 1988, trying to narrow down the choices for a facility and an Asia strategy. The size and liberal trade policies of the ASEAN group (viz., Malaysia, Indonesia, Singapore, Thailand, and the Philippines) led to plans to set up a plant to manufacture polyethylene in Southeast Asia to serve primarily that regional market. The company's officials had had preliminary talks with government officials from the various countries in the region and finally decided to set up a plant either in Indonesia or Malaysia. Both countries are producing natural gas, a necessary production input, and possess known reserves that will last for at least another 30 years. The problem is to choose where the company should set up its plant and how it should raise the $4 million needed to finance this project.

The following is some of the information available on each country and the requirements likely to be demanded by each government.

Malaysia is basically an agricultural country, with about 30 percent of its population in the industrial sector. The government encourages the local private sector and foreign firms to set up businesses in line with its economic policy of utilizing local resources in both agriculture and manufacturing industries. The education standard in the country is high and is enabling Malaysia to modernize with fewer difficulties than in many other less developed nations. Moreover, Malaysia has much of the infrastructure needed to accommodate industrialization.

This case was written by Margarita Siman and Ahmad Sabri Ismail, with revisions by Professor Robert Grosse. It is intended for use in class discussion, 1984 (rev. 1987).

Numerical Solution to Masasi Case *(in $ millions)*

	Malaysia	Indonesia
Sales	$10	$10
Labor cost	3	2
Materials	3	2.5
Indirect cost	3	4
Net income before taxes	1	1.5
Tax	0 (for 3 years) 0.55 (after 3 years)	0.675
Net income after taxes	1 (for 3 years) 0.45 (after 3 years)	0.825

The local currency of the country is fairly stable, with an exchange rate around 2.30 Malaysian dollars per U.S. dollar. As an incentive for foreign manufacturing investment, the government gives foreign investors an income tax holiday for three years, provided that the manufacturing facility is set up in a designated location.

By comparison, *Indonesia,* which is also an agricultural country, has a larger reserve of natural gas. The labor cost in the country is 33 percent lower than in Malaysia. The government requires that 90 percent of company managers be local nationals; the Malaysian government demands only 80 percent. Both governments require that local resources be used when available and that a minimum of 50 percent of the output be exported. Indonesia demands that at least 80 percent of capital be raised abroad, whereas Malaysia stipulates that a minimum of 40 percent of the capital come from foreign sources. The Indonesian rupiah is devaluing at the rate of 25 percent per year. Currently, the rupiah exchanges at the rate of 100 rupiahs per U.S. dollar. Indonesia also has a 45 percent corporate tax rate and charges a further 20 percent tax on remittance of profits. Malaysia imposes a corporate income tax of 55 percent after the tax holiday period, with no dividend withholding tax. The interest rate for loans to Masasi in Indonesia is 17 percent, whereas the Malaysian rate is 15 percent.

Masasi would be able to secure a loan in the international (eurodollar) loan market at a rate of 13 percent. The opportunity cost of capital used by the Indonesian government to evaluate foreign investment projects is 20 percent, whereas the Malaysian officials use a rate of 30 percent. The company expects to sell about $10 million worth of polyethylene in a typical year's operation. Annual labor cost is expected to be $2 million in Indonesia and $3 million in Malaysia. Cost of materials is estimated to be $2.5 million in Indonesia and $3 million in Malaysia. The indirect cost in Indonesia would be about $4 million, while in Malaysia it is expected to be $3 million. Transportation is cheaper and faster in Malaysia. Both countries propose to allow the company to operate for 10 years without permitting other foreign firms to enter the market for polyethylene.

PART

3

The New United Motor Manufacturing Company, located in California, is a strategic alliance between General Motors and Toyota.
Courtesy of New United Motor Manufacturing, Inc.

318

Managing the MNE

Many American companies are using offshore assembly to reduce their costs.
Milt and Joan Mann/Cameramann International, Ltd.

Chapter

12

Culture and Ethics

Culture and ethics are important to the international business person. MNEs deal in a variety of different cultures and must do so effectively. Culture affects both their strategic and operating decisions. And managers come to different problems and opportunities wearing their own cultural masks. This chapter looks at how culture affects MNEs' competitive advantages and everyday management decision making. The chapter also looks closely at business ethics in the international arena. In some situations, the ethics are clear and ethical behavior easy to accomplish. In others, what is ethical is not so evident. The main goals of the chapter are to:

1. Examine how the competitive advantages of MNEs are affected by cultural variables.

2. Learn about the practical school and the cross-cultural school of thought regarding the universality of management practices.

3. Note how different cultural variables affect management decision making.

4. Learn how to use the self-reference criterion to one's advantage when making cross-cultural decisions.

5. Examine business ethics in international business, with special reference to the international portability of ethics concepts.

6. Become sensitive to the situational factors affecting management behavior and how these may be interpreted in the ethics sense.

INTRODUCTION

What is culture? Why is it important in international business? These questions have become increasingly important over the past few years. They have to do with the implementation of strategy, or how firms accomplish their business objectives. "Culture" can either facilitate or hinder business effectiveness. It does this by affecting which business decisions are made, how they are made, and how they are implemented. As expected, culture also affects management communications—an especially important matter for the MNE that operates across various cultures with management and technical staff that are culturally diversified.

Consistent with the unifying theme of this book, this chapter begins with a discussion of cultural influences on the competitive advantages of MNEs. Managing in multicultural environments is then discussed and illustrations of cultural differences affecting managerial effectiveness are presented. The analysis of culture concludes with a close look at a prescription for cross-cultural management decision making.

The issue of business ethics is becoming increasingly important both domestically and internationally. It is also an issue that is closely related to culture. Later in the chapter, business ethics are discussed. The format for this discussion centers on an extended case analysis involving Eastern Airlines and drug smuggling from South America into the United States. Hopefully, this discussion will illustrate that ethics can at times be difficult to define, that situations can become complex and lacking in clarity as to which of several parties may be more responsible than others for resolving ethical problems, and that, at the margin, realistic trade-offs between ethics and economics may well have to be addressed.

CULTURE AND THE COMPETITIVE ADVANTAGES OF MNES

In Chapter 2, considerable attention was given to the concept of competitive advantages. Thirteen such advantages were listed (in Table 2–4) and discussed. Comments on how to "take advantage" of these competitive advantages were made, and alternative methods for exploiting competitive advantages through alternative forms of foreign involvement were analyzed. Let's return to some of these topics of Chapter 2 and put them into a cultural perspective. But first, we need a working definition of culture.

Anthropologists might well define **culture** as consisting of behavioral patterns, values or beliefs, art forms, institutions, and so on, which are characteristic of a "community of social expression." For our purposes, this is not a very workable definition of culture.

E. T. Hall, for years a prominent researcher on culture and management, identifies several key features of culture—that is, culture is acquired, or learned; various aspects of culture, such as values and behaviors, are interrelated; and culture pertains to groups of people and defines the boundaries among different groups.[1] For present purposes, we should note culture includes values and behavior patterns, is a product of conditioning, involves groups of people, and distinguishes one group from others. Culture affects what people see in a situation, what these observations may mean in terms of imputed intentions or motives, and the responses deemed appropriate. Culturally distinctive groups are not necessarily countries. And, individuals may belong to several different culturally defined groups simultaneously—with any single cultural influence varying depending on the time, the issue, and so forth. For example, one may be German, Christian, and young. Being identified with each of these groups may likely result in differing values and behaviors regarding differing issues and times.

Proprietary Technology

The competitive advantage of **proprietary technology** relates to culture in several ways. The cultural characteristics of a particular society affect product design itself, for example, by determining use conditions and expectations regarding product longevity (i.e., useful life). Witness the trend toward "low maintenance" products in the United States. Note how Germans, in general, have a more evident "lifetime of value" standard, especially for big-ticket items, than do Americans. Culture affects process technology too. For example, India's Mahatma Gandhi's outlook toward the use of machinery was negative. Gandhi felt labor-saving machines often put workers "on the streets to die of starvation."[2] One could argue that the incidence of innovation in product and process technologies is also culturally affected. In the United States, the market-oriented entrepreneur is intrinsic to the decentralized, capitalistic economic system. Historically, the U.S. environment has been the most prolific spawning ground of new products that the world has known. In contrast, Japan has traditionally purchased advanced technologies and then worked to perfect them in terms of product quality and cost minimization via process technology enhancements.

    Cultural risk is certainly important to both the development and the transfer of product and process technologies. Some products can be successful in one foreign market and not another—or substantial product adaptation may be required to make them successful. Process technology may have to be adjusted to reflect a cultural nuance—such as the long midday lunch break in the traditional Latin American firm and the effect it would have on the operation of a printing company or any other business in which extensive setup time is required prior to a production run. Firms that overlook the need to adapt to the local culture do so at considerable risk to their competitive potential. Successful adaptation may also be difficult to accomplish in firms whose corporate culture is monolithic or ostensibly risk averse.

Goodwill

Regarding **goodwill,** cultural risk is probably most evident in the potential for misreading the extent and durability of the franchise allegedly developed via time and experience in the home market as that franchise is commercially exploited in the foreign market. Mistakes can be made in market segmentation strategy, pricing strategy, and so on. The franchise may or may not be transferable. Products bearing labels of the European fashion houses—such as Pierre Cardin and Gino Pompeii—sell in upscale market segments around the globe. Chrysler, on the other hand, eventually withdrew from direct participation in European markets. Why couldn't Chrysler transfer its U.S. franchise successfully? The answer lay, in part, in the production cost increases associated with its need to move quickly in upgrading process technologies at its (former) European subsidiaries—as illustrated in the United Kingdom, where Chrysler (i.e., its subsidiary Rootes) "bought out" the old piece rate practice by paying workers time-measured wages well in excess of industry norms. Also, the Chrysler brand name had no special appeal for Europeans.

Scale Economies in Operations and Finance

Scale economies in production, purchasing, distribution, and financing were listed in Chapter 2 as potential sources for competitive advantages. The first of these is probably the most vulnerable to cultural risk. Large-scale production operations may be bound by product market limitations, such as extensive segmentation reflecting, for example, cultural diversities within the customer base that affect product use, or resource market limitations, such as the lack of an industrial plant-oriented culture among the workers. On this latter point, there is a famous case involving a Colombia-based textile manufacturer that established a modern plant in a rural area near Medellin and encountered excessive absenteeism and other problems involving personnel behavior, including widespread instances of fathers beating daughters who were employed at the plant, because the daughters brought home more money than the fathers did. People living in rural/peasant communities had difficulty in adjusting to an industrial setting, and the company had difficulty in adjusting to the rural/peasant setting. The period of transition was very costly. (Think, for a moment, how you as a manager, would deal with such a situation.)

There is some exposure to cultural risk in purchasing and distribution. Lot sizes may be affected by changes in process technology. The availability, price, and quality of raw materials and vendor-supplied components may be culturally influenced. The propensity of dockworkers, or perhaps miners, to go on strike may be relevant here—as may be the work ethic or the industrial culture. Shopping habits affect distribution and are often culturally influenced. For example, people living in the smaller towns and villages of Europe and in Japan prefer almost daily shopping. This leads to a more atomized distribution channel structure and possible losses of scale economies.

The scale economy that is probably least vulnerable to cultural risk is financing. Money is generally fungible internationally. Some funds-sourcing strategies relate to impersonal international capital and money markets and are thus generally not exposed to cultural nuances. Others, however, can relate to a wide range of types of funding sources, such as "building societies" in Great Britain and the *financieras* prevalent in Latin America. Such financing can vary considerably country by country, reflecting local values and practices. The use of debt can also reflect local values and practices. In Japan, for instance, a 4-to-1 debt to equity ratio—unheard of in the West—is not at all unusual.

Government Protection

Perhaps surprisingly, **government protection** can be substantially culture-bound. Witness the free-market philosophy so predominant in the United States and the difficulties some industries and unions have had in convincing the U.S. government to protect domestic markets through import restrictions. The idea of protectionism is foreign to the culture of numerous American citizens. On the other hand, developing countries historically often agree to erect import restrictions to protect growing domestic industries. Multinationals setting up plants in such countries could often expect this kind of support for local production. Those investing in developing countries might also expect to find varying degrees of hostility among host country personnel, including government officials. For U.S. MNEs, the "ugly American" syndrome can be very real—and nearly impossible to overcome.

Human Resource Management

Because it deals directly with people, **human resource management** is significantly culture-bound. For example, personnel practices and policies concerned with promotion, compensation, layoffs, and unionization vary considerably across (and even within) countries. In Japan, promotions are often based on age and seniority; in the United States, on seniority and equivalent capability (if the company is unionized) or merit (if the company is not unionized). Compensation is likewise based on age and seniority in Japan and on seniority or merit in the United States. As a form of employee compensation, profit sharing is frequently found and substantial in Japan but hardly evident in the United States and Western Europe. Layoffs of workers fly in the face of management's commitments and self-esteem in Japan; they are commonplace in the United States. Unions are often company specific in Japan, industry specific in the United States, trade specific in the United Kingdom, and politically specific in France. Thus, it is nearly impossible for the MNE to generalize cross-culturally regarding human resource management. However, there has been some movement recently toward similarities in practices as markets have become increasingly competitive in the open, global economy.

The challenge for the MNE is to learn not only how to accommodate differences in practices within the technological, financial, marketing, and managerial constraints facing them but also how to transfer practices that have been found especially productive in one locale to other locales—a difficult but potentially rewarding initiative.

Scale Economies in Advertising

Technology (e.g., the media available), government regulation, and culture all influence **scale economies in advertising.** Such economies rely on the repetition of standardized advertising appeals. The amount, content, and delivery of advertising messages may well have to accommodate cultural nuances, however. Advertising is much less prevalent in Iran today, for example, than it was in the days of the shah. Some messages may be irrelevant, or perhaps even offensive, depending on the cultural setting. The "Coke adds life" theme, which is designed to promote consumption by showing how Coke fits in nearly everywhere, would probably be ineffective in Buddhist settings—which typically value the suppression of desires.

Message delivery involves the use of media. Some media are culturally inappropriate for promoting certain types of products. Feminine hygiene products are advertised on television in the United States, for example, but not in Latin America. In some countries, the use of particular media may have important political implications. Terpstra reports, for example, that the two leading newspapers in Colombia, *El Tiempo* and *Espectador,* support different political groups and that the smart promoter might do well to advertise in both.[3] The "bottom line" here is that purchase decisions are made by people, and therefore the motivation to buy may well reflect people-specific characteristics. Such characteristics sometimes manifest a transnational homogeneity—when they reflect income level, for instance. Often, however, cultural influences are dominant in defining them. Only when the former situation exists can scale economies in advertising be realized.

Multinational Sourcing and Marketing Capabilities

Culture also affects multinational sourcing and marketing capabilities, two competitive advantages that are distinctive to MNEs. The **multinational sourcing** advantage implements a set of intermediate production, purchasing, and/or logistic relationships. The establishment of these relationships (e.g., purchase contracts) incorporates management's appraisals of the performance risks it has identified. As time unfolds, events with a low probability of occurrence may indeed take place. There might be a civil war, for example, or U.S. longshoremen might refuse to unload cargo from Soviet or Iraqi ships. Similarly, unanticipated events may occur that change the basic premises underlying the production, sourcing, or marketing patterns originally defined (e.g., U.S. consumers may again prefer big, or small, cars), thus denying the benefits expected from those patterns. Such events could result from cultural change or from management's misreading of the cultural environment. Similar comments might be made regarding **multinational marketing** networks.

The key point is that sourcing and marketing capabilities relate to both resource and sales markets and how these are linked through the MNE. These capabilities allow the MNE to locate the most profitable resource and sales (product) markets and to link them systematically. Culture is a concern relevant to the ongoing, efficient operation of these linkages.

Managerial Experience

Managerial experience in several countries, another competitive advantage distinctive to MNEs, is both dependent on and constrained by cultural variations. Being able to understand different cultures and being able to conduct effective cross-cultural operations are the competitive requirements unique to MNEs. The cultural differences evidenced internationally can provide the very basis for an MNE's ability to generate a competitive position. The learning curve effect, which energizes the MNE system and provides the competitive edge, is itself predicated on the successful transfer of management know-how among parent and subsidiaries. Cultural heterogeneity, however, complicates the transfer of such know-how and adds a special risk dimension to the transfer process. Some firms avoid this risk by not transferring management know-how to certain areas. For example, Kujawa reports that not all Japanese firms operating in the United States bring in Japanese systems of people management because they often have less risky alternatives (e.g., unique process technologies) for achieving the competitive success of their U.S.-based subsidiaries. On the other hand, some Japanese firms were successful in the U.S. market because of their ability to take advantage of the management expertise developed at home. For these firms, the cultural disparity between the United States and Japan relevant to industrial relations provided the very opportunity they needed for competitive success.[4]

International Diversification

International diversification is essentially a portfolio concept used to reduce risk and cost. It is pertinent to the global, MNE level; that is, it is the corporate headquarters that manages the "portfolio." The strategy is not culturally neutral, however. Its success ultimately turns on the profitable operation of the units contained in the portfolio. This situation returns us to the whole host of considerations regarding culture and competitiveness that have already been discussed.

ADDED DIMENSION

La Casa del Whopper

Consider Burger King's experience in adjusting to Venezuelan tastes and preferences at its restaurants in Caracas. The hamburger buns don't come with sesame seeds on them anymore; the Venezuelans kept brushing them off. Catsup is sweeter, and milk shakes are sweeter and creamier. The menu includes soft ice cream—which is everyone's favorite dessert in Latin America. Latins are late diners, so the Caracas Burger Kings stay open as late as 1:30 A.M. Everything else, however, is standard Burger King. For example, frozen french fries (which are imported, since Venezuela doesn't grow the "right kind" of potatoes) are prepared according to parent company specifications.

The managing director of the Venezuelan Burger Kings feels that the Latin American fast-foods markets are at the stage reached by the U.S. markets in the 1950s. But he expects the Latin American markets to develop fast, especially over the next 10 years, and he feels that Burger King's best growth opportunities are in international markets. At the start of 1991, about 13 percent of Burger King's 6,200 restaurants operated outside the United States, up from 10 percent in 1987.

Burger King has learned that cultural adaptation must relate to business enhancement and that simply adapting to local cultures may be counterproductive. For example, Burger King originally served wine in its French restaurants, but customers tended to linger and visit over their glasses of wine. This affected table turnover and revenues. You can't buy wine at a French Burger King anymore! ■

Sources: Mimi Whitefield, "La Casa del Whopper Goes South," *Miami Herald*, November 29, 1982, p. 5; and information provided by Burger King Corporation, Miami, Florida, January 22, 1987 and May 7, 1991.

MANAGING IN THE MULTICULTURAL ENVIRONMENT

There are two schools of thought regarding managing multiculturally. One, the practical school of thought, contends that good managers function the same regardless of the cultural environment. Cultural differences don't really matter. The other, the cross-cultural school, argues that management behavior and effectiveness are affected by the culture in which managers operate.[5] The preceding discussion on culture and competitive advantages supports the cross-cultural school perspective. Let's explore both of these schools of thought more deeply.

The Practical School

According to Black and Porter, the "practical" school of thought is so named because practicing managers (in the United States) are most often selected for overseas assignments with little or no regard for their cultural awareness and sensitivities. The key criteria are whether or not the manager was successful in the domestic operation, and, of course, is willing to accept the foreign assignment. The practical school contends good management practices are effective everywhere.[6]

Miller, in 1973, was the first to provide evidence that MNEs actually possessed the practical school orientation.[7] Later studies by Tung (1981) and Black (1988) showed approximately 70 percent of Americans appointed to foreign management assignments had no special preparation and training.[8] This behavior would only be rational where decision makers felt no training was necessary, that is, where success in a prior assignment was sufficient to ensure success in a foreign assignment. This is the practical school in action. Several comparative management scholars, such as Negandhi and Prasad,[9] have also long contended that culture does not have a major role to play in managerial effectiveness.

A major research finding reported by Black and Porter in 1991 raised serious doubts about the efficacy of the practical school approach. Black and Porter conducted a statistical analysis of American and local managers' behaviors and the relationship of these behaviors to job performance in the United States and in the foreign country. They found U.S. managers behaved essentially the same in the United States and in the foreign country, but there was no positive correlation between these behaviors and successful job performance in the foreign country (as there was in the United States).[10] This is contrary to practical school thinking.

The Cross-Cultural School

The roots of the cross-cultural school also date back many years. Farmer and Richman, in their 1965 classic *Comparative Management and Economic Progress,* presented and defended the view that the effectiveness of managers' performances varied in accordance with the cultural context in which the managers' behaviors occurred.[11] In other words, culture mattered.

Ouchi's 1982 popular report of his research on the correlation between corporations' profitability and their "Z-ness", or presence of Japanese management-like practices, and on the competitive superiority of Japanese management practices, further supports the cross-cultural school.[12] More recently, others have identified links among culture, management behavior, and corporate competitiveness. Abbeglen and Stalk, for example, identify elements in the Japanese work ethic, group orientation, and so on, as constituting what some contend is a "benign conspiracy" underpinning Japanese firms' competitiveness.[13]

Reconciling the Two Schools of Thought

For our purposes, it seems safe to say culture matters. But, there are also commonalities pertaining to managerial effectiveness that are independent of culture. These commonalities are embedded in the identity of the management performance necessary for success. For example, studies conducted by management scholars in both the 1970s and 1980s have found successful managers at home and abroad shared high, common values regarding productivity and ability, and found that certain skills, such as effective interpersonal and communication skills, and certain behaviors, such as flexibility, respect, and sensitivity, were common to successful managers regardless of the cultural context.[14]

This all says some elements of the management process (e.g., listening and communicating) and some management attitudes and behaviors that are process related (e.g., valuing ability and training) seem to be universal. But management behavior and decision making often have to be conditioned to accommodate cultural differences if they are to be successful. To illustrate, *Nation's Business* reported that (inexperienced) American tractor exporters, in negotiating with potential Japanese buyers, thrice lowered their export price in the face of silence by the Japanese, who were not rejecting any proposal by their silence, but were merely "thinking over" the proposal, a reportedly typical Japanese "motivating" practice.[15] Surveys, such as those reported on by Ricks, Fu, and Arpan in their classic *International Business Blunders,* are replete with other examples of management mistakes based on management insensitivities to cultural differences.[16]

This all suggests, then, that management must (1) be aware that culture differences matter, (2) be generally knowledgeable about the types of cultural differences that can affect management effectiveness when operating cross-culturally, and (3) be able to make decisions incorporating necessary and relevant cultural factors. The first of these three points has been addressed in the preceding discussion. We now turn to the latter two.

Cultural Differences Affecting Managerial Effectiveness

There are many ways to categorize culturally related behavior. Hofstede has identified four dimensions of national culture that have important management implications. These are "power distance" (the extent to which a society accepts an unequal distribution of power among people within an organization), "uncertainty avoidance" (a society's tolerance for uncertainty and the extent to which it will diminish uncertainty by supporting career stability, eliminating or reducing deviant ideas and actions, and so on), "individualism/collectivism" (social Darwinism—discussed later—versus group identification and responsibility), and "masculinity/femininity" (the extent to which a society espouses male values, such as assertiveness and the acquisition of material goods, and not female values, such as caring for others and the quality of life).[17]

Hofstede goes on to relate differences among societies on these four dimensions to the implications of these differences for supervisor/subordinate relationships (for example, the larger the power distance, the greater subordinates' dependence needs), the role of laws and rules as such apply to different classes of people within a society, the use of status symbols, the need for consensus (where uncertainty avoidance is strong), and so on.[18]

Hofstede's work encouraged managers to look at national cultures in ways that differed from those of the past—and this was an important contribution by Hofstede. But, let's look too at some of these more traditional perspectives, which typically include (among others) communication and education, achievement motivation, attitudes toward work, group identification, concepts of time, and hierarchical relationships.

Communication and Education

Gift-giving, which is a form of communication, can be quite culture-bound—as are other forms of communication. Cordiality and friendliness, for example, are expressed via the handshake of Westerners when people meet. Respect and social position are dominant in the greetings of Japanese, who bow before each other. Indeed, the angle of the bow will vary by the amount of respect due. The point to remember, according to Ronen, is that language (either spoken or silent) conveys social reality as well as providing for communication.[19] This is clearly evident in the dialogue presented in Figure 12–1. (Note the role of "power distance.")

FIGURE 12–1

Communication
Perceptions—Beware!

Behavior	Perception
American: How long will it take you to finish this report?	**American:** I asked him to participate. **Greek:** His behavior makes no sense. He is the boss. Why doesn't he tell me?
Greek: I don't know. How long should it take?	**American:** He refuses to take responsibility. **Greek:** I asked him for an order.
American: You are in the best position to analyze time requirements.	**American:** I press him to take responsibility for his actions. **Greek:** What nonsense: I'd better give him an answer.
Greek: Ten days.	**American:** He lacks the ability to estimate time; this time estimate is totally inadequate.
American: Take 15. Is it agreed? You will do it in 15 days?	**American:** I offer a contract. **Greek:** These are my orders: 15 days.

Source: From *Interpersonal Behavior* by H. C. Triandis. Copyright © 1977 by Wadsworth Publishing Company, Inc. Reprinted by permission of Brooks/Cole Publishing Company, Pacific Grove, California 93950.

Formal education is also typically viewed as culture-bound. It is not valued in some societies, possibly little valued in certain subgroups within societies, and highly valued in others. Educational systems and vehicles also vary widely across countries and cultures. Business schools, for example, are less prevalent outside the United States and Canada. They are a fairly recent addendum to the educational systems in other countries. Literacy levels and social/technical competencies usually correlate positively with the value placed on education.

Achievement Motivation

McClelland's benchmark study *The Achieving Society* provided a host of basic insights into **achievement motivation.**[20] McClelland reported that behavior patterns follow thought patterns—that is, people behave according to how they think. If people think about achievement, they have a desire or need for achievement and will seek to be achievers. McClelland noted that achievers universally exhibited three distinguishing characteristics: taking personal responsibility for solving problems, setting moderate achievement goals and taking moderate risks, and needing performance feedback. These characteristics, according to McClelland, position achievers as likely business executives.

The competitive, entrepreneurial business environment provides achievers with opportunities to "take command" by setting a strategy and implementing it, to be aggressive and take chances in the marketplace, and to value profits—which are, in fact, market-generated feedback on the appropriateness of the achiever's actions. Taking a broader perspective, a society whose business function responds to the needs of achievers will attract achievers to the enterprise sector and will thus be an achieving society. Moreover, a society that responds in this way to achievers creates an environment conducive to the economically effective application and growth of achievement motivation in general. The whole system feeds on and favors itself.

In support of his conclusions, McClelland observed and recorded the incidence of achievement orientation in different societies and found a strong, positive correlation between a high need for achievement and high economic growth. He found such a correlation when analyzing a society through time and when comparing different societies at a given point in time. For a business manager in an MNE context, achievement orientation is very important. It correlates with economic growth and expanding profit opportunities and with societal interests in economic achievement. It identifies foreign markets that are likely to be more accommodative of business success and, conversely, less antagonistic toward business in general.

Attitudes toward Work

Attitudes toward work are closely related to achievement motivation. The ideas are slightly different, however. Attitudes toward work include the "work ethic," the allocation of different types of work among different groups within the society, and even the relationship between labor and capital.

The **Protestant work ethic** is often cited as one of the driving forces in the development of the U.S. economy. This contention rests on the fact that in its early days the United States was populated via a large influx of immigrants from the United Kingdom, Holland, and other European countries. Many of these immigrants reflected a sociocultural heritage based on Puritan, Calvinist, or Lutheran doctrines that differed from Catholicism in several important relevant respects. In a classic essay written near the end of the large-scale European immigration into the United States, Fullerton noted that in Protestantism the person-God relationship is direct and individualism is emphasized in the struggle for salvation. The idea of work in this view pertains to discipline—that is, the fortification of the individual against temptation. Work is commanded by God and is an end in itself. Fullerton contrasted this perspective with the situation he saw in Catholicism, where the church mediates, as it were, between a person and God (e.g., via the sacrament of penance) and is itself populated by religious clerics who establish standards for the laity. The result was, in the Protestant view, that the daily living of Catholics was too casual and that the work of Catholics did not directly equate with prayer.[21]

Given these differences, one might expect that the commitment to work will differ considerably between societies embracing the Protestant view of work and those embracing the Catholic view. Management in a U.S. MNE operating in a Latin country may be well advised to temper its expectations, and structure its operations, to accommodate the different concept of work likely to be held by its Latin employees.

Attitudes toward work, to be sure, are also influenced by factors other than religion. Geography and climate, for example, are important influences. Temperature extremes, whether hot or cold, affect living patterns—including work-related activities. Attitudes toward work may also differ between private sector and public sector employment and may vary with the size of the enterprise. Harris and Moran report, for example, that in France there is little incentive to be productive in the government bureaucracy and in public concerns but that French workers in the private sector

have the reputation of being productive. Part of the explanation . . . may lie in the French tradition of craftsmanship. A large proportion of the French work force has been traditionally employed in small, independent businesses where there is widespread respect for a job well done. Many Frenchmen take pride in work that is done well because traditionally they have not been employed in huge, impersonal industrial concerns.[22]

Further evidence of the productivity differences between privately owned and publicly owned enterprises is seen in "privatization" trends, especially in the United Kingdom and in some of the continental European countries, where some public enterprises that had become noncompetitive and required government subsidies have been sold to private interests.

Attitudes toward work reflect the distribution of different kinds of work among different segments within a society. Social class distinctions may well determine who does manual labor—indeed, they may even bestow a "right" over such work by a specific class. In England, for example, class consciousness has greatly influenced labor-management relations. Historically, the factory-level work group was quite independent. It had its own leadership and its own allocation of effort and income, and it contracted with management on piece payment rates and production schedules.

Attitudes toward work are readily seen as affecting a variety of management decisions, such as staffing, production scheduling, equipment utilization, and process technology, as management seeks to work efficiently and competitively within whatever constraints society presents. The links among attitudes, constraints, and the choice of management options may be more direct, however. Some options may just be ill-advised, if not downright unacceptable. In the Hindu culture, for example, the use of laborsaving machinery was opposed early on by Mahatma Gandhi, who noted:

Men go on "saving labour" till thousands are without work and thrown on the streets to die of starvation. I want to save time and labour, not for a fraction of mankind, but for all.[23]

Moreover, if the Hindu's goal in existence is the liberation of the soul from the body, and this in turn is accomplished through the development of "wantless-ness," can Hindus embrace an economic system stressing wants and the satisfaction of wants or appreciate technology and machinery whose function is solely to satisfy material wants?[24] If you plan to do business in India, you might well read up on Gandhi and Hinduism (among other things).

Group Identification

Group identification, a hallmark of the "Japanese management style," which both fascinated and perplexed European and U.S. managers in the 1970s and 1980s, is generally credited with delivering substantial productivity gains. Japanese workers are seen as intensely loyal to their work groups and committed to group success. Individual interests and values give way to those espoused by the group. Harmony and hard work characterize the workplace. Labor-management relations are essentially nonadversarial in this model. New equipment and work methods are introduced without workers fearing for their jobs. Some roots of the model—including the development of communities and the difficulties of living off the land—can be found in the social structure of imperial Japan. Other roots are more recent—such as the paternalism that developed among the business class in response to the emigration of farmers into industrial centers.

In contrast, **social Darwinism** and the **rugged individualist** are often used to typify the keys to economic growth in the United States. Concepts of opportunity and entrepreneurship go hand in hand with "survival of the fittest." The Protestant ethic, the "frontier," and an abundance of natural resources (including fertile land) all favored the growth of individualism. It's not difficult to see why Americans have a hard time understanding Japanese business.

There are also other dimensions of group identification that are important to the international manager. For example, different ethnic groups, or subcultures, often exist within a society (e.g., the Flemish and Walloons in Belgium), and relations among these groups may not be harmonious. Staffing problems may result from the existence of such groups, as may difficulties in crossing market segments.

Concepts of Time

Cultures vary considerably in how they view time. In the United States, punctuality is valued. Typically, time is of the essence (as are those favoring strong uncertainty avoidance in Hofstede's model). Executives are often "time driven." Their day is defined in terms of a series of time slots through which they are programmed. Some executives even take courses in "time management." Other societies hold quite different views of time. In some African cultures, for example, time is not a constraint. Lateness is considered acceptable behavior. Time bends to accommodate behavior. People who are pressed by time are not

---

ADDED DIMENSION

Progress or Poverty—Land Reform in Mexico

Farming in Mexico is clearly inefficient. Nearly a third of the population lives on farms but produces only 8 percent of the gross national product. The problem dates back to the 1910 Mexican revolution, when the big *haciendas* were broken up and the land parcelled out to Indians. The *ejidos*, or Indian communal farms, then emerged where *ejido* farmers farmed the land and passed on farming rights to their children. After a few generations, the *ejidos* became very crowded. They were inefficient and unable to raise capital. Then along came one person with an idea.

Alberto Santos, Chairman of a Mexican cookie making concern, entered into a joint venture with an *ejido* to grow wheat for the company's cookies. The *ejido* provided the land and labor; the company the capital and technology. Both parties would share in the profits. Farming equipment was purchased and sprinkling systems installed. Modern agribusiness techniques were implemented. Productivity exploded!

Subsequently, the Mexican government has promoted similar joint ventures. It wants to break the rigidities in Mexico that have constrained the country's economic development. The Mexican cigarette company, Cigatam (a Philip Morris licensee) has invested $20 million to expand tobacco growing at the *ejidos*. Tropicana and Procigo (a Mexican juice company) recently put $13 million into orange groves on *ejido* land. ∎

Source: Claire Poole, "Land and Life!," *Forbes*, April 29, 1991, pp. 46–46.

trusted. Latins are famous for their "tomorrow" attitude. The stereotype is one of laziness, but in fact the origin of the attitude is an uncertain future. Why stress a timely behavior when the circumstances of tomorrow may well require a different behavior?

Time orientation is important in understanding people and how they behave—as Figure 12–2 illustrates. Many Americans, for example, are future oriented. Peasant-dominated societies are more concerned with the here and now. The Chinese and other Oriental cultures are very concerned with the past. Different views of time affect interpersonal relationships, the pace with which business can be conducted—and even product definition. Where time is valued, you'll probably see timesaving products. Household appliances generally originate in the United States, where family members, not household servants, perform the routine cleaning and cooking chores and where the demands on these people are typically seen as endless. "Time" influences business decisions in a variety of ways.

Hierarchical Relationships

Culture also affects **hierarchical relationships.** Vertical organization structures of six or more layers are often evident in the United States, and decision-making and authority levels are allocated by hierarchical standing. In Japan, functional organizations are typically flatter and communication is more horizontal. Participation in decision making is less a function of responsibility than it is of knowledge. In the Latin cultures, people and personalities dominate. Key people, the chiefs (or "jefes") control decision making. The worker's task is to perform routine jobs and to call on the jefe for decisions. This leads to an inordinate amount of paper-shuffling and to a lack of initiative among employ-

FIGURE 12–2

Time and Conflict (a continuation of the dialogue in Figure 12–1)

Behavior	Attribution
In fact, the report needed 30 days of regular work. So the Greek worked day and night, but at the end of the 15th day he still needed to do one more day's work.	
American: Where is the report?	**American:** I am making sure he fulfills his contract. **Greek:** He is asking for the report.
Greek: It will be ready tomorrow.	[Both make the attribution that the report is not ready.]
American: But we had agreed it would be ready today.	**American:** I must teach him to fulfill a contract. **Greek:** The stupid, incompetent boss! Not only does he give me the wrong orders, but he doesn't even appreciate that I did a 30-day job in 16 days.
[The Greek hands in his resignation.]	[The American is surprised.] **Greek:** I can't work for such a man.

Source: From *Interpersonal Behavior* by H. C. Triandis. Copyright © 1977 by Wadsworth Publishing Company, Inc. Reprinted by permission of Brooks/Cole Publishing Company, Pacific Grove, California 93950.

ees at the lower skill levels. It also leads to economic and social dependences of workers on their jefes and therefore to paternalism.

Hierarchical relationships are thus seen to affect reporting and control, communication, documentation, attitudes toward paternalism, the locus of initiative, and so on. Interestingly, workers at a Spanish subsidiary of a U.S. multinational, in a dispute with management, refused to eat the lunch provided by the company or to use company-provided transportation to get home. These actions, which the workers took at some cost, registered the workers' denial of their jefes' paternalism. They were a slap in the face of the Spanish management. Managers in the U.S. parent had a hard time understanding their significance.

The preceding illustrates that cultural characteristics vary considerably across different societies and that the potential of these characteristics for affecting business decisions and success is significant.

Making Decisions

If we accept that there are cultural differences and that these differences need to be taken into consideration by management when making decisions, the question then arises as to how this might be most effectively accomplished. This issue is addressed to some extent in Chapter 18 on personnel management and training. The chapter confirms the emergence of the truly international manager. If the modern international manager is of necessity cosmopolitan, and if key (international) decisions are made by or with important inputs from various managers and technical specialists from around the globe, as relevant, these decisions will likely be sensitive to cross-cultural elements.

This says simply that decision making must be **culturally adaptive,** that is, that decisions must accommodate the cultural environment. Local customs can affect everything from product design to marketing to production technology. They have to be addressed so that both strategy and operations reflect their impact.

Decision makers must also be culturally adaptive, that is, they can't just rely on "practical school" behavior that is based on a **self-reference criterion** (SRC). We use an SRC when we impose our own standards or expectations when observing or being affected by others' behaviors. For example, many U.S. companies have a hard time setting up marketing organizations in Japan. They often blame the Japanese government and the Ministry of International Trade and Industry (MITI) for holding back on the required approvals. They think the U.S. government should negotiate with the Japanese government to eliminate or streamline this approval process, thus ensuring them a successful entry into the Japanese market. There is likely more to it than this, however. Given the demographics of the country, distribution is highly fragmented in Japan. Moreover, distributors—from wholesalers to retailers—are often already associated with Japanese firms that will be the American firm's competitors. Japanese companies just don't walk away from these relationships. They are fiercely loyal to suppliers and/or distributors. Success in getting into the Japanese market entails much more than getting beyond government barriers. This simple example illustrates the SRC is really a "blinder" hindering cultural adaptation.

Lee, in a classic on dealing with the SRC, outlines a four-step procedure for isolating and eliminating the SRC in business decision making.

1. Define the business problem or goal from the home country perspective.
2. Define the same problem or goal from the local perspective.

3. Compare the two definitions and note the differences, that is, the SRC influence.

4. Eliminate the SRC difference, redefine the problem or goal, and proceed towards some optimal solution.[25]

To illustrate this procedure, Jain uses the example of designing an automobile for the Pakistani market. The U.S. perspective identifies an auto as a necessity item, designed for high speed, performance, and comfort. In Pakistan, the auto is hardly affordable and then by but few. Moreover, it must be durable, efficient, and not ostentatious (since materialistic living is frowned upon). Comparing the U.S. and Pakistani perspectives brings out important differences on the role and function of an automobile. In Pakistan, the auto should be inexpensive, easily maintained, highly fuel efficient, and simple in design.[26]

It is important to note here that the SRC is a beneficial starting point when making decisions across cultures. It provides those making decisions with comfortable "benchmarks" against which to identify and hopefully better understand the impact of cultural traits on managerial decisions.

BUSINESS ETHICS

When considering business ethics in the international business arena, the issue of bribery usually comes to mind first. Bribery is important in international business for several reasons. For one, it is often culturally defined. *La Mordida* (the "bite") is an accepted custom in several Latin societies. It is a payment to someone to secure a sale, an approval by some government agency, or whatever. In most industrially advanced societies, such *mordidas* don't exist. Second, when excessive and when used for inappropriate purposes, bribes are seen by all as illegal and unethical. The Recruit scandal in the late 1980s in Japan where a company bought political favors by paying large sums of money to selected legislators and government officials was so pervasive and obscene, the Takeshita Government was brought down. Third, home country rules prohibiting bribes can seriously affect the competitiveness of some MNEs in societies where bribes are necessary to the conduct of business. All too often, executives of U.S. MNEs note that they are hindered because local firms and other MNEs are able to secure local government favor by paying off certain local officials. Differential tax treatments regarding such expenditures are also relevant. For example, for U.S. MNEs, bribes anywhere are not a deductible business expense; for Japanese MNEs, they are deductible (everywhere); for German MNEs, they are not if the bribes were domestic, but they are if foreign.

Chapter 15, "Accounting and Taxation," discusses the U.S. Foreign Corrupt Practices Act and U.S. MNEs obligations under the Act. It should be noted here though that the Act makes bribes illegal, but allows for "grease" payments to low-level officials to cut through bureaucratic delays and obstructions to doing business in a timely fashion. A firm could give a special inducement to a port authority, for example, to move product from a warehouse to a truck within some desired time period.

Business Ethics—The Broader International Context

The issue of bribery is important but it is only one of several that are important in international business. The issues multiply when one considers that countries' legal systems are themselves reflective of those countries' ethical standards, that differences in laws and standards exist, and that MNEs operate in different countries with different laws and ethical standards.

Consider or question, for example, the firm that sells children's sleepwear in foreign countries that does not meet safety (fire hazard) standards in its own country. Consider too the firm that transfers high-pollution (toxic-producing) production to developing countries where environmental legislation and controls are not in place. Consider the firm that locates production in societies where the working classes are politically oppressed and economically disadvantaged.

Your thoughts on each of these may vary depending on your own sense of ethics. But, surely most of you would be opposed to selling unsafe sleepwear anywhere. Many would be opposed to foreign direct investments made to avoid local environmental controls. Probably some of you would be opposed to locating production in areas where wages reflected workers being economically disadvantaged. Many Americans, for example, felt that Occidental Petroleum's activities in the Soviet Union during the Stalin era were ethically questionable, and many also questioned the ethics of American firms' participation in South Africa during the time of *apartheid*. Others may well feel, in this latter instance, for example, the best thing MNEs could do for politically oppressed and economically disadvantaged workers would be to give these workers jobs! The issues here are not legal issues. Firms were operating in all instances within the legal confines of the different societies involved. But the ethics can be questionable.

Let's look at a real live case and see where we feel the ethical issues lie and how we feel about them.

The Eastern Airlines Drug-Smuggling Case[27]

Smuggling drugs from Latin America into the United States via Eastern Airlines became all too common in the latter 1980s. Cocaine would be packed into an airplane's wheel wells, bathroom panels, legitimate cargo, and the flooring of shipping containers.[28] The Eastern baggage handlers and ramp supervisors involved in the smuggling ring would wait until the regular baggage cleared customs, then remove the coke-filled baggage from hiding places and mix it with luggage in the domestic arrival area—to be collected by accomplices for further distribution.[29]

The huge profits available from drug trafficking obviously provided a basis for the corruption of the Eastern Airlines staff involved. But, there was more to it than just money. Staff were threatened. At times, new hires in Miami were greeted with a "bullet-in-the-palm" by smuggling ringleaders. In Colombia, employees were coerced by death threats to "look the other way" as drugs were put onto aircraft. Eastern employees actually received death threats. Several Colombia-based officials and employees at Eastern and other airlines flying similar routes were murdered; others found mini-coffins outside their homes. They all resigned.[30]

Some observers would contend that Eastern's labor-management difficulties at this time likely complicated the drug smuggling problem. Employees who were distrustful of management and likely contentious regarding management initiatives directed towards employees on the drug smuggling issue, would probably not be especially cooperative in helping shut down the problem.

Eastern, of course, paid dearly for these problems. In 1985, Eastern was fined $1.2 million. By 1989, the (proposed) figure for current infractions had grown to $13 million. In addition, the airline contended it lost some $7 million annually due to passenger losses stemming from the aircraft delays and cancellations caused by U.S. Customs' searches and seizures of aircraft.[31]

One could well contend that both Eastern Airlines and its employees were big losers in the drug war.

The Management Involvement and Response   Eastern Airlines management knew as far back as 1984 its flights were being used to smuggle drugs into the United States. In 1985, some 22 drug busts were made aboard Eastern Airlines' planes, and an Eastern aircraft was eventually impounded. Some observers felt it was the seizure of the aircraft that really got management's attention to the drug trafficking problem. Later that year, U.S. Drug Enforcement Agency (DEA) officials busted cocaine traffickers using Eastern on two occasions. Eastern security agents also then began cooperating with DEA officials and a large number of Eastern employees were indicted in early 1986.[32]

Management's initial attitude toward drug smuggling was consistent with that of other carriers and was simply that drug smuggling was not Eastern's problem. It was a police problem. Eastern eventually responded, however, by installing a special security system costing $3 million per year. The system included training a 17-person security force, installing surveillance cameras at selected airports, and establishing special baggage-handling procedures for passengers. Additionally, Eastern temporarily suspended flights to Barranquilla, Colombia, while it implemented improved security procedures, attempted to drug-proof planes by removing plastic panels secured with screws with metal panels that were riveted in place, installed a drug "hotline" for employees to call in tips, and fired and otherwise disciplined employees involved in drug smuggling or infractions of security procedures.[33]

But the drug smuggling problems still persisted. In 1988, for example, eight Eastern Airlines' planes were seized at Miami International Airport carrying in excess of a total of 1,000 pounds of cocaine.[34]

The U.S. Government's Role   For years the U.S. government has focused on the supply side of the drug problem. Lacking sufficient funding, however, interdiction was not originally successful. In the early 1980s, stepped-up funding and interdiction efforts successfully curtailed the activities of drug runners using small planes and fast boats. This led drug smugglers to use commercial aircraft to transport ingeniously hidden drugs along with regular cargo and passengers' baggage. This led to Eastern's problems.

The Anti-Drug Act of 1986 identified commercial carriers as an integral part of the drug transshipment problem, and provided for substantial financial penalties, even for carriers who were unwitting collaborators in transporting drugs. This, of course, got the attention of all commercial shippers and justified their increased costs in developing responses to be in compliance with the Act.[35]

Evaluating the Eastern Airlines Case   This case raises a lot of interesting questions pertinent to the ethics issue. Did Eastern "ask" for drug smugglers to use its flights? Why did drug smugglers turn to using such flights? Was Eastern responsible for this? Was management's original attitude inappropriate in the face of the growing drug-smuggling problem? Why did management change its attitude? Who is paying for Eastern's enhanced security procedures? Can a firm afford to be proactive on problems such as this? Should it be proactive? Since the drug problem is so pervasive, should the U.S. government have funded commercial carriers' responses to reduce the trafficking? What were the responsibilities of governments and government agencies in other countries where drug trafficking begins or transshipments are accomplished?

Answers to these questions will likely vary depending on one's knowledge and values.

CONCLUSIONS

This chapter is concerned with what culture is and why culture is important in international business. It is also concerned with business ethics. Culture was defined as distinctive of groups of people and consisting of acquired, interrelated values and behaviors.

All of the MNE's 13 potential competitive advantages are affected, in varying degrees, by diversity in cultural environments. Culture can influence *proprietary technology,* for example, as related to product design by affecting product use conditions. Process technology may need adaptation as it is transferred from one country to another. Different cultural environments were identified as giving rise to competitive advantages—the United States, for example, has traditionally been very receptive to product innovations. Americans, according to the stereotype, are typically willing to try new things. It was noted that the transferability of *goodwill* is dubious and depends on homogeneous strands of cross-cultural similarities between markets.

Of the five advantages related to scale economies, the advantages in production and advertising are probably the most susceptible to cultural risk. To the extent that culture affects market size and segmentation or the behavior of in-plant personnel, it has an impact on *scale economies in production.* The amount, content, and delivery of advertising messages, and hence *scale economies in advertising,* are affected by cultural nuances. Culture may also affect the availability, price and quality of raw materials or vendor-supplied components, and thus *scale economies in purchasing and distribution. Scale economies in financing,* when related to the international money and capital markets, are not generally vulnerable to cultural risk. Financial institutions, however, can vary substantially country by country and often reflect cultural attitudes to savings and lending. The use of debt itself may be regarded as highly desirable in some cultures and as socially unacceptable in others.

Government protection, which is a public policy statement and should reflect public interests and values, is typically culturally influenced. The United States, for example, has eschewed trade protectionism for at least the past 50 years.

Human resource management, which deals directly with people and their behavior in the workplace, is obviously culturally affected. If, for example, a group of production managers were transferred from either Italy or Germany to a factory in Japan or Canada, the adjustments required of all parties would be fairly extensive.

Multinational sourcing and marketing capabilities lead into the establishment by the MNE of transnational purchasing, intermediate production, and/or logistic relationships and marketing patterns that are themselves dependent on the given set of existing or anticipated conditions. Many of these conditions can be influenced by people and are culture-bound.

The competitive edge provided by *managerial experience in several countries* is rooted in cultural differences. If all environments were totally homogeneous, the ability of MNE management to bring in superior (e.g., more productive) practices would give it no advantage over local management. It is the differences in experiences internationally and the capacity to learn from one situation to be more effective in another that can give the MNE an advantage over purely local firms. Similarly, *international diversification,* to be an effective strategy, requires success in simultaneously operating in different political, economic, and cultural environments.

Two approaches to managing in a multicultural environment were discussed—the practical school, which says good management practices are effective everywhere, and the cross-cultural school, which says managers' performances vary with the cultural context within which managers function. The two schools come together if we acknowledge that managers everywhere share common values and certain skills, but adjust the management process and some managerial behaviors to accommodate cultural differences across operating environments.

Some important cultural differences affecting managerial effectiveness were then discussed. These included Hofstede's power distance, uncertainty avoidance, individualism/collectivism, and masculinity/femininity characterizations regarding different societies and their effects on management. They also included commentary on the more commonly identified cultural factors affecting management decision making, such as communications, education, achievement motivation, attitudes toward work, group identification, concepts of time, and hierarchical relationships.

The section on culture closed with a normative discussion on the need to be aware of the self-reference criterion (SRC) when making cross-cultural decisions. The SRC was identified as an important tool in analyzing cross-cultural problems and opportunities.

Business ethics were discussed initially in terms of the bribery issue so typical of international businesspeoples' concerns. Bribes are generally considered wrong in all societies, but nonetheless exist in some. "Grease payments," which are endemic to almost all developing countries, were differentiated from bribes. Needing to avoid bribes was noted as putting MNEs from some countries at a competitive disadvantage since local firms and other MNEs may well participate in making bribes.

Business ethics in the broader international context was then identified as concerned with the issues arising from doing business across two or more different countries, each with its own laws and sense of ethics. Some of these issues appear straightforward, and there is considerable agreement by parties in all societies as to appropriate business behavior. Others may well reflect differences in values across different societies. The Eastern Airlines drug-smuggling case was presented to illustrate the difficulties inherent in identifying and criticizing behavior felt to be either ethical or unethical.

QUESTIONS

1. Define the term *culture.* How can culture be ubiquitous and yet distinguishing?
2. Give an example of a business practice that you feel reflects cultural origins.
3. Give an example of a cultural difference between two environments and show how it affects business.
4. After initially transferring its operating policies from the United States to France, Burger King (*a*) adjusted them to suit its own needs in light of the local cultural environment or (*b*) adjusted them to accommodate the local

environment. With which of these two explanations do you agree? Could you agree with both?

5. How does culture relate to competitive advantage? Give an example of cultural differences destroying an MNE's competitive advantage. Give an example of cultural differences enhancing an MNE's competitive advantage.

6. Contrast the position of the practical school with that of the cross-cultural school as to the universality of effective management practices. Can you come up with examples of different practices that appear to be consistent with each school?

7. What is an SRC? Have you ever used an SRC when examining the behavior of others? How can international businesspeople put the SRC to work for them?

8. Distinguish between bribes and "grease payments." Why are bribes almost universally seen as unethical, whereas grease payments are acceptable as a necessary way of doing business? Can a grease payment ever become a bribe?

9. Are ethical standards transferable internationally?

10. Eastern Airlines had some real problems in dealing with drug smugglers, as did the U.S. government. What are the ethical issues involved here for Eastern? For the U.S. government?

REFERENCES

Adler, Nancy J. *International Dimensions of Organizational Behavior.* Boston: PWS-Kent Publishing Company, 1991.

Adler, Nancy J., and John L. Graham. "Cross-Cultural Interaction: The International Comparison Fallacy." *Journal of International Business Studies,* Fall 1989, pp. 515–37.

Graham, J. L., and D. Andrews. "A Holistic Analysis of Cross-Cultural Business Negotiations." *Journal of Business Communications,* Fall 1985, pp. 63–77.

Jamieson, I. "The Concept of Culture and Its Relevance for an Analysis of Business Enterprise in Different Societies." *International Studies of Management and Organization* 12, no. 4 (1982–83), pp. 75–105.

Moller, J. Orstrom. *Technology and Culture in a European Context.* Copenhagen: Copenhagen Business School, Institute of International Economics and Management, 1991.

Ronen, Simcha. *Comparative and Multinational Management.* New York: John Wiley & Sons, 1986.

Shibagaki, Kazuo, Malcom Trevor, and Tetsuo Abo (eds.). *Japanese and European Management: Their International Adaptability.* Tokyo: University of Tokyo Press, 1989.

NOTES

[1] E. T. Hall, *Beyond Culture* (Garden City, NY: Doubleday, 1977), p. 16.

[2] D. P. Mukerji, "Mahatma Gandhi's Views on Machines and Technology," in *Culture and Management,* ed. Ross A. Weber (Homewood, Ill.: Richard D. Irwin, 1969), p. 113. Reprinted from *International Social Science Bulletin 6,* No. 3 (Paris: UNESCO, 1954), pp. 411–23.

[3] Vern Terpstra, *International Dimensions of Marketing* (Boston: Kent Publishing, 1982), p. 162.

[4]Duane Kujawa, "Technology Strategy and Industrial Relations: Case Studies of Japanese Multinationals in the United States," *Journal of International Business Studies,* Winter 1983, pp. 9–22; and Duane Kujawa, "Flexible Production Systems and Japanese Multinationals' Experiences in the U.S. Automotive Industry: Strategic Imperatives and Strategic Dividends" (Miami: International Business & Banking Institute, University of Miami, Discussion Paper Series, 1990).

[5]J. Stewart Black and Lyman W. Porter, "Managerial Behaviors and Job Performance: A Successful Manager in Los Angeles May Not Succeed in Hong Kong," *Journal of International Business Studies,* First Quarter 1991, pp. 99–113.

[6]Ibid., pp. 101–2.

[7]Edward L. Miller, "The Selection Decision for an International Assignment: A Study of the Decision Maker's Behavior," *Journal of International Business Studies,* Spring 1973, pp. 49–65.

[8]Rosalie Tung, "Selection and Training of Personnel for Overseas Assignments," *Columbia Journal of World Business,* vol. 16 (1981), pp. 68–78; and J. Stewart Black, "Workrole Transition: A Study of American Expatriate Managers in Japan," *Journal of International Business Studies,* Summer 1988, pp. 274–91.

[9]Anant R. Negandhi and S. B. Prasad, *Comparative Management* (New York: Appleton-Century-Crofts, 1971).

[10]Black and Porter, "Behaviors."

[11]Richard N. Farmer and Barry M. Richman, *Comparative Management and Economic Progress* (Homewood, Ill.: Richard D. Irwin, 1965).

[12]William G. Ouchi, *Theory Z: How American Business Can Meet the Japanese Challenge* (New York: Avon Books, 1982).

[13]James C. Abbeglen and George Stalk, Jr., *Kaisha: The Japanese Corporation* (New York: Basic Books, Inc., 1985).

[14]See, for example, George W. England and R. Lee, "The Relationship between Managerial Values and Managerial Success in the United States, Japan, India, and Australia," *Journal of Applied Psychology,* vol. 59 (1974), pp. 411–19; Bernard M. Bass and Phillip C. Berger, *Assessment of Managers: An International Comparison* (New York: Free Press, 1979); Frank Hawes and Daniel Kealey, "An Empirical Study of Canadian Technical Assistance," *International Journal of Intercultural Relations,* vol. 5 (1981), pp. 239–58; and Brent Ruben and Daniel Kealey, "Behavioral Assessment of Communication Competency and the Prediction of Cross-Cultural Adaptation," *International Journal of Intercultural Relations,* vol. 3 (1979), pp. 15–47.

[15]"Blunders Abroad," *Nation's Business,* March 1989, p. 54.

[16]David Ricks, Marilyn Y. C. Fu, and Jeffrey S. Arpan, *International Business Blunders* (Columbus, Ohio: Grid, 1974).

[17]Geert Hofstede, "Managing Differences in the Multicultural Organization," in *Organizational Psychology,* ed. David Kolb *et al* (Englewood Cliffs, N.J.: Prentice Hall, Inc., 1984), pp. 309–31. (Note: This a reprint of Hofstede's original article by the same name, which appeared in *Organizational Dynamics,* Summer 1980.)

[18]Ibid.

[19]Simcha Ronen, *Comparative and Multinational Management* (New York: John Wiley & Sons, 1986), p. 97.

[20]David C. McClelland, *The Achieving Society* (Princeton, N.J.: D. Van Nostrand, 1961).

[21]Kemper Fullerton, "Calvinism and Capitalism," *Harvard Theological Review* 21 (1928), pp. 163–91. Reprinted in Ross A. Weber, ed., *Culture and Management* (Homewood, Ill.: Richard D. Irwin, 1969), pp. 91–111.

[22]Philip R. Harris and Robert T. Moran, *Managing Cultural Differences* (Houston: Gulf Publishing, 1979), p. 223.

[23]Mukerji, "Mahatma Gandhi's Views."

[24]Ibid., p. 114.

[25]James A. Lee, "Cultural Analysis in Overseas Operations," *Harvard Business Review,* March–April 1966, p. 110. For an extended discussion on Lee's model and the SRC, see Subash C. Jain, *International Marketing Management* (Boston: Kent Publishing Company, 1984), pp. 208–11.

[26]Jain, *Marketing,* pp. 209–11.

[27]This case benefits from research conducted by Donald R. Major, a doctoral student at the University of Miami's Graduate School of International Studies.

[28]"Drug War Drains Airline, Ships," *The Miami Herald,* January 16, 1989, p. 6.

[29]"The Eastern Connection; Coke Was a Frequent Flier," *Newsweek,* February 24, 1986, p. 8.

[30]"Drug War" and "Old Foes Are New Allies in Drug War," *The Miami Herald,* January 23, 1989, "Business Monday" sec., p. 8.

[31]"Drug War."

[32]Ibid.

[33]Ibid. and "Firm Turns to Army-Style Surveillance," *The Miami Herald,* January 16, 1989, p. 6.

[34]"Drug War."

[35]Ibid.

NUMMI

NUMMI stands for New United Motor Manufacturing, Inc., a 50–50 joint venture between Toyota Motor Corporation and General Motors Corporation—automobile companies that are, respectively, the third largest and the largest in the world. NUMMI, which began production in late 1984, assembles smaller-sized cars designed by Toyota. It is located in Fremont, California, and employs about 2,500 people. The plant receives components and parts from Toyota plants and suppliers in Japan and from suppliers in the United States. The cars it assembles are sold to marketing organizations belonging to each of its parent companies.

Why a "NUMMI"?

NUMMI was conceived during the early 1980s, an admittedly tumultuous time for the auto industry in America. High energy prices and changing consumer preferences had resulted in an expanding demand for smaller, high-quality, more fuel-efficient cars. Japanese auto producers, Toyota among them, were operating under a program of Japanese export quotas on cars shipped to the United States, a program intended (1) to give U.S.-based producers "breathing time" to adjust their production to meet market needs and federal standards on increased fuel efficiency and (2) to encourage Japanese auto companies to establish production in the United States.

One could speculate at length about the factors that motivated Toyota and General Motors (GM) to join together to form NUMMI. At the time, however, articles in the press focused on two important considerations.

Toyota found the idea of producing in the United States attractive for short-term reasons, such as the quota, and for long-term reasons, such as its own business philosophy and the global competitive environment facing the auto industry. At the same time, it was interested in lowering the risks associated with beginning U.S. production by bringing in a partner knowledgeable about U.S. marketing and labor-management practices and by learning how to manage successfully in the United States. General Motors, on the other hand, was comparatively inexperienced in small-car production and in the shop floor, worker-

This case was written by Professor Duane Kujawa. Information on NUMMI's operations was obtained by the author during on-site research in September 1986. The research was part of a larger research project directed by Professor Tetsuo Abo at the University of Tokyo's Institute of Social Science and funded by the Toyota Foundation in Japan. The support from Professor Abo and the Toyota Foundation is gratefully acknowledged, as is the cooperation of New United Motor Manufacturing, Inc.

management, and vendor-supplier relationships that were needed to make such production cost competitive. It saw the joint venture with Toyota as an opportunity to participate, in a substantial way, with one of the world's foremost cost-competitive producers of high-quality, small cars—and to learn from the experience and transfer what it learned to other GM operations. From this perspective, General Motors' participation in NUMMI would serve to enhance GM's potential for future success in small-car production.

Thus, there were sound business reasons for creating NUMMI. Lowering the risks associated with possible future financial and operating commitments of impressive magnitudes motivated both Toyota and GM to come together in NUMMI.

But NUMMI involved other risks—risks that were intrinsic to its very nature. Could Toyota's Japan-based management system be implemented successfully in the United States? NUMMI would be breaking new ground and creating a distinctive, hybrid corporate culture reflecting both Japanese and American culturally based traits and culturally influenced institutions. At the beginning, neither GM nor Toyota was really sure that an experiment like NUMMI could succeed.

The GM-Toyota Contractual Relationship and Toyota's Responsibility for Running the Plant

The joint-venture agreement between GM and Toyota gave Toyota the responsibility for operating the plant and established an eight-person board of directors consisting of four Toyota representatives and four GM representatives. Although the board is the ultimate decision-making body, it cannot by itself change the joint-venture contract. Toyota runs the plant, and this situation can be changed only if both Toyota and GM agree.

In implementing its responsibility for running the plant, Toyota has drawn on its experience with its production system in its Japanese plants, an experience that reflects substantial and compelling Toyota-specific and "Japanese" influences and characteristics. Those influences and characteristics determine the entire NUMMI system, a system that differs noticeably from that found in "traditional" U.S. auto plants. To enable us to place differences in perspective, let us note first some of the fundamental features of the traditional U.S. system as seen in auto and other types of plants over the years.[1]

The "Traditional" U.S. System

The automobile assembly line concept was built around the idea of engineering the production job down to a series of discrete worker tasks. The simpler these tasks were, the better, since that made it possible to use less-expensive workers. Production engineering made these workers more productive by providing them with specific operating methods and tools, many of special design. Production engineering also determined output standards and time standards against which to measure worker "efficiency." The quality control department checked to see whether the product produced was within what was felt to be a tolerable quality range. Training was limited to what was necessary to make the worker more effective on his or her present job.

The traditional U.S. auto plant was a unionized plant, and its work practices reflected a variety of influences regarding workers' and unions' interests in job control and income protection. For example, there were typically a large number of job classifications and wage levels reflecting the various tasks that workers performed. An employee usually worked strictly within his or her job classification.

Critics of the traditional system felt that it was "dehumanizing" and that it permitted no personal identification between the worker and the job, the product, or the company.

Relationships with suppliers were typically subject to periodic review and "rebidding." This meant that vendors would prepare proposals, which might or might not be accepted, to supply certain components, made to the buyer's specifications and design configuration, for a particular model year. The relationship was tenuous and often temporary. If a new vendor came in with a lower price and was deemed reliable, a new supply relationship was created. Critics saw this behavior as denying the benefits of experience and promoting an orientation toward short-term profit on the part of vendors. Both of these effects were seen as impairing product quality. Vendors shipped on a periodic basis, and buyers routinely performed receiving inspection and testing before putting these shipments into their inventory.

Before leaving the U.S. system, it is important to note that many of its practices have distinctively American roots. Scientific management principles have long been part of the U.S. industrial culture. They pertain to the procedures for engineering a job down to its simplest tasks. Social Darwinism (the "survival of the fittest") comes into play when workers' interests and vendors' interests are constantly subjected to competitive and impersonal market tests. "Extended hierarchical relationships" come into play when workers are just "hands" that need to be managed and supported from above. The distribution of power reflects these relationships.

Toyota's Plant Management Approach at NUMMI

Visualize an automobile assembly line such as that shown in the photo of the line at NUMMI. As the line moves along, teams of employees work together on the car, installing, for example, the battery and battery cables or certain dashboard components.

Each team is responsible for its increment of work on each car. Quite importantly, each team is also responsible for assigning specific tasks among its members, and these assignments may rotate hourly, daily, weekly, or whatever—as the team may wish. Each team sets its own task sequence and is responsible for the quality of its work.

If a team is having difficulty with the number of tasks it has to complete during the time it has the car, the allocation of tasks within the team or among teams may be changed. The key is to have each team working productively on each car during its allotted time.

The members of each NUMMI team generally get together about 10 or 15 minutes before the starting time to exercise as a group and to socialize. These activities take place at a "team room," which is right on the shop floor. The team room also serves as a meeting place when work-related issues need attention. Each team uses a structured, systematic technique for identifying and resolving any scheduling and quality problems that it may face.

As expected, training is important and varied at NUMMI. Workers must be able to do all the jobs within their team's jurisdiction. They are also encouraged to work occasionally on other teams and to learn the jobs of those teams too. There is only one pay grade, or job classification, for production workers at NUMMI. All production workers are paid the same wage after 18 months of

Photo courtesy of New United Motor Manufacturing, Inc.

service. There are also three higher pay classifications—one for maintenance technicians, the others for tool and die and tool and die tryout personnel.

NUMMI utilizes the "just-in-time" inventory system that Toyota developed in Japan. All components, parts, and subassemblies flow together in a continuous process paced by the main assembly line. Suppliers deliver their products to the NUMMI plant on a nearly continuous basis—in some cases, every few hours or so. There is minimal receiving inventory and little receiving testing or inspection of supplier-provided parts.

NUMMI works with qualified suppliers on a long-term basis. The team approach is again key here. Suppliers work on the design and quality of their products, with substantial assistance from NUMMI when required. Purchase relationships are of indefinite duration. Suppliers know what is expected of them in terms of product schedule and quality. They also know that NUMMI will help them solve problems.

Some Cultural Dimensions of NUMMI's Approach

Ringi is the Japanese participatory approach to decision making. Communication with the objective of understanding is a hallmark of *Ringi*. This approach underlies NUMMI's team system. A corollary of the Japanese participatory approach is that problems are identified and solved at the bottom levels in the hierarchy—which possess a detailed knowledge of whatever the situation demands. Management does not impose solutions; workers don't pass problems up.

Kaizen is the Japanese concept of constant improvement. The plant is a "living" institution. It is constantly learning and changing. Work teams always focus on how to improve what they are doing. Job rotation and cross-training, which give workers a more complete perspective on the production process, are relevant here.

The concept of "purity of intent" is rooted in Japanese culture.[2] Individuals are seen as being meant to think for themselves and to take action, sometimes significant action, if that is felt to be needed. For example, any NUMMI worker can stop the assembly line if he or she feels that this is necessary for safety, quality, or other important purposes. And management would recognize the action as acceptable even if it turned out to be the wrong thing to do, since the worker's intent was correct. From the management perspective, however, the support of management and the other team members ensure that the action would never turn out to be the wrong thing to do.

How Has NUMMI Been Doing?

Before assessing NUMMI's performance, it is important to note that there are really four partners in this joint venture—not just Toyota and GM. The United Automobile Workers (UAW) and the employees themselves are also very important partners. The UAW has been especially accommodative in developing "new" ways of doing things. For example, it has accepted wage systems and pay classifications that depart considerably from the traditional ones. The work environment at NUMMI is much less adversarial than that of its predecessor. The evidence is solid on this: At any given time, five or six grievances (i.e., workers' complaints against management that allege a violation of the labor agreement) are usually outstanding at NUMMI. Yet a few years back, when the same plant was run by a U.S. auto company (and eventually shut down), the outstanding grievances typically totaled at least 1,000. Absenteeism at NUMMI is about 5 to 6 percent; it was 20 percent or more under the prior operator. Interestingly, about 80 percent of the workers now covered by the labor agreement at NUMMI also worked at the plant under the prior operator.

How has NUMMI been doing? Quite well, apparently, in terms of its union-management relations and in terms of its employee relations. Moreover, the Toyota production system and methods of work force organization have been implemented at NUMMI and are operating well.

Compared to Toyota plants in Japan, NUMMI is also doing quite well. Product quality at NUMMI is as high as that at Toyota's plants in Japan. Worker efficiency is close to that of Toyota's plants in Japan and higher than was originally expected. Because employee turnover rates are higher in California than in Japan and because NUMMI's work force has less experience with the Toyota system than has Toyota's work force in Japan, management feels that worker efficiency at NUMMI is about as high as possible.

NOTES

[1] The author stresses that the discussion of conditions in U.S. plants is indeed about "traditional" conditions. Note should be taken here that, in contrast to "traditional" conditions, many cooperative innovations, developed by both the union and management, have been finding their way into U.S. auto plants.

[2] S. Prakash Sethi, Nobuaki Namiki, and Carl L. Swanson, *The False Promise of the Japanese Miracle* (Marshfield, Mass.: Pitman Publishers, 1984), p. 15.

Chapter

13

Strategy and Organization Structure

Strategy involves goal setting and the planning needed to attain goals. Organization structure involves grouping activities and allocating management decision-making authority among different operating units, or among levels of management within units. This chapter looks at organization structure from several different perspectives, including the relationship between strategy and organization structure, the three "classic" MNE strategies/structures—ethnocentric (single power center), polycentric (many power centers), and geocentric (diffused power)— the different structures that were created and subsequently replaced as the MNE itself evolved into a mature, globalized competitive entity, and the more complex organization forms and relationships that characterize MNEs today. The main goals of the chapter are to:

1. Define organization structure and note its relationship to both strategy and environment.

2. Review (briefly) the essence of strategy management and planning in the MNE.

3. Determine the rationales for and the key organizational features of ethnocentric, polycentric, and geocentric structures.

4. Examine the different organization forms that characterized MNEs as MNEs evolved, and the rationales behind those structures.

5. Investigate the impact of today's highly competitive global environment on MNEs' operating structures and organizational relationships.

INTRODUCTION

There was considerable discussion in Chapter 5, "Developing a Global Strategy," on the importance of strategy and control to competitive advantage, the assignment of strategy to strategic business units (SBUs), and multinational firms' four basic, generic strategies—i.e., broad-line competition, global focus, national focus, and protected niche. This chapter builds on the content of that chapter and deals with strategy and organization structure, that is, the manner in which firms—at both the MNE and SBU levels—group activities and allocate authority for decision making among different, specified operating units or among levels of management within units.

Topics discussed in this chapter include strategy, the basic nature of the strategic management process, the kinds of decisions typically taken at the MNE level that impact organization structure significantly, the generic types of strategy and structure combinations employed by firms involved in international business, the evolution of organizational structure within the MNE, and some important organizational issues confronting MNEs in an increasingly competitive operating environment.

STRATEGY DEFINED

Strategy

Strategy involves goal setting and the planning needed to attain goals.[1] It also involves translating plans into programs and monitoring programs to make sure they remain goal directed. Strategy is pertinent to two levels within the enterprise: the corporate level and the strategic business unit (SBU) level.

At the corporate level, two primary considerations in setting strategy are synergy and balance. The different SBUs in the corporate "portfolio" must realize some operational benefit, or **synergy,** derived from their common corporate parentage. For example, automatic welding technology (including the use of robots) developed for use in Nissan's plants in Japan is also used at the Nissan plant in Tennessee.

Alternatively, or in addition, different SBUs may complement, or **balance,** one another in terms of cash needs or cash flows. For example, stable and profitable cigarette sales produce substantial revenues for the tobacco operations at RJR Nabisco that provide the financial resources needed to implement the firm's current global product diversification strategy. In this sense, tobacco sales in the United States can be seen as enabling the food products group to expand in Europe or Latin America.

For the corporate level to serve some competitively meaningful role, either synergy or balance must be present. If synergy or balance were not present, the SBU would bear the burden of sustaining the corporate level without receiving any benefit in return. In such circumstances, the corporate structure, serving no economic or commercial purpose, would be forced by a competitive marketplace to disintegrate.

Strategy at the SBU level is operations driven. It is concerned with competition, technology, production, logistics, marketing, taxes, and so on. Scale economies, learning curve effects, and similar phenomena are especially pertinent. Managers at the SBU levels are more market driven, more concerned with the typical management functions, and are typically responsible for the "bottom line." Consider the Burger King franchisee in Venezuela. Management there is on the "firing line" day in and day out, but it relies heavily on Burger King U.S., the franchisor, for direction on product quality control, production techniques, new products, and so on.

STRATEGIC MANAGEMENT AND PLANNING IN THE MNE

Chapter 5, "Developing a Global Strategy," deals with strategy alternatives, but it doesn't cover the strategic management process as experienced in multinational firms. This section addresses this topic. The strategic management and planning process is looked at first, and then strategic issues pertinent to MNEs are discussed. The process, we admit, is not so distinctive when comparing MNEs to purely domestic firms. However, in contrast, the issues are indeed distinctive.

Strategic Management — The Basics[2]

Strategic management is a process that can be conceptualized in terms of six fundamental steps, as shown in Figure 13–1.

Formulating the mission statement defines why the organization exists. Business organizations exist to make profits, but typically their mission statements go beyond this purpose and indicate how the firm will pursue profits compared to how other firms might do so. "Flying the friendly skies of United" suggests, for example, that United Airlines wants to compete on the basis of high-quality service. The **mission statement** thus begins to define the firm.

Determining strategic objectives and formulating the master strategy answer three basic questions:[3] Where are we? Where do we want to be? How do we get there? These answers, in turn, build on a detailed analysis of the firm's internal strengths and weaknesses and of the external opportunities and threats that confront it. (The literature refers to this as the **SWOT analysis.**) Consistent with the mission statement and in light of the SWOT analysis, the firm then sets its **strategic objectives** and its **master strategy**—the basic blueprint on how to accomplish the strategic objectives.

Setting the organization and implementing the operating plan constitute the implementation phase of the strategic management process. Setting the organization involves organizational structuring. It allocates the tasks that must be done to implement the master strategy, and it defines responsibilities and allocates power within the organization. Implementing the **operating plan** involves short-term planning, setting operating targets, determining budgets, and so on.

FIGURE 13–1

The Strategic Management Process

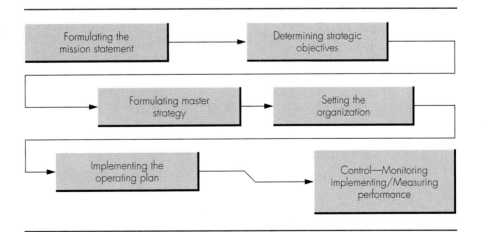

ADDED DIMENSION

Matsushita's Mission—and the Beginning of Strategy Implementation

Mission statements and master strategies can be vague concepts at first. To clarify the concepts a bit, let's look at what Matsushita, the maker of Panasonic and Quasar products, is and what it says about its mission.

Today, Matsushita is "home" to 150,000 employees worldwide. It produces and sells over 14,000 products in more than 130 countries. Its global sales total over $22 billion. Traditionally Matsushita manufactured consumer electronics products, but as a result of its pursuit of new products and technologies, it now serves industrial, office, and communications markets as well.

Matsushita's basic mission statement is its creed:

Through our industrial activities, we strive to foster progress, to promote the general welfare of society, and to devote ourselves to furthering the development of world culture.

Matsushita's more specific mission is to focus on "key areas of technological growth which will have a tremendous impact on society in the near future." These are communications and information processing technologies, semiconductor components and materials technologies, advanced video and audio technologies, and production engineering technologies, such as robotics and factory automation.

Visualize Matsushita as the high-tech, R&D-oriented company that it is, and from a global perspective, try to identify broadly the strengths and weaknesses a company of this kind might have in addressing such issues as new product development and the understanding of specific market segments. ■

Source: Information abstracted from *Matsushita Electric Corporation of America*, an undated brochure provided by company officials.

Control, the final step in the strategic management process, consists of monitoring strategy implementation, measuring performance against pre-established standards, and taking corrective action when necessary. (Various approaches to strategic control are discussed in Chapter 5.)

Strategic Issues in the MNE

Strategic issues are those that have long-term implications. Most often they therefore involve risk assessment and risk taking. What are these issues from the MNE perspective? The more important issues are identified in the discussion that follows.

MNEs must decide which countries and regions are most appropriate for business expansion. And then, how should this expansion be implemented—that is, which product(s) should be marketed and/or produced in the country? What is the best entry form—e.g., exporting, local production via a wholly owned subsidiary, joint venture (with a foreign or domestic partner), or a licensing relationship?

MNEs must also decide on a product strategy.

What are its global products?

What is the extent of product adaptation required by local markets?

How can the MNE network best respond to the production synergies evident from product standardization while yet responding to the distinctive consumer characteristics that local markets may well dictate?

Where should MNEs do their financial sourcing? New York, London, Tokyo . . . ?

How should it handle risks, such as exchange risks and political risks?

When and under what circumstances should the MNE pull out of a country?

Returning to entry strategy and form—when are strategic alliances appropriate, and should such alliances ever be made with governmentally owned companies?

What should the executive development programs consist of at both corporate and subsidiary levels?

Several other questions are certainly pertinent.

How distinctive, or universal, are the market determinants of product, promotion, distribution, and other policies?

What products, product cores, and component parts can be produced most economically on an internationally integrated basis? On a country or regional basis?

If scale economies in production and marketing are optimal for relatively small markets, what opportunities for product differentiation and competitiveness exist?

How can the product and the production and marketing functions be disaggregated to allow for an effective blending of scale economies and learning curve effects and the differentiation necessary to respond to market peculiarities?

These questions, most of which are decided at the MNE level, cover a variety of fundamental issues. Some of these issues are pertinent to the MNE because they involve crossing country, market, or cultural boundaries; others, because they involve dealing in international markets (e.g., foreign exchange or capital markets). One thing is certain: these issues surely present the MNE with a more complex business environment. But they also provide the MNE with business opportunities that it alone is strategically poised to benefit from.

THREE CLASSIC STRATEGIES/ STRUCTURES— ETHNOCENTRIC, POLYCENTRIC, AND GEOCENTRIC

Rutenberg sees the "two economic reasons that sustain most international diversification" as experience curves (synergy) and risk spreading (balance).[4] Experience curves, in the extreme, would lead to globally centralized power—or ethnocentric organization. Risk spreading, on the other hand, requires a portfolio of reasonably unrelated, globally distributed subsidiaries—a polycentric organization.[5] Why do these two strategies lead to these particular structures, and what do the strategies mean operationally?

The Ethnocentric Organization

The Rationale for Ethnocentrism   Experience curve effects result in declining costs of operations (e.g., production, marketing, and distribution). These effects require standardization, which allows repetition to result in increased efficiency. In the aerospace industry, an 80 percent experience curve seems to be the historical standard in manufacturing. This means that every time cumulative production doubles, costs of production decline to 80 percent of the previous level. The **experience curve effect** is thus readily seen as an important competitive weapon. Standardized production lowers costs of production and enhances profit margins and competitiveness. For the MNE, competitive success entails effectively transferring what was learned in one location to other locations. Doing this positions the MNE further down the experience curve and gives it a competitive advantage over firms operating only in local markets. In Chapter 2, this effect was labeled "managerial experience in several countries."

Ethnocentrism in Operation   The strategy/structure implications here are fairly straightforward. The multinational enterprise operates on global product mandates and is typically organized at the top on a product division basis. This is a niche strategy made viable by the presence of a globally identifiable market segment that allows for standardization in production (for example) and, for the MNE able to transfer experience internationally, the delivery of a competitive edge.

Ethnocentrism, as a management core strategy, carries with it distinctive organizational and operational characteristics.[6] As already noted, the organization is divisionalized at the top on a product basis. The divisions manage their own inventories and logistic flows internationally. Products are designed for the home (parent company) market and manufactured in large factories located where costs are lowest. These factories serve both domestic and export markets. In this environment, products are not likely to be adapted, in any substantial way, to reflect foreign market differences. Both internal and external pressures exist for uniform, global product pricing. The finance function is typically controlled at the MNE level, and profits remitted to the parent company are the bottom line in evaluating foreign investment opportunities.

Ethnocentrism, like any strategy, has the potential for generating certain kinds of problems as it is being implemented. In its eagerness to take advantage of experience effects, management may overlook market niches that are best served by products adapted to satisfy localized preferences. Moreover, these overlooked niches may be where future market growth is concentrated—to the potential detriment of the firm's predominant position in its well-established market. That experience curve benefits are proportionately larger in the earlier stages of production (i.e., with newer products) magnifies the significance of this problem.

Another potential difficulty may arise when customers in a particular area or country see representatives of the various company product groups operating under different policies. Ethnocentrism can result in customers' perceptions of a disorganized company presence, and, more important, in their disaffection with one company division because its policies appear less beneficial to the customer than the policies of another company division. Yet a third problem of ethnocentrism is that it can lead to management self-assuredness that is overly insular. This, in turn, can lead to difficulties in certain social and operating areas, such as government relations and industrial relations.[7]

The Polycentric Organization

The Rationale for Polycentrism   In contrast to the ethnocentric MNE, the **polycentric organization** finds that marketing or production considerations favor geographic diversification. Nuances of local markets mandate a unique

**IB
ILLUSTRATION**

**What Went Wrong at Westinghouse? (A Classic Case of an
Organization Outgrowing Ethnocentrism!)**

During the 1970s, Westinghouse consistently lagged General Electric in foreign sales and profits. Early in the decade, it decided to close the gap and,
perhaps surprisingly, eliminated its international division in favor of four new
divisions with global product mandates. This put foreign sales on an equal
footing with domestic sales and was designed to take advantage of the international ubiquity of product technology.

The change was fairly successful. Foreign sales grew significantly during
1971–76, as did product lines. To encourage even more growth, Westinghouse reorganized again in 1976 when it established 37 SBUs with product-
specific, global responsibilities.

Then some interesting problems surfaced!

A Saudi Arabian customer, for instance, was dealing with 24 Westinghouse
sales representatives—each from a different SBU. He underscored his confusion with this query: "Who speaks for Westinghouse?" In another situation,
a Westinghouse subsidiary in one country had excess cash, while another
Westinghouse subsidiary in the same country, but in a different division, was
borrowing locally at very high rates. The company also lost some important
deals because of its inability to put together project packages, which cut
across SBU lines, as competitive as those offered by its European and Japanese rivals. The bottom line here was that from 1976 to 1978 foreign sales fell
from 31 percent to 24 percent of total sales. ■

Sources: Hugh D. Menzies, "Westinghouse Takes Aim at the World," *Fortune*, January 14, 1980, pp. 48–53; "Westinghouse's Third Big Step
Is Overseas," *Business Week*, October 2, 1971, pp. 64–67; and various Westinghouse Electric Corporation annual reports.

product strategy for each market. Alternatively, the production technology may
be such that optimum scale economies are realized with small production
runs, especially with regard to total market size, or that scale economies are
insufficient to offset the freight and other costs that exporting to the market
would entail. Hence, in the extreme case, the polycentric MNE consists of a set
of freestanding SBUs that have very little, if anything, to offer one another
operationally.

Polycentrism in Operation   What, then, are the benefits to these SBUs of their
common affiliation with the parent company? Actually, the benefits can be significant, but they must be appraised at the MNE level. They arise from portfolio
effects on the one hand and, on the other hand, from profit maximization on a
global basis. This latter point relates to the ability of the SBUs in a polycentric
organization to price more aggressively in different, geographically segmented
markets.

How do portfolio effects operate to the benefit of the MNE? In marketing, for
example, demand conditions may well vary from country to country. A slump in
France may be offset by a boom in England. This results in less variation in total
MNE earnings and a lower cost of capital. Demand for certain products may

develop and mature in different countries at different times. This allows MNEs to extend product life cycles. In manufacturing, the production structure of the polycentric MNE is more atomized than that of the ethnocentric MNE. Thus, risks are diversified in the polycentric structure and, because of portfolio effects, are lower than otherwise at the MNE level. For example, a strike has less effect on overall production in the polycentric MNE than in the ethnocentric MNE. This difference would also hold true for the demise of an important supplier or a shift to a more contentious political environment.

The key point with regard to profit maximization in the polycentric structure is that maximum profits result from the freedom to price according to what individual markets will bear. (Picture a market in which you could price your product according to its "value" to each customer. You would vary your price by customer and would thus be enriched. In fact, your supply curve would exactly coincide with the market demand curve. Happiness!) This strategy is viable, of course, only where geographically defined markets are indeed distinctive.

The polycentric organization has its drawbacks too. Since the SBUs are separated, and perhaps jealously so, there is little communication among them and little opportunity for them to learn from one another. Potential synergies are never realized. Moreover, if one accepts the notion that product markets are becoming increasingly internationalized, the geographically segmented customer base essential for polycentrism could be seen as a generally vanishing phenomenon. Where does this leave the polycentric organization? In the forefront of a difficult, but necessary, adjustment process!

The Geocentric Organization

The Rationale for Geocentrism   An alternative to the ethnocentric and polycentric organizations is the **geocentric organization.** It has a global perspective, and it seeks to maximize total global returns to the MNE and all its units. It is especially relevant to the global matrix structure, to be discussed later, and is especially pertinent to the multiproduct firm with a niche strategy turning on the firm's ability to deal successfully with distinctive markets that require unique products—all of this balanced against the firm's multiproduct capabilities and its desire to benefit from scale economies.

Geocentrism in Operation   The geocentric organization is typically a matrix organization. The markets of the MNE are distinctive enough to require a distinctive product response from it. This denies the opportunity to benefit from ethnocentrism. On the other hand, enough commonalities exist—for example, in the customer base or in component parts or product cores—to permit scale economies and experience curve effects. This denies the opportunity to benefit from polycentrism. Geocentrism, then, is a global concept attuned to local market needs.

The geocentric organization is often defined as a hybrid that includes elements of geographic and product structures. Its objective is to blend these two elements into a competitive, profitable market presence. Hence the matrix structure—and a critical need for internal communication and for a corporate-wide perspective on what constitutes success. These are difficult needs to address—especially if the MNE has traditionally been ethnocentric (centralized power) or polycentric (dispersed power). Often the need for geocentrism evolves as product markets mature. Market trends are, in a sense, forcing that

ADDED DIMENSION

Ford Motor Company—From Poly to Geo and Beyond!

Prior to the 1970s, Ford–US, Ford–UK, and Ford–Germany were really separate and distinctive operating units. They all designed and built cars for their local, or close-by, markets. Then as the 1970s unfolded, Ford realized scale economies in design and production were becoming available as production technologies were being developed that meant larger production runs at lower total production costs, and consumers' tastes were converging, especially regarding the European Community and, to a lesser extent, Europe and the United States in the small-car segment of the U.S. market.

During the 1980s, the commonalities in consumers' preferences solidified substantially within Europe, forcing added integration between Ford's German and British operations, and among other Ford plants established in France, Belgium, and Spain to supply components and assemblies to Ford–UK and Ford–Germany. In reality, the polycentric structure of pre-1970 times is gone. Today, Ford of Europe is the effective organizational entity! ∎

evolution. The transition from ethnocentrism or polycentrism to geocentrism is thus typically a real phenomenon addressed by many MNEs, but a totally geocentric firm may be hard to find. The transition is certainly not a simple one.

The above commentary on ethnocentrism, polycentrism, and geocentrism in MNEs is highlighted in Figure 13–2.

Having identified some of the environmental pressures (both internal and external to the MNE) influencing organization structure in the generic categories of ethnocentric, polycentric, and geocentric, the discussion now turns to a more detailed description of alternative organization structures.

STRUCTURAL CHANGE AND THE EVOLUTION OF THE MNE

Much of the growth of multinational enterprises in the manufacturing and service sectors has taken place in the past four decades. The pattern of that growth was traced to some extent in the earlier chapters, especially Chapters 2 and 3, in the discussions of the international product cycle relative to international trade and foreign direct investment. Further consideration of the product-life-cycle (PLC) model, as it illustrates organizational change and key strategy points, would certainly be useful in the present context. Let's turn back the clock to the mid-1950s or so and examine, from the starting point, the roots and growth process of what has become the modern MNE. (To facilitate discussion, the following focuses only on firms in the manufacturing sector.)

Setting the Stage

Following World War II and into the 1950s, income levels advanced substantially in the United States—giving rise to significant and expanding levels of discretionary spending by U.S. citizens. Producers increasingly responded by offering products that were destined to satisfy new and expanding market segments of

FIGURE 13–2

The Three Classic
Strategies/Structures
Compared

Basic Rationale	Key Features/Implications
The Ethnocentric MNE Cost cutting via learning curve effects transmitted by parent to subsidiaries	Company strives for globally standardized products and production processes Company targets on market niches that are similar internationally Strong headquarters involvement at all levels Company too often overlooks new markets—extensive communication needed (hard to provide cross-culturally and over long distances)
The Polycentric MNE Cost/risk reduction via portfolio effects at the parent level	Company (including subsidiaries) thrives on product and market distinctiveness in different countries Company enjoys maximum freedom in product pricing (because markets are separate and distinctive internationally) Internal communication not important; few internal transfers of knowledge internationally Long-term prognosis for the polycentric MNE is negative—product markets becoming increasingly similar internationally
The Geocentric MNE Ethnocentric and polycentric pressures balanced in favor of optimizing the MNE system	Company is typically organized on a matrix basis—product and geographic divisions Best structure for handling changing market preferences and new products Internal communication critical Key personnel developed over the long term and on a global experience basis

distinctive tastes and preferences. This, in turn, led to product differentiation as a basis for competitive strategy and to market segments in which income levels were important determinants of demand characteristics. These market segments, almost by definition, were not initially highly competitive, and for these and other reasons oligopolistic market structures were spawned—a small number of producers served (shared) the market and enjoyed above-average returns.

At this point, there was nothing international about the firm. It was busy learning about and responding to domestic market opportunities. Organizations were often structured on a product or functional basis, with power centers likely to be located in engineering and manufacturing, or perhaps even marketing. Organization charts were typically like those presented here. The **functional structure,** shown in Figure 13–3, was usually the first one to be implemented.

FIGURE 13-3
Functional Structure

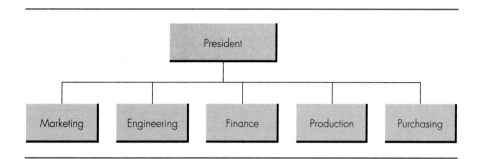

There was a single product or product line, and management power clearly ascended the pyramidal organization structure. The functional structure facilitated internal technical and marketing coordination. As more numerous and more distinctive market niches developed, so too did product lines and the need for the firm to move to a **product structure** (see Figure 13-4). This organizational form allowed the firm to segmentize internal operations so as to match them with product and market differences. It continued to facilitate internal coordination. As with the functional structure, power in the product structure was hierarchically defined.

Fortuitous Exports

At this time, products that were successful in the U.S. market were also found to be in demand in foreign markets, such as in Canada and Western Europe, where income levels and income-related tastes and preferences were similar to those in the United States. Research showed that exports to these markets were often unsolicited—which implied that intermediaries, typically either foreign or domestic firms that were specialists in exporting, with knowledge of what U.S. producers were bringing to markets and what would sell overseas (mainly in advanced industrial societies) were creating export markets by requesting products from U.S. suppliers.[8]

FIGURE 13-4
Product Structure

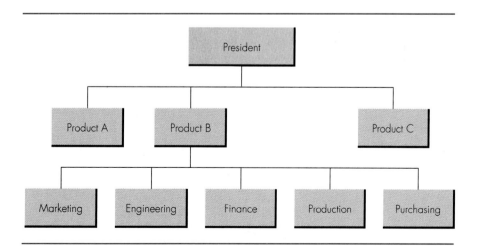

Firms were not systematically exploiting export markets during this period. Exports were handled by the domestic divisions and frequently were just viewed as orders placed by yet another customer—that happened to be located in New York, London, or some other port city—and was handling the shipping of products to customers in foreign markets. At this point, there was still nothing international about the firm from the organizational perspective. But from the operational and financial perspectives, the firm began to become dependent on exports.

Deliberate Exports

As **accidental exports** attracted the attention of management, firms became involved in direct exporting. Exports had become important. They accounted for a goodly share of production and profits. Company sales representatives began calling on overseas customers, but product modifications to secure foreign sales were minimal, and sales contracts were typically denominated in dollars. In these earlier times, exports by U.S. pharmaceutical companies, for example, typically involved products packaged for the U.S. market and were priced in dollars.

By now, the firm had established an **export department,** often within marketing, which was initially concerned with logistics—packaging, shipping, letters of credit, insurance, and so on (see Figure 13–5). The customers of this department were often viewed as less familiar and less reliable than those of the domestic divisions, so that to some extent the department had to negotiate with the domestic divisions to secure product for export sales. Thus, foreign sales were not given as high a priority as domestic sales. In fact, during periods of robust home demand when production was pushing capacity limits, it was not unusual for exports to be cut so that domestic customers could be satisfied. A modern-day illustration of this greater emphasis on the domestic market is provided by the steel minimills in the United States, which often export excess supply rather than sell off inventory at depressed prices at home—a practice that would spoil their domestic market.

But with the continued expansion of foreign sales, often accompanied by intensifying home front competition as other domestic producers cut into the

FIGURE 13–5

The Export Department—
Exports Worthwhile but Not
Significant

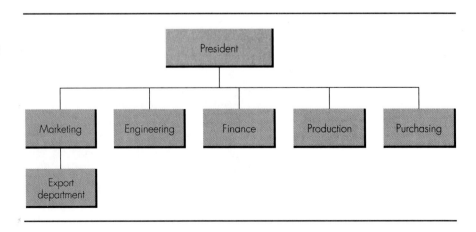

firm's innovative lead, corporate attitudes began to change. In some cases, the result was the establishment of an **international division** (still concerned only with exports) that operated on a par with the domestic divisions and had some influence over product design, availability, and price in the export markets (see Figure 13–6). Gradually, the international division accumulated some power. From being a product and schedule "taker," this division now had influence over production schedules and product allocation and was able to justify minor product modifications necessary to export success. The Singer Company and its famous sewing machine operations grew this way. The accompanying organization charts typify this evolution.

The conclusions at this point are several. Perhaps the most important is that exports are affecting the bottom line in a measurable way. Organizationally, the international division has credibility. Now the firm's strategy is to serve both domestic and foreign markets with domestically based production. Both domestic and export markets are valued for their profit contributions. This means that more funds are available for R&D, for capital investment, and for dividends. These funds strengthen the firm regardless of where it operates. Thus, success in the export market is seen as important for success in the domestic market. Serving both domestic and foreign markets rather than just domestic markets often results in scale economies in production or research and engineering and thus lower product unit costs. Export market success enhances domestic market success in this regard too.

Expanded Competition and the Competitive Response

Competition continued to build in the domestic market as other firms imitated the success formulas of the original firms. For the same reason, competition developed in the export markets too. Domestically, the innovative firms had responded by defining market segments more precisely and by bringing more varied products to the marketplace. The result was that product lines grew, enabling these firms to enjoy some level of monopoly profits over a now extended period of time. In the foreign markets, the vulnerability of the MNE, in this earlier period, was enhanced because far-flung logistic and management networks were costly and because products sold overseas were not fully adapted

FIGURE 13–6

The International Department—Exports Important: A Substantial Part of Company Sales

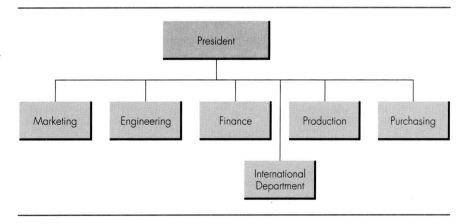

to the consumer preferences of the foreign market. Competitors producing in Western Europe and Canada, for example, were able to imitate the competitive essence of a product and yet package the product to meet distinctive preferences of foreign consumers. They produced and marketed within their local markets (which were export markets to the MNE). The U.S. MNEs were at a product disadvantage—and possibly a cost disadvantage too, since they faced tariffs, shipping costs, and other charges not experienced by the foreign competition. They responded by opening plants in their export markets.

These direct foreign investments were significant in many ways. They allowed the U.S. MNEs to get inside tariff barriers, and they eliminated transcontinental shipping and insurance costs. Perhaps more important, they facilitated significant product adaptation—a fine tuning of product design in response to distinctive use conditions in foreign markets. Quite important too, as these overseas subsidiaries gained experience, the "new" products developed to meet increasingly competitive domestic markets were channeled into overseas markets. This gave the subsidiaries competitive strengths reflective of the positive synergistic effects associated with multinational enterprise.

Structural Implications of Foreign Direct Investment

Putting plants overseas affected the "mind-set" of MNE management in several important ways. The balance sheet exposure of having assets placed in foreign countries required closer attention to foreign operations by top management. The transfer (export) of product and/or process technologies, required initially to get the foreign plant on line, and the ongoing transfer of component parts between the parent and the **foreign subsidiary** meant, in some cases, substantial attention to foreign operations by lower-level management and technical staff. The firm's marketing activities, which began with exporting, were adapting now to new logistics patterns and enhanced sales potentials. The production and distribution pipeline was shorter now, and the firm was able to be more price competitive. The subsidiary's sales revenues were definitely denominated in local currency, as were many of the costs of its operations. Parent company nationals were probably on assignment at the subsidiary. Local management had considerable control now over production, marketing, and other functions and had more flexibility to respond effectively to competitive opportunities in the marketplace. The firm's strategic objectives at this time were to establish a solid market presence by building on the technical, financial, and managerial expertise provided by the parent, and eventually to expand market share.

Organizationally, these early days of foreign direct investment saw a group of geographically defined subsidiaries reporting to the parent through an international division (see Figure 13–7). Often this international division was organizationally parallel to the product or functional divisions. The structure was a hybrid, with responsibilities allocated between domestic and international via a set of nondistinctive categories. It was a logical structure, though, in terms of historical evolution. The international division was already in place before the subsidiaries were established. Its roots went back to the days of deliberate exports. The accompanying organization chart typifies the international division within a general product division structure with manufacturing subsidiaries in several countries.

FIGURE 13–7

Foreign Direct
Investment—The Early Days

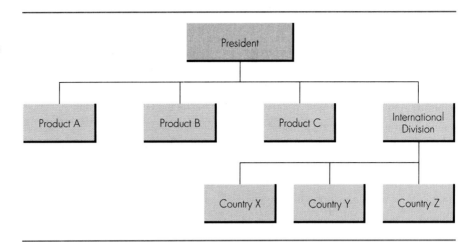

The Drive to Structural Maturity

As scale economies in production grew and as markets were developed outside the traditional geographic domain of each subsidiary, the business effectiveness of the geographically defined subsidiary declined. (In some MNEs, subsidiaries in different countries could even be found competing with one another in some third markets—note the discussion presented earlier in the highlighted feature "What Went Wrong at Westinghouse?".) If product lines were fairly narrow, product groups with both domestic and foreign jurisdictions were typically formed (see Figure 13–8). If broad product lines were the rule, the **matrix structure** was the answer. In this case, country- or subcountry-level managers reported to both area and product managers (see Figure 13–9). It was their job to balance global or regional rationalization needs against local market needs or nuances. They were "company specialists" rather than just market or technical specialists. The organization charts in Figures 13–8 and 13–9 illustrate these two structures.

Some companies, it should be noted, do not prefer the matrix-type structure—and rightly so. Single-product companies and companies with a dominant, distinctive product (such as Coca-Cola) need not evolve into the matrix structure. Product proliferation, on the other hand, leads almost invariably to a

FIGURE 13–8

The Global Structure—
Narrow Product Line

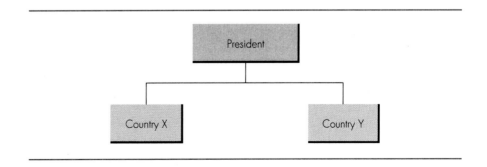

FIGURE 13–9

The Global Matrix Structure

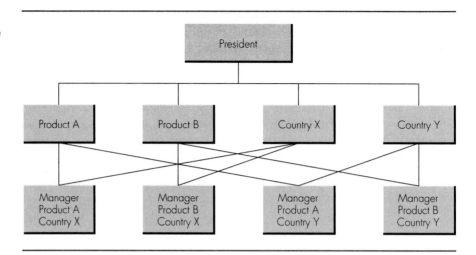

matrix organization. The strategy implications here are fairly straightforward. The subsidiary is an extension of the parent, and it benefits from the parent's market dominance in a single or narrow product line. The multiproduct firm, on the other hand, must find the niche that requires product uniqueness but still allows it to gain from positive linkages among its products and markets. Success here involves fine tuning and considerable knowledge of both company capabilities and market opportunities. The matrix structure makes possible the "team" response required for success in situations where no one person has all the knowledge or all the information needed.

The Driving Force of the Market—The Rationale of Change

The preceding discussion on the evolution of the MNE and the accompanying structural changes might appear to imply that management is consistently reactive, that it merely adapts to changes in its competitive environments—at times, even begrudgingly. This conclusion would be fairly accurate for the emergent MNE. It does not mean, however, that change is made without intelligence or that management's behavior is without a rationale. The marketplace conveys a lot of information!

By participating in and paying attention to the market, management receives important feedback on the commercial propriety of its behavior. Accidental exports, for example, give the firm important information—not only on the marketability of the product overseas, but also on market potential, pricing strategy, characteristics of customers (including their motivations for buying), locations of customers, distribution channels, and so on. Also, quite importantly, most business organizations are justifiably cautious. They just don't throw funding into projects unless there is a reasonable expectation of success. Success in an initially limited market justifies (and helps fund) expansion. It gives the project, and the project team, credibility. It allows management to compete intelligently with other potential users of the firm's limited funds. Put somewhat differently, it would be fair to say structure does not change without reason.

Changes in the marketplace provides a rationale for changing structure. The successful (lasting) firm responds properly to those changes.

No One Universally Best Organization Structure

The preceding discussion may be interpreted by some to suggest the matrix organization structure, ostensibly compatible with the geocentric approach, is superior to the others. One cannot draw this conclusion. The best structure will be a function of firm size, extent of foreign operations, product nature, product line, availability of financial and/or human resources, etc.

For example, the small firm—a new entrant to the market—would likely reflect the early stages of organizational development for international operations. The simple product or functional structure would most likely be appropriate. The size of the export market would in this case determine whether the firm had an export department. Large firms develop new products too, and depending on such strategy determinents as the scale economies in production and the willingness of the firm to take risks (as the new product is introduced globally), an ethnocentric, global product structure may well be the best organization structure for bringing these new products to market successfully.

IMPACT OF INCREASED GLOBAL COMPETITION ON STRATEGY AND ORGANIZATION STRUCTURE

During the past decade or so the global marketplace has become increasingly competitive. Multinational enterprises have emerged from Europe, Asia, Latin America, etc., to challenge the market supremacy of the traditional leaders. The business world is today substantially characterized by global competition, shorter-than-ever product life cycles, powerful MNEs with significant financial and R&D capabilities and globally distributed production and marketing organizations, generally favorable national economic policies increasingly supportive of market mechanisms, and high-tech information networks that result in efficient, nearly instantaneous communications.

The MNE strategy implications of these environmental factors are several. One is that the lead-time required for bringing new products to (global) markets must be as short as possible, as must the response time needed by the MNE to answer competitors' initiatives in new product introductions, other marketing innovations, production and logistics cost-cutting efforts, etc. Another implication is that MNEs must compete in markets that are increasingly risky. This chapter looks at two of the more important ways in which MNEs have responded organizationally to these strategic considerations: internally via enhanced organizational flexibility and externally via the forming of joint ventures.

Enhanced Organizational Flexibility

The geocentric, matrix organization structure just discussed is an important organizational concept and form. But today there must be more to an organization than simple functional and product overlaps as competitive pressures call on the firm for increasingly timely, effective competitive responses and initiatives. The MNEs need to coordinate internally more successfully than ever, and do this in the face of increasingly globally diffused activities and capabilities.

Martinez and Jarillo have recently examined empirical studies on MNEs regarding the evolution of MNEs' organizations and internal coordination mechanisms as product markets have become increasingly competitive and resource markets increasingly geographically diversified. Their findings show that coordination mechanisms other than formal organization structure and the allocation of decision-making within a hierarchial structure (that is, the centralization/decentralization issue) have evolved in more recent times. These other coordination mechanisms include formalized and standardized policies, rules, and job descriptions, and the implementation of strategic planning and control procedures. They also include the more subtle forms of mechanisms such as the development of international task forces, teams, and committees, extensive informal personnel contacts, such as via meetings, conferences, management transfers, etc., and enhanced socialization via the building of an organizational culture characterized by shared objectives and values.[9]

Martinez and Jarillo examined a total of 85 research articles. Figure 13–10 displays a frequency distribution showing their findings as to the use of these different coordination mechanisms during different time periods. Their study clearly shows that MNEs are increasingly using other more flexible and informal coordination mechanisms in the more recent, highly competitive times.

Joint Ventures

MNEs form joint ventures with either other MNEs or local firms typically for strategic reasons. They seek to access important technology, for instance, or to enter certain markets, or to enter markets more quickly than otherwise. Dow Chemical and Eli Lilly recently formed an international joint venture, "Dow-elanco", to expand their product base in agricultural chemicals and to have a market share large enough to justify future R&D expenditures.

FIGURE 13–10

Evolution of the Studies on Mechanisms of Coordination, as Used by MNCs

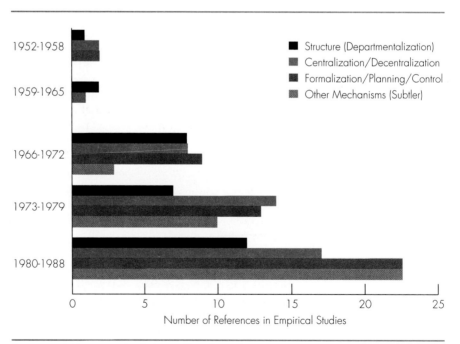

Source: Jon I. Martinez and J. Carlos Jarillo, "The Evolution of Research on Coordination Mechanisms in Multinational Corporations," *Journal of International Business Studies,* Fall 1989, p. 496.

Geringer defines a joint venture as a legal entity jointly owned by two or more legally distinct organizations which share in the joint venture's decision-making activities.[10] The joint venture (JV) is a separate organization from those of its owners. Linkages, however, certainly exist between the JV and the owners (firms). The ownership linkage is evidenced by the composition of the JV board of directors. There are likely management contracts and licenses between the JV and its owners too. These contracts define the relationships among the different parties, including the allocation of control and the nature of any coordination mechanisms.

The challenge to those firms involved in international JVs, according to Geringer and Hebert, is to have coordination and control (via contractual and/or more subtle coordination mechanisms as identified above) vis-á-vis the joint venture without burdening the JV with an administrative or organizational hierarchy whose costs (including inefficiencies introduced into the JV) outweigh the gains from the successful implementation of the JV's strategy.[11] Firms involved in JVs today are becoming increasingly aware of this challenge.

CONCLUSIONS

Strategy consists of two main parts: formulation and implementation. Formulation is based on SWOT analysis. Implementation requires people, money, organization, and so on—the structure through which strategy operates. Strategy involves setting goals and doing the planning necessary to attain goals. It operates at the corporate and SBU levels. At the former level, the main concerns are synergy and balance; at the latter level, operating effectiveness and efficiency are the main concerns. Structure, at its best, is the institutional embodiment of strategy implementation.

The strategic management process was defined as consisting of six components: formulating the mission statement, determining strategic objectives, formulating the master strategy, setting the organization, implementing the operating plan, and applying a control system. Various strategic issues pertinent to the MNE were identified. Some of these issues arose because the MNE crossed country, market, and cultural boundaries—such issues as market selection, entry strategy, and ownership strategy. Others arose because the MNE was operating through international markets with characteristics peculiar to themselves, such as the foreign exchange and capital markets. The complexity of operating multinationally presents the MNE with both a challenge and an opportunity. It makes success difficult, but it also makes success defensible (at least over some intermediate period).

Three classic strategies/structures were discussed. The ethnocentric organization relies on scale economies and learning curve effects to develop and sustain a low-cost competitive strategy. The polycentric organization, on the other hand, lacks opportunities for scale economies and learning curve effects because it has to deal with diverse and distinctive geographically defined markets. This often results in multiple power centers within the MNE and, as time and technology unfold, in resistance to changes that are necessary to meet competitive threats. The geocentric organization is an alternative to both ethnocentrism and polycentrism. It balances market needs favoring distinctive approaches against the firm's multiproduct capabilities and its desire to benefit from scale economies and learning curves. The geocentric organization is typically a matrix organization.

The evolution of the MNE provides an illustrative, and relevant, example of the interplay between strategy and structure. Highlights of this evolutionary process included fortuitous exports and the development of an operating and financial dependence on foreign markets. Deliberate exporting followed, which meant that foreign sales had become an objective in their own right. By this time, an export department had probably been established to facilitate logistics matters. Afterward, in many cases, exporting became more significant and product modifications, special pricing strategies, and the like were developed to enhance foreign sales. The export department then gave way to the international division—a more internally influential unit. Exports were now affecting the bottom line in a substantial way.

As competition expanded in both domestic and foreign markets, firms implemented several defensive strategies, including product line expansion at home (and later abroad) and direct investment in foreign markets. This latter strategy enabled the MNE to produce within tariff walls and to eliminate heavy shipping costs. Very important, it allowed product modification—the fine tuning of product specifications to the incomes, tastes, and use conditions peculiar to the foreign market. Drastic organizational change accompanied foreign direct investment. Within the MNE, not only were marketing and logistics changed, but production, engineering, personnel, accounting, finance, and so on, were redefined to include multinational operations. Initially, the geographic definition of operations gave rise to geographically defined organizational structures.

As the mature multinational evolved, as product lines expanded overseas (in the same way that they expanded domestically), and as competitive conditions became increasingly difficult, many firms moved to the global matrix structure—a team-based approach to blending company capabilities with market opportunities.

The chapter concluded with a review of the evidence showing MNEs are developing more complex, informal internal control and coordination mechanisms in the face of increasing competition and other factors. It was noted too that joint ventures are typically formed for strategic reasons, and that they offer distinctive challenges to the owners in terms of organizational fit and coordination.

QUESTIONS

1. Of what relevance to strategy are synergy and balance? Can you give some examples of synergy in MNEs? Of balance? If neither synergy nor balance were present in a particular MNE, could the corporate level be justified? Could it be sustained?

2. What are the six components of the strategic management process? How do these components relate to Matsushita and to the text discussion of Matsushita? Why are they important?

3. What is the driving force behind the ethnocentric organization? Give three examples of companies that behave ethnocentrically.

4. What is the driving force behind the polycentric organization? Give the theoretical argument behind the statement that global profit maximization is most likely to occur in the polycentric organization.

5. How does geocentrism differ from ethnocentrism and polycentrism? Is geocentrism the strategy/structure of the future?

6. What were the internal, organizational effects of fortuitous exports? Of deliberate exports?

7. Why would the international division have more power than the export department? In this context, what is "power"? What does power mean in terms of the firm's future direction?

8. Why does direct foreign investment affect the organization structure so significantly? How does it affect the organization structure?

9. What went wrong at Westinghouse?

10. In terms of organization structure, how are MNEs responding to today's highly competitive environment?

REFERENCES

Abegglen, James C., and George Stalk, Jr. *Kaisha: The Japanese Corporation*. New York: Basic Books, 1985.

Bartlett, Christopher A., and Sumantra Ghoshal. *Managing Across Borders: The Transnational Solution*. Boston: Harvard Business School Press, 1989.

Bartlett, Christopher A., Yves L. Doz, and Gunnar Hedlund. *Managing the Global Firm*. New York: Routledge, Chapman & Hall, 1990.

Contractor, Farok J., and Peter Lorange (eds.). *Cooperative Strategies in International Business*. Lexington, Mass.: Lexington Books, 1988.

Garland, John, Richard Farmer, and Marilyn Taylor. *International Dimensions of Business Policy and Strategy*. Boston: Kent Publishing, 1990.

Gates, Stephen R., and William G. Egelhoff. "Centralization in Headquarters-subsidiary Relationships." *Journal of International Business Studies,* Summer 1986, pp. 71–92.

Kiggundu, Moses N. *Managing Organizations in Developing Countries: An Operational and Strategic Approach*. West Hartford, Conn.: Kumarian Press, Inc., 1989.

Kujawa, Duane. *Japanese Multinationals in the United States: Case Studies*. New York: Praeger Publishers, 1986.

Mascarenhas, Briance. "International Strategies of Non-Dominant Firms." *Journal of International Business Studies,* Spring 1986, pp. 1–26.

NOTES

[1] For an extensive report on strategic management, especially as it pertains to the MNE, see William H. Davidson, *Global Strategic Management* (New York: John Wiley & Sons, 1982).

[2] This account of the strategic management process was adapted from James M. Higgins, *Organizational Policy and Strategic Management,* 2nd ed. (Hinsdale, Ill.: Dryden Press, 1983).

[3] Ibid., p. 65.

[4] David P. Rutenberg, *Multinational Management* (Boston: Little, Brown, 1982), p. 12.

[5] For the original presentation on ethnocentric, polycentric, and geocentric MNE structures and strategies, see Howard V. Perlmutter, "L'Entreprise

internationale—trois conceptions," *Revue Economique et Sociale,* May 1965. (A translation appears in *Quarterly Journal of AISEC International,* August 1967.)

[6]See, for example, Rutenberg, *Multinational Management,* pp. 16–18.

[7]See, for example, International Labour Office, *Social and Labour Practices of Some U.S.-Based Multinationals in the Metal Trades* (Geneva: ILO, 1977); and Rutenberg, *Multinational Management.*

[8]Claude L. Simpson, Jr., and Duane Kujawa, "The Export Decision Process: An Empirical Inquiry," *Journal of International Business Studies,* Spring 1974, pp. 107–17.

[9]Jon J. Martinez and J. Carlos Jarillo, "The Evolution of Research on Coordination Mechanisms in Multinational Corporations," *Journal of International Business Studies,* Fall 1989, pp. 489–514.

[10]J. M. Geringer, *Joint Venture Partner Selection: Strategies for Developed Countries* (Westport, Conn.: Quorum Books, 1988).

[11]J. Michael Geringer and Louis Hebert, "Control and Performance of International Joint Ventures," *Journal of International Business Studies,* Summer 1989, p. 248.

Windmere Corporation

Windmere manufactures and markets a diversified line of consumer electrical products. Sales in 1989 totalled $179 million, nearly three-and-one-half times the 1980 figure of $50 million.

In 1990, Windmere's product line consisted of several models of hair (blower) dryers, hair curlers, curling irons, lighted makeup mirrors, shavers and related personal beauty products, electronic air cleaners, oscillating fans, nail dryers, and wand-type massagers. These products are marketed under a variety of brand names, such as Signature, Pro, Windmere, Boss, Solid Gold, Prelude, Mirror-Go-Lightly, Fabergé, Brut, and Ronson.

Time and Change

In 1973, Windmere marketed only two products: "permanent lash clusters" and the 1,000-watt Pro hairstyling dryer. From 1973 to 1989, its product line expanded enormously and its sales (of consumer products) grew 600-fold—from $306,000 in 1973 to the $179 million of 1989. Indeed, during this period Windmere grew at a rate nearly 10 times that of the consumer electrical products industry in general. This was an impressive accomplishment.

The Hong Kong Connection

From the very beginning, Windmere sourced its electrical personal care products in Hong Kong. Indeed, from the early 1970s on, the company purchased products from different factories and trading companies in the old British crown colony.

Windmere's founder and current board chairman, Belvin Friedson, personally developed this strategy and personally established the commercial contacts in Hong Kong. The idea was really quite simple. Hair care consumer products were fairly standardized and could be produced quite cheaply in Hong Kong, with its comparatively low labor costs. In fact, many producers there were capable of making such products. They sold directly to buyers and also through Hong Kong-based trading companies.

The arm's-length buying arrangement was a learning experience for Windmere. It soon became evident to Friedson that quality control, scheduling, and other considerations, including Windmere's developing satisfaction with sourcing

This case was written by Professors Duane Kujawa and Harold Strauss, School of Business Administration, University of Miami, Coral Gables, Florida. The authors gratefully acknowledge the cooperation and assistance of Windmere Corporation, and especially Windmere's president, David Friedson, in providing company-specific information.

in Hong Kong and its desire to expand its activities there, required that it secure a longer-term relationship with its suppliers. Accordingly, Durable Electrical Metal Factory, Ltd., a Hong Kong-based, independent manufacturer that had emerged as one of Windmere's more important suppliers, joined Windmere in establishing several joint ventures. Durable-Belson, for example, was set up in 1975 as a manufacturing joint venture. In 1977, two other joint ventures were established: Dubel Industrial, Ltd., an injection molding operation, and Kamwon Electrical Factory, Ltd., an electrical products manufacturer. Subsequently, Windmere acquired 50 percent ownership of Durable itself.

Similarly, K. C. Lau & Co., Ltd., a trading company with which Windmere had developed a good working relationship, was acquired in 1978. This too was done for control reasons—but there were also reasons that went beyond scheduling, documentation, and financial considerations.

Windmere had learned that operating without the aid of a Hong Kong-based trading company resulted in higher prices and poorer goods and services. It worked with several trading companies, but was displeased with nearly all of them. This was because Windmere was dissatisfied with certain Hong Kong "business practices," such as paying trading companies or their key personnel "face money" or kickbacks that were over and above the normal commissions earned. The company felt that operating through a controlled trading company would ensure a more honest, dependable relationship. It also felt that a controlled trading company could help expand Kamwon's and Durable's businesses more effectively. Subsequently, K. C. Lau & Co. was merged into PPC Industries, Ltd., another trading company and a wholly owned subsidiary of Windmere.

By 1980, Windmere had thus put into place the basic operating structure that it felt was necessary to be competitive and to grow as a provider of low-cost, high-quality consumer electrical products to markets in the United States.

Establishing Production in the People's Republic of China

As Windmere's marketing success and its sourcing needs expanded, the company began to look beyond Hong Kong—where labor was becoming increasingly expensive and seasonally scarce. Lai Kin, the managing director of its Durable joint venture, set up an assembly operation in Canton in the People's Republic of China (PRC) in 1980. Labor rates were much lower there—but so were productivity and product quality. David Friedson, Windmere's president, put it this way:

At this time, the modernization of China had begun, but it was in a rudimentary form. The authorities in Canton could not understand our needs, and the workers had no concept of what [factory] work meant. Productivity was extremely low; the defect rate of products was extremely high; and the experiment was doomed to failure. At the insistence of Mr. Lai we allowed the experiment to continue because we thought we would lose face with the Chinese if we withdrew.[1]

Lai's persistence led to a second attempt to establish operations in the PRC. Man Fung Village, which is in the Shenzhen Special Economic Zone and lies about 35 miles north of Hong Kong, was the scene of a special challenge in 1981. Durable transferred a production line, complete with workers and equipment, from Hong Kong to an old theater in Man Fung Village to demonstrate what the Hong Kong Chinese could do in terms of efficiency and productivity. The mayor and people of Man Fung Village were impressed with this demonstration. They committed themselves to duplicating what they saw in that old theater.

Early the next year, the village put up some facilities and about 100 workers signed up to work there. Durable provided equipment, middle management, supervision, and training.

The rest is history!

Within a few years, the operation employed 2,700 workers and was the largest employer in the Shenzhen Zone. Moreover, Durable's workers were making about double the standard wage for government jobs in China. They were able to build large two-story villas that were beyond the reach of the average Chinese worker. Compensation typically totaled over $65 a month, including bonuses, which, even with transportation costs factored in, resulted in a cost savings of about 50 percent compared to Hong Kong-based production.[2] Interestingly, with the success of the Man Fung operation, Durable felt that it could close its Canton plant without "losing face."

Windmere's president, David Friedson, states that, in the company's opinion,

China provides us with the best value in labor for producing the kinds of products that we produce. This is based on the actual cost of labor as well as other benefits, such as free land and buildings the Government provides and the close proximity to our Hong Kong facilities.[3]

By 1988, nearly 75 percent of Durable's output was produced in China. It was capped at that level, however, since Windmere didn't want to "become wholly dependent on a single source."[4] In January 1989, Windmere expanded its ownership interest in Durable to 80 percent. An organization chart depicting the relationships among Windmere's major affiliates and divisions is presented in Figure 1.

Recent Developments

In the last few years, Windmere has added several products that can take advantage of its low-cost production in Hong Kong and the PRC. In 1986, for example, Windmere acquired the Mirror-Go-Lightly line from Jerdon Industries. It expected sales to be $3 million or more that year. In early 1987, Windmere introduced the Clothes Shaver (a device to remove lint and fuzz from wools and linens), which was expected to add another $3 million in sales. The Crimper, a heated styling element introduced in late 1986, was expected to generate yet another $3 million in sales. Plac Trac, a new approach to home plaque removal and dental care, was added in 1989, as was the Guardian line of electric shock protection personal care products.

As 1989 came to a close, Windmere was positioning itself as a newly emergent low cost, world class manufacturer of small consumer appliances. It had expanded distribution in the United States and was establishing the "Windmere" brand name worldwide.[5] Windmere Europe and Windmere Latin America, two new marketing divisions, had been established. Moreover, Durable was now manufacturing for "third parties," such as Rival, Sunbeam, and Hamilton Beach. Sales to such third parties were $20 million in 1990.

FIGURE 1

Organization
Structure—Windmere
Corporation

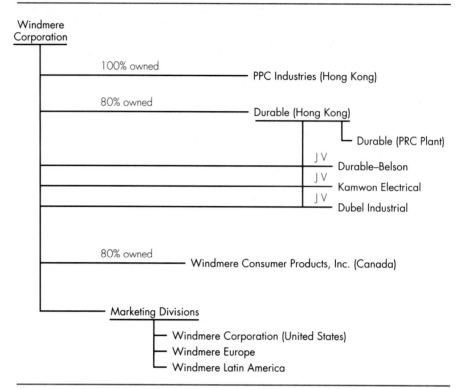

Note: The structure depicted here pertains to the material presented in the case and is useful in understanding the relationships discussed in the case. It is not an "official" organization chart provided by the company.

NOTES

[1]Letter from David M. Friedson to Dr. Harold Strauss, dated August 13, 1984.

[2]Michael Browning, "Dade Capitalist Brings Holiday Joy to Chinese," *Miami Herald,* January 30, 1984, pp. 1A and 11A.

[3]Letter from Friedson to Strauss.

[4]"Strong Rebound: Windmere Back in the Black after Heated Court Battle," *Barron's/Investment News & Views,* February 9, 1987, p. 45.

[5]Shearson Lehman Hutton, "Report on Windmere," April 28, 1989.

Chapter

14

Marketing Management

Marketing management in the MNE has two major kinds of concerns. At the operations (business unit) level, it addresses the traditional "four Ps" (product, price, place, and promotion) as they operate in different environments—technical, social, legal, economic, and so on. At the MNE level, it addresses the MNE's potential for competitive strengths in marketing and what the MNE must do to benefit from that potential. This chapter focuses on these concerns. The main goals of the chapter are to:

1. Develop an appreciation for the complexity of marketing management in the MNE—especially with regard to the effects of environmental nuances on the MNE's internal operations and competitive strengths.

2. Review the evolution of marketing management within the MNE.

3. Examine how the international marketing environment provides opportunities for MNEs, specifically in connection with:
   a. Product influences and pressures for product adaptation or standardization.
   b. Pricing concerns and the basis for setting an optimal pricing strategy.
   c. The transferability of experiences among markets and the importance of place.
   d. Promotion influences and promotion as an MNE competitive advantage.

INTRODUCTION

As suggested in some of the earlier chapters, marketing in the multinational enterprise can be especially challenging and complex.

The Extractive Industries

For MNEs in the extractive industries dealing with commodities that follow global pricing trends, marketing will probably involve long-term contracts with provisions stipulating consistency in product quality, timely delivery, and periodic price adjustments based on changes in some price index. For example, Intercor, the coal mining joint venture of Exxon and the Colombian government, sells premium-quality bituminous coal, mainly to electric utility companies in Europe. Sales contracts, which specify quality standards, quantities, and delivery dates, are typically for five or more years. Prices are keyed to spot market prices—which will probably vary during the term of the contract.

The Service Industries

In services, the product is "produced" at the time of sale or consumption. The buyer/seller relationship is personalized, and therefore substantially influenced by environmental, including cultural, factors. Thus, an advertising agency such as J. Walter Thompson would approach potential clients in Japan with considerable deference to age and seniority and an appreciation for the participative, consensus-style decision making typically found in larger Japanese firms. This would require an extensive and patient selling effort.

The Manufacturing Industries

In manufacturing, the MNE is also often quite marketing intensive. On the one hand, it may seek to maintain competitiveness by extending product life cycles through advertising, packaging, branding, distribution, and the like. On the other hand, it monitors changing market needs and may respond to them by introducing new products. Heinz catsup, for example, has been around for nearly a century, but its plastic, squeezable bottle is less than seven years old. The new sales generated by this ostensibly simple packaging innovation have helped Heinz capture over 50 percent of the U.S. catsup market. Over a third of the company's revenues now come from products new to Heinz in the past decade—such as Weight Watchers frozen dinners and Chico-San rice cakes. Heinz has capitalized on recent trends toward nutritious dieting and natural foods. It is benefitting from its experiences with these trends in the United States as these trends expand in Europe.

Complexity of Marketing Management in MNEs

Marketing management is typically seen as involving functional expertise that is especially pertinent at the SBU level. But there is more to this in an MNE context. At the international level, the MNE/SBU tries to identify and implement marketing strategies and programs that benefit in one area from experiences gained in other areas or that can effect positive scale economies by allocating fixed costs (for example, in R&D related to product development) over two or more markets. At this level, marketing management can be dealing both with a number of products that are in various life-cycle stages in a single market area and with single products that are in various life-cycle stages, depending on the market area. This means that strategies, staffing, and other functions are more complicated and demanding both within individual markets and internationally.

Keegan identifies three basic approaches to global marketing management. The first is the "standardized" approach, in which products, distribution channels, promotional activities, etc., are standardized to the greatest extent possible—thus contributing to low-cost operations. A second is the "decentralized" approach in which local, market-specific factors need to be addressed in product planning and promotion, or else sales and profits will suffer inordinately. The third is the "integrative" approach, which draws on the advantages offered by both standardization and decentralization—i.e., it requires adaptation to meet local market needs, but looks also to standardize products, promotions, etc., to minimize costs. Finding this "balance" at the point of maximizing long-term profits is naturally a difficult challenge.[1]

The key points here are that marketing management is more complex in the MNE than in the non-MNE and that MNE/SBUs with global marketing responsibilities must respond to two major issues—one dealing with the environmental variations and similarities that affect marketing strategies and programs, the other focusing on the internal operations that can give rise to competitive strengths unique to the MNE (see Figure 14–1). Responding to these issues effectively is international marketing management's challenge.

This chapter considers both issues. The environmental analysis is especially important to the MNE in dealing with the unification or fragmentation influences[2] that affect product, place, price, or promotion—the traditional four Ps of marketing. The internal analysis is important in implementing marketing programs that successfully utilize opportunities to benefit from scale economies in production, R&D, and so on, as well as opportunities to benefit from experiences in one market that make the firm more effective (profitable) in other markets. First, we discuss marketing management and the expanding importance of environmental and internal analyses as the MNE evolves from emergent to mature. Then we examine the four Ps, fairly extensively, in the context of the international marketing environment.

FIGURE 14–1

Marketing Management in the MNE

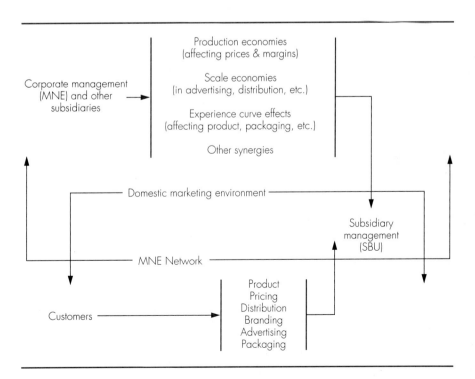

MARKETING MANAGEMENT AND THE EVOLUTION OF THE MNE

Accidental Exporting

As noted in Chapter 13, "Strategy and Organization Structure," many of today's large MNEs began their international involvement via accidental, or fortuitous, exporting in the 1950s and early 1960s. In those days, export marketing management was fairly simple. The product was determined to suit the domestic market, as was the price. There was no deliberate promotional program aimed at foreign markets, and often distribution was either the buyer's responsibility or just involved shipment to the domestically based exporter that was buying the product. The same packaging and warranty policies that were used in domestic sales were also used in foreign sales.

Deliberate Exporting

As foreign sales grew, deliberate exports displaced accidental exports and the producer's participation in international marketing began to expand. Sales representatives were assigned to foreign markets and producer-developed distribution channels were now used. Logistics received increasing management attention. Product pricing strategies became more market based, but this presented some special problems. One of these problems concerned the cost add-ons associated with exporting, such as shipping, insurance, tariffs, and packaging; another concerned the currency required. (In these times, exports were nearly always denominated in dollars. This put currency risk on the foreign customer.) Operating margins were required to cover the cost add-ons. Prices had to be high enough to do this while still leaving room for profits. What product adaptation there was at this time generally centered on technical modifications to meet foreign use conditions. Foreign marketing research was embryonic. Follow-up service was just being developed, and its absence presented a real barrier to more successful market penetration—a situation not unlike the one facing many of the U.S. firms that sought to export to Japan in the mid-1980s and early 1990s.

When a firm established an international department, marketing management grew in importance. Extensive foreign sales offices were set up, as were warehouses and repair centers. Exports were now a substantial portion of total sales and there was increasing integration between domestic and foreign marketing groups on product planning, production scheduling, and so on. Foreign marketing research expanded, and the firm was beginning to look for synergies in product design and promotional appeal between the domestic and foreign markets.

Producing in Foreign Markets

With the onset of foreign direct investment, marketing activities and the importance of marketing management increased dramatically. (For many firms, this took place in the late 1960s.) The defensive nature of this initial investment (recall the discussion on this subject in Chapter 13) meant that foreign markets were becoming very competitive for firms that were merely exporting to them. Producing overseas gave rise to new products that were designed to closely fit foreign market needs. Marketing research for foreign markets blossomed. Distribution channels were shortened and redefined. Given the heightened competition, promotional activities (including advertising) expanded. Competitive pricing strategies became commonplace, as did pricing in local currencies. Margins were tighter. Firms began looking for competitive advantages through scale economies in marketing via product R&D, distribution, advertising, and so on.

Marketing and the Mature MNE

Over time, the management response to these kinds of competitive pressures culminated in what by the mid-1970s had come to be called the **mature MNE.** In this organizational form, effective international marketing management is crucial. Such management involves coordinating, among the parent and its subsidiaries, product development and new product introduction strategies, taking advantage of experiences in one market to improve positions in other markets, benefiting from scale economies in production and marketing, and so on—while paying close attention to the distinctiveness of some markets and what this implies with regard to decentralized, market-specific strategies and operations. It may also involve the MNE entering strategic alliances, of varied forms, to enhance competitive advantages by reducing the lead times from product definition, to production, to marketing.

This discussion of marketing and the MNE underscores the effect of the environment on the MNE's marketing strategies and decisions. The changing environment facing the MNE results in both structural and operational changes within the MNE. Understanding international marketing management requires a more detailed knowledge of these varied environmental influences—our next subject.

THE INTERNATIONAL MARKETING ENVIRONMENT AND ITS CHALLENGES TO MNES

The world is indeed complex, and a review of each market—nuance by nuance—would be impossible to accomplish in a text such as this. The decision-oriented nature of management suggests that a more appropriate approach to the environment would be to focus on decision topics and to center on concepts. Marketing's **four Ps**—product, price, place, and promotion—require management decisions and make up the **marketing mix,** a term that identifies marketing both strategically and operationally. Our discussion of the environment centers on the four Ps.

Product

Producers view products as having a distinctive configuration that is definable and reproducible. The **product** can be anything from an American Express card, which is governed by a set of policies determining its use while limiting the company's exposure and risk, to a Mazda Miata sports car, which is produced by means of a deliberate and controlled process to guarantee product quality and costs. Consumers, however, view products as satisfying needs. To many, the American Express card provides global liquidity and connotes a sense of personal financial maturity and the Miata reinforces a self-image of youthfulness and excitement. Marketing management's first task is to identify consumer needs and define their product impact (e.g., how these needs influence product design).

Research indicates that consumer needs are usually determined by economic (e.g., income) and sociocultural (e.g., legal, religious, cultural) factors. The American Express card and the Miata, for example, are popular with high-income consumers and have a sort of "universal," cross-country appeal. Within country markets, consumers and nonconsumers of these products would correlate well with high and low income levels, respectively. In contrast, some products—foods, clothing, shelter, and the like—are often more culture based. To illustrate, beer can vary considerably depending on culturally accepted variations in consumers' tastes and preferences. The Dutch and Canadians, for example, like heavier beers; the Germans strongly prefer regional or local beer brands; the Japanese lately prefer "dry" beers; and the Irish, of course, like a heavy, dark, sweet "stout."

To some extent, **culture-based products** tend to be "necessities" (Wouldn't most college students consider beer a necessity?) and **income-based products** tend to be "discretionary" purchases. Given these market-based characteristics of consumer buying behavior, rising or high income levels facilitate a product policy that transcends country or cultural barriers. Cultural characteristics, on the other hand, make for a variety of discrete markets, which, in turn, leads to a fragmented product policy—that is, the design of different products to serve different markets.

Actually, a variety of factors—some compelling, others not—exert fragmentation, or decentralization, influences on product design and packaging. *For discussion purposes,* let us begin with the idea that a product can be the same (i.e., standardized) in the foreign market as it is in the home market, and put the burden of justifying **product modification** on foreign market factors. What could justify product modification?

Technical Factors   All products must be technically consistent with their environments. A classic example is the voltage of electric current which may vary (e.g., from 110 volts in the United States to 220 volts in Europe). Another is the use of different measurements by different countries, such as feet and pounds instead of meters and kilograms. Production technology may differ from one country to another. The availability of capital equipment or highly skilled workers may also vary country by country. These differences, in turn, may affect

---

product design or quality. Certain raw materials may be unavailable locally. Import restrictions or economic factors may force products and production processes to be altered so that available raw materials can be utilized.

Use Conditions   Products may be used in drastically different conditions from one market to another. Western Europe's long history of urban development, with villages and cities having narrow roads to accommodate the horses and buggies of days gone by, has certainly influenced automobile size. The bumpy brick roads often found in older towns and the often poorly maintained roads in rural areas mean that more durable autos and tires have to be built. Climatic conditions, transportation capabilities, and storage facilities all influence product configuration.

Legal Environment   The variations in laws from country to country affect products in numerous ways. Many countries have safety and pollution control standards. Products must be modified to meet these standards—for example, automobiles imported into the United States since the mid-1960s, when special safety regulations went into effect. (It might be noted that British Leyland Motor Corporation's Austin-Healey sports car was withdrawn from the U.S. market at that time because management decided not to adjust its classic design to meet the new safety requirements.) Foods and drugs are also usually heavily regulated areas, as is noise abatement. Terpstra reports, for example, that British lawn mowers are kept off the German market because they do not meet Germany's stringent noise control laws and that countries differ considerably in the amount of sugar, fruit, and juice they allow in jam, the amount of water they allow in canned fruit and vegetables, and the preservatives they allow in cereals.[3] (For the 12 countries comprising the European Community, many of the legal barriers causing segmented markets were eliminated in 1992.) Developing countries frequently limit the number of models of a product and the prices at which products may be sold. Any of these legally imposed constraints obviously affect product design.

Use conditions and the technical and legal environments leave a firm that wants to serve a particular market little room for discretion. Other factors—both economic and sociocultural—allow firms varying degrees of discretion with regard to product adaptation. These factors include income levels and income dispersion, educational levels, and consumer tastes and preferences.

Income   What people earn determines what they can afford. Regardless of overall income level, many countries are similar in that they all have a high-income stratum that has the discretionary income to afford the big-ticket item. Certain items, then, such as French perfumes, are used in all of these countries by persons with high incomes. Key variables here, aside from income levels and income structure, include the size of the various income groups and their effective purchasing power. Country markets may, in some cases, be dominated by higher or lower-income classes. In such cases, the kinds of products or product variations that will sell in the high-income countries differ considerably from the kinds that will sell in the low-income countries.

It is not unusual, for instance, for stripped-down versions of products sold in high-income areas to be marketed in low-income areas. For example, Singer sells a line of sewing machines in parts of Africa that are often simple and handpowered; in Europe, it sells a line of electrical machines with insertable cams to automate complicated patterns. Income levels and the dispersion of income help define market size, which, in turn, influences the selection of process technology and product configuration.

Education   The general level of education affects product decisions both directly and indirectly. A highly literate market, for example, would typically demand more complex products. Product sophistication should match consumer sophistication. Computers and other electronic apparatus find limited markets where illiteracy prevails, as, in general, do products with complicated maintenance requirements, such as chain saws.

Consumer Tastes and Preferences   What consumers desire is often related to culture—as discussed in Chapter 12, "Culture and Ethics." Toyota learned this the hard way in 1956, when it designed a small car for the Japanese market that it thought would be adaptable to the U.S. market.[4] The home market version had a 20-horsepower engine and a top speed of 62 miles per hour. It weighed nearly three quarters of a ton, and it was not fuel efficient as compared to other small cars being sold in the United States. The lack of fuel efficiency turned off small-car lovers, the smallness was unappealing to consumers who wanted style, and the performance characteristics were just not attractive. The car, which was marketed under the name Toyopet (a self-deprecating name at best), presented a confused message to American consumers and flopped. No firm can afford to ignore consumer tastes and preferences.

The history of the MNE, brief as it is, contains numerous examples of firms that have misread local market preferences for products of certain sizes, configurations, colors, and so on.[5] For example, Campbell Soup, an American company, had difficulty in adjusting its products to suit the tastes of its European consumers. Knorr Soup, a European company, found it difficult to break into the U.S. market with its dehydrated soups in the face of the preference of U.S. consumers for soup in liquid form.

MNEs' Responses   Firms must decide whether or how they want to respond to the aforementioned economic and sociocultural factors. What would Campbell sell in Europe if it had not sweetened its tomato soup? Marginal analysis would be the appropriate method to employ here. What would be the sales revenues and costs if the product were not adapted to accommodate local influences? What would they be if it were? What alternative approaches might be taken? Which alternative is the most profitable? Interestingly, one could argue that product analysis by the MNE should always seek to favor standardization, since it is in standardization that the MNE has competitive strengths vis-à-vis other firms. In this sense, MNEs can be seen as market leaders in market segments where tastes and preferences are converging internationally and where products (or product cores) are thus being standardized internationally.

Price

Setting a product price is a difficult task at best. Ideally, the firm prefers as few constraints as possible on its product pricing. The only constraint that most firms want to accept is that imposed by competition, but even then the typical corporate strategy is to reduce or eliminate the effect of competition on pricing, for example, through the implementation of a strategy involving product differentiation. Firms want to set prices so that they can maximize profits under the given market conditions. Multinationals have more than this to deal with, however. Price strategy for a global market must accommodate considerations that would not exist otherwise, or at least would be less pressing. These considerations include price escalation when exporting, transfer pricing, dumping, price controls, and price differentials among segmented markets. Each of these considerations is explained in the text that follows.

Price Escalation when Exporting   The term **price escalation when exporting** refers to the percentage add-ons to the ex-factory price of a product by the middlemen that make up the distribution network and by tariffs, as the product goes from domestic producer to foreign customer. The ex-factory price is amplified by the combined amount of these add-ons, multiplied by one another. Distribution channels are typically lengthier when exporting than when selling domestically. For the MNE exporting an end product, price escalation cuts into sales and profits by biasing the product's final price upward. For the MNE exporting component parts or subassemblies, on the other hand, although price escalation still exists, it is not as big a problem. There is less price escalation for components and subassemblies than for end products, and the effect is thus less than otherwise. The value added by the foreign-based production is not exposed to price escalation. Also, the MNE typically handles the international distribution of components and subassemblies in-house (via commercial shippers), where costs are not subject to percentage add-ons.

Transfer Pricing   What a subsidiary is charged by another subsidiary or the parent company for the intracompany sale of a product or part is termed the **transfer price.** For the exporting unit, the transfer price affects sales revenues; for the importing unit, it affects costs. The transfer price also affects the amount of money that flows between the exporting and importing units (the goods transferred have to be paid for), the amount of the tariffs paid on the transferred items, and the amount of the profits (or losses) realized at each unit (since transferred goods are part of the cost of goods sold at the importing unit and part of the total income received at the exporting unit). If firms were totally free to set transfer prices as they wished and were not concerned about where funds were accumulated in the MNE network, they would probably do the following on parts or products sent to subsidiaries:

1. Set prices high in countries where income taxes are high.
2. Set prices low where imports come in at high tariffs.
3. Set prices high where the parent company has a problem in getting profits out of the country where a subsidiary is located.
4. Set prices low if income taxes in the parent country are high.

In reality, the MNE is not really free to set transfer prices in whatever manner it wishes, because governments are generally concerned about the amounts of income taxes and tariffs collected. At best, the price set by the company is justifiable, reasonable, and acceptable to the government. Typically, an arm's-length price, one that would be set between two unrelated firms in a competitive marketplace, is deemed acceptable. Alternatively, the price may be negotiable

IB ILLUSTRATION

As an International Trade Commissioner, How Would You Vote?

The International Trade Commission (ITC) voted 2–1 that imported sweaters from Hong Kong, Korea, and Taiwan are being sold in the United States at less than "fair value." Thus, the U.S. Customs Service is to collect antidumping duties (i.e., duties assessed as a percentage of the merchandise cost above the normal tariff) ranging from 5.86 percent on imports of man-made fiber sweaters from Hong Kong to 115.5 percent on imports from a specific firm in Hong Kong—Prosperity Clothing, Ltd./Eastern Enterprises, Ltd.—because the firm did not cooperate with the ITC anti-dumping investigation.

The U.S. National Knitwear and Sportswear Association praised the ITC's decision since it would "provide a welcome boost for the beleaguered domestic sweater industry." On the other hand, the American Association of Exporters and Importers objected and noted the ". . . sweater business has changed dramatically . . . from a basics business to a fast-changing, fashion-forward business." A spokesperson for the Association recently noted: "Imports have filled a void for high-quality and novelty sweaters; they have not damaged a domestic industry." With special duties affecting imports from Hong Kong, Korea, and Taiwan, consumers will be injured. The sweaters they want just won't be available at attractive prices. ■

Source: *Women's Wear Daily,* September 6, 1990, p. 23.

between the company and the government agency involved—and be pegged at a justifiable and reasonable level. At worst, from the company's perspective, the government sets the price at whatever level it wants to and collects taxes and tariffs accordingly. Deliberate attempts by MNEs to present their records in a fraudulent manner to evade taxes or tariffs are, of course, illegal—criminal acts. For internal accounting and control purposes, however, a company can use whatever transfer prices it wants to use.

Dumping   Another major concern that affects the pricing strategies of MNEs is **dumping.** The General Agreement on Tariffs and Trade (GATT) forbids selling products in export markets at less than the prices for which they are sold in the home market. This restriction is meant to preclude the introduction of disruptive, predatory pricing practices whereby, for example, an exporter could establish a monopoly in a foreign market by pricing deceptively low to drive competitors out of that market—and then increase its prices at will. Under GATT, a country can erect a retaliatory tariff to offset dumping. (Chapter 9 discussed some of these issues.)

Price Controls   Governments, especially governments in developing countries, have been known to set product prices. But from time to time, **price controls**

IB ILLUSTRATION

Who Is Protecting Whom?

The U.S. International Trade Commission (ITC) recently voted that the U.S. "high content flat panel display industry" was materially injured by Japanese imports. The case now goes to the Commerce Department, which has eight months to make a determination that "dumping" did in fact occur. It then comes back to the ITC for a final decision. The full process takes a year. In the meantime, producers of flat panels—U.S. and Japanese—will continue to slug it out in the marketplace.

An interesting twist to the case is that America's most successful computer makers are lined up in support of the Japanese. These include IBM, Apple, Compaq, and Tandy. They buy flat panel displays from the Japanese, whom they say are the only ones capable of supplying them with the volume and quality needed. If antidumping duties were applied, the U.S. computer firms would either have to discontinue models using the panels, or shift production of laptop computers offshore.

If duties are applied, who is the winner? Certainly not the Japanese producers. Is it the American computer manufacturer? Or the American consumer? How about the American firms producing flat panel displays? ∎

Source: *Electronic News*, August 13, 1990, p. 1 and September 3, 1990, p. 1.

also appear even in developed countries—in the United States, for example, in the early 1970s. Price controls can present some real problems. Some MNEs have abandoned foreign markets because of their inability to price products at profitable levels. Price controls are typically evident in markets where there are inflationary pressures, and they are usually applied in both product and resource markets. As a result of local political pressures, wages are sometimes allowed to advance, while the firm is not allowed to pass this cost increase along in the form of a higher product price. Profits become squeezed. In such situations, the firm's short-run options are quite limited. It can continue to press the government to approve a product price increase, or, it can downgrade the cost (and quality) of the product, a risky strategy in a competitive market. Being the low-cost producer in the market, a long-term strategy provides the best hedge, but even that may not be sufficient in an especially difficult situation.

The Pricing Strategies of MNEs Unless a firm deals in commodities that sell on world markets at world prices (e.g., oil, copper, or coal), it wants to maintain separate prices that correspond to the specific cost and competitive conditions of its various markets. Apart from the aforementioned situations that interfere with the firm's ability to implement this pricing strategy, competitive market forces themselves may compromise the firm's ability to maintain price differentials among (otherwise) segmented markets. Markets that were heretofore effectively separated may now have greater elements of commonality—such as might result when tariffs between countries are lowered or eliminated, when shipping costs between markets decline, when consumer tastes change and become similar between markets, or when the customer is itself a multinational enterprise that buys from the firm in several geographic markets. As MNEs grew during the decade of the 1970s, for example, Citicorp found that its geographically independent, nation-based subsidiaries were ill-equipped to serve the needs of MNEs effectively. A basic problem was that each Citicorp subsidiary was charging clients according to local market norms—the result being that subsidiaries of MNEs were being charged more than the parent company was paying in the home country. The MNEs pushed for (and succeeded in getting) homogeneous, company-specific pricing on a global basis.[6]

Pricing, as illustrated above, can be very complex. At best, the firm wants to remain unconstrained so that it can price to meet the firm's objectives and the requirements of individual markets. Nonmarket elements, such as governments, that constrain the firm's pricing behavior detract from the desirability of serving the markets where they exist. Changes in market-based elements, such as consumer tastes and the emergence of MNEs as customers, may well force the firm to change its pricing strategy, perhaps by segmenting a market on the basis of something other than geography. Examples of such segmentation include product differentiation according to consumers' incomes or tastes, quantity discounts for large-volume buyers, and variations in branding, packaging, or distribution. Barcardi rum, for example, sells Anejo (premium), Bacardi (standard), and Castillo (low grade), with some variations, in the United States and many other countries, both rich and poor. In each market, the sales and profit margins associated with each grade of rum will vary depending on income distribution, tastes and preferences, the extent of competition in each segment, and so on.

Place

The concept of **place** is considerably more complicated for a firm that functions on a multinational basis than for a firm that functions on a purely domestic basis. Place is both strategically and operationally important to the MNE. In the strategic sense, the importance of place arises because for some products there are global markets that typically follow a lead (single country) market. In the operational sense, place encompasses both global logistic networks and in-country distribution management.

The Strategy Perspective Place is traditionally viewed as the location of the market served by the firm. For the international firm, place issues invariably focused on foreign marketing research and on the difficulties of doing such research. These matters are still important to the MNE. Forecasting foreign market potential, for example, is necessary for a host of important decisions—especially the decision to serve the market in the first place. Data must be collected and interpreted country by country—an extremely difficult task. Consider, though, the advantage that the experienced MNE, with experienced staff on location in the foreign market, has over the new entrant to that market.

Place, as a strategy variable at the MNE level, pertains to the location of the new product introduction, or the **lead market,** and to the interrelationships among markets that allow the MNE to benefit from experiences in one market that can make it more competitive in other markets. To an MNE, lead markets are typically the higher-income markets, where, as previously discussed, market size and market segments, with distinctive buying patterns influenced by income levels, tastes, and preferences, encourage innovation (i.e., bringing new products to market) and reward successful innovation (e.g., with substantial profits).

In the 1950s and 1960s, the United States was the most important lead market and the home country of most of the multinationals in manufacturing industries. In those years of the emergent MNEs, there was even concern that domination of foreign economies by American MNEs would lead to global U.S. hegemony.[7] Then income levels expanded in Japan, Western Europe, and Canada, and MNEs based in these countries established themselves in foreign markets. By the 1990s, their successes in product innovation resulted in competitive advantages both at home and in other countries (including the United States).

Today, the mature multinational views the concept of the lead market somewhat differently. The ethnocentric MNE probably still views the home market as the lead market. The home market is its experience base and is seen as essential to the firm's long-run success. For the polycentric MNE, however, there are several distinctive, comparatively isolated important markets. Such an MNE is, by definition, fragmented. Each market has its own decision center and a rather provincial perspective.

The lead market concept is most meaningful to the geocentric MNE. It has distinctive characteristics that provide the geocentric firm with opportunities to excel internationally. The lead market is the one that can give the geocentric firm the greatest overall, global competitive advantage. Thus, the lead market is typically the one that offers the firm the greatest opportunity for quick market

---

ADDED DIMENSION

Kodak's Successful Instamatic Camera Failure

In 1963, Kodak introduced its then revolutionary Instamatic camera simultaneously in 28 country markets. Sales were immediately fantastic. During the first two years after the Instamatic was introduced, almost 5 million units were sold outside the United States—the first time in the company's history that the international sales of a new product exceeded sales in the home market.

But Kodak had its problems too. Sales had been seriously underestimated. Production lagged demand significantly in the first few years. Kodak *lost* a lot of business! Moreover, its competitors benefited from seeing Kodak's market success with the Instamatic and had time to respond to that success by bringing out competitive products. To prevent this, of course, Kodak could have built up huge inventories of Instamatics prior to the global launch. But this would have been a costly strategy—and prior to the launch, a risky one. Alternatively, Kodak could have introduced the product on a sequential basis in each of its markets. But this strategy too would have had its own set of benefits and risks. ∎

Source: This highlighted feature is based on David P. Rutenberg, *Multinational Management* (Boston: Little, Brown, 1982), pp. 260–61.

penetration and large-scale operations. The potential positive learning curve effects or scale economies would be most fully realized in such situations—to the benefit of subsidiaries in **follow-on markets** which can learn from the lead market experience, and to the benefit of the total MNE, which has now established a durable, competitive presence in a major market capable of giving financial and technical support to activities in other markets. A third criterion, then, addressed in the selection of a lead market is the extent to which experience in that market is relevant to potential experiences in other markets. If such a relationship exists, the lead market has special value pertinent to an MNE's competitive success.

Figures 14–2 and 14–3 display graphically the lead market/follow-on market concept. By way of illustration, two products—color TVs and VCRs—are depicted in terms of their market absorption patterns (that is, the patterns of each product's sales through time) in several national markets. Figure 14–2 shows the patterns for color TVs in the U.S., German, and British markets. The figure depicts the U.S. market as the lead market (where the product was initially introduced—at time 0). As time passed, an increasing percentage of the U.S. market purchased color TVs until, finally, a market saturation point was reached. Sales of color TVs are shown as beginning in the German and British markets later than time 0. Eventually, sales in these markets also reach their saturation points. A similar set of **market absorption curves** is presented in Figure 14–3 for videocassette recorders (VCRs).

FIGURE 14–2

Market Absorption Curves:
Color TVs

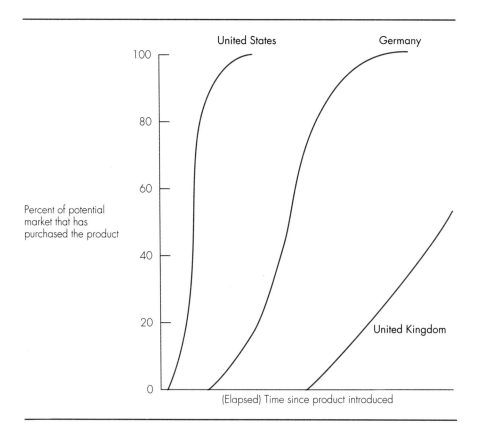

Let's look at the value of the information shown in Figures 14–2 and 14–3 to the firm that is experienced in consumer electronic products and is planning to introduce a new product, say a compact video camera. (Recall that the curves reflect actual experiences with the other two products.) The slopes of the curves reflect the rates of sales growth in each market and assist the firm in planning production capacity and production rates. The proximity of the different country curves gives the firm solid expectations on global market growth, including the rate and country-by-country distribution of that growth. Depending on the specific data represented by the curves as well as the relevant scale economies, shipping costs, tariffs, and so on, and the expected competitive reactions, the firm may decide, for example, to export from the United States to the German market during the latter stages of U.S. market penetration and the earlier stages of German market development. Similarly, it may want to use German production to satisfy the initial British demand. If the economics of production and distribution required it, parallel production facilities would eventually be operating in all three countries.

The data are useful to the firm for even more than decisions on capacity planning, market entry, and production allocation. For example, the slope of each curve can be influenced, depending on industry and company practices regarding pricing, advertising, and so on. The distances between the country-specific curves can be reduced, depending on the firm's market entry and timing strategies. MNEs have options regarding pricing, promotion, markets, and so on

FIGURE 14–3

Market Absorption Curves: Videocassette Recorders (VCRs)

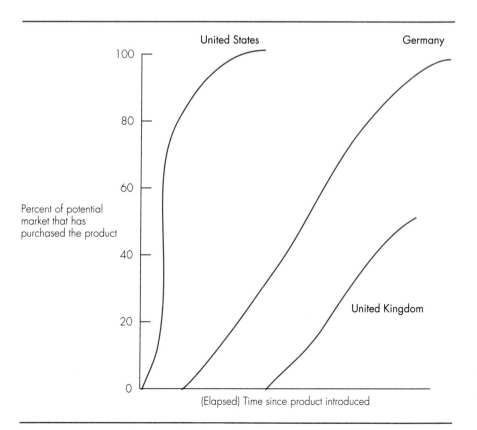

that can alter the patterns and locations of the curves to fit their profit and strategy objectives more precisely.

General Electric was a pioneer in the use of market absorption curves. Today, many companies use them, including Westinghouse, Sony, Panasonic, Siemans, and Philips.

The Operations Perspective "Place" as an operations variable pertains to the MNE's establishment and management of global logistic networks and to its management of distribution within a country market.

The logistic problems confronting emergent MNEs initially centered on exporting—moving the product from the domestically located factory to a foreign market. As direct foreign investment occurred, "captive" exports of parts and subassemblies, from parent to subsidiary, grew in volume. In the mature MNE, the logistics function is much more complex. To be competitive, the firm must source wherever costs are lowest to support globally distributed production centers serving both domestic and export markets.

Figure 14–4 presents the **global logistic network** of the Helicopter Division of France's Société Nationale Industrielle Aerospatiale. The fairly extensive network involves the shipment of components (rotors) and subassemblies (air-

FIGURE 14–4

Global Logistic Network: Société Nationale Industrielle Aerospatiale, Helicopter Division

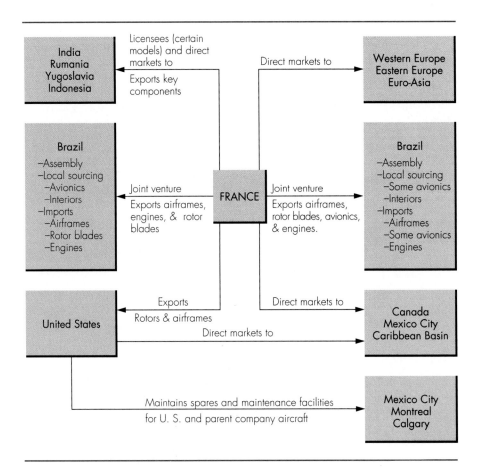

frames) between plants in France and plants in the United States and Brazil. Fully assembled helicopters are shipped from Brazil to markets in South America and from the United States to customers in Mexico, Canada, and the Caribbean Basin. The U.S. subsidiary, Aerospatiale Helicopter Corporation (AHC), also maintains spares and maintenance bases in Mexico and Canada—where parts from both the parent and AHC are inventoried. The U.S. subsidiary purchases engines and avionics from U.S. suppliers (Lycoming and Collins, respectively) and manufactures and installs its own interiors. A similar sourcing pattern exists at the Brazilian subsidiary. The French parent markets fully assembled helicopters throughout Western Europe and parts of Asia. Sales in Eastern Europe are accomplished through licensees in Rumania and Yugoslavia and in parts of Asia through licensees in India and Indonesia. These licensees import components and subassemblies, including engines and avionics, from France and provide locally manufactured interiors.

More complicated patterns of logistics networks could be presented, but the conclusions would remain the same: (1) intracorporate product transfers combined with local sourcing can be intricate and costly to establish and maintain, and (2) their efficient management is essential to the competitiveness of the firm. Viewed slightly differently, one could conceptualize that geographically distributed production facilities provide the MNE with cost efficiencies that enhance competitiveness and profitability but that the movement of parts and products among these facilities results in distribution costs that diminish the cost savings resulting from these location advantages. The value of effective, internal communication pertains to both the establishment and the operation of geographically distributed facilities. The whole "problem" is best resolved through linear programming, with the optimal solution considering not only direct shipping and packaging costs but also inventory charges and the scale economies realized in production when a single production site serves multiple markets.

On this last point, an interesting illustration was provided by Ford Motor's international sourcing patterns on four-cylinder engines. Early in the 1970s, Ford-Britain put a new four-cylinder engine plant on-stream to serve both the British and U.S. markets. As demand in the UK grew, production for the U.S. market was shifted to a new Ford-Brazil plant. Eventually, as both Brazilian and U.S. demand grew, production was shifted to a new Ford-U.S. plant.[8]

Decisions regarding distribution systems within countries must consider a set of variables totally different from those related to global logistic networks, where costs and timing are the key concerns. With **in-country distribution,** cost and timing are again important, but local conditions, institutions, and cultural influences are also important.

One approach to in-country distribution is to secure the services of distributors outside the firm which are, in turn, responsible for the selling of the product in their respective countries or local markets. In this instance, the MNE is accessing the foreign market through indirect exporting. It is effectively buying local expertise, but it can no longer determine distribution costs, ensure product quality, and maintain timely delivery schedules. (The classic case of the French wine producer that exported to the United States through local agents comes to mind here. The U.S. importing company let thousands of bottles sit in a New York warehouse during a winter freeze. The wine was ruined, but the importer sold it anyway—at depressed prices. It took the French vintner several decades to overcome the bad product image caused by this importer's indiscretion.)

Indirect exporting may be the only sensible approach, however, for smaller MNEs or for MNEs serving smaller markets. Moreover, the loss of control will vary, depending on just which form of indirect exporting is selected. The loss is greatest when ownership of the product is transferred to a buyer that, in turn, exports the product to the foreign market. Examples here include **export commission agents,** which buy on behalf of foreign clients; **export merchants,** which buy for their own account and then sell to foreign customers; and **international trading companies,** which, like export merchants, buy for their own account but then often sell in the foreign market through their parent companies. The Japanese *sogo sosha,* such firms as Mitsui and C. Itoh, are classic examples of international trading companies. More recently, however, such firms as General Electric and Kmart have established international trading companies. In the United States, the Export Trading Company Act, passed in 1982, enables small and medium-sized U.S. firms—companies that are often too small to go after foreign markets—to combine export operations in a separate **export trading company,** exempt from antitrust law so long as this does not adversely affect their competitive practices in the domestic market. Bank holding companies are permitted to hold stock in export trading companies—a privilege that is designed to make financial services more readily available to potential customers.

Indirect exporting may also involve using agents that export on behalf of a supplier without taking title to the exported goods. Such agents include **manufacturer's export agents** and **export management companies**—firms that represent several noncompeting manufacturers overseas and often even provide shipping and promotional services. (International trading companies and export management companies, it should be mentioned, may buy and sell for their own account and may operate on a commission basis.)

Most MNEs serve their major foreign markets through direct exporting or foreign-based production. During direct exporting, these firms may or may not procure logistics support, such as that offered by freight forwarders, customs brokers, and distributors. Similarly, foreign-based production to serve foreign markets would probably involve local distributors, wholesalers, and retailers. Whether or not to use such intermediaries is essentially a "make or buy" decision that turns on comparative costs, operating margins, or other expectations related to sales or profits. These factors are, in turn, likely to be influenced by local conditions, institutions, and culture.

For example, in some countries, like Japan, distribution systems are multi-tiered and complex, while in developing countries, they are often "lean," that is, with few specialized middlemen except in the larger cities.[9] Both wholesaling and retailing are generally more atomized outside the United States than within the United States. This may require the MNE to work with several, parallel channels within a country market, and to stand prepared to provide channel participants with inventory and technical support on a timely basis. If the firm were a U.S. MNE, this would represent a different way of doing business than it was accustomed to at home.

Promotion

When a firm is dealing with the four Ps of marketing, **promotion** is probably the one in which the environmental influence is greatest. Promotion seeks to activate the motivation to purchase by conveying the information that the firm needs to get across the desirability of its product. Promotion typically deals with advertising, personal selling, and sales promotion—which usually involves brochures, displays, exhibitions, samples, and so on. However, promotion does not exist alone. Place and price, for example, are often closely related to promotion, as are product design features and product quality. How often have we heard that a product "sells itself" or that there is a 20 percent price discount during a special promotional period? Promotion, as noted, more often just relates to advertising, personal selling, and sales promotion. Promotion is normally place specific and therefore very culture-bound.

Promotion Practices Vary Internationally   In many countries, legislation or industry practices significantly affect advertising. In the United States, for example, such products as liquor and cigarettes cannot be advertised on television, and advertising messages, regardless of media, are subject to "truth in advertising" standards. In Sweden and Great Britain, among other countries, advertising is subject to a "purchase" tax just like that paid on a product purchased in a store. In some countries, governments must preapprove advertisements for certain kinds of products. In yet others, certain media, such as television, may not be available for advertising. Restrictions of these kinds often lead to what the MNE may consider creative forms of advertising, such as billboard advertising at local soccer fields.

Global surveys related to advertising show considerable differences among countries in both media selection and per capita advertising outlays.[10] In the United States, for example, 32 percent of all advertising outlays are spent on print media; in Japan, 35 percent; and in Australia, 49 percent. In the United States, 22 percent of all advertising outlays are spent on the TV media; in Australia; 34 percent, and in Canada, 17 percent. In Venezuela, advertising expenditures absorb about 1.0 percent of GNP (gross national product), which is about 40 percent of advertising's share of GNP in the United States. Among the factors affecting these distributions are living standards, infrastructural development, and regulation.

Because of language, ethnic, and religious differences among customers, **personal selling,** by its very nature, is largely country- or subcountry-bound. This is especially true for consumer goods firms, whose personal selling is mainly concentrated among the wholesalers and retailers with which the firm deals. For firms dealing with intermediate goods, economic factors typically become more important in the purchase decision. Such firms often put together selling teams so that all the relevant expertise—marketing, technical, financial, and so on—can be brought to bear on the purchase decision. One could also argue that mature intermediate products will involve personal selling that is more culture- or country-bound than the selling of innovative products, whose producers have more control or influence over the purchase decision.

The Promotion Strategies of MNEs   For the multinational enterprise seeking to obtain and implement competitive advantages, the question of the global standardization of promotional strategies and campaigns is quite important. To some extent, scale economies do exist, for example, in advertising—that is, in advertising research, copy preparation, and so on. The big plus, however, is the experience effect. A successful promotional campaign in one market may indeed bode well for similar successes in other markets. As mentioned earlier, income-related influences on consumers' tastes and preferences often override cultural and country-related influences in the product-specific areas that are more likely dominated by MNEs. Cross-cultural and cross-country similarities that correspond to similarities in income levels provide a rationale for similarities in promotional campaigns. To the extent that an MNE can transform a promotional program in one country into a competitively superior or more timely program in another country, it will be benefiting from an experience effect. The business world is replete with examples of this process. Marketing-intensive firms such as Coca-Cola, Heinz, Ford Motor, and Exxon have successfully developed and implemented international promotional programs.

CONCLUSIONS

International marketing management varies considerably, depending on the product and the market. For the global MNE, the challenge is to create and sustain a competitive edge based on experiences elsewhere or on scale economies that are unavailable to other firms.

International marketing management has changed considerably within the MNE as the MNE has grown and matured. In the early years, product and price were set by domestic demand conditions and exports were mainly fortuitous. Later, firms became more deliberate regarding exports. Technical adaptation to foreign product markets began, as did more direct involvement in the logistics function. As export markets grew, international departments, foreign marketing activities, and production integration between foreign and domestic markets evolved. Direct foreign investment, itself occasioned by the need for enhanced competitiveness in foreign markets, expanded the nature of the marketing function dramatically. New products were introduced. Pricing strategies became more market specific, and promotion and distribution were subjected to closer local control. In today's mature MNE, the keys to success are parent-subsidiary coordination on production and marketing issues and close attention to the distinctive characteristics of local markets. This contention was examined more closely as each of the major decision-making areas of marketing management—categorized in terms of marketing's traditional four Ps—was discussed.

Product is defined by the nature of consumers' needs and is substantially influenced by both culture and income levels. Culture and the local economic and institutional settings make for the fragmentation of products; higher and rising income levels generally make for the unification of products. More specifically, technical factors often result in product modifications to meet local market needs. Use conditions, climate, transportation capabilities, and storage facilities, which may differ from market to market, also lead to product adaptations—as do legal, income, educational, and consumer influences and maintenance requirements.

Most firms, including MNEs, want as much freedom as possible with regard to *price,* so that they can price according to market conditions and, hopefully, maximize revenues and profits. The product pricing of the MNE must accommodate a set of considerations broader than the set of conditions that must be accommodated by the exclusively domestic firm. Price escalation when exporting—the result of the percentage add-ons of channel participants and tariffs—multiplies ex-factory price increases. Transfer pricing on items that move between units within the MNE can affect overall revenues, the direction of revenue flows, and the taxes and duties paid in different countries. Transfer prices are generally closely scrutinized by governments. Dumping, which involves selling at unfairly low prices in foreign markets, is prohibited by GATT. Price controls are another concern of the MNE. At one time or another, many countries set product and resource prices—leaving the MNE with few short-run options. Finally, the problem of maintaining price differentials among markets that are otherwise segmented is also germane to the MNE. While markets maintain a geographic separation, certain segments across geographic boundaries may be developing into homogeneous markets. This presents the MNE with a pricing problem as it seeks to maintain price differentials among location-specific and product-specific markets.

Place is important to the MNE as both a strategy variable and an operations concern. In the strategic context, MNEs have the capability to identify lead markets that provide them with internationally transferable experiences and integrated production practices that result in competitive advantages. As an operations concern, global logistics networks can be very complex in mature MNEs and their efficient and timely operation can contribute to the competitive advantages of MNEs. In-country distribution systems are similarly important, but they are influenced to a greater extent by local conditions, institutions, and cultures. Firms may engage in indirect exporting—thus buying local expertise at the cost of losing control. They may export directly and they may produce and distribute within the foreign market—thus requiring flexibility and adaptation as operational hallmarks and management characteristics.

Promotion is probably the most environmentally influenced of the four Ps. It can take on many forms, and it can follow from decisions made regarding product, price, and place. However, promotion generally pertains to advertising and personal selling—both of which are substantially influenced by market-specific factors. Personal selling, by its very nature, is fairly culture-bound. For the MNE, the challenge is to find promotional strategies and programs that are transferable internationally. Cost savings is one incentive here, but the experience effect as related to the potential effectiveness of programs is considerably more important.

QUESTIONS

1. What are the two major issues confronting marketing management in the MNE? How does marketing management in the MNE differ from marketing management in a purely domestic firm, if at all?

2. How have the emergence and maturation of the multinational enterprise influenced the development of the international marketing management function? The domestic marketing management function?

3. Rising personal income generally expands discretionary purchasing power. How does this fact benefit the global marketing presence of the MNE?

4. Identify the main factors influencing product design among MNEs—especially the factors that exert fragmentation pressures. What should the MNE be doing in the face of such pressure?

5. Identify the main factors influencing the pricing strategy of MNEs. Is the maintenance of price differentials among segmented markets unique to MNEs? What similarities and differences might exist between a domestic firm that is trying to maintain a market segmentation strategy via product differentiation and an MNE that is trying to maintain a market segmentation strategy across geographically segmented markets for a single product?

6. How does the GATT influence MNEs' pricing strategies? What are some of the inherent problems associated with any country's attempt to control dumping?

7. What are the major features of the lead market concept as a tool for strategic marketing planning?

8. How does the operations variable "place" affect the competitive strategy of MNEs? Characterize the importance of logistics in MNE competitive strategy as the MNE has evolved from emergent to mature.

9. What are the main points with regard to in-country distribution that an MNE must consider? What are the trade-offs with regard to in-country distribution strategy that the MNE has to evaluate?

10. Why is the question of the globally standardized advertising campaign relevant to an MNE?

REFERENCES

Al-Eryani, Mohammad F.; Pervaiz Alam; and Syed H. Akhter. "Transfer Pricing Determinants of U.S. Multinationals." *Journal of International Business Studies,* Third Quarter 1990, pp. 409–26.

Boddewyn, Jean J. "Comparative Marketing: The First 25 Years." *Journal of International Business Studies,* Spring–Summer 1981, pp. 61–80.

Cateora, Philip. *International Marketing.* Homewood, Ill.: Richard D. Irwin, 1990.

Douglas, Susan P., and Dong Kee Rhee. "Examining Generic Competitive Strategy Types in U.S. and European Markets." *Journal of International Business Studies,* Fall 1989, pp. 411–36.

Doyle, Peter; John Saunders; and Veronica Wong. "A Comparative Study of Japanese Marketing Strategies in the British Market." *Journal of International Business Studies,* Spring 1986, pp. 27–46.

Gillespie, Kate, and Dana Alden. "Consumer Product Export Opportunities to Liberalizing LDCs: A Life-Cycle Approach." *Journal of International Business Studies,* Spring 1989, pp. 93–112.

Kashani, Kamran, and John A. Quelch. "Can Sales Promotion Go Global?" *Business Horizons,* May–June 1990, pp. 37–43.

Levitt, Theodore. "The Globalization of Markets." *Harvard Business Review,* May–June 1983, pp. 92–102.

Norburn, David; Sue Birley; Mark Dunn; and Adrian Payne. "A Four Nation Study of the Relationship Between Marketing Effectiveness, Corporate Culture, Corporate Values, and Market Orientation." *Journal of International Business Studies,* Third Quarter 1990, pp. 451–68.

NOTES

[1] Warren Keegan, *Global Marketing Management* (Englewood Cliffs, N.J.: Prentice-Hall, Inc., 1990), pp. 489–93.

[2] Unification and fragmentation influences refer to concepts initially identified by John Fayerweather. A unification influence facilitates the global strategy and competitive distinctiveness of MNEs. A fragmentation influence requires a location-specific response from the firm. See John Fayerweather, *International Business Strategy and Administration* (Cambridge, Mass.: Ballinger Publishing, 1982), pp. 300–27.

[3] Vern Terpstra, *International Dimensions of Marketing* (Boston: PWS-Kent Publishing, 1988), p. 87. Some of the other examples in this section are also noted in this reference.

[4] "Toyota Concern to Build Car to Sell for $1,250," *New York Times*, February 9, 1956, p. 2.

[5] For numerous examples, see David Ricks, *Big Business Blunders* (Homewood, Ill.: Richard D. Irwin, 1983).

[6] David P. Rutenberg, *Multinational Management* (Boston: Little, Brown, 1982), chap. 1, "Organizational Structures and Tensions" (First National City Bank case), pp. 1–9.

[7] This concern was first expressed in Jean-Jacques Servan-Schreiber, *The American Challenge* (New York: Atheneum Publishers, 1968).

[8] Information obtained during interviews with Ford Motor Company's world headquarters staff, Dearborn, Michigan, in 1971 and 1972. See also "Cleveland Plant to Manufacture Pinto Engine Castings," *Iron News*, November 1971, p. 4; and "Ford to Build Mavericks in Brazil; Plans $150 Million Investment," *The Wall Street Journal*, March 3, 1972, p. 3.

[9] Philip R. Cateora, *International Marketing* (Homewood, Ill.: Richard D. Irwin, Inc., 1990), pp. 570–71.

[10] Keegan, *Global Marketing Management*, pp. 489–95. (Some of the percentages were calculated from data presented in Keegan.)

Monster Chomp Cookies in Brazil

Beatrice Companies, Inc. is a highly diversified producer of processed foods, beverages, consumer products, chemicals, and other products in 30 countries, with sales offices and licensees in over 120 more. In 1984, Beatrice's sales were about $12 billion worldwide, with U.S. sales accounting for about three quarters of that amount. In that year, less than 5 percent of Beatrice's sales were made in Latin America, although the company was then a market leader in most of the products it sold in the region.

Beatrice Enters Brazil

Beatrice entered the Brazilian market in 1983, through its acquisition of 80 percent ownership in an existing local firm, Ailiram, S. A. Ailiram was a local manufacturer of cookies and candies in the São Paulo state, selling mainly to retail stores outside the city of São Paulo. Ailiram's cookies were very similar to those sold by dozens of other Brazilian firms—plain, fairly undifferentiated, round cookies and biscuits made of wheat flour and sugar. The company was formed in 1945, and by 1983 it had grown to include two manufacturing plants and 1,000 employees. Beatrice intended to use Ailiram as a base for entering the national Brazilian market, first by pursuing sales to supermarkets—a fast-growing segment for food product distribution—in the city of São Paulo, then by expanding product lines and distribution throughout the whole country.

Soon after the acquisition, managers of the subsidiary were planning a strategy to break into the highly competitive market for sales of cookies to supermarkets. A survey showed that about a dozen other companies already sold similar products to leading supermarkets and that Ailiram would have very little chance to displace any of them unless it produced a new type of cookie.

The Creation of Monster Chomp

On a trip to the United States, one Ailiram executive noticed the highly successful Monster Chomp cookies that were sold there. She felt that this product would have good sales potential in Brazil since cookies of this kind were not being sold in that country. Ailiram's attempt to sell to supermarkets would be greatly enhanced by the appealing packaging of Monstrinho Creck cookies. These would sell at the top end of the cookie market, where only a few other brands were

---

This case is reprinted from *Case Studies in International Business for ESL*, by Christine Grosse and Robert Grosse, Prentice Hall, 1988. Reprinted by permission of Prentice Hall. Eleven additional cases on international business are available in this same source.

competing. By successfully selling Monstrinho Creck cookies, Ailiram would establish an image of high-quality, innovative products and demonstrate to supermarkets that it knew how to mass-market cookies. Both of these goals had been set by Beatrice, which wanted to compete nationally throughout Brazil in both cookie and candy markets.

The Monster Chomps sold in the United States were much thicker and softer than the cookies normally sold in Brazil. Ailiram's managers felt that cookies had to be hard and flat in order to meet Brazilian children's tastes—but that their shape could be unusual. Thus, they decided to produce a hard, flat cookie that looked as if a monster had taken a bite out of it. The flavors initially chosen were chocolate, vanilla, and coconut.

A completely new package design was chosen to appeal to children between the ages of 5 and 12. (A survey showed that children up to the age of 10 accounted for almost 50 percent of Brazilian cookie consumption.) The package, shown in the accompanying illustrations, depicts a friendly monster with a chomp out of a cookie on its front. On the back of the package, some child's

TABLE 1

Monstrinho Creck
Cookies—Eight-Month
Forecast, 1984

	May	June	July	Aug.	Sept.	Oct.	Nov.	Dec.
Price index	100							166
Retail price (200 grams)	600							
Ailiram sales price (net, 200 grams, Cr$)	400	423	456	484	512	545	578	615
Ailiram sales price (net, 1 kilogram, Cr$)	2,000	2,115	2,280	2,420	2,560	2,725	2,890	3,075
Ailiram sales (tons)	120	350	280	300	330	350	330	300
Net trade sales (Cr$ millions)	240	740	638	726	845	954	954	923

game is shown and a lesson about safety or some other constructive message is presented. Thus, the package provides both an appealing, funny advertisement and an educational lesson.

The advertising campaign to introduce Monstrinho Creck in the São Paulo area was quite expensive. Initial estimates were for a total marketing cost of about U.S.$500,000. As shown in Tables 1 and 2, this expense would virtually eliminate any profit for the first year of sales. Subsequently, prospects appeared very good for a growing profit margin and greater sales. The expected return on sales of 13–15 percent is similar to that of other Beatrice products, but this expected return does not take into account for the high risk of doing business in Brazil at present (i.e., during the debt crisis of the 1980s).

TABLE 2

Monstrinho Creck Cookies—Three-Year Forecast

	1984 (8 mos.)	1985	1986
Price index	100	180	260
Exchange rate (average, Cr$)	1,600/U.S.$	2,880/U.S.$	4,160/U.S.$
Avg. Ailiram sales price (net, 1 kilogram, Cr$)	2,551	4,592	6,631
Ailiram sales (tons)	2,360	6,065	7,670

	1984 (8 mos.)		1985		1986	
	Cr$ mil.	Percent	Cr$ mil.	Percent	Cr$ mil.	Percent
Net trade sales	6,020	100.0	27,850	100.0	50,860	100.0
Cost	3,492	58.0	15,875	57.0	28,990	57.0
Gross margin	2,528	42.0	11,975	43.0	21,870	43.0
Advertising	491	8.2	1,453	5.2	2,107	4.1
Sales promotion, trade	122	2.0	29	0.1	–	–
Sales promotion, consumer	50	0.8	111	0.4	51	0.1
Sales promotion, merchandising	71	1.2	278	1.0	334	0.7
Market research	49	0.8	79	0.3	51	0.1
Total marketing expenses	783	13.0	1,950	7.0	2,543	5.0
Gross contribution	1,745	29.0	10,025	36.0	19,327	38.0
Sales expense	1,264	21.0	5,292	19.0	9,663	19.0
Administrative expense	289	4.8	1,114	4.0	2,034	4.0
Total sales and administrative expense	1,553	25.8	6,406	23.0	11,697	23.0
Profit contribution	192	3.2	3,619	13.0	7,630	15.0

15

Accounting and Taxation

Accounting systems vary considerably country by country. This presents problems for MNEs that have to report operations on a consolidated basis in the system of the parent company's country. Moreover, parent companies must account for foreign purchases and sales and report foreign operations on their own books. Tax systems differ country by country, and MNEs want to avoid being "double-taxed" on profits that subsidiaries earn and send home. This chapter covers such issues. The main goals of the chapter are to:

1. Explain how and why accounting and taxation are different in MNEs than in domestic companies.

2. Explore why countries differ regarding accounting systems.

3. Describe how MNEs account for foreign purchases and sales and report foreign operations on the parent's books.

4. Describe how MNEs report foreign and domestic operations on a consolidated basis, including
   a. The definition and handling of conversion and translation gains and losses.
   b. U.S. financial standards on consolidations and disclosures.

5. Examine how income deferral and foreign tax credits work to the benefit of the MNE.

6. Examine accounting/management information systems in MNEs.

7. Explain how MNEs achieve compliance with the U.S. Foreign Corrupt Practices Act.

INTRODUCTION

Accounting and tax matters are typically seen as administrative concerns. Financial reporting requires adherence to a set of prescribed procedures and standards. Tax laws mandate a certain type of record-keeping and reporting and the payment of taxes to the appropriate authorities. For the purely domestic firm, accounting and tax matters do not usually result in competitive advantages—although every manager certainly wants to keep as much profit as possible by minimizing taxes.

Accounting Differences of MNEs

For the MNE, the situation is somewhat different. Accounting and tax matters are obviously more complex, and they can have a direct effect on the MNE's profitability and competitiveness. The astute handling of taxes can, for example, result in legitimate tax avoidance and increased profits or deferred taxes. Why locate profits in France, which has a 42 percent tax rate, in contrast to Taiwan, where the rate is 25 percent? Also, timely and accurate MNE system-wide financial reporting can lead to more informed management (and better management decisions) and more informed investors (which, hopefully, makes the firm a more attractive investment). Enhanced profits and more effective management should make the firm more competitive. Relationships among competitiveness, multinational operations, international accounting, and taxation will be visited at various points in this chapter.

Financial accounting systems differ country by country, and managers in multinational firms must be aware of these differences to know what information their accounting records are really conveying. For similar reasons, managers must be aware of the special circumstances and rules affecting the handling of international transactions and the parent company's consolidated statements reporting on the MNE's global situation. Financial accounting at the subsidiary and parent levels reflects not only traditional accounting practices but also laws and regulations regarding disclosure (with publicly held companies) and taxation. Variations in accounting practices and in exchange rates, which alter the unit of measurement, complicate the financial accounting systems of MNEs.

In addition to financial accounting systems, most firms utilize managerial accounting systems or managerial information systems that reflect, in some cases, slight modifications to financial accounting data already generated or, in other cases, the collection and presentation of additional data useful for managerial control purposes. This chapter deals with managerial accounting when the firm is operating cross-nationally and cross-culturally. (In general, management control systems are discussed in Chapter 16 in the section on control.)

Tax Differences of MNEs

Tax laws also differ country by country. Moreover, tax laws must address the location of income and define the territorial extent of the jurisdiction of the taxing authorities. Taxation at just the domestic level can be quite complex. It can be even more complex at the international level. This chapter presents some highlights regarding taxation in the MNE and MNEs' strategies for avoiding or reducing taxes. It discusses key tax topics relating to multinational operations, such as deferral, Subpart F income, and foreign tax credits. It also discusses the tax advantages of using a foreign sales corporation. A final section of the chapter deals with management responsibilities under the U.S. Foreign Corrupt Practices Act.

ACCOUNTING

Because accounting systems deal with numbers, they are perceived as being precise. And in the sense that they report specific numerical measurements, they are precise. But the purpose of an accounting system is to convey information—and measurement of activity in monetary terms is simply the mechanism used to achieve this purpose. What is to be measured, how it is to be measured, and how often it is to be measured are important questions that an accounting system must address. Answering them involves people and judgments. An **accounting system** is thus a contrived system. Its objectives, rules, and methods are established by people with needs that they hope the system will fulfill. It is, in brief, place specific.

Country Differences in Accounting Systems

Consistent with this perspective, Zeff's classic *Forging Accounting Principles in Five Countries* demonstrated that such influences as theory, practice, and social, political, and economic conditions come together to determine an accounting system.[1] Early on Choi and Mueller identified 15 such conditions, some of which follow.[2]

1. *Type of Economy Involved.* Inventory methods, audit functions, and cost accounting techniques are affected by whether the economy involved is agrarian, extractive, or industrialized.

2. *Legal System.* Code law countries favor codification of accounting principles and procedures; common law countries are typified by private, professional organizations that establish accounting policies.

3. *Political System.* In centrally controlled economies of communist states, profit and the private ownership of fixed assets and land may not even exist. Political systems are also known to have exported accounting practices, as in the British Commonwealth countries and in former Dutch and French possessions.

4. *Social Climate.* Concepts of public disclosure and social responsibility have had considerable influence on accounting practices in the United States; in Switzerland, which requires substantially less public disclosure than the United States, the influence of such concepts is far smaller. In some Latin countries, accounting is equated with bookkeeping and seen as socially unimportant.

5. *General Levels of Education and Facilitating Processes.* People need to know mathematics if the quantitative information in an accounting system is to be used effectively. Computerization requires the presence of electronic data processing installations.

As expected, accounting practices are found to vary country by country. For example, disclosure of the cost of sales is a reporting requirement in Brazil and the United States, a minority practice in the United Kingdom, seldom found in Sweden, and not permitted in Germany.[3] (Periodic reports published by major accounting firms and available in most university libraries present highlights of accounting practices in selected countries.)

Accounting for International Transactions

Firms active in international business often deal in foreign currencies. Exports and imports, for example, may well be denominated in foreign currency and entail trade credit of 30, 60, or 90 days or longer. Dividends paid by a foreign subsidiary are denominated in the home currency of that subsidiary

FIGURE 15–1

Accounting for Foreign
Currency Transactions: The
Three Alternative
Situations—Export Sale
Illustration

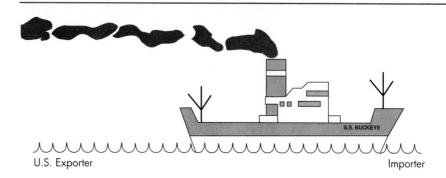

U.S. Exporter   Importer

1. Foreign currency received at time of sales and sold for dollars

1,600 DM's

2. Trade credit extended to importer — no hedge

Account Receivable
1,600 DM's

Account Payable
1,600 DM's

3. Trade credit extended to importer — hedged

Account Receivable
1,600 DM's

Account Payable
1,600 DM's

Forward Exchange Contract
Sell 1,600 DM's at 1.7 DM per $ when received in the future

and are usually declared weeks prior to actual payment. Debt denominated in foreign currency entails predictable servicing requirements that involve purchasing foreign currency for delivery at some known future date. Such **international transactions** have to be reflected in the company's accounting records.

Three alternative situations may be involved in accounting for transactions denominated in foreign currency. To understand these alternatives, consider the export sale illustrated in Figure 15–1.

Alternative 1: Immediate Payment The exporting firm does not hold the foreign currency beyond the date of its receipt, which is also the date the sale is made. Financial accounting standards in the United States require that assets, liabilities, sales, and expenses denominated initially in foreign currency be reflected in the accounts in the dollar equivalent on the date they arise. In the present case, the foreign currency would be converted into dollars in the exporter's accounts on the date the sale is made. The exporter's accounts would also reflect the net dollars received when the foreign exchange is sold.

To illustrate, consider an export sale to a German buyer for 1,600 deutsche marks (DMs). On the date of sale, the DM is trading at 1.6 DM per dollar. Neglecting bank charges for selling the DMs, the sale generates $1,000 in revenues for the exporter. Excluding the credit to finished goods inventory and the debit to cost of goods sold, the debit and credit entries are simply as follows:

Dr: Cash $1,000
Cr: Sales Revenues $1,000

Alternative 2: Trade Credit In this case, the exporter is willing to accept payment for the goods in foreign currency at some future date *and* does not cover this exposure with a forward market transaction. The accounting principle identified in alternative 1 would still hold as far as initial entries are concerned. Thus, the entries on the date of sale are as follows:

Dr: Account Receivable $1,000
Cr: Sales Revenues $1,000

(Note that the account debited is Account Receivable and not Cash. This reflects the fact that the sale was made on trade credit.)

During the period of time for which the trade credit was extended, the DM depreciates to 1.8 DM per dollar. This lowers the dollar value of the sale of the export to $889 at the time the receivable is collected. (Don't forget that the sale, by contract, is for precisely 1,600 DMs.) Settlement of the account thus involves a **conversion loss** (that is, a loss when an account is settled), which is reflected on the exporter's books in this way:

Dr: Cash $889
Dr: Foreign Exchange Transactions $111
Cr: Account Receivable $1,000

The Foreign Exchange Transactions account is debited for foreign exchange losses and credited for foreign exchange gains. It is an income statement account that is closed out to profit and loss at the end of the accounting period.

To complicate matters a bit, consider the same case but with the exporter's accounting period ending during the time period in which the trade credit is extended—and after the DM depreciation. To reflect conditions as factually as possible, the foreign exchange loss is reflected in the end-of-period reports as follows:

Dr: Foreign Exchange Transactions $111
Cr: Account Receivable $111

The foreign exchange loss in this case is termed a **translation loss** (that is, a loss on a transaction that has yet to be settled). Later, when the export is paid for, the following accounting entries are made:

Dr: Cash $889
Cr: Account Receivable $889

Can you Figure This One Out?

On December 15, 1990, Keebler Co., a wholly owned U.S. subsidiary of the British firm United Biscuits (Holdings), Ltd., declared a dividend of $2 per share, payable on January 15, 1991. The British parent holds 1 million shares. (All of these figures are hypothetical.) Assuming that the applicable accounting rules are like those described for the U.S. exporter in the accompanying text, that United Biscuits closed its fiscal year on December 31, that from December 16 to December 28, 1990, the British pound went from $1.92 to $1.94 and that there was no forward market hedge on the dividend receivable, what accounting entries would United Biscuits show on its books on December 15, 1990, December 31, 1990, and January 15, 1991? What entries would Keebler Co. show on these same dates? ■

Alternative 3: Trade Credit—Hedged   This alternative is like alternative 2, except that the exposure of the foreign exchange receivable because of the export is exactly offset by a forward exchange contract requiring the sale of 1,600 DMs. The initial entries related to the sale of the goods and the account receivable would remain precisely as shown above. However, subsequent entries will reflect the forward market transaction. No accounting entries are made to record the forward contract at the time the contract is made (i.e., at the time of the sale). Assuming that the forward contract rate is 1.7 DM per dollar, the dollars collected by the exporter (when the DMs are received per the export sale and paid out to complete the forward contract) total $941. The accounting principle is that forward contracts offsetting specific foreign currency receivables or payables are included in the dollar basis of the original foreign currency transaction. Hence, the subsequent accounting entries are as follows:

```
Dr: Cash . . . . . . . . . . . . . . . . . . . . . . . . . . . . . . . .   $941
Dr: Foreign Exchange Transactions . . . . . . . . . . . . . . . . . . . . .   $59
Cr: Account Receivable . . . . . . . . . . . . . . . . . . . . . . . . . .           $1,000
```

In this instance, the foreign exchange loss (debit) has been reduced to $59 because of the forward exchange contract. If the contract had been written at a rate of 1.6 DM per dollar, there would be no foreign exchange transactions loss at all.

In their 1979 international survey of accounting practices, Fitzgerald, Stickler, and Watts reported that the U.S. accounting practices described in connection with alternatives 1, 2, and 3 are consistent with the accounting practices followed in most other advanced industrial societies.[4] In 1988, Kubin confirmed this was still the situation.[5]

Consolidations

A **consolidated statement** is a single balance sheet or income statement that combines the financial accounts of the parent and its subsidiaries. All MNEs, U.S. or otherwise, prepare consolidated statements, so that managers, lenders, investors, and others can understand the overall financial situation of the firm. **Consolidation** is required of publicly held U.S. firms. It is a tedious process requiring adherence to specific procedures and is performed at the parent company level. Before consolidation is discussed in more detail, some basic definitions and concepts must be understood. (Recall that we are mainly concerned with the situation pertinent to the *U.S.* MNE. The situation would be different for other parent-company nationalities.)

A consolidated statement pertains only to a parent and its subsidiaries. For accounting purposes, a **subsidiary** is a foreign corporation more than 50 percent of whose common stock is owned by the parent (implying parental control). Technically, if the parent owns 50 percent or less of the foreign entity's common stock, that entity is an **affiliate,** not a subsidiary. The foreign entity is considered a **branch** if it is not incorporated in the foreign country but exists as an office or extension of the parent and is legally constituted as a branch. If affiliates and branches are not consolidated per se, how are they handled at the MNE level? This question is important, and answering it necessitates a brief digression from our discussion of consolidation.

The parent company's books (nonconsolidated) carry any foreign entity (subsidiary, affiliate, or branch) as an investment reflected on the asset side of the balance sheet. A branch is reflected in the plant and equipment accounts, for example, depending on what buildings, furniture, and so on are physically in place at the foreign entity. An affiliate or subsidiary is shown in a specific investment account, such as Investments in Foreign Companies.

Income from a foreign branch is considered the same as income to the parent since the branch is simply an extension of the parent. Income from an affiliate can be handled by either the cost method or the equity method, depending on the level of parent company ownership. If parent ownership is below 20 percent, the **cost method** must be used—that is, the affiliate's income is recognized on the parent's books only when the parent receives it in the form of dividends. When such income occurs, income is credited and cash is debited. If parent ownership is 20 percent or more (meaning the foreign entity can be an affiliate or a subsidiary and is not just a financial investment), the **equity method** is used—that is, the parent's investment account is increased by the income that the foreign entity earns, in proportion to the parent's ownership share, whether or not that income is paid out in dividends. In this case, income at the affiliate, as allocated to the parent, is credited and the investment account is debited. When a dividend is paid out of the earnings, the investment account is credited and cash is debited. Figure 15–2 illustrates these alternative methods for handling income.

Preparing a Consolidated Report

A **consolidated report** involves the line-by-line summary of the balance sheet and income statement accounts of both the parent and its subsidiaries. A first step in this process is to restate subsidiaries' accounts, if necessary, to reflect the generally accepted accounting principles used by the parent company. In preparing a consolidated report, accounts denominated in foreign currencies at subsidiaries have to be translated into the currency of the parent company's country, and the question of which exchange rate should be used to do this has to be resolved. For the United States, the rule is to use the exchange rate applicable to dividend payments by the subsidiary. In some cases, this rate is a market rate used for all foreign exchange transactions; in others, where exchange restrictions or multiple rates exist, it is the dividend rate that is or would be applied.

FIGURE 15–2

Accounting for
Income—Parent Company's
Books

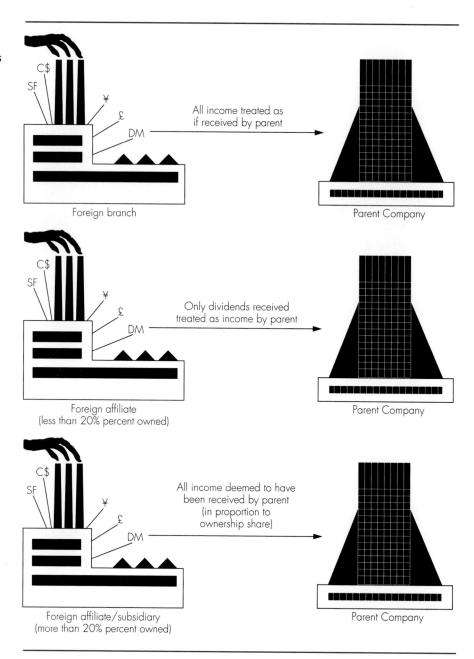

Foreign branch

All income treated as
if received by parent

Parent Company

Foreign affiliate
(less than 20% percent owned)

Only dividends received
treated as income by parent

Parent Company

Foreign affiliate/subsidiary
(more than 20% percent owned)

All income deemed to have
been received by parent
(in proportion to
ownership share)

Parent Company

Another question arises when the exchange rate used varies through time, that is, when there has been a devaluation or revaluation between the currency of the subsidiary country and the currency of the parent country. Two kinds of accounting-related management problems are generated by exchange-rate changes. One has to do with conversion gains and losses; the other, with translation gains and losses.

Conversion Gains/Losses   When the subsidiary has assets or liabilities that require payment or receipt in a foreign currency and the value of that currency changes relative to the currency of the subsidiary's home country, conversion gains or losses are generated. The values of accounts so affected change in terms of the subsidiary's currency, and these changes alter real future cash flows at the subsidiary level. The situation discussed here is illustrated below in the case of Sympático, S.A., a Mexican subsidiary of New York-based Friendly Industries, Inc. Half of Sympático's accounts receivable are due from customers in the United States and are dollar based, as is the parent company loan. The remainder of Sympático's accounts receivable are based in Mexican pesos. The peso, in our illustration, has devalued from 3,000 to 3,750 pesos per dollar during the 1991 fiscal year. To keep it simple, let's assume that Sympático's performance in FY1991 was "flat." Indeed, had it not been for the devaluation, Sympático's books at the close of FY1991 and FY1990 would be identical.

SYMPÁTICO, S.A.
Balance Sheet
(thousands of pesos)

	End of Fiscal Year	
	1990	**1991**
Assets		
Cash.	45,000	45,000
Accounts receivable		
Peso-denominated	60,000	60,000
Dollar-denominated	60,000	75,000
Plant and equipment	180,000	180,000
Liabilities		
Accounts payable.	90,000	90,000
Bank loan	75,000	75,000
Parent company loan	45,000	56,250
Net worth.	135,000	138,750

At the close of FY1991, Sympático had to adjust the peso value of its accounts receivable to reflect the 15 million added pesos it would receive when it converts the $20,000 account receivable as it is collected. Likewise, the $15,000 loan from Friendly remains at $15,000 regardless of the peso/dollar value. Sympático will now need 56.25 million pesos to pay it off, not the 45 million pesos reflected in the 1990 statement. The net effect of these two adjustments is shown in a 3.75 million peso increase in net worth (in this case).

Once the subsidiaries' accounts have been adjusted by the parent to reflect potential conversion gains/losses, the preparation of the consolidated statements can proceed. The basic rules for U.S. MNEs are fairly simple: assets and liabilities, balance sheet items, are translated at the rate of exchange in effect on the date of the consolidated statement; revenues and expenses, income statement items, are translated at the average rate of exchange in effect during the reporting period.

To illustrate, let's return to our example of Sympático, S.A. and Friendly Industries, Inc.—but let's show Sympático as having made some profits during FY1991.

SYMPÁTICO, S.A.
Income Statement
January 1, 1991 through December 31, 1991
(thousands of pesos)

Revenues		$675,000
Expenses		
Cost of goods sold	$405,000	
Selling and administrative costs.	135,000	
Interest on debt	33,750	
Depreciation—buildings	16,875	
General management costs	16,875	
Total expenses		607,500
Operating income		67,500
Income taxes		33,750
Net income		33,750

If the deterioration in the dollar value of the peso occurred at an even rate during 1991, the average rate of exchange would be the midpoint between the January 1, 1991 rate of 3,000 pesos/dollar and the December 31, 1991 rate of 3,750 pesos/dollar, or 3,375 pesos/dollar. This 3,375 pesos/dollar rate would be the one used to translate Sympático's income statement accounts. Note that this rate is applied to all accounts, even those whose values reflected on the income statement are based on historical costs–"depreciation" and perhaps "costs of goods sold." To illustrate, two income statements for Friendly Industries are presented below—one for the parent alone, the other for the parent and the subsidiary on a consolidated basis.

FRIENDLY INDUSTRIES, INC.
Income Statement
January 1, 1991 through December 31, 1991
(thousands of dollars)

	Parent Company		Consolidated	
Revenues		$36,000		$36,200
Expenses				
Cost of goods sold	$18,000		$18,120	
Selling and administrative				
costs	5,000		5,040	
Interest.	2,000		2,010	
Depreciation	3,000		3,005	
General management	1,000		1,005	
Total expenses		29,000		29,180
Operating income		7,000		7,020
Income taxes		3,000		3,010
Net income		$ 4,000		$ 4,010

It should be noted that the adjusted balance sheet items—accounts receivable and the parent company loan—do not directly affect the income statements of either the parent or the subsidiary. The exchange rate change will increase the interest in pesos that Sympático pays to service its debt to the parent company. This interest is included in the interest expense indicated on the income statements.

Translation Gains/Losses   Balance sheet consolidation is a bit more complicated than income statement consolidation, although mid-1980s changes approved by the U.S. Financial Accounting Standards Board have substantially simplified the consolidation procedures of MNEs. The exchange rate used is the rate in effect on the date of the consolidated balance sheet. Prior to consolidation, as noted above, the books at the subsidiary level must be adjusted to reflect changes in assets or liabilities due to an exchange-rate change. Thus, Sympático had to change its accounts receivable and parent company loan accounts to show their changed peso values when the peso went from 3,000 to 3,750 per dollar. These changes resulted in a 3,750,000 peso credit adjustment to Sympático's net worth. They will have an identical impact on the company's consolidated net worth. Indeed, since exchange-rate changes alter the values of asset and liability accounts reported on a consolidated basis and since companies typically show a positive net worth where assets exceed liabilities in value, adjustments will have to be made to the consolidated net worth accounts.

These adjustments offset the net effect or residual resulting from the inequality between assets and liabilities and from the fact that all of the subsidiary's asset and liability accounts are translated to the consolidated balance sheet at the same rate of exchange. These are translation gains/losses resulting from consolidation. There are thus two sources of adjustments to consolidated net worth—those resulting from *conversion gains/losses* as the subsidiary adjusts its own books to reflect changes in the subsidiary's own local-currency value of assets and liabilities based on currencies other than its own, and those resulting from *translation gains/losses* as the structure of accounts (i.e., assets exceed liabilities) and the translation rules regarding the use of a single exchange rate result in residuals that have to be recorded in the consolidated statement.

Consolidation Illustrated

Let's proceed by illustrating these principles in our case with Friendly Industries. As a first step, Sympático's balance sheet, changed to show the situation where Sympático actually earned 33.75 million pesos profit during FY1991, appears below. (For simplicity, the 33.75 million peso increase in net worth is balanced by a similar increase in cash.)

SYMPÁTICO, S.A.
Balance Sheet
December 31, 1991
(thousands of pesos)

Assets

Cash	$ 78,750
Accounts receivable (total).	135,000
Plant and equipment	180,000

Liabilities

Accounts payable	90,000
Bank loan.	75,000
Parent company loan	56,250

Net worth	172,500

Before consolidation, any intracompany transactions are netted out. For example, Sympático's parent company loan, a liability, is offset by an asset on the parent's (nonconsolidated) books reflecting the loan due from Sympático. Similarly, Friendly's investment account showing its ownership of Sympático is netted out against Sympático's net worth account balance reflecting Friendly's ownership position. Assuming that Friendly, the parent, had a flat year in 1991, the consolidated balance sheets for FY1990 and FY1991 might thus look as follows:

FRIENDLY INDUSTRIES, INC.
Consolidated Balance Sheet
(thousands of dollars)

	End of Fiscal Year	
	1990	1991
Assets		
Cash.	$ 815	$ 821
Accounts receivable	3,040	3,036
Plant and equipment	16,060	16,048
Liabilities		
Accounts payable.	630	624
Bank loans.	825	820
Long-term debt	10,000	10,000
Net worth		
Common stock.	3,600	3,600
Earned surplus.	4,860	4,860
Cumulative translation adjustment	0	1

The net result of the consolidation is a onetime $1,000 credit to the net worth account Cumulative Translation Adjustment. The $1,000 credit can be explained by looking at the changes in the dollar basis of each individual account at the end of FY1990 and FY1991. Recall that such changes can be caused by exchange-rate changes resulting in (1) conversion gains or losses, (2) translation gains or losses, and (3) changes in the subsidiary's accounts owing to operations during the period (the 33.75 million peso increase in cash in the present example). The changes in Friendly's accounts can be explained as follows:

Account	Change	Comment
Cash	$ 6,000 dr	Gain of 33.75 million pesos during fiscal year yields a dollar gain of $9,000. Translation loss on 45 million pesos is $3,000.
Accounts Receivable	4,000 cr	Conversion gain of $4,000 on 15 million peso write-up on dollar-based receivables. Translation loss on 120 million pesos is $8,000.
Plant and Equipment	12,000 cr	Translation loss on 180 million pesos is $12,000.
Accounts Payable	6,000 dr	Translation gain on 90 million pesos is $6,000.
Bank Loan	5,000 dr	Translation gain on 75 million pesos is $5,000.
Cumulative Translation Adjustment	1,000 cr	Entry to balance out net effect of conversion and translation gains/losses.

Note that the sum of the debit changes equals the sum of the credit changes, so that the net effect of the changes is zero. This follows since the entry to Cumulative Translation Adjustment is a balancing entry. This is always the way in which residual gains or losses derived during consolidation are handled.

U.S. Financial Accounting Standards on Consolidation and Disclosures

The accounting procedures just discussed regarding consolidations are those required of U.S. MNEs by Financial Accounting Standard 52. Specifically, FAS 52 requires that

1. A subsidiary's books be kept in the **functional currency** of the subsidiary, that is, its home currency (pesos, in Sympático's case).
2. Changes in a subsidiary's foreign-currency assets and liabilities be reflected in changes in its functional currency records.
3. The exchange rate on the balance sheet date be used to translate assets and liabilities from the subsidiary's functional currency accounts into the parent's **reporting currency** accounts (dollars, in Friendly's case).
4. A **weighted-average exchange rate** be used to translate income statement accounts from the functional currency into the reporting currency.
5. Net gains or losses arising from consolidation be reported directly as charges or credits to a special account in stockholders' equity (that is, to Cumulative Translation Adjustment in the Friendly case).

An exception to these rules occurs, however, when the subsidiary is operating in a hyperinflationary environment or when its operations, financing, and cash flow are highly dependent on the parent. The parent's currency then serves as both the functional currency and the reporting currency. In such a situation, assets carried at historical costs—fixed assets and, in some instances, inventories—are translated at historical rates of exchange. Other balance sheet items continue to be translated at current rates.

Income statement accounts similarly differentiate between accounts that are carried at historical costs and those that are not. In the former instance, such accounts use historical costs and the historical exchange rates that were in effect when the purchases were made. In the latter, such accounts continue to use the average exchange rate for the period. Translation gains or losses are taken as periodic charges or credits to income. They are not taken directly to equity.

The importance of understanding FAS 52 is underscored by Choi's observation that the current-rate translation basis (notwithstanding the exceptions noted) required by FAS 52 in the United States is also the method that is used most frequently in Japan and Europe.[6]

Financial accounting disclosure, including disclosure of foreign operations, is accomplished by means of the consolidated statements reporting just discussed. Reporting just on foreign operations is another matter. For U.S. firms, FAS 14 is the controlling policy statement. FAS 14 requires financial reporting by business segments, including geographic segments. To illustrate, Table 15–1 presents a financial report pertaining to the Coca-Cola Company's global operations.

Accounting practices and standards could be treated in considerably greater depth. Here, however, we have confined ourselves to presenting some important concepts that should help managers better understand some of the fundamental accounting implications of multinational operations.

Managerial Accounting/Information Systems

Accounting information systems pertaining to management decision making can be varied and complex. Such systems are conditioned by many influences—the nature of the financial reports; the records needed to prepare the financial reports and the usefulness of such records (or the ease with which they can be

TABLE 15–1

The Coca-Cola Company's
1989 Performance by
Geographic Profit Centers
(in millions of U.S. dollars)

	Identifiable Operating Assets	Net Operating Revenue	Operating Income
European Community	$1,342.8	$1,855.1	$ 540.6
Northeast Europe and Africa	328.8	425.2	147.3
Latin America	515.4	646.2	226.7
Pacific and Canada	652.7	1,959.5	612.8
Corporate	1,036.4	57.6	(269.8)
Total United States	2,476.0	4,022.2	468.2
Total The Coca-Cola Company and subsidiaries	$6,352.1	$8,965.8	$1,725.8

Source: The Coca-Cola Company, *1989 Annual Report,* p. 58.

modified) for decision-making purposes; product configuration; process technology; local financial practices; the legal, cultural, and social environments; and so on.

The key issue regarding an appropriate **management information system (MIS)** is essentially similar to the issue already discussed on product configuration and advertising in Chapter 14. That issue is to determine the appropriate balance between a **universal MIS**—uniform, easily understood at all management levels, and efficient to produce—and an MIS that is substantially adapted in each instance to fit the nuances of discrete, local environments.

For the ethnocentric MNE, the universal MIS is the ideal. Decisions at the parent level dominate the MNE network, and the parent generally imposes operating standards that determine operations everywhere. Parent company managers insist on information flows that are easily understood and consistent in their measurement of activities at all subsidiaries. Note that this is not a bad MIS policy for the ethnocentric MNE. It is in agreement with the firm's corporate strategies and functional policies. The fact that the firm dominates a global market, and that the parent is the source of this dominance, allows it to disregard local influences on operations. Production, marketing, and other functions are carried on in the same way at both the parent and subsidiary levels. For example, IBM's personal computer plant in Mexico operates under production standards and an MIS similar to those that are in place in its U.S. personal computer plants.

For the polycentric MNE, a universal MIS makes little sense. Operations decisions and key managerial decisions are made at the subsidiary level. There is little need to accumulate information for use at the parent level. For example, Ford-Germany's cars have differed substantially from Ford's U.S. cars, and Ford's U.S. and German markets have been geographically segmented. Installing a global MIS would be of questionable value to Ford—and, in fact, the parent and its European subsidiaries were fairly autonomous, with infrequent information exchanges below the board of directors level, until some product integration policies came on line in the early 1970s.

For the geocentric MNE, the need is to find the balance between an MIS that consistently portrays operations at all subsidiaries and one that accommodates local nuances giving real meaning to the data and information transmitted. For example, H. J. Heinz has manufactured powdered baby food in Italy which was packaged in the United States and sold in the People's Republic of China (PRC). (This was an interim arrangement pending completion of a baby-food processing and packaging plant in the PRC.) In this case, Heinz had to transmit a lot of information internationally and also to develop the information base it needed in order to successfully market a product in China. For the geocentric MNE, such as Heinz, finding the appropriate balance between global information needs and local market information needs is a compelling necessity.

The theory of the MNE discussed in Chapter 2 revealed that MNEs have several competitive advantages over purely local firms. The effective transmission and implementation of these advantages within the parent-subsidiary MNE network gives the MNE units their competitiveness. This means that management at all levels must have some fundamental, universal understanding regarding technology, operations, and so on. This, in turn, requires information feedback, effective management communication, and the like. The MIS must contain some measurements that are common to all locales. Where local nuances obviate this possibility, extra care must be taken to train managers in what their MIS is really telling them.

TAXATION AND THE MNE

The issue of taxation is especially important to the MNE since the MNE operates in multiple taxing jurisdictions (i.e., countries) and has options for avoiding or deferring taxation in certain countries. Income, which is typically taxed at the source, has more than a single source when it is generated at the subsidiary level. The country in which the subsidiary is located views the subsidiary as a source; the country in which the parent is located views the MNE structure as a source. In some cases, U.S. MNEs can defer U.S. income taxes by retaining profits at the subsidiary level; in other cases, they cannot. Through foreign sales corporations, U.S. firms can defer taxes. In all cases, however, the U.S. Internal Revenue Service has the upper hand. It has the final word on how much a firm's taxes are. This section discusses these and related topics.

Income Taxes – The General Case

The after-tax income to the parent generated by profits at the subsidiary can vary considerably, depending on the handling of foreign taxes in the country of the parent company. The payment of the foreign tax by the subsidiary can be ignored (resulting, effectively, in double taxation), acknowledged as an income deduction (as it is in the United States for income taxes paid to state governments), or recognized as a dollar-for-dollar tax credit. Table 15–2 illustrates the use of these alternative approaches and their bottom-line results.

The example in Table 15–2 gives quite different results, depending on how the taxes paid by the subsidiary are handled by the tax authorities at the parent company level. The net, after-tax income to the parent ranges from $20,000 to $50,000! Fortunately for business executives who want to minimize taxes, bilateral tax treaties between the United States and a large number of other countries (including Germany, France, the United Kingdom, and other countries where large amounts of U.S. direct investment are in place) allow for a U.S. tax credit for foreign income taxes paid by subsidiaries. It seems reasonable too that if the parent company's country is to allow tax credits for taxes paid by subsidiaries in other countries, the books of those subsidiaries should be "reconstructed" to conform to the depreciation and other tax-related rules of that country. Most tax

TABLE 15–2

Alternative Methods for
Recognizing Taxes Paid at
the Subsidiary by the Parent
Company's Home Country

Item	Double Taxation	Income Deduction	Tax Credit
Operating income	$100,000	$100,000	$100,000
Subsidiary's taxes	30,000	30,000	30,000
After-tax income	70,000	70,000	70,000
Parent's taxes	50,000	35,000	20,000
Net after-tax income to parent	$ 20,000	$ 35,000	$ 50,000

Note: The applicable income tax rate at the subsidiary is 30 percent; at the parent, 50 percent.

authorities, including the U.S. Internal Revenue Service (IRS), reserve the final word on taxes, and Section 482 of the U.S. Tax Code allows the IRS to reconstruct a company's records, if necessary, and to assess the tax due. This assessment, of course, can be appealed to the U.S. Tax Court. Assuming that the tax accounting rules have already been accommodated, let's look at a concrete example to illustrate how tax credits work.

Taxation Illustrated

Magna Corporation's wholly owned French subsidiary, Monser, S.A., has closed its fiscal year with pretax profits of 8 million francs. Monser's dividend payout ratio is 50 percent, and the French income tax rate is 25 percent. Magna's U.S. federal income tax rate is 34 percent, and the rate of exchange is FF 5 per dollar. To complicate matters a little, let's also assume that there is a 10 percent French tax on dividend remittances to foreigners. The actual funds received by Magna can be determined in this way:

Monser's pretax profit	FF 8,000,000
French income taxes	2,000,000
Monser's after-tax profit	6,000,000
Dividends declared (50 percent)	3,000,000
Less: Dividend remittance tax	300,000
Dividends received by Magna	
In French francs	2,700,000
In U.S. dollars	540,000

Since Magna prepares its own income statement, dividends received from a subsidiary represent taxable income, and since there is a tax treaty between the United States and France that allows for a tax credit on foreign taxes paid, the taxes that Magna was imputed to have paid in France on its portion of Monser's income can be deducted from Magna's U.S. tax bill. (Recall that in the absence of a tax treaty, there would be no tax credit for foreign taxes paid.) This may sound more complicated than it really is. Let's return to our example.

Magna received a net-of-all-taxes dividend of $540,000 from Monser. The taxes that this $540,000 bore were the $60,000 (FF 300,000) that Monser paid in dividend remittance taxes, *plus* the French income taxes of $200,000 (FF 1,000,000) that Monser paid on the FF 4 million that it had to generate in pretax income in France to fund payment of the dividend. These taxes are important since if local taxing authorities give a credit for foreign taxes paid, the dividend at the parent's level must be "grossed up" to include these taxes. The **grossed-up dividend** thus represents the total taxable income imputed to have

TABLE 15–3

Corporate Income Tax Rates in Selected Countries as a Percentage of Taxable Income*

Country	Tax Rate	Country	Tax Rate
Denmark	40%	Philippines	35%
France	42	United Kingdom	35
Venezuela	50	United States	34
Turkey	46	Argentina	20
Belgium	41	Japan	37.5
Mexico	36	Taiwan	25
Singapore	32	Liechtenstein	15
Italy	36		

*Rates are for the middle of 1990, except for the United Kingdom, where the rate is as of March 31, 1990. Tax and tax rates may vary with definitions of "Taxable Income," which may differ according to sources and deductibles allowed, with levels of earnings and with uses of earnings, e.g., distributed as dividends or undistributed. Rates shown are maximums.

Source: Data were collected from various sections in Price Waterhouse's *Corporate Taxes: A Worldwide Summary,* 1990 Edition.

been received by the parent. The system has to work this way if the foreign taxes are subsequently credited against U.S. taxes due. Let's return again to our example.

Net dividends received by Magna	$540,000
Plus: Dividend remittance tax	60,000
Plus: French taxes paid by Monser on dividend received by Magna	200,000
Grossed-up dividend to Magna	800,000
U.S. income tax on grossed-up dividend	272,000
Less: Foreign tax credit	260,000
U.S. taxes payable—preliminary determination	$ 12,000

The last line, U.S. taxes payable, is a preliminary determination in that this amount can still be offset by unused foreign tax credits on income from Magna's subsidiaries in other countries or by unused foreign tax credits generated from foreign operations in the past seven years. In no instance, however, can unused foreign tax credits be used to reduce taxes on domestically produced income. The rationale for grossing up the dividend to include the foreign taxes paid on it is that if one tax is to be a credit against the other, they both have to be applied to the same income base. If this were not the case in our example, Magna's initial tax determination would be 34 percent of $540,000, or $183,600. A U.S. tax of $183,600 would be wholly offset by French income taxes of $200,000. That all U.S. taxes could be eliminated in the face of a foreign income tax rate lower than the U.S. rate (i.e., 25 percent/34 percent) is irrational.

Income Taxes—A Special Case

Income tax rates for businesses vary considerably country by country—as Table 15–3 illustrates. In fact, some countries don't tax business income at all and other countries don't tax income from foreign sources. The former include Bermuda and the Cayman Islands; the latter include Panama and Liberia. Wouldn't the astute MNE set up a holding company in one of these countries to receive the dividends of its subsidiaries, which it could then divert (as investments) to other subsidiaries? (If such a holding company never paid a dividend to the U.S. parent, the parent company could defer U.S. income taxes forever.) Many U.S. MNEs pursued this practice prior to the passage of the Revenue Act of 1962. President Kennedy was outspoken in his opposition to the practice, which, although legal, effectively exempted multinationals from paying U.S. income taxes on foreign earnings (for the time being). The provisions of the Revenue Act of 1962 that eliminated the practice were the policy response to his initiatives.

The act specifically defined a **controlled foreign corporation (CFC)** and Subpart F income to isolate and tax holding company earnings. A CFC is a foreign corporation that is 50 percent or more owned by U.S. "shareholders"—defined as U.S. citizens (including corporations) holding 10 percent or more of the common stock. (Thus, a U.S. citizen that owned less than 10 percent did not qualify as a U.S. "shareholder" for the purposes of this act.)

Subpart F income is defined as the income received by a foreign-base company. A **foreign-base company,** in turn, is a CFC that derives income from investments, sales, services, or shipping. Subpart F income is deemed to have been received by the U.S. parent of the CFC. It is not deferred, unlike the operating income that a subsidiary derives from the actual conduct of a business and does not pay to the parent as dividends—as with Monser and Magna. There is one exception, however—the **10/70 rule.** This rule recognizes that subsidiaries may have income from numerous sources: production and sales, investments, and so on. The 10/70 rule stipulates that if less than 10 percent of a CFC's income is Subpart F income, then full deferral applies. If more than 70 percent of a CFC's income is Subpart F income, then none of it is deferred. (If Subpart F income constitutes between 10 percent and 70 percent of the CFC's income, then the CFC's income is allocated between deferred and not deferred in the same ratio as its origin.)

If Monser were a holding company and if its 8 million franc income were from dividends, management fees, and royalties, those 8 million francs, equal to $1.6 million, would immediately be taxable income to Magna—whether or not Monser declared any dividend. The initial U.S. tax would be $544,000, but $400,000 of this would be offset by income taxes paid in France by Monser. (Note that there would be no U.S. tax credit for dividend remittance taxes, since in this instance Monser paid no dividend to Magna.)

The Foreign Sales Corporation

Several countries have established schemes for subsidizing exports by "relieving" export profits or revenues of taxes. In many European countries, for instance, firms that export are rebated by governments for the taxes their export products carried. A major business tax in Europe is the **value-added tax (VAT).** This tax is applied to the value added by each producer/processor/distributor as a product progresses through the stages of production and distribution. It is applied to both intermediate products and final products. The total value-added taxes paid on a product are returned by the government to the exporter, thus making exports more price competitive in world markets than they would be otherwise. In the United States, channeling exports through a **foreign sales corporation (FSC)** can, like the VAT, result in tax advantages.

A U.S. company can establish an FSC to handle its exports and to accumulate profits on its export sales. Approximately 65 percent of the profits of the FSC will be tax exempt. Certain procedures and restrictions apply, however. The FSC, for example, must be physically located outside the United States or in a U.S. possession other than Puerto Rico, and it must actually participate in the conduct of export business. It cannot be a mere "shell." It must maintain an office, keep records, participate in sales solicitations and negotiations, and handle order processing, billings, and collections. The parent and its FSC are free to establish transfer prices on export goods as they see fit; however, profits at the FSC are limited to the larger of 1.83 percent of the total revenues generated by exports or 23 percent of the total income of the FSC and its parent.[7]

Dividends remitted by the FSC to its parent corporation are totally tax-free at the parent level. At most, therefore, 65 percent of the profits at the FSC (which equals 65 percent of 23 percent of the combined, total corporate profits, or 15 percent of the total corporate profits) are tax exempt. Since countries where an FSC is located can also tax the FSC's profits, the preferred location for FSCs is the U.S. Virgin Islands, where U.S. tax laws are in effect.

There are other special situations where tax laws authorize tax benefits and advantages—for example, the FSC for small businesses, which does not require an offshore location. Inquiries on these and other tax-related issues should always be directed to a competent authority, such as a tax accountant.

Taxation—The Management Impact

How do the tax matters just discussed relate to management? In many ways, tax considerations are one of several important inputs into management decision making. They are certainly relevant to the strategic management function at the corporate, MNE level, especially with regard to decisions on ownership structures, plant location, production allocation, target market selection, and financing. The astute manager will incorporate tax effects on cash flow projections when building the data base appropriate to the planning function.

At the SBU level, tax concerns need to be addressed (perhaps jointly in some cases by both SBU-level and corporate-level managers) in decisions on

---

ADDED DIMENSION

Do Foreign-Owned Firms in the United States Pay Their Fair Share?

The U.S. Internal Revenue Service (IRS) recently completed a study that showed profits, as measured by return on assets, reported by foreign-owned firms in the United States were consistently and substantially below those reported by U.S. companies. The data base used covered the period 1979–1987.

There may be several factors influencing these findings in the direction observed. One is that much of the direct foreign investment in the United States is new. It usually takes a while for firms to get beyond start-up costs and turn profitable. In addition, debt taken on by subsidiaries is a favored financing alternative for both U.S. and non-U.S. MNEs alike. This would tend to attenuate profits in the early years.

Nonetheless, some U.S. legislators have expressed concern over MNEs' transfer pricing schemes that draw profits out of their U.S. subsidiaries. The Japanese have been especially identified regarding this allegation. They are, in many ways, the most ethnocentric of all the foreign direct investors in America. On the other hand, Japanese firms in America are fairly new, and they generally have big future growth plans for their U.S. subsidiaries. Why drain funds from these subsidiaries then?

What do you think? ■

---

intracorporate product transfers and transfer prices, personnel assignments, cash management and short-term financing arrangements, dividend policy, export strategy, profit planning, and accounting systems.

The foregoing illustrates that many factors affect an MNE's tax strategy. Frequently, the more ethnocentric manager will be concerned with individual "strategies" that aim at tax reduction as a primary objective such as transfer pricing to locate profits in low tax jurisdictions, delaying dividends to delay paying income taxes at the parent, or loading high tax areas with MNE-benefitting operations and expenses (such as R&D expenses). In the polycentric structure, management is only concerned with tax avoidance at the subsidiary level. The geocentric manager sees taxes as only one of a variety of factors affecting MNE decision-making. Moving funds, for example, from subsidiary to parent would be influenced by funding needs at both levels, the movement of such funds on the cost of capital, tax effects, and so on. Moving funds in the geocentric MNE may well be determined via a linear programming approach where tax minimization is but one of several objective functions.

MANAGEMENT RESPONSIBILITIES UNDER THE FOREIGN CORRUPT PRACTICES ACT

During the 1970s, there was considerable public concern in the United States (and elsewhere) over unethical business practices—bribes to secure sales contracts, falsification of corporate records, and so on. Many of these practices, engaged in outside the United States, involved dealings between representatives of U.S. corporations and officials of foreign governments. In response, legislation was enacted in 1977 to mandate corporate control over firms' activities in this regard.

The **Foreign Corrupt Practices Act** forbids bribes and similar questionable conduct, requires that funds not be made available for the payment of bribes and other questionable financial activities, and mandates that companies develop and apply internal accounting and control procedures to support the requirements of the act. A compelling feature of the act is that its penalties for noncompliance include not only fines for both companies and company officials but also *imprisonment of company officials.*

The Omnibus Trade and Competitiveness Act of 1988 amended the Foreign Corrupt Practices Act of 1977. It defined more specifically the type of business acts that are not permissible under the law (thus clearing up considerable ambiguity), and provided for substantially increased fines for violations. To illustrate, payments to foreign agents must now be to agents who are knowingly engaged in illegal conduct (such as bribery), and fines can reach as much as $2 million per company per violation.

Although the internal accounting and control procedures mandated by the act are costly, they may save money too by reducing the potential for fraudulent activities. When the act was first passed, many observers felt that its antibribery provisions would put U.S. firms at a competitive disadvantage overseas. A 1984 study, however, suggests that this has not been the case. The act has caused no loss of foreign sales by U.S. firms.[8]

CONCLUSIONS

Accounting and tax matters are especially challenging to MNE management. They are both complex and rewarding. Properly approached and implemented, accounting systems and tax strategies—especially those that pertain to the transfer and evaluation of management expertise and the minimization of cash outflows stemming from taxes—can support the competitive presence of MNEs both at home and abroad.

Accounting systems were seen to reflect environmental influences, such as the legal climate and levels of education, and to vary somewhat country by country. Accounting for international transactions was discussed, as was consolidation accounting. The rules germane to each of these activities are fairly complex, and the record-keeping is tedious. Management's responsibility is to acquire knowledge of the rules and to ensure that they are followed.

The taxation of MNEs varies, depending on the answers to a variety of questions. Is there a tax treaty between the home and host countries? What are its provisions? Is the foreign entity an operating company, or is it simply a holding company? What are the levels of taxes abroad, and of the dividends remitted to the parent? What is the overall foreign tax credit limitation? Can export income be channeled through a foreign sales corporation? The questions can go on and on.

Management in the United States has special responsibilities under the Foreign Corrupt Practices Act. The most difficult one to address is the requirement for internal accounting and managerial controls to ensure compliance with the act. Managers who fail to comply can face a jail sentence.

QUESTIONS

1. Explain how accounting and tax matters can affect the competitiveness of an MNE.
2. Distinguish between financial accounting and managerial accounting/information systems; between accounting for international transactions and accounting for consolidations.

3. Identify three environmental factors that have influenced the development of indigenous financial accounting systems. Identify specific results of these influences.

4. Explain the differences between the "trade credit" and the "trade credit—hedged" cases when accounting for international transactions.

5. Distinguish between a parent company's financial statements and the consolidated statements. Where does an investment in a subsidiary appear on the parent's books? On the consolidated statements?

6. What is FAS 52? What are its major provisions?

7. Distinguish between a conversion gain/loss and a translation gain/loss. Of what significance is the difference between the two?

8. In the Magna Corporation example, change the French income tax rate to 30 percent. What will Magna's U.S. taxes then be?

9. Distinguish between Subpart F income and ordinary income. Why is this distinction necessary?

10. Identify some management problems that must be resolved when a foreign sales corporation is established. Of what benefit is a foreign sales corporation?

REFERENCES

AlHashim, Dhia D., and Jeffrey S. Arpan. *International Dimensions of Accounting.* Boston: PWS-Kent Publishing Co., 1988.

Bavishi, Vinod B. *International Accounting and Auditing Trends.* Vols. 1 and 2. Princeton, N.J.: Center for International Financial Analysis and Research, Inc., 1989.

Belkaoui, Ahmed. *The New Environment in International Accounting: Issues and Practices.* Westport, Conn.: Quorum Books, 1988.

Beresford, Dennis R. "What's the FASB Doing about International Accounting Standards?" *Financial Executive,* May–June 1990, pp. 17–23.

Corporate Taxes: A Worldwide Summary. New York: Price Waterhouse, 1990.

Kostin, Edward B., ed. *International Tax Summaries 1990: A Guide for Planning and Decisions.* Coopers & Lybrand International Tax Network. Somerset, N.J.: John Wiley & Sons, Inc., 1990.

Militzer, Ken, and Ilona Ontscherenki. "The Value Added Tax: Its Impact on Saving." *Business Economics,* April 1990, pp. 32–37.

Morehead, Jere W., and Sandra G. Gustavson II. "Complying with the Amended Foreign Corrupt Practices Act." *Risk Management,* April 1990, pp. 76–82.

United Nations. *International Accounting and Reporting Issues.* New York: UN, 1990.

Walter, Ingo. *Secret Money: The Shadowy World of Tax Evasion, Capital Flight, and Fraud.* Lexington, Mass.: Lexington Books, 1985.

NOTES

[1]Steven A. Zeff, *Forging Accounting Principles in Five Countries: A History and an Analysis of Trends* (Champaign, Ill.: Stipes Publishing, 1972).

[2]Frederick D. S. Choi and Gerhard G. Mueller, *An Introduction to Multinational Accounting* (Englewood Cliffs, N.J.: Prentice Hall, 1978), pp. 24–28.

[3]Konrad W. Kubin, "Comparative Accounting Systems," in *Handbook of International Management,* ed. Ingo Walter, (New York: John Wiley & Sons, 1988), chap. 23, pp. 23–4.

[4]R. D. Fitzgerald, A. D. Stickler, and T. R. Watts, *International Survey of Accounting Principles and Reporting Practices* (New York: Price Waterhouse International, 1979).

[5]Kubin, "Systems," p. 23–5.

[6]Frederick D. S. Choi, "Accounting for Multinational Operations," in *Handbook of International Management,* ed. Ingo Walter (New York: John Wiley & Sons, 1988), chap. 22.

[7]Detailed information on foreign sales corporations can be found in analyses of the Tax Reform Act of 1984 prepared by most major accounting firms and by Commerce Clearing House.

[8]J. L. Graham, "The Foreign Corrupt Practices Act: A New Perspective," *Journal of International Business Studies,* Winter 1984, pp. 107–23.

Hurricane Canoe Corporation

Hurricane Canoe Corporation (HCC) is a major U.S. canoe manufacturer located in Orlando, Florida. The firm is not large by overall U.S. industrial standards, but it is the second largest canoe builder in the world. With annual sales of about $200 million and assets of nearly $100 million in North America and Europe, HCC is clearly beyond the small-business stage. Its sales growth has exceeded 20 percent per year since 1978, and its prospects for continued success appear good.

Most of HCC's growth has come through expansion of its distribution network. The firm's main products have remained basically the same over the years: canoes, paddles, safety and camping gear, and some specialty clothing. Its diversification has been primarily geographic (rather than through new products), though some of its sales outlets have added other firms' canoes and canoe rentals to their product lines. HCC's U.S. operations reported sales of $72.7 million and profits before taxes of $11.4 million in 1991 (exclusive of management fees and royalties from foreign operations).

Hurricane Canoe began its foreign operations in the late 1960s by establishing a sales office in Montreal, Quebec, Canada. Canoeists in Canada rank among the most avid in the world, and HCC had great expectations for Canadian sales of its high-performance Kevlar and ABS boats. These expectations were borne out by sales of hundreds, then thousands, of boats in the first eight years of the Canadian operation. Subsequently, HCC established a wholly owned assembly operation in Windsor, Ontario, Canada, which currently produces one third of HCC's North American output. At present, 75 percent of the Windsor operation's output is sold in Canada and the balance is exported to the United States at a price to HCC-owned distributors of cost plus 10 percent. Pretax profits in Canada last year were $5.8 million on sales of $45 million.

After several years of small-volume exports to European purchasers, Hurricane Canoe established a regional sales office in Frankfurt, Federal Republic of Germany, to serve the Common Market. This wholly owned subsidiary established ties with unaffiliated distributors throughout Western Europe. Selling canoes and peripheral equipment manufactured in both the United States and Canada, the Frankfurt office showed a pretax profit last year of $16.8 million on sales of $48.8 million. During the past five years, sales of the Frankfurt office have been growing phenomenally—25 percent per year.

This case was written by Professor Robert Grosse.

TABLE 1

Tax Rates (percent)

	United States	Canada	Germany	Denmark	Spain
Corporate income tax	34	45	56/36*	50	35
Dividend withholding tax	0	25	25	30	15
Royalties and fees withholding tax	0	30	25	0	15

*In Germany, the corporate income tax rate is 56 percent on undistributed profits and 36 percent on distributed profits (i.e., dividends paid out).

In 1978, HCC formed a joint venture with Kirk and Steuergard, S.A. (K & S), of Denmark, the world's leading manufacturer of Olympic-style canoes. In return for a 49 percent contribution of capital, technology, and management, HCC received 49 percent ownership and exclusive distribution rights for K & S boats in North America. This $5 million investment in Copenhagen was a sizable commitment of funds, but the investment was paid back within three years and profits continue to grow rapidly. Last year, the joint venture's sales and pretax profits were $25 million and $6.9 million, respectively. Currently, this affiliate is capitalized at $9.7 million.

Hurricane Canoe's most recent foreign venture is a 100-percent-owned assembly plant near Barcelona, Spain. HCC saw low-cost assembly, plus tariff-free access to the Common Market, as adequate justification for the investment. HCC spent $4.5 million during the start-up phase of operations, and at year-end 1991 it had assets worth $2.9 million in the Barcelona plant. In the past year, the sales of this plant were a modest $6.5 million and initial operating problems led to a loss of $1.2 million.

Hurricane Canoe's policies require that each subsidiary remit 50 percent of its after-tax earnings to the parent company. Each affiliate—that is, the Danish joint venture—pays out 50 percent of pretax earnings in dividends. A management fee totaling 2 percent of sales is charged to all wholly owned subsidiaries. A royalty totaling 5 percent of sales is charged to all manufacturing affiliates.

Tax-rate data for the countries within which Hurricane Canoe operates are presented in Table 1. Using these data as necessary, complete Table 2 to figure Hurricane Canoe's U.S. income taxes last year. From a total tax perspective, what costs are HCC bearing to maintain its ethnocentric 50 percent dividend payout ratio from overseas operations in the face of rapid growth and high cash needs in its European operations? (As a basis for comparison, assume that no dividends are paid out by the operations in Germany and Denmark and that the Canadian subsidiary requires that two thirds of its after-tax profits be reinvested in Windsor.)

TABLE 2

U.S. Income Tax Calculations (in millions of U.S. dollars)

	United States	Canada	Germany	Denmark	Spain
Country level					
Sales	72.7	45.0	48.8	25/12.3	6.5
Pretax profit	11.4	5.8	16.8	6.9/3.4	−1.2
Income tax	_____	_____	_____	_____	_____
After-tax profit	_____	_____	_____	_____	_____
Dividends		_____	_____	_____	_____
Parent level (consolidated, except as noted)					
Gross dividends		_____	_____	_____	_____
Less: Dividend withholding tax		_____	_____	_____	_____
Net dividends	_____	_____	_____	_____	_____
Management fees		_____	_____	_____	_____
Royalties		_____	_____	_____	_____
Total fees and royalties		_____	_____	_____	_____
Less: Fee/royalty withholding tax		_____	_____	_____	_____
Net fees and royalties	_____	_____	_____	_____	_____
Grossed-up income		_____	_____	_____	_____
U.S. tax—initial		_____	_____	_____	_____
Less: Foreign tax credit		_____	_____	_____	_____
U.S. tax due (by country)	_____	_____	_____	_____	_____
Total U.S. tax due	_____				

Chapter

16

Financial Management and Control in the International Firm

This chapter discusses the opportunities and problems that face multinational firms because they operate in a multicurrency world. Basically, it is an extension of corporate finance to the international level. The capital budgeting process is reviewed, with attention given to foreign exchange risk and political risk and also to opportunities for financing with nondomestic sources of funds. Short-term asset management is similarly covered, with emphasis on centralized international cash management. The choice of debt versus equity for financing the MNE's activities is considered, and the special financing advantages available to the international firm are pointed out. Finally, a more comprehensive look at foreign exchange risk management complements the one in Chapter 6. The main goals of the chapter are to:

1. Elaborate the differences from traditional capital budgeting analysis that occur because of the international nature of the firm.

2. Explain the concept of political risk and discuss methods for dealing with it.

3. Show how the MNE can make financial structure decisions based both on its total capitalization and on market conditions in the countries where it operates.

4. Elaborate the differences from traditional working capital management that occur because of the international nature of the firm.

5. Define transaction, translation, and economic exchange risk and present methods for dealing with each.

6. Show how financial controls can be established in the MNE.

INTRODUCTION

Any firm with affiliates in at least two countries (or even with a simple sales office abroad) is faced with the need to deal with differences in the financial environments of these countries—differences in their tax systems, their currency systems, and numerous other areas. Can you imagine trying to keep the books of a company such as Johnson & Johnson, which is required to maintain financial records according to the different accounting standards in the dozens of countries where it operates, plus records for use in internal control? Beyond the chores of record-keeping, the firm operating at this level obtains opportunities to transfer funds (and products) between countries, to utilize financial markets in each country to serve its global needs, and to diversify its risks internationally. Increasing numbers of MNEs, such as Sears and General Electric, are building internal financial institutions so that they can take advantage of these opportunities around the world. This chapter explores the opportunities and problems of firms in such an environment.

The issue of measuring an MNE's tax liabilities was covered in the previous chapter; what matters here is the firm's ability to arbitrage tax jurisdictions (that is, to reduce global taxes paid by incurring expenses in high-tax countries and showing higher profits in lower-tax countries) and in general to deal with taxation in each country of operation. Similarly, national financial markets and the euromarkets were discussed in Chapter 7; here the emphasis is on using these markets to optimize the financial position of the multinational firm. The issue of exchange risk was treated in Chapter 6; what remains is to consider such risk in the context of a firm that does repeated international business and maintains long-term assets abroad. Finally, consideration is given to the full set of financial issues in a firm whose subsidiaries in different countries are competing for use of the available financial resources. This chapter treats the topic of multinational financial management as a whole.

The chapter is structured to cover major issues in corporate finance as they are relevant in the international context. Basic financial management can be divided into two broad headings: (1) choice and management of *sources* of funds and (2) choice and management of *uses* of funds. At the international level, exchange risk management must be added. Figure 16–1 depicts the topics that constitute the substance of the chapter. Overall financial management requires *control* over each type of decision depicted in the figure—especially since financial managers in each affiliate may be making decisions that affect the total corporation's financial position.

The next three sections explore aspects of long-term asset and liability management. Then working capital management is covered. Next, a section is devoted to a more extensive presentation of exchange risk management than that given in Chapter 6. Finally, the problem of financial control is discussed.

The main uses of funds in a business can be divided into long-term capital projects and such short-term assets as cash, securities, accounts receivable, and inventories. Long-term overseas projects are our first subject for discussion.

CAPITAL BUDGETING IN THE MULTINATIONAL ENTERPRISE

Capital project evaluation follows much the same reasoning in an international firm as in a domestic firm, though additional variables and risks must be considered. Specifically, foreign projects must be evaluated for exchange risk, political risk, different financing costs, and any problems associated with the transfer of products, services, or funds due to government controls in any of the

FIGURE 16–1

Financial Management in
the MNE

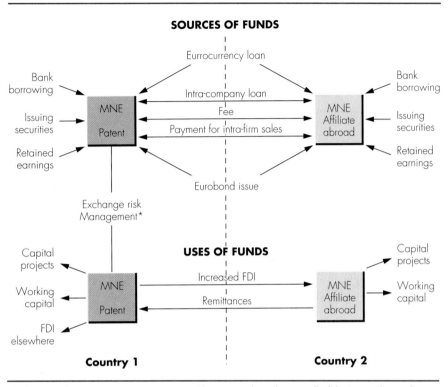

*Exchange risk management is a company-wide concern that relates to all of the issues shown above.

relevant countries. To see how these factors appear in the analysis, consider the following example of a food processing plant to be constructed by a U.S.-based company in Shapironia.

The company has developed the following pro forma income statement for the proposed investment project:

Proposed Shapironia Processing Plant
Pro Forma Income Statement, Typical Year
(in local currency)

Sales	10,000,000
Cost of goods sold	
Local materials	1,000,000
Imported materials	2,000,000
Labor	3,000,000
Overhead expenses	600,000
Interest on loan from parent firm	400,000
Net income before tax	3,000,000
Local tax—50%	1,500,000
Net income after tax	1,500,000

Assuming that the investment made by the parent firm is 4 million in local currency, the project appears to have a simple return on capital of about 38 percent per year (1,500,000/4,000,000). As long as the firm's cost of capital is less than 38 percent, the project is worth undertaking.[1] The normal, domestic concerns apply to this project evaluation—that is, the estimate is only as good as the forecasts of costs and sales. In addition, this foreign project faces potentially important considerations, such as exchange risk, currency inconvertibility and other political risks, and preferential local-borrowing opportunities.

Exchange risk will affect the U.S. dollar value of the profits earned, potentially raising or lowering them substantially. For example, if the local-currency value rises by 10 percent in relation to the dollar, net income after tax will rise (in dollar terms) by 10 percent, other things equal. However, if imported materials come from the United States, then that cost (in local currency) will fall. Similarly, if the loan is made in dollars, then interest cost (in local-currency terms) will fall. Sales, if any are exported from Shapironia, may decrease due to the exchange-rate change.[2] In sum, a rise in the value of the local currency relative to the U.S. dollar will tend to cause an increase in dollar profits from the affiliate—and such profits will tend to fall if the local currency devalues relative to the dollar.

Political risk (defined below) constitutes another concern in the attempt to evaluate this project properly. If the host government decides to restrict profit remittances, then no matter how profitable the project, the MNE will not be able to utilize its earnings elsewhere in the firm or to distribute them to shareholders. This problem is known as **currency inconvertibility,** regardless of whether the cause is a political decision or simply an economic reality. If discontent with the Shapironia government leads to strikes or to violent confrontation between the government and opposition groups, then the plant may be damaged or its production curtailed. Not all political risk is negative—if the government chooses to reduce corporate taxes to stimulate greater investment, then the project may generate greater profitability than that shown above. In sum, political risks need to be considered when the full set of the project's financial implications is being judged.

Borrowing costs may not be the same in Shapironia and the United States. Thus, if the firm uses its **weighted-average cost of capital*** in capital budgeting decisions, this project should be adjusted to account for any locally subsidized borrowing opportunity that may exist. Many countries (and states or provinces within countries) offer low-interest loans to corporate investors in order to attract production facilities and jobs. If this is true in Shapironia and if the firm chooses to borrow some funds locally, then the subsidized capital cost should be reflected in the capital budget.[3] The project as shown uses an intracompany loan, whose interest may be charged at the parent's actual cost of funds or marked up (or down) to achieve greater (or lesser) transfer of funds to the parent.

Finally, it should be recalled that the capital budget measures the project's *incremental impact* on the whole firm. Thus, if there are export sales from the

---

*The weighted-average cost of capital is the firm's cost of obtaining funds from the various sources available. Each source of funds is weighted (multiplied) by the percentage of total capital that it provides. Thus, the WACC is: W_1 (cost of using retained earnings) + W_2 (cost of bank borrowing) + W_3 (cost of other source of funds), where each cost is stated as an annual percentage rate, and each W is the percentage of total capital from that source.

parent to this new affiliate, those new sales must be counted in the evaluation. If the project replaces sales that were formerly exported to Shapironia, those lost sales must be counted. Any other intracompany impacts should also be measured in the project evaluation. This means that the project should be judged in comparison with other alternatives available to the firm serving the Shapironia market. If exports from the United States offer a greater incremental profitability than the proposed plant, then that alternative should be chosen. In summary, the incremental gains to the firm from the proposed project should be compared with the potential gains from other international business alternatives that may also be available.

POLITICAL RISK MANAGEMENT

Definition

Political risk is the decrease or increase in a firm's value that may occur because of unexpected changes in the external, political environment.

Political risk generally refers to a full range of environmental factors that may affect the firm's performance in a particular country. Normal business risks are excluded from this category, but most of the other factors that are outside the firm's control are included. Thus, political risk includes the risk that a government may alter its policies toward the firm or its products (e.g., through price controls), thus lowering or raising profitability or asset values. Political risk also includes the risk of civil war, foreign war, riots, strikes, and other violent social acts that disrupt business. Efforts to harm foreign firms or the particular firm through kidnappings, assassinations, sabotage, or other means fall into this category. Although expropriation of the firm's assets by the host government occurs very infrequently, it constitutes a major political risk. Remember that political risks are not only negative—when a government changes its policies to the firm's advantage (e.g., by lowering taxes or providing some kind of subsidy), this positive outcome also constitutes political risk. Since most decision makers are concerned with "what could go wrong?", political risk discussions usually focus on the negative side.

All of these factors are considered political risks because they can all lead to losses (or gains) by the firm for reasons unforeseeable and uncontrollable by it and because they all constitute discontinuities in the firm's external environment. In other words, political risks must involve *changes* in the environment that can affect the firm. Therefore, an *existing* government policy that disallows profit remittances is not a political risk; it is a business condition in the particular country. The possibility of expropriation can be considered virtually a nonrisk for most manufacturing investments in most countries; almost all expropriations since World War II have taken place in extractive industries (e.g., oil, copper, bauxite) and in a handful of less developed countries (primarily in Latin America and the Middle East).

Political risks may be "macrorisks" or "microrisks." A **macrorisk** applies to all foreign firms doing business in a particular country. For example, the changes in taxation or profit remittance rules that often occur in LDCs generally apply to all the foreign firms in those countries. A **microrisk,** on the other hand, applies specifically to one firm or one group of firms. For example, Saudi Arabia's decision to nationalize its oil industry in 1974 constituted a risk for foreign oil companies there, but that risk did not carry over into the manufacturing sector. Even more firm-specific was the campaign by several public interest groups against Nestlé during the 1980s, when Nestlé was accused of promoting its infant formula in poor LDCs in a manner that overstated the benefits and understated the risks. Similarly, ITT's reported involvement in attempts to overthrow the Allende government in Chile in the early 1970s caused substantial government reprisals at that time in Chile and continuing wariness on the part of Latin American governments with respect to ITT activities.[4] This political risk is company specific.

What exactly is at risk? The answer to this question clearly depends on the type of firm and on its activity in the country. A manufacturing plant typically exposes physical facilities, people, and money to political risk. A sales office may leave only a small number of people and a small amount of equipment at risk. An international bank loan may expose only money to political risk. The correct measure of exposure is that part of the firm's worldwide business that could be affected by unexpected political events or policies in the given country. To determine an appropriate strategy for dealing with this risk, the firm must establish the importance of the risk to its overall operations.

The full scope of the issues involved in political risk is so broad that it cannot be presented in detail here. Kobrin (1982) encompasses the range of "potentially significant managerial contingencies generated by political events and processes" in his definition of political risk. Brewer (1985) sees political risk as "uncertainty about the political environment of business and its effects on individual firms," that is, as a measure of the effects of politics on business. Every definition of political risk focuses on the potential impact of political factors on company performance.

Measures of Political Risk

A number of very large firms and banks go to great lengths to measure political risks in this businesses. Texaco and Royal Dutch Shell, for example, maintain corporate staff groups of political risk analysts who keep up with political conditions in countries where the firms do business and try to anticipate important changes in those conditions. Similarly, Bankers Trust Corporation and a handful of other multinational banks operate "country risk" staffs that track political and economic conditions abroad and try to assess their implications for the banks' loan portfolios. Instead of accumulating very detailed knowledge about a large number of countries, many firms create country ranking systems, which they use to compare political risk internationally (and presumably to avoid very risky nations).

Several independent services create political risk and country risk ratings. A typical one is *Euromoney* magazine's annual Country Risk Rating, which is based on a measure of different countries' access to international credit. Figure 16–2 presents the ratings for 1990.

Unfortunately, it is not possible to know the future, so political risk forecasters are doomed to failure as crystal ball analysts. However, some value can be gained from their efforts if these are viewed as an attempt to keep in touch with conditions in the various countries so that signals of policy changes are not overlooked. The fall of the shah of Iran and the overthrow of the Somoza regime in Nicaragua were the two events that led to widespread focus on political risk analysis in MNEs during the past decade. It is not possible to predict the next major upheaval of this kind. However, it may be possible to anticipate that a country will increase taxes or be unable to make payment on its foreign debt.

FIGURE 16–2

The Euromoney Country Risk Ratings, 1990

Rank		Country	Rating (0-100)		
1990	1989		1990 (During)	1990 (Before)	1989
1	3	West Germany	92.1	94.1	93.0
2	1	Japan	91.9	93.4	95.0
3	na	Luxembourg	91.1	91.5	na
4 =	10	Austria	89.9	90.7	88.0
4 =	8	Netherlands	89.9	90.1	89.0
4 =	6	France	89.9	91.1	90.0
7	1	Switzerland	87.6	88.1	95.0
8	8	Sweden	87.4	88.4	89.0
9	10	Finland	86.2	86.5	88.0
10	6	Canada	85.8	86.3	90.0
11 =	22	Ireland	85.7	86.3	75.0
11 =	17	Denmark	85.7	86.2	83.0
11 =	4	USA	85.7	88.4	92.0
14	10	Belgium	85.4	85.9	88.0
15	13	Norway	84.9	85.1	87.0
16	16	Singapore	84.8	85.2	84.0
17	13	Italy	83.6	84.6	87.0
18	5	UK	83.5	84.5	91.0
19	na	United Germany	82.7	85.0	na
20	20	South Korea	82.0	83.0	79.0
21	15	Spain	81.9	82.5	85.0
22 =	25	Taiwan	79.2	80.0	72.0
22 =	21	Portugal	79.2	79.9	77.0
24	29	Malaysia	75.8	76.6	68.0
25	19	Australia	74.4	76.4	82.0
26	28	Malta	73.9	74.4	69.0
27	17	New Zealand	73.5	74.9	83.0
28	25	Thailand	72.2	72.8	72.0
29	29	Brunei	72.1	71.2	68.0
30	27	Hong Kong	71.2	72.8	70.0
31	31	Cyprus	70.0	71.9	67.0
32	23	Iceland	69.0	69.1	74.0
33	44	Mauritius	66.5	66.8	59.0
34	31	East Germany	66.4	68.0	67.0
35	39	Indonesia	65.7	65.6	62.0
36	31	Bermuda	65.2	65.2	67.0
37	31	China	65.1	65.4	67.0
38	31	Greece	64.7	65.5	67.0
39	53	Nauru	63.1	63.2	54.0
40	38	Czechoslovakia	61.7	62.0	63.0
41	39	Hungary	60.8	61.4	62.0
42	51	Botswana	60.3	60.5	55.0
43	66	Uruguay	60.1	60.1	42.0
44 =	39	Bahrain	60.0	77.6	62.0
44 =	37	Saudi Arabia	60.0	71.2	65.0
46	47	Oman	59.0	65.9	57.0
47	31	India	58.7	59.2	67.0
48	63	Mexico	58.6	57.1	44.0
49	62	Fiji	57.0	58.0	45.0
50	43	UAE	56.0	67.7	61.0

FIGURE 16–2

continued

Rank			Rating (0-100)		
1990	1989	Country	1990 (During)	1990 (Before)	1989
51	49	Barbados	55.3	55.3	56.0
52	60	South Africa	55.0	55.0	46.0
53	69	Chile	54.4	54.7	41.0
54	39	Turkey	54.0	66.6	62.0
55	23	USSR	53.4	54.5	74.0
56	86	Paraguay	53.0	53.6	35.0
57	58	Pakistan	52.7	53.9	49.0
58	56	Solomon Islands	52.4	52.8	51.0
59	88	Panama	50.8	51.2	34.0
60	46	Tunisia	50.0	54.0	58.0
61	49	Israel	49.9	61.6	56.0
62	60	Papua New Guinea	48.5	48.6	46.0
63	54	Trinidad & Tobago	47.6	47.8	52.0
64	66	Algeria	47.0	47.8	42.0
65	59	Venezuela	46.1	44.9	47.0
66	69	Zimbabwe	46.0	47.6	41.0
67 =	93	Brazil	45.0	45.7	32.0
67 =	80	Colombia	45.0	45.5	37.0
67 =	63	Swaziland	45.0	45.3	44.0
67 =	54	Vanuatu	45.0	45.5	52.0
71	47	Qatar	44.8	67.7	57.0
72	66	Romania	43.3	44.1	42.0
73	65	Kenya	43.2	44.2	43.0
74	75	Poland	43.0	43.4	38.0
75	57	Morocco	42.5	48.5	50.0
76	93	Sri Lanka	42.4	47.3	32.0
77	82	Yugoslavia	42.2	43.5	36.0
78	75	Philippines	41.4	42.4	38.0
79	80	Malawi	40.0	40.5	37.0
80	75	Egypt	39.6	46.6	38.0
81	75	Bangladesh	39.3	40.3	38.0
82	82	Jamaica	39.0	39.5	36.0
83	na	Belize	38.0	38.5	na
84	90	Senegal	37.8	38.2	33.0
85	72	Cameroon	37.0	36.0	40.0
86	na	Rwanda	36.9	37.4	na
87	na	Mali	36.8	37.1	na
88	82	Lesotho	36.0	36.4	36.0
89	72	Gabon	35.8	34.8	40.0
90	90	Costa Rica	35.0	35.9	33.0
91	51	Bulgaria	34.7	35.0	55.0
92	75	Ghana	33.9	35.8	38.0
93	90	Iran	33.8	36.8	33.0
94	99	Tanzania	33.7	34.7	30.0
95	101	Argentina	33.3	34.0	28.0
96	82	Nigeria	33.0	31.5	36.0
97	74	Jordan	31.0	39.7	39.0
98	98	Ecuador	30.0	30.9	31.0
99 =	na	Sierra Leone	28.9	29.3	na
99 =	na	Gambia	28.9	29.6	na

FIGURE 16–2

concluded

Rank			Rating (0-100)		
1990	1989	Country	1990 (During)	1990 (Before)	1989
99=	109	Peru	28.9	29.3	25.0
102	88	Libya	28.7	33.4	34.0
103	93	Niger	28.6	29.9	32.0
104	109	Bolivia	28.3	28.3	25.0
105	86	Dominican Republic	28.0	28.4	35.0
106	44	Kuwait	27.9	77.1	59.0
107	105	Congo	27.4	26.3	27.0
108	na	Chad	27.2	27.7	na
109	na	Albania	27.0	27.0	na
110=	93	Honduras	26.0	26.4	32.0
110=	93	Guatemala	26.0	26.6	32.0
112	105	El Salvador	25.7	26.1	27.0
113	116	Angola	25.6	25.0	23.0
114=	na	Madagascar	25.4	25.6	na
114=	101	Cuba	25.4	25.6	28.0
116=	na	Djibouti	25.2	25.4	na
116=	69	Ivory Coast	25.2	25.9	41.0
118	105	Myanmar (Burma)	25.0	25.1	27.0
119	115	Haiti	23.2	23.2	24.0
120	109	Zambia	23.0	23.8	25.0
121	101	Mauritania	22.8	24.1	28.0
122	99	Syria	22.3	28.3	30.0
123	118	Zaïre	21.5	21.0	20.0
124	120	Lebanon	19.6	19.6	17.0
125=	109	Guyana	19.4	19.6	25.0
125=	109	Uganda	19.4	19.6	25.0
127	109	Ethopia	19.3	19.5	25.0
128	na	Namibia	18.9	18.9	na
129	101	Iraq	18.4	22.3	28.0
130	117	Liberia	17.3	17.3	21.0
131=	na	Nicaragua	14.5	14.5	na
131=	119	Sudan	14.5	17.3	18.0
133	108	Mozambique	13.6	13.6	26.0

The Euromoney country risk method: A cross section of specialists was asked to give views on each country with particular reference to one or more of the factors we detail. These take the form of three broad categories: analytical indicators 40%; credit indicators 20%; and market indicators 40%.

Analytical Indicators 40%: This is made up of political risk 15%; economic risk 10%; and economic indicators 15%. The economic indicators consist of three key ratios: the debt service-to-export ratio, as a measure of liquidity, while the balance-of-payments-to-GNP and the external-debt-to-GNP are used as measures of solvency. Inevitably these ratios are historical, so the prospective view of economic performance to 1991, as judged by a panel of economists, is represented by the economic risk factor. The political risk factor is a measure of stability and to an extent the potential effects of any instability, as judged by political risk specialists.

Credit Indicators 20%: This category is made up of payment record 15% and ease of rescheduling 5%. Both these factors show the historical creditworthiness of a country. Ease of rescheduling indicates a country's general creditworthiness in the face of temporary liquidity problems.

Market Indicators 40%: These consist of access to bond markets (FRN, straight and Yankee) 15%; selldown on short-term paper 10%; and access to, and discount available on, forfaiting 15%.

Clearly, each factor we have used in our risk rating contains varying elements of other factors: for instance, the market is perceptive and takes political, analytical and credit indicators very seriously, while a country's economic stability may be dependent on the market's favour.

Source: *Euromoney*, September 1989, p. 206.

The opening of the Soviet bloc countries now provides a huge possible set of opportunities for international firms. Political risk assessment is vitally needed for firms to decide on their resource commitments to Poland, Czechoslovakia, the Soviet Union, etc. If political risk analysts pursue such more modest but more realistic goals, they may indeed offer useful inputs into corporate decision making.

The analysts currently measure political risks in ways ranging from estimates of the probability that governments will be overthrown to nonquantitative commentaries on the styles of decision making employed by national leaders. Most of the political risk analysis done today evaluates macrorisk, since the available models do not readily handle highly idiosyncratic company-specific factors.[5] Each firm must then assess the bearing of the macrorisk evaluations on its own specific circumstances.

Political Risk and Financial Decision Making

How can political risks be incorporated into a firm's decision making? At the level of capital budgeting, either cash flows or a discount factor can be adjusted to account for such risks. Models have been developed to do exactly that.[6] While no model can incorporate such an imprecise factor with complete accuracy, at least there can be no argument that political risk should be taken into account.

Consider how political risk is generally used in decision making in large firms today. In surveys of both industrial corporations and banks (e.g., Kobrin 1982, Grosse and Stack 1984, and Mascarenhas and Sand 1985), it has been found that some individual or group within the firm assesses political risk and that this assessment is then used in corporate investment or lending decisions. The sequence of events pictured in Figure 16–3 illustrates the basic method of incorporating political risk into the decision-making process. Notice that political factors are combined with economic factors to create an evaluation of the overall environment in the host country. The actual lending or investment decision is also influenced by several other key factors; and indeed political risk may be viewed as relatively unimportant in many cases.

Methods for Dealing with Political Risk

Given that there is no way to forecast political risks with certainty, what can a firm do to cope with it? The methods for dealing with political risk are very similar to the methods for dealing with exchange risk, discussed in Chapter 6. These methods are (1) avoidance, (2) transfer, (3) adaptation, and (4) diversification.

Avoidance   The firm can *avoid* political risk by minimizing activities in or with countries that are perceived to be highly risky and by using a higher discount factor (that is, a higher required rate of return, which reflects a higher cost of capital) for projects in riskier countries. This strategy may not be feasible unless the firm develops some measure of risk that it can apply to projects in the various countries of interest to it. Such a measure may fail to achieve its purpose if some unexpected risk appears. For example, the United States, generally viewed as the least politically risky country in the world, created a huge political risk for its grain exporters by restricting their shipments to the Soviet Union during the Afghanistan crisis of 1979–80. Similarly, U.S. manufacturers of oil

FIGURE 16–3

Political Risk in the
Investment/Lending Process

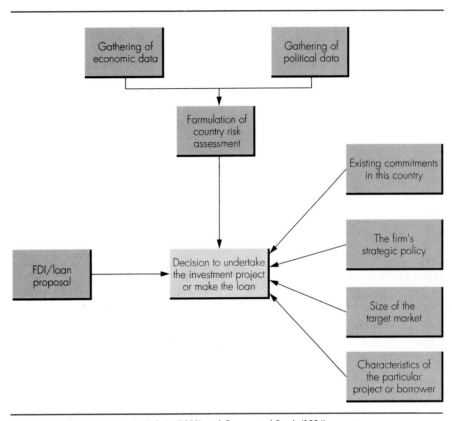

Source: Based on statements in Kobrin (1982) and Grosse and Stack (1984).

pipelines and electronic equipment have repeatedly faced unpredictable U.S. government policies with regard to their sales to Eastern-bloc purchasers. In sum, a firm may follow the strategy of political risk avoidance, yet still be harmed by political risks.

Risk Transfer   Most developed countries offer political risk insurance to their exporters, and often to their direct investors. This is a form of political risk *transfer*. In the United States, the Eximbank offers policies to exporters that cover such political risks as war, civil unrest, and currency inconvertibility.[7] In addition, the Overseas Private Investment Corporation (OPIC) offers insurance policies to U.S. foreign investors to cover such risks as expropriation, civil or foreign war damages, and currency inconvertibility.[8] In Great Britain, similar policies are offered by the Export Credit Guarantee Department (EGDC); in Germany, by an agency called Hermes; and in Canada, by the Export Development Council (EDC). At the multilateral level, the World Bank operates a Multilateral Investment Guarantee Agency, which offers insurance policies analogous to those of OPIC. In each case, some or all of the political risks encountered by a firm may be transferred to the government agency, in exchange for the payment of insurance premia.

Adaptation   A third method for dealing with political risk is to *adapt* the firm's activities to reduce such risk. Just as assets in a currency that is exposed to exchange risk can be hedged by incurring liabilities in the same currency, so assets exposed in a given country can be hedged with liabilities in the same country. A factory in Egypt can be hedged against political risk by financing its operation through local borrowing or by incurring local accounts payable. Notice that political risk must be hedged through liabilities (or assets, depending on the exposure) *located in* the host country, whereas exchange risk may be hedged in the eurocurrency markets, regardless of the country of location.

Many other means of adapting the firm's business to reduce political risk can be devised. One possibility is to support social and charitable activities in the host country, to demonstrate the firm's good corporate citizenship. Another method is to support political parties and politicians (particularly the ones in power), such that their views of the foreign firm become more favorable. The fundamental goal of this strategy is to alter the firm's activities appropriately, so that the probability of negative government actions is reduced.

Diversification   The fourth method for dealing with political risk is to *diversify* across national borders, so that problems in one country do not debilitate the firm. Then, if a strike or a war causes the firm to cease operations in one country, facilities in other countries will still allow it to remain in business. With such possibilities in mind, firms that assemble clothing or electronic products in less developed countries often set up plants in two or more countries. Similarly, if taxes are raised in one country, production or funds may be moved to another country to avoid the extra cost. Diversification does not reduce the political risk in any given country; it just allows the firm to survive politically risky events by operating in other countries and reduces the overall risk.

As with exchange risk, the four strategies for protecting against political risk are not mutually exclusive. They may be used separately or in combination, depending on the availability and cost of each strategy in a particular country.

DEBT/EQUITY CONSIDERATIONS

Financial structure in a multinational enterprise is complicated by the fact that the "normal" **debt/equity ratio** differs from industry to industry and from country to country. For example, the average debt/equity ratio in large Japanese companies is about 2.3 to 1. In the United States, this ratio is generally far less than 1, averaging about 0.6 for nonfinancial industries as a whole.[9] As a rule, the total financial structure of an MNE follows the standards of the home country financial market, since shares are usually traded there. On the other hand, a U.S. company's affiliate in Japan may be able to operate successfully with far higher leverage than that of the parent, given local conditions in Japan. Thus, the financial structure of foreign affiliates may differ from that of the firm overall or of the parent in particular. The only limitation is that the financial structure of the affiliate must not cause the financial structure of the entire firm to deviate from acceptable standards in the home country.

The funding sources available to a foreign affiliate of an MNE include debt and equity from the parent and local financing in the host country. Figure 16–4 presents a view of these sources that expands on the view presented in Figure 16–1. The sources of credit to the MNE are divided between short- and long-

FIGURE 16–4

International Sources of Credit (including markets and intrafirm transfers)

Borrowing	Domestic inside the Firm	Domestic Market	Foreign inside the Firm	Foreign Market	Euromarket
Direct, short-term	Intrafirm loans, transfer pricing, royalties, fees, service charges	Commercial paper	International intrafirm loans, international transfer pricing, dividends, royalties, fees		Eurocommercial paper
Intermediated, short-term		Short-term bank loans, discounted receivables	International back-to-back loans	Short-term bank loans, discounted receivables	Euro short-term loans
Direct, long-term	Intrafirm loans, invested in affiliates	Stock issue Bond issue	International intrafirm long-term loans, FDI	Stock issue Bond issue	Eurobonds, Euroequity
Intermediated, long-term		Long-term bank loans	International back-to-back loans	Long-term bank loans	Euro long-term loans

Direct means borrowing from owners of wealth (e.g., investors); intermediated means borrowing from a financial intermediary (e.g., a bank).

term loans and between direct provision of funds and intermediated provision of funds, through a bank or some other financial institution.

The entire MNE may choose to meet its external financing needs by borrowing through an affiliate in a low-interest country, if such funding is available and if exchange-rate protection still leaves financing costs lower than those in other currencies. As already noted, since the MNE is evaluated by investors in the home country, the firm's overall debt/equity structure must satisfy the financial community in that country. However, if the firm sells shares of an affiliate in the host country's financial market, then the debt/equity position of the affiliate is an important issue.

For a wholly owned foreign subsidiary that does not sell shares in the host country, the debt/equity ratio should be determined by overall corporate needs. If funding is available at low cost (adjusted for expected exchange-rate change), then local borrowing is appropriate. If a substantial amount of assets are exposed locally, then local borrowing provides a hedge to both exchange and political risks. If the local currency is expected to devalue substantially, then even if local interest rates are high, it may make sense to borrow locally—assuming that the expected postdevaluation interest costs would be lower than the home-country costs.

Local equity financing may be forced on the firm if the host government demands partial local ownership of foreign enterprises. This situation exists today in many less developed countries and in most of the formerly communist countries. In this case, the affiliate's debt/equity ratio may be skewed toward equity, especially if the parent seeks to avoid sending funds into that country. That is, financing for the affiliate would come from the local partner's equity investment plus retained earnings, and other funding would be sought only after these sources were used up.

In countries with restrictions on funds transfers, such as profit and royalty remittances, equity financing would again be sensible—using those funds that cannot be taken out of the country. That is, if funds are blocked from transfer abroad, then the MNE must reinvest them locally; investing the funds in the existing operation (i.e., profit reinvestment) may offer greater benefit than placing them in local financial instruments, such as bank deposits or government securities. This strategy is widely used by multinationals—though most of them would prefer the freedom to take their funds out of the host country.

Finally, notice that *if* the MNE is able to lower its total borrowing costs by utilizing foreign sources of funds, it has gained an advantage relative to domestic firms that limit themselves to domestic financial markets in any country. If the MNE has a lower weighted-average cost of capital for any given capital budget, then the MNE will undertake more projects than the purely domestic firm (or will be more profitable in the same projects).

WORKING CAPITAL MANAGEMENT

The MNE can use working capital decisions to reduce currency and political exposures, cut down on the firm's total liabilities, maximize returns on available funds, and minimize the cost of obtaining financing. Each of the main categories of working capital—cash, accounts receivable and payable, short-term loans, and inventories—can be used to pursue these goals.

Cash Management

Consider a multinational firm such as Nestlé (based in Switzerland), whose network of affiliates extends around the world. Each affiliate has its own customers and suppliers, as well as financial ties to the rest of the company. Viewing the company as a single unit for purposes of cash management can yield far better results than would be obtained if each affiliate managed its cash independently. For example, much less foreign exchange protection is generally needed if all of the affiliates are evaluated together than if each affiliate hedges its own position. The French subsidiary may have a large amount of accounts payable in francs that can be hedged simply by placing the German affiliate's excess cash into French franc assets, such as eurofranc deposits. Similarly, the Canadian subsidiary may possess a large amount of Canadian dollar assets that can be hedged by having the U.S. company contract some liabilities (e.g., purchasing equipment) denominated in Canadian dollars. The whole company may coordinate its borrowing efforts through the British subsidiary that uses the London eurocurrency market.

Centralized cash management offers five kinds of potential gains to the MNE:

1. By pooling the cash holdings of affiliates where possible, it can hold a smaller total amount of cash, thus reducing its financing needs.
2. By centralizing cash management, it can have one group of people specialize in the performance of this task, thus achieving better decisions and economies of scale.

3. By reducing the amount of cash in any affiliate, it can reduce political risks as well as financial costs.

4. It can net out intracompany accounts when there are multiple payables and receivables among affiliates, thus reducing the amount of money actually transferred among affiliates.

5. Its central cash management group can ensure that cash management decisions aim at corporate goals rather than the goals of individual affiliates, when these might conflict.

The first kind of gain occurs simply because of better use of the cash held by the firm. If each affiliate holds enough cash to meet its transactions needs, its precautionary needs, and its speculative needs (following the Keynesian categories of money demand), then far more cash is likely to be held than is needed *company-wide*. A domestic company centralizes the cash management function at one location (usually the home office) and an MNE can do the same. The key difference between the two is that the MNE will often be restricted in its ability to shift funds among affiliates internationally, so less centralization is possible at the MNE level. Any reduction in cash holdings, however, enables the firm to reduce its financing needs, thus lowering costs.

The second kind of gain relates to the development of management skills. By centralizing the cash management function, even if funds are left for the most part in the affiliates, the firm can utilize the skills of a specialized group of cash managers. Gains from this group's decision making should include economies of scale in borrowing, since the group can borrow to meet the entire company's needs and then distribute funds to affiliates as required. Also, the group should develop detailed knowledge of financial opportunities worldwide, thus enabling the firm to borrow at lower cost or lower risk than firms without such expertise.

If the MNE reduces its total assets through centralized cash management, it also reduces both its exchange risk and its political risk, in that fewer assets are at risk worldwide. The political risk of a country does not change, but the exposure of the company to that risk decreases. Political risk may also be hedged or transferred by the decision makers in the cash management group, who have greater access to protection tools than do managers in any one affiliate.

Whether or not actual cash is placed in a central location, such a location can be used to keep track of financial flows within the MNE. When accounts among affiliates lead to partially or totally offsetting transfers, the cash management center can *net* the transfers and move only the final sum required. For example, if Nestlé France sells $1 million of products to Nestlé U.S., it will incur an account receivable, say in 180 days. Simultaneously, the home office in Switzerland may borrow $1 million from Nestlé U.S. If Nestlé Switzerland sells some products to the French affiliate, the bill could be denominated in dollars, to partially or completely offset the other two liabilities. Thus, this fourth kind of gain from international cash management involves (and is called) **multilateral netting of accounts.** Figure 16–5 shows these three transactions, as well as other methods of shifting funds among affiliates in the MNE. Notice that the funds transfer methods depicted in the figure may be used not only to carry out the transactions discussed above but also to transfer funds to a desirable location in order to minimize taxes or to avoid exchange and political risk in any country. If Nestlé wants to shift more funds to the United States in order to expand its

FIGURE 16–5

Some Methods of Moving Funds in the MNE

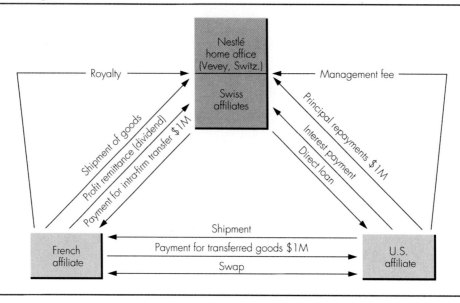

operations there, it can lend or invest more from the home office, swap assets between affiliates (e.g., accounts receivable from the United States for cash from France), remit less from the U.S. affiliate, and even use New York as a cash management center, shifting available cash from other affiliates to that central location for redistribution as needed.

The fifth kind of gain from centralized cash management relates to business strategy. Placing the cash management function in one location, either at the home office or at a location closely monitored by the home office, makes better control possible. In this way, the firm can assure that cash management decisions are made to meet global corporate needs rather than to improve an affiliate's position, possibly at the expense of the rest of the company. This is especially true with respect to hedging, which should be decided at the corporate level, since virtually every affiliate is likely to have assets or liabilities in another currency that are partially or totally hedged by balance sheet items of other subsidiaries.

While the benefits of centralized cash management are easy to see and potentially very large, it also presents some problems. Most important, if freedom to manage cash is taken away from the affiliate manager, some of the affiliate's ability to improve its performance is also taken away. The evaluation of each affiliate must recognize this point. (This idea is discussed further in the section on controls.)

Another problem with internationally centralized cash management arises when national rules restrict financial transfers into or out of some countries. Virtually all less developed countries and many developed ones limit funds outflows through exchange controls or taxation. Some countries specifically disallow international netting of payments. Because of such restrictions, international cash management today requires a great deal of knowledge about national financial constraints, and often requires a decentralized strategy of funds transfers because of these constraints.

Accounts Receivable

Accounts receivable (A/R) management may be divided according to the type of customer: A/R due from outside customers and A/R due from other affiliates of the firm. Receivables due from outside customers are the typical source of exchange risk, which can be handled as discussed in Chapter 6. Receivables due from other affiliates can be priced and timed to maximize the gains for the MNE, if a central policy is devised.

To deal with the exchange risk created by contracts with outside customers, the MNE can use any number of hedging strategies. In addition, the MNE can substantially reduce the expected cost by setting appropriate credit terms (to discourage late payments, or penalize them to account for expected devaluation of the receivable) and by pricing to account for expected exchange-rate changes. The key to managing foreign-currency accounts receivable is to plan the currency and price *before* contracting, that is, before creating the receivable. One way to eliminate exposed accounts receivable is to discount them by creating banker's acceptances, factoring, or forfaiting. (These three discounting methods are discussed in Chapter 19.)

Intracompany accounts receivable can be managed to serve a variety of company goals. Assume, for example, that the firm wants to move as much money as possible from a foreign affiliate to the home office. One way to do this is to have the foreign affiliate prepay any intrafirm purchases, and conversely to have the parent delay any payments due to the affiliate. Another is to price the intrafirm shipment so that greater profit is shown at the home office. (Some legal limitations on the use of these transfer strategies exist in most countries; for example, prepayments are limited to at most 90 days in many countries.)[10]

To move funds from a foreign affiliate to the parent firm, the parent can charge a high **transfer price** for sales to the affiliate. The transfer price is simply the price paid by the affiliate for an intrafirm sale of some product or service. If the product is a computer that costs the firm $1,000 to manufacture, the transfer price might be $1,000—in which case the manufacturing affiliate earns no profit. If the foreign affiliate is just a sales office, it might sell the computer to an outside customer for $3,000. Figure 16–6 depicts the transactions involved. Now, ignoring transportation costs and taxes, the foreign affiliate shows a profit of $2,000 on the sale. The firm could just as easily have charged $3,000 to the foreign sales office for the computer, leaving the entire $2,000 profit in the manufacturing affiliate. Or the firm could have charged some transfer price between $1,000 and $3,000, to share the profits between affiliates. The "optimal" transfer price would move the funds wherever the firm desires, subject to government constraints and the costs of carrying out the transfer. Important criteria for choosing transfer prices are the tax rates in each country, government-imposed price restrictions, and the risks of holding funds in a given currency and country. This simplified example is intended to offer a view of the basic issue in transfer pricing, rather than to say that either of the two extreme prices is "optimal," or even legally possible.

All in all, the management of accounts receivable is an area of great opportunity for the MNE, and one in which the purely domestic firm does not have the same options.

FIGURE 16–6

Transfer Pricing in the MNE

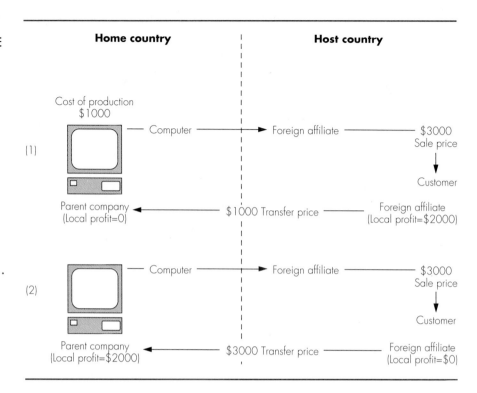

Inventories

Inventory management in an MNE parallels inventory management in a domestic firm. In addition, its concerns include physical risk reduction through diversification of location (if inventories are held in more than one country) and exchange risk increase due to denominating inventories in different currencies. Like centralized cash management, centralized inventory management offers cost-reducing opportunities to the MNE. If the firm produces the same product in more than one country, it can reduce the level of the inventories it needs globally by shipping products from locations where extra inventory exists to locations where inventory is drawn down.

Diversification of inventories across countries cannot be overemphasized as a potential advantage of the MNE. If for any reason the firm's production or shipment in one country is curtailed, the MNE with multiple production sites can serve various markets from other sources. Financially, the firm's cost would be lowest at one particular site at any given time. Strategically, its ability to ship from several sites reduces its risk of sales losses due to the strikes, other production problems, and adverse political developments that may arise in any one country.

Accounts and Notes Payable

To some extent, accounts and notes payable can be managed in the same way as accounts receivable. That is, for accounts and notes payable from one affiliate of the firm to another, the firm can use the timing and pricing of transfers to move funds where and when desired. Payables to outside suppliers and lenders are a key source of foreign exchange risk, which can be managed as discussed previously. Except for dealing with exchange risk, foreign payables can be managed as in the domestic firm, with the aim of minimizing the cost of making necessary payments.

EXCHANGE RISK MANAGEMENT

Exchange risk has been discussed primarily in relation to *transactions* denominated in foreign currency. In addition, exchange risk exists in the translation of financial statements and, in principle, for future, so-far unspecified activities of the firm. Three kinds of exchange risk should be differentiated: (1) transaction risk, (2) translation risk, and (3) economic risk. Each of these kinds of risks is important to the MNE, and each leads to somewhat different conclusions for hedging strategies.

Transaction Risk

When a specific contracted asset or liability is denominated in a foreign currency, it is subject to **transaction risk,** or the risk of change in its home-currency value during the time to maturity. Accounts payable and receivable, loans, and bank deposits denominated in foreign currencies are examples of items that are subject to such exchange risk. Each foreign-currency transaction can be hedged (or not) with some offsetting transaction in the same currency and with the same maturity.

Translation Risk

Translation risk is the risk of value changes in foreign-currency assets and liabilities on the balance sheet—whether or not the transactions occur during the accounting period. For example, the plant and equipment of foreign subsidiaries is subject to valuation change even if no purchase or sale of such facilities takes place during the accounting period. Because balance sheet information is reported to U.S. securities regulators and in financial statements published in the United States, valuation changes in the foreign operations of U.S. firms become public knowledge. Loss in the values of foreign-currency assets, regardless of its impact on company earnings, may negatively affect investors' perceptions of a firm. To avoid the appearance of weakness due to the devaluation of foreign assets, firms often try to hedge their balance sheets through financial contracts (such as forward contracts or money market hedges). This issue has been discussed in Chapter 15; conclusions as to the desirability of **balance sheet hedging** are ambiguous. On the one hand, since investor decisions may be based on valuation changes in foreign-currency assets, the firm should hedge to avoid investor preoccupation with such changes; on the other hand, since the valuation of foreign-currency assets may not affect the economic viability of the project, it would be a waste of effort for the firm to deal with such changes.[11]

Economic Risk

Economic risk is the risk of unexpected changes in future cash flows from foreign operations (and from activities denominated in foreign currencies, wherever they occur). Such risk is most important to the firm, since future cash flows are the basis for the firm's value. Unfortunately for the manager, it is not possible to know with certainty the full set of future cash flows that will occur. So a hedging strategy cannot be perfectly matched with such cash flows. To deal with economic risk, the firm may choose to follow a generalized strategy of hedging transactions when they are contracted and trying to balance foreign currency assets and liabilities as they appear on the balance sheet. Or the firm may choose not to hedge at all, on the assumption that future currency fluctuation will be approximately offset by price changes in each country (i.e., that purchasing power parity will approximately hold). Despite the inherent difficulty of predicting future foreign exchange exposures, ultimately the firm should be concerned about economic (foreign exchange) risk as the key variable in exchange risk management.

In fact, all three kinds of foreign exchange risk play important parts in the management of an international firm. No single hedging strategy can cover them all, so the MNE manager must devise plans for dealing with each. Fortunately, both transaction and economic risk deal with future cash lows, so the management of these two kinds of risk can be combined fairly readily. For example, the firm can hedge all occasional exports denominated in foreign currencies and seek local-currency financing for the entire production of its foreign affiliates. Then, if it does not employ balance sheet hedging (as suggested above), it can follow a consistent and simple hedging strategy. Judging from the immense volume of material dealing with corporate foreign exchange management strategies, it is safe to say that MNEs generally do *not* follow such simple strategies. Instead, they combine some hedging with some speculation in an effort to maximize their results from foreign exchange dealings.[12]

An Example of Exchange Risk Management

Consider the situation facing a U.S.-based firm such as American Express Company when its subsidiary in the United Kingdom reports the purchase of £5 million of office equipment (mainly furniture and computer terminals) for the subsidiary's tourist service offices throughout that country. This equipment is to be paid for in 180 days in British pounds. The strategies for dealing with exchange risk in this transaction depend on the whole firm's position in British pounds. The problem can be analyzed as follows.

First, if American Express already has an existing asset exposure in Great Britain, because of its subsidiary's ongoing activities, that position may partially or wholly cover the new transaction. In other words, if American Express-U.K. has a balance sheet that shows net sterling (pound) assets, typically because foreign subsidiaries have some dollar liabilities, then the new account payable may partially offset that asset exposure.

Second, the same results may occur even if the British subsidiary has been operated to cover ongoing exchange risk there. In the event that American Express has placed funds in euro-British pound deposits in one of its other subsidiaries (e.g., in France or Germany), the new account payable may offset the existing exposure. *Note that the exposure is still not covered unless the maturity of the existing asset matches the 6-month maturity of the new liability.*

Third, American Express can look for some financial hedging technique to avoid the exchange risk. For example, some new asset such as a bank deposit or short-term security could be purchased with a maturity of 180 days and value of £5 million. Or a forward contract could be arranged with a bank to sell dollars and buy pounds in 180 days. Through the London International Financial Futures Exchange (LIFFE) or through one of the U.S. futures exchanges, American Express could arrange a futures contract or option contract to hedge the account payable. The alternatives are numerous, but the basic goal is to find some British pound asset that matures in 180 days, worth £5 million, to hedge the new liability that calls for a cash outflow of £5 million in 180 days.

The following table lists relevant financial information if American Express were making this hedging decision on March 1, 1991.

Spot exchange rate	$US 1.9105 / £1
180-day forward exchange rate	$US 1.8627 / £1
180-day LIBOR in pounds	12.125% / year
180-day LIBOR in dollars	6.8125% / year
6-month sterling call option strike price The options cost $US 875 per contract at the CME, with £31,250 per contract.	$US 1.925 / £1
6-month sterling futures contract rate The futures contracts have £62,500 per contract.	$US 1.87 / £1
American Express has a (hypothetical) weighted average cost of capital of 13% per year.	

American Express can use this information to evaluate various financial hedges for the sterling account payable.

First, the firm can use a simple forward contract to hedge the exposure. A forward contract to buy British pounds would cost about $US 9.3 million in 6 months, as shown below:

$$£5,000,000 \times \$US 1.8627/£ = \$US 9,313,500.$$

This forward contract completely hedges the account payable, because it will result in receipt of £5 million in 180 days from the bank, which will be used to pay the supplier of office equipment.

A second alternative would be to place funds now into a pound-denominated investment that matures in 6 months. The choice shown above is a euro-sterling account that pays 12.125 percent per year for the 6-month period. The dollar value of pounds for AMEX to buy today can be calculated by discounting the future pounds that are needed to a present value of pounds that must be deposited today to achieve that sum in 6 months. The calculations are as follows:

$$£5,000,000 / (1.060625) = £ 4,714,202.$$

This first step shows that the interest earned in the eurosterling deposit for 180 days will be 6.0625 percent, and that £ 4,714,202 must be deposited today to reach the value needed to pay the account payable. Next, the dollars that must be used today to buy these pounds is:

$$£ 4,714,202 \times \$US 1.9105/£ = \$US 9,006,483.$$

It should not be surprising that the hedging cost is lower for this alternative, since the funds must be paid *now* rather than in 180 days. To compare the two choices, they must be placed in the same time period. This requires discounting the forward contract value, using the relevant cost of capital as the discount rate.

$$\$US 9,313,500 / (1.065) = \$US 8,745,070.$$

This results in a lower cost of hedging in the forward market, if the weighted average cost of capital is used as the appropriate discount factor.

A third alternative is to use a futures contract hedge in the LIFFE or the Chicago Mercantile Exchange (CME). Using the CME's quotes, we see that American Express could buy future pounds for $US 1.87 per pound in contracts worth ₤ 62,500 per contract. Multiple contracts could be bought, so that with 80 contracts the company could obtain the needed ₤ 5 million. However, since the exchange rate is *worse* than the forward rate (i.e., it costs more dollars to buy the pounds), AMEX will not consider a future hedge.*

Each of these financial hedges can protect American Express against foreign exchange risk. The company will want to choose the least costly hedge in this case—namely, the forward market hedge. In other situations one or another of these three alternatives will be the most beneficial to the firm. Beyond these choices, American Express should consider the possibility of structuring its business such that British pound assets (e.g., accounts receivable, investments, etc.) could be used to hedge liabilities such as this purchase of equipment. A broad range of hedging techniques are shown in the box below.

---

*The *option* contract can also be used to hedge this transaction. American Express could buy 160 call options as listed in the example, for a total premium of $US 140,000. For this price American Express would receive the right to buy pounds at the strike price of $US 192.5 per pound—a much worse price than the forward and futures contracts. (Actually, options for lower strike prices are available at much higher premia.) The option does not look attractive, unless American Express wants to speculate that the pound will go down in value even below the forward contract price. If this were to happen, by *not* exercising the options, AMEX could just buy pounds in the spot market in 180 days and benefit from the lower price. The option is generally useful if the firm wants to speculate or if the original commercial contract may not be fulfilled, so that the pounds may not be needed after all.

ADDED DIMENSION

Exchange Risk Hedging Techniques

To Hedge an Exposed Liability	To Hedge an Exposed Asset
Buy fx in the forward market	Sell fx in the forward market
Buy fx in the futures market	Sell fx in the futures market
Buy fx call options	Buy fx put options
Invest/deposit in a fx instrument	Borrow in a fx instrument
Incur accounts receivable in fx	Incur accounts payable in fx
Swap liabilities with another firm	Swap assets with another firm
Obtain any other fx asset	Obtain any other fx liability

In each instance, the hedge must produce an equal-value asset (liability) in the same currency with equal maturity to offset the exposed liability (asset).

CONTROL: IDENTIFYING OBJECTIVES, EVALUATING AFFILIATE PERFORMANCE, AND MAKING PERFORMANCE CONSISTENT WITH GOALS

Control is the fundamental part of management that involves developing profit plans for the firm and its divisions, then deciding what to do when actual operating results differ from those planned. For a foreign investment project, the financial control process generally begins with putting together a set of pro forma financial statements (income statement, balance sheet, cash flow report), such as the income statement shown at the beginning of this chapter. Then detailed budgets are developed for individual divisions, allocating the full capital budget to the specific purposes for which it will be used. During the time period after the creation of these plans, the firm's management observes the results and any deviations from the budgets. Usually, of course, actual results differ from budgeted ones. Finally, the firm develops a management plan for dealing with the deviations and implements it. The process is cyclical—as each planning period ends, another begins—and new budgets and managerial contingencies may be developed.

In the multinational firm, the potential for substantial home office control over affiliates exists because major capital budgeting usually requires more resources than those available in an affiliate—and home office assistance is needed to carry out capital projects. In addition, financial reporting to the parent company provides an informational basis for controls, which may or may not be exercised, depending on the extent of the firm's decentralization. And finally, because the people assigned to manage foreign affiliates are usually well known to the home office managers, there is an informal, personal contact that ties affiliates to the home office. All of this goes to say that the home office has the potential to impose substantial controls on the activities of foreign affiliates.

The process described so far is substantially equivalent to the one used to evaluate and control domestic divisions in a firm. But foreign affiliates face a wide range of additional factors that may affect their performance, and these factors should be taken into consideration when setting the goals and judging the performance of affiliates. How should the managers of foreign affiliates be evaluated for their financial performance? If they are evaluated in local-currency terms, then the home office must worry about hedging foreign-currency exposures and about remitting or reinvesting profits. If they are evaluated in home-currency terms, then their managers must deal with exchange risk and remittance policy. If they are limited in their financial dealings due to centralized cash and foreign exchange management policies, but they are evaluated in home-currency terms, then it must be recognized that their options are limited. On another issue, if transfer prices are set to move funds to the home office, then foreign profitability will look worse than it would if these prices were set to keep more funds in the affiliates. Correct evaluation of the performance of affiliate managers must take into account the constraints imposed on the affiliates.

Most managers and outside analysts agree that foreign affiliates must be evaluated in home-currency terms, since home-currency investors judge the firm as a whole. What the firm must do is create an evaluation scheme that produces home-currency performance measures, adjusted to account for the limitations placed on the affiliate by the home office.[13]

CONCLUSIONS

Financial management in a multinational firm encompasses concerns and opportunities greatly expanded from those encompassed by financial management in a domestic firm. Foremost among these concerns and opportunities is foreign exchange risk management, which is considered in several chapters of this book. Ultimately, foreign exchange risk management seeks to maximize the present value of future cash flows into the firm, just as most other aspects of financial management seek to do.

The issue of political risk arises when the firm operates in more than one national legal jurisdiction. The MNE possesses the ability to avoid total dependence on national authorities for its ability to operate; when the national government in one country places limitations on the MNE, the MNE can turn to other countries for sales, production, and so on. This asymmetry in bargaining power will be seen again when the government/business relationship is explored in Chapters 21–23. The MNE cannot avoid political risks completely, but it can reduce them through hedging, insuring, and diversifying strategies.

The capital structure of a multinational firm is limited primarily by the existing norms in the firm's home country, but that does not stop the firm from using different structures in host countries, as local conditions dictate. Extensive borrowing may be used in high-risk countries, to reduce political and economic exposures of assets. It may also be used in low-interest countries whose currencies are not free to adjust to eliminate interest differentials. This strategy may create highly leveraged affiliates, but it can be used to finance many other parts of the MNE more cheaply than local borrowing elsewhere. Also, locally subsidized financing often presents opportunities for borrowing that may lower the MNE's average cost of capital.

Working capital management presents a wealth of opportunities for minimizing financing costs and maximizing returns on available funds through the use of foreign markets and euromarkets. From centralized cash management, to multilateral netting of accounts payable, to pooling inventories, the MNE has far more flexibility than purely domestic firms. Because of its ability to move funds internationally, the MNE can arbitrage tax and other regulatory jurisdictions to minimize taxes and other costs of operation.

All in all, international finance is one of the most exciting, dynamic areas of corporate management at the international level—but it is also one of the most complex.

QUESTIONS

1. What are the main pros and cons related to the centralization of cash management in a multinational enterprise?
2. Define political risk. How may it affect a multinational firm?
3. Explain the difference between transaction and translation risk in foreign exchange risk management.
4. What competitive advantages does an MNE possess relative to local firms in terms of international financing opportunities?
5. How can a firm such as United Technologies, which has subsidiaries in Mexico and Argentina, protect these affiliates against both political and foreign exchange risk?

6. How can an MNE utilize intracompany accounts (such as loans, fees, and product shipments) to deal with exchange risk?

7. What is a transfer price? In dealing with its American affiliates, what transfer pricing policy should Nissan use to keep more funds in its Japanese affiliates?

8. What does it mean to say that the cost of capital is lower in Japan than in the United States? If this is true, how can U.S.-based MNEs that have affiliates in Japan take advantage of the situation?

9. Explain why economic risk, not translation or transaction risk, is the measure of foreign exchange risk that the MNE manager should be concerned about.

10. Should the managers of an MNE's foreign affiliates bear the responsibility for exchange risk management, or should this task be centralized? Explain your choice carefully.

REFERENCES

Brewer, Thomas, ed. *Political Risks in International Business.* New York: Praeger Publishers, 1985.

Business International Corporation. *Financing Foreign Operations.* New York: Business International Corporation, current edition.

De la Torre, José, and David Neckar. "Forecasting Political Risks for International Operations," *International Journal of Forecasting* (Vol. 4, 1988).

Eiteman, David, and Arthur Stonehill. *Multinational Business Finance.* Reading, Mass.: Addison Wesley, 5th ed., 1989.

Grosse, Robert, and John Stack. "Noneconomic Risk Evaluation in Multinational Banks," *Management International Review* (1/1984).

Hekman, Christine. "A Financial Model of Foreign Exchange Exposure," *Journal of International Business Studies,* Summer 1985.

Kobrin, Steven. *Managing Political Risk Assessment.* Berkeley: University of California Press, 1982.

Lessard, Donald, and Peter Lorange. "Currency Changes and Management Control: Resolving the Centralization/Decentralization Dilemma," *Accounting Review,* July 1977.

Mascarenhas, Briance, and Ole Christian Sand. "Country-Risk Assessment Systems in Banks: Patterns and Performance," *Journal of International Business Studies* (Spring 1985).

Robins, Sidney, and Robert Stobaugh. *Money in the Multinational Enterprise.* New York: Basic Books, 1973.

Rutenberg, David. "Maneuvering Liquid Assets in a Multinational Company: Formulation and Deterministic Solution Procedures," *Management Science,* June 1970.

Shapiro, Alan. *Multinational Financial Management.* Boston: Allyn & Bacon, 3rd ed., 1989.

NOTES

[1] A full set of the measures used in capital budgeting appears in basic finance texts, such as Brealey and Myers, *Principles of Corporate Finance,* 3rd ed. (McGraw-Hill, 1988).

[2] However, if the local-currency price goes up due to the currency revaluation and demand is price inelastic, then the total revenue received may go up even if the quantity sold declines.

[3] Low-cost financing may be available locally even without government subsidy. In most countries, capital controls limit the ability of foreigners to borrow locally. Thus, in Japan, where interest rates are below those in the United States, a firm with local operations may take advantage of these rates.

[4] See, for example, "The ITT Affair," in Prakash Sethi, *Up Against the Corporate Wall* (Palisades, Calif.: Goodyear Publishing, 1976).

[5] Useful surveys of political risk models appear in Kobrin (1982), Brewer (1985), and de la Torre and Neckar (1988).

[6] See, for example, Shapiro (1989), chap. 14.

[7] *Eximbank Program Summary* (Washington, D.C.: Office of Public Affairs, Export-Import Bank of the United States, n.d.).

[8] See Alan C. Brennglass, *The Overseas Private Investment Corporation* (New York: Praeger Publishers, 1983); and Business International Corporation, "Investment Guarantees," in *Financing Foreign Operations* (New York: Business International Corporation, current edition).

[9] Calculated from *Business Week,* March 22, 1985, p. 134; and Ravi Sarathy and S. Chatterjee, "The Divergence of Japanese and U.S. Corporate Financial Structure," *Journal of International Business Studies,* Winter 1984.

[10] See Business International Corporation, *Financing Foreign Operations,* for information about restrictions on financial transfers in over 50 countries.

[11] See, for example, Dennis Logue and George Oldfield, "Managing Foreign Assets when Foreign Exchange Markets Are Efficient," *Financial Management,* Summer 1977.

[12] See, for example, Nick Gilbert, "Hedging Trims the Costs," *Euromoney,* February 1985, pp. 141–44; and Derek Bamber, "How SKF International Keeps a Grip on 18 Currencies," *Euromoney,* September 1982, pp. 341–51.

[13] See, for example, Lessard and Lorange (1977) and Robins and Stobaugh (1973).

Bill Smythe & Co.

A firm from any country that decides to set up a foreign subsidiary for manufacturing, sales, shipping, or other business activity, generally faces an important challenge in dealing with the foreign-currency aspects of the business. American firms in particular tend to have difficulty with this situation, because they often operate in dollars exclusively in their U.S. operations. European firms, on the other hand, commonly are used to working in at least two or three currencies, and in many cases with the European Currency Unit as well. So, especially for American firms, the need to understand and deal with foreign currencies is a fundamental business problem of the 1980s.

One industry that has long been associated with international business is the production of textiles, for example, men's and women's clothing. From the ancient silk trade that formed an important part of the activities of the British East and West India Companies to modern offshore assembly of blue jeans in Taiwan, trade in textiles has extended throughout the world. Even with this international component, the production of clothing in most countries remains primarily domestic. That is, due to differences in costs, tastes, and government regulations, clothes sold locally are generally also produced locally.

The clothing business in the United States historically has been a very inward-looking industry. Most clothing is made from domestically produced fibers, either natural (such as cotton or wool) or synthetic (such as nylon or polyester). Although a large percentage of the natural fiber is imported today, most clothing is still made of primarily domestically manufactured material. Very little of the United States' domestic production is exported; several American companies, however, have foreign subsidiaries that produce locally in various foreign markets.

One way that domestic firms have been able to survive international competition is through successful lobbying for protection against imports. The textile industry in the United States has been one of the most adept at gaining government protection, mainly through the international Multifibre Agreement. This accord among producing and consuming nations gives the importing countries essentially unlimited power to restrict imports of both raw materials and assembled clothing in order to protect domestic producers. The Multifibre Agreement is a major exception to the rules of the General Agreement on Tariffs and Trade (GATT) that promote freer trade among such member nations as the United States and its European trading partners.

This case was written by Professor Robert Grosse as a basis for class discussion, 1987.

About the Company

Bill Smythe & Co. was founded in 1951 by a Philadelphia shop foreman, Bill Smythe. He had spent five years working for a small men's shirt manufacturer in Yeadon, Pennsylvania, that went out of business due to inadequate sales and rising costs. With his knowledge of the manufacturing process and his determination to succeed through better marketing than his predecessor, Smythe set up his shop in a West Philadelphia industrial district and began to produce a line of high-quality men's shirts and women's blouses. His initial customers were many of the same clients served by the previous company.

Within a year of opening the shop, Smythe decided to expand his marketing efforts. Sales were fairly stable but barely enough to pay the bills until he set up a licensing agreement with one of the leading designers of high-fashion women's clothing. This agreement enabled him to produce blouses under the designer's name and to obtain access to several large department stores as clients. Even after paying the licensing fee, Smythe's earnings rose substantially.

By 1960 Bill Smythe & Co. was selling over 200,000 shirts and blouses per year. The original 5 employees had grown to 11, and the shop now took up 4,000 square feet of operating space. At this point Smythe had licensing agreements with three fashion designers for making both shirts and blouses. The branded lines made up over three fourths of his total sales. In looking over the business, Smythe decided that his next step should be to expand into additional product lines.

The process of growth continued during the 1960s. The firm added lines including handkerchiefs, undergarments, and jackets—though the last line was discontinued in 1968 when consistently poor sales led Smythe to drop it. By the end of the decade, Bill Smythe & Co. had become a fairly large producer of shirts and blouses in the northeastern United States, with export sales into Canada. Despite the efforts to diversify, sales were dominated by Smythe's two original lines.

By that time, competition from foreign producers was beginning to affect sales. Smythe found that Italian and Spanish firms, in particular, were making unbranded shirts that undercut his prices by almost 30 percent, and some of these firms were producing brand-name shirts at a similar price advantage. By coincidence, Smythe discovered that one of the Italian firms was run by a high school classmate, Joe Todarello, who had returned to his parents' native country and entered the business there. When his friend mentioned that his father wanted to sell the firm, Smythe quickly offered to buy it and keep his friend as general manager. This arrangement was concluded in 1977. It turned out very well, with the Italian subsidiary bringing in about 22 percent of total company sales within four years of the acquisition.

Although he had never thought about the problem in any detail, Smythe began to realize that changes in the lira/dollar exchange rate were altering his costs and profits in a serous way in the early 1980s. He was especially unhappy with the loan that he had used to finance most of the purchase of the Italian firm. The loan was made in dollars to the Italian subsidiary with Smythe & Co.'s guarantee, but the subsidiary was paying it off through profits earned. With the demise of the Bretton Woods system of fixed exchange rates in 1971, the lira had been devaluing in spurts against the U.S. dollar (thus raising the financing cost with each devaluation). Figure 1 shows this situation. When the dollar began to decline relative to the deutsche mark and the Japanese yen in 1985, the lira

FIGURE 1

Lira/Dollar Exchange Rates*,
1970–1986

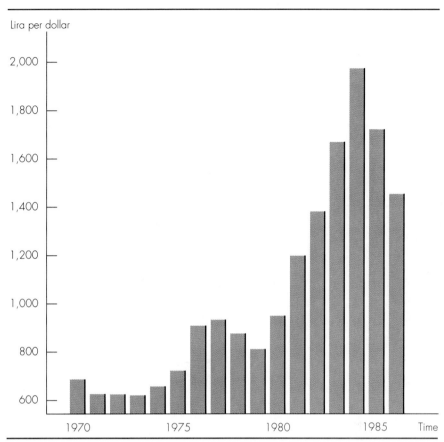

*Lira per dollar, end-of-year market rate.

strengthened somewhat, but the downward trend seemed likely to continue. Smythe found that his earnings in Italy declined precipitously from 1981 to 84 (due to depressed sales as well as currency devaluation). In 1985 sales rose, but operating profits remained weak. In 1986 earnings (counted in dollars) rose sharply as operating costs in Italy stabilized and the U.S. dollar weakened.

Current Concerns

Bill Smythe sat uncomfortably in his living room in December of 1986, looking over the projected earnings statement (Table 1) drawn up by Joe Todarello. While the numbers in lira appeared clear and justifiable, Smythe was totally unable to come to grips with the problem of exchange risk and projecting dollar values of the various cash flows. Moreover, he felt that some attention should be paid to the possibility of restrictions on the firm's shipments of materials and finished shirts and blouses between Italy and the United States. He had asked Todarello to describe the currency situation in 1985 and 1986. Table 2 was Todarello's response.

The projections show a stable growth of lira earnings and cash flow. Dollar cash flows are negative, reflecting the continued purchase of materials and

TABLE 1

SMYTHE ITALIA
Pro Forma Income Statement
1987 to 1991
(in billions of lira)

	1987	1988	1989	1990	1991
Revenues:	21.2	27.0	36.4	45.9	60.4
Local sales	15.8	20.4	28.5	35.7	49.2
Export sales	2.3	3.9	4.5	6.8	8.2
Earnings on investments	3.1	2.7	3.4	3.4	3.0
Expenses:	18.4	22.9	29.3	37.3	47.8
Labor	5.2	6.8	8.8	11.5	14.9
Local materials	6.1	7.9	10.3	13.4	17.4
Imported materials	1.9	2.1	2.9	3.5	4.2
Licensing fees	0.9	1.1	1.4	1.8	2.4
Supervisory fees	0.7	0.9	1.1	1.4	1.9
Operating overhead	1.5	1.8	2.3	2.9	3.9
Interest expense	2.1	2.3	2.5	2.8	3.1
Net income before taxes	2.8	4.1	7.1	8.6	12.6
Corporate income tax (45%)	1.3	1.8	3.2	3.9	5.7
Net income after taxes*	1.5	2.3	3.9	4.7	6.9

*Note: Tax of 30 percent is payable on any profit remitted to the U.S. parent.

TABLE 2

SMYTHE ITALIA
Flow of Funds Statement
December 1986
(values in $ U.S. equivalents)

Cash flow	Currency		
	Lira	Dollars	Marks
Next month	82,000	−39,000	8,000
In 2 months	79,000	−43,000	8,000
3 to 6 months	360,000	−195,000	34,000
7 to 12 months	540,000	−295,000	52,000
13 to 18 months	570,000	−295,000	57,000
19 to 24 months	580,000	−310,000	57,000
Year 3 and after (per year)	1,180,000	−600,000	120,000

equipment from the U.S. parent company. Profit remittances are *not* included in the calculations. Export sales to a German department store, which began in 1984, are listed as German mark cash inflows, also growing at a stable rate. Export sales from the Italian subsidiary to the U.S. parent company are shown as lira cash inflows, since they are billed in lira by the subsidiary.

Chapter

17

Industrial Relations

Industrial relations are often regarded as place specific and therefore not especially relevant to MNEs and their competitive strategies. This perspective is inaccurate. MNEs possess internal strengths that they can use to improve their industrial relations management at the levels of both the parent and the subsidiary. Moreover, MNEs must consider the effects of industrial relations environments on some of their key strategic management concerns. This chapter examines these topics. The main goals of the chapter are to:

1. Explore the international aspects of industrial relations from the standpoints of MNEs, labor, and society.

2. Present the industrial relations systems approach to characterizing industrial relations environments.

3. Describe the international activities of trade unions.

4. Examine the management of industrial relations within MNEs.

5. Explain how industrial relations concerns affect certain strategic management decisions, such as those pertaining to production allocation, production smoothing, and disinvestment.

WHAT ARE INDUSTRIAL RELATIONS?

In the following chapter, "Personnel Management," the focus is on the relationship of individual employees to their employers. In this chapter, the focus is on collective employee-employer relationships. Such relationships vary considerably country by country and industry by industry, and this variability can provide the MNE with important problems and opportunities. These will be discussed later. Let's begin, however, by reviewing some key aspects of **industrial relations,** especially in the United States. Knowledge of the U.S. industrial relations system will provide us with a basis for noting and understanding differences between U.S. industrial relations and industrial relations in other countries.

Industrial Relations in the United States

In the United States, we typically view industrial relations within the context of union-management relations and of a collective agreement or **labor contract.** Industrial relations, then, involve both substance (i.e., the terms of the contract) and procedure (i.e., determining and administering the contract).

Among the topics usually covered in labor contracts are job classifications, wages, wage supplements (such as shift differentials and overtime pay premiums), fringe benefits (such as health insurance and the retirement program), holidays, vacations, promotion and layoff procedures, a no-strike/no-layoff commitment, union recognition and security, and management rights. Other topics, such as cost-of-living wage supplements and the procedures to follow with regard to plant closings, may also be covered. Typically, the contract includes rules regarding its administration. These rules identify the structure of the in-plant union representation and the procedure to be followed in handling complaints (or grievances)—so as to resolve them in a timely fashion consistent with the substantive provisions of the contract.

Laws enacted by the U.S. government have established rules regarding bargaining unit determination (whom will the contract cover?), union recognition, and the conduct of the parties during collective bargaining. The size or scope of the **bargaining unit** is usually decided by the National Labor Relations Board (NLRB) in an administrative ruling based on employee and employer petitions, historical precedents relating to the common interests of groups of workers, the nature of the tasks identified in the proposed unit, and so on. Voting by the employees in the proposed unit decides whether there will be a union and, if so, which union it will be. If there is strong employee support for a union and management concurs, the NLRB may determine a bargaining unit and then certify a union without an election.

U.S. law also requires that both management and union bargain in good faith (this means, for example, that information necessary to the successful conduct of the bargaining must be shared and that there must be give-and-take during the negotiations) and that bargaining be conducted only over topics related to the terms and conditions of employment. Overall, the thrust of U.S. labor law has been to lower the potential for labor-management conflict by establishing rational, democratic procedures related to union recognition; by limiting the substance of collective bargaining to worker-related interests and issues; and by requiring the parties to the collective bargaining process to be reasonably open, accessible, and forthcoming.

Perceptions of the Stakeholders

We see from this that industrial relations are important in several respects. From management's perspective, industrial relations determine labor costs, the facility with which work processes are changed, and the potential for conflict in resolving differences held by the union, the firm, or the employees. From the union's perspective, industrial relations determine the extent of shared decision making on matters that concern workers and on the level of income and financial security enjoyed by those whom the contract covers. Government and society value successful industrial relations too. Such issues as the frequency and duration of strikes that interrupt commerce, the cost-push pressures of wages on product prices, and worker participation in decision making typically relate to broader social interests in productivity, competitiveness, inflation, employment growth, and industrial democracy.

In the following section, the international dimensions of industrial relations pertinent to MNEs and their operations will be discussed, as will important public policy issues regarding the effects of MNEs on employment and industrial relations. Subsequent sections cover key features of the industrial relations environment—worker representation, the nature of the labor-management agreement, wage determination, industrial conflict, and so on—that are evidenced in several countries. In addition, the activities of unions and government-related organizations at the transnational level are characterized and discussed. The chapter concludes with a section on the management of industrial relations in an MNE context and on the impact of industrial relations on strategic management.

WHAT'S INTERNATIONAL ABOUT INDUSTRIAL RELATIONS?

Like industrial relations at the national or domestic level, industrial relations at the international level are important to companies, management, unions, workers, society, and government.

Ethnocentric, Polycentric, and Geocentric Views

The ethnocentric MNE, which mandates the behavior of subsidiaries, typically has problems regarding industrial relations. The cultural, legal, and factual contexts that drive industrial relations are too crucial to be managed from the distance of the parent company. As a result, local management is usually given, perhaps begrudgingly at first, considerable autonomy in its industrial relations.

If one considers the multinational enterprise (MNE) to be simply a collection of reasonably freestanding, national production and marketing units, then industrial relations would, at a minimum, be as important to the MNE as to a purely domestic company. This is the polycentric view. Key elements in the competitive success and profitability of either type of firm—production wages, work methods, benefit levels, and so on—would be determined by means of the industrial relations process. But there is really more to industrial relations than this for the MNE—as will be shown later.

The mature multinational enterprise is more than a collection of freestanding, national subsidiaries. Because of its transnational linkages in terms of technological (including management expertise) and financial flows and because of its ability to identify and utilize product and resource markets advantageously, the geocentric MNE is quite different from the non-MNE in its industrial relations. Here are some illustrations:

> Opel (General Motors' German subsidiary) negotiates an *increase* in the basic workweek hours with Belgian unions as it adds a second shift at its Belgian assembly plant. The intent of management is to keep the costs of production there competitive with the costs of production at a similar

Opel plant in Germany. The intent of the Belgian workers is to expand employment and enhance job security.

A U.S. electronics firm cuts back its U.S. manufacturing output 10 percent by laying off a portion of its U.S. workers. Its French subsidiary picks up the resulting product market slack. By cutting back employment in the United States, the firm avoids the large payments to workers that French law would have required if the cutback had been made by the French subsidiary.

Workers at a German company's British subsidiary go out on strike to support their demand for improved wages. Operations at the company's German plants continue, providing substantial cash inflows (revenues) to the entire MNE system. The British workers completely forgo their cash inflows—their wages—during the strike. The company is less severely pressed financially than these workers are and can sustain a long strike if need be.

Ford of Europe integrates production among several European subsidiaries. For certain models of cars, the engines could be British-made, the power train and some stampings German-made, the wheels and other stampings Belgian-made, and so on. A strike by workers in Belgium could shut down assembly plants in Britain and Germany. This gives the Belgian workers operational leverage vis-à-vis management and enhances their power in collective bargaining. A similar conclusion would hold for workers in Britain or Germany.

These examples show how the multinationally distributed operations and markets of the MNE affect the economics and stability of the workplace and the relative bargaining power of the parties involved in industrial relations. These effects, in turn, can have a significant impact on unions and on worker-related social issues.

Labor's View of MNEs

Organized labor usually operates within the context of a nationally defined industrial relations system. It is the product of a specific cultural and legal heritage. As the above examples indicate, the MNE may determine or influence labor's interests transnationally, but unions and workers are less transnationally mobile than the MNE. They see the MNE, then, as having options that they do not have. They see it as having the potential for:

Forcing workers in one country, faced by competition from workers in other countries, to "bid down" their wages and benefits in order to get or keep jobs.

Taking advantage of differences in legally required benefits for workers by adjusting operations in countries where the costs of such adjustments are lowest and thus forcing excessive dislocation burdens on workers in these low-benefit countries.

Outlasting workers in the event of a strike in one country because cash inflows to the MNE are at least partially maintained by operations in countries where there is no strike.

In the Ford of Europe example above, the bargaining leverage gained by the unions because of transnational production integration may be only a short-run benefit, as the company might position future production facilities in worker and union environments that are less threatening to it.

Social Issues and MNEs

From a broad public policy perspective on the international dimensions of industrial relations, the MNEs have been both criticized and praised. Critics contend that by opening plants abroad, the MNEs have exported jobs from the United States and destroyed the diverse industrial base that it needs to sustain its economic well-being.[1] They argue that MNEs have compromised the national security of the United States by locating high-technology operations overseas and by licensing foreign firms to produce high-technology products. It has also been argued that MNEs, by the very nature of their operations, negate the national interest expressed in the U.S. National Labor Relations Act, in maintaining the balance of power between management and unions that successful collective bargaining requires.[2] On the other hand, supporters of the MNEs contend that overall employment has grown faster in MNEs than in non-MNEs[3] and that workers in MNEs receive higher salaries than workers in non-MNEs.

A key issue in the public policy area arises from the ability of MNEs to respond quickly to new market opportunities wherever they arise, whereas workers are unable to suddenly relocate geographically or acquire new needed skills. This is the adjustment problem. Most industrialized countries offer adjustment assistance funds to retrain and relocate workers affected by changes in products and markets. This says that these countries value the economic benefits that are realized when firms develop new products and markets and that society in general should provide a "cushion" to workers adversely affected by such developments. Some countries, as noted earlier, penalize firms for laying off workers by requiring large severance payments. This says that these countries do not want workers and society to be forced into a costly adjustment process unless the threshold value of the economic benefits realized in this way is above a legally defined minimum. A problem here is that marketplace competition may make adjustment compelling anyway. What could result from penalizing layoffs is "hidden unemployment" as workers are kept on the job in the face of declining production or product prices and state-provided subsidies keep firms afloat and jobs intact. This is a problem today in some of the state-owned enterprises in France and the United Kingdom. It is a big problem in the newly market-oriented countries in Eastern Europe—such as Poland and Czechoslovakia. Finally, the more aggressive countries underwrite or legislate benefits to firms that invest in them or trade internationally so that they may get to keep jobs and earn foreign exchange. These benefits take such forms as tax rebates on exports, low-interest loans, government-funded R&D, and special purchase agreements. Policies of this kind distort comparative advantage and invite political retaliation.

THE DIVERSITY OF THE INDUSTRIAL RELATIONS FACING MNES

Since MNEs have generally concentrated their manufacturing[4] investments in the more industrialized countries, where larger markets and higher income levels exist, two of these countries—the United Kingdom and Germany—have been contrasted with the United States to illustrate the diversity among country-bound industrial relations systems. Japan's industrial relations system has also been considered, because of the positive influence of its work force management techniques and industrial relations on its industrial prowess and its competitive successes. To help us focus on the business-related features of these industrial relations systems, our discussion is organized around selected key industrial relations issues as evidenced in each system.

Worker Representation

United States   In the United States, the union, if certified, becomes the exclusive bargaining agent for the employees in the bargaining unit. It negotiates with the company on the contract terms, and it monitors management's compliance with the contract. Depending on what the contract stipulates and on what state law may require, workers may or may not have to join the union or pay union dues as a condition for continued employment. Collective bargaining typically occurs at the company and plant levels, with some notable exceptions involving multicompany bargaining, for example, in trucking and the building trades, where the level is regional, and in the steel industry, where it is national.

United Kingdom   Work groups within a plant often express a sense of solidarity and negotiate with management on matters that they feel are important. They elect someone from their ranks to be their chief spokesperson, or steward. Workers also often belong to a union, which is organized on a geographic basis and includes members at many firms in a local area. Collective bargaining is conducted with a company's representatives by a council of representatives of the unions in the area. It may also be conducted by a **steward's council** representing only workers at the company. This dualism, which is in sharp contrast with the exclusive jurisdiction that prevails in the United States, allows for conflict between the unions and the stewards. For example, the union council may accept an agreement with management and the company stewards may reject it. Major work stoppages have resulted in cases of this kind. Labor negotiations are conducted at the company level with the larger firms in an area, or at the industry level for an area if the firms are fairly small.

Germany   Union membership is purely voluntary, and there is only one union for laborers in each major industry. Collective bargaining, conducted between the union and the employers' federation for the industry, covers major terms of employment, such as wages. Firms that are federation members apply the labor agreement to their workers. Nonfederation firms may or may not implement their industry agreements, depending on a variety of factors—the tightness of the labor market, the desires and solidarity of their workers, and so on. Secondary conditions of employment (such as the scheduling of vacations and workshifts) are negotiated at the company and/or plant levels between management and legally established **works councils**—whose members are elected by the company's workers and may or may not be union members.

Works councils in Germany are legally empowered to "codetermine" with management issues related to worker safety procedures and other in-plant practices. These works councils are made up of management and employee representatives. Some employees are also elected to serve as employee representatives on **boards of supervision.** These boards, which operate in some respects like boards of directors, appoint and evaluate top management. Works councils and the presence of employees on boards of supervision are the results of the widespread German codetermination movement.

Japan Unions in Japan are typically characterized as **enterprise unions.** There are over 70,000 of them, and they usually include all the hourly and salaried employees of the firm. Workers view themselves as employees first— and because they are employees, they belong to the enterprise union. Collective bargaining is accomplished at the enterprise level. Enterprise unions in the same industry affiliate to form industrial federations, which are generally loosely knit and do not themselves engage in collective bargaining. The federations typically coordinate the bargaining policies and timing of enterprise unions during *Shunto,* the so-called Spring Wage Offensive.

Labor-management relations in Japan reflect the often close, mutually supportive identification between the worker and the company. The larger firms, for example, offer "lifetime" employment (i.e., up to retirement age) and structure their operations, and changes in operations, to accommodate that commitment. Workers, on their part, dedicate themselves to the company and the company's competitive success.

The Labor Agreement

United States The **labor agreement** is a contract that can be enforced in court, if need be. It is in effect for a fixed period of time, and its terms and conditions apply to all of the workers covered by it. Therefore, the employees of an individual bargaining unit have no individualized right to bargain with management for their own wages and benefits. Legislation at the national level abolishes this right for such workers.

The content of the contract, which is typically fairly extensive, covers the various topics identified earlier. Disputes regarding the proper application of the contract's provisions are typically resolved by means of the grievance system specified in the contract itself. This usually means that binding arbitration, where an impartial, outside party makes the final decision, is the last step in the grievance procedure.

United Kingdom The labor agreement is not a legally binding contract. It is an "understanding" among the parties that basically means, given the present circumstances, these are the acceptable terms and conditions of employment. Violations of the agreement by unions or stewards' groups carry no legal penalties since these entities are not recognized in law. They have no legal status or identity.

The content of the United Kingdom labor agreement is generally less extensive than that of the U.S. contract. Such agreements may contain provisions defining the structure of the relationships among the parties. Separate wage provisions are then negotiated; their duration is effectively open-ended. Procedures for handling complaints are often spelled out in the labor agreement, but there is no provision for arbitration. In fact, complaints are typically handled by the shop steward, who was probably not formally involved in the negotiations establishing these procedures, and resolved, if need be, by industrial action (i.e., a strike) before the procedures have been completed.

Germany Workers in an industry may be covered by several fixed-term contracts, each of which has a different expiration date. There is typically a wage structure agreement that spells out the job classifications and the relative wage levels for the different jobs. The tariff, or wage, agreement sets out the actual wages to be paid. Another agreement may specify the amount of indemnification paid a worker who loses his job because of automation or a sales decline. Yet another agreement covers general working conditions, such as work times, personal leave, vacations, and overtime pay. The provisions of each agreement are limited to the issues that it alone addresses.

Conflicts over the application of an agreement can be negotiated between management and the individual involved, perhaps with the participation of a union representative and/or the works council. The final resolution of complaints is handled in German labor courts, if necessary. In contrast to the U.S. situation, individual workers covered by labor contracts may still negotiate individually or collectively with management to secure wages and benefits superior to those defined in the contract. By statute, their individual rights here are not preempted.

Japan   Union and company representatives review annually the labor agreement and it is changed if the parties agree that this should be done. Typically, labor agreements cover wages, bonuses, working conditions, grievances, personnel affairs, and welfare issues. **Shunto,** the Spring Wage Offensive, is an annual, enterprise-level bargaining over wages and the summer bonus that is coordinated closely at the industry level. The practice of *Shunto* acknowledges that wage gains at the enterprise level are constrained by the labor costs of a firm's competitors. *Shunto* attempts, in effect, to extend wage bargaining to cover all of the firms in an industry. There may be yet another round of bargaining when unions negotiate the year-end bonus.

The provisions of the Japanese labor agreement are often general and vague, and they even include employment conditions that are legally required. Disputes about the rights conveyed in such agreements are often settled between the parties in an amicable manner involving compromise. The disputes can be taken, however, to an agreed-upon private third party for mediation and, if necessary, arbitration. Japanese labor law establishes labor relations commissions that can also mediate and arbitrate disputes, and the courts can do this too.

Industrial Conflict

The two most common forms of industrial conflict are strikes and lockouts. **Strikes** can result from two types of disputes: those relating to rights that workers feel are theirs because of contracts or past practices and those relating to interests that workers have regarding the setting of wages, benefits, and other terms and conditions of employment. **Lockouts,** in which employers close the plant and thus keep employees from working, don't occur nearly as often as strikes. Other forms of industrial conflict include "work to rule" (i.e., a slowdown, "going by the book"), industrial sabotage, and the occupation of plants by workers.

United States   As noted, most labor agreements contain provisions barring strikes. The very existence of the agreement signifies that both management and the union have defined their mutual interests. The contract conveys certain rights to both parties (e.g., the wages to be received and the ability of management to reassign workers). The grievance system, which typically includes binding arbitration, is also defined in the contract. This procedure resolves whatever disputes over rights may arise.

Strikes and lockouts during the term of the contract are usually forbidden. One effect of all this is that once a contract is in place, strikes and lockouts are typically illegal and rare. Such actions, however, are not rare after a contract expires and when a new contract is being negotiated. They then involve the entire bargaining unit. At such times the parties are seeking to define their interests. Typically, "wildcat" strikes—strikes that occur during the term of a contract—result from allegedly onerous management practices or working conditions related to specific work groups and are not endorsed by the union. Such strikes are usually brief. Other forms of industrial conflict seldom occur.

Business unionism, which characterizes the pragmatic, enterprise-oriented focus of the U.S. labor movement, acknowledges that an ongoing, hopefully profitable, firm is in the best interests of the union and the workers. Likewise, socially accepted values, such as those relating to private property and the concept of the contract, help explain U.S. labor's reluctance to destroy equipment, occupy a factory, or provide less in the way of labor services than the labor agreement calls for.

United Kingdom Labor in the United Kingdom is typically more strike prone than labor in the United States. The social philosophy of **voluntarism,** a keystone concept of the British labor movement, asserts that workers alone will define and pursue their self-interest. From this, it follows that the right to "industrial action," such as a strike or "work to rule," must be unconstrained (e.g., by law). Labor agreements do not prohibit the right to strike, and strikes often occur during impasses in bargaining and in support of workers' grievances. Such strikes are typically brief, and they often involve small work groups.

The dual worker representation structure (i.e., the shop stewards and the unions) has been known to complicate both collective bargaining and grievance handling in the United Kingdom and to result in fragmented bargaining relationships—and, in so doing, to enhance the propensity of workers to strike and to extend the duration of strikes. Lockouts, especially those involving company workers other than those in a work group that is out on strike, are not uncommon. Workers extend the idea of voluntarism to mean not only that they will take care of themselves but also that management will take care of itself. There is more class consciousness on the part of both labor and management in the United Kingdom than in the United States, and the work environment is probably more adverse to the efficient settlement of labor-management disputes.

Germany Labor laws prohibit strikes and lockouts when an agreement is in effect. This means that conflicts (such as strikes) over rights are illegal. Conflicts over interests, which occur when an old contract has expired and a new one is being negotiated, are legal. Focus and clarity are given to the issues in collective bargaining and the potential for strikes is reduced by the fact that there are several labor agreements in an industry, with different termination dates and covering different terms and conditions of employment.

This structure is apparently consistent with the preference of Germans for orderly, well-defined work relationships. Nevertheless, at times some strikes have occurred when an existing contract was in effect. These strikes were illegal. The issues, however, were usually not rights but interests. For example, in the early 1980s, unanticipated inflation was damaging workers' living standards, and strikes were conducted to increase wages accordingly—even though a wage agreement was currently in effect.

Japan   Strikes and lockouts at the enterprise level are rare. Strikes of exceedingly brief duration (perhaps a half-day or so) are typically scheduled during *Shunto* to demonstrate workers' support for their representatives' demands in industry-wide negotiations. The issues over which there may be industrial conflict between management and the union are also fairly limited. For one thing, the provisions of the labor contract supersede an individual worker's terms and conditions of employment that are not equal to or better than what the contract mandates. For another, the law establishes standards for minimum wages, hours, overtime, rest periods, vacations, sick leave, sanitary conditions, and discharge notice that are set at the comparatively high levels of other advanced societies.

One result of all this is that the overwhelming majority of strikes are over economic issues, brief, and, since they usually relate to *Shunto,* anticipated. The Japanese social philosophy of *Wa* implies that individuals subordinate individual interests and identities to those of the group. Social harmony and teamwork are derived from this. Significant (i.e., other than ceremonial) conflict is the antithesis of *Wa.*

Cross-Country Comparisons

Management in the multinational enterprise is concerned with several aspects of the industrial relations systems in and across which it operates. These aspects are basically the same as those with which management in the domestic enterprise is concerned, but the MNE can treat them as variables in its strategic planning since its operations transcend typically place-bound industrial relations. This management perspective will be developed more fully toward the end of this chapter. However, some of the groundwork can be put in place now. The key question is: How do the countries compare on certain issues important to management, such as wages and benefits, the potential for productivity improvement, and production continuity?

Wages and Benefits   The importance of the level of wages and benefits is obvious. Major business decisions and significant financial commitments often turn on a comparative analysis of wage and benefit costs. But what about the propensity of these costs to change? What about the pace of these changes relative to inflation in general?

Wages in the United States have traditionally been among the highest in the world. Changes in basic wage rates, within the union-management context, are reflected in labor contracts. Such changes are programmed over a period of time—most often a three-year period. Cost-of-living wage increases must by definition lag inflation, and typically they do not fully offset the amount of inflation. Cost-of-living formulas defined in the labor contract define and control such increases.

In the United Kingdom, wages are almost constantly subject to scrutiny, and if workers or unions feel that higher wages are necessary or desirable, a new round of wage bargaining can occur at any time. The structure of the work force representation may be a factor here too. In the UK, shop-level work groups can initiate new wage demands and attempt to make them effective. In comparable U.S. industrial settings, the more broadly constituted union bargaining unit is the single collective bargaining entity. Wage escalation within that unit is not constantly at issue, as it is in the United Kingdom where a militant and aggressive work group may secure higher wages, which, in turn, leads to demands from other work groups within the firm for the reestablishment of the wage parity differentials that they have traditionally merited and enjoyed. The potential for a firm to be caught in a wage cost/product price squeeze appears to be substantially higher in the United Kingdom than in the United States.

In Germany, wages set in industry-wide negotiations are paid by all firms in the industry. The firms also pay wage increments, depending on the labor market conditions they face, their profitability, or the intensity of their workers' demands. Strikes in support of wage increments are illegal when an industry-wide agreement (which covers wage minimums at firms party to industry-wide bargaining) is in effect. Moreover, the social and cultural environment is not usually supportive of random strikes over economic issues by small, shop-level groups. German labor contracts do not contain provisions for cost-of-living wage increases. Wage increases lag inflation.

In Japan, industry-wide wage bargaining occurs during *Shunto* and the unions' wage increase targets reflect the recent inflation experience. Pattern-setting unions in each industry lead the way during *Shunto*. These unions are usually in firms with strong financial positions, and other unions in other firms push to imitate the wages they negotiate. Cost-of-living increases are part of *Shunto*'s wage targets. These increases lag inflation, but the pattern wage, which is based on the most profitable firm's ability to pay, may, if extended, put other firms at a cost disadvantage. **Pattern-bargaining,** incidentally, is also common in some U.S. industries (e.g., automobiles and aerospace).

Productivity Improvements   The use of new and better tools and equipment, changes in the way the work force is managed, and so on, are intended to enhance productivity. A crucial element here is the management incentive to innovate, or take risks, for this purpose—for example, by spending large sums of money for new machinery that management foresees as lowering production costs. Here the prospects for increasing profits justify the cost of the new equipment. Management's right not to share decision making on such changes with unions becomes relevant, as do the timing and the methods by which the firm's workers come to share in the benefits of the productivity improvements.

In the United States and Germany, management can initiate process improvements, peg the affected workers' wages according to the prescribed job evaluation system, and benefit (profit) substantially from the new equipment. In Japan, a similar situation obtains, but wages, which to a greater extent reflect age and seniority considerations, are not likely to be increased because of a new job assignment. In all three countries, unions bargain for higher wages based, among other things, on the firm's profitability. But the profitability must be demonstrated first. The company does profit from productivity improvement, at least for a while—probably for a few years.

In contrast, in the United Kingdom, an equipment change is often accompanied by the negotiation of a **gain-sharing agreement** acceptable to the work group affected. A wage increase for this group can lead to demands for wage increases by other groups that seek to maintain parity, or customary wage differentials, among the firm's workers. The overall costs of these wage increases must be measured against the cost saving anticipated if new equipment is installed. In this case, the benefits of the productivity improvements are immediately shared with the workers and the firm's incentive to innovate is dampened.

Strikes and Lockouts   Because they interrupt production, strikes and lockouts are costly. Whether or not a firm produces, its fixed costs, such as rent, interest on loans, and management salaries, continue. Without production, sales revenues are reduced (either immediately or eventually, depending on inventories). Industrial conflict per se has costs (to all parties) associated with it. If such conflict can be anticipated, these costs can sometimes be reduced by building up inventories of the firm's product or, if the conflict is expected at a supplier, by building up inventories of the supplier's product. Cross-country comparisons on strike experiences are difficult to interpret.[5] For example, if work stoppages per 100,000 employees in the United States and the United Kingdom are compared, it is found that the United Kingdom has twice as many work stoppages but that the number of lost workdays because of such stoppages in the United States is about double the number in the United Kingdom. The random or unplanned-for strike is, however, widely recognized as being more evident in the United Kingdom than in the United States.

Although the intent of the above data on work stoppages is not to malign the British industrial relations system, when compared to Japan, Germany, or the United States, the United Kingdom does appear less attractive to enterprises on three counts. This conclusion is not the purpose of our discussion, however. The point we wish to make is that industrial relations environments can vary substantially and can thereby affect a firm's profitability differently. The management challenge is to align the firm's operations with the industrial relations environment that offers the best fit.

ADDED DIMENSION

How Would You Handle This One?

A few years back, a large U.S.-based automaker sent some financial auditors to its British subsidiary. During the course of their audit, they found that the compensation paid some in-process inspectors was being charged to quality control instead of to production. They then reallocated that compensation to production. Had the inspectors not been "in-process" but "final" inspectors, charging their compensation to quality control would have been OK.

When the in-process inspectors heard of this reallocation of costs, they walked off the job in protest. This was because the pay for production inspectors was less than the pay for quality control inspectors and they felt their pay would be cut. In support of the inspectors, other workers walked out and the entire plant had to close down. ∎

Theories on Industrial Relations Systems

Industrial relations systems vary so much country by country that it is difficult to see what commonalities exist among them. One of the first widely accepted attempts to conceptualize a cross-country theory of industrial relations was presented by Dunlop in the 1950s.[6] In his theory, Dunlop identifies elements common to all industrial relations systems and a schematic framework on the interactions among these elements. Figure 17–1 presents this framework. Dunlop identifies rules, or outputs, as common to all industrial relations systems. They have to exist—and they have to be determined by someone or some group, that is, the *actors*. In some societies, such as totalitarian states, government may unilaterally determine these rules. In others, such as the industrial democracies in the West, all three actors—workers, management, and government—participate. The influence of each actor may vary, however, depending on the rules at issue. For example, safety rules usually receive special attention by workers, management, and government alike. Installing new equipment and work methods will probably be management's prerogative.

The nature of the rules is also affected by the *contexts* within which they are expected to operate. Variations in product and process technologies, market structures relating to both product and resource markets, and ideology or culture relevant to the workplace may affect the kinds of *rules* as well as the intensity of the actors' interests regarding them. Substantive rules define the nature of the outputs (wages, vacations, etc.). Relational rules define how the actors behave toward one another (e.g., no strikes or lockouts).

Dunlop's framework is a fairly static one, but it is useful in sorting out and developing an initial understanding of how any system operates and how changes might work their way through a system. Let's look at a few illustrations of recent socio-political changes and the structure of Dunlop's model.

During the 1980s, Poland's Solidarity Union represented a different ideology than that presented to workers by Poland's communist government. It persisted in developing and promoting this ideology, based on principles of political democracy and unionism free from government control (i.e., different relational rules). During 1989–90, Solidarity was at the forefront of social and institutional change in Poland as democratic pluralism replaced communist totalitarianism as the controlling socio-political ideology. The roles of all the actors changed dramatically as the adjustment to a more market-based context has evolved.

The reunification of Germany in 1990 resulted in important changes in German industrial relations and the German economy. The communist-sponsored

FIGURE 17–1

Dunlop's Industrial Relations System: Elements and Relationships

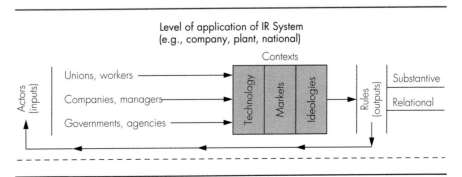

unions in East Germany were dissolved and the industrial union structure of West Germany was applied to workers in the East. Wages accelerated in the East, but worker skills and other factors affecting worker productivity did not change so quickly. Unemployment expanded in the East, as did migration from the East to the West. The German government is investing considerable sums of money in the East in the 1990s to rebuild the social infrastructure necessary for the expansion of private-sector activities to expand productivity and employment. In Germany, ideology and market changes have resulted in adjustments by government, union, and company actors and changes in both substantive and relational rules.

Other theories have been presented, such as that by Clegg, who sought to identify trade union behavior within the context of a systematic behavior pattern.[7] His "trade unionism under collective bargaining" theory rationalizes such aspects of unionism as membership, structure, and governance in terms of the nature and scope of the collective bargaining in which the union participates. Clegg's theory is also useful in understanding the workings of an industrial relations system.

THE INTERNATIONAL STRUCTURE OF TRADE UNION ACTIVITIES

Trade unions are active internationally via three basic avenues—tripartite intergovernmental organizations, affiliation with unions from other countries, and an extension of their contacts with domestic firms and their home country government.

Intergovernmental Organizations

ILO   The **International Labour Office (ILO)** is a United Nations affiliate (located in Geneva) composed of government, industry, and union representatives. Through the years, the ILO has sought to define and promote fair labor standards regarding safety, health and other working conditions, and freedom of association and other workers' rights. Through its research and publishing programs, it reports on wages and working conditions by country and industry.

In the early 1970s, the ILO published a pioneering study on the social policy implications of the global activities of MNEs.[8] Among the topics covered by the study were investment concentration by area and industry, capital and technology transfers, international trade, manpower effects, working conditions, and industrial relations effects. The study concluded by noting the different views and concerns of employers and workers and recommending that the social problems and benefits specific to MNEs, as opposed to those of national firms, be identified and studied further.

In the latter 1970s, the ILO conducted a series of industry-specific studies on U.S. and non-U.S. MNEs in Western Europe to document these views and concerns. In 1980–81, it published a series of country studies on the employment effects of MNEs—jobs lost and gained because of MNEs and the quality of jobs (e.g., skill levels) within MNEs.[9] It concluded that MNEs were significant employers in many countries, and for a few countries, including the United States, the data implied that employment was growing faster in MNEs than in non-MNEs and that the internal structure of employment was shifting more quickly toward white-collar workers in MNEs than in non-MNEs. The tendency of MNEs to be more R&D intensive than non-MNEs was seen as a key factor affecting the differences between them in employment growth and stability. The ILO sponsored a second study on MNEs' employment effects in the United States in 1989. This later study looked not only at the jobs issues, but also industrial relations and public policy effects.[10]

OECD   In 1976, the **Organization for Economic Cooperation and Development (OECD),** a government, industry, and union group located in Paris, established a set of voluntary guidelines for MNEs. These guidelines, which are still in effect, note that MNEs are obliged to respect the laws, regulations, and administrative practices of member countries and that countries are obliged to provide national treatment to MNEs within their borders. These mutual obligations of MNEs and countries appear simple, but they can become quite complex. The classic case in this regard, which occurred in 1976, involved a disagreement between the Belgian government and the Belgian subsidiary of the Badger Company over whether Badger's parent, the U.S.-based Raytheon Corporation, was responsible for the legally required indemnification payments to Belgian workers who were laid off (permanently) when Badger's Belgian office was closed.[11] The government contended that Badger's Belgian subsidiary lacked sufficient funds for this purpose because of the parent's transfer pricing and transnational work allocation patterns. Here the obligation to respect national laws provided Belgium with a rationale for extending its influence to the parent company in another country.

Transnational Union Affiliations

Windmuller classifies international trade union affiliations into four categories: global, regional, specialized, and industrial internationals.[12] The global international category includes trade union organizations that cut across regional, specialized, and industrial groups. Such organizations, which can be found in nearly every country, are mainly concerned with political and missionary activities.

The International Confederation of Free Trade Unions (ICFTU) is the most important **global international** for MNEs, since its membership is heavily concentrated in North America and Western Europe—areas that are also significant to MNEs. Most of the **regional internationals** are subdivisions of the globals, and their activities are regional applications of what the globals do. **Specialized internationals**—for example, the Worker Group in the ILO, the Trade Union Advisory Committee in the OECD and the European Trade Unions Congress, which represents workers' interests at the European Community level—function as components of intergovernmental agencies and lobby within these agencies.

The **industrial internationals** are also affiliates of the global internationals. In the ICFTU, they are termed the International Trade Secretariats (ITSs), and there is a separate ITS for each major industry group—for example, the International Metalworkers' Federation (IMF) in the metal trades. Unions at the country level in the metal trades belong to the IMF and to industry-specific departments in the IMF—for example, the Automotive Department.

Of special interest to the MNE, **worldwide company councils** have been formed under the auspices of the ITSs. A case in point is the General Motors Council in the IMF, which consists of union representatives from GM plants all over the world. The GM Council meets periodically to share information about working conditions, collective bargaining, and so on. Unions can use this information to push for comparable treatment in country-level bargaining. The international structure of the ITS provides a union vehicle that parallels the international structure of the MNE. On occasion, an ITS representative has sought to intervene at the global headquarters of an MNE on behalf of a member union having difficulty in its dealings with a subsidiary of the MNE at the national level.

During the 1970s, when the worldwide company councils were developed, there was considerable speculation that these councils would be vehicles for transnational collective bargaining with MNEs. However, transnational bargaining is precluded by such factors as the diverse legal and cultural environments affecting national unions. In the early 1990s, **industrial regionals** in Europe grew in importance as new industrial policies at the European Community were being debated and formed. The European Metalworkers' Federation, for example, seeks to influence EC policies affecting metalworkers' unions in the various European countries.

Extension of Domestic Contacts

Some U.S. unions have responded to the U.S. MNE by trying to bargain with it as a global, headquarters operation. The International Union of Electrical Workers (IUE), for example, invited union representatives from General Electric's foreign plants to participate with it in its collective bargaining. These representatives were just observers, however, and were not directly party to any negotiations. U.S. labor law is the controlling factor here, since it limits collective bargaining to matters related to the U.S. bargaining unit.[13]

Similarly, during collective bargaining several years ago, the IUE proposed that General Electric cease transferring work from its U.S. operations to its foreign operations. The company contended that this proposal was without merit and refused to consider it or to provide the union with details on its foreign operations. The union then filed an unfair labor practice charge with the NLRB. The board's general counsel denied the charge and noted that the union had not substantiated its allegation that work transfers were in fact occurring.[14] Overall, unions have not been successful in their attempts to prohibit or limit, through collective bargaining, the foreign sourcing practices of MNEs (i.e., manufacturing abroad for the U.S. market).

The AFL-CIO has been active in promoting U.S. public policy changes that would limit the ability of U.S. MNEs to export capital and technology and to import production. However, this effort has not been particularly successful.

The U.S.-Canada situation is a special case in the extension of U.S. union activities internationally. A Canadian region is an integral component of many U.S. **international unions.** This binationalism in union structure has facilitated the binational coordination of collective bargaining with MNEs having U.S. and Canadian operations and of subsequent contract administration activities. Canadian nationalism has resulted in some Canadian regions becoming autonomous unions, but close coordination with the U.S. counterparts of these unions has been maintained. The 1989 U.S.–Canada Free Trade Agreement has required unions on both sides of the border to coordinate collective bargaining even more closely. If Mexico and the United States form a free trade area, as suggested by the presidents of both countries in 1990, U.S. unions will not be able to coordinate activities as closely as they have with the Canadian unions. The U.S.

and Mexico do not share a common union heritage nor have similar union structures as do the U.S. and Canada. One might thus expect the U.S. union movement to be quite active on the public policy front, and generally opposed to the idea of a U.S.-Mexico free trade area, as the potential for such an agreement is debated and U.S. unions seek to protect their members' economic interests.

THE MANAGEMENT OF INDUSTRIAL RELATIONS IN THE MULTINATIONAL ENTERPRISE

Earlier material substantiated the view that industrial relations systems differ considerably country by country and are place-bound. Successful MNE management recognizes this and allows subsidiaries considerable autonomy in managing their worker relationships. This approach is consistent with generally accepted management principles regarding line/staff relations and decentralization of decision making supportive of operating responsibilities at the subsidiary level. One MNE's view on the local autonomy experienced in industrial relations is provided by George McCullough, an industrial relations executive at Exxon.

My company operates in 137 countries. The variations in our labor relations processes, the manner in which we go about collective bargaining, and the differences in items included in collective agreements are staggering. Even in two countries like Holland and Belgium, where the proximity between Rotterdam and Antwerp has caused us to consolidate some management functions, the labor relations processes are totally independent of each other and the contracts bear little resemblance.[15]

Studies on the locus of decision making in MNE industrial relations operations invariably conclude that the local management makes the operating decisions and is responsible for implementing those decisions. Even in the Japanese multinationals, industrial relations, in the context of a union-management relationship, is the subsidiary's responsibility. Japanese management frequently defers to the expertise and opinions of local management. A single exception to such local autonomy is the handling of pension issues by MNEs. Approval of pensions, which may involve a future liability of the parent company, is often required at the parent level prior to acceptance at the subsidiary.

Most large MNEs have an **industrial relations staff** at the parent company level. The activities of this staff relate to both operational and strategic matters. These activities include advising and participating in personnel selection and development at both the subsidiary and headquarters levels.

Advising — The Subsidiary Level

The MNE industrial relations staff represents a pool of expertise that is available to subsidiary management. It is not only experienced in industrial relations per se but also knowledgeable about plant operations and workplace management. It can be called on for opinions and suggestions on such local matters as bargaining strategies and tactics or the development of a new job evaluation system.

The MNE industrial relations staff also monitors industrial relations at the subsidiary to ensure that wages, benefits, and working conditions relate solely to local labor market needs—thereby guarding against the emergence of a global settlement pattern, which would probably saddle the company with greater labor costs than those of its competitors. A related function of the headquarters staff is to provide information useful to subsidiary management during labor negotiations—especially when the local union supports its claims by citing ITS-generated data on company-specific conditions in other countries.

Advising—The Headquarters Level

The MNE industrial relations staff counsels the production, marketing, finance, and similar groups at the headquarters level. Budgeting and financial pro formas of subsidiary operations include estimates of labor costs. Forecasts of changes in these labor costs are often provided by the MNE industrial relations staff in consultation with local management. In the event of strikes or lockouts at a subsidiary, the industrial relations staff can provide advice to the MNE-level production, logistics, purchasing, and marketing groups on the anticipated duration of the conflict. If the MNE's production pattern is transnationally integrated, such advice would be especially significant, since operations at other subsidiaries are affected by such a conflict. Alternatively, if headquarters management is weighing the possibility of replacing production at a struck subsidiary by production at another subsidiary, it would probably value an appraisal of the anticipated duration of the conflict.

Senior line management at the MNE level often solicits interpretations by the industrial relations staff of significant events at the subsidiaries. Such interpretations prepare it to participate with and respond to subsidiary management in the making of line management decisions.

Personnel Selection and Development

Management personnel are typically selected by the person to whom they will report. Typically, the person above the one who makes such a selection approves or rejects the selection decision. The top industrial relations executive at a subsidiary would be selected by the subsidiary's managing director, and that selection would be approved or rejected by the headquarters-level executive to whom the managing director reports. Typically, the head of the MNE industrial relations staff consults with senior line management at the MNE on such selection decisions.

The involvement of the MNE industrial relations staff is even more extensive than this, however. Career path and progression planning for key personnel is a fairly continuous process that includes individual development programs, identification of training needs, and so on. The MNE industrial relations staff participates in such planning as it affects key industrial relations personnel at the subsidiaries. Indeed, it may on occasion organize and conduct special training seminars for industrial relations managers from several of the MNE's subsidiaries.

THE INDUSTRIAL RELATIONS COMPONENT IN STRATEGIC DECISION MAKING IN THE MULTINATIONAL ENTERPRISE

Strategic decisions are often regarded as those that establish the longer-run direction of the firm and that provide the basis for operating decisions. From the industrial relations perspective, four strategic decision-making areas appear especially relevant—foreign direct investment, production allocation, production smoothing, and disinvestment.

Foreign Direct Investment

Historically, the foreign direct investments of U.S. MNEs (in the manufacturing sector) were defensive in nature. They were made to protect a foreign market presence originally obtained through exports. As foreign competition developed and profit margins were eroded, the firm sought to establish a plant within the market that it intended to continue serving. Its success often depended on its ability to transfer established management and production techniques from the parent to the subsidiary and to minimize overall production and marketing costs.

Of special importance, then, were those labor-related elements in the foreign environment that affected production costs and product availability. Critical assessments of alternative production sites typically included data on present and anticipated employee compensation costs and days worked per year (exclusive of holidays, vacations, and absenteeism). Wages and benefits are higher in Holland than in Hungary, for example. Days worked per employee per year may be lower in Germany than in the United Kingdom. All of these factors affect (product) unit labor costs. Potentially relevant factors are worker militancy and management's ability to initiate changes in workplace technology and work force organization. In these respects, Germany might be favored over the United Kingdom or France.

The key here is for management to identify all of the pertinent industrial relations factors and to evaluate its foreign direct investment alternatives in light of those factors. The final outcome may well involve more than just a go or no-go decision. It may involve the nature of the work to be performed at the proposed plant or the kind and amount of production equipment that will be used. It may involve participation by the local government in securing attractive financial support or trade union concessions that will render the proposed facility more profitable. When Ford Motor opened a plant in Belgium in the mid-1960s, for example, the provincial government helped secure a written five-year peace commitment from the local trade unions. When Volkswagen decided to open a plant in Pennsylvania in the mid-1970s, the United Auto Workers (UAW) agreed that Volkswagen's wages could be lower than those of other U.S. automakers. In the mid-1980s, the principals involved in the General Motors/Toyota NUMMI joint venture agreed to recognize the UAW as the plant workers' exclusive bargaining representative. The UAW, in turn, eventually negotiated an innovative contract to enhance productivity at the plant.

Production Allocation

With respect to industrial relations, **production allocation** decisions are similar to foreign direct investment decisions. Indeed, some might contend that the latter are, in effect, initial production allocation decisions. New product and equipment cycles, however, do afford MNEs the opportunity to reevaluate, and perhaps renegotiate, their industrial relations environments. In some instances, unions have, in effect, bargained down on wages and benefits to keep jobs, or governments have offered special incentives.

Offshore production decisions by MNEs are also production allocation decisions. However, such decisions are special in some ways. They are made largely because of labor cost differences, and they result from the MNE's unique resource market scanning capabilities. The selection of the specific operations to be performed offshore turns substantially on the labor intensiveness involved. The parent-subsidiary logistics involved are usually inventory intensive and time consuming. Thus, the offshore production concept, including the labor element, is not especially flexible. Labor, which is usually the most flexible factor of

ADDED DIMENSION

Who's the Culprit in This One?

When an economic recession recently occurred, a large MNE in the electronics industry had to cut back production in all of its major markets. It ordered a 10 percent employment reduction at all of its plants in those markets.

Some subsidiaries, however, were faced with paying large "redundancy" or discharge payments to workers that were let go. Management at these subsidiaries complained about this. The parent then changed its order and allocated cutbacks at the plants in different countries to minimize the total MNE-system costs resulting from discharge payments. As a result, most of the cutbacks in employment were made in the United States, where no such payments were required. In Western Europe, where the required payments were quite high, there were small cutbacks or none at all. ■

production, is not so in this context. The firm that engages in offshore production may do well to also maintain a domestic production capability that can respond more quickly to demand changes and competitive conditions in the domestic product market.

Before transferring production to an offshore facility, the firm is required by U.S. labor law to negotiate with the union over the effects of the relocation decision on the workers who constitute the bargaining unit. Since that decision apparently turns on economic factors, and since collective bargaining is concerned with economic factors, enlightened management may well negotiate with the union over the relocation decision and not just over its effects. Negotiations of this kind could well result in the weakening or elimination of the relocation rationale.

It is interesting to note the historical differences here among the U.S., Japanese, and European MNEs. In contrast to the U.S. MNEs, the Japanese are not required by law to negotiate with a union on the employment effects of transferring production to an offshore facility. But the Japanese would not transfer such production without examining domestic employment effects, discussing the situation with the employees involved, and doing everything possible to reduce negative effects. European MNEs, on the other hand, have not favored offshore production. They imported workers from nearby, low-wage countries instead. The interests of these workers and their effects on local, native workers were addressed within the employee and union representation structures already in place.

Production Smoothing

Rutenberg identifies **production smoothing** as a special variation on production allocation and notes:

In each nation, production smoothing problems and opportunities are different. A unique feature of the multinational corporation is that headquarters can alter the flow of products between nations to smooth production ... [that is, force a] reallocation of markets to factories to achieve optimal production smoothing for a multiproduct, multifactory corporation.[16]

He identifies three types of factories that are crucial to a production smoothing strategy and relevant to industrial relations: lowest unit cost factories, flexible multi-item factories, and seasonal factories.

The **lowest unit cost factory** produces standardized items and operates at full capacity. In such factories, productivity is the key consideration. Lowest unit cost factories can be either capital intensive or labor intensive. If they are capital intensive, the union enjoys some leverage vis-à-vis management since comparatively high fixed costs will continue in the event of a strike. In such factories, one management strategy is to treat workers as salaried staff to encourage their closer identification with the company; another is to pay workers on a piece rate basis. If they are labor intensive, the offshore manufacturing plant becomes a viable consideration.

The **flexible multi-item factory** is one in which new items are produced. The equipment in such factories is general purpose, and the work force is usually highly skilled. Job enrichment, Rutenberg suggests, appears appropriate to factories of this sort. Worker assignments and job categories cannot be rigidly defined. Some industrial relations environments, such as Japan, seem well suited to the flexible factory.

The **seasonal factory** probably operates a few months out of the year. In such factories, a work force buildup is followed by layoffs. Rutenberg suggests that seasonal factories be located in areas accustomed to seasonal work—in northern Finland, for example, where variations in weather conditions have preconditioned society to accept seasonal changes in labor demand. In such cases, even unions tend to accommodate the cyclical employment pattern.

Expanding on Rutenberg's scheme, there appears to be a fourth type of factory relevant to production smoothing. It is a variant on the flexible, multi-item factory model. In this instance, the flexible factory is so named because it can adjust output volume in any one product while experiencing low adjustment costs. To illustrate, Japanese car manufacturers, such as Toyota, limited exports to the United States during the 1990–91 recession rather than cut back on the U.S. domestic production of Toyota cars manufactured in the United States. Toyota's workers in Japan were much more flexible than those in the United States regarding the handling of a drop in product demand. For example, it would not be unusual for some of them to work at dealers selling Toyota products. American auto workers are not that flexible.

This discussion on production smoothing can be best summarized via the Labor Flexibility/Production Variation Matrix presented in Figure 17–2. Quadrants I and III are the ideal ones to operate in. Variations in production are most efficiently handled in locations where labor is highly flexible (quadrant I). For example, Japanese production is noted for its flexibility. Robots can be efficiently reprogrammed (preserving capital investment), workers have high skill levels and can perform effectively on various assignments, unions are not concerned with job demarcation systems, workers are willing to relocate if necessary, and so on. Where low variation is anticipated, low labor flexibility locations offer the best opportunity for low-cost operations (i.e., the low unit cost factory). Large

FIGURE 17–2

Labor Flexibility/Production
Variation Matrix

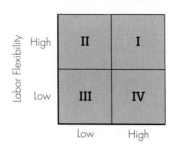

Variation in production scheduling

amounts of fixed capital can be employed to secure scale economies, or production can be located in low wage areas when skill needs are low.

In contrast, the firm is usually disadvantaged cost-wise when production variation is low but labor is highly flexible (quadrant II). The high human asset (skill) levels of flexible workers generally sit idle when production is standardized and routinized. Yet, the wage levels must be high enough to service these high human asset values. Similarly, high variation in production coupled with low labor flexibility results in high costs (quadrant IV). This could be the result, for example, of workers' low skill levels and the application of insufficient talents and/or knowledge to changing job demands, or of institutional, worker-related barriers to worker flexibility, such as a requirement to pay overtime wage premiums when workers perform jobs outside of their permanent job classifications.

Production smoothing allows the MNE to implement competitive advantages, for example, by locating production facilities in environments characterized by quadrants I and III, and then varying production in the quadrant I factory as demand varies over product and business cycles, or during structural changes, while keeping production at the quadrant III factory level at optimum scale output.

Disinvestment

A **disinvestment** decision—that is, a decision to close or sell off a plant—is not easily or routinely taken. The prevailing wisdom, however, is that management should move swiftly and decisively in such matters, that it is best not to have a difficult situation linger. This wisdom must confront the reality that in many countries, especially in Western Europe, legally constituted works councils have the right to be informed of the subsidiary's economic health and prospects and that substantial indemnification payments to laid-off workers are often legally required. Therefore, any disinvestment proposal should be carefully analyzed and its attractiveness discounted by the anticipated indemnification costs. The disinvestment procedure should be planned carefully, and the legal rights of workers to information must be addressed. Contingency plans should be developed to cover the adverse publicity that usually accompanies disinvestment decisions, and even the possibility that workers may forcibly occupy the plant and attract additional headlines.

CONCLUSIONS

International industrial relations are more complex and diverse than industrial relations in a single country. Industrial relations are not necessarily more difficult to manage at the subsidiary level than at the domestic level, however, and the very diversity of international industrial relations may present opportunities to the MNE—especially in terms of strategic management.

The role and function of the MNE industrial relations staff require a special awareness and sensitivity. The personnel of this staff must be knowledgeable about the different foreign industrial relations systems and the critical trends and events that affect subsidiary operations, and they must be sensitive to the effective allocation of authority and power between the MNE and subsidiary management levels. Sometimes only a fine line separates advising from controlling.

Different as industrial relations systems are, they all share a common general structure. They are all concerned with the determination and application of workplace rules. The basic actors—management, union, and government—participate in varying degrees in this rule-setting. Models, such as those developed by Dunlop, are useful starting points in learning about any specific industrial relations system.

QUESTIONS

1. Are industrial relations more or less significant to an MNE than to a purely domestic company?
2. What options or advantages not possessed by a purely domestic counterpart might the subsidiary of an MNE have in its industrial relations?
3. Compare the productivity incentives for management in the British and Japanese industrial relations systems.
4. Compare the productivity incentives for management in the British and American industrial relations systems.
5. If you could pick specific features (rules, practices, etc.) from the American, German, and Japanese industrial relations systems and put them into one "ideal" system, which would you pick, and why?
6. What purposes are served by an MNE industrial relations staff?
7. Why should industrial relations operating decisions be made by subsidiary-level management?
8. What do industrial relations imply for strategic management decisions regarding production allocation?
9. With regard to a plant location decision, what key characteristics of the industrial relations environment would an MNE take into consideration? Which of these characteristics would be of concern to an MNE but not to a purely domestic company?
10. How does industrial relations management in MNEs relate to the competitive advantages of MNEs?

REFERENCES

Bean, R. *Comparative Industrial Relations: An Introduction to Cross-National Perspectives.* New York: St. Martin's Press, 1985. See, especially, "Industrial Relations in Multinational Enterprises," chap. 8, pp. 184–207.

Ferner, Anthony. *Governments, Managers, and Industrial Relations: Public Enterprises and Their Political Environments.* Cambridge, Mass.: Basil Blackwell, Inc., 1988.

Harvey, Charles and Turner, John (eds.). *Labour and Business in Modern Britain.* Savage, Md.: Rowan & Littlefield, 1989.

Kujawa, Duane. "U.S. Labor, Multinational Enterprise and the National Interest," *Law and Policy in International Business,* 1978 (no. 3), pp. 941–68.

_____ . *American Public Opinion on Japanese Direct Investment* (with Daniel Bob). New York: Japan Society, 1988.

_____ . "Technology Strategy and Industrial Relations: Case Studies of Japanese Multinationals in the United States," *Journal of International Business Studies,* Winter 1983, pp. 9–22.

Local Production of Japanese Automobile and Electronics Firms in the United States: The "Application" and "Adaptation" of Japanese Style Management. Tokyo: University of Tokyo, Institute of Social Science, Research Report No. 23, March 1990.

Sisson, Keith. *The Management of Collective Bargaining: An International Perspective.* Oxford, England: Basil Blackwell, 1987.

Spalding, Hobart A. *Organized Labor in Latin America.* New York: New York University Press, 1977.

NOTES

[1] An early summary of these views is presented in Nat Goldfinger, "An American Trade Union View of International Trade and Investment," in *American Labor and the Multinational Corporation,* ed. Duane Kujawa (New York: Praeger Publishers, 1973), pp. 28–53.

[2] Duane Kujawa, "U.S. Labor, Multinational Enterprise, and the National Interest: A Proposal for Labor Law Reform," *Law and Policy in International Business,* 1978 (no. 3), pp. 941–68.

[3] For a general review of the evidence on these issues, see *Employment Effects of Multinational Enterprises in Industrialized Countries* (Geneva: International Labour Office, 1981).

[4] The reader should note that workers' and unions' interests in MNEs focus more on firms in the manufacturing sector than on firms in the mining or extractive industries. The foreign situs of a mine may merely reflect the simple fact that that is where the ore is. Locating a plant abroad, however, is seen as a decision that turns on less absolute considerations.

[5] The observations on strike effects in this paragraph are based on data presented in Hugh Clegg, *Trade Unionism under Collective Bargaining* (Oxford: Basil Blackwell & Mott, 1978), p. 69.

[6] John Dunlop, *Industrial Relations Systems* (New York: Henry Holt, 1958).

[7] Clegg, *Trade Unionism,* passim.

[8]*Multinational Enterprises and Social Policy* (Geneva: International Labour Office, 1973).

[9]For the summary study, see *Employment Effects of Multinational Enterprises in Industrialized Countries* (Geneva: International Labour Office, 1981).

[10]Duncan C. Campbell and Roger G. McElrath, *The Employment Effects of Multinationals in the United States* (Philadelphia: Industrial Research Unit, Wharton School, University of Pennsylvania, December 1989).

[11]R. G. Blainpain, *The Badger Case and the OECD Guidelines for Multinational Enterprises* (Deventer, the Netherlands: Kluwer, 1977).

[12]John P. Windmuller, "International Trade Union Organizations: Structure, Function, Limitations," in *International Labor,* ed. Sol Barkin et al., (New York: Harper & Row, 1967).

[13]Herbert R. Northrup and Richard L. Rowan, *Multinational Collective Bargaining Attempts* (Philadelphia: Industrial Research Unit, Wharton School, University of Pennsylvania, 1979), p. 120.

[14]Duane Kujawa, "Foreign Sourcing Decisions and the Duty to Bargain under the NLRA," *Law and Policy in International Business,* 1972 (no. 3), pp. 523–24.

[15]George B. McCullough, "Comment," in *Multinationals, Unions, and Labor Relations in Industrialized Countries,* eds. Robert F. Banks and Jack Stieber (Ithaca, N.Y.: New York State School of Industrial and Labor Relations, Cornell University, 1977), p. 150.

[16]David P. Rutenberg, *Multinational Management* (Boston: Little, Brown, 1982), p. 182.

Volkswagen of America (A)

Volkswagen of America (referred to hereafter as Volkswagen) is the U.S. subsidiary of Volkswagenwerk, A.G., headquartered in Wolfsburg, Germany. Volkswagenwerk is Germany's largest automobile manufacturer. Its worldwide production capacity is about 2.5 million units—about one third of which it produces outside Germany.[1] In addition to its U.S. operations, Volkswagenwerk has assembly plants in Nigeria, Belgium, and Yugoslavia and produces motor vehicles and components in Brazil, Mexico, Argentina, Peru, and South Africa.

During the 1980s, labor-management relations at Volkswagen of America have generally been quiescent and constructive. But this was not always the case—especially in the start-up years. Let's take a look at what happened then.

Investment Considerations

Volkswagenwerk's first plant in the United States opened in 1969. It produced air conditioners for German-made VW "beetles" sold in the United States. In January 1976, Volkswagenwerk's Supervisory Board (analogous, to some extent, to a U.S. firm's board of directors) authorized management to begin negotiations on establishing an assembly plant in the United States.

The issue over opening such a plant had been debated in the German company for several years. There was concern by worker representatives and others on the Supervisory Board about the employment effects in Germany if cars then being made in German plants and exported were assembled abroad.[2] The timing of the decision coincided with an investigation by the U.S. Treasury Department of an allegation pressed by the United Auto Workers (UAW) that Volkswagenwerk had dumped cars in the United States in 1974 and 1975—that is, priced cars cheaper in the United States than in Germany. Commenting on both the decision and the Treasury Department's investigation, a spokesman for the Supervisory Board noted:

We all realize that Volkswagens made in Germany are just too expensive, after repeated dollar devaluations, to meet the American and foreign competition in the United States. If we don't assemble there, we'll lose the American market. [Regarding the dumping complaint,] such a finding could force a reconsideration of the decision to go to the United States—and it would have enormous political repercussions in the Government too .... If a special penalty duty were assessed on every Volkswagen, ...

This case and the (B) case which follows were written by Duane Kujawa using information provided in discussions with Volkswagen company and union officials and collected from public sources.

the company would be forced to raise prices by so much that sales in the United States would collapse and our dealer network would fall apart.[3]

The deterioration of Volkswagen's U.S. market position was also ascribed to higher fuel prices that were reflected in higher shipping costs associated with exporting from Germany, higher German labor costs, and the upward revaluation of the German currency during the 1971–75 period. Labor costs for Volkswagenwerk advanced 40 percent from 1973 to 1976.[4] This brought German labor costs, consisting of wages and benefits, up to parity with those of U.S. auto workers. Moreover, because of differences in vacations, holidays, and so on, German workers spent considerably less time on the job in a typical year than did their U.S. counterparts. The result was that a U.S. Volkswagen plant could operate with direct labor costs about 10 percent lower than labor costs in Germany.[5]

Later in 1976, Volkswagenwerk's Supervisory Board approved a decision to manufacture autos in Westmoreland County, Pennsylvania. The chairman of the Management Board stated that a U.S. assembly plant would "lower manufacturing costs, neutralize the effect of international currency changes, and attain greater flexibility in supplying . . . American dealers."[6]

Obtaining a Labor Contract at Westmoreland

When Volkswagenwerk invested in the Westmoreland plant, it adopted a neutral approach toward the organizing of that facility by the UAW. The German parent had had a long-lasting, constructive relationship with the German union in the metalworking industry (I G Metall), and union members sat on its Supervisory Board. The parent had advised Volkswagen's management not to oppose the UAW's organizing efforts. The parent management did not deal directly with the UAW, however, and avoided giving further direction to Volkswagen's management on the conduct of its labor relations.

In May 1978, the UAW petitioned the National Labor Relations Board (NLRB) to conduct a representation election for hourly workers at Westmoreland. The hourly employment level was then about 900, and nearly 80 percent of the hourly workers had signed petition cards. No other union competed with the UAW, and Volkswagen's management did not oppose the UAW's organizing efforts. The election was held in June, and the UAW received 98 percent of the 885 ballots cast.[7]

Volkswagen immediately commenced collective bargaining with the UAW, and a tentative contract was soon agreed upon. A UAW spokesperson noted that the proposed contract included lower wage rates than those paid by the "Big Three" automakers but that most of the other items in the contract were "nearly identical to existing contracts with Detroit automakers."[8] The UAW president hailed the tentative contract as "an excellent example for other foreign auto manufacturers who may open manufacturing or assembly operations in the United States."[9]

But members of UAW Local 2055 at the Westmoreland plant rejected the proposed contract overwhelmingly. Moreover, they began a "wildcat" strike and moved immediately to picket the plant site. The key issue was that the wages called for would be substantially lower than those paid by the Detroit auto firms. The Westmoreland workers were also reportedly of the opinion that the proposed agreement shortchanged them on vacations, delayed for too long (one year) the start of Volkswagen's payments to a layoff fund, and denied workers the right to refuse heavy overtime.[10]

NOTES

[1]"Volkswagenwerk, AG," in *The World Directory of Multinational Enterprises,* ed. John N. Stopford, John H. Dunning, and Klaus O. Haberich (New York: Facts on File, 1980), pp. 1126–27.

[2]"Inflation and Jobless Rate Stir West German Concern," *New York Times,* May 19, 1976, p. 64.

[3]"Volkswagen Said to Plan Assembly Plant in U.S.," *New York Times,* April 23, 1976, p. 1.

[4]"Volkswagen Is Investigating Two Sites in the Northeast for an Assembly Plant," *The Wall Street Journal,* October 6, 1976, p. 3.

[5]Ibid.; "VW Delays Start-Up Date at Its Facility in New Stanton; Parts Problems Develop," *The Wall Street Journal,* January 8, 1976, p. 2; and interview with the industrial relations director, Volkswagenwerk, AG, San Diego, California, June 1976.

[6]"VW Delays," p. 2.

[7]"Volkswagen Workers in Pennsylvania Pick UAW as Their Union," *The Wall Street Journal,* June 12, 1978, p. 21.

[8]"VW's American Unit, UAW Agree to Terms of Tentative Contract," *The Wall Street Journal,* October 6, 1978, p. 31.

[9]Ibid.

[10]"Strike at VW Disturbs Foreign Auto-Makers Weighing U.S. Plants," *The Wall Street Journal,* October 13, 1978, p. 1.

Volkswagen of America (B)

In late 1987, Volkswagen of America announced it would close the Westmoreland County plant at the end of the 1988 model run. As with most major decisions, the rationale here was complex, but the proximate cause was quite simple: VW cars produced in America were not competitive—the plant was a money loser. Interestingly, some analysts called the decision a victory for the Japanese auto firms who had been fighting Germany in the United States for nine years.[1]

During the 1970s and 1980s, Volkswagen lost considerable market share in the United States—from 7 percent to 2 percent. By 1987, the Westmoreland plant was operating at one-third capacity and losing $120 million annually.[2] The reasons for Volkswagen's demise were many. Some observers contended the company just didn't have the right product. There were concerns too about product quality and product availability. Some felt Volkswagen's products were just too expensive in light of the competitive prices of Japanese-made cars. Most likely each of these reasons had some impact on defining the company's competitive position and the decision to close the Westmoreland plant.

Interestingly, observers such as *Automotive News* concluded Volkswagen's relations with the United Auto Workers (UAW) did not affect the decision to close the Westmoreland plant.[3] Labor costs were an important issue though. They were high (even with the comparatively "weak" dollar seen by most Western European countries and some Asian countries such as Japan) compared to costs at other Volkswagen plants located in low wage countries such as Brazil and Mexico. The plan was to serve the U.S. market with exports from these countries that will take up the slack occasioned by the closing of the Westmoreland plant.

Several points are worth mentioning here. One is that automotive assembly plants traditionally need a production volume of about 220,000—240,000 units per year to be operating with optimum scale economies. These plants are of the prerobotics, preflexible production type. The Westmoreland plant was one of these. Production volume at Westmoreland had declined to 73,000 units per year in 1987. On a per unit output basis, the capital costs at Westmoreland rendered total production costs uncompetitive. This is an example of the quadrant III type company discussed in Figure 17–2.

In contrast to Volkswagen's situation, Japanese auto plants that use robots and other flexible production features need a plant output of only 80,000 to 120,000 units per year to be operating at maximum efficiency. The Japanese plants fit into quadrant I in Figure 17–2.

How has the quadrant III approach affected plant workers compared to how a quadrant I approach would? Would workers still be "competitive?" Would they still have their jobs?

In the Volkswagen of America (A) case, the production was transferred from the high-cost German environment to the more cost-competitive U.S. environment. Now, production was being transferred from the high-cost U.S. environment to more cost-competitive environments in Brazil and Mexico. This has to be frustrating from the perspectives of American workers and American unions. What could the UAW and the Westmoreland plant's employees have done to affect this scenario of competing for jobs with workers in low-wage countries? Should they lower their own wages? Are there limits here? How about work-rules? Could they be changed to make the workers more productive? Does management have a leadership role to play here? Maybe the union and workers should lobby for a political solution, such as high tariffs on auto imports from low-wage countries. Who would be the winners and losers on this one?

In any event, Volkswagen sold the tooling and production equipment at the Westmoreland plant to First Automobile Works of Changchun, China in mid-1989. In early 1991, Sony Corporation bought the plant.

NOTES

[1]"Volkswagen Goes Back to the Drawing Board," *International Management*, February 1988, p. 43.

[2]Ibid., and "VW to Shut U.S. Plant by End of 1988 Run," *Automotive News*, November 23, 1987, pp. 1 and 53.

[3]Matt DeLorenzo, "Anatomy of a Plant: Westmoreland Closing Holds a Lesson for All Transplants," *Automotive News*, November 30, 1987, p. 8.

Personnel Management

Personnel management within the MNE shapes the conduit through which the implementation of competitive advantages flows. For the mature MNE, which relies on timely and accurate transnational flows of information and directives, the effectiveness of the personnel management function is crucial. The mature MNE requires personnel skilled in the company's operations, in the environments across and within which the MNE functions, and in the art of cross-cultural communication. This chapter examines these needs and covers the entire range of interests and issues pertaining to international personnel management. The main goals of the chapter are to:

1. Describe how and why personnel management in MNEs differs from personnel management in purely domestic firms.

2. Examine the relationship between personnel management and the competitiveness of MNEs.

3. Examine the statistics on the use of foreign nationals (expatriates).

4. Explain the criteria for choosing between local and foreign nationals.

5. Explore issues pertinent to expatriates, such as selection, training, compensation, taxation, repatriation, and promotion.

6. Discuss the present demand for foreign assignments.

INTRODUCTION

All businesses function through people, and the effective management of people has become increasingly recognized as fundamental to business success. For the domestic, unicultural firm, people management embodies a varied set of activities. Typically, it includes such personnel practices as recruitment, selection, compensation, career-path planning, promotion, training, and performance motivation. These practices are important to the multinational, multicultural firm too. But they are more complicated in the MNE setting, and there are other personnel practices that are unique to MNEs.

Personnel Management Issues in MNEs

Selection, for example, involves questions at both the parent and subsidiary levels as to whether local nationals or home country nationals should be used. Should Nestlé, for example, rely primarily on Swiss nationals in its home office and on American nationals at its U.S. subsidiary? Are there positions at the subsidiary that Swiss nationals would probably be more suited for? Are there positions from which Swiss nationals should be excluded? Compensation for persons assigned outside their home countries involves packages that cover the added costs of living abroad—for housing, taxes, and so on. People who accept overseas assignments are concerned about how the home office views such assignments and about the advancement opportunities that will be open to them upon their return. Is an overseas assignment an "out of sight, out of mind" situation? Training for a foreign post may well involve an introduction to the cultural, social, and political conditions in the country of assignment. It may well involve training for the entire family of the assignee.

These and other differences between foreign and domestic assignments will be discussed in this chapter. The topics covered include the relationship between the personnel function and the competitiveness of MNEs, the definition of expatriate management, the extent to which expatriates are used and the purposes for which they are used, the use of local nationals versus the use of expatriates, selection and training for foreign assignments, the repatriation and promotion of expatriates, and, quite important, compensation and taxation issues pertinent to an overseas assignment.

PERSONNEL MANAGEMENT AND THE COMPETITIVENESS OF MNES

Traditional View Being Challenged

The traditional view has been that personnel management is a "facilitative" function—something that has to be done well to accommodate the more important success-related strategies pertaining to marketing, production, finance, and so on. Today, this view is being seriously questioned. One challenge to the traditional view originates from the emergence of high-tech companies that value highly skilled employees as human capital assets. Another challenge originates from our growing understanding of and ability to adapt Japanese management practices that view employees as key ingredients in attaining low-cost, high-quality product strategies.[1] Indeed, several industries are totally revamping their personnel practices to utilize the brain power as well as the muscle power of their workers. General Motors' Saturn Plant, for example, departs radically from GM's historical management-labor relations in this regard. At Saturn, "operating teams" (workers) are responsible for defining and solving production problems and for quality control as they work to assemble a car.

A third challenge to the traditional view originates from the emergence of the mature, *geocentric* MNE, which relies on the effective, transnational flow of information and directives—accomplished by people—that balance local com petitive needs and strengths with those required or available elsewhere in the MNE system. Such information flows require personnel who are skilled in the company and its way of operating, in the environments within and across which the MNE functions, and in the art of communication—including cross-cultural communication. Developing these personnel requires overseas assignments and responsibilities.

Personnel Management and the Competitiveness of MNEs

Since personnel management in the MNE shapes the conduit through which the implementation of competitive advantages flow, it has a great impact on the effectiveness of the firm in the marketplace. The challenge of personnel man agement is to ensure effectiveness at minimum cost by finding the right balance between the parent's people needs and the subsidiary's people needs and to staff these needs at both the parent and subsidiary levels with a continuing flow of knowledgeable, motivated personnel. Reaching these objectives is no easy task—and mistakes can be costly. The personnel manager in the MNE is thus seen as a special kind of person—a specialist in legal matters, such as equal employment opportunity and taxation related to foreign assignments; an expert regarding the personnel functions, such as recruitment, motivation, and com pensation; and a highly knowledgeable person on company-specific matters, such as technology and competitive strengths and even the values and prefer ences of key executives.

DEFINITION AND USE OF EXPATRIATES

Parent company nationals and third-country nationals assigned to subsidiaries and foreign nationals assigned to parent companies are typically referred to as **expatriates.** They are the major focus of this chapter. Expatriates are generally found in technical and managerial assignments, and their numbers have histor ically been significant. For example, Hays reported that over 200,000 U.S. citizens worked abroad in the early 1970s, and the U.S. Department of Commerce's 1984 "benchmark" survey on direct foreign investment in the United States reported that an estimated 50,000 foreign citizens were employed by foreign firms in the United States.[2] While the numbers of expatriates working aborad are not tracked on a routine basis and there are no official figures regarding them, the rapid growth in foreign direct investment in the United States during the latter 1970s, 1980s, and early 1990s, and the continued expansion of U.S. MNEs abroad during this period suggest that the numbers of foreign nationals working outside their home countries have probably increased during the 1980s. Indeed, Britain's ICI and Holland's Philips alone employed a total of 2,300 expatriates in the mid- 1980s.[3]

Variations in the Use of Expatriates

Studies by Franko indicate that an MNE's use of expatriate personnel is high during the initial stages of foreign operations to accomplish technology trans fers, including production and management technologies. The number of ex patriates declines as the firm's local managers and technical staff assimilate this knowledge. It expands again as local operations become increasingly integrated into a global operational framework.[4] These views suggest that as a product's life cycle evolves, the need for expatriates expands (at the subsidiary level) in the early stage and then diminishes in the later stages. Finally, with the mature MNE the need for expatriates arises at both the subsidiary and parent company levels. These views are also consistent with the staffing needs of those MNEs that develop from *ethnocentric* to *geocentric* as the intrafirm relationship evolves from a parent-to-subsidiary technology transfer process to an integrated, system-wide need for the development and application of MNE-specific competitive advantages. These views also imply an expanding need for an awareness at the global management level based on country-by-country knowledge pertaining to a variety of employment-related concerns, such as laws regarding race, age and sex discrimination, compensation practices, and taxes.

The Ashridge Research Management Group reported in a 1989 study that many multinationals, such as Electrolux and ICI, were deliberately developing "international managers"—people who could serve in any foreign location and also play a leadership role in determining future corporate strategy. Part of the development process for international managers involved short-term (i.e., for a few months to a few years) assignments at subsidiaries.[5]

Incidence of the Use of Expatriates

Studies of foreign MNEs in the United States have shed some light on the incidence of the use of expatriates. Of 100 foreign MNEs studied by the U.S. Department of Commerce in 1975–76, about one third reported that their CEOs were expatriates and that, at levels below the CEO, expatriates often occupied only a few management positions. In addition, expatriates held technical positions. Moreover, mode of entry and parent nationality were found to be factors affecting the use of expatriates. Expatriates were more likely to be used in start-up cases than in takeover situations and at Japanese-owned subsidiaries.[6] Kujawa, in a study of Japanese multinationals in the United States published in 1986, reported extensive use of Japanese expatriates. These expatriates, at Honda in Ohio and at Murata in Georgia, for example, were needed to implement and monitor Japanese management practices related to statistical quality control techniques and continued technology transfers from the Japanese parent to the U.S. subsidiary.[7]

A recent study by Tung and Miller suggests U.S. multinationals are less prone to use expatriates than are European or Japanese multinationals. Their 1989 survey of U.S. business executives found, for example, that only about one in twenty U.S. executives felt an international assignment or experience was important for promotion into top management. Other studies, they noted, showed this perception was in stark contrast to the practices found in Japanese and European multinationals where international experience was essential for promotion.[8]

We can conclude this section, then, by noting the use of expatriates likely varies by product life cycle, the extent of the firm's geocentrism, the level of the (potential) expatriate position in the management structure, and the parent company nationality. But there is also the question of balance. Where should the line be drawn between the use of local nationals and expatriates? To this the discussion turns.

LOCAL NATIONALS VERSUS EXPATRIATES

The question of using local nationals or expatriates can be asked at both the parent company and subsidiary levels. The answer invariably turns on the perceived benefits to be gained by using expatriates balanced against the added costs required to maintain expatriate staff. Benefits are usually derived by bringing in technical or managerial expertise not available locally, including special knowledge about the firm itself. More effective communication and more consistent, trustworthy management behavior may be other objectives in assigning expatriates overseas. Measured against these benefits are differing types of costs. Table 18–1 lists some of the pros and cons associated with choosing between local nationals and expatriates.

Cost Considerations

Studies have shown that it can be very expensive to use expatriates. Most firms use the rule of thumb that an expatriate costs at least three times as much as a local national. The reasons for the higher costs are several. Expatriates may be taxed twice on their income, especially their unearned income—in both the home and host countries. They may have home leave, family maintenance, and extra educational expenses. Also, and quite important, some areas just cost more than others to live in, especially if the expatriate's consumption pattern is not consistent with local, or native, supply patterns. For an expatriate, living costs among the different cities of the world are reasonably high and can vary substantially. Table 18–2 shows what it would cost for an American family of four to live in selected cities outside the United States. Not only do the overall costs vary considerably (at the limits), but the individual cost components also vary considerably. For example, the cost of housing ranges from $8,635 in Mexico City to $69,624 in Hong Kong and taxes range from $10,770 in Hong Kong to $74,106 in Brussels! Clearly, expatriates are expensive to put in place and to maintain. The contributions they make while on foreign assignments have to justify such expenditures.

TABLE 18–1

Factors Affecting the Choice between Local Nationals and Expatriates

Factors Favoring Expatriates
Expatriates possess technical and managerial skills.
Using expatriates enhances communications between the parent and the subsidiary.
The presence of expatriates promotes the foreign or MNE image.
Parent/subsidiary relations are facilitated by the presence of expatriates familiar with the corporate culture.
The assignment of expatriates is part of their professional development program, and it improves senior management's decision making—as discussed in the context of the "international manager."

Factors Favoring Local Nationals
The total compensation paid to local nationals is usually considerably less than that paid to expatriates.
No host country cultural adaptation is necessary when local nationals are used.
Using local nationals is consistent with a promote-from-within policy.
No work permits are needed with local nationals.
Using local nationals promotes a local image.
Using expatriates with special employment contracts rather than using local nationals may block promotional opportunities for local nationals and thus run afoul of local equal employment opportunity regulations.

TABLE 18–2

Living Costs of American
Expatriates: For a Family of
Four in Selected Cities, 1990

City	Housing	Transportation	Taxes	Goods and Services	Total
Hong Kong	$69,624	$21,113	$10,770	$16,904	$118,411
Tokyo	69,611	10,988	27,589	32,499	140,687
Geneva	45,788	11,461	40,367	35,143	132,759
Brussels	18,470	10,504	74,106	27,128	130,208
Frankfurt	23,844	10,657	50,197	28,253	112,951
Sydney	20,495	16,171	30,023	22,304	88,993
Paris	30,105	9,479	37,408	25,944	102,936
Amsterdam	20,794	9,592	37,237	25,503	93,126
London	27,979	11,640	19,572	25,371	84,562
Mexico City	8,635	3,056	13,183	10,710	35,584

Source: Base-line data prepared by Runzheimer & Co., Rochester, Wisconsin, and presented in *Business Week*, January 16, 1984, p. 99. Data adjusted to reflect inflation and changes in currency exchange rates during 1984–1990.

In addition to out-of-pocket costs and the reasons suggested in Table 18–1, there are other reasons why firms use expatriates only when necessary. These reasons and some of the positive aspects of overseas assignments are discussed in the sections that follow.

Effectiveness Considerations

Several final points, however, should be noted regarding the use of local nationals versus the use of expatriates. First, when an expatriate is assigned overseas to fill a skill void, be it technical or managerial, it is often a prime responsibility of that person to train a local national to take his or her place. Second, some overseas positions are appropriate only for local nationals since these positions are highly culture-bound. Industrial relations management is an example. Other positions, such as the senior management position, seem to favor the use of an expatriate in order to facilitate communication and ensure control. Third, as MNEs are maturing into truly global enterprises, the need to integrate top management on a cross-national basis is expanding. Global firms need a global perspective at the top. The fact is, however, that top management and boards of directors have been slow to change and typically are not becoming multinational in their composition. This may change in the future as the "international manager" concept expands.

Host Country Considerations

Host countries, especially developing countries, generally favor the use of local nationals. Their reasons include increasing employment in general (jobs), advancing skill levels via on-the-job training and experience, and saving foreign exchange (where relevant). Nonetheless, these countries accept the use of expatriates when this is justified by legitimate business need. At times, though, MNE-host country friction can make securing local work-permits for expatriates difficult and time consuming.

Even without such friction, regulations regarding the use of expatriates can be complex and costly to the MNE. The Bahamas, for example, will not approve the use of any expatriate until the position to be filled has been advertised and it can be demonstrated that no qualified person is available locally. The MNE also pays an annual work permit fee that can amount to thousands of dollars for each expatriate on assignment in the Bahamas.

To cite another situation, Brazil requires that the MNE document the need for an expatriate with the Ministry of Labor and submit to the ministry a copy of the expatriate's résumé, university diploma, and employment contract (between the MNE and the expatriate). Moreover, Brazil limits the number of foreign nationals employed to one third of the total number of employees and limits the compensation paid to foreign nationals as a group to one third of the compensation paid to all employees.

SELECTION AND TRAINING OF EXPATRIATES

An overseas assignment that ends traumatically for an expatriate hurts both the individual and the firm. A valued employee may be demoralized. Crucial time may be lost. Important supplier, customer, or governmental relations may be soured. Recognizing that an expatriate's job is likely to be more demanding than a similar job at the home base, the firm usually takes extra care in the selection and preparation of an expatriate for a foreign assignment. Nonetheless, a study reported in the *Economist* in 1984 noted that one in three American expatriates assigned abroad returned home sooner than originally planned. For European expatriates, the ratio was one in seven.[9] A 1981 study of 80 American MNEs found that at half of these companies 10 to 20 percent of the expatriates were called home or fired because of their inability to perform effectively on a foreign assignment.[10] A similar study, focusing on expatriates in 35 Japanese MNEs, reported that at over three quarters of these companies less than 5 percent of the expatriates were called home.[11] It appears that some companies, especially American MNEs (and perhaps others), have something to learn.

The talents and skills that are needed in an overseas assignment include those typically identified with a domestic assignment—technical competence, educational achievement, initiative, creativity, independence, emotional maturity, ability to communicate, and so on. In an overseas assignment, several other talents and skills can be added to this list—for example, knowledge of a foreign language, cultural adaptability and empathy, and social flexibility (of the expatriate, and the expatriate's spouse and family). When the talents and skills required for a foreign assignment are lacking, special training programs are used. Studies generally confirm these points, but as Tung reports, the selection and training of expatriate personnel depend on just what their overseas positions are—chief executive officer (CEO), other manager, technical specialist, or operative.[12]

Selection

In her benchmark 1980 study of 80 U.S. MNEs, Tung found that the importance of certain key attributes related to the selection decision varied considerably, depending on the position being filled at the subsidiary. Selected data regarding these findings are presented in Table 18–3. In the selection decision for a CEO, the criteria emphasized managerial talent, maturity and emotional stability, initiative and creativity, experience in the company, adaptability and flexibility in a new environment, and technical knowledge. For managers other than CEOs, maturity and emotional stability, technical knowledge of the business, managerial talent, and initiative and creativity were emphasized over other criteria.

The criteria were considerably less extensive for technical specialists, where technical knowledge and initiative and creativity were emphasized; and for

TABLE 18-3

Selection Criteria for
Expatriate Personnel: Survey
of U.S. MNEs (n = 80)

Criterion	CEO	Other Manager	Technical Specialist	Operator
Experience in company	83%	68%	58%	37%
Managerial talent	96	86	16	18
Initiative, creativity	84	82	82	52
Technical knowledge of business	79	91	89	68
Maturity, emotional stability	94	98	75	86
Knowledge of language of host country	26	42	25	46
Adaptability, flexibility in new environment	83	76	46	62
Spouse's and family's adaptability	61	63	40	49

Note: The percentages reflect those respondents who felt that the criterion was used and that it was very important in the selection decision.
Source: Data abstracted from Rosalie L. Tung, "Selection and Training of Personnel for Overseas Assignments," *Columbia Journal of World Business*, Spring 1981, p. 75.

operators, where only maturity and emotional stability were emphasized. In general, CEOs and other managers were more often seen as needing managerial experience and skills, personal and family flexibility, company experience, and communicative ability. Technical specialists and operatives were generally scored less frequently on all of these points. All four categories were scored quite frequently (that is, in over 70 percent of the MNEs surveyed) regarding technical skills, maturity, and emotional stability. Except for technical specialists, expatriates were required to display an interest in overseas work by a majority of the companies studied.[13]

How does gender affect the selection outcome? Some societies and cultures have been traditionally male dominated—e.g., Japan and many of the Latin American countries. Multinationals have been sensitive to this, but in many instances have selected women to serve on expatriate assignments. But, there is a long way to go yet on this issue. Part of the problem is that more females need to be included in the upper management and technical support positions at home from which the multinationals draw to fill expatriate slots abroad.

Training

Training programs seek to prepare potential expatriates for the situations and problems unique to an overseas assignment. For this reason, such programs are country specific and are quite often tailored to individual needs and time constraints. Among the topics typically covered are a cultural orientation, the social and religious setting, political and social issues, language training, home country/host country relations, and the legal environment.

In Tung's aforementioned benchmark survey of 80 U.S. MNEs, responses were collected on the training activities pertaining to a foreign assignment. Of the firms surveyed, only 32 percent were found to have formal training programs.[14] The types of programs reported are shown in Table 18–4. About half of the companies with programs noted environmental/cultural orientation programs for CEOs and other managers. For these personnel, language training was often provided. Recall that language competence was discussed earlier as not being important in the selection decisions of many firms. Apparently firms do view language competence as important, but other criteria in the selection

TABLE 18–4

Frequency of Training Programs: Survey of U.S. Multinationals (n = 26)

Type of Training	CEO	Other Manager	Technical Specialist	Operative
Environmental	52%	54%	44%	31%
Cultural	42	41	31	24
Language	60	59	36	24

Source: Adapted from Rosalie L. Tung, "Selection and Training of Personnel for Overseas Assignments," *Columbia Journal of World Business*, Spring 1981, p. 76.

process override this criterion. Firms will train the selected expatriate in the needed language. Note too that the incidence of special training drops off sharply for the technical specialists and the operatives. This may reflect an anticipated brief duration of foreign assignment for the technical specialist (the "troubleshooter") and a somewhat company-confined assignment for operatives and thus, generally speaking, a lesser need for relational skills. In contrast to her findings on the low incidence of formal training in U.S. MNEs, Tung reported that over half of the 35 Japanese MNEs she studied had formal programs stressing environmental and language training.[15]

Larger firms, in which the frequency of moving personnel into expatriate positions is high enough to sustain the costs of developing training programs, are more often involved in training activities. Smaller firms, which use expatriates less often, are more likely not to be involved in developing and conducting special training programs. In smaller firms, moreover, the geographic diversity of overseas assignments, the pressures of time and money, and a lack of knowledge of their training needs at a given point in time generally preclude the extensive training of expatriates by companies specialized in such training.

Studies have shown that failures on overseas assignments can often be traced to difficulties encountered by spouses and other family members in adapting to local environmental/cultural nuances.[16] In this regard, training can be especially beneficial. Larger firms, again, are the ones that can afford such training. They are also the ones that define their career-path programs for key personnel far enough in advance to incorporate such training into their expatriate assignments. General Motors, for example, maintains "management progression and succession charts" for key managerial employees in both domestic and foreign positions. These charts identify future positions for such employees and the further developmental activities that are required for promotion into those positions. The positions may be anywhere in the world that General Motors operates. Dow Chemical, British Petroleum, and other large MNEs maintain similar information on key executives.

COMPENSATION AND TAXATION

Motivation and performance on the job are closely related to the reward structure. "Pay for performance" is perhaps more evident in more companies today than ever before, given the trend toward increasingly competitive markets. How does an overseas assignment relate to one's income needs? How does it relate to one's performance on the job and to one's potential for visibility and preparation for advancement? The first question is addressed in this section. Overall, however, it is linked with several other questions. What special considerations

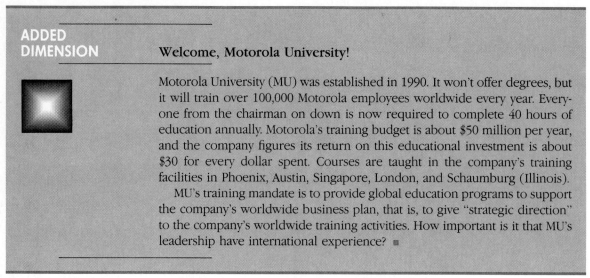

Source: Brian S. Moskal, "Just a Degree of Confidence," *Industry Week*, February 19, 1990, pp. 65–66.

affect the compensation paid expatriates? What currency-related problems might exist? How about income taxes for expatriates? These and other questions are addressed in the following text.

Compensation—Labor Market Factors

Several important factors, some obvious, others more subtle, influence the total compensation package pertinent to expatriate personnel.

The base salary paid an expatriate must be competitive with what that person would receive on a domestic assignment. The salaries paid expatriate personnel must reflect the labor markets in which they participate. For example, an American expatriate engineer on assignment in Singapore has alternative employment opportunities in the United States. The salary paid this person has to be competitive with the salaries paid engineers in the United States (not engineers in Singapore). Otherwise, the MNE would not be able to hire, or retain, expatriate engineers. For similar reasons, the major fringe benefits provided expatriates, such as retirement benefits and medical and life insurance, must be competitive with those afforded domestic personnel in the home country.

If the salaries and benefits of expatriates are competitive with salaries and benefits at home, they will probably differ from and be typically better than those obtained by local nationals on assignment at a subsidiary. This does not disrupt local pay and benefit scales, since the expatriate is recognized as providing special services to the company that are typically unavailable locally—that is, for which there is no local labor market counterpart and therefore no locally established, comparative compensation level. Where expatriate assets of this kind are less apparent, the fact of being an expatriate is sufficiently distinctive and on this ground alone local personnel generally accept the necessity of "special" salaries and fringes. In contrast, if the subsidiaries of MNEs pay local nationals salaries that are higher than those that local companies pay local nationals in comparable positions, labor market problems can be created as other local employers move to match the compensation levels at the MNEs and as the MNEs subsequently respond by establishing yet higher total compensation costs and thus reestablishing pay differentials. The labor cost spiral benefits no one. To ward off that possibility, MNEs have been especially deliberate in setting salaries for local personnel that are essentially responsive to local labor market conditions.[17]

Compensation—Cost-of-Living Considerations

Cost-of-living considerations are a second set of factors influencing the compensation levels of expatriate personnel. If the MNE is to be competitive in securing personnel for expatriate assignments, it must offer a compensation package that reimburses expatriates for the added costs associated with living abroad. Otherwise, the net compensation of an expatriate assignment would be lower than that of a domestic assignment.

What are these cost-of-living considerations? Taxation at the foreign locale is certainly one of them. Others relate to bona fide added personal expenses arising from an expatriate assignment. Examples are the travel costs associated with an expatriate's need to manage personal investments in the home country; the cost of hiring someone to manage such investments, such as a real estate agent in the case of a home rental; and the cost of attending to other important personal matters, such as the care of an elderly parent.

Some added costs of living arise, not from a geographic relocation per se, but from lifestyle values and needs. For example, overseas housing, education, recreation, security, and so forth must meet the expatriate's home country expectations and alternatives. There are also the home leave requirements of the expatriate and his or her family. The cost of living abroad may also be affected by a spouse's inability to secure professional employment in a foreign country or to the inability of older children to obtain part-time employment and the income thus generated. Such forgone family income requires indemnification. To encourage expatriates to accept assignments abroad and to complete the terms and conditions of the contracts governing such assignments, especially time-on-the-job provisions, bonuses may be included. This practice is apparently more common in construction (turnkey) projects and in natural resource development projects than in manufacturing operations.

All of these cost-of-living requirements add up. Shehzad reports (1984), for example, that the total cost of an American manager on assignment in Tokyo and in Ireland will be, respectively, six times and three times the cost of a manager in the United States.[18] Tung and Miller (1989) note the costs of expatriates run two to three times their base salary levels, and these costs can only be justified for "fast track" managers and technical specialists.[19]

Compensation—Currency Factors

The currency of compensation is an important concern too. Expatriates "live" in two countries. They have to meet day-to-day living expenses in the currency of the country of assignment, but they also have expenses that must be met in the currency of the home country—expenses for savings and investments, life insurance premiums, a child's education, and so on. For these reasons, expatriates' compensation packages are typically split into local-currency and home-currency payments. The latter are deposited by the parent in the employee's account in the home country; the former are typically paid by the subsidiary.

What happens in the event of exchange-rate changes? If local inflation pushes up the local-currency cost of living and the exchange rate does not reflect this deterioration in the value of the local currency, the home country cost of maintaining an expatriate's local standard of living will rise. This will necessitate an adjustment in the compensation package provided by the expatriate's home country. On the other hand, if the local currency devalues on foreign exchange markets to reflect the internal inflation, the home-currency costs borne by the expatriate will not rise and the compensation package will not require adjustment. For example, expatriates' employment contracts with U.S. MNEs are dollar based. Their dollar value is a constant. They have cost-of-living provisions, however, to compensate for situations where inflation increases local living costs in the absence of offsetting exchange-rate changes.

Taxes

Income taxes, which exist in nearly every country, are always paid by expatriates in the countries where they work. However, special tax considerations may significantly affect individual cases. Some countries, for example, tax expatriates only on the income they receive in the host country. When salaries are split between local and home currencies, local taxes are paid only on the former. In the United Kingdom, 50 percent of the income earned by a non-British citizen working for a foreign company is exempt from British income taxes. Some countries, such as the United States, require that the unearned income of expatriates (e.g., interest and dividend income) be taxed as if it had been earned in their own countries.

Tax policy affecting U.S. expatriates is governed by U.S. tax law, as most recently amended by the **Tax Reform Act of 1986.** Beginning in 1987, for example, a U.S. citizen has been allowed to exempt the first $70,000 of income earned abroad from federal income tax. This income deduction comes off the top of the expatriate's reportable income and may put the expatriate in a lower marginal tax bracket than would otherwise be the case. Of course, if the effective foreign income tax rate is higher than the U.S. rate, the U.S. national on assignment overseas derives no benefit from the deduction.

Unearned income, as noted earlier, is taxable income in full. It benefits from no foreign income exclusion. If there is a tax treaty, however, between the United States and the host country where the expatriate works, the foreign income taxes paid on unearned income are creditable against U.S. taxes due on this income. The net effect is that the expatriate pays the higher of the U.S. or the foreign tax rate.

Certain residency requirements must be met for a U.S. taxpayer overseas to qualify for the foreign earned income credit. The taxpayer must have a tax home that has shifted to the foreign country and must be a **bona fide resident** of the foreign country for an entire year or *physically present* overseas for a minimum of 330 consecutive days. The tax home is the place of employment, and the shift to the foreign location must be indefinite, that is, for a duration of at least two years. For a person to qualify as a bona fide resident of a foreign country, U.S. tax law requires an indefinite period of employment and the establishment of a permanent family residence outside the United States. Of course, the residency requirements of the foreign country must also be met. A bona fide resident of a foreign country can travel into and out of the United States at will. There is no

---

**IB
ILLUSTRATION**

Can You Figure This One Out?

Jesse Jones, an American citizen, is employed by the American firm Patriotics, Inc. He is assigned to its French subsidiary, Ex-Patriotics, S.A. Jesse's salary is $240,000 per year. Jesse also earns $8,000 annually on bank interest on his savings accounts in France.

Assume that France, in this hypothetical case, taxes Jesse's earned and unearned income at an effective rate of 50 percent. Also assume that France allows no income deductions and thus taxes Jesse's entire income at this rate. In the United States, Jesse qualifies for the $70,000 earned income exclusion. For simplicity, assume that there are no deductions here too and that Jesse's effective tax rate in the United States is 28 percent.

What are Jesse's taxes in France? (Answer: $124,000.) What is Jesse's U.S. taxable income? (Answer: $178,000.) What are his U.S. taxes payable before the foreign tax credit? After the foreign tax credit? (Answers: $49,840; zero.) If France dropped its income tax rate to 20 percent, what U.S. taxes would Jesse pay after applying the foreign tax credit? (Answer: $240.) ∎

---

minimum number of days per year that the person must stay out of the United States—as with the physically present overseas category.

The income taxes paid by expatriates reflect a complicated set of laws and personal as well as corporate considerations. Advance planning is important, and the use of tax counsel is not unusual. In fact, many of the larger MNEs routinely provide such counsel to expatriate personnel on a periodic basis. Dow Chemical, for example, provides such counseling both to U.S. nationals on assignment at foreign subsidiaries and to foreign nationals on assignment in the United States.

REPATRIATION AND PROMOTION

Repatriation occurs when the expatriate returns from an assignment at the parent or subsidiary located in a foreign country. It is a major event in any person's career, and it would be expected to occur during a period of high personal expectations with regard to promotion and solid career-path progress. Such expectations are especially likely to be held by expatriates who are parent country nationals. The extent to which expectations of this kind have been met is a matter of record—and the record shows that the pattern has changed as the MNE has grown and matured.

The Early Experiences

During the late 1960s and the 1970s, a period of rapid growth in the number of MNEs, many parent-level expatriates on assignment at subsidiaries found the going rough. One reason was that many of these assignments were responses to problems at the subsidiaries that required expertise available only at the parent. The assignments arose too quickly to allow for adequate preparation of either

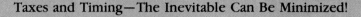

ADDED DIMENSION

Taxes and Timing—The Inevitable Can Be Minimized!

Tax analysis and planning can be a tedious exercise at best. Yet, it is so important—especially for the expatriate. For example, some countries have a de minimus rule requiring a minimum period of assignment during any tax (typically calendar) year. If the expatriate's minimum period of assignment is 60 days, effecting patriation prior to March 1 would save paying foreign taxes that year. Moreover, if the income earned abroad then were less than $70,000, no U.S. income taxes would be paid on that amount either.

Stock options provide another example. If the expatriate participates in a qualified incentive stock option plan (ISO), U.S. tax law may allow for deferral of a capital gain when the option is exercised (obviously at a market price above the option price). Deferral is not allowed in Germany, Mexico, and many other countries. The gain is taxable—often at high foreign marginal tax rates. The expatriate may be better off converting that option after arriving home! A third example pertains to the four-year deferral of capital gains resulting from the sale of a U.S. residence. If a new home is not bought within these four years, the gain is taxed. The employer (which would likely have to reimburse the expatriate for these taxes) may be well advised to bring the expatriate home before the time limit expires. ■

Source: Jeffrey M. Kadet and Robert J. Gaughan, Jr., "Oversee Expatriate Returns to Curtail Taxes," *Personnel Journal*, July 1987, pp. 71–76.

the expatriate or the expatriate's family.[20] The result was frustration. Moreover, little consideration was given to the position that the expatriate would hold upon returning to the parent company. The literature of the period identified several problems or concerns pertinent to the repatriation of expatriates:

1. "The career-path holiday"[21]

   Expatriates on foreign assignments are on a career-path holiday. Little or no concern is expressed for how they will fit into the organization upon their return.

2. "The isolation syndrome"[22]

   The expatriate feels isolated—personally and professionally. Communication with the home office is difficult since no one (or few) appreciate the difficulties of operating abroad.

3. "Missing the management progression mainstream"[23]

   Advancement relates to exposure and significance. The foreign assignment isolates the assignee, and often the employer judges overseas experience as unrelated to what is important for advancement.

4. "Play it again, Sam!"[24]

   Repatriated expatriates are often placed in a holding pattern upon their return home, since no appropriate positions have been defined for them. In some cases, this means proving yourself all over again to the parent organization.

5. "And now, the letdown!"[25]

   Senior-level foreign assignments generally require a lot of autonomous, almost entrepreneurial, decision making and interactions with others, such as high-level government officials. The new job at home is likely to be more constrained both in external contacts and in the scope of management responsibility. The personal adjustments required can be difficult.

6. "The high opportunity cost of staying on"[26]

   Repatriated executives put into a parent company holding pattern find that they can earn more money and be challenged again by taking positions at other companies.

These concerns, which could themselves be costly, along with the (U.S.) tax disincentives of the latter 1970s and early 1980s, which greatly reduced the foreign earned income exclusion, resulted in a substantial curtailment of the use of expatriates by U.S. MNEs.

The Changing Rationale   The role and treatment of the expatriate have changed dramatically as the structure and operations of MNEs have evolved. During the emergent years of the MNE, management could generally be characterized as fairly ethnocentric and certainly as inexperienced regarding the handling of overseas personnel assignments. Foreign subsidiaries were seen as appendages—conduits through which flowed products, technical expertise, financial resources, and marketing prowess generated by the parent company. Expatriates were in fact operating downstream with regard to development of competitive advantages. Their positions were not as important or powerful as those at home. Moreover, a tight competitive environment accompanied the onset of defensive direct foreign investment. Firms had to set up plants overseas, and to do so quickly. This time compression exacerbated the already difficult situation that expatriates were experiencing because of their firms' inexperience in handling them. A lot of mistakes were made that complicated the role, if not the life, of expatriates. Family problems, for example, led many expatriates to want to return home. Also, as discussed above, the professional experiences of those on assignment overseas often led to personal frustration and to a questioning of the desirability of expatriate assignments.

In the polycentric structures, where considerable autonomy was exercised at local levels, the expatriate's role, if any, was quite limited. For example, prior to the integration of automobile production between the United States and Western Europe and within Western Europe, Ford Motor Company's subsidiaries were substantially autonomous. They used few, if any, expatriate personnel. Indeed, at one time in the 1960s, the only managerial personnel link between Ford of England and the U.S. parent was the presence of Henry Ford II on the former's board of directors. Nonetheless, expatriates could be found in polycentric MNEs. Some were located in the finance and treasury functions. Others were holdovers from an ethnocentric period. In fact, some expatriate managers worked deliberately to isolate the subsidiary from parent company control.[27] These managers liked to be their "own boss" and enjoyed working and living abroad.

Historically, subsidiaries of European MNEs were fairly autonomous from their parent organizations. Expatriate managers were schooled over long periods of time, however, and were substantially conversant with corporate values

---

**IB
ILLUSTRATION**

A Global Product Brings People Together at Bank of America

Bank of America's System Engineering group (BASE) is responsible for aligning technical expertise with overall business strategies and is providing the bank's World Business Division with managerial and technical support in the development of International Banking Systems (IBS), an on-line computer system that supplies current financial information to account officers and corporate customers, facilitates electronic global monetary transfers, provides treasury department support for foreign exchange and money market activities, and so forth.

The IBS was originally developed in England, Germany, Holland, and Belgium. It is now operational in all overseas divisions and in the United States. Bank of America regards its implementation of the IBS as one of its "most significant strategic decisions." The IBS allows the bank to deliver comprehensive, integrated electronic banking services to customers worldwide.

BASE, headquartered in San Francisco, coordinates closely with the bank's strategic planning and control functions there. The IBS was originally developed in only a few European countries, and was extended to cover global operations. Applications specialists who are already using the IBS were instrumental in implementing it elsewhere. BASE and IBS personnel with experience in the new system assisted colleagues in other countries in getting on-line while streamlining their own operations. IBS allows bankers around the world to coordinate activities with a single global customer, such as an MNE. ∎

Source: BankAmerica Corporation, 1984 *Annual Report*, pp. 2–8.

and methods. There was little ongoing communication between these managers and the managers at the parent.[28] This was especially evident with Europeans in senior management assignments at the U.S. subsidiaries of European MNEs.[29]

The Recent Experiences

Today's mature MNEs have expatriate policies and programs that are more established and effective than those of earlier times. For example, career-path planning, which is routinely done for executives in the larger MNEs, identifies postexpatriate placement alternatives prior to an expatriate assignment. The larger firms are also more likely to have special training programs for personnel accepting expatriate assignments and for their spouses.

The enhanced concern of the MNE for the expatriate reflects, to some degree, the expatriate's enhanced importance to the competitive success of the enterprise. Since the mature MNE seeks competitive advantages that result from, among other factors, the integration of information and expertise across geographic boundaries, the people who embody multinational knowledge are especially valuable to it. Where these people were originally from is perhaps incidental to their value. It is their experiences and expertise that enhance their value.

ADDED
DIMENSION

Traits of the Modern International Manager

Jacques Maisonrouge, president of IBM World Trade Corporation, expressed some fairly strong beliefs about today's international manager:

One major consequence of this internationalization of business has been the increased need for international managers; that is, for managers who, aside from having all the qualities that make good managers of national companies, are also mobile, adaptable, and at ease in cultures other than their own. In addition, because they will undoubtedly work outside their home countries at some point in their careers, they should have one or two foreign languages; an understanding of the sociopolitical environment in which they will be working; and a world view that inhibits the growth of chauvinism.

... tomorrow's managers will have to demonstrate more awareness of the world around them [and] more flexibility of mind ... than ever before. In a world where new knowledge continues to accumulate rapidly, the most valuable managers of all will be those who have learned *how* to learn. ∎

Source: J. G. Maisonrouge, "Education of a Modern International Manager," *Journal of International Business Studies*, Spring–Summer 1983, pp. 143–44.

Some examples might be useful here. In the global MNE, R&D may be conducted in various national centers and then pooled at the corporate level. National Semiconductor, for example, conducts research in the United States, Japan, and Israel. It coordinates projects among centers in these three countries to integrate their findings and come up with product and process improvements that are applicable worldwide. The personnel involved at these centers are more project oriented than location oriented and may or may not be local nationals.

Marketing research is handled on a geographically decentralized basis but is pulled together at some central point as product definition is evaluated in terms of manufacturing processes and production allocation. Honda, for example, conducts marketing research on motorcycles in numerous countries. This work involves both local nationals and Japanese expatriates. Honda pulls its findings together to decide on a specific motorcycle design and subsequently defines which organizational units worldwide will be responsible for production.

Operations management or industrial engineering in different geographic segments can pool expertise and develop, for example, operating systems with global applicability. Ciba-Geigy, a large Swiss chemical company with major operations in the United States and Europe, routinely integrates operations technology between the two areas. Process engineers and managers in both areas communicate continuously, and often U.S. personnel are on assignment in Europe and European personnel in the United States.

The point here is that people from different countries with different experiences are valuable at the global level of the MNE. The situation today is very different from what it was in the earlier years, when subsidiaries were appendages. The globally integrated MNE is a different entity and has different personnel needs.

Foreign Assignments in High Demand

People are certainly aware of the increasing potential for professional success associated with overseas assignments. The expatriate assignment is becoming increasingly attractive to many executives. Kenny, Kindler & Hunt, a New York executive recruiting firm, reports that fast-track executives are seeking overseas assignments to show that they can operate effectively at the general management level. In a survey that it conducted in 1983 where 37 percent of the 125 managers polled were willing to take overseas jobs—up from 10 percent a decade earlier[30]—Heidrick & Struggles, another executive recruiter, reported that managers who in the past had shunned overseas jobs that got them "two-years into oblivion," or forgotten at the parent, were now seeking such jobs.[31] These findings comport well with a statement by the vice president of PepsiCo's international division that "his group is the primary farm team for top company talent."[32]

Business schools in America, Europe, and Asia are increasingly concerned with educating the international manager. MBA and specialty degree programs, such as the Master of International Business Studies (MIBS) degree at the University of South Carolina and the Master of International Management (MIM) degree at Thunderbird (the American Graduate School of International Management in Arizona), are becoming increasingly popular. Enrollments in these programs are expanding, and more universities (e.g., Wharton, UCLA, Miami, etc.) are developing academic programs geared towards education for international business. These programs and their expanding enrollments support the thesis that international business employment opportunities are increasing.

CONCLUSIONS

Many important personnel management issues are pertinent to the MNE. One of these is the use of expatriate managers and technical specialists.

Benefits/Costs

Many pros and cons are associated with the use of expatriates. Two pros seem especially relevant, however. Expatriates can provide special expertise that is not otherwise available at a specific location—and they can often provide it quickly and in a manner consistent with company mores. Using expatriates, however, is very costly. Obviously the benefits derived from their special expertise must exceed the added costs of using them.

Historically, a fairly large percentage of expatriate assignments have ended in failure—with the expatriate returning home prematurely. This expensive experience raises questions as to the adequacy of the standards that have been used to select and train them.

Selection

The criteria used in selecting expatriates have varied considerably, depending on the overseas position involved. CEOs and other managers have been required to possess managerial experience and skills, personal and family flexibility, company experience, and communicative ability. Highly valued traits of technical specialists and operatives have included emotional stability and maturity. Training for expatriates has often been country specific, with topics including cultural, religious, political, and social issues; language proficiency; home country/host country relations; and the legal environment. Training for CEOs and other managers has been more extensive than that for technical specialists and operatives. Larger firms have typically employed more sophisticated selection procedures and training programs than those employed by smaller firms.

Compensation

The compensation paid expatriates must be competitive with what they would receive if they were employed at home. It must also cover the added costs of living abroad and of maintaining both a domestic and a foreign presence. Examples of the former are housing, educational expenses, forgone income that might be earned by a spouse or by children, and security expenses. Examples of the latter are travel expenses, the extra costs of maintaining investments at home, and extra taxes. The compensation of expatriates is also complicated by split payroll policies that result in partial compensation payments in both home and host country currencies, by inflation in the country of assignment and by changes in exchange rates.

Taxes

Expatriates always pay income taxes where they work, in the countries that have income taxes. Special considerations derived from their expatriate status may lower their tax bills, however. A U.S. national on assignment abroad is allowed a substantial foreign earned income exemption by the Tax Reform Act of 1986. An expatriate's unearned income is never exempt from U.S. taxation. Foreign taxes paid on such income by an expatriate, however, can be credited against any U.S. taxes due. To be eligible for the foreign earned income credit, an expatriate must meet certain residency requirements.

Repatriation

In the early days of the MNE, expatriate repatriation was often a disappointing experience. Firms were inexperienced in dealing with expatriates, and the competitive pressures of the times allowed for no hesitancy in moving needed people overseas. Mistakes were made. Those who had been on assignment overseas often fared miserably upon their return to the home operation. For these and other reasons, especially reasons related to the taxation policies then in effect, the incidence of expatriate assignments declined.

The Increased Importance and Attractiveness of Expatriate Assignments

As MNEs matured and their operations and marketing became more globally integrated, the status and value of the expatriate were enhanced. The future even for U.S. MNEs seems especially promising in this respect. Career-path planning and other MNE activities reduced the uncertainties associated with expatriate assignments, especially the uncertainties related to repatriation. Perhaps more important, the attractiveness of expatriate assignments increased as MNEs became more dependent on personnel with multinational experiences that would contribute to strategies of global competitive effectiveness. Consequently, larger numbers of executives and technical personnel have come to view overseas assignments as positive aspects of their professional development.

QUESTIONS

1. Identify the links between personnel management and the competitiveness of MNEs. How do expatriate personnel relate to the transfer of management-based technologies, such as those pertaining to experience curves, and product and process technologies?

2. What is an expatriate? Does the use of expatriates correlate with the product life cycle? If so, how? How would the use of expatriates vary among ethnocentric, polycentric, and geocentric MNEs?

3. What are the main pros and cons of using expatriates as compared with using local nationals?

4. What are the most important selection criteria for selecting expatriates for overseas positions? How and why do these criteria vary with the nature of the overseas position?

5. What special training programs might be beneficial for expatriates and their families pending an overseas assignment? What is the likelihood that such programs would be found in a U.S. multinational? Why?

6. What major factors affect the compensation paid to expatriates? With regard to influences on compensation, how do expatriates differ from local personnel?

7. How are exchange-rate changes accommodated in the compensation packages of expatriate personnel? How might such packages be administered in the face of currency nonconvertibility?

8. Describe the provisions of the U.S. tax law that pertain to foreign earned income and unearned income. What is the rationale for these provisions?

9. Why did U.S. MNEs have difficult early experiences in the handling of their expatriate personnel?

10. Compare the role and significance of the expatriate in the competitive strategies of the emergent MNEs and the mature MNEs. What role do expatriates play in the competitiveness of MNEs today? What effect does this role have on the desires of personnel to include overseas experiences in their career ladders? Why?

REFERENCES

Adler, Nancy J. *International Dimensions of Organizational Behavior.* Boston: PWS–Kent Publishing, 1991. See, especially, chap. 5, "Multinational Teams"; chap. 8, "Cross-Cultural Transitions: Expatriate Employee Entry and Reentry"; and chap. 9, "A Portable Life: The Expatriate Spouse."

Dowling, Peter J. and Randall S. Schuler. *International Dimensions of Human Resource Development.* Boston: PWS–Kent Publishing Co., 1990.

Edstrom, Anders, and Jay Galbraith. "Transfer of Managers as Coordination and Control Strategy in Multinational Organizations." *Administrative Science Quarterly,* June 1977, pp. 248–63. (A classic.)

Gerber, Beverly. "A Global Approach to Training." *Training,* September 1989, pp. 42–47.

Grub, Phillip D.; Fariborz Ghadar; and Dara Khambata, eds. *The Multinational Enterprise in Transition.* Princeton, N.J.: Darwin Press, 1986. See chap. 5, "International Personnel Management."

Kiggundu, Moses N. *Managing Organizations in Developing Countries: An Operational and Strategic Approach.* West Hartford, CT: Kumarian Press, Inc., 1989.

Maisonrouge, J. G. "The Education of the Modern International Manager." *Journal of International Business Studies,* Spring–Summer 1983, pp. 141–46.

Ronen, Simcha. *Comparative and Multinational Management.* New York: John Wiley & Sons, 1986. See chap. 12, "Staffing the MNC Foreign Subsidiary."

Rossman, Marlene L. *The International Businesswoman of the 1990s: A Guide to Success in the Global Marketplace.* New York: Praeger Publishers, Inc., 1990.

Tung, Rosalie L. "Career Issues in International Assignments." *The Academy of Management Executive,* August 1988, pp. 244–47.

NOTES

[1] For evidence, see Duane Kujawa, "Technology Strategy and Industrial Relations: Case Studies of Japanese Multinationals in the United States," *Journal of International Business Studies,* Winter 1983, pp. 9–22; and Duane Kujawa, *Japanese Multinationals in the United States: Case Studies* (New York: Praeger Publishers, 1986), pp. 40–88.

[2] Richard D. Hays, "Expatriate Selection: Insuring Success and Avoiding Failure," *Journal of International Business Studies,* Spring 1974, p. 25; and U.S. Department of Commerce, *Foreign Direct Investment in the United States,* vol. 1 (Washington, D.C.: U.S. Government Printing Office, 1976), p. 20.

[3] As reported in "Mad Dogs and Expatriates," *Economist,* March 3, 1984, p. 69.

[4] Lawrence G. Franko, "Who Manages Multinational Enterprise?" *Columbia Journal of World Business,* Summer 1973, pp. 30ff.

[5] Kevin Barham and Clive Rassam, *Shaping the Corporate Future* (Ashridge, CO: Ashridge Management Group, 1989).

[6] U.S. Department of Commerce, *Foreign Direct Investment,* vol. 5, appendix 1, "Management and Employment Practices of Direct Foreign Investors in the United States," pp. I-63–I-64.

[7] Kujawa, *Japanese Multinationals,* pp. 40–59.

[8] Rosalie L. Tung and Edwin L. Miller, "Managing in the Twenty-first Century: The Need for Global Orientation," *Management International Review,* Vol. 30, 1990/1, pp. 5–18.

[9] "Mad Dogs and Expatriates."

[10] Rosalie L. Tung, "Selection and Training of Personnel for Overseas Assignments," *Columbia Journal of World Business,* Spring 1981, pp. 68–78.

[11] Rosalie L. Tung, "Human Resource Planning in Japanese Multinationals: A Model for U.S. Firms?" *Journal of International Business Studies,* Fall 1984, p. 141.

[12] Tung, "Selection and Training," p. 69.

[13] Ibid., p. 75.

[14] Ibid., p. 76.

[15] Tung, "Human Resource Planning," p. 142.

[16] See, for example, Hays, "Expatriate Selection," pp. 30–36.

[17] Ehrenfried Pausenberger, "The Conduct of International Enterprises in Developing Countries," *Intereconomics,* November–December 1980, p. 297.

[18] N. Shehzad, "The American Expatriate Manager's Role and Future in Today's World," *Human Resource Planning,* 1984, pp. 55–61.

[19] Tung and Miller, "Managing," p. 10.

[20]Llewellyn Clague and Neil B. Krupp, "International Personnel: The Repatriation Problem," *Personnel Administrator,* April 1978, pp. 29–33; and Cecil G. Howard, "Integrating Returning Expatriates into the Domestic Organization," *Personnel Administrator,* January 1979, pp. 62–65.

[21]Ibid.

[22]Lee Smith, "The Hazards of Coming Home," *Dun's Review,* October 1975, pp. 71–73.

[23]Howard, "Integrating Returning Expatriates."

[24]"How to Ease Reentry after Overseas Duty," *Business Week,* June 11, 1979, pp. 82–83.

[25]Smith, "Hazards of Coming Home."

[26]D. W. Kendall, "Repatriation: An Ending and a Beginning," *Business Horizons,* November–December 1981, pp. 21–25.

[27]Published evidence on such a point is difficult to find. However, the authors have conducted a considerable number of company-specific case studies in which expatriate executives have attested to these views. One example, involving expatriate management at Chrysler Corporation's then Spanish subsidiary and the parent's desire to wrest managerial control from a local team consisting of both local nationals and expatriates, is briefly reported in Duane Kujawa, *International Labor Relations Management in the Automotive Industry* (New York: Praeger Publishers, 1971), p. 31.

[28]For evidence, see Lawrence G. Franko, *The European Multinationals* (Stamford, Conn.: Greylock Publishers, 1976), pp. 187–98.

[29]U.S. Department of Commerce, *Foreign Direct Investment,* vol. 5, appendix 1, "Management and Employment Practices," pp. I-60–I-65.

[30]"Overseas Work Appeals to More U.S. Managers as a Wise Career Move," *The Wall Street Journal,* July 19, 1983, p. 1.

[31]Ibid.

[32]Ibid.

Ernesto Gracias por Nada

Ernesto Gracias por Nada had served as president of Ace Synthetics Caribbean (ASYNCA) for two years, and today was his "big day." He was resigning his position with Ace to join Plasticos, S.A. as executive vice president, strategic planning. Ernesto had been working on this move for over a year.

Plasticos was Ace's major customer in the Caribbean and Central America. It bought petrochemical-based feedstocks from Ace that it molded, extruded, or otherwise fabricated into plastic piping, conduit, and sheet used in the construction industry. Both ASYNCA and Plasticos were subsidiaries of U.S. multinationals long active in Latin America. Both were known to be progressive companies. But how often does the president of a major subsidiary resign? What happened at Ace that made Ernesto want to leave? What could Plasticos do for him that Ace couldn't?

Ernesto joined Ace in 1975, nearly 17 years ago. He had just completed his MBA at ESAN, a graduate business school in Lima, Peru. He was 32 then. Ernesto also held a bachelor's degree in chemical engineering from a university near his boyhood home in Rosario, Argentina. Prior to attending ESAN, he had worked for several engineering consulting firms on projects in Argentina, Ecuador, Jamaica, the Dominican Republic, and Peru. The people he worked with were quick to recognize his technical competence and his strong interest in management. Most of them believed that a distinguished career lay ahead of him.

Ace's Organization Structure

Ace Synthetics organized its Latin American Division in 1965 to enhance its focus on several growing, important markets in that region. During the latter half of the 1960s, Ace Synthetics Latin America (ASYNLA) was essentially a marketing organization selling intermediate products produced in upscale, highly capital-intensive plants in the United States. Its marketing success resulted in local production where market size—from a regional, multicountry perspective—could justify direct investment. During the 1970s, Ace put up plants in Brazil, Mexico, Argentina, Chile, and Colombia.

In the early 1980s, ASYNLA "spun off" several operating companies whose responsibilities included both producing certain products locally and marketing all Ace products within their respective countries. Hence, Ace Synthetics Brazil

---

Note: This case is based on a real person and real companies and events known to the case-writer, Duane Kujawa. Fictitious names have been used for all the parties, however, for purposes of anonymity.

(ASYNBRA), Ace Synthetics Mexico (ASYNMEX), Ace Synthetics Argentina (ASYNAR), Ace Synthetics Chile (ASYNCHI), and Ace Synthetics Colombia (ASYNCO) came into being. ASYNCA was also formed then and was given marketing responsibilities for all Ace products in all the Caribbean and Central American countries. ASYNLA was restructured to perform as a regional headquarters organization responsible for all of Latin America and as a marketing organization covering those Latin American countries where no other subsidiary had responsibility—for example, Ecuador, Bolivia, Uruguay, and Peru. At this time, ASYNLA was relocated from its New Jersey-based parent company office to Coral Gables, Florida.

Ace relied on a matrix structure to provide it with operational flexibility and market continuity. Its major organizational units were product based as well as geographic. The Organic Chemicals Group, for example, had world-wide responsibility for organic chemical production, and it was also responsible for the sale of all Ace products (regardless of their production sites) wherever organic chemical plants were located. (Recall that plants were located in major markets.) Area-specific marketing groups such as ASYNCA handled all of the Ace products marketed in their regions.

In this structure, business plans were developed via a committee process involving those responsible for the production of certain products and those responsible for the territories in which those products were marketed. Decisions on production level, production allocation, and pricing, for example, were recognized as interdependent and as requiring diverse managerial inputs. The matrix structure also allowed for the ongoing close coordination among all the organizational subunits, including production, marketing, R&D, and finance, that was required for maximum long-term profitability.

Ace's Key Personnel Policies

Ace's matrix structure required the internal development of managerial/technical personnel. Committee decisions rested not only on accurate inputs from each member but also on knowledge of the broader, system-wide considerations on which decisions were ultimately based. These considerations, in turn, required personnel who were knowledgeable about Ace's overall operations and committed to maximizing returns at the overall corporate level.

For these reasons, Ace hired in only at the lower-level entry positions. Individuals needed to grow within the organization by accepting diverse and increasingly responsible positions that expanded their knowledge of how Ace operated overall, while allowing for progressively stringent testing of their technical and managerial mettle.

Every year, Ace evaluated the performance of its key personnel and forced a rank-ordering of these people reflecting their performance effectiveness. The top 20 percent were given substantial merit pay increases and positioned for subsequent promotion into even more responsible and rewarding positions. The middle 60 percent were given average raises. The bottom 20 percent got no raise and were often encouraged to leave. Ace's compensation policy was to reward performance while encouraging performance improvement.

Ace preferred to use cash compensation as much as possible. It felt that this was a stronger performance motivator than indirect payments, such as fringe benefits. Many viewed Ace's retirement bonus as the ultimate cash reward. Key employees received a cash bonus equal to three years' salary when they retired. This typically amounted to several hundred thousand dollars and was in addition to the regular retirement program benefits.

Ernesto's Case

Ever since Ernesto joined Ace, he had received superior performance ratings. He was always in the top 20 percent, and he had progressed fairly rapidly up the company's hierarchy. He was initially a technical sales representative in an Argentina-based group responsible for polymer sales. He was appointed head of the polymer marketing group in Peru within two years, and two years after that appointment, he was put in charge of polymer sales for all of Argentina. Four years later, he moved to the Coral Gables regional office as director of polymer sales at ASYNLA. In 1985, he was promoted to director of marketing, Organic Chemicals Group, at ASYNLA. As before, his performance was outstanding.

By 1988, Ernesto had spent five years at Coral Gables. Company policy now required that he return to Latin America since he was not on the Ace-U.S. payroll. During his five years at Coral Gables, he was treated like all Ace-U.S. management personnel in terms of pay scale and basic benefits. In addition, as an expatriate manager, he was given extra compensation to cover schooling costs for his children, travel during an extended annual home leave, and so on.

The five-year limit was imposed for several reasons. One reason was that five years seemed more than adequate from a professional development standpoint. A second was that expatriates were expensive, so there had to be good grounds for continuing to pay the added costs associated with their status. Yet another was that such expatriates from Latin American countries were ultimately more valuable to the company if they returned to Latin America, where their assets, including their linguistic and cultural affinities, could be put to optimum use.

Ernesto was first offered a position as executive vice president at ASYNVEN. He turned it down, claiming hardship on his family if he were to relocate just then. A month later, he requested advancement into the Ace-U.S. organization. His request was denied. Shortly thereafter, Ernesto was offered and accepted the president's position at ASYNCA. Within three months, he and his family had relocated to San Jose, Costa Rica.

Ernesto felt that he had been treated unfairly by Ace. Other Latin American executives confided that they too felt that Ace had treated them as "second-class citizens," since their career paths had been essentially confined to Latin America. Ernesto and others like him were highly results-oriented and had been compensated handsomely over the years. They had all developed substantial investments in the United States. (These investments reflected a variety of concerns, not the least of which was the long-term currency hedge that such investments provided in the face of nearly continuously declining Latin American currency values.) Moreover, a Latin American on assignment in a Latin American country did not receive the special three-year salary bonus upon retiring.

Ernesto arrived in San Jose determined to recover what he felt was a financial loss occasioned by Ace's failure to recognize him on an equal basis with parent country nationals. It took him about two years to identify Plasticos as his "target" and to negotiate his salary and benefit package.

19

Export-Import Management

This chapter describes how export-import transactions are carried out and demonstrates how a firm can benefit from being involved in international trade. It illuminates the main participants, instruments, and practices in international trade. The perspectives of small firms, large MNEs, and importers are presented in separate sections to show the opportunities available to each. The main goals of the chapter are to:

1. Explain how relatively simple export-import transactions, including documentation, work.

2. Show how domestic and multinational firms can benefit from exporting.

3. Demonstrate the gains available to the firm from using imports in its business strategy.

4. Explain a wide variety of the most important trade financing procedures.

INTRODUCTION

International trade was probably the first form of international business, and it certainly involves the largest number of participants in international business today. The value of international banking transactions far surpasses that of trade, whose value in turn exceeds that of foreign direct investment, foreign portfolio investment, contractual arrangements such as licensing, intergovernment transfers, and other forms of international business. The participants in many of these business activities tend to be large, established companies and banks. In the area of exports and imports, on the other hand, there is a huge variety of participants, ranging from one-person companies that buy products from manufacturers for export, all the way to major multinational enterprises such as General Electric, which constructs and exports nuclear power plants and a great variety of other products to many countries.

Exporting can be used as a marginal activity by a company that sells some product in one country and agrees to ship that product overseas on request. Similarly, importing may be used to obtain an input needed for manufacturing when domestic supplies are inadequate. In each of these cases, the international aspect of the business may be relatively unimportant to the firm, but it exists anyway. Then if the firm discovers that overseas sales (or imported parts) begin to count for a major part of total sales, it may place some specific focus on developing a strategy for exports and imports.

This entry into international business through exporting or importing is not a *necessary* condition, since a firm may just as well decide to invest overseas in a low-cost location, in order to maintain its market share for a product facing serious price competition. In this case, initial international business occurs through foreign direct investment. The key point is that, generally speaking, exporting or importing is a type of international business open to virtually any size or kind of firm, whereas other types of international activity, such as foreign direct investment and overseas franchising, tend to demand greater capital, management time, and other company resources.

Multinational firms have the potential for using exports and imports both to move products among their affiliates in different countries and to deal with outside customers and suppliers. MNEs that do this face many opportunities for benefiting from low-cost overseas suppliers (including their own affiliates), for selling excess inventories from an affiliate in one country to customers in another, and even for shipping some products to a subsidiary that produces others, in order to offer a full product line to local customers. On the whole, MNEs can use international trade to pursue many business goals more efficiently or effectively than do purely domestic firms.

Many companies fail to consider *imports* as a means of supplying their needs for parts, components, and even finished products. Perhaps this bias is due to the managers' main focus on sales (and hence on potential exports). Or perhaps it follows the typical government-led emphasis on exports to improve a country's balance of trade. Since imports as well as exports may contribute to a company's business success, they should not be ignored. Reducing the cost of production inputs (through importing) adds to the bottom line, just as increasing the volume of sales does.

This chapter is organized to illuminate the main participants, instruments, and practices in international trade first and then to explore managerial issues. The next section lays out the basic export/import transaction. Then the perspectives of small firms, MNEs, and importers are considered in separate sections. After that, the specific issue of financing exports and imports is discussed. Finally, the ways in which exporting and importing can utilize (or create) the firm's competitive advantages are reconsidered.

A BASIC EXPORT-IMPORT TRANSACTION

The Participants

Although there is probably no such thing as a "typical" **export-import transaction,** we can consider a number of frequently used instruments and features of such transactions as a basic model, to which other alternatives can be attached or compared. Figure 19–1 depicts a transaction in which an importer and exporter agree on a sale and they each use a bank to handle the financial arrangements. Other intermediaries—an insurance company, a transportation company, and customs in the importing country—are also shown.

The transaction would probably take place somewhat as follows. First, the exporter would look for a foreign buyer for its products. (Alternatively, a foreign buyer might come to the exporter and request a shipment.) When the exporter finds a buyer—not necessarily an easy task—the transaction can proceed. The two firms negotiate for terms, such as the price, the quantity to be delivered, the delivery date, and the payment date. When an agreement is reached, some kind of bill of sale can be drawn up, depending on what the two parties determine. The negotiations will probably include a demand by the exporter to have some guarantee of payment made on the importer's behalf—for example, a letter of credit from a bank that the exporter chooses. (The financial aspects are discussed at length in the "Trade Financing" section.) These negotiations, if successful, result in an export-import transaction.

In addition to the payment documents, the transaction usually involves an insurance contract on the goods shipped (to protect against losses from damage in shipping) and a contract with some transportation company to ship the goods from the exporter to customs in the importer's country. The goods must be

FIGURE 19–1

A Simple Export-Import Transaction

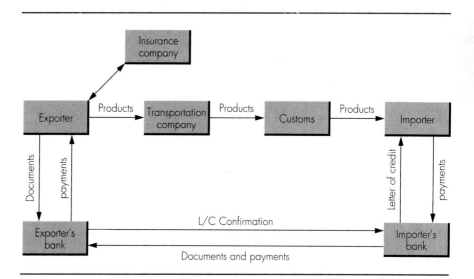

cleared by customs inspectors in the receiving country, after which the importer or another transportation company may pick them up for delivery to the importer's facility.

This highly simplified transaction illustrates some central concerns of the parties involved in international trade. The exporter wants to assure payment as soon and as certainly as possible. The importer wants to make sure that the goods arrive on time and in good condition. Each bank wants to make sure that payment takes place on time and, of course, that it earns its fees for providing the letter of credit or other services (in addition to interest on any financing that it offers). The insurance company wants to make sure that the cargo is delivered as contracted in the sale. And finally, the transportation company wants to make sure that the exporter (or importer) pays for the shipment as contracted. These concerns are listed in concise fashion in Table 19–1. Notice that the concerns are more or less inverse for the exporter (who wants earlier payment and later shipment) and the importer (who wants later payment and earlier delivery). The other parties mainly want to see the transaction completed as contracted, since their income generally comes from fees based on the value of the shipment.

The Documentation

To carry out the export-import transaction already described, a substantial amount of documentation is required. The documents most often used include the letter of credit, the bank draft, the bill of lading or combined transport document, the commercial invoice, the insurance certificate, and the certificate of origin. Let us consider each of these documents in turn.

An (export) **letter of credit (L/C)** is a contract between an importer and a bank that transfers liability for paying the exporter from the importer to the (supposedly more creditworthy) importer's bank. From the issuing bank's point

TABLE 19–1

Export-Import Participants and Their Concerns

Participant	Concerns	Items Affecting Income	Risks
Exporter	Early payment, guaranteed payment	Revenues, production costs, transport costs, financing costs	Nonpayment, delays, damage to goods
Importer	Timely arrival of goods, safe arrival of goods, latest payment allowable	Product cost, import-related fees and expenses, financing costs	Delays, fraud, damage to goods
Exporter's bank	Documents in order, payment received from importer's bank	Fees, contract-processing costs	Nonpayment, incorrect documents
Importer's bank	Documents in order, payment received from importer	Fees, contract-processing costs	Nonpayment, incorrect documents
Insurance company	Payment of premiums, safe arrival of goods	Premiums, contract-processing costs	Damage to goods, incorrect documents
Transport company	Payment of shipping charges	Fees, contract-processing costs	Damage to goods, delays

of view, the L/C represents a contingent liability: if the terms stated in the letter of credit are met, then the bank agrees to pay the exporter. As seen in Figure 19–2, the terms of the L/C specify the presentation of appropriate documents (in this case, a commercial invoice, a customs invoice, a packing list, a bill of lading, and a 60-day bank draft) but do not refer to the quality (i.e., acceptability) of the merchandise.

As long as the bank that issues the L/C (Marine Midland International Bank) is presented with the required documents before expiration of the L/C, the bank is obligated to pay the exporter. If the importer fails to pay the bank, then the bank must deal with that problem as a separate contract. Similarly, if the importer fails to receive acceptable merchandise for any reason, that problem must be dealt with as a separate contract not involving the bank (e.g., damages to merchandise are covered by insurance and fraud by the exporter is a failure to uphold the initial commercial contract). Multiple contracts are involved in the simple export-import transaction; the L/C in particular requires only that the specified documents be in order for the exporter to receive payment from the bank—all other contractual obligations are generally separate from this one.[1]

Notice that the document shown in Figure 19–2 is called an "irrevocable commercial letter of credit." The word *irrevocable* refers to the fact that, once drawn up for the importer and accepted by the exporter, the L/C may not be amended by either party without prior approval by both. The L/C is also "commercial," because it refers to a commercial transaction. This type of L/C is called "documentary," because it requires that documents be presented in order to carry out payment. It is the most commonly used means of guaranteeing payment in international trade between unrelated firms. If the paying bank is not in the exporter's country, the exporter many demand that a bank in that country offer a "confirmation" of the L/C. In that event, the responsibility for paying the exporter falls on the confirming bank, which in turn will seek payment from the importer's bank, which in turn will seek payment from the importer. (In this example, the Hongkong & Shanghai Banking Corporation only offers "advice" to the exporter, XYZ Trading Company. This bank could be asked to confirm the transaction and take responsibility as noted.)

The **bank draft,** also called a bill of exchange, is similar to a simple check in its use as the means of payment for an export-import transaction. If the transaction is payable on sight, the draft becomes a check when the exporter presents it (plus the L/C and other documents). If the transaction is payable at some fixed time after acceptance of the documents, the draft is akin to a postdated (delayed-reaction) check, cashable only at the specified date. The latter is called a **time draft,** and the former a **sight draft.** Figure 19–3 is a time draft, payable in 60 days from the account of ABC Company at Marine Midland International Bank.

When a letter of credit is used to guarantee payment to the exporter, the draft remains the vehicle through which payment is made, but it becomes relatively unimportant because the bank issuing (or confirming) the L/C has taken responsibility to pay the exporter, whether or not the importer's account contains sufficient funds. If the draft is used alone (i.e., without a letter of credit), it becomes all-important as the means of payment. (Payment by draft alone, of course, is less expensive to the importer than using an L/C as well.)

When a draft is used without a letter of credit, some form of instructions must accompany it to explain to the various parties involved what other documents

FIGURE 19–2

APPLICATION & AGREEMENT FOR IRREVOCABLE COMMERCIAL LETTER OF CREDIT	L/C No _____ (For Bank Use Only) DATE __June 19,19__

To: MARINE MIDLAND INTERNATIONAL BANK
777 Brickell Avenue, Suite 1201
Miami, Florida 33131
Please issue for our account an irrevocable Letter of Credit (herein called Credit) as set forth below by:

☐ AIRMAIL ☐ AIRMAIL, WITH SHORT PRELIMINARY TELEGRAPHIC ADVICE ☒ FULL TELEGRAPHIC ADVICE

Advising Bank (Please leave blank unless Advising Bank has been specified)	For Account of
The Hongkong & Shanghai Banking Corp. 18 Rue de la Paix 75002, Paris France	ABC Company 100 Madison Street New York, New York

In Favor of (Beneficiary)	Amount
XYZ Trading Co., Ltd. P.O. Box 260-09 Paris, France	In Numbers US$45,000.00 In Words Forty-five thousand and 00/100 U.S. Dollars
	Drafts must be presented for negotiation or presented to drawee on or before Expiration Date September,1 19

Available by drafts at _____60 days sight_____ drawn, at your option, on you or your correspondent
for ___100___ % of the invoice value. _(Please indicate Sight or Tenor)

When accompanied by the following documents, as checked:

C H E C K   R E Q U I R E D   D O C U M E N T S

☒ Commercial invoice ___1___ original and ___2___ copies.
☒ Customer invoice ___1___ original and ___2___ copies.
☐ Insurance Policy and/or Certificate _____
☐ Including War Risk _____ _(If other insurance is required, please state risks)

☒ Other documents __Packing list in duplicate__
_____
_____

☐ Air Waybill consigned to _____
☒ On Board Ocean Bill of Lading (if more than one original has been issued all are required)
Issued to Order of **MARINE MIDLAND INTERNATIONAL BANK** _____
Marked: Notify: __ABC Company, 100 Madison Street, New York, N.Y.__
_____

Freight: ☒ Collect ☐ Paid

Covering: Merchandise described in the invoice as (Mention commodity only in generic terms omitting details as to grade, quality, etc.) __Purse accessories__

Shipping Terms
(Check One) ☐ FAS ☒ FOB ☐ C&F ☐ CIF ☐ OTHER
_____ _(Specify City, Port or Airport)

Shipment From: Paris, France To: New York, USA Latest: August 21, 19	Credit Transferable ☐ Yes ☒ No	Partial Shipments ☒ Permitted ☐ Not Permitted	Transshipments ☐ Permitted ☒ Not Permitted

☒ Documents and/or Draft(s) must be presented to negotiating or paying bank within ___10___ days after the date of issuance of documents evidencing shipment but on or before the expiration of the Credit. (*Note: If number of days left blank it will automatically be considered 21 days.*)

☒ Insurance effected by ourselves. We agree to keep insurance coverage in force until this transaction is completed. All banking charges outside the U.S.A. are for ☒ Beneficiary's account ☐ Our account
☐ Other instructions _____
_____

Disposition of Documents: ☒ To Us ☐ Other _____
Unless Otherwise Instructed You May Authorize Your Correspondent To Forward All Drafts and Documents In One Airmail.

MMIB-60 (Rev s8 85)

FIGURE 19–3

A Commercial Draft

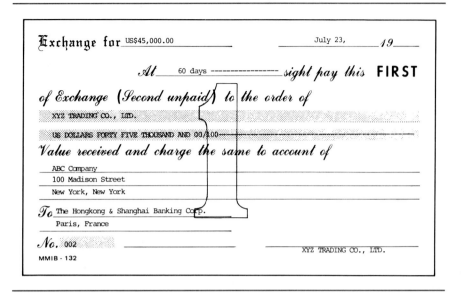

and goods are involved in the transaction. (This type of transaction is called a **documentary collection.**) If the draft is payable on sight, then the instruction letter specifies that documents will be released to the importer upon payment of the draft (abbreviated D/P). If the draft is payable at a later date (i.e., a time draft), then instructions specify that the documents will be released to the importer upon acceptance of the draft (abbreviated D/A). Notice that in the case of a sight draft, the importer actually pays the exporter before receiving the goods—so the exporter's main risk is that it may ship the goods to customs in the importer's country and subsequently need to retrieve them if the importer fails to complete the transaction by paying the draft. (Payment on sight occurs when the importer receives the documents after the exporter ships the goods and sends the documents to the importer.) In the case of a time draft, once the draft is accepted by the importer (it becomes a "collection"), the exporter surrenders the merchandise, with only the draft as its claim on future payment. Both sight and time drafts accompanied by instructions and other documents (but no L/C) are called **documentary drafts.**

A **bill of lading** issued by a shipping company or its agent is used as evidence of a contract for shipping the merchandise and as a claim to ownership of the goods. The exporter owns the goods until the importer accepts the documents, at which point ownership shifts to the importer. The bill of lading serves as a receipt of the exporter, showing that it delivered the merchandise to the shipping company for transportation to the importer. The bill of lading does *not* require the carrier to inspect the merchandise; it only requires that the carrier accept the containers stated by the exporter to contain the specified merchandise.

If the goods are shipped by airplane or by more than one means of transport, alternative documents may replace the bill of lading. An **airway bill** is used in shipment by air. A **combined transport document** is used for shipments that involve more than one mode of transportation (e.g., a truck to the port, then a ship).[2]

TABLE 19–2

Common International Trade
Documents

Instrument	Seller or Issuer	Buyer	Reason for Use
Letter of credit (L/C)	Commercial bank	Importer	To guarantee payment to the exporter
Bank draft	Drawn on a commercial bank	Payable to exporter	It is the means of payment
Bill of lading	Shipping company	Exporter	To prove that the exporter delivered the goods as agreed
Combined transport document	Shipping company	Exporter	To prove that the exporter & each transport company delivered the goods as agreed
Commercial invoice	Exporter	Importer	To describe precisely the merchandise and terms of sale
Insurance certificate	Insurance company	Exporter	To prove that the shipment is insured and on what terms
Certificate of origin	Government of shipping country	Exporter	To prove the country where the merchandise was produced, for customs purposes

Another document usually involved in an export-import shipment is the **commercial invoice,** which is written by the exporter to describe precisely the merchandise and terms of the sale. This document resembles the shipping invoice used in domestic shipments.

Some proof of *insurance* is generally included. The **insurance certificate** will explain what type of coverage is being used (e.g., fire, theft, water) and will name the insuror and the exporter whose property is being insured.

In order to assess tariffs and other government-imposed restrictions on trade, the shipment may require a **certificate of origin,** stating the country in which the goods were produced. This document is necessary when shipping to European Community countries, where tariffs are charged on goods originating outside the Community but not on goods produced in member countries.

Table 19–2 summarizes the documents discussed above, noting the parties involved and the reasons for their use. The above discussion is not intended to cover all the documents used in export-import transactions, but rather to point out the ones that are most widely used. In every transaction of this kind, it is necessary to check with each country's government before shipping, in order to verify what documents are necessary.

EXPORT MANAGEMENT FOR THE DOMESTIC FIRM

This section examines exporting as a part of the business of a nonmultinational firm. Such a firm may be large or small, but it is one that does *not* do substantial international business—that is, its competitive advantages do not include experience in foreign markets. This type of firm must consider exports to be a kind of new business, just like production of a new product or entry into a new market segment in the domestic market. The appropriate products must be selected, buyers must be found, production and transportation costs must be estimated, promotional strategy must be created, and the business must be incorporated into the organization effectively. While each of these matters deserves detailed study, they are discussed here only to point out some of the most important considerations.

Exporting within Corporate Strategy

Figure 19–4 offers a view of **exporting** in a corporate strategy context. It depicts exporting as a means of entry into foreign markets. Other alternatives include foreign direct investment and contractual arrangements such as licensing and franchising. The company can set its strategy by assessing its competitive advantages and disadvantages (step 1), then proceeding to explore foreign markets that offer a potential for sales.

The target markets can be chosen on the basis of expected sales, competition from other suppliers, government restrictions, costs of getting the product to those markets, and any other factors that may be relevant. Although there are over 160 countries in the world, it is most likely that the firm will be able to limit its initial search to a very small number of markets—probably based not only on incomes but also on proximity and cultural affinity.

Once a country has been chosen (step 2), the strategy must be developed to select products and a market entry vehicle. If the firm makes only one product or a narrow product line, then product selection is not an issue. For the diversified firm, it may be appropriate to introduce different products into different national markets. Product selection is based on competitive conditions in the chosen market for the range of products made by the firm, the costs of making and transporting the products, and the risks involved (step 3). In any event, once a product has been selected, the firm can proceed to explore ways of getting that product to the foreign market.

Depending on the firm's set of competitive advantages and the conditions in a given national market, each of the market-serving alternatives can be evaluated (as discussed in Chapter 2). Assuming that the firm has no experience with other international business, and because the costs and risks of exporting are usually low, exporting most likely will be chosen (step 4).

Nevertheless, the other market-serving alternatives should be considered carefully. Direct investment certainly can give the firm a greater local visibility in the host country, and it avoids the risk that the government may impose barriers to imports in the future. However, direct investment is much more costly than exporting in most situations. Likewise, licensing should be considered, especially if the firm's technology is capable of being protected and if import restrictions are significant. And, of course, other strategic alliances such as joint marketing agreements or joint production ventures should also be evaluated in terms of their impacts on costs, revenues, and the strategic position of the firm relative to key competitors.

Assuming that exporting does appear superior to the other choices and that the company does decide to pursue the given market (rather than eliminate it from consideration), a detailed business plan can be created and executed (step 5, as discussed below).

Finally, after observing the results of the strategy for some period of time (step 6), adjustments can be made or the strategy can be rejected in favor of

FIGURE 19–4

Foreign Business Strategy

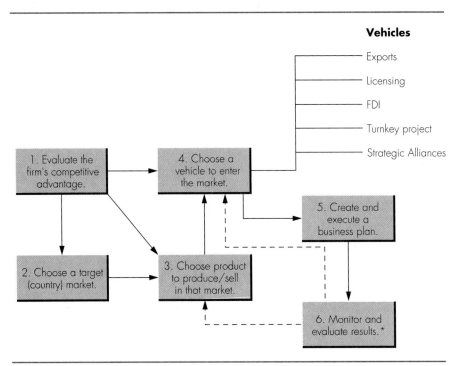

*The dashed lines show that performance evaluation may lead to changes in the products selected or in the market entry vehicle (or even to exit from the market) if the results justify such strategic shifts.

another. Altogether, Figure 19–4 presents a logical structure for thinking about foreign market entry, through exports or other means that may be available to the firm.

The Business Plan

The detailed business plan mentioned above as step 5 should cover the usual marketing considerations such as pricing, promotion, and distribution—and also the organization of the firm to handle this new business.

Pricing may be aimed to cover the incremental costs of producing extra products for export,[3] or to cover the full costs of production (including fixed costs), or to equate marginal revenue to marginal cost. Other goals, such as revenue maximization or loss minimization, could be sought too. The point is that pricing for overseas sales may be based on criteria different from those used in pricing for domestic sales.

Another consideration to keep in mind is that if the exchange rate changes, prices in domestic currency will change in terms of the foreign currency. Such a change may be helpful or harmful to the firm, but it definitely should be taken into account when a pricing strategy for export sales is being set. For a target country whose currency is devaluing relative to the home country currency, the firm's export prices will need to be lowered if it wants to maintain the same host country prices. For a country whose currency is revaluing relative to the home country currency, the firm's product will become less expensive unless export prices are raised to offset the exchange-rate change.

A firm exporting to several foreign markets would like to price separately in each market, charging higher prices in markets that will bear them. This strategy can create problems, however, since customers in a low-price country could try to resell the product in high-price countries—competing with the firm itself! Also, this type of price discrimination may lead the authorities in high-price markets to penalize the firm for monopolistic practices.

Promotion may be extended abroad or adapted to the host country environment, as discussed in Chapter 14. If exports are solicited from abroad, then initially no promotion is required. If the firm wants to expand its export business, then some promotional effort will be required. If the market entry mode chosen is exporting through distributors, then promotion must be done among potential distributors, rather than focusing only on final customers.

Distribution to the foreign market will require new arrangements with transportation companies, insurers, and so on, because the transactions will cross national borders and thus cross national legal jurisdictions. While no single distribution method can be singled out as best for all cases, the pros and cons of each method can be evaluated, just as in the domestic market. The key differences are that costs are generally higher because distances are longer and risks are greater because of the additional national economies and legal jurisdictions involved.

Organizational issues relate to the fit of international sales into the company's total business (as discussed to some extent in Chapter 13). Generally, exports are handled by an existing division when they are small in value. As exports grow, at some point it may make sense to assign responsibility elsewhere for foreign sales—by establishing an international division or otherwise reorganizing the firm. Basically, the goals are to communicate with prospective customers in the host country about product availability and to control the export activity so that it does not disrupt other company business.

EXPORT MANAGEMENT STRATEGY FOR THE MNE

Once the company has become multinational, or is willing to consider establishing overseas operations, a new set of alternatives arises. Now it may be possible to export some products from the home country to the target country and to produce other products in the target market. When the MNE introduces new products at home, it may simultaneously introduce them in the host market, through either exports or local production in the existing facility there. When cost or regulatory difficulties arise in one country, it may be possible to move production to the less-constrained country, resulting in either imports or local production for each market served. The MNE may also export parts or other production inputs from an affiliate in one country to another affiliate in another country for assembly—in this case serving the host country market only indirectly, through products manufactured by the host country affiliate. In general, the MNE possesses a greatly expanded set of choices in comparison with the domestic firm in any country.

Returning to Figure 19–4, the MNE again begins with an inventory of its competitive advantages and disadvantages to see what products and markets are worth exploring. Now it can divide target markets into those where it already has some operations—and thus where additional products can be introduced—and those that are new to it. In a market where the MNE already has operations, it has a competitive advantage (relative to other foreign firms without local operations) in knowledge of demand conditions and in knowledge of the legal, cultural, and cost barriers to serving that market. In a market where the MNE does not yet have operations, it faces barriers similar to those confronting the non-MNE, except that the MNE has had experience in dealing with new entry in other markets (such as dealing with tariffs and import licensing) that may be transferable to the new market. The knowledge advantage from previous international business gives the MNE an edge over other firms in market entry in both situations. Thus, the MNE's choice of a target market depends both on market characteristics in potential host countries and on the firm's existing array of foreign affiliates.

The MNE's choice of products to sell in the target market once again depends on the firm's previous activities in that market. Some products may have already been introduced there. Others may be appropriate for local production rather than export from the home country (or from an affiliate in another country). Having considered such factors, the firm can choose products based on expected demand in the target market, on the costs of getting the products to customers, and on the risks involved.

The choice among exports, local production, and other market-serving alternatives has already been discussed. For the MNE, it is important to note that some products may be supplied to a particular country through one vehicle and other products through other vehicles.

When the MNE manager arrives at step 5 of the decision-making process, a specific business plan must be designed, once again recognizing the interrelations between the new project and the firm's existing activities. The new export venture must be evaluated on the basis of its *incremental* contribution to the firm's sales and profits. If the exports simply replace products previously manufactured by the company in the target country, then they are justified only if they lower the costs or risks of producing and delivering the products to customers. If the exports represent entry into a new market, then they may be evaluated as in the case of the non-MNE.

If the exports are sold from one affiliate to another in the same firm, the issue of **transfer pricing** arises. By pricing intrafirm shipments higher or lower, the firm may transfer more or less funds to the shipping affiliate. While this issue does not necessarily affect the decision to export, it does constitute a vehicle for moving funds to desired locations within the MNE—a strategic consideration that may be very important when there are exchange controls and other restrictions on company financial dealings.

Organizationally, the export function in the MNE is often assigned to an international division or added onto each product division as needed. The need for internal control over export decisions becomes more and more important as exports, local production, and other alternatives are used to serve markets in various countries. The key concern is that export sales must not simply replace existing company business (e.g., through local production or licensing) but must generate additional profits to the firm by raising revenues, lowering costs, or lowering risks.[4]

IMPORT MANAGEMENT

While attention generally is focused on exporting as the relevant aspect of international trade for the firm to pursue, there is no reason why **importing** cannot be equally important. In fact, some firms do their entire business as import intermediaries, finding suppliers overseas and customers domestically for various products. Both the MNE and the non-MNE can utilize importing to obtain lower-cost or unavailable products from abroad.

Both the MNE and the domestic firm can make importing part of the purchasing function. Simple product availability may be the initial reason for seeking a foreign supplier—if the needed product is not available from domestic suppliers, then imports must be used. The decision to import may also be based on comparative cost differences between domestic and foreign suppliers and on the risk-reducing goal of obtaining multiple suppliers, including one or more from abroad. In general, the use of imports in the firm's total business can serve a variety of goals, each of which improves its position in the market.

The multinational firm can not only use imports as a source of supplies from other firms; it can also import from affiliates abroad. Very important for many MNEs today is the use of *offshore assembly* (for example, of televisions, stereos, and other electronic products), which requires import into the home country from an assembly plant overseas. Also important for MNEs is the possibility of supplying the home market from a foreign affiliate in the event of a strike, machinery breakdown, or any other type of production problem in the home country. Thus, MNEs need to consider the risk-reducing aspect of importing at least as much as the cost-reducing aspect.

TRADE FINANCING

In the simple export-import transaction discussed above, **trade financing** was included when the importer used a letter of credit, allowing payment to be postponed for some period of time, such as 180 days. Realistically, both the importer and the exporter may need pretrade and posttrade financing. The importer may need **pretrade financing** if it is required to make partial or total prepayment to the exporter or if it is required to place a deposit with the government before receiving permission to import. Even after shipment, the importer may need credit during the period before it is paid for sale of the merchandise. The exporter may need pretrade working capital financing. Later, if the exporter accepts payment by a time draft or any other future means of payment, it may also need financing for the period after shipment but before payment by the importer. Common means of financing these needs are shown in Table 19–3.

The exporter may obtain pretrade financing by requiring the importer to prepay the shipment. Alternatively, the exporter may seek a working capital loan from a commercial bank or some other financial institution. One type of working capital loan, called a **back-to-back L/C,** uses the letter of credit issued by the importer's bank as security for a loan made to the exporter. A second letter

TABLE 19–3

Simple Trade Financing Techniques

	Pretrade Financing	Posttrade Financing
Exporter	Prepayment Back-to-back L/C Working capital loan	Sale of receivables (e.g., banker's acceptance) Bank loan Sight draft and letter of credit Documentary collection payable on sight
Importer	Bank loan to cover prepayment	Letter of credit and time draft Bank loan Sale on consignment Sale on open account

**IB
ILLUSTRATION**

Pyrotek Goes International

Pyrotek Corporation is a small, family-run company based in Dallas, Texas, that manufactures and sells fire extinguishers for use in office buildings, hotels, and industrial settings. The firm has been in business for over 10 years, and it has established a viable market niche with a dozen fairly large clients and about 100 smaller clients. Three members of the Wyler family and five other employees constitute the entire work force of Pyrotek. In 1990, the company had sales of about $12 million, virtually all of which were made in the United States. Only three rival firms are perceived to provide competition for Pyrotek, although several larger suppliers do produce fire extinguishers for major hotel chains, restaurants, and other potential Pyrotek customers.

Pyrotek's main competitor recently reduced its prices on the basic carbon dioxide and foam extinguishers that make up most of the market. Facing this challenge, Mr. Wyler began to look for new suppliers of the metal tubing, valves, and fittings that the firm uses to make fire extinguishers. In addition, sales were increasing to the point where Pyrotek could not continue to expand without installing new manufacturing capacity of its own. Based on these two pressures, Mr. Wyler was able to find a brass foundry in Birmingham, Alabama, that agreed to contract on a long-term basis to produce much of the needed valves and fittings and to assemble the fire extinguishers. The deal included an option for Pyrotek to buy 25 percent of the stock in the foundry over a period of five years.

This step solved the problem of expansion for the firm, but it left the cost/price issue unchanged. At almost the same time as the foundry deal was closed, Mr. Wyler was contacted by a Taiwanese firm that manufactured brass and copper casings. This firm was trying to attract American customers for its products. It offered a price of $US 0.65 per casing (the shell of the fire extinguisher), a considerably lower price than the $US 1.20 that Pyrotek was paying its existing suppliers. With no experience in international business, Mr. Wyler was extremely hesitant to enter into a contract. However, he was also quite aware of the "Asian challenge" facing American manufacturers and of the successes that several U.S. auto and electronics firms had had in dealing with Asian suppliers.

He decided to "hedge" his bet by purchasing only about 10 percent of his needs from this new supplier. After an initial order of 3,000 casings, Mr. Wyler was totally satisfied with the quality and delivery conditions of the shipment, and today Pyrotek imports approximately one half of its supplies from Taiwan. The firm is now actively seeking additional Asian suppliers for its other components. ∎

of credit is issued by the exporter's bank, drawn on the exporter's account, and paid to its supplier. The exporter's bank may offer this type of credit more readily than a straight loan because the importer's L/C provides evidence of a reasonable likelihood that the exporter will be able to pay back the credit.

The importer may not need to worry about pretrade financing unless the shipment is prepaid or the government requires a deposit before issuing an import license to permit the transaction. In either case, the likely means of financing (other than using internal sources of funds) is a bank loan.

For **posttrade financing,** the exporter has various alternatives. It can seek another bank loan to cover the period until payment by the importer. Often it can discount the receivable through the creation of a **banker's acceptance.** Many L/Cs are drawn up to conform to the rules for creating banker's acceptances that can be discounted at a Federal Reserve bank in the United States.[5] If the L/C meets these rules, many banks are willing to purchase the L/C and draft from the exporter at a discount, at which point the documents become a banker's acceptance. (The discount rate for banker's acceptances varies all the time; the current rate can be found daily in the "Money Market Rates" column of *The Wall Street Journal.*) To avoid having to deal with posttrade financing, the exporter can push the problem onto the importer by demanding payment on sight (i.e., at shipment).

The importer will generally use a letter of credit plus a time draft for posttrade financing. If this financing lasts until the importer receives payment from its customers, all of its financing needs are satisfied. If not, the importer would seek other means, such as a bank loan. Perhaps the importer can push the problem onto the exporter by demanding sale on **consignment** (where payment is made to the exporter only when the importer sells the goods to a final customer) or on **open account** with no fixed date required for payment. This last option is usually available only to importers that are legally tied to their exporters, such as subsidiaries of the same company.

These means of financing export-import transactions are not the only ones available, but they do account for most of the business of this kind that is done today. Additional financing is available from an array of nonbank institutions that offer services complementing or substituting for bank lending. Four of the most important ones are (1) government loans and loan guarantees, (2) factoring, (3) forfaiting, and (4) countertrade.

Government Loans and Loan Guarantees

In one form or another, every country today offers *government support* to its exporters. Japan offers low-interest loans to exporting firms; France rebates part of the taxes that exporters have paid on exported products; Brazil allows exporters to exchange foreign-currency earnings at a favorable exchange rate; and other governments do one or more of these things.[6]

The United States offers its exporters two of the above types of support. First, it allows firms that incorporate an overseas export sales subsidiary as a **foreign sales corporation (FSC)** to reduce the taxes paid on their export earnings by as much as 50 percent.[7] Although this is not a "loan" in strict terms, it is a means of reducing the cost of export sales that affects the exporter in a manner similar to that of a low-interest loan. Second, the United States offers exporters support through the loans and guarantees provided by the Export-Import Bank of the United States (Eximbank).

Broadly speaking, **Eximbank** offers U.S. exporters a variety of programs that reduce their costs and risks in dealing with foreign clients. Short-term loan guarantees (actually provided by the Foreign Credit Insurance Association under Eximbank's supervision) enable exporters to obtain credit in cases where commercial banks would not offer it. Similarly, Eximbank offers medium- and long-term loans and guarantees that enable exporters to finance their foreign sales, generally in cases where bank financing would be difficult or impossible to obtain. Eximbank also provides a program of insurance against the political risks that could confront an exporter (e.g., war, government policy changes, currency inconvertibility). Each of these programs is discussed in detail in Eximbank's publications.[8]

Factoring

For financing the period between the shipment of its merchandise and payment by the importer, an exporter may turn to a factoring company, or factor. This arrangement is a direct alternative to acceptance financing. A factor will buy the exporter's receivables at a discount and assume the risk of nonpayment by the importer, as well as the right to payment of the receivables.

Factoring involves a greater commitment from the exporter than does acceptance financing, because a factoring contract generally calls for the exporter to sell *all* receivables to the factor during the contract period. Since factoring is a contractual arrangement between the exporter and the factor, the terms of the contract may include virtually anything that the two parties agree to do. Typically, the factor will agree to buy all export accounts receivable from the exporter at a specified discount and to assume all of the responsibility for collecting from the importer. In return, the factor receives the discounted receivables, on which it gains effective interest when it is paid their full value by the importer. The factor also charges a fee for performing this service.[9]

The choice to an exporter between use of a factor and use of a bank as intermediary in the export-import transaction depends on (1) the cost of using each intermediary; (2) the amount of business being committed; and (3) the flexibility desired.

Forfaiting

Another method of trade financing that is quite similar to factoring and the use of banker's acceptances is **forfaiting.** Forfaiting was developed to handle large capital goods exports from Western firms to Eastern-bloc countries. Like factoring, forfaiting is a means of nonrecourse export finance. As with factoring, the exporter sells its receivable (for an export shipment) at a discount to a forfaiting firm, which accepts the risk of nonpayment by the importer and the right to payment under the exporter's sales contract. However, the forfaiting firm obtains a guarantee (or aval) from the government of the importing country, which accepts responsibility for payment as contracted.

Forfaiting originally gained acceptability among some West European banks, especially in Switzerland, during the 1960s. For export sales to communist countries, these banks (through their forfaiting subsidiaries) began to purchase the payment contracts from exporting companies when suitable guarantees of payment by the host government could be arranged. The banks agreed to purchase these contracts "à forfait," that is, without recourse to the exporting firm. Thus, full nonpayment risk was shifted to the forfaiter, which accepted the guarantee of the host government (or a government bank) as sufficient to justify the transaction. Since the forfaiter operated regularly as an analyst and acceptor of host government risk, it was presumably better able than the exporter to assess and manage that risk. Although forfaiting remains primarily oriented toward financing exports to Eastern Europe, this kind of trade financing is now more broadly available for large transactions involving medium- and long-term payment by the importer. Figure 19–5 depicts the relationships involved in forfaiting.

The costs of forfaiting to the exporter are multiple, and generally they are justifiable only if the transaction is too complex to be handled through the banker's acceptance method. These costs commonly include: (1) a charge for political and transfer risks, about ½ percent to 5 percent per year; (2) a charge for the use of money and for the covering of interest rate risks— generally the eurocurrency rate, LIBOR; and (3) a charge for administrative work, about ½ percent per year.[10]

Countertrade

Finally, the exporter may be able to use **countertrade**—the exchange of goods for goods. Due to the unavailability or very high cost of foreign exchange, many importers are constrained from making purchases from abroad. Countertrade eliminates this bottleneck. (Of course, since the exchange of goods for goods is just barter, countertrade is characterized by all of the inefficiencies and bottle-necks associated with barter.) However, it transforms the exporter's problem of financing the sale into the problem of using or selling the goods received in payment. Moreover, this problem is often complicated by the fact that the goods received in countertrade may be shipped later than the original exports—so that the exporter requires financing during the interim.

Though no standard form of countertrade has yet been developed, two broad categories of countertrade transactions can be distinguished. The first category, for which the label **counterpurchase** is often used, involves commercial compensation by the importer in the short or medium term. (For example, the Soviet Union purchased construction machinery from the Japanese firm Komatsu in return for Komatsu's agreement to buy Siberian timber. Also, Occidental Petroleum contracted to sell phosphate rock in exchange for molten sulphur with Poland. Many more East-West counterpurchase agreements appear in Table 23–5.) The second category, labeled a **buy-back agreement,** involves long-term repayment and often compensation with industrial products. The compensation may be raw materials or intermediate goods (i.e., industrial products)—or it

FIGURE 19–5

Forfaiting

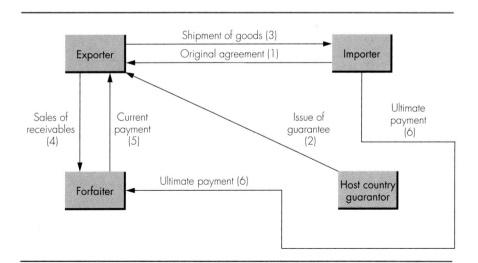

Why Countertrade Is Increasing

Countertrade grew rapidly during the 1980s and appears to be flourishing in the early 1990s as well. The reasons for this persistence of an apparently suboptimal business activity are numerous. First and foremost, when many countries continue to face balance-of-payments problems—specifically deficits that use up available foreign exchange reserves—these countries look to means of obtaining desired imports without having to pay with foreign currency. Countertrade fits the bill. Second, given that firms from many countries do not have experience in selling overseas, countertrade requirements can force foreign MNEs to do the overseas marketing for them, and thus gain access to new markets. Third, when goods are sold in countertrade deals, they may not be priced explicitly in currency terms. This fact may permit a country to sell goods at discount or dumping prices, when they otherwise would be restricted or when direct selling would force cartel (e.g., oil, sugar, coffee, etc.) prices down. Fourth, because of protectionist pressures in many countries, countertrade can be used to force importers to accept the country's exports, thus (supposedly) maintaining jobs and incomes in the host country. These and other factors are resulting in increased countertrade at the same time as international business is becoming more open around the world. ■

may be output from the technique or installation that was sold by the Western exporter. (For example, Fiat, S.A. built an automobile plant in the Soviet Union and received payment in a number of shipments of finished cars. Similarly, after the U.S. government forced U.S. suppliers out of the market in 1980, the German, French, British, and Italian governments subsidized companies from their countries to construct a $US 4 billion natural gas pipeline in the Soviet Union; the Soviet Union is paying for this project with natural gas today.) Transactions in both of these categories involve all goods and no money; hence the term *countertrade* or *barter* conveys the appropriate idea.

Countertrade presents serious constraints to the exporter, relative to other means of trade financing. First, there is the problem of trying to value the products to be received in payment. Second, there is the problem of disposing of these goods. Third, if payment is not simultaneous with the exporter's shipment, then some other form of financing will still be necessary (even if it is generated internally by the exporter). And fourth, the exporter assumes all of the political risk of dealing with the importer. These difficulties may outweigh the value of the possible export sale. The value of countertrade transactions has been estimated to be less than 15 percent of exports to Eastern Europe and a much smaller percentage of the exports among other countries.[11] Countertrade involving U.S. firms was estimated to constitute less than 6 percent of total exports and 0.1 percent of imports in 1984; 80 percent of this trade was related to U.S. military sales to foreign customers.[12]

CONCLUSIONS

Exports and imports accounted for about $2.900 billion worth of sales in 1989, clearly a huge part of total international business. Companies ranging from very small middlemen to giant multinational enterprises participate in export-import transactions, though of course large firms dominate in terms of the value of their shipments.

Even a simple export-import transaction generally requires a large number of participants, ranging from the exporter and importer all the way to transportation companies, insurers, and banks. Although the mechanics of such a transaction were described above, the actual documents and participants may differ from the description given, depending on the countries (i.e., national laws) involved, on the type of shipment, and on many other factors. It is fair to say, however, that most export-import transactions are variants of the process described here.

Like FDI (and local production), licensing, franchising, and so on, exporting can be viewed as a means of foreign market entry. Exporting can be selected to achieve least-cost supply for the foreign market, or to reduce the risk of having all sales in one country, or to establish a base for further production, such as offshore assembly. All in all, exporting can be a dynamic strategic activity that affects even domestic competitiveness, not just a means for disposing of excess production that a firm may be stuck with in its home country.

Domestic firms can utilize exports both to absorb products that cannot be sold locally and to expand business in new markets. For the domestic firm, probably the key problem in international trade is finding buyers abroad; when that has been done, the problems of financing, distribution, and organization can be dealt with.

As compared with domestic firms, multinational firms have many more possibilities for using exports. In addition to exporting to outside buyers, MNEs can export to their own subsidiaries overseas. An MNE can produce the same product in two countries; then, if any difficulty that constrains production occurs in either country, the MNE can import from the other country. An MNE can have an affiliate in one country produce some products, and then it can fill out the product line of that affiliate with shipments from another affiliate in another country.

Importing is an often neglected part of international trade strategy. Any firm may find that it can obtain production inputs from abroad more cheaply or when suppliers are not available locally. Also, by sourcing abroad (using foreign suppliers) and at home, a firm can diversify its suppliers and avoid dependence on local firms only. Each of these possibilities provides a competitive advantage to the importing firm.

While not necessarily the most important part of an export-import transaction, financing does play an important role in such transactions. Traditionally, commercial banks have offered most of this financing, in the form of letters of credit and banker's acceptances. Recently, such forms as countertrade and forfaiting have come into greater use. Factoring also continues to play a role in trade financing. MNEs gain a useful competitive advantage over local firms in any country through their export financing, because MNEs can use high or low transfer prices to move funds wherever desired, they can delay or advance payment to move funds at a desired time, and they face no risk of nonpayment by their importing subsidiaries (although the host country may restrict the affiliate's ability to pay).

QUESTIONS

1. Describe a basic export-import transaction, including the various participants and the various types of documentation.

2. When trying to enter a new national market, how would you choose among exports, FDI (plus local production), licensing, and other market-serving possibilities? That is, what criteria would you use?

3. Explain how a letter of credit works. Who is responsible for paying the exporter? What happens if the importer does not pay as contracted, even through all other parts of the transaction were performed as stipulated?

4. What competitive advantages does a multinational enterprise gain by operating a network of affiliates that export among themselves?

5. What benefits does the domestic firm gain from exporting? How do these benefits differ from the benefits gain by an MNE?

6. What benefits does the domestic firm gain from importing? How do these benefits differ from the benefits gained by an MNE?

7. Explain how forfaiting works. Why would a firm use forfaiting rather than other means of financing an export sale?

8. Countertrading has become quite popular in trade with Eastern Europe. Why is it *not* likely to replace traditional bank financing as the main source of trade finance?

9. Create a market entry strategy for Nabisco Brands Corporation, which wants to enter the market for cookies in Japan. Assume that the company does not have any affiliates in Japan. Discuss the choice of entry mode, product selection, and business plan.

10. What reasons might a U.S. company have for exporting its electronic products to customers in Mexico even though production costs are lower there and tariffs are fairly high there?

REFERENCES

Aggarwal, Raj. "International Business through Barter and Countertrade," *Long Range Planning* June 1989.

Crédit Suisse. *Forfaiting.* Zurich: Finanz AG, 1986.

Eiteman, David, and Arthur Stonehill. *Multinational Business Finance.* 5th ed. Reading, Mass.: Addison-Wesley Publishing, 1988.

Guild, Ian, and Rhodri Harris. *Forfaiting.* London: Euromoney Publications, 1985.

Haar, Jerry, and Marta Ortiz-Buonafins. *Import Marketing.* Lexington, Mass.: Lexington Books, 1989.

International Chamber of Commerce. *Guide to Documentary Credit Operations.* Paris: ICC, 1978.

Khoury, Sarkis. "Countertrade: Forms, Motives, Pitfalls, and Negotiation Requisites," *Journal of Business Research,* June 1984.

Morgan Guaranty Trust Company. *Financing Exports and Imports.* New York: Morgan Guaranty, n.d.

Root, Franklin. *Entry Strategies for International Markets.* Lexington, Mass.: Lexington Books, 1987.

NOTES

[1]Letters of credit are frequently subject to legal action by parties involved in the export-import process. Much of the terminology and conditions in L/Cs has been standardized and codified in *Uniform Customs and Practices 400,* published by the International Chamber of Commerce.

[2]Examples of each of these documents and of the others can be found in International Chamber of Commerce, *Guide to Documentary Credit Operations* (Paris: ICC, 1978).

[3]Pricing to cover only marginal costs may be viewed as *dumping* by the host country, so the firm may be required to select a price higher than this.

[4]Exports can lower risk by replacing local production in a country that experiences political or economic upheaval. They can also supplement local production, providing a portfolio of supply sources and thus again reducing risk.

[5]The banker's acceptance is considered "eligible" if it matures in less than 270 days. That is, the acceptance may be discounted at any Federal Reserve bank by the paying bank or any secondary purchaser of the acceptance.

[6]An overview of federal export subsidy programs appears in Business International Corporation, *Financing Foreign Operations,* "Commercial Banks" (New York: Business International Corporation, latest edition). Also see Robert D. Frazer and Associates, *International Banking and Finance,* vol. 1 (Washington, D.C.: R&H Publishers, latest edition); and Burke Dillon and Luis Duran-Downing, *Officially-Supported Export Credits* (Washington, D.C.: Intl Monetary Fund, 1988).

[7]See the Foreign Sales Corporation Act of 1984, which appears in the *Internal Revenue Code* (Washington, D.C.: U.S. Government Printing Office, 1984), sections 921–27.

[8]See, for example, *EXIMBANK Program Summary* (Washington, D.C.: Export-Import Bank of the United States, current edition).

[9]The factor's fee can be viewed as a charge for accepting the risk of nonpayment, and the discount can be viewed as a charge for making funds available immediately to the exporter; but both charges really contribute to the total cost, which the factor receives to cover the two needs of the exporter.

[10]All costs are as estimated by Crédit Suisse, *Forfaiting* (Zurich: Finanz AG, 1986).

[11]Organization for Economic Cooperation and Development, *East-West Trade: Recent Developments in Countertrade* (Paris: OECD, 1981), pp. 10–11.

[12]U.S. International Trade Commission, *Assessment of the Effects of Barter and Countertrade Transactions on U.S. Industries,* publication no. 1766 (Washington, D.C.: USITC, October 1985).

ACME Rockets, Inc.

James King, the president of ACME Rockets, Inc., recently returned to his hometown of Milwaukee, Wisconsin, from a model toy exhibition in Toronto. There he had talked extensively with several other company presidents about their common problem of stagnant sales in North America. One of his new Canadian acquaintances from the exhibition had presented a strong case for pursuing sales in foreign markets, especially in the European Community. This person reasoned that he had successfully and relatively easily entered the U.S. market by exporting his wooden toys—so extending this experience to other foreign markets should be manageable. Since trade barriers were declining in most of the world, opportunities were opening up for small and large exporters. All of the participants in this discussion were running companies with less than 100 employees and sales in the range of $US 10–75 million per year; so they faced similar problems of limited managerial time and limited financial resources.

King saw the possibility of selling in Europe as a very desirable alternative to continuing to beef up his advertising efforts in the United States, in an attempt to boost sagging sales. His company's model rockets, ranging from $3 toys to $250 intricately-designed models for science projects, were producing an adequate income for the company, but the market seemed to have become saturated in the past three years after an initial rapid growth during the first five years of operation. (ACME's financial statements are presented later in this case.)

Mr. King had founded ACME after working for several years for a large consumer goods manufacturer. Originally, he had studied mechanical engineering and had planned to go to work for a company such as Lockheed or Boeing. When he discovered his greater interest in sales and business administration rather than in industrial design, he took the position in sales of consumer goods. Realizing that he wanted to pursue a business of his own, and with six years of experience under his belt, King decided to take the plunge. Using his engineering background, he decided to try making higher-quality model rockets than the ones commonly available in toy and hobby stores. Remembering Wile E. Coyote's zany gadgets for outracing the Road Runner, he named his company ACME Rockets.

The day after the toy exhibition, Mr. King met with his management team of four department heads in their regular weekly strategy session. He raised the

This case was written by Prof. James Sood and Prof. Robert Grosse as a basis for class discussion. 1991.

issue of pursuing export markets in Europe as well as expanding ACME's efforts in Canada. The sales manager, Jan Vlcek, was enthusiastic about this idea, since he liked the thought of traveling through Europe to examine the markets. Sandy Rogers, the financial manager, reacted in almost the opposite manner. She saw the likelihood of spending lots of money chasing foreign markets as imprudent, when U.S. opportunities still could be pursued much more aggressively. (While it was certainly true that ACME did not sit on a pile of cash for this purpose, the company was far from broke.) The production manager saw the idea as a possibility for unloading the excess inventory that currently sat in ACME's warehouse, as well as an outlet for more rockets that could push the plant toward fuller capacity. The personnel manager, Jose Romero, was somewhat concerned about the cultural differences in Europe that might create a barrier to ACME's products or to its advertising methods. He nevertheless thought that the idea should be examined in more detail.

In the following week's meeting, Mr. King brought up the issue of exporting to the European Community again. He asked each of his managers to suggest points that should be studied in coming to a decision about the feasibility of this new direction for ACME. The first point raised was about customers—where would they be and how could they be approached? With the resources available to ACME, it would not be possible to mount a large-scale project evaluation effort. Sandy Rogers suggested that talking with other members of the Milwaukee Chamber of Commerce would give them some ideas about how other local firms did their overseas marketing. She also thought that someone from the Chicago World Trade Center might be able to offer more insights.

Jan Vlcek felt somewhat overwhelmed with the prospect of leading the new marketing effort. He was already fully occupied with the existing promotional efforts of ACME in the United States, and he did not relish the thought of expanding his hectic schedule. On the other hand he wanted to explore the prospect of selling in Europe, so he faced a difficult situation. Jose Romero recognized Vlcek's reticence in the discussion and proposed that an outside consultant be hired to help with the newly-labeled "European Marketing Plan." By giving Vlcek the authority to approve the consultant, he would be able to maintain his control over the marketing function while benefitting from the consultant's work. This proposal brightened Vlcek's outlook considerably.

When the meeting concluded, James King felt quite pleased with his colleagues' support for the new venture. He subsequently asked Vlcek to check around Milwaukee for a consulting firm to carry out the marketing study. This effort resulted in the venture's first setback: the large, well-known management consulting firms all wanted more than $50,000 to carry out such a study, even before getting down to the details of ACME's needs. Vlcek then recommended that they ask a marketing professor at the local business school for help, since he had a friend in another company who had used this method before to get a marketing survey done. Sandy Rogers immediately thought of her favorite marketing professor, Bruce Madison, from the executive MBA program that she had taken last year.

Professor Madison turned out to be happy to offer his help, at a much lower cost than that of the large consulting firms. Given his teaching duties at the university, he offered to carry out an initial market study that would identify potential types of customers, rules on importing, and channels of distribution in Europe. He would then recommend steps for ACME to take so that a more detailed plan could be created. This effort would cost the company $10,000, which included the final report and four weeks of research by Professor Madison and a research assistant.

Professor Madison recommended that ACME get in touch with one or more market research firms in London for a more detailed analysis of the European Community market for the firm's model rockets. Almost without hesitation, James King agreed to the proposed market study and asked Professor Madison to get started.

Professor Madison's Market Study

Professor Madison first decided to determine the production capacity of the firm. Klaus Schneider, the production manager, explained to him that ACME had been operating during the past year at about 80 percent of capacity with its one 8-hour shift of workers in the Milwaukee plant. The capacity of the plant could be expanded by asking the existing production workers to work overtime, or by beginning a second shift.

Next, Professor Madison looked at the financial condition of ACME. The income statement indeed portrayed a stagnant situation for the past several years, though fortunately ACME was earning a solid profit each year. The balance sheet was a bit weak, with more than $3 million in short-term liabilities and a fairly large balance of uncollected receivables. In his view the company was solvent, but not in a position to pursue any major expansion activities.

Finally, Professor Madison talked with Jan Vlcek about ACME's current marketing strategy. Not surprisingly, Vlcek was rather reluctant to discuss the situation, given both the recent leveling off of sales and his lack of experience in international marketing. Professor Madison tried to defuse Vlcek's evident antagonism toward an outsider who was trying to impose a marketing strategy on ACME. After complimenting Vlcek on the marketing success that ACME had achieved under his leadership, Professor Madison asked why the firm had encountered a slowdown in growth over the past several years. Vlcek explained that he had, indeed, tried to stimulate a new upswing in U.S. sales, but that competition from other established makers of model airplanes and rockets (such as Mattel and Lionel) had frustrated the effort. The domestic market was quite saturated. This led Professor Madison to conclude that overseas markets could very well be an appropriate focus for ACME at this time.

Based on these pieces of information, Professor Madison reasoned that an effort to push ACME's sales into Europe would definitely be an appropriate strategy (though he also saw room for improvement in the domestic marketing efforts of the firm). He assigned his student assistant to search the international trade information available in Milwaukee to identify firms that could export for ACME to Europe. He also asked the student to try to find names and addresses of distributors in Europe who would be able to sell the model rockets in those countries.

A review of the rules applicable to imports into the European Community showed no apparent limitation against the model rockets; and it appeared that a tariff of at most 7 percent ad valorem would be encountered in any of the EC countries. Professor Madison put this information into his report, along with a recommendation for ACME to consult with a law firm in the chosen target country to make sure than no other restrictions existed. He did not recommend a particular European country as the target market, since he viewed this as a decision for James King to make. He did suggest that the United Kingdom would be a logical choice, because of its language and cultural similarities to the United States. He also suggested that ACME give careful consideration to Germany, because it is the largest economy in Europe.

As far as channels of distribution were concerned, Professor Madison found that no large toy store chains existed across Europe (similar to Toys "R" Us or Lionel Toy World). Thus, sales of model rockets would have to be either to individual toy or hobby stores or to distributors who would seek out retail stores as clients. Clearly at this point, the only viable way for ACME to proceed was to consider wholesale distributors who would act on ACME's behalf to contract with retail stores.

Also related to European distribution, ACME would have to create new promotional materials and instructions for the model rockets in several languages, assuming that sales were to be pursued in France, Germany, Italy, and elsewhere in Europe. This problem could be ignored initially until buyers were identified, but it ultimately would require significant expense to redo the printed materials that accompany ACME's products.

At the end of the month, Professor Madison delivered his report to James King, along with his recommendation that ACME begin immediately to look for European distributors for the model rockets. Mr. King was happy with the optimistic outlook of the report, but he still did not see clearly how to proceed.

ACME's Financial Statements

	Simplified Income Statements, 1985–91 (in $US millions)						
	1985	1986	1987	1988	1989	1990	1991
Net sales	4.16	6.47	8.30	10.13	12.54	12.98	13.25
Cost of goods sold	2.87	4.66	5.81	6.98	8.90	9.10	9.54
Gross profit	1.29	1.81	2.49	3.15	3.64	3.88	3.71
Operating expenses	1.17	1.54	2.02	2.52	2.88	3.18	3.08
Profit before taxes	0.12	0.27	0.47	0.63	0.76	0.70	0.63
Federal income taxes	0.04	0.09	0.15	0.19	0.27	0.23	0.20
Net profit after tax	0.08	0.18	0.32	0.44	0.49	0.47	0.43

Balance Sheet, December 31, 1991 ($US millions)

Cash	0.316
Accounts receivable	2.748
Inventory	1.958
Plant and equipment	2.933
TOTAL ASSETS	7.955
Accounts payable	0.861
Notes payable	1.163
Accrued taxes	0.410
Short-term debt	0.812
Long-term debt, current portion	0.237
Long-term debt	1.453
Shareholders' equity	3.019
TOTAL LIABILITIES AND SHAREHOLDERS' EQUITY	7.955

Technology and the MNE

This chapter focuses on technology—the single most important competitive advantage in business today. It begins by defining technology according to its product, process, and managerial applications. It then considers both company management and government regulatory views concerning the transfer of technology within the firm across national borders. Most of the chapter is devoted to demonstrating how technology can be a competitive advantage and how firms can obtain, utilize, and protect a technological advantage. The main goals of the chapter are to:

1. Define technology and technology transfer.

2. Show how firms can benefit from the use of product, process, and management technology.

3. Analyze the choice of whether to exploit technology within the firm or sell/license that technology to other firms.

4. Explain how a firm can protect its proprietary technology.

5. Point out the concerns of governments in industrial and less developed countries with respect to the use of technology by MNEs.

INTRODUCTION

Technology is the single most important competitive advantage of firms in the world today. From new products, to knowledge of markets, to industrial processes, technology is a fundamental factor in the success of both domestic and international firms. This chapter begins by defining technology itself, and then it explores the use of technology as a competitive advantage of the MNE. Firms need to select technologies that provide optimal competitive gains, then decide how to implement those technologies, and then try to protect their technological advantages. A fundamental problem is deciding how to obtain desired technology—through R&D or through acquisition from another firm.

The transfer of technology among countries within the MNE network and through markets outside the firm is a second focus of our analysis. Dealing with governments in both industrial countries and LDCs on the issue of technology transfer has become a major problem for MNE managers. In industrial countries, technology protection and the generation of new technology are the main areas of concern. In the LDCs, on the other hand, restrictions on technological transfers through limits on royalties, lack of patent protection, and other legal constraints on company activities compel MNE managers to seek strategies that overcome or at least recognize these constraints and incorporate ways of accommodating them.

Definition[1]

The business literature generally refers to at least three types of technology: product, process, and management.[2] **Product technology** is the knowledge used to produce any product—the information that specifies the product's characteristics and uses. **Process technology** is the knowledge used in production to organize the inputs and operate the machinery—it relates to the techniques and process by which a given product or service is produced. **Management technology** is the knowledge used in operating a business—the managerial skills that enable a firm to compete by using its resources effectively. Each of these types of technology can create a competitive advantage for the firm that possesses it. That is, although all firms possess each type of technology, an advantage accrues to firms that are able to obtain *superior* technology.

Given that technology is industrial knowledge, we want to consider its creation, its introduction into markets, and its spread into different markets and applications. These three stages of technology development may be labeled invention, innovation, and diffusion. **Invention** is the creation of new knowledge that may have application to business or industry. An invention may be as extraordinary as the light bulb or as commonplace as a new type of laundry soap. **Innovation** is the introduction of the new knowledge into the marketplace. A fairly recent innovation is the microcomputer-based spreadsheet capability that allows financial forecasting for business (e.g., by using the Lotus 1–2–3 program). Most inventions never become innovations, that is, they never reach the stage of commercialization. For every successful innovation, there are hundreds of inventions that never become commercialized. **Diffusion** is the spread of the new knowledge throughout the market, including markets in different countries, and to different product applications. It may take place through a company's affiliates in different locations and businesses or through purchase or copying by competitors. Proprietary drugs are typically diffused by the initiating firm's sale of the product through its affiliates and distributors around the world.

An aspect of technology that should be noted at the outset is its nature as a **public good**—a good that can be used repeatedly without being used up. Technology is a form of knowledge that is not destroyed when it is transferred between people or firms. This aspect of technology is the source of both competitive strength for a firm that successfully innovates and of social concern for countries that wish to have the benefits of innovation made available to their populations at as low a cost as possible. The cost of creating a technology is not zero, and that cost is borne by the innovating firm;[3] the cost of diffusing that technology is generally relatively low—and innovating firms do not like to let their hard-earned technological gains be given away to the public without earning a good return. This issue of social versus private valuation of technology is discussed below.

Technology Transfer

Technology transfer is the diffusion of technology from the place of its introduction to other markets around the world. This diffusion may take place through market transactions, with one firm selling a product, process, or skill to another, or it may be carried out within a firm through its network of affiliates. Since technology has become recognized as an extremely important base for competition worldwide, governments are quite concerned with obtaining up-to-date technology at the lowest possible cost. Innovating companies, on the other hand, wish to protect their technology as much as possible so that they can reap its benefits. Clearly, the interests of firms and governments may diverge in this matter, and technology transfer has become a major issue of debate with respect to the MNE.

Within the multinational firm, technology transfer is also an internal managerial concern. Informing managers, technical staff, and workers in different locations about new technologies is far from costless; and the firm must carry out such transfers efficiently and adjust structurally and operationally in order to derive maximum benefits from the exploitation of these technologies. Part of corporate strategy must be the determination of and the effective transmission of key technology to the people, subsidiaries, and locations that can use it best.

Technology Appropriability

Technology may well represent the key competitive advantage that the innovating firm possesses. After having invested human and financial capital in developing proprietary technology, such a firm will naturally seek to protect it. Looking at the effort of the innovating firm to maximize its returns from proprietary technology (viz, knowledge possessed by the innovating firm that is unavailable to other firms in the marketplace), Magee (1977) coined the term *appropriability*. **Appropriability** is the ability of the innovating firm to protect its technology from competitors and to obtain economic benefits from that technology. The knowledge required to construct a nuclear power plant is very specialized and therefore highly appropriable. On the other hand, the knowledge required to produce a certain food flavor is often quite simple once the ingredients are known—so the innovating firm seeks protection such as a patent, or, as with Coca-Cola, it tries to keep the "formula" secret from competitors. Such knowledge is appropriable only if it can be hidden from rival firms or denied to them through legal means such as patents. The more appropriable the technology, the better able the innovating firm will be to guard it and transfer it internally (that is, to *internalize* the technology).

TECHNOLOGY AS A COMPETITIVE ADVANTAGE

The success of multinational firms during the 20th century has very often depended on a base of **proprietary technology.** In this section, we look first at some empirical evidence about the importance of technology in international competition. Second, we consider the problem of obtaining technology that could give the firm competitive advantages. Third, we consider ways in which a firm can utilize the advantages generated by proprietary technology.

Success of MNEs Based on Technological Advantage

Technology was demonstrated to be a key production factor in international business through a large number of research efforts conducted during the 1960s. The search for an explanation of Leontief's paradox (namely, that although the United States was relatively capital rich, its manufactured exports were less capital intensive and more labor intensive than its import-competing goods) led several investigators to focus on the **technology intensity** of U.S. exports. The studies of Gruber, Mehta, and Vernon (1967), Hufbauer (1966), and Keesing (1966) were discussed in Chapter 3. Those studies concluded that technology intensity was an important explanatory variable for U.S. exports; that is, technology was highly positively correlated with U.S. exports and thus that U.S. exports were technology intensive and not paradoxically labor intensive.

Studies of U.S. foreign direct investment have produced similar results: U.S. firms with a higher degree of technology intensity (measured, for example, as R&D expenditures relative to sales or as the number of scientists and engineers employed relative to the total number of employees) tend to establish more affiliates abroad than do less technology-intensive firms. Gruber et al. (1967), Horst (1972), Caves (1974), and others have lent support to this point. Hence, greater technology intensity seems to lead to greater multinationality. (This correlation was shown clearly in Chapter 2, Table 2–2, which lists top-performing U.S.-based firms, almost all of which are highly multinational and most of which are more or much more technology intensive than the U.S. industry average.)

Each of the preceding measures of the importance of technology in international business supports the general principle that technology is a fundamental "factor of production" that enables firms to compete successfully against foreign and domestic competitors. This does not mean that all firms must be technology intensive in order to succeed; rather, it means that technology is one factor that can create a sustainable competitive advantage for its possessor. The next step is to explore when and how technology can be used in competition. This is something that the studies mentioned above failed to do, since their emphasis was macroeconomic. We want to know how to obtain the technology that leads to an advantage and how to utilize that advantage in business activities. Our next step, therefore, is to focus on these microlevel (company-specific) concerns.

How to Acquire a Technology Advantage

The basic decision for a firm when it is considering the acquisition of any needed input is whether to make that input internally or to buy it from an outside supplier (or to do both). When the input is a known machine or a component, the choice will be whether or not to manufacture it. When the input is a skill, such as knowledge of a particular market, the choice will be whether to hire a specialist or to sell to an intermediary firm that deals with final customers. When the input is process or product technology, the choice will be whether to try to create the knowledge by carrying out R&D or to buy the knowledge from another firm through a license or some other contractual form.

The last of these choices is much more difficult than the first two because so much uncertainty is involved. If the firm chooses to undertake R&D to create product or process technology, there is no way to ensure that the result will meet the need. R&D is risky by its very nature, since it requires creativity on the part of the research person or team and since it leads to output that may be very efficient, very inefficient, or of no use at all in dealing with the problem at hand. So, while the **make-versus-buy decision** can be made on a fairly concrete basis for inputs whose technology and costs are known, the decision to produce technology by carrying out R&D has a much less concrete basis and necessarily leads to substantial uncertainty.

IB ILLUSTRATION

Pfizer's R&D Strategy

Pfizer, a U.S.-based pharmaceuticals firm, chooses to invest in its own R&D for the creation of new ethical drugs (i.e., proprietary pharmaceuticals). Pfizer's choice is to internalize the entire process of R&D, production, and sale as much as possible, and thus to reap maximum revenues and profits. This firm sets limits on its research spending by comparing the expected costs of research projects with the size of the potential market for the new product being sought.

In the area of antiarthritic drugs, for example, Pfizer sought to develop a product that could be administered once a day rather than every few hours. In the pharmaceuticals industry, the process of R&D plus product testing and submitting to regulatory approvals until a new drug is commercialized is generally believed to cost at least $100 million. Only after forecasting that its expected sales would substantially exceed this amount did Pfizer choose to undertake the research that led to the product Feldene. Pfizer does not become involved in R&D for a product whose potential market it judges to be smaller than $100 million. (Notice that the R&D being considered is fairly well targeted on a potential product, rather than open-ended as in the case of university research, which depends largely on the preferences of the individual researchers.)

From Pfizer's perspective, a second limitation on R&D spending is the shortage of highly qualified research scientists to work on possible projects. Even if dozens of the new products that Pfizer is considering for development appear viable, the number of people—inside the firm, in universities, and in other firms—who are qualified and available to do the necessary research is quite limited. This also limits the amount of R&D spending done by Pfizer.

For these two practical reasons (expected market size and availability of research scientists), an optimal amount of R&D can be proximately established despite the claim that research results are unpredictable. That overly simple claim of unpredictability obviously fails to come to grips with the problem, whereas pragmatic reasoning defines the problem clearly and focuses on the real limitations that exist on R&D. ■

Moving a step further, when a firm depends on technology as a key competitive advantage, the need to generate new technology on a continuing basis becomes paramount. In such industries as pharmaceuticals, computers, and telecommunications, R&D is a critical function in each firm. In industries of this kind, the question becomes: How much R&D should the firm do? Since there is no simple, direct relation between R&D expenditure and successful new product development, there is no simple answer to the question. However, since products in these industries do become obsolete, the firm that does not introduce new products will in all likelihood be unable to compete. Then what level of R&D is in some sense "optimal"?[4]

The best answer is, "It depends." It depends on how large the firm is, how diversified its products and markets are, how financially sound it is, how appropriable its technology is, and many other factors. A small firm that competes on the basis of its ability to create new products must carry out extensive R&D. A very large MNE, on the other hand, may be able to use a comparatively small research team, aimed mainly at learning about new technology developments and deciding whether to incorporate them into the firm's business. If such a firm chooses a particular innovation as one to acquire, then the decision becomes whether to buy it from the producer, or to undertake R&D in an effort to copy it, or even to try to buy the innovating firm. This kind of **follow-the-leader strategy** has been pursued successfully by many firms in a variety of industries. Of course, a firm that pursues the follower strategy loses the opportunity to take full advantage of innovations achieved by other firms. Hoffmann-La Roche, for example, would have earned far less if it had depended on another firm to develop its highly successful tranquilizers, Valium and Librium. Also, there are spillover effects of R&D efforts that may lead to the creation of additional new products or processes. These benefits would be lost to a firm that chose not to carry out the basic research itself and pursued the follow-the-leader strategy. (Internal "new venture teams" are used by 3M to carry out R&D on projects proposed by company employees—projects that are then pursued as relatively independent efforts until results are achieved and the decision to go to market is made.)[5]

Notice that the multinational firm gains an advantage in R&D because of its ability to spread its R&D expenses over a global market rather than depending solely on domestic sales to recoup them. Also, the MNE has broader access to technical talent in many countries.

How to Utilize a Technology Advantage

Each firm is different from any other firm, if only because it employs different people with different skills. At the simplest level, **technology advantage** is any superior business knowledge held by people in one firm that is not held by people in another firm. As discussed in detail in Chapter 2, each firm should try to take maximum advantage of its technological edge over other firms. How can this be done? (The problem of *protecting* the firm's technology is discussed later.)

Consider Hoffmann-La Roche & Co.,[6] the Swiss-based multinational pharmaceutical firm. This firm innovated the two drugs chlordiazepoxide and diazepam (whose Hoffmann-La Roche brand names are Librium and Valium) in the early 1960s. Librium and Valium became two of the most successful tranquilizers in history. In order to protect the proprietary technology embodied in these drugs,

Hoffmann-La Roche took out patents in each of the countries where it sold them. Patents gave the firm long-term legal protection against competitors that might seek to copy the patented products. In most countries, patent protection lasts well over 10 years. (In the United States, for example, it lasts 17 years.) By registering Valium and Librium for patent protection around the world, Hoffmann-La Roche effectively gained a period of time in which it was the sole producer of the two drugs. Thus, the firm was able to sell enough Valium and Librium at a high enough price to repay the research costs of developing them and many less successful drugs, plus to pay for additional research to create new drugs for future sales. Because patent protection lasts for only a fixed period of time, additional R&D (and, hopefully, the creation of more successful products) must be part of the firm's strategy.

Hoffmann-La Roche sells Valium, Librium, and its other products through its own network of affiliates around the world. In a small number of cases, generally under government pressure, the firm has also licensed local companies to produce its proprietary drugs. Mostly, however, its sales take place through subsidiaries that it manages and owns. This is an example of internalized technology. (Also, the technology is *embodied* in products, which are then sold to customers.)

As a second example, consider Arthur Andersen & Co., the U.S.-based multinational accounting and management consulting firm. This firm's knowledge of accounting rules and practices and of business strategy is superior to that of many U.S. firms and many firms in other countries. Its proprietary technology is not in product or process technology, but rather in management knowledge.

Arthur Andersen is organized as a partnership, with individual accountants and consultants acting as both owners and managers. A legal entity called a "société coopérative" was formed in Switzerland, and it functions as a legal link among Arthur Andersen's widespread affiliates throughout the world and to the home office in Chicago. The main strategic links among Arthur Andersen affiliates are partners from affiliates in one country who are made partners in affiliates in other countries. By linking firms across countries through individual partners, Arthur Andersen is able to transfer its technology as embodied in its people. Thus, in its overseas activities, Arthur Andersen usually operates as a linked set of partners, although the legal entity is sometimes a corporation in which the parent firm owns some or all of the shares. In 1985, for example, Arthur Andersen acquired the Philippine firm SGV Group, with over 3,000 employees, via the Swiss Société Coopérative. (The Philippine firm itself has affiliates in Thailand, Taiwan, Malaysia, and Indonesia.)

Arthur Andersen sells its knowledge as a service to other firms and to individuals. Its main businesses are auditing, tax accounting, and management consulting. Each service is sold to outside clients, a number of which are multinational firms, that can benefit from Arthur Andersen's knowledge of tax and other accounting rules in many countries.

These two examples show that there are numerous means for taking advantage of proprietary technology and that these means are very dependent on the kind of business involved. The possibilities include internalizing knowledge through a network of subsidiaries, working through partnerships (as discussed above), licensing local producers, and selling the use of the company name through a franchise. Let us examine these alternatives to see what company and product characteristics suit each of them best.

Internalizing   First, there is the strategy of internalizing all technology. This translates into international business by requiring the firm to use local affiliates around the world to sell its products or services, and perhaps to use exports to some smaller or less important markets. **Internalization** tends to be best under these conditions:

1. The firm makes new *products* that cannot be copied easily by competitors.
2. Important economies of scale that the firm achieves on *products* would be lost if outside firms also used the technology and served part of the total market.
3. The *firm* depends greatly on the sale of the product or service that uses the technology.
4. The *firm* is so small that it does not have the personnel to both use the technology internally and sell it to outsiders; or the firm is so large that it can easily exploit the technology through its own affiliates.
5. The firm considers its *technology* to be more valuable than do potential buyers of the technology.
6. The *technology* is costly to transfer from one firm to another.

These conditions illustrate the kinds of situation-specific issues that a firm must take into account if it wants to properly utilize its technology advantage. They point out some of the company-specific, product-specific, and knowledge-specific considerations that (in these cases) would justify internalizing technology.

Recall the example of Polaroid Land cameras from Chapter 3. The key technology in that case was the knowledge necessary to produce high-quality, instant-developing film. Because no other firm was able to re-create equivalent technology, Polaroid gained a lasting competitive advantage in the photography market. There is no doubt that such firms as Eastman Kodak, Agfa-Gavaert, and Fuji have better distribution networks worldwide and perhaps other advantages over Polaroid. However, as long as Polaroid can keep the instant-developing segment of the photography market to itself, it will be able to compete successfully. By continuing to innovate and improve its film, Polaroid has been able to keep patent protection on its best technology through the years. The particular characteristics of this case, taken from our list above, are that (1) the product cannot be copied by competitors, (2) the firm is highly dependent on its technology for its success, and (3) the firm is large enough to exploit the technology through its own affiliates around the world. These conditions justify the internalization of instant-developing film technology in Polaroid Corporation and the sale of only the final product (i.e., *not* the knowledge by itself) to customers.

Externalizing   As a second possible strategy for utilizing proprietary technology, the firm could contract with other firms under a licensing agreement, management contract, or other income-producing arrangement that involves the sale of the technology rather than the sale of a final product embodying the technology. This strategy (of **externalization**) would be appropriate in these conditions:

1. The firm's *products* are easily copied, but rival firms would still be willing to buy its product- or process-specific knowledge.
2. The firm's *products* are not central to its ability to survive in competition.

3. The *firm* has greater skill in creating the technology than in producing and marketing the final products.

4. The *firm's* financial and personnel capabilities make it desirable to let another firm incur the cost of producing the products.

5. The firm cannot protect its *technology* with a patent, and it could lose the benefits of that technology unless it contracted for the technology's use by rival firms.

6. The *technology* is not costly to transfer between firms.

Each of these conditions tends to justify the sale of proprietary technology to other firms rather than (just) internalizing it in final products. Broadly, these product-, firm-, and technology-specific conditions relate to situations in which the technology is embodied in products that are not the lifeblood of the firm or to situations in which the technology itself, rather than the final product, is the most valuable factor.

The sale of "intermediate goods"—either components that embody proprietary technology or knowledge in the form of plans, blueprints, books, or other technical information formats—is common in many industries. The entire industry of management consulting is a form of externalizing business knowledge and skills. The management consultant possesses skills useful for running a firm, but chooses to sell those skills contractually to various firms without actually joining any of them. (Many times such a consultant *is* eventually hired by one of the client firms, when the skills are perceived as sufficiently valuable to justify this step!) Similarly, public accounting and economic forecasting are businesses that sell knowledge for further use by firms producing final products or services. Arthur Andersen is an example of such businesses. Even in manufacturing, there are many consultants and capital equipment manufacturers that work independently from companies, selling their knowledge on onetime or repeated contractual terms to different firms.

Franchising Another interesting example of technology transfer through intermediate goods rather than final products is **franchising.** Many hotel chains, restaurants, and other service firms create a company or brand name that comes to connote good quality, rapid service, and so on. Once the name becomes established, its possessor can sell its use to other firms. This contractual arrangement is called franchising. McDonald's, Burger King, Hilton, Holiday Inns, Avis, and Hertz are just a few of the best-known franchisors.

The franchisor generally sells the franchisee the right to use its name plus some array of products and services. For example, franchisees contract with Burger King to buy plastic packaging, napkins, some food ingredients, and kitchen equipment used in cooking the hamburgers and other products sold in the restaurants that bear the Burger King name. Burger King maintains the right to control the quality of the franchise (e.g., through quality control of products and pricing strategy), so that franchisees cannot tarnish the company's image. In return for the use of Burger King's name and for these services, the franchisee must pay the company a fee based on the volume of sales. In this arrangement, the technology being transferred includes some production (of hamburgers) technology, some marketing skills, and some management policies.

ADDED DIMENSION

The International Product Cycle

Another way to look at the use of technology as a competitive advantage comes from Vernon's international product cycle analysis. By studying the stage of any product in the cycle in a given country, the firm can select a strategy that exploits its advantages. For example, when personal computers became extremely popular in the United States (about 1982), competition became fierce and these computers advanced quickly from the new product stage to the maturing product stage. At that time, the personal computer was still in the new product stage in Argentina. Thus, IBM or Apple Computer had opportunities to operate as new product producers in the Argentine market, selling with very little competition and facing a very price-inelastic demand. In the United States, on the other hand, these firms had to lower their prices and work on new software and hardware developments to maintain their market positions. The maturing product stage of the cycle required these actions, as well as increasing efforts to lower production costs. In fact, both IBM and Apple have turned to offshore, low-cost supply sources for such components as memory chips and peripheral equipment.

The international product cycle offers insights not only for high-tech industries but also for standardized products. Once production technology has become standardized, the firm must search for low-cost production sites and low-cost distribution channels. By taking a global perspective, a firm in an industry whose technology is fairly standardized, such as shirt or shoe manufacturing, can select production sites that offer cost advantages *and* markets in which particular shirts or shoes can compete. ∎

A Continuous R&D Process

A general method of targeting research that avoids the dilemma of huge uncertainty in new product development, and one that many firms have selected, is to build incrementally on proven technology through a **continuous R&D** process. That is, the firms follow a strategy of developing modifications for the basic product or process, without undertaking major basic research in areas unrelated to the successful original innovation. Clearly, this is the strategy that IBM has followed in the development of its personal computer. Virtually all of the components used in making the first IBM PC were innovations that IBM or other companies had made in other applications. The PC itself is thus an amalgam of existing technologies, packaged in a valuable way and marketed very successfully. (IBM's competitive advantages in reliability and service, as well as its huge capital resources, enabled it to apply known technology to the product and to market the product with phenomenal success.)[7]

Dow Chemical Corporation is another MNE that follows the incremental approach to developing technology. Dow uses what are called **skunk works** (a term coined at Lockheed Aircraft Corporation in California), or small project teams that work on new applications of existing technologies or on the development of new technologies for specific uses. The skunk works are viewed as separate from the mainstream of the firm's production and sales activities, but the firm supports them in order to maintain an active presence in R&D. By remaining small, the skunk works allow the project teams to function more or less as entrepreneurs, though with potential substantial backing from the corporation in the event of a promising development. Because the skunk works generally focus on clearly defined new products or processes, they can be viewed as incremental builders on existing technology.

Using Strategic Alliances Another means of utilizing a technological advantage is through a strategic alliance such as a coproduction agreement, joint research project, or turnkey venture. Both Westinghouse Electric Company (USA) and Siemens, A.G. (Germany) possess advanced technology in factory automation; they formed a joint production agreement in 1988 to manufacture more than 20 such products, including robots. This strategic alliance is intended to give each company greater access to the other's home market, while leaving both free to compete in other product areas.

Joint research projects have proliferated in the computer industry in recent years, as firms increasingly choose to pool R&D resources to reduce the in-house cost of designing new memory chips, processor chips, and other equipment. IBM, AT&T, and MIT have formed a research consortium to explore the field of high-temperature superconductivity, for example. Turnkey ventures are less-frequent, though they similarly leverage the technology of the possessor firm by contracting with an outside supplier of some other key ingredient to the business. The example of Exxon's coal project in Colombia (see Chapter 11) illustrates a venture in which Exxon supplies the technology and international marketing of the coal, while Colombia provides access to the natural resource, manpower for local facilities, and an agreement to take over the entire project in 30 years.[8]

All of these strategic alliances enable a firm that possesses technology to enjoy some benefit from, while allowing the partner access to, that technology in exchange for some key input such as funding, additional technology, market access, etc. The crucial consideration in such alliances is to avoid jeopardizing the firm's competitive advantages through sharing the technology. If the partner gains enough from the joint project, that firm may in the future become a competitor against the original partner, unless the technology is protected adequately.

CONTROL OF PROPRIETARY TECHNOLOGY

So far, we have examined the use of technology as a competitive advantage in international business. An important aspect of this advantage is its ability to be dissipated, that is, to be acquired by other firms and thus reduced in value to the original possessor. The next problem we will consider, therefore, is the *protection* of proprietary technology.

Whether the knowledge in question is production or management technology, there is a potential for rival firms to copy it. In some cases, the rival firm may assimilate the technology by simply looking at the innovation. In other cases, the technology may be complex or difficult to transfer, so the rival firm needs to spend substantial money to obtain it. In any case, the technology can be dissipated and the competitive advantage lost. A protection method is needed.

Methods for Protecting Technology

Once again, the appropriate strategy depends on the type of technology. If the knowledge possessed by the firm is a manufacturing process that produces a new product, that process and the product can be protected with a **patent** in most countries. If the knowledge is embodied in a book or manual that can be sold, then a **copyright** will protect the document against copying, though the knowledge itself will need patent protection as well. If the knowledge is embodied in the product, and it implies a high standard of quality or service, then often a **trademark** can be obtained for protection.

Three of the legal devices that protect proprietary technology are defined below.

Trademark   "A technical trademark is a distinctive mark, word, design, or picture which is affixed to goods so that purchasers may identify their origin. In general, a trademark must be fanciful, arbitrary, unique, and nondescriptive."

Copyright   "A copyright protects literary, musical, dramatic, pictorial, audio, and audiovisual works, but it is only the form of the work that is protected rather than ideas, concepts, or methods of operation. . . . The copyright holder is given exclusive right to reproduce, perform, or display the work, subject to what is known as 'fair use.' . . . The life of a copyright under [U.S. law] is 50 years beyond the death of the last surviving author."

Patent   "Patent law represents a balancing of society's interest in promoting free competition against its interest in encouraging innovation by rewarding inventors with temporary monopoly rights. . . . A patent may be granted to any person on any new and useful invention of (1) a process, (2) a machine, (3) a product, (4) a composition of matter, (5) a new and useful improvement of a prior patented invention, (6) a growing plant, or (7) a design."[9] (Note the Hoffmann-La Roche example above.)

The trademark, copyright, and patent laws offer protection to innovating firms if their technology fits into one of the categories stated above. They do not protect all kinds of innovation, and in different countries the rules and enforcement vary widely even for technology of these three types.

Other methods for protecting technology include *hiding* it from competitors. This strategy works especially well when the key aspect of the technology is simple to understand but embodied in the product in a complex manner. Then, unless competitors can obtain the "formula" for using the technology, the proprietor can preserve its advantage. Another method is to require employees developing new products to sign an agreement prohibiting their use of the new technology outside the firm, so that they cannot leave the proprietor firm and use their knowledge of the new technology to compete against it.

Yet another method for protecting technology is simply to exploit it quickly, gain a large market share where it is used, and thereby discourage market entry by other firms. This strategy enables the firm to move quickly along the experience curve, lowering costs and creating a larger entry barrier as time passes.

Problems of Protecting Technology

Despite the methods of protection discussed above, there are still many situations in which adequate protection may not be available. For example, the Four Tigers of Asia (Hong Kong, South Korea, Singapore, and Taiwan) are notorious for producing imitations of branded, patented, copyrighted, and otherwise protected products.[10] From computers to videodiscs, from audio cassettes to textbooks, a huge market exists in every country, particularly since interpretation of the law is required to judge whether an imitation is legal or not.

A problem that often thwarts the firm's efforts to protect its technology is **industrial espionage.** This method of obtaining technology from the possessor firm is also illegal, and it also occurs frequently. In a highly publicized case, IBM successfully sued Hitachi Corporation for stealing company documents containing proprietary information about a new mainframe computer introduced in 1981.[11] A scientist who had left his employment at IBM enabled Hitachi to obtain extensive documentation about the computer, thus placing Hitachi in a substantially better competitive position. While the espionage was detected and prosecuted in this case, much undetected espionage undoubtedly takes place.

A problem with which multinational firms in particular have to deal is the *difference in rules on technology use and technology transfer in different countries.* Less developed countries often afford foreign MNEs less protection on their technology than is afforded by industrialized countries. The Andean Pact countries in Latin America, for example, do not allow patents for many proprietary products brought in by MNEs, and these countries do not allow local subsidiaries to pay royalties to parent companies for the use of technology.

A problem for firms involved with joint ventures or other contractual links with other firms is the *difficulty of constraining partners* to apply shared knowledge only to the application under contract. In this type of situation, the firm supplying its technology to a joint project often finds that the partner is able to appropriate the technology for uses that the supplier cannot control or profit from. Thus, some of the value of the technology is lost to the supplier firm.

A final problem related to the protection of proprietary technology is the *mobility of employees.* Even if a firm successfully uses patents and copyrights on its technology, its competitive advantage may be lost if key employees (such as the scientists or managers who introduced the technology) leave the firm to work elsewhere. Since these people cannot leave their brains behind when they leave one company to join another, a tremendous amount of technology transfer takes place at relatively low cost through job mobility.

COUNTRY-SPECIFIC CONCERNS IN TECHNOLOGY USE AND TRANSFER

In Industrial Countries

The generation and use of technology in industrialized countries tends to be very market based, with the government playing the role of referee and rulemaker. Table 20–1 lists a few of the government rules related to technology in a selected group of developed nations. Note that patent life is fairly consistent among these countries (in the range of 17–20 years), as is the lack of limitations on intercountry transfer of technology. In fact, the main "limitation" is on the use of royalties to pay for technology transfer; these are limited to 6–10 percent of the firm's sales in a few countries. Perhaps a more important restriction is the immigration laws in most developed countries, which make it difficult to transfer skilled employees to different countries.

Despite the tendency of the governments in developed countries to allow market activity to determine technological advancement and diffusion, as shown in this table, another factor needs to be considered. The governments in each of the countries shown spend billions of dollars each year on military and other government-sponsored research. In fact, the U.S. government accounts for (i.e., finances) approximately 46 percent of R&D spending in the United States today

TABLE 20-1

Industrial Country Rules Relating to Technology Use and Transfer

Selected Countries	Limits on Royalties	Unpatentable Items	Patent Duration	Trademark Duration	Highest Tax Bracket on Royalties (%)
Canada	None	Chemicals for food & medicine; theories	17 years	15 years, renewable	25%
France	6% of sales unless tech is approved	Nonindustrial items; animals; plants; computer programs; medical treatments	20 years	10 years, renewable	33.3
Germany	10% of sales	Medical treatments; computer programs	20 years	10 years, renewable	25
Italy	None	Theories	20 years	20 years, renewable	21
Japan	None, but generally 8% of sales	Nuclear transformations	20 years	10 years, renewable	20
United Kingdom	None, but generally 7% of sales	Scientific discoveries; artistic creations; animals; plants; medical treatments	20 years	7 years, renewable	25
United States	None	Noncommercial items	17 years	20 years, renewable	46

Source: Business International Corporation, *Investing, Licensing, and Trading Conditions* (New York: Business International Corporation, 1989–90).

(though industry carries out 73 percent of the actual R&D).[12] Viewed in this light, governments are clearly major players in the creation and diffusion of technology.

Companies doing business in industrial countries find that R&D is subsidized either through tax benefits or through direct government spending on company research. R&D is seldom restricted, except in cases where public health or safety is perceived to be at risk—for example, recombinant DNA research ("gene-splicing") or research on nuclear reactions.

When transferring technology between countries, a firm can usually choose among exporting, direct investment, and local licensing on the basis of market conditions, without concern for government intervention. In that case, the decision can be based on the factors discussed above, such as the technology's importance to the firm, its ease of transferability to other firms, and the size of the host country market.

Legal protection of proprietary technology is widely available in industrial countries, although industrial espionage and some illegal copying still take place in many industries. The countries of the European Community have standardized most of their rules on technology usage and transfer, and these rules differ fairly little from the rules in Japan and the United States. One major difference is in the amount and targeting of government spending on R&D in each country.

Another factor that firms operating in industrial countries need to consider is the level of competition and the length of product cycles. As modern telecommunications and transportation have virtually eliminated the distances between developed countries, innovations in any one country tend to be copied or transferred within MNEs very rapidly. Increasingly in the 1990s, firms introduce new products into several markets simultaneously, without waiting for the traditional international product cycle to follow its course. One can conclude that the diffusion process of proprietary technology is becoming more and more rapid and that innovating firms must be aware of the shortening life spans of their products.

In many cases, R&D by firms from industrial countries has become international. Large MNEs such as General Electric and IBM operate research facilities in several countries, benefiting from breakthroughs that take place in each country and spreading them to affiliates elsewhere. Several studies over the past few years have demonstrated the increasing internationalization of the R&D function within MNEs.[13]

Pfizer Corporation carries out basic research on new chemical entities in the United States, the United Kingdom, and Japan. It also has a large product development laboratory in France and numerous development facilities in other countries for the local product testing required by their governments. The Pfizer strategy is to maintain key research facilities in locations that have concentrations of research scientists and a relatively high likelihood of new product developments by many firms. Minor product adaptation is done when needed in Pfizer's plants around the world, but major research work is concentrated in the three large centers.

<table>
<tr><td>In Less Developed
Countries</td><td>The generation and transfer of technology are far more restricted in less developed countries than in industrial countries. Less R&D takes place in LDCs, and more government policies constrain the use and transfer of proprietary technology. Table 20–2 shows some of the important government policies that influence technology use by multinational firms in LDCs. In comparison with industrial countries, LDCs offer less patent protection, place more limitations on international transfer of technology, and present greater demands for participation in the process of technology creation and diffusion. This should not be surprising, since these countries face a "technology gap" between their economies and the economies of industrial countries, and they see a need to catch up. Among the ways in which they attempt to catch up is to get MNEs to engage in greater local R&D activity and to transfer skills to local people—both of which are policies widely used today.</td></tr>
</table>

Multinational firms, for their part, generally find that local R&D in less developed countries is relatively inefficient (or not even viable) because there are far fewer skilled scientists, engineers, and managers in such countries than in industrial countries. Therefore, MNEs tend to concentrate their basic research in developed nations and to carry out a minimum of product development (often adaptation to local conditions) in the LDCs that require it. Moreover, as emphasized in Vernon's international product cycle, firms prefer to do R&D in or near their large markets, so that they can respond to customer preferences and government policies. This is another reason for the small amount of MNE research done in LDCs.

The choice among exporting, direct investment, and licensing is often mandated by the less developed countries. Often they simply do not allow direct investment in a particular industry, or they require the licensing of local firms. In other situations, they require local investment (i.e., FDI) and do not permit

TABLE 20–2

Less Developed Country Rules Relating to Technology Use and Transfer

Selected Countries	Limits on Royalties	Unpatentable Items	Patent Duration	Trademark Duration	Highest Tax Bracket on Royalties (%)
Argentina	None	Pharmaceuticals; non-industrial items	5, 10, 15 years	10 years, renewable	45%
Brazil	1–5% of sales to unrelated firms only	Pharmaceuticals; foods; chemicals	15 years	10 years, renewable	25
Egypt	None	Any substance; only production processes are patentable	15 years, renewable	10 years, renewable	40
India	8% of sales	Foods, drugs, agri. chemicals; semiconductors	14 years*	7 years, renewable	30
Korea	None	Food, drink, medicine, chemicals	15 years	10 years, renewable	25
Mexico	None, but generally 7% of sales	Foods, drugs, agri. chem.	14 years	5 years, renewable	40
Nigeria	1% of sales	Plants, animals, biol. processes	20 years	7 years, renewable	15
Singapore	None	n.a.	Only U.K. patents are valid	U.K. or Singapore registered, 7 years	32
Venezuela	5% of sales; no royalties to foreign parent firms	Foods; medicines; chemicals; financial instruments	15 years	15 years, renewable	50

*India allows patents for 10 years on food processes and medicines. Also, technical service fees are taxed at 30% rather than the normal 40% on royalties.

Source: Business International Corporation, *Investing, Licensing, and Trading Conditions* (New York: Business International Corporation, 1989–90).

imports. Thus, the MNE manager's choice of the market entry method, and consequently of the technology transfer method, is often forced by the host government. Similarly, operating conditions often include continued pressures to increase technology transfer into the country, as the box on IBM in Mexico shows.

Even after the firm brings a new product or process into an LDC, the legal protection for proprietary knowledge is often either unavailable or less assured than in industrial countries. Many LDC host countries refuse to grant patent protection for some products, reasoning that the technology is not new, or that it should not be proprietary, or that the MNE has already earned a reasonable return on its patent in industrial countries. Any of these arguments leads to less protection for the technology than that available in industrial countries.

The competitive situation is far less pressing in many LDCs than in developed countries, so that in LDCs technology tends to diffuse more slowly, and a technological advantage can be maintained for a longer period of time. Even when patents expire, local firms are often not quick to acquire the technology and compete with the originating firm. Because of a lack of competitive pressure, MNEs often continue to use production processes in LDCs even after they have been replaced by modernized processes in the MNEs' facilities elsewhere.

IB
ILLUSTRATION

IBM in Mexico*

IBM has operated in Mexico as an importer of mainframe and minicomputers since the 1950s. Manufacture of minicomputers was begun near Guadalajara in 1981; at the time, all IBM facilities abroad were wholly owned by the company. Mexico is a relatively small market for IBM, accounting for annual sales of only 90,000 PCs in 1986, valued at approximately U.S. $200 million. On the other hand, Mexico's proximity to the United States and the availability of low-cost labor presented an important opportunity to IBM for reducing production costs of its computers that are sold elsewhere.

Mexico has, since 1973, required that all FDI projects accept a minimum of 51 percent local ownership. But, as with IBM in Guadalajara, this rule has been broken when the government found compelling reasons to permit greater foreign ownership (typically due to the investment's introduction of new technology, creation of many jobs, and/or generation of significant exports). Nonetheless, the Mexican government has largely held to the minority joint-venture law, even during the 1980s foreign debt crisis.

Mexico passed legislation in 1981 to require foreign computer manufacturers to meet the 1973 rule on 51 percent minimum local ownership and to increase their Mexican local content beyond rules established for most other industries. The stated goal was to achieve 70 percent local supply of the nation's computer needs by 1986. In addition, computer manufacturers were required to meet minimum export requirements to generate foreign exchange for Mexico.

In 1984, IBM proposed to construct a PC plant at the site of its existing minicomputer facility near Guadalajara, to invest about U.S. $40 million, and to produce about 100,000 personal computers per year, 75 percent of which would be exported. The firm sought 100 percent ownership of the plant, presenting its case that the project would create many major benefits for Mexico (namely, about 80 direct new jobs and over 800 indirect ones; transfer of high-tech job skills into Mexico; new direct investment of U.S. $7 million; and exports of 75,000 personal computers per year). The government initially rejected the proposal, on the grounds that IBM did not propose to use sufficient local content in the plant, and thus would be importing too much in parts and materials. It appears as well that the other foreign firms that were producing PCs locally successfully lobbied the government to refuse 100 percent ownership to IBM, since they all had accepted minority positions.

A year later, with Mexico increasingly hobbled by its more than U.S. $100 billion indebtedness to foreign banks and other foreign lenders, IBM twice more resubmitted the proposal, each time increasing its commitment to purchase local inputs, to increase investment more than tenfold, and to raise the level of exports, but to retain 100 percent ownership. On the third occasion, with the enhanced offer and the promise of more technology and the establishment of secondary and tertiary enterprises, the Mexican government found itself much less able to resist the clear balance-of-payments and employment benefits to be produced by the project, and agreement was reached.

The final agreement called for IBM to invest a total of U.S. $91 million. This money was distributed among expansion of the Guadalajara plant ($7 million), investment in local research and development ($35 million), development of local suppliers ($20 million), expansion of its purchasing and distribution network ($13 million), contribution to a government-sponsored semiconductor technology center ($12 million), and the remainder to begin local university partnerships and other linkages to local computer-related activities. Also, IBM agreed to achieve 82 percent local content by the fourth year of operation and to export 92 percent of the PCs produced in Mexico. The firm retains 100 percent ownership of the plant.

This example demonstrates both the importance of technology transfer to the host country and the bargaining relationship between the LDC government and the foreign MNE. ■

*Taken from Jack N. Behrman and Robert Grosse, *International Business and Governments* (Columbia, S.C.: University of South Carolina Press, 1990).

Finally, for the past two decades governments of LDCs have been pressuring the MNEs to use **appropriate technology.**[14] This is generally considered to mean less capital-intensive and more labor-intensive technology in LDCs with an overabundance of labor and a scarcity of capital. Long and heated debates have taken place between companies and governments, and the United Nations has even tried to create a Code of Conduct on Technology Transfer that would push MNEs into using technology that offers maximum benefits to LDC host countries. There has been no clear outcome as yet, but at least a better definition of "appropriate technology" has been developed. It is now defined as product, process, or managerial knowledge that is optimally adapted to local conditions.[15]

CONCLUSIONS

Technology is knowledge that has application in an industrial (business) setting. Such knowledge may be created through research and development or simply through experience in doing business, from which the firm develops managerial skills. It can also be purchased from innovating firms. Technology may be used through internal transfer and deployment within the firm or through sale to outside firms via licensing or some other contractual means. Ultimately, the competitive advantage obtained from technology may be dissipated, due to copying by other firms or to their creation of comparable knowledge.

Technology is at the heart of the multinational enterprise. Whether it be product, process, or managerial technology, the MNE usually depends on it for competitive advantage. This kind of firm benefits from technological advances made by an affiliate in one country that can be transferred within the firm to affiliates in other countries. Production technology can be created through R&D in several countries, benefiting from the spillover effects of the activities of other firms there. The knowledge of market and supply conditions in many countries is itself a technological advantage possessed by MNEs.

Control over the use and diffusion of proprietary technology is a difficult task for the multinational manager. There are many protection measures, and these are sometimes effective in preserving the competitive advantage of proprietary technology. Eventually, however, all technology becomes diffused or outmoded, and the proprietor firm needs to develop or acquire new technology to create new competitive advantages.

Each country has established rules governing the use and transfer of technology by firms operating there. Developed countries tend to offer relatively few restrictions on the creation and dissemination of technology. LDCs generally limit the MNE's use of technology by imposing restrictions on licensing agreements, limiting patent protection, and otherwise trying to restrict the competitive advantage that the MNE derives from technology. The future will probably bring greater government attempts to control the use and transfer of technology, since the benefits of technology are important to countries as well as companies.

QUESTIONS

1. What is technology? How is it used by multinational enterprises in competition?
2. Explain the concept of a "public good." Why does this concept cause problems for innovating firms? How do governments view this issue? How does management?
3. By what methods can technology be transferred internationally? What are the key costs and benefits to an MNE for each transfer method?
4. How can an MNE create a technological advantage over other firms? Give several examples.
5. What is R&D? What is the optimal level of investment in R&D for a multinational firm?
6. Explain several methods that a firm can use to protect its proprietary technology.
7. What are the main kinds of problems that make it difficult for a firm to maintain its competitive advantage based on proprietary technology?
8. How do industrial countries and LDCs differ in their approaches to regulating technology use and transfer?
9. How can an MNE best deal with the regulatory structure facing technology in the less developed countries?
10. What would be a viable strategy for a firm such as Hoffmann-La Roche in international competition, given that its key proprietary pharmaceuticals have passed the period of patent protection?

REFERENCES

Baranson, Jack. *Technology and the Multinationals.* Lexington, Mass.: D. C. Heath, 1978.

Behrman, Jack N., and W. A. Fischer. *Overseas R&D Activities of Transnational Companies.* Cambridge, Mass.: Oelgeschlager, Gunn, and Hain, 1980.

Caves, Richard. *Multinational Enterprise and Economic Analysis.* Cambridge: Cambridge University Press, 1982. Chapter 7.

Chudson, Walter. *The International Transfer of Commercial Technology to Developing Countries.* New York: UNITAR, 1971.

Contractor, Farok. *International Technology Licensing: Compensation Costs and Negotiation.* Lexington, Mass.: D. C. Heath, 1981.

Davidson, William, and Donald McFetridge. "Key Characteristics in the Choice of International Technology Transfer Mode." *Journal of International Business Studies,* Summer 1985.

Emmanuel, Arghiri. *Appropriate or Underdeveloped Technology?* New York: John Wiley & Sons, 1982.

Guile, Bruce, and Harvey Brooks (eds.). *Technology and Global Industry.* Washington, D. C.: National Academy Press, 1987.

Magee, Steven. "Information and Multinational Corporations: An Appropriability Theory of Direct Foreign Investment." In *The New International Economic Order.* ed. J. Bhagwati. Cambridge, Mass.: MIT Press, 1977.

National Science Foundation. *National Patterns of Science and Technology Resources.* Washington, D. C.: National Science Foundation, 1990.

Organization for Economic Cooperation and Development. *Appropriate Technology.* Paris, OECD, 1976.

Teece, David. *The Multinational Corporation and the Resource Cost of International Technology Transfer.* Cambridge, Mass.: Ballinger Publishing, 1976.

Tinnin, David. "How IBM Stung Hitachi." *Fortune,* March 7, 1983.

NOTES

[1] Technology is "industrial science, the science or systematic knowledge of the industrial arts, especially of the more important manufactures" (*Webster's New International Dictionary,* 2nd ed.). *Webster's* identifies two key points in this definition. First, technology relates to industry; that is, it is the application of science to business. Second, it relates to systematic knowledge of the various parts of industry such as production but also distribution, R&D, and even marketing and finance.

[2] Jack Baranson, *Technology and the Multinationals* (Lexington, Mass.: D. C. Heath, 1978), defines three types of technology: product, process, and managerial. Walter Chudson in *The International Transfer of Commercial Technology to Developing Countries* (New York: UNITAR, 1971), similarly defines technology as having three forms: product design, production techniques, and managerial functions.

[3] See, for example, David Teece, *The Multinational Corporation and the Resource Cost of International Technology Transfer* (Cambridge, Mass.: Ballinger, 1976).

[4] See, for example, Henry Grabowski and Dennis Mueller, "Industrial Research and Development, Intangible Capital Stocks, and Firm Profit Rates," *Bell Journal of Economics,* Autumn 1978; and E. L. Reynard, "A Method for Relating Research Spending to Net Profits," *Research Management,* July 1979.

[5] Thomas Peters and Robert Waterman, *In Search of Excellence* (New York: Harper & Row, 1980), pp. 223–34.

[6] Thomas Gladwin and Ingo Walter, *Survival of the MNE,* pp. 300–304; and the Harvard Business School case "Hoffmann-La Roche A.G."

[7] "IBM: Colossus of Armonk," *Creative Computing,* November 1984, pp. 298–306.

[8] Examples such as these, along with useful descriptions of the projects, appear regularly in the bimonthly magazine, *Mergers & Acquisitions.*

[9]Harold Lusk, Charles Hewitt, John Donnell, and James Barnes, *Business Law and the Regulatory Environment,* 5th ed. (Homewood, Ill.: Richard D. Irwin, 1982), pp. 984, 987, and 990.

[10]See, for example, "Where Trademarks are up for Grabs," *The Wall Street Journal,* December 5, 1989, p. B1.

[11]David Tinnin, "How IBM Stung Hitachi," *Fortune,* March 7, 1983.

[12]National Science Foundation, *National Patterns of Science and Technology Resources* (Washington, D. C.: NSF, 1990), p. 3.

[13]See, for example, Robert Ronstadt, *Research and Development Abroad by U.S. Multinationals* (New York: Praeger Publishers, 1977); and Jack N. Behrman and William A. Fischer, *Overseas R&D Activities of Transnational Companies* (Cambridge, Mass.: Oelgeschlager, Gunn, and Hain, 1980).

[14]See, for example, Henry Norman and Patricia Blair, "The Coming Growth in Appropriate Technology," *Harvard Business Review,* November–December 1982.

[15]Organization for Economic Cooperation and Development, *Appropriate Technology* (Paris: OECD, 1976), Chap. 1.

Miracle Corporation

Introduction

Staring out the window of his room in a downtown Washington hotel at the jets taking off and landing at National Airport, Dirk Roberts pondered tomorrow's presentation to the executive committee. Dirk was Miracle Corporation's Coordinator of International Investments and Strategic Planning and had lately been working on one of the most challenging projects he had seen in his eight years with the firm. Dirk had just returned from a meeting with Mexico's Assistant Undersecretary for Economic Development, Dr. Roberto Estaphan, and was returning to Miracle's St. Louis headquarters the following morning. That afternoon he was to make a presentation to the Executive Committee for Strategic Development on the details of the meeting with Dr. Estaphan and offer recommendations as to how Miracle should organize itself vis-à-vis its proposed Mexican investment.

Company Information

Miracle was in the business of manufacturing electronic test equipment for the automotive repair industry. Miracle had annual sales in the $300–$350 million range and employed 130 employees at its plant in St. Louis. It also had a 20 person research center in Michigan to track technological developments in the automotive industry.

Electronic test equipment is the auto industry equivalent to the diagnostic equipment found in hospitals and doctors' offices. Without some means of accurately measuring the performance of automotive engine components, valuable repair time could be lost speculating on the reasons an engine is running incorrectly. As automotive technology advanced with the advent of semiconductor technology, there was a need for more complicated testing equipment to track faults in vehicles' electrical, carburetion, fuel injection, and ignition systems. Vehicle emissions regulations also created a demand for measurement equipment. Fifty percent of Miracle's sales were exhaust emissions analyzers to automotive service establishments. This segment of their business had taken off as a result of Miracle being the first manufacturer to have an analyzer certified for use in California (home of the most stringent emissions control laws in the U.S.) in 1984. As "green" awareness rose, other states and communities had since followed California's lead in adopting strict vehicle emissions controls and this business segment was growing rapidly.

This case was written by Prof. Frank Dubois as a basis for class discussion, 1991.

The firm also sold and leased highly-sophisticated engine test and measurement equipment to automotive dealerships and other repair shops. This represented about 30 percent of sales. The final 20 percent of sales was composed of sales of hand-held test equipment such as timing lights to check engine timing, multimeters to check electrical faults, and dwell and RPM meters.

Miracle's customers for emissions analyzers and engine test equipment could be split into two segments. The primary market was auto dealerships. Dealers' service departments required state-of-the-art test equipment as a result of their need to diagnose new vehicle models brought in for warranty claims. Since repairs were made under warranty and generated no revenue to the car's manufacturer, dealers were given various forms of incentives (in the form of low interest loans and discounts) to minimize the warranty costs that were reimbursed to the dealer as part of the franchise agreement. Having the latest test equipment allowed dealers to track faults and make repairs quickly. Dealers were generally allowed to trade in their old equipment for new equipment as new car technology came on line. Quite often the old equipment was returned to the factory for refurbishment and then sold to Miracle's other major market: the general service auto shop.

The general service shops owed their existence to a reluctance on the part of a large segment of the driving population to have post-warranty service done at dealerships. Repair costs were typically lower and it was often possible to cultivate a personal relationship with the mechanic that serviced your car. Mechanics in the general service shops were generally working for independent entrepreneurs who were not required to do low-margin warranty work and were under less pressure to generate revenue. Because of their focus on repairs to older vehicles, these shops did not have to invest in state-of-the-art test equipment and could not make do with older equipment.

Miracle also had a distribution arrangement with the leading automotive equipment vendor in the U.S., Pop-Off Corporation. This arrangement had been quite lucrative for both parties and as a result, Miracle had an 80 percent share of the U.S. market for this equipment. Miracle produced equipment for sale under its own brand name in the U.S. and Canada and was an original equipment manufacturer for Pop-Off, manufacturing products under the Pop-Off label. Pop-Off distributed automotive tools and other products through independent franchisee's who were given exclusive rights to sell products to automotive service establishments using a showroom-on-wheels concept. Pop-Off vendors owned large panel trucks stocked with a large assortment of tools and equipment. These trucks could be seen making the rounds of automotive service establishments in every city in the U.S. and Canada. Most vendors carried at least two or three of Miracle's lower priced hand-held test equipment, e.g., battery testers, timing lights, mini-engine analyzers, and multimeters. More costly items such as integrated engine analyzers costing as much as $10,000 and emissions test equipment had to be special ordered with delivery times of two to six weeks depending on the backlog and the degree of customization the customer wanted.

In addition to sales to Pop-Off, Miracle had a contract with a major retail chain to manufacture hand-held test equipment for the do-it-yourself consumer market. This contract represented about 10 percent of Miracle's sales revenue. Export sales were dominated by the emissions analyzers and were growing rapidly as a result of international efforts to control vehicle emissions. There were also export sales through the relationship with Pop-Off and the company hoped that it could increase this component of its business.

The auto test equipment industry was quite small with only three other major competitors in the U.S. Competition was generally on product performance and after sales service and not on price. Miracle felt that they were the market leader as a result of their early entry into the emissions analyzer market. Sales revenue from this segment provided funds to improve the performance capabilities of their equipment and to keep up with changes in automotive technology. The major competitive threat facing Miracle was competition from the Far East with comparably priced products specifically designed for the high performance, small displacement engines found in Japanese imports. The less expensive hand-held items such as battery testers and timing lights were taking a beating from imports from Taiwan, Hong Kong, South Korea, and Singapore. As a result, Pop-Off was putting pressure on Miracle to either reduce costs or increase product performance. In addition, the small test equipment account for the retail chain was coming up for renewal next year. The executive committee was worried that unless quick action was taken to reduce manufacturing costs and lower prices while maintaining profit margins, both the Pop-Off and the retail accounts would be lost and the future of Miracle would be in peril. Miracle's stock price was already starting to show weakness as a result of a financial analyst's sell recommendation on Cable TV's "Nightly Business Report."

Investment in Mexico

Miracle's executive committee had decided that the time was right to explore investment in a manufacturing platform in Mexico. There was interest in a Mexican location because of U.S. tariff regulations and the possibility of the two countries negotiating a free trade agreement sometime in the 1990s. Many other U.S. companies were shifting operations to Mexico in response to competitive pressures. Even Japanese and European firms were setting up operations across the border to serve the U.S. market. There was a consensus among Miracle's executive committee that the best way to maintain market share and remain competitive during the economic slump of the early 1990s was to shift a portion of production to a site in Northern Mexico into a facility known as a *Maquila-dora*. Mexico was chosen as a site because the company was worried about losing control over the operation and had relatively little experience in the international environment. Most Maquiladoras were located less than a one day drive from the border and the corporate Lear jet would facilitate one day trips on the part of upper management.

Maquiladoras are offshore manufacturing facilities that operate under terms of U.S. tariff laws 806.3 and 807.0. Under the terms of these laws, a firm can export from the U.S. to Mexico, parts and components for further processing and assembly and pays duty upon import back into the U.S. only on the value-added in Mexico. In other words, the value of the product for U.S. Customs purposes is the difference between its value leaving the U.S. and its value upon return to the U.S. In addition, labor rates in Mexico averaged approximately $1.50 per hour versus $7.80 per hour in the U.S.

The problem with the project from Dirk's perspective involved the location of the project, the characteristics of the products that would be produced there, and the type of processing technology that would be transferred to the Maqui-ladora. Dr. Estaphan had remarked that the Mexican government did not look favorably upon the transfer of less than state-of-the-art equipment into Mexico unless it was absolutely necessary. The Mexican government was proud of the accomplishments of Ford's automotive manufacturing plant in Hermosillo and wanted as many new investments as possible to follow Ford's lead in transferring modern technology. Modern technology contributed to spin-offs in terms of training and development of supporting industries. Dr. Estaphan also stated that the Mexican government was willing to offer lower tax rates to those firms that used modern equipment in their Mexican facilities. The government would lower tax rates even further for firms that chose manufacturing locations some distance from the border. There were serious social and environmental problems along the border and the Mexican government was trying to encourage new Maquiladoras to set up in the underdeveloped interior.

Characteristics of the Manufacturing Process

Miracle's main plant was in St. Louis. All manufacturing took place in this plant. As a result of automation of most of the major process functions, the plant's capital to labor ratio was very high and Dirk was worried that transferring some of the production process technology might be inappropriate in a low-wage site. The assembly line for the hand-held test equipment relied on a significant investment in plant and equipment to support a very high output rate. There was, however, a hand assembly component to the production process. For much of this work, Miracle relied on low-skilled hourly labor.

An exception was the manufacturing line for the integrated engine analyzers and emissions test equipment. Since production volumes for this product were quite low, Miracle had in place a much less sophisticated production process. Products were assembled using relatively standardized components such as printed circuit boards and power supplies that were sourced internally. Workers assembled the final product in batches using general purpose equipment. At this stage of the process there was a need for very highly skilled employees because of the different variations of the product that could be manufactured. Most of the employees working on this line had been with the firm for over 10 years and the company had invested heavily in their training as technology grew more sophisticated. Management was pleased that various attempts to unionize their direct labor force had not been successful.

Notwithstanding the impact on the St. Louis workforce, Dirk was also worried about the effects of Mexican manufacturing on the firm's ability to meet delivery commitments. Miracle prided itself on its ability to ship 99 percent of its engine analyzers on schedule. Since the cost of the engine analyzers precluded keeping a very large inventory, the ability to meet due dates reliably was critical to winning orders. Because of the lower investment in hand-held test equipment large stocks of finished goods inventory were kept to ensure a steady supply of distributors. The company found that demand for these products was inversely related to business cycles. Demand increased during downturns because people kept their cars longer and there was greater need for repair services. [However, the 1990 recession coupled with Operation Desert Shield had hit Miracle's business hard, particularly in communities surrounding major military installations. Many auto repair shops noticed a reluctance on the part of military wives to take over the traditionally "male" job of automotive upkeep.][1]

With this information in mind Dirk proceeded to sketch out recommendations to the executive committee.

QUESTIONS

1. What arguments should Dirk make in his presentation to the executive committee with respect to the technology transfer question?

2. What considerations should be taken into account in deciding between locations on the border or in inland Mexico? What locations would you suggest?

3. What types of products are most amenable to production in a Maquiladora? Can you identify any of Miracle's products or components that might be best manufactured in Mexico?

4. Do you think that U.S. tariff regulations should provide incentives for firms to move manufacturing outside of the U.S.?

4

The European Community, the World's Largest single market, has been headquartered in Brussels since 1957.
Worlview

DOING BUSINESS IN . . .

A new era began with the tearing down of the Berlin Wall in November 1989. The impact of this event on international business is wide-reaching and still unfolding.
Fotex/Journalism Services, Inc.

Chapter

21

Industrialized Countries

Chapters 21–23 examine issues related to doing business in each of three types of country: industrialized, less developed, and formerly communist. This chapter begins the sequence with a discussion of some general characteristics of industrialized countries and of common problems and opportunities that occur when doing international business there. First, criteria are offered to distinguish industrialized countries from the rest of the world. Then specific aspects of the economies and government systems of industrialized countries are presented to give an idea of the kinds of international business that are most likely to be appropriate in these countries. Subsequent sections focus on government concerns and policies that relate to international firms and on company strategies that can be used to deal with the policy environment. Finally, entry and operating strategies are presented. The main goals of this chapter are to:

1. Demonstrate important characteristics of industrialized countries.

2. Show what kinds of international business are common and appropriate in such countries.

3. Examine the role of governments in industrialized countries and show how firms can deal with these governments.

4. Consider entry and operating strategies that international firms can use in industrialized countries.

5. Illustrate the general issues with the case of Japan.

INTRODUCTION

Definition of Industrialized Countries

The countries considered in this chapter are the developed nations of Western Europe and North America, plus Japan, Australia, and New Zealand. They are called **industrialized countries (ICs)** because their economies have become dominated by industrial production (and services) rather than agriculture. They all have relatively high standards of living, compared to the rest of the world, and they all use market-based economic systems (as opposed to communism). Table 21–1 lists the countries that are considered industrialized today and provides several measures of their economic performance, such as per capita incomes, unemployment, and real economic growth rates. Notice that Scandinavia, the United States, and Switzerland have the highest incomes and that Japan (which was substantially behind the others after World War II) has the greatest growth rates. The economic performance of the industrialized countries is significantly better than that of the communist countries. (In 1988 per capita GDP was $US 8,850 in the Soviet Union, $US 8,220 for Eastern Europe as a whole, and $US 320 in China.) It is tremendously better than that of the less developed countries (LDCs)—although such individual LDCs as Hong Kong, Korea, and Singapore have achieved very impressive economic records during the past decade or so, and several oil-exporting LDCs with small populations, such as Kuwait and the United Arab Emirates, have high per capita incomes. (In 1987, per capita GDP averaged $US 290 in low-income LDCs, $US 1,810 in middle-income LDCs, and

TABLE 21–1

Selected Characteristics of Industrialized Countries

Country	GNP per Capita ($U.S., 1988)	Growth Rate of GNP per Capita*	Average Annual Infla. (%/yr.)**	Average Unemployment (%) 1990	Current Account BOP, 1988 ($ mill.)	Mfg. as % of Total GDP 1988
Canada	16,960	2.7	4.6	7.7	−8,258	23
United States	19,840	1.6	4.0	5.3	−126,620	22
Australia	12,340	1.7	7.8	6.9	−11,256	18
Japan	21,020	4.3	1.3	2.2	79,590	29
New Zealand	10,000	0.8	11.4	7.2	−780	23
Austria	15,470	2.9	4.0	3.2	−642	32
Belgium	14,490	2.5	4.8	8.7	3,334	24
Denmark	18,450	1.8	6.3	9.3	−1,819	25
Finland	18,590	3.2	7.1	3.8	−3,006	29
France	16,090	2.5	7.1	9.3	−3,522	27
Germany	18,480	2.5	2.8	6.1	48,499	44
Ireland	7,750	2.0	8.0	14.9	625	n.a.
Italy	13,330	3.0	11.0	12.2	−5,363	27
Netherlands	14,520	1.9	2.0	6.8	5,282	24
Norway	19,990	3.5	5.6	5.0	−3,671	21
Spain	7,740	2.3	10.1	16.1	−3,730	27
Sweden	19,300	1.8	7.5	1.6	−2,567	30
Switzerland	27,500	1.5	3.8	0.6	8,326	n.a.
United Kingdom	12,810	1.8	5.7	6.1	−26,590	27

*For the period 1965–1988.
**For the period 1980–1988.
Sources: World Bank, *World Development Report, 1990* (Washington, D.C.: World Bank, 1990). For unemployment data: OECD, *OECD Economic Outlook* (June 1990) p. 123.

$US 2,710 in upper middle-income LDCs.) More detailed comparisons can be made by looking at Table 21–1 along with its counterparts in the next two chapters, Tables 22–1 and 23–1.

In addition to the macroeconomic indicators shown in Table 21–1, many other measures of development distinguish the industrialized countries from the rest of the world. For example, all of the industrialized countries have well-developed securities markets in which private sector and government borrowers and lenders participate. While the markets in the United States and the United Kingdom are the largest and most influential in international financial dealings, even tiny Luxembourg has stock and bond markets and other financial markets. Broad financial systems of this kind are usually lacking in less developed countries and in the formerly communist countries.[1]

Industrialized countries generally possess an advanced system of *distribution*—roads, railroads, airports, and navigable waterways. These pathways for the transportation of products and people enable companies to get their products to customers and to move raw materials and intermediate goods to processing locations. Similarly, advanced *communications* networks allow rapid and efficient transmission of information through telephone, telex, television, radio, and print media. Also, the systems of *education* in industrialized countries generally offer high-level training in the skills needed to function in an industrial setting—particularly engineering, sciences, and business administration. Each of these types of infrastructure exists in less developed countries as well as industrialized ones. The key difference is their very wide availability and high quality in the developed countries as compared with the LDCs.

Main Forms of International Business in Industrialized Countries

Not surprisingly, the main forms of international business discussed throughout this book are the ones used among the industrialized countries. As noted earlier, about two thirds of world exports and imports take place among developed nations (which comprise one sixth of the world's population), and an even larger portion of total foreign direct investment occurs among them. International banking activity likewise involves mostly banks and clients in North America, Europe, and Japan—despite the emphasis of public debate on LDC debt during the economic crisis (especially in Latin America) of the 1980s. Table 21–2 shows some aggregate measures of the international business that occurs in the developed-country members of the **OECD (Organization for Economic Co-operation and Development).**[2] Note that by far the bulk of international business worldwide occurs among industrialized countries and that foreign direct investment is more concentrated among these countries than is international trade (or lending).

With this base of information, we can proceed to discuss major factors that company managers should consider when doing business in industrial countries. The next section describes a variety of attributes of industrial countries as they pertain to international firms. The third section focuses specifically on the regulatory structure and government policies that affect international firms in these countries. The fourth section suggests entry and operating strategies for multinational firms. Some strategies for dealing with the host and home country governments are sketched in the fifth section. Then current international business activities and concerns in a particular industrialized country—Japan—are presented. The final section provides a summary and some conclusions.

TABLE 21–2

International Business among Industrialized Countries

From ICs to	Exports 1988 ($U.S. billions)	Av. Annual FDI Flow 1980–1987 ($U.S. billions)	Commercial Bank Loans Outstanding 1989** ($U.S. billions)
ICs	1,463.5	55.1	1,925.8
Latin America	78.2	6.2	117.8
Africa	47.3	2.0	18.5
Asia	201.1	7.9	96.4
Oil-exporting LDCs*	68.1	1.1	27.8
Communist	34.8	n.a.	86.5

*These countries also are counted in the regional totals shown.
**Liabilities of borrowers in each group of countries owed to foreign commercial banks.
Sources: International Monetary Fund, *Direction of Trade Yearbook* (1989); Bank for International Settlements, semiannual international lending report (1989); U.S. Department of Commerce, International Trade Commission, *Direct Investment Update: Trends in International Direct Investment*, September 1989, p. 15.

KEY CHARACTERISTICS RELATING TO MNEs

The Concept and Function of the Marketplace

All industrialized nations use the free market as one acceptable means of organizing economic activity—subject to fewer or greater government constraints, depending on the country. This assertion is more or less a definition; the only countries that have high per capita incomes, well-developed economic infrastructures, and other characteristics similar to those of the industrialized nations are a few formerly communist countries, such as the Soviet Union and Czechoslovakia. Those countries have recently begun to move to a **market-based economy.** While these distinctions are intended primarily to distinguish countries on the basis of economic development, in fact the formerly communist countries are quite varied between high-income and low-income countries, between industrial and agricultural countries, and so on. Nonetheless, we will retain the common classification of industrialized countries as those that use a market-based economy and have achieved relatively high levels of per capita income and other measures of development.

Even the industrialized countries vary fairly widely in the degree of private sector and public sector (i.e., government) participation in business. France and Italy have placed ownership and control of a large number of companies and industries in the hands of government managers, in contrast with the United States and Germany, where very few government-owned companies exist except for some public utilities.

The key point is that industrialized countries view the market as a legitimate means of organizing economic activity. By allowing markets to function, and firms to compete, these countries reap the gains from the efficient use of resources. This contrasts with the remaining communist countries, such as China, in which the government largely allocates economic resources according to various nonmarket criteria and in which resource allocation has generally been relatively inefficient.

Recall that economic activity can be organized by markets, by governments, *and* by large firms that internalize business activities. As noted in Chapter 2, the MNE is itself a means of organizing economic activity internationally, because it carries out production, resource transfers, distribution, and consumption. Sometimes large firms operating internally can carry out business activities more efficiently than small, competitive firms; thus, they add an element of efficiency to the market. Since the vast majority of multinational enterprises are headquartered in ICs, and both earn their income and employ their staffs there, these countries do not view MNEs nearly as critically as do many LDCs. Consequently, MNEs as well as markets are allowed to function with substantial freedom in ICs, as contrasted with LDCs.

Although these generalizations are reasonably accurate, still many differences exist in the degree of freedom of markets and MNEs in different ICs. As mentioned, France's government owns and operates numerous corporations, whereas the United States owns and operates almost none. The Japanese economic system favors private ownership of firms but tends to limit competition in favor of company/government cooperation to avoid extensive layoffs of employees or company failures. In contrast, the British government owns a substantial portion of industry but permits fairly open competition, with much less company/government cooperation. The Western European countries have generally been willing to allow corporate mergers and acquisitions to create large companies capable of competing with the Americans and the Japanese, whereas the United States has followed a strong antitrust policy for most of the 20th century. In sum, although the ICs all utilize the marketplace as a base for their economies, they each follow a somewhat different model for doing so.

Cultural Differences

Despite the many similarities in the economic systems of developed countries, major differences due to cultural factors still exist among them. For example, doing business in Japan may appear to parallel doing business in the United States, but many U.S. companies find it much more complicated. Although consumers in the United States and Japan have similar levels of income and education, huge differences exist in tastes, in business practices, and in many other aspects of business. U.S. firms trying to enter the Japanese market have often found a need to obtain some "inside" help from a Japanese company that knows the local distribution system and can get products to customers. Numerous stories about the problems of U.S. firms trying to do business in Japan appear in *The Wall Street Journal* every year; these stories generally point out that the traditional inward-looking Japanese business system makes it very difficult for foreigners to enter. Many other cultural factors—not the least of which is language—effectively limit the access of foreign firms to the Japanese market. Each of these factors raises a barrier to business among industrialized countries, which thus cannot be viewed as homogeneous markets, despite their similarities.

Government Involvement in Business

Governments in every country own some or many companies, particularly in such industries as electric and telephone utilities, banking, and petroleum. For the most part, IC governments own fewer companies than governments in LDCs or communist countries. During the 1980s, the tendency was toward even less government ownership in ICs, as shown by the sale of shares in such national companies as:

In Great Britain—British Telecom, British Petroleum, British Gas, and British Airways.

In Japan—Nippon Telephone and Telegraph.

IB
ILLUSTRATION   Privatization in Europe

During the 1980s a massive sweep of privatizations took place in most of the Common Market countries. Begun by the Thatcher administration's sale of British Telecom and a dozen other high-profile state-owned companies, privatization has become a signal of European governments' willingness to use the free market to build the region's economies.

Once the bastion of protectionism in Europe, France has moved aggressively into the privatization mainstream with the sales of several major state-owned firms. Saint-Gobain, a diversified company with a concentration in glassmaking, was sold in 1987 through a widely-promoted campaign to attract small investors from all parts of France. This company had been nationalized in 1982 under the socialist government that also nationalized the banking system. After several years of losses and low profits, Saint-Gobain began to improve profitability in 1986, and then was sold to the public in 1987 for $US 1.9 billion.

France's government followed this sale with the denationalization of several banks and other major industrial and service firms. Although the initial steps into privatization were taken by the Conservative government of Premier Jacques Chirac, this policy continues to be followed into the 1990s. As the European Community drops more of the restrictions on internal business, all the national governments will have to consider more ways to assist their national firms to compete in the regional market. Privatization is one vehicle that permits firms to pursue market-based strategies without being subjected to the non-economic demands that are placed on government-owned companies. ■

In France—Paribas (a major financial holding company), Saint-Gobain (industrial equipment), and Assurances Générales (insurance).

In Italy—Montedison (a very large chemical company), Alfa-Romeo.

In Germany—the government-owned portion of Volkswagenwerk.

Despite this trend, many companies with total or partial government ownership still exist in Western Europe. A measure of overall government participation in the economy appears in Figure 21–1. This measure shows aggregate government spending on defense, education, health, social security, economic services, and general administration. On average, the government sector accounts for less than one third of economic activity in industrial countries. On top of this, government-owned companies account for another 10 percent of GDP in most Western European countries.

Perhaps the most important issue raised by the existence of government-owned (or state-owned) companies that compete with privately owned ones is that of the nature of competition. How can a private firm compete with one that

FIGURE 21-1

Government Participation in the Economy (central government expenditures as a percentage of GDP)

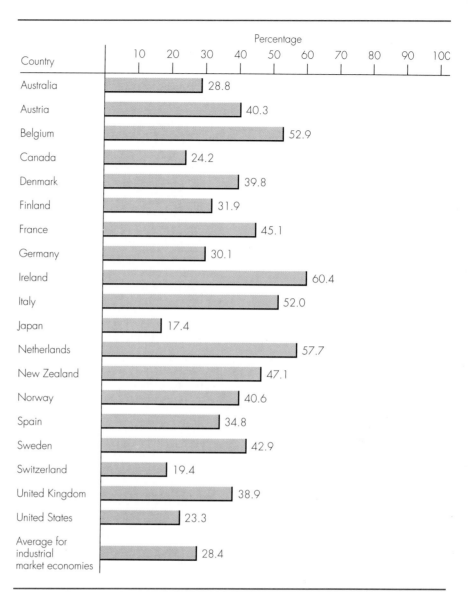

Source: World Bank, *World Development Report 1989*, p. 223.

is backed by the resources and rule-making power of a government? In another light, how can a government company compete with private companies when it must serve both political and economic goals, and hence must usually sacrifice some efficiency for political reasons? As global competition increases among firms from many countries, concern about the practices of state-owned companies that are not limited by profit considerations (because governments can subsidize them) will continue to intensify.

A second form of government involvement in business is subsidization of local firms and/or restriction of foreign firms. In every country, governments show some sort of favoritism to local firms and institutions, while discriminating against foreign firms. From limits on deposit taking by foreign-owned banks to government purchasing practices that favor local suppliers over foreign ones (such as the "buy American" policy in the United States), antiforeign bias exists everywhere. In the 1990s, increasing efforts are being made to force governments to treat foreign firms fairly in business, following a principle, established in 1976 by the OECD, that calls for "national treatment of non-nationals."[3] That is, the OECD called on its member countries to give equal treatment under the law to foreign and domestic firms. Although a trend toward more equal treatment exists, the fact remains that antiforeign rules and practices still occur in the business systems of industrialized countries.

GOVERNMENT CONCERNS AND POLICIES RELATED TO MNEs

Except for IC policies that have been established to protect local businesses against foreign competition, most of the IC policies that affect MNEs are aimed at regulating business in general. For example, antitrust rules seek to maintain competitiveness in the economy, and they limit monopolistic practices such as unfair pricing by MNEs and local firms alike. Similarly, pollution control is a major concern in most countries, and in dealing with this concern, the ICs have established rules that limit company practices regardless of the nationality of the firm. The following paragraphs discuss several major concerns of IC governments that relate to MNEs, beginning with the concerns that tend to be most significant to the government/business relationship. In each case the concern has led to some policies, which are discussed as well. Table 21–3 shows these concerns and policies. The listing in the table is intended to be in order of

TABLE 21–3

Industrial Country Concerns and Policies toward MNEs

Concern	Company Activities	Government Policies	International Agreements
Employment	Importation of products and people, anti-union behavior, production switching	Immigration limits, labor protection laws, investment incentives	OECD Code of Conduct, ILO Tripartite Agreement
Balance of payments	Importing and exporting, transfer pricing, remittances, loans	Nontariff barriers, requirement of arm's-length pricing, taxes on transfers	GATT, OECD Code
Taxation	Transfer pricing, arbitrary booking of sales and expenses	Corporate income tax, remittance taxes, double-tax treaties	OECD Code
Antitrust	Dumping, overpricing, collusion	Sherman and Clayton Acts	EEC Treaty articles 85 and 86; OECD Code
Sovereignty	Overseas decision making, production shifting	Attempts to extend jurisdiction extraterritorially	OECD Code
Information disclosure	Multicountry operations, transborder information transfer	Information demanded on foreign operations	OECD Code

importance, with the most important concern at the top. However, the actual significance of any concern depends on the country and on its economic/political situation at a particular time.

Employment

Employment, and its consequent impact on national income, is generally the single most important concern of home and host governments dealing with MNEs. If MNEs hire local people when they enter a country, and produce output that raises GNP, then they are viewed positively by the host government. If they displace local workers through imports of their products, or through layoffs at their local plants, offices, and so on, then they are viewed negatively. If MNEs move their production out of a country because of labor problems or high costs, then they are certainly viewed negatively.

As discussed in Chapter 11, it is often very difficult to measure the overall impact of an MNE on employment in a given country. Since one cannot turn back time and see what would have happened if the MNE had been absent from a given situation, generally no precise measure of that "what if" result is possible. Thus, employment impacts tend to be measured in the manner stated above; and when a company changes its employment pattern, it is scrutinized carefully by both home and host governments.

Government policies that deal with employment include a variety of limitations on employment practices. The most common rules relate to immigration. Every country restricts foreign nationals from receiving visas to enter the country for employment (because this would presumably keep a local person from being employed). The United States is among the strictest in limiting entry by foreign nationals for employment purposes. The European Community, on the other hand, has established rules permitting nationals of any member country to seek employment freely in another member country, in order to create a single Community-wide labor market.[4] (Nationals of other countries still face substantial restrictions on entry into any European Community country for employment.)

MNEs are greatly affected by the limitations on hiring and firing that exist in most countries. Throughout Europe, national laws require payment of substantial severance benefits to employees who are laid off by a firm. In France, for example, compensation equal to 42–70 percent of a year's wages is required when a firm terminates a person's employment. In addition, most countries require demonstration of a just cause for terminating employment, rather than allowing employers the power to lay off workers or managers for any reason. Even the United States has been increasing such restrictions.[5] Rules of this kind raise the cost of layoffs in general, and they raise the cost to MNEs of moving operations from one (national) location to another if layoffs are involved.

At the multilateral level, both the International Labour Office (ILO) and the OECD have enacted guidelines for the treatment of workers by multinational firms. The ILO's "Tripartite Declaration" and the OECD's "Guidelines" describe acceptable behavior for MNEs. The prescriptions in these documents are so general that they have had very little impact on company decisions. However, since both documents call for fair and reasonable treatment of workers and for the upholding by MNEs of the labor laws in the countries where they operate, these documents reinforce the efforts of countries to ensure that MNEs engage in the labor practices desired.

The Balance of Payments

The *balance of payments* impacts of MNE activities are another top concern of IC governments. MNEs transfer funds repeatedly between parent and affiliates and among affiliates in different countries. Every transfer of this kind has a different impact on the sending versus the receiving country, and of course raises a different concern for each of their governments. MNEs ship products and services among affiliates, again giving rise to BOP impacts that concern national governments. Virtually every link between MNE affiliates in different countries, even down to transborder telephone calls, leads to direct or indirect BOP impacts.

Industrialized countries use a wide variety of limitations on imports and subsidies for exports, as discussed in Chapter 9. While the GATT negotiations have reduced tariff protection on manufactured goods to very low levels over several decades, nontariff barriers and restrictions on imports of agricultural goods and services still limit trade in many ways. Due to a tremendous bilateral trade deficit with Japan over the past decade, the U.S. government, for example, has "jawboned" (threatened to set up tariff or quota barriers if foreign importers do not "voluntarily" limit their sales to the United States) the Japanese into reducing their sales of autos and televisions in this country. This tactic has stimulated such Japanese MNEs as Toyota, Honda, Sanyo, and Toshiba to avoid **de facto protectionism** by establishing manufacturing subsidiaries in the United States.

Limitations on funds transfers are much fewer among the ICs than among the LDCs. Even so, each industrial country has on occasion limited its residents' ability to take funds abroad through some form of exchange controls. The countries with the largest trade deficits, such as France and Italy, have been most prone to use such controls, though the United States in the late 1960s limited funds transfers by MNEs to their foreign affiliates. In the early 1990s, with a huge U.S. trade deficit, no exchange controls have been enacted, though the Federal Reserve has been accused by some foreign governments of allowing interest rates to remain high to attract foreign capital into the United States.

At the transnational level, the GATT has become a substantial forum for reducing barriers to the exports and imports of MNEs (and other firms) and for harmonizing the treatment of trade. The GATT does not, however, attempt to guide trade in any particular direction, as do national laws in each country. Concerning financial flows, the OECD Guidelines call for MNEs not to undertake transactions that destabilize national BOP positions. Adherence to this guideline is particularly difficult, since any cross-border financial transaction has opposite effects on the countries involved (i.e., it may be good for one country and bad for the other). In sum, no clear international accord exists with regard to financial flows—though some analysts have called for a GATT-type organization to deal with them.

Taxation

Taxation is a third major concern of IC governments in dealing with MNEs. Each government would like to tax MNE activities in its jurisdiction, but MNEs have the ability to move funds around through a variety of financial transfers. The home country would like to tax earnings of foreign affiliates that are based on value added by the parent firm, but host governments have first access to those earnings. Host governments are worried about parent companies charging their affiliates high transfer prices, royalties, and other fees, so that little profit is shown in host countries and little tax paid there. To the governments, this is largely a zero-sum game—because of treaties that reduce **double taxation** of company income; if one receives more tax payments from an MNE, the other receives less. The central issue is fairness; each government should be able to tax the company activities within its jurisdiction based on the **fair value** of those activities. Even apart from the fact that each government would probably prefer to receive as much tax as possible, it must be admitted that measures of fair value are at best arbitrary.

The main tax policies used in industrialized countries are national corporate income taxes that apply to all firms within the jurisdiction, that is, parent companies and local affiliates of foreign firms. When profits are remitted to parent companies abroad, the home country allows some kind of tax reduction (credit or deduction) to account for taxes paid abroad. Profit remittances (dividends) are generally taxed by the host country, as are payments of royalties and fees to the parent company. The MNE usually has substantial leeway to place available funds in such instruments as eurocurrency deposits, so that funds transfers are not the central concern of governments. It is the MNE's ability to declare more (or less) taxable income in selected jurisdictions that creates the tension with governments; for example, the firm can book more sales in low-tax jurisdictions and more costs in high-tax jurisdictions.

The taxes actually paid by MNEs vary widely from country to country and across industries. Because of government incentive policies, the United States taxes such industries as oil exploration and capital-intensive manufacturing less than other industries.[6] Because of similar incentives, companies that locate their plants and offices in specified zones in Great Britain, France, and Italy pay lower taxes than other firms in those countries. For the most part, such policies are not directed toward MNEs alone, but they do alter the tax environment faced by MNEs.

The OECD Guidelines call for MNEs to use arm's-length transfer prices and to otherwise fairly value their transactions so that taxes are properly determined and paid to the governments concerned. Double-taxation treaties between countries try to avoid overtaxing MNEs relative to local firms in each country by allowing for coordinated taxing of earnings by home and host governments. As yet, no single policy for taxation of MNEs has been established in multilateral agreements.

Antitrust Regulation and Competition

Antitrust (or, viewed from the other side, *competition*) is another major concern of IC governments. Historically, the most restrictive legislation to limit monopolistic practices, that is, to ensure competition in the market, has been enacted by the United States. European countries and Japan have tended to encourage company combinations that lead to larger firms, which are then expected to be better able to compete in oligopolistic markets. While these countries usually do not object to large company size, they do seek to limit abusive practices, such as discriminatory pricing and collusion between firms to monopolize a market.

The main legislative vehicles of antitrust regulation include the Sherman and Clayton Acts in the United States, the Antimonopoly Law of 1947 in Japan, and Articles 85 and 86 of the European Community Treaty (plus individual national laws in Europe). **Dumping** is a particular monopolistic practice that led to government action in the 1980s, when Japanese firms took leading market positions in many industries and countries. To constrain Japanese MNEs from dumping their products at prices below cost, U.S. and Western European governments enacted penalty tariffs, fines, and so on. If additional industries become dominated by groups of MNEs, the industrialized countries will undoubtedly pay more and more attention to antitrust problems.

Other Concerns

The four concerns considered above are not always the most important, but they arise repeatedly in discussions about regulating MNEs and they are often central to both company and government interests. Additional concerns, such as the protection of local firms and the involvement of government-owned companies, were discussed in the previous section. A handful of other concerns merit mention here.

First, the issue of **sovereignty** should be noted. While this concern figures much more importantly among the LDCs, it has important implications in ICs as well. Canada, for example, has traditionally pursued a very difficult path between allowing U.S.-based MNEs to dominate the economy and limiting their activities and creating economic tensions with the United States. In the late 1970s and early 80s, Canada used the Foreign Investment Review Agency to evaluate foreign direct investment proposals, and the Agency rejected a large number of them. In 1985, this protectionist policy was replaced by the "Investment Canada" program, which sought to attract more direct investment (and consequent jobs and income) and allowed more foreign control of the economy.[7] Although not going to Canada's earlier extreme, all industrialized countries limit foreign ownership and other forms of participation in key industries such as national defense, telecommunications services, and postal service. Each of these limitations can be viewed as an attempt by the national government to preserve sovereignty over the national economy.

A second concern is **information disclosure.** Each country requires disclosure of some types of information by firms doing business there. MNEs are constantly being asked to provide information about foreign operations to national governments that want to assess taxes, to limit unfair practices, and even to protect consumers and investors. MNEs often argue that the information requested is overly expensive to collect and report and/or that it could be used by competitors if disclosed. A related concern is **information transfer** across national borders. National governments are seeking to judge the importance of transborder data flows, especially within MNEs. Such transfers place information that could be sensitive to national interests in the hands of company decision makers in other countries; the full implications of this concern remain to be seen.[8]

Additional concerns such as pollution control, consumer protection, and labor protection sometimes present major hurdles for MNE managers, but they are usually not aimed specifically at MNEs; rather, they are directed at all firms operating in the given country.

ENTRY AND OPERATING STRATEGIES FOR MNEs

Entry Strategies

General entry strategies were presented in Chapter 2, and specific strategies for exporters in Chapter 19. This section raises a few additional points with respect to entry into industrialized countries. While conditions differ to some extent across industrialized countries, the main factor in determining **entry strategy** is usually *competition*. That is, the choice of a country, a product, and an entry mode (see Figure 19–1) depends on the kind of competition faced by the firm in each country.

In the television industry, for example, competition takes place among a half-dozen or so major manufacturers, whose plants are located in countries or regions with low-cost labor, plus many additional firms that buy televisions from the primary manufacturers and sell them through retail outlets, sometimes under their own brand names. Entry into the market of, say, Belgium, would most likely be through exports from a low-cost factory in another country. Whether the exports will be sold by the manufacturer itself or through a secondary firm and its retail network must still be determined. Sony, Panasonic, General Electric/RCA, and Siemens have entered through the establishment of sales offices and through direct sales to retailers, in both cases under their own brand names. Other firms sell televisions to retail stores, which place their own brands on the TVs and market them through their own channels. Virtually no manufacture of televisions takes place in Belgium.

There are no restrictions on foreign-owned television firms that want to enter the Belgian market. Such firms must follow the same rules as local firms and must compete with imports or local production. Since competition is very strong in this industry, a firm might consider setting up local production in exchange for government protection in some form. Such a strategy would probably be wasted, however, because the European Community countries would continue to have free access to the Belgian market and because any subsidy offered to one firm would be protested by other suppliers. Since the principle of free competition is clearly established in Belgium, a television maker would be concerned mainly with minimizing the delivered cost of getting the TVs to the market and with maintaining the quality of the product relative to the others that are available. Seeking government protection would most likely not be a viable strategy in this case.

The choice between entering with an owned affiliate versus contracting with another firm to make the product or deliver the service raises another interesting problem. If we assume that the firm is from North America or Japan, then producing in, say, the French market constitutes an entry into the European Community (EC). If the firm does not specify the contract carefully enough, the French contractee may be able to use the product or service in other EC countries in ways detrimental to the supplier firm's overall strategy.

For example, if a small Japanese manufacturer of computer circuit boards chooses to produce and sell in France through a licensee, that licensee may want to serve the entire European Community. Unless the contract is written restrictively enough, the licensee may have the right to do so—even if the Japanese manufacturer wants to set up its own plant in Italy or elsewhere in the EC for a similar purpose. The initial manufacturer may find that France's participation in the EC requires an "EC strategy," rather than a strategy for the French market alone.

In fact, for the competitive reasons just discussed, the OECD countries can be divided usefully into North America, the European Community, and Japan (ignoring Australia and New Zealand). Within each of these areas, there are few legal barriers to trade and other transborder business activities—and transportation costs are very low compared to the costs of interregional transport. In addition, there are few cultural barriers between the United States and Canada in North America, though there are often important cultural barriers between countries in Europe. Another barrier to interregional business that should be noted is the difference in time zones; North America crosses six of them, and the European Community crosses three. Japan, by contrast, is in only one, and that one has very little overlap of business hours with the other two regions. None of these points is an absolute barrier to interregional business, but they all tend to make firms view North America, Europe, and Japan as three markets.[9]

Operating Strategies

Assuming that the entry strategy chosen is an owned affiliate, the firm must next consider the operating details. Given that government protection is not likely to be a viable option in many cases, the firm will need to compete on the basis of cost, product differentiation, or market segmentation. All three of these strategies have been discussed previously, and here examples are given to illustrate them.

Cost minimization strategies have been followed widely by domestic firms as well as MNEs. During the past half-century, many U.S. firms have moved production from the industrial Northeast to lower-cost locations in the South. During the late 1970s and the 1980s, dozens of European and Japanese firms set up manufacturing in South Carolina, Georgia, and other Southern states, because these states had a cost advantage over Michigan, Pennsylvania, and other Northern states, but they still offered access to the entire U.S. market.

For similar reasons, Monsanto, Dow, Ciba-Geigy, ICI, and several other multinational chemical companies have chosen to manufacture basic chemicals in Northern Ireland. This politically risky location has the advantages of low-cost labor (relative to the rest of the EC) and of a government incentive program that further reduces costs. In this case, where production costs are the key competitive variable, firms have been able to operate a European Community strategy with a supply of basic chemicals from their plants in Northern Ireland. Of course, such other costs as transportation and communication are also low, in comparison with what they would be from production sites outside the EC.

The strategy of **product differentiation** plays a very important role in the industrialized countries, where consumers have relatively large amounts of discretionary income to spend on both necessities and luxury items. Not only can McDonald's, Burger King, and Wendy's succeed as fast-food outlets, but with different foods and pricing strategies, so can Wimpy's, Kentucky Fried Chicken, and Arby's. Entry into the U.S. market for this type of store still offers possibilities to additional participants, as long as they can sufficiently differentiate their menus and other characteristics to attract customers. The fast-food concept swept the United States first, but the other ICs have accepted it as well—so opportunities exist in Tokyo and Rome too.

Product differentiation by country or region is a strategy followed by such automobile manufacturers as General Motors and Ford. These two companies have introduced models in their European affiliates different from those they sell in the United States and Japan. Both Ford and GM have introduced "world cars" that they sell in both European countries and North America, but they also produce many models that they sell within only one or a few countries. In fact, they sell virtually all of their North American models only in the Western Hemisphere, and GM imports none of its Opel and Vauxhall models into this area.

Finally, **market segmentation** is a useful strategy in industrialized countries, whose markets are generally much larger than those in LDCs. Even when large competitors dominate markets for thousands of products, smaller firms or competitors not yet in the market can often find a niche for their sales.

DEALING WITH THE GOVERNMENTS OF INDUSTRIALIZED COUNTRIES

Much of the discussion in this chapter has focused on the central importance of competition in determining business opportunities and problems in the industrialized countries. It is also true, however, that the governments of industrialized countries do impose highly detailed rules on some industries (such as defense-related ones) and that they operate companies in others (such as utilities). Also, the government sector typically constitutes more than one fourth of the total economy, so the government is a huge consumer in each industrialized nation. This section looks at some of the central issues of government/business relations during the current decade.

Probably the most contentious issues in the 1980s in government/MNE relations were:

- MNE decisions to locate production facilities, often made to minimize costs, that shift production and jobs away from high-cost countries.
- MNE financial policies that affect a country's BOP and taxes, such as transfer pricing and other funds transfer strategies.
- MNE allocations of markets to affiliates, which are then limited to serving only some markets and thus may not be responsive to national efforts to stimulate exports or to restrict dealings with specific countries.
- Overshadowing all of the above points, the multinationality of MNEs versus the uninationality of governments, which some governments argue creates unequal bargaining power in favor of MNEs.

Successful dealings with host and home governments require careful consideration of both sides of these issues. The MNE manager, while needing to pursue the goals of the firm, must be aware of the government's goals as well—and aware of the government's sovereign right to set rules that seek to achieve those goals.

The MNE's decision to move production to low-cost locations has become a more and more crucial issue in the 1990s. U.S.-based firms have faced substantial criticism for using **offshore production** in the electronics, clothing, automobile, and many other industries. Because MNEs can consider many national locations for production, while governments can regulate only one, there is an essential imbalance in positions between the two. A fundamental step for MNEs is to demonstrate clearly either (*a*) that employment is not lost through offshore manufacture but merely shifted into other tasks (e.g., the production of other products or more white-collar activities in the firm) or (*b*) that the employment would have been lost anyway, due to less costly foreign production by firms of other countries. Both of these contentions are difficult to prove, so the tension between government and MNE remains.

On the issue of **financial transfers,** for example, the MNE manager typically wants to minimize the tax burden paid on transfers and to take advantage of the ability to move funds where they are needed in the firm. But when a country faces a balance of payments problem due to a trade deficit and/or capital outflows based on expectations that the currency will devalue, the MNE's funds transfers may add to the problem. There is no simple solution to this conflict, though the MNE can seek to improve government relations by exporting to other affiliates, importing less into the country, reducing funds outflows, and generally looking for ways to help the BOP of the country. Such a strategy might ward off government policies that would constrain the MNE much more significantly.

Market allocation by MNEs limits a government's ability to push companies into greater exporting or other domestic or overseas activities. Typically, the MNE will use a local subsidiary to supply the local market but not to supply its operations in other countries. If the Canadian government wants to stimulate exports, it would probably find it difficult to convince the affiliates of U.S. companies that they should ship products to the United States, whose needs the parent firm is already supplying. This problem becomes especially acute when the affiliate is a joint venture and the partner firm perceives itself as constrained from exports that would add to the joint venture's profitability. Again, the issue is not simple to manage. Perhaps the best alternative for the MNE is to consider ways in which the affiliate could export without too greatly affecting the firm's global strategy. Then government relations might be enhanced at a low cost to the firm.

Finally, the basic issue is **multinationality.** An MNE is bound to follow the rules in any country where it does business. However, it is not tied down by the laws and conditions in one country, because it also does business in other countries. When difficulties arise in one country, the MNE may be able to shift some or all of its business activities to another country. Since a government cannot pursue an MNE into another nation's jurisdiction, a situation of unequal power exists. However, as Vernon (1977), Behrman & Grosse (1990), and others have noted, MNEs are not free to ignore governments; if an MNE wants to do business within a government's jurisdiction, it will have to follow the demands of that government. Sovereignty is not at bay. As additional questions about the transnational dealings of MNEs arise, MNE managers will need to develop responsive strategies to government demands, rather than utilizing multinationality as a tool to avoid them.

AN EXAMPLE— COMPETING IN JAPAN

Overview

Since Japanese and American firms will continue to become more directly competitive in the years ahead and since both Japan and the United States are highly desirable target markets in terms of size and per capita incomes, managers from both countries will benefit from a better understanding of the functioning of each other's business system. This section lays a simple foundation for starting to understand the Japanese system; additional insights about human resource management in Japanese firms were offered in Chapters 17 and 18; and several excellent references to the issues are cited at the end of this chapter.

Since a detailed analysis of Japan's business system is not possible here, our approach is to discuss several key aspects of Japanese business that confront foreign firms seeking to operate in Japan. First, we discuss the largest and most important companies and industry groups; next, we note key aspects of Japan's indicative planning process (i.e., the government/business relationship); and finally, we consider some competitive strategies for foreign firms.

Major Local Competitors

Major local competitors for virtually any foreign firm operating in Japan are the nine largest trading companies, the **Sogo Shosha,** and their related networks of firms. These few firms account for about one fourth of Japan's GNP and for about half of Japan's imports and exports. Table 21–4 lists the nine Sogo Shosha and some of their characteristics. These firms follow in the tradition of the pre-World War II **Zaibatsu,** Japanese holding companies that owned or otherwise controlled hundreds of affiliated firms in manufacturing, finance, and other business areas. The Zaibatsu dominated Japanese business at that time, but they were forcibly dissolved as a result of the war and the subsequent Allied occupation. While many of the Zaibatsu were effectively split up, a few retained business ties and in the 1950s redeveloped some of their ownership ties. This led to the reconstitution of the two largest groups around their original core firms, Mitsubishi and Mitsui.

Additional networks of firms formed around a number of large industrial corporations, such as C. Itoh and Marubeni in textiles and Nissho-Iwai in metals, as well as around banks, such as Fuyo (Fuji) and Sanwa. All of these groups once again established their **Keiretsu,** affiliating large numbers of suppliers, intermediaries, and other related firms into industrial power centers. A distinguishing characteristic of the postwar groups has been their extensive expansion into international business, through the creation of trading companies, the Sogo Shosha. Today, the dominant form of business entity in Japan is the industrial group, linked by ownership and business ties to a Sogo Shosha rather than to a family-related Zaibatsu. The Sogo Shosha function as marketing arms for the affiliated firms of the Keiretsu, seeking sales at home and abroad as opportunities

TABLE 21–4

The Nine Largest Sogo Shosha in Japan

Name	1988 Sales ($ million)	Major Industries
Mitsui & Co. Ltd.	113,083	Chemicals, energy, steel, food products
Mitsubishi Corp.	102,126	Oil, industrial products, financial services, computers, communications
C. Itoh & Co.	90,963	Banking, electronics, textiles, oil
Sumitomo Corp.	88,966	Steel, chemicals, precious metals, communications
Marubeni Corp.	87,033	Textiles, machinery, steel, food products
Nissho Iwai Corp.	56,166	Banking, steel, aircraft, machinery, ships, lumber, rolling stock
Toyo Menka Kaisha Ltd.	28,837	Cotton, food products, machinery, electronics
Nichimen Corp.	28,240	Banking, lumber, computers, machinery
*Kanematsu-Gosha	23,246	Banking, textiles, machinery, electronics, oil

*1989
Source: Business Rankings Annual: 1989; Dun & Bradstreet, 1990.

are uncovered. Figure 21–2 sketches some of the relationships among members of the largest Keiretsu, the Mitsubishi group of companies. Note that the central components of the chain are the trading company, which provides markets and information for the group; the banks, which provide financing for the group; and a large number of manufacturing companies, which provide the main products sold by the group.

The Japanese trading companies and their associated Keiretsu pose a very real threat to potential foreign competitors, since they control a large portion of Japan's distribution channels and they operate cooperatively among many of the country's manufacturers, banks, and so on.

Government/Business Relations

Relations between the government and private sector firms have developed far more cooperatively in Japan than in the United States. While the private sector does own and operate most of Japan's business system, government policy is often used to support chosen industries and firms. Historically, government policy has been inward-looking as far as production is concerned and outward-looking as far as sources of supply are concerned. (Since Japan is not blessed with many fossil fuels or other minerals, oil, coal, iron, and so on must be imported—and export markets must generate funds to pay for these imports.)

The government agency responsible for implementing Japan's industrial policy is **MITI,** the Ministry of International Trade and Industry. After World War II, this agency was given responsibility for instituting a plan of economic development focusing on four major industries: electric power, steel, shipbuilding, and fertilizers. By setting up a system of incentives to prompt investment in these industries and to assist the successful firms in entering export markets—and also a strict system of protection against competitive imports—MITI contributed substantially to Japan's "economic miracle" after the war. During the 1950s and 1960s, GNP grew about twice as fast in Japan as in the most dynamic of the other industrial countries.

In more recent years, MITI has maintained its role as a primary agent of indicative industrial policy, offering incentives to push business into desired activities, especially to stimulate investment in targeted industries, such as chemicals and computers. The policies of protectionism have been largely dismantled, so that Japan is now no more protectionist than other industrial nations.

MITI has historically dealt with business as a partner in development, rather than as an antagonist or opponent. (There is frequent movement of managers from private sector corporations into MITI and from MITI back to the private sector.) MITI tends to be highly supportive of the private sector rather than distrustful of it. This cooperative relationship has been noted widely as a reason for Japan's superior ability to put national economic resources into leading ("sunrise") industries and to avoid overcommitment to declining ("sunset") industries. MITI officials frequently meet with company managers in selected firms and industries to discuss business needs, government goals, and ways to cooperate. All in all, Japan's system of indicative planning has functioned very successfully during the past 40 years.

Successful Competitive Strategies

Foreign firms entering Japan in the 1980s found that the legal restrictions were not overwhelming but that the cultural barriers were. The language is a major hurdle—Japanese is only remotely related to the Indo-European languages, such

FIGURE 21–2

The Mitsubishi Keiretsu

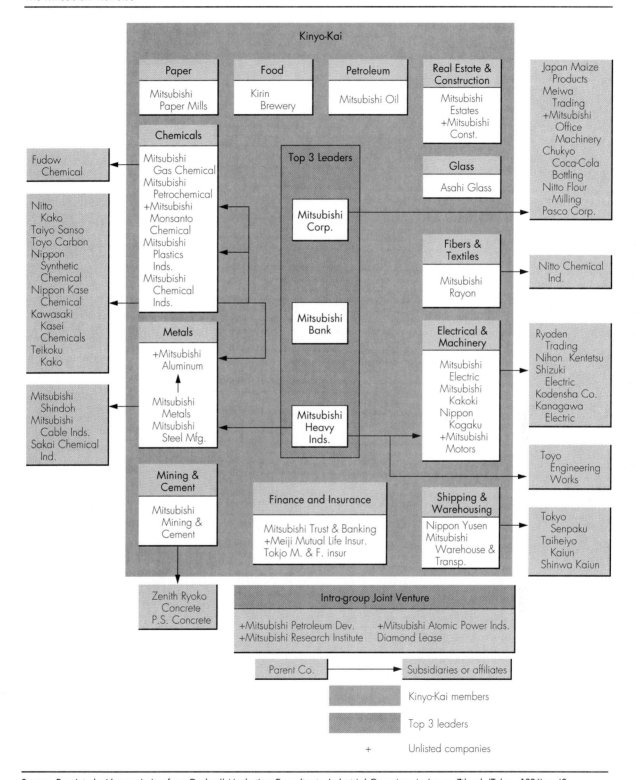

Source: Reprinted with permission from Dodwell Marketing Consultants, *Industrial Groupings in Japan*, 7th ed. (Tokyo, 1986) p. 48.

as English, French, and German—and the highly homogeneous society is quite inwardly biased. Japanese consumers tend to prefer to buy from domestic suppliers and to reject foreign goods in general. This presents a huge barrier to the foreign exporter or direct investor.

One extensively used strategy has been the **joint venture** with a Japanese partner. By linking up with a local firm that belongs to one of the key Keiretsu, a foreign firm can obtain distribution and promotion support that would be totally unavailable to the independent firm. By taking on a Japanese name, the foreign firm may avoid the negative customer reaction that prevails throughout the country. And finally, by truly working with a Japanese partner, the foreign firm may be able to absorb some of the managerial and technical expertise that has enabled many Japanese firms to succeed around the world in recent years.

Another strategy that has proven successful in Japan is the **licensing** of a Japanese firm to use the foreign firm's proprietary technology. After World War II, when the Japanese government restricted domestic industries to local participants, this was the only way (except for exporting) that the Japanese market could be entered. Foreign direct investment has been permitted more and more freely since the 1960s, but licensing continues to offer a low-cost alternative. The main advantage of licensing is that it allows immediate market entry without the start-up costs of setting up production, distribution and so on. The main disadvantages are that earnings are limited to the licensing fee, and that the proprietary technology must be given up to the licensee.

A **sequential entry strategy** might offer better results. In this strategy, the firm uses licensing to gain some knowledge about the Japanese market and subsequently sets up its own local manufacture or service facilities. (IBM initially entered the Japanese market through licensing agreements with various local firms in the 1950s. When the prohibition on FDI was lifted, IBM was able to enter with its own operations, and today it is one of the most successful foreign firms in Japan.)

Another strategy that has become very common during the past decade is the formation of **strategic alliances** with Japanese firms to gain market entry. These agreements include joint marketing accords, in which the foreign company sells its (branded) products through the Japanese partner and the Japanese firm sells its products in Europe and/or North America through the foreign partner. This kind of arrangement has been followed by a number of pharmaceuticals companies such as Eli Lilly (with Fujisawa), Merck, and SmithKline. Nissan similarly markets Volkswagens in Japan, while Volkswagen sells Nissan four-wheel drive vehicles in Europe. Other strategic alliances include joint production facilities (PPG and Asahi Glass), joint research projects (GE with Toshiba and Hitachi), and other associations that can be devised and organized.

In sum, all of the basic market entry strategies that have been discussed in this book are now generally possible in Japan. The difficulties that most foreign firms have encountered lie much more in the areas of product acceptability, distribution, promotion, and so on—fundamental business considerations—than in the area of government regulation. Japan's market, while very large and very affluent, presents major barriers of cultural and geographic distance from the experience of European and American firms.

CONCLUSIONS

Doing business in other industrialized countries is the main concern of most MNEs today. Problems in LDCs or formerly communist countries may be more visible and more difficult, but most of the international business carried out today is between industrialized nations. These countries have market-based economies that permit many MNE activities. In fact, the main problem generally faced by firms in the industrialized countries is competition from other firms.

While government-owned companies do exist in every IC, the private sector plays a very large role in the economy. Government policies tend to be pro-competition; they limit the activities of business mainly in order to assure that both local firms and MNEs deal fairly in employment, pricing, taxpaying, and so on. In industrialized countries, dealing with governments is largely the same for both local and foreign firms. A key concern in government relations is that MNEs are multinational, while governments are only uninational. This concern has led governments to share information about MNEs among themselves, to harmonize some of their policies that relate to MNEs, and to require that MNEs provide more information about their operations.

Strategies for doing business in ICs focus mainly on creating solid competitive positions. The basic strategies include cost minimization, product differentiation, and market segmentation.

QUESTIONS

1. Define "industrialized country." Does Norway fit into your definition? Does Spain? How about Kuwait? What would be an appropriate definition of industrialization?

2. Which countries are the most developed today? Which ones do you think will be the most developed by the year 2000? Why?

3. What are the general differences between the French and U.S. business systems, and what are the particular differences between these systems with respect to the treatment of MNEs?

4. How do IC governments participate directly in business? What implications does this situation have for the MNE manager?

5. Name four main concerns of IC governments in dealing with foreign multinational firms. What can the firms do to minimize tensions with the host government with regard to each of these concerns?

6. Name four main concerns of IC governments in dealing with MNEs based in their own countries. What can the firms do to minimize tensions with the home government with regard to each of these concerns?

7. What problems would arise for multinational firms if transborder transmission of information were restricted, as has been proposed in recent government discussions? How could MNEs cope with these problems?

8. Present three broad operating strategies for MNE affiliates in industrialized countries. Which of these strategies would have been appropriate for Monsanto Chemical Corporation when it was seeking to enter the European Community?

9. Explain the imbalance of power between MNEs and national governments due to the fact that the MNEs can operate in several countries, whereas the national governments are limited to their own jurisdictions.

10. Create a market entry strategy for a small German textile manufacturing company that wants to enter the U.S. market for synthetic fabrics. Make necessary (reasonable) assumptions so that your answer covers the organizational form of the venture, the channels of distribution, the structure of decision making in the firm, financial concerns, and any other issues that you feel are important.

REFERENCES

Behrman, Jack, and Robert Grosse. *International Business and Governments.* Columbia, S.C.: University of South Carolina Press, 1990.

Bergsten, C. Fred; Thomas Horst; and Theodore Moran. *American Multinationals and American Interests.* Washington, D.C.: Brookings Institution, 1978.

Boyer, Edward. "How Japan Manages Declining Industries," *Fortune,* January 10, 1983.

Gladwin, Thomas, and Ingo Walter. *Multinationals under Fire.* New York: John Wiley & Sons, 1980.

Grosse, Robert. *Foreign Investment Codes and the Location of Direct Investment.* New York: Praeger Publishers, 1980.

Hirschmeier, J., and T. Yui. *The Development of Japanese Business.* 2nd ed. London: Allen & Unwin, 1981.

Ohmae, Kenichi. *The Borderless World.* New York: Harper Business, 1990.

Organization for Economic Cooperation and Development. *Declaration on International Investment and Multinational Enterprises.* Paris: OECD, 1976.

Safarian, A. E. *Governments and Multinationals: Policies in the Developed Countries.* Washington, D.C.: British-North American Committee, 1983.

United Nations. *National Legislation and Regulations Relating to Transnational Corporations.* New York: UN Center on Transnational Corporations, 1983.

Vernon, Raymond. *Storm over the Multinationals.* Cambridge, Mass.: Harvard University Press, 1977.

NOTES

[1] Until recently it also was possible to distinguish the industrialized countries from the other groups because of their freely-elected, democratic governments. Since the international debt crisis of the early 1980s and the fall of the Berlin Wall, now most of the countries in all 3 groups are democracies.

[2] The OECD is an organization that groups the industrialized countries of the world plus a few LDCs, such as Turkey, Yugoslavia, and Portugal. The organization provides a forum for the rich countries to cooperate on issues of concern—improving education and social services, harmonizing policies such as those on MNEs, and so on. The OECD was founded in the early 1950s and is headquartered in Paris.

[3] Organization for Economic Cooperation and Development, *Declaration on International Investment and Multinational Enterprises* (Paris: OECD, 1976), sec. 2.

[4] This, of course, is easier said than done. Language and other cultural differences hinder the creation of a true Community-wide labor market.

[5]See "Beyond Unions," *Business Week,* July 8, 1985, pp. 72 ff.

[6]See *The Miami Herald,* May 26, 1985, p. 3F, for a listing of the taxes paid by 200 of the largest corporations in the United States in 1984.

[7]See the "Investment Canada Act," *Investment Canada Regulations.* Ottawa: Government of Canada, 1986 [S.C., 1985, c. 20.].

[8]The issue of regulating transborder transfers of information has led to OECD and United Nations efforts to establish a code of conduct. See, for example, the United Nations Center on Transnational Corporations, *The CTC Reporter* (latest issue).

[9]The overwhelming concentration of international business in these three groups of countries is analyzed in Kenichi Ohmae, *Triad Power* (New York: The Free Press, 1985).

Morioka Manufacturing

During the 1970s and 1980s, worldwide attention focused on the successes of Japanese firms doing business in the United States, Europe, and elsewhere. Nissan, Toyota, Honda, NEC, Sanyo, Panasonic, and numerous other Japanese brand names have become household words throughout the world. Only two or three decades ago, the largest and most successful international firms came almost exclusively from the United States and Western Europe. How have the Japanese attained such an impressive position in world markets?

As we have already seen in "The U.S. Auto Industry Case," the Japanese auto manufacturers are currently exceeding their American and European competitors in labor productivity and in reducing production costs. In addition, in many industries the quality of Japanese products is perceived to be better than that of firms from other countries. Companies that want to compete successfully against the Japanese will need to achieve similar results in their own business activities. The purpose of this case is to focus attention on the issue of labor productivity, using the Japanese model as a basis for the discussion.

Japanese-style management has been widely analyzed, from its emphasis on long-term employment to its concept of consultative decision making. The central issue in all of the analyses is that Japanese firms appear to pay more attention to *human resources* (i.e., the people who work in the firm) than do firms from other countries. Among the policies used by Japanese firms for human-resource management are these four key elements:

1. Long-term employment.
2. Slow performance evaluation and promotion.
3. Generalist career paths.
4. Consultative decision making.

Since World War II, large industrial corporations in Japan have followed a practice of hiring their employees and managers directly from high school or college, then keeping them employed throughout their careers within the same firm. Very little mobility exists between companies, since Japanese society has come to expect that a person will remain with the same employer until retirement. A very positive aspect of this practice is that it provides job stability for everyone in the firm, so that individuals tend to identify their own interests more with the company, which must perform well if their jobs are to be protected.

This case was written by Prof. Robert Grosse as a basis for class discussion, 1988.

Also, the company can justify expenditures on the training of employees, knowing that they will remain and offer benefits to the company from their increased skills. The negative aspect (from a Western point of view) is that few socially acceptable choices exist for someone who wishes to change companies during a career, regardless of the reason.

By giving careful evaluation to each employee and manager, Japanese firms demonstrate a sense of caring for the person. Also, by promoting managers through the ranks of management very slowly, the firm conveys to all that long-term performance is what counts. Even after the long initial period, ranks tend to be equal among people with similar seniority, though tasks and compensation become differentiated according to performance. People "save face" by maintaining equal rank with others in their cohort through the years, even while the firm can be managed capably by assigning the key decisions to those who demonstrate the greatest ability to handle them.

A third characteristic of Japanese human-resource management is the use of a generalist career path. That is, Japanese workers and managers are trained in one area of specialization when they join the firm, then rotated among assignments and specializations during their careers so that everyone learns several job skills. Someone hired as a financial analyst may be shifted into the personnel department after four or five years, and then into government-business relations after that. A worker who spends all or most of his time on an assembly line may be moved into repair work and subsequently into another type of assembly-line activity. This policy enhances the flexibility of the firm, because people can be shifted from job to job. It also enables the firm to operate more efficiently by imparting more skills to managers and workers. Thus, no one becomes over-specialized, and everyone spends some time in areas outside of the initial area of specialization, although a worker or manager may return to a preferred specialty after spending time working in other areas.

Finally (in this brief sketch), Japanese firms use a system of consultative decision making, which attempts to pass information about important company activities from the top managers all the way down to the lowest-ranking workers. In particular, decisions that will affect people in any area of the firm are discussed with those people *before* the decision is made, so that the affected workers and managers can voice their opinions and concerns before a problem arises. (For example, an auto company will distribute information about a proposed new assembly line, so that workers affected by the change will be able to see its impact on them and discuss it with their superiors before the change is made.) Because top managers have been rotated through several functional areas of the company, they tend to understand the concerns of people at lower levels and to be responsive to them. Because all employees involved in the decision have the opportunity to raise concerns about potential problems, the firm can avoid errors that otherwise would occur. Ultimately, top management must take responsibility for decisions, so this process does not imply that everyone has equal say in decision making. It is the conscious effort to create communication from bottom to top and top to bottom in the firm, and the fact that this information flow enables managers to make better decisions, that is so crucial here.

Other aspects of Japanese human-resource management could be noted, but those already discussed give a good idea of the basic differences between those firms and their competitors from other countries. One of the major subjects of discussion by managers in the United States during the past few years has been the possibility of transferring some of the Japanese style to U.S. firms. Are people from different countries and cultures similar enough that Japanese practices can be used elsewhere? An illustration of these issues follows.

The Case

The Morioka Manufacturing Company (also known as 2M) is a fairly typical large Japanese corporation that makes abrasives for automobile and industrial clutches, grinding and sanding machines, and specialized polishing equipment. In 1985 the company had about a 70 percent market share in Japan, and had gained almost 25 percent shares in most Western European countries and in North America. Total worldwide sales were over 250 billion yen in 1984.

2M has been evaluating a proposal to acquire a factory formerly operated by Bendix Corporation in California. The factory produced industrial clutches, which Bendix sold to a variety of companies for use in industrial machinery. Because the factory shut down only last year, almost half of the 300 workers formerly employed there would be available to work for 2M. Mr. Yoshi Hajima, the director of 2M's International Division, was wondering about the advisability of investing in the United States at all. He knew that the political pressure on Japan to import more U.S. goods and to invest in the United States to provide more American jobs was strong and most likely would continue through the rest of the decade. 2M could face limitations on its exports to the U.S. market at any time. Since that market now provided about 40 percent of the company's world-wide sales, maintaining U.S. business was critical.

The Bendix factory was not completely outmoded, but it would require substantial investment to upgrade the machinery. The location in California was not a problem for U.S. sales because of the excellent transportation system in the United States. In fact, there was only one negative aspect of the whole idea: Hajima had seen various studies that showed an enormous productivity gap between output per worker in Japan and in the United States. He was not excited about the prospect of dealing with the Americans, even though there was no current threat of a union fight (that is, an effort by workers to organize a union to demand better treatment by management). Other Japanese firms had successfully invested in the U.S. market, though very few of them had achieved anything near the productivity levels of their Japanese operations.

Hajima was most concerned about the need to establish a positive, enjoyable atmosphere in the workplace. He had grown up in such an environment, and he felt complete loyalty to the company that had supported him. He wondered if the U.S. workers, with their average annual turnover rate of almost 10 percent in the chemical industry, could possibly achieve a harmonious relationship with managers and staff that would lead to some degree of company loyalty at 2M in California. He was somewhat encouraged by the telephone conversation he had with a friend at Mitsui's office in San Francisco. The friend had found that the American workers at Mitsui were generally very happy to try many of the Japanese practices, and indeed turnover there was much lower than in comparable U.S. firms. Still, Mr. Hajima was skeptical.

Perhaps the largest difference between the Americans and the Japanese workers with whom Hajima was familiar was the American social preference for rugged individualists versus the Japanese emphasis on commitment to the team (or company) and group achievement. He did not think that the Americans would readily join company-sponsored social groups or do group exercises before work, as in Japan. Though quality circles had shown some promise of acceptance and positive results in American firms, Mr. Hajima did not believe that this was enough to generate the needed level of commitment to the firm. With only a fair understanding of English, he felt quite uncomfortable in trying to assess the situation and reach a decision.

Chapter

22

Less Developed Countries

This chapter examines business conditions and opportunities for international firms that seek to operate in less developed countries (LDCs). First, the characteristics of LDCs are presented; this is no simple task, since LDCs include countries ranging from relatively high-income Korea and Singapore all the way to very low-income Bangladesh and Ethiopia, with governments ranging from elected socialist and capitalist regimes to military dictatorships. In general, the aspects of these countries that are relevant to international firms are emphasized. Major emphasis is placed on the role of government in the economy, including both policies toward business and the widespread use of government-owned companies. Specific entry and operating strategies for international firms seeking to operate in LDCs are suggested and analyzed. The main goals of the chapter are to:

1. Demonstrate important characteristics of less developed countries for international firms.

2. Show what kinds of international business are common and appropriate in these countries.

3. Examine LDC concerns and government policies that relate to foreign MNEs.

4. Consider the entry and operating strategies that international firms can use in these countries.

INTRODUCTION

While no brief discussion of business conditions, policies, and opportunities in less developed countries (LDCs) can hope to offer detailed insights into particular countries, this chapter aims to raise the key issues facing foreign firms that want to do business in the nonindustrialized countries of Latin America, Africa, and Asia. Business conditions are far from uniform in these countries, which range from newly industrializing nations such as Singapore and Taiwan in Asia to the poorest, least developed African nations such as Ethiopia and Uganda, with most of Latin America somewhere in between. International firms in these countries engage in the full range of business activities, though a large part of their activities involve extractive industries and manufacturing assembly operations for exporting products to the industrialized countries.

This section provides a definition of less developed countries and a brief commentary on the main kinds of international business found in such countries. The next section discusses key aspects of LDC political and economic environments that particularly relate to MNE activities. The third section focuses on government policies and practices in dealing with foreign MNEs. In the fourth and fifth sections, company strategies for entering and operating in LDCs are presented.

Definitions of Less Developed Countries

In principle, a **less developed country (LDC)** is one that is at a lower level of economic development than some other countries. This oversimplified definition just recognizes that some countries are poorer than others, and classifies them according to such measures as per capita income, average life expectancy, and average level of education. Since economic development continues to occur in all countries, the absolute measures of poverty, health, education, and so on continue to improve, though some countries must still be in the bottom part of the distribution and others in the top part. That is, the measures of economic development themselves change as standards of living rise worldwide—but some countries must still be below the world average.

The World Bank uses a classification scheme that groups countries into four categories: low-income, lower middle-income, upper middle-income, and high-income economies. Table 22–1 describes selected countries from all three LDC categories along several dimensions.

Another classification scheme has been used by the United Nations, which grouped countries into developed economies, socialist economies, and developing countries. These categories group low- and middle-income countries together, with the exception of Eastern Europe and China, which were listed as socialist economies. The developed economies here are equivalent to the high-income economies in the World Bank grouping. This scheme simplifies the categories, but it also obscures the different situation of the key group of oil-exporting developing countries by placing them together with all other LDCs—and it fails to reflect the democratization of Eastern Europe.

Finally, a new classification—**newly industrializing countries (NICs)**—has arisen to describe the LDCs that have moved farthest along the road to industrialization. Most of these are Southeast Asian countries that have succeeded in attracting large amounts of foreign investment in manufacturing. MNEs from Japan, Europe, and North America (as well as locally based MNEs) use facilities in these countries to assemble electronic equipment, clothing, machinery, and various other products. The attraction of these countries lies in their relatively high levels of education, low wages, and industrious work forces,

TABLE 22-1

Selection of Countries Classified as LDCs by the World Bank

Country	GDP per Capita, 1988 (U.S. $)	Growth Rate of GDP per Capita*	Average Annual Inflation (%/year)†	Average Unemployment (%) 1988	Current Account BOP, 1988 ($ millions)	Manufacturing as Percent of Total GDP, 1988
Low-Income						
Ethiopia	100	1.4	2.1	n.a.	−389	12
Uganda	240	1.4	100.7	n.a.	−163	6
Nigeria	270	−1.1	11.6	n.a.	−1,024	18
India	290	5.2	7.4	n.a.	6,870‡	19
Kenya	330	4.2	9.6	n.a.	−454	12
China	340	10.3	4.9	2.0	−3,760	33
Haiti	400	−0.2	7.9	n.a.	−53	15
Indonesia	480	5.1	8.5	n.a.	−1,189	19
Lower Middle-Income						
Bolivia	620	−1.6	482.8	20.7	−306	17
Philippines	650	0.1	15.6	9.6	−406	25
Egypt	680	5.7	10.6	n.a.	−1,868	14
Nicaragua	890	−0.3	86.6	24.4§	n.a.	24
Mexico	2,110	0.5	73.8	18.0	−2,905	26
Brazil	2,240	2.9	188.7	3.7§	4,448	29
Upper Middle-Income						
S. Africa	2,320	1.3	13.9	21.5	1,292	25
Argentina	2,520	−0.2	290.5	6.1	−1,615	31
S. Korea	4,080	9.9	5.0	2.5	14,161	32
Libya	n.a.	n.a.	n.a.	n.a.	−2,259	n.a.
High-Income						
Saudi Arabia	5,190	−3.3	−4.2	n.a.	−9,583	8
Singapore	9,180	5.7	1.2	6.5||	1,660	30
Kuwait	9,990	−1.1	−3.9	n.a.	4,713	10
Israel	10,220	3.2	136.6	6.4	−678	n.a.
U. Arab Emirates	15,900	−4.5	0.1	n.a.	2,700	9

*Average annual rates during the period 1980–1988.

†Average annual inflation during the period 1980–1988.

‡World Bank estimate.

§Urban unemployment, 1987.

|| 1986 unemployment.

Source: World Bank, *World Development Report, 1990* (Washington, D.C.: World Bank, 1990); *Foreign Economic Trends and Their Implications for the U.S.,* (Washington, D.C.: U.S. Department of Commerce, 1990); Economic Commission for Latin America and the Caribbean, *Statistical Handbook for Latin America and the Caribbean* (New York: ECLA, 1989).

all of which make local manufacturing profitable for domestic and foreign firms. Indeed, the phenomenal success of such ventures has led some people to contend that these countries, which they call the "Asian Challenge," will rival the United States and Japan for supremacy in manufacturing during the coming years.[1] Table 22-2 illuminates some key characteristics of the NICs.

TABLE 22-2

Development Indicators for
NICs (newly industrializing
countries)

Country	GDP per Capita, 1988 (U.S. $)	Annual Growth Rate of GDP per Capita 1980–1988	Exports as % of GDP, 1988	FDI as % of GDP, 1988
		Indicator		
Brazil	2,240	2.9	10.4	0.8
Hong Kong	7,860	7.3	140.9	0.6
Singapore	9,180	5.7	165.7	4.5
South Korea	4,080	9.9	35.4	0.4

Source: World Bank, *World Development Report, 1990* (Washington, D.C.:World Bank, 1990); and International Monetary Fund, *Direction of Trade Statistics Yearbook, 1989* (Washington, D.C.: IMF, 1989).

Each of the classification schemes has useful aspects. Which scheme is best really depends on the type of presentation desired. For our purposes, it should be noted that important differences exist among oil-exporting LDCs, NICs, and other less developed countries, and that one should be aware of these differences when using World Bank, United Nations, or other sources of information.

Main Kinds of International Business in LDCs

The international business activities carried out in LDCs are at least as varied as those carried out in developed countries. These activities include exporting and importing, foreign direct investment, such contractual arrangements as licensing and franchising; and international banking. The most striking characteristic of much of this business is that it is generally far more *regulated* in LDCs than in industrialized countries. The limitations placed on foreign business in LDCs far surpass those imposed by industrialized countries. This point will be discussed in some detail in the section on "Government Policies."

Another striking characteristic of international business in less developed countries is its relatively small size—LDCs comprise more than 80 percent of the world's population but only about 25 percent of international business. Tables in Chapters 2 and 3 illuminate this issue to some degree, showing that LDC exports and imports each constitute slightly less than one third of the world total. (This measure can be divided between oil-exporting countries and other LDCs. In the early 1990s, the former had a substantial trade surplus and the latter faced a substantial trade deficit.)

As far as foreign direct investment is concerned, Table 22–3 shows the distribution of FDI in the countries listed previously. Probably not surprisingly, the largest amounts of FDI go to the largest economies, although the Southeast Asian NICs have attracted a disproportionate amount to their relatively small countries. Of total worldwide FDI, just under 25 percent is in LDCs, and about one third of that is in manufacturing. The service sector has become the second largest recipient of FDI in LDCs. It replaced mining after the wave of nationalizations of oil properties and other mining ventures of MNEs during the 1960s and 1970s.

Although the use of **offshore assembly** to reduce production costs is becoming more and more popular, such manufacturing counts for only a small part of total FDI at present. Even if we assume that all U.S. FDI in Hong Kong, Singapore, South Korea, and Taiwan is for offshore assembly, it only constitutes about $U.S. 4.2 billion of the total $U.S. 29 billion in LDC manufacturing. The trend is dramatically upward, however, as shown by the fact that as recently as

TABLE 22-3

Flows of Foreign Direct Investment in Selected Less Developed Countries (in millions of SDRs)

Country	1966–1971	1972–1977	1978–1983	1984–1988
Ethiopia	65	83	–	–*
Uganda	24	–2	–	–
India	–42	–29	–	–*
Haiti	0	33	48	25
China	226	–	–	4,618†
Kenya	–	142	327	74
Bolivia	28	52	171	44
Indonesia	308	1,054	1,331	1,487
Egypt	–	130	2,922	4,479
Nigeria	683	1,822	1,021	1,899
Nicaragua	134	61	15	2*
South Korea	136	419	–15	1,396
Brazil	922	6,155	11,181	3,447†
Mexico	1,466	2,746	7,444	6,582
South Africa	1,240	448	–1,529	–319
Israel	178	375	–366	388
Singapore	299	2,350	4,681	3,979
Libya	383	–1,631	–3,250	–50*
Saudi Arabia	–3	–1,730	17,207	5,131†
Kuwait	–	–	–438	–656

*Data through 1986.
†Data through 1987.
Source: International Monetary Fund, *Balance of Payments Statistics* (Washington, D.C.: IMF Publications Unit, 1969, 1977, 1981, 1986, and 1989).

1970 U.S. manufacturing FDI in those countries was less than $U.S. 270 million out of an LDC total of $U.S. 5.5 billion.[2]

International bank lending to LDCs also grew dramatically during the 1970s and early 1980s. Table 22–4 shows the change in commercial bank loans to developing countries from 1976 to 1989. Notice that the most internationally indebted countries are the large Latin American borrowers, followed by the newly industrializing countries. (This is somewhat misleading, because Hong Kong and Singapore are offshore banking centers, where large volumes of eurocurrency transactions take place separate from borrowing for domestic uses.) The countries that are least economically developed have attracted the least commercial bank financing (given their relatively low abilities to generate foreign exchange to repay such loans). The Latin American countries experienced huge decreases in foreign credits during the 1980s, as they were unable to service that debt incurred earlier. Finally, note that the Arab OPEC countries incurred substantial foreign debt during 1982–1989. This was certainly associated with the decline in the price of oil since 1981.

KEY CHARACTERISTICS OF LDCS RELATING TO MNES

Government Involvement in Business

As in the industrial countries, the government sector in LDCs constitutes a substantial percentage of the total economy. Figure 22–1 shows estimates of the size of the public sector in selected LDCs. In fact, on average the government's activities account for a *smaller* portion of GDP than in the industrial countries (even when state-owned companies are included). This situation needs to be contrasted with the *regulatory* environment that confronts private-sector firms in DCs and LDCs.

TABLE 22–4

Commercial Bank External Claims on Borrowers in LDCs, Selected Years (in millions of U.S. dollars of loans outstanding)

Country	December 1976	June 1982	December 1986	December 1989
Ethiopia	18	41	135	163
Uganda	7	57	62	66
Nigeria	284	6,714	–	7,302
India	571	1,577	6,705	10,571
Kenya	102	830	828	1,365
China	506	1,295	6,552	17,977
Haiti	39	59	64	105
Indonesia	4,010	8,155	15,944	18,808
Bolivia	448	1,053	590	278
Philippines	2,953	–	13,857	9,666
Egypt	1,264	5,350	6,525	6,084
Nicaragua	634	796	503	388
Mexico	17,885	64,395	70,840	59,746
Brazil	18,461	55,300	69,400	60,944
South Africa	7,624	14,125	15,618	13,854
Argentina	3,260	–	31,063	27,054
South Korea	3,701	19,994	15,618	23,291
Libya	148	830	698	910
Saudi Arabia	1,053	5,268	5,392	5,852
Singapore	9,168	33,690	87,545	108,806
Kuwait	939	6,274	5,840	5,683
Israel	2,033	6,126	5,243	3,507
United Arab Emirates	1,172	4,449	4,201	4,129
Hong Kong	7,485	34,003	99,051	136,968

Source: Bank for International Settlements, "Maturity Distribution of International Bank Lending" (Basel, Switzerland, June 1977, December 1982, June 1987, and July 1990).

While such industrialized countries as France and Sweden have a very great degree of government participation in business through government-owned companies and highly regulated industries, most industrialized countries allow firms substantial freedom to operate as the market dictates. Among LDCs, contrarily, the exceptions are the few Asian nations that allow broad competitive freedom to the market, while the rule is that LDC governments place many limits on company activities and participate actively in the market through government-owned or -controlled companies. In most LDCs, a national airline dominates or monopolizes that industry (for example, Aeromexico in Mexico, Varig in Brazil, and Air India in India), a national oil company controls that industry (for example, YPF in Argentina, the National Iranian Oil Company in Iran, and Nigerian National Petroleum Corporation in Nigeria), and a national bank (in addition to the central bank) controls or greatly influences local financial markets (for example, Banco de la Nación in Peru; Arab Banking Corporation in Kuwait, Libya, and the United Arab Emirates; and the Bank of Korea and Korea Development Bank in Korea)—all in addition to government-controlled postal service and electric, telephone, and water utilities.

Even beyond these industries, the government in an LDC often operates through an owned or controlled company that competes with private firms in other industries. A national automobile company (for example, Hindustan Motors in India) may compete with General Motors, Toyota, Ford, and others in the local market. A national food processing company or cooperative (such as Food Corporation of India and the National Cereals and Produce Board of Kenya)

**IB
ILLUSTRATION**

A Continuing Saga: The LDC Debt Problem

Balance of payments problems have repeatedly caused severe difficulties for less developed countries that depend on imported machinery, medicines, foods, and other products and services. When capital flight and/or downturns in prices of raw materials (that are key exports for many LDCs) cause foreign exchange shortages to occur, the countries are faced with a need to protect those foreign currency inflows that can be obtained and to reduce the demand for foreign exchange used in importing and paying claims to foreigners (such as foreign debt service).

During the 1970s many LDCs (and communist countries) built up large debts to foreign lenders. These lenders were principally the commercial banks that were trying to recycle dollars earned by OPEC countries when they pushed the price of oil up dramatically in 1973–74 and 1979–80. (This story is told in more detail in Chapter 24.) Especially in Latin America, governments and state-owned companies borrowed extensively in the euromarkets during this period, to the point where total foreign indebtedness of many countries exceeded their abilities to generate foreign exchange to repay it. The table, "Total External Debt in Latin America 1970–1990," presents an overview of this phenomenon for several major debtor countries.

Total External Debt in Latin America
1970–1990

Year	Argentina	Brazil	Chile	Mexico	Venezuela
1970	5.1	5.1	2.6	6.0	1.0
1973	6.4	13.8	3.2	8.6	4.6
1974	8.0	18.9	4.5	12.8	5.3
1975	7.9	23.3	4.8	16.9	5.7
1980	27.2	71.0	12.0	57.4	29.3
1982	38.0	88.2	17.3	82.0	31.3
1983	43.6	91.2	17.9	89.3	34.0
1985	51.0	105.5	20.3	96.9	35.7
1989	64.7	111.3	18.2	95.6	33.1
1990	68.1	114.5	17.7	92.9	33.2

There is plenty of blame to be shared for this problem. It is the borrowing countries' fault for taking out more loans than they could repay. It is the lending banks' fault for not being prudent enough in their lending policies to realize that the countries were borrowing more than they could repay. It is the OPEC countries' fault for shocking the world economy with their cartel practice of hiking prices to take advantage of their monopoly power—and then not being able to spend the new earnings fast enough to keep global supply and demand of funds in balance. It is the Fed's fault for not providing a cushion for the commercial banks during the oil crises, and instead encouraging them to find new borrowers such as the LDC governments to "recycle the petrodollars"—and then not supporting them when the debt crisis unfolded. In sum, no one organization or group can be blamed for this problem.

Today companies are finding that it is more important than ever in the LDCs to structure their activities such that they do not cause a drain of foreign exchange from these countries. Even as LDC governments pursue the perestroika-led economic opening around the world, they must continue to limit firms' access to foreign exchange when shortages occur. Most Latin American countries have embarked on policies of permitting the sale of their foreign currency debts in exchange for new local currency that can be invested in the local economy (that is, *debt-equity swaps*). These countries are actively seeking offshore assembly plants that generate net export earnings. They are opening up their economies to foreign-owned firms; but simultaneously they are looking for ways to limit the outflow of foreign exchange. This situation presents a new and exciting challenge to INC managers. ∎

often competes with Borden, Kraft, United Brands, and others both domestically and in other countries. The list may extend to dozens of industries, depending on the country.

Finally, the government in an LDC may exercise considerable control over the private firms in an industry by setting rules that limit their power to import, transfer funds, hire and fire, and so on. In this manner, LDC governments attempt to guide business in directions deemed desirable—though of course they do not always succeed in forcing the expected results.

In all of the above ways, LDC governments participate actively in the business systems of their countries. To foreign MNEs seeking to enter such markets, these conditions present challenges different from those in the industrialized countries. In industries monopolized by the government, foreign firms can operate *only* through contracts with the government to provide needed products or services used by the national monopoly. In industries where a government company competes with private sector firms, the rules of competition are different from those in a wholly private market, and the managers of foreign companies need to understand the key differences. In other industries, managers of foreign companies need to deal with the regulatory structure in a way that satisfies the local government and still leads to acceptable profitability for the firm. The challenge is to maintain the acceptability of the foreign firm to the government while carrying out some business activity that has value to the firm as well.

Dual Economies

Much has been said in the literature on economic development about the existence of **dual economies** in LDCs.[3] That is, the economic environment in many LDCs contains two separate and distinct groups: people who belong to a traditional society and do not participate in international business or even in the national market economy and people who belong to the market economy, which includes manufacturing and other modern industry, with its links to foreign business.

In Latin America, the Indian populations of the Andean and Central American countries typify the traditional societies, with very low per capita incomes, often living in remote areas far from cities, and with few ties to the market economy,

FIGURE 22–1

Government Participation in the Economy (Central Government Expenditures as a Percentage of GDP, 1988)

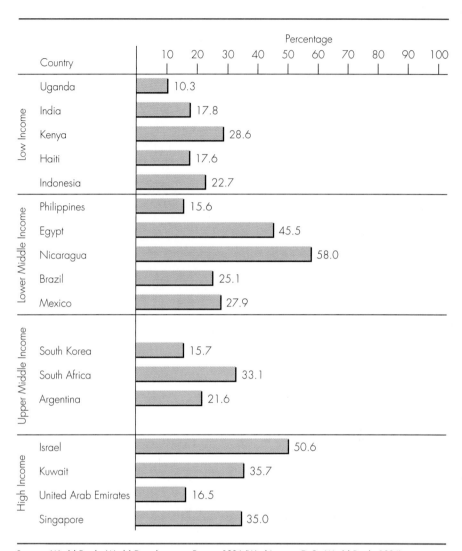

Source: World Bank, *World Development Report 1986* (Washington, D.C.: World Bank, 1986).

which predominates in a few cities of each country. In political science terms, these people represent the **periphery,** which fails to benefit substantially from the economic development of the **center,** that is, the cities. The populations of Latin American cities (of both European and Indian descent), while far from a wealthy class overall, include a wealthy elite group as well as middle-income and poor groups. The entire urban area generally has access to foreign products and to a functioning market economy; hence it is the center of economic development.

The multinational enterprise usually deals only with the **market sector** of a dual economy, that is, with the urban centers and more specifically with the middle and upper classes (which have sufficient purchasing power to buy foreign goods or sufficient education to work in the factories or offices of foreign firms). This presents quite a difficult social problem for the MNE to deal with, since the government officials who determine policy toward business generally come from the urban centers, while a large percentage of the population may exist on the periphery. The response of most MNEs has been to operate in the market sector and let the government worry about the **traditional sector.** This response has subjected MNEs to great criticism by LDC analysts and policymakers. Unfortunately, these firms are expert at producing and selling goods and services but not at redistributing income or choosing a country's economic development strategy. Because MNEs are a part of economic development, however, their managers must come to grips with such problems. Possible strategies are discussed below.

Political Risk

A third key characteristic of LDCs in general that tends to affect foreign firms is the high degree of political risk. Broadly speaking, less developed countries tend to present foreign companies with much more frequent and greater shifts in policy than do developed countries. While it is not every day that a shah is overthrown or a president deposed, the amount of political instability tends to be far higher in LDCs than in industrialized nations. Also, the frequent changes in political orientation—from leftist to conservative to centrist—tend to result in policy changes ranging from nationalizations to tax holiday incentives. The often unstable political environments lead MNE managers to perceive greater political risk in LDCs than in industrialized countries even if the instability does not have substantial effects on business activities.[4]

GOVERNMENT POLICIES

Important Government Concerns

As contrasted with governments in industrialized countries, LDC governments tend to focus their concerns on crucial development issues such as poverty, political instability, and social strife. Where European and North American countries seek to ensure a fair distribution of the benefits of MNE activities through taxation and antitrust rules, the Latin American, African, and Asian countries look for access to technology, capital, and managerial skills. In another view, the industrialized nations are largely concerned with sharing the benefits of MNEs fairly, whereas the LDCs are concerned with gaining more of those benefits and minimizing the costs of doing so. (It must be recognized, of course, that most of the world's multinational enterprises come from the industrialized countries and thus are "foreign" to the LDCs.)

The result of these concerns is a range of policies in LDCs that attempt to extract as much value as possible from MNE activities without driving away the firms that are providing the benefits. Table 22–5 lists a set of important concerns of LDCs in dealing with foreign firms and notes some of the policies that LDCs are using currently. Each of the concerns is discussed separately below.

Sovereignty   Since the 1960s, a fundamental concern of LDCs, especially those that are former colonies of European countries, has been the demonstration of **sovereignty**—that is, control over the national economy. Many of the most serious problems for foreign companies arose during the late 1960s and early 1970s, when LDC governments expropriated a number of oil, copper, and other raw materials investments and demanded that other investments be partially sold to local investors. Chile, for example, expropriated the copper mines of Anaconda, Kennecott, and Cerro de Pasco in 1969 and several other foreign

TABLE 22–5

LDC Relations with MNEs

Issues of Concern to the Government	Policy Reactions of LDCs
Sovereignty	Expropriation
	Require joint ventures
	"Unbundle" capital, technology, management, distribution, etc.
Lack of financial capital	Capital controls
Lack of technology	Technology controls
	Incentives for local R&D
Lack of infrastructure	Local content requirements
Lack of access to developed-country markets	Stimulate offshore assembly
	Encourage countertrade
Unemployment	Local labor requirements
All the concerns of the developed countries	

(primarily U.S.) investments during the Allende regime, from 1970 to 1973. Even more striking were the oil company nationalizations during the mid-1970s, following the OPEC embargo and price hike in 1973. Most of the Middle East countries nationalized the properties of foreign oil companies during that period, as did Venezuela and Ecuador in Latin America.[5] (**Expropriation** implies forced loss of MNE property with inadequate or no compensation. **Nationalization** refers to forced sale of MNE property to local purchasers with compensation.) Very few expropriations have occurred worldwide since 1980. In fact, Chile began following a free-market policy in 1973, and has welcomed MNE participation in the economy since then.

Another policy that became widely used to gain more local ownership of MNE activities was the requirement of a **fade-out** of foreign ownership over some time period. Instead of demanding that the MNE sell its local affiliate to nationals immediately, a number of LDCs set rules requiring the sale of 51 percent or more of foreign-owned businesses over a period of 10 to 20 years. The Andean Pact countries utilized this policy up until 1987. A somewhat similar policy, implemented by Mexico, India, and Nigeria, requires new investments to take joint-venture partners with some prescribed minimum ownership (51 percent local ownership in Mexico; 60 percent in India; and 40 or 60 percent in Nigeria, depending on the industry). Each of these policies could be considered a partial nationalization, since the intent is to have local investors gain control over the affiliate.

Expropriation and nationalization have not been the only responses of LDCs to their concern about controlling the national economy. Many of the policies enacted by LDCs in the past two decades have aimed at **unbundling** the MNE into components that have value to the host country. For example, in order to force MNEs to transfer managerial skills to local people, LDCs have limited the use of expatriate managers in MNE affiliates and required local nationals to be employed. Similarly, to gain access to technology, LDCs have tried to force MNEs to sell their proprietary technology to local firms and have disallowed the payment of royalties to parent firms, so that the country will not pay (through transfer of funds abroad) for technology developed by the MNE elsewhere. Without totally disallowing the entry of MNEs, many LDCs have sought to obtain the valuable pieces of the firm separately.

Lack of Financial Capital   Another concern of LDCs is a relative lack of financial capital for investment in productive activities. More specifically, this refers to a shortage of foreign currencies that could be used to buy foreign products necessary for supporting the local economy and to a lack of domestic long-term capital markets that could provide financing as well. While a government can print as much money as it wants, it cannot print the dollars or deutsche marks that are needed to buy machinery to run local factories. Nor can a government simply create long-term financial markets without substantial private sector participation and support, both of which are generally lacking in an LDC.

No simple solution exists to this problem. Many countries try to implement **capital controls** to limit transfers of funds abroad (which drain the country of foreign exchange). When capital controls are implemented, typically a black market arises for the purchase of foreign exchange and the problem continues.[6] Transfers of funds abroad are also taxed by host governments, thus reducing their profitability. This policy has some usefulness, though it does not stop the capital from moving. Many efforts have been undertaken to stimulate the development of capital markets in LDCs; thus far, successes have largely been limited to offshore eurocurrency markets such as those in the Bahamas and the Cayman Islands, neither of which has provided any major amount of local access to the markets for local development. On the other hand, Singapore and Hong Kong are examples of offshore financial markets that *have* significantly aided local development; and some larger LDCs such as Brazil and Mexico *are* operating sizable local stock and bond markets.

The real basis of the problem is that investors, domestic and foreign, try to move their funds to safe and high-yielding investments. When an LDC demonstrates an unstable political climate, or a debt crisis that makes foreign exchange very scarce, these investors will try to place their funds abroad—and they occasionally cause such a massive **capital flight** that the crisis is exacerbated.[7] In addition to seeking funds from MNEs, less developed countries go to the private credit markets for international bank loans and bond issues, and they attempt to raise their borrowing needs from international organizations such as the IMF and the World Bank.

Lack of Technology   All countries have come to view technology as a critical factor of production.[8] That is, no country is willing to follow simple comparative advantage and specialize solely in the production of raw materials, even if such specialization is dictated by cost conditions. Rather, every country seeks access to current technology in manufacturing, so that the economy can be diversified and not dependent on a narrow range of products (especially raw materials). Consequently, LDC governments want to obtain a continuing flow of current technology from suppliers such as MNEs at the lowest cost and to the greatest degree possible.

The policies used to achieve this goal range from refusal to recognize patents (which is intended to gain access to technology without paying for it) to incentives for local R&D. The Andean Pact countries do not allow payments to parent firms for technology transferred to local affiliates, although they still maintain patent protection. Most LDCs offer one form of subsidy or another to attract MNEs to do some local product development (the "D" of R&D), recognizing that basic research is usually centralized in one or two locations in the firm. In late 1984, Brazil required that all computers (except mainframes) sold in the country be produced locally by local firms. This attempt to force the development of a domestic capability in such a key high-tech industry has led to great turmoil in the Brazilian computer industry, with IBM, Burroughs, and other MNEs still not certain of the full implications for their activities in Brazil.[9]

Lack of Infrastructure   Not only do most LDCs lack major domestic companies in manufacturing industries; they also lack the necessary **infrastructure** to support such industries. That is, good roads, accessible electric power, good telephone service, up-to-date educational institutions, and other utilities and public services are often lacking in LDCs. These facilities tend to be extremely sensitive politically, and foreign firms are often not permitted to provide the services rendered by such facilities, though they may supply equipment and other inputs to construct the facilities.

The most common strategy used by LDCs to create the necessary infrastructure is to contract with MNEs to set up the telephone system, port, or power plant and then either to buy the project under a turnkey arrangement or to let the MNE remain as an adviser and perhaps licensor of the government-owned project. During the past several years, more and more LDCs are *privatizing* some of their utility firms, often selling ownership to foreign MNEs.

Another tactic used by governments is to require MNEs and other firms that operate locally to obtain a substantial percentage of their inputs locally. In this manner, MNEs are compelled to carry out as much of the production process as necessary to reach the local content limit and/or to buy inputs from local suppliers. Thus, other local businesses are stimulated and a larger industrial sector is created. The supplier firms form part of the local infrastructure needed by MNEs to produce locally. The Venezuelan government, for example, requires that automobile firms obtain at least 40 percent of their sales value from local sources, either their own local production or purchases from local suppliers. General Motors, Toyota, and Jeep have expanded their local assembly operations to achieve the necessary level of local content under this rule.

Lack of Access to Developed-Country Markets   Even when LDCs make products that can be competitive in world markets, they face another disadvantage relative to MNEs. LDC firms generally lack the knowledge of market conditions in the industrialized countries that they need to build distribution networks there. The enormous competitive advantage gained by an MNE that operates a distribution network in several countries and passes information among its affiliates cannot be overemphasized. Without such networks, the LDC raw material supplier or manufacturer faces little chance of success in competing with the MNEs.

In response to this problem, a number of policies have been tried. One interesting example during the 1980s, a result of the Latin American debt crisis, was Colombia's requirement that any firm importing specified products into the country also had to find some product or service of equal value to export. This effort to balance trade and reduce the dollar outflow from Colombia was a form of barter or countertrade that attempted to gain the country better access to the markets of other countries.[10] Another example is the attempt made by many countries, especially in Southeast Asia and Mexico, to attract offshore assembly by MNEs. By positioning itself as a location for assembly of manufactured goods, the LDC gains not only new production and employment but also access to the developed-country markets via the MNE that takes the assembled goods and sells them abroad.

Unemployment   Unemployment is the last concern of LDCs that will be discussed here—though certainly not the last of the many difficulties faced by LDCs in seeking to improve their economic conditions. Rates of unemployment and underemployment in LDCs are estimated to be anywhere from a manageable 2–3 percent in such countries as Korea and Singapore all the way to 25 percent or more in such countries as Jamaica; and these rates are not even available from Ethiopia and Uganda. Thus, most LDCs experience far more unemployment than industrialized nations.[11] This issue represents a continuing critical problem for most LDCs, which look to MNEs as one source of additional jobs.

The main policy tool utilized by LDCs to push MNEs to hire as many locals as possible is the local labor requirement, under which limits are set on the use of expatriate staff. Typically, labor is required to be all local and management is required to be 90 to 95 percent local, depending on the country. Also typically, the MNEs have no trouble achieving these targets because they seldom transfer production workers overseas and because the high cost of using expatriates makes hiring local managers very desirable. The use of expatriate managers was a serious point of contention in the 1960s and 70s, when MNEs used far more of them, but most MNEs now have enough local managers in most countries to avoid conflict on this score.

A criticism of MNE employment practices in LDCs is that they are too capital intensive in countries where the abundant supply of labor calls for more labor-intensive production. This issue was discussed in Chapter 11 and will not be treated again here. In the present context, we are concerned with the fact that LDC governments are interested in stimulating MNEs to utilize more labor-intensive production and other activities. No specific policies to carry out this task are in wide use, probably because no one has been able to decide what **appropriate technology** really is. (For instance, more labor-intensive technology and production often leads to more costly products, which are not competitive in international markets.)

The Concerns of the Developed Countries   The previous categories covered only problems peculiar to LDCs. In addition, the less developed countries, like the industrialized countries, are concerned with their balances of payments, the distribution of the costs and benefits of MNE activities, and tax issues. Rather than repeat what has already appeared in Chapter 21, this section concludes with the reminder that the problems presented there also concern the LDCs.

Table 22–6 reviews the categories of problems specific to LDCs by presenting a selected listing of policies in 11 LDCs.

TABLE 22–6

Selected Policies in 11 LDCs

Country	Ownership Rules	Financial Controls	Technology Controls	Local Content Requirement	FDI Incentives
Brazil	No majority ownership in select industries	Foreign exchange and remittance controls	Technology transfer strictly regulated; some bans	Imposed in select industries; incentives	For investment in select regions
Chile	None	Limited exchange controls; few remittance restrictions	None	None, except in auto industry	Few; for mining, oil, technology
Egypt	Few legal limits; few 100% foreign firms exist	Foreign exchange controls; remittance limits	Some controls	None, but encouraged	Substantial
India	Most firms 40% limit	Foreign exchange controls; remittances scrutinized	Close scrutiny	Maximum use encouraged	Numerous and varied
Indonesia	Foreign firms must fade out to 49% in 15 years	None	Foreign ventures must bring technology and training	None	None
Israel	None	Some exchange controls	No approval necessary	None	Wide range in selected development areas
Korea	Foreign ownership restricted but not prohibited	Foreign exchange controls	Liberal licensing rules; technological imports encouraged	Generally quite high	Wide range
Mexico	Limited to 49% foreign in select industries	Foreign exchange controls	Must be registered	Strict rules under review due to entry into GATT	For export-oriented ventures
Nigeria	Some industries restricted	Some foreign exchange controls and remittance limits	Approval required	Tax incentives	For pioneer industries
South Africa	None	Foreign exchange controls; remittance restrictions	Licenses easily obtained	In auto industry	Area incentives
Venezuela	Majority ownership in select industries	Limited foreign exchange controls	Limited rules	In autos, some other industries	Some, generally in mixed participation, national countries

Source: Business International Corporation, *Investing, Licensing, and Trading Conditions* (New York: Business International Corporation, 1990).

Broad Development Policies and Their Implications for MNEs

Solutions to the specific problems presented above are often offered in broad, macroeconomic treatments of the development process that follow Keynesian, Marxist, monetarist, or other models. The Keynesian view, for example, calls for government spending to stimulate production and national income and for government policies that encourage exports and reduce imports. The Marxist view, on the other hand, calls for government control over the entire economy and for participation by foreign firms only as suppliers of products or services that the country cannot obtain elsewhere. The monetarist view focuses on the use of monetary policy as the key tool in shaping economic development. This view is espoused by many University of Chicago economists, whose policies have been a key basis for the development of Chile since 1973.[12] Other broad development perspectives have also been followed.

But even such perspectives change with changes in a country's economic situation. Chile, for example, shifted from fairly Keynesian policies in the 1960s, to Marxist policies under the Allende government, to monetarist policies under the subsequent military government, and again somewhat Keynesian policies under elected governments in the 1990s.

In the international sectors of their economies, LDCs have pursued two broad policies in the post–World War II period: import-substituting growth and export-led growth. **Import substitution** calls for policies subsidizing the local production of goods that are being imported and for limiting the importation of products that have been successfully introduced into local production. In the extreme, import substitution could lead to complete self-sufficiency, though the cost of producing some products locally (for example, mainframe computers, airplanes, and nuclear power plants) would be so high that the country would be better off if it continued to import them. The intent of import substitution is to alter a country's comparative advantages by subsidizing the start-up of industries that could in time become cost effective—that is, less expensive than if their products were imported. Thus, available foreign exchange could be used to import products that could not be produced locally without great cost, and the country would be better off.

Export promotion calls for subsidizing the production and export of whatever products can be made locally and sold competitively in international markets. This development strategy has the same general goal as import substitution, namely the creation of economically viable local industries that add income and employment to the country. Export promotion is a more outward-looking strategy, however, because it focuses on the production of exportable goods whose foreign exchange earnings can be used for further imports.

Foreign MNEs should be aware of the policy orientation of the host government as regards these two views of international business. The import-substituting country will most likely use high tariffs and other import barriers as a part of its international business policy. On the other hand, the export-promoting country will typically subsidize production and sale of exports, without limiting (to the same degree) imports that the firm may want to bring in. Over at least the past few decades, export-promoting countries have allowed foreign firms more opportunities to participate in the local economy, whereas import-substituting countries have reserved much more of the economy to local firms and have placed much more stringent limits on the activities of foreign MNEs. The broad trend of the early 1990s in LDCs clearly favors export-led growth.

ENTRY AND OPERATING STRATEGIES FOR MNES

Entry Strategies

The possible **entry strategies** for doing business in LDCs do not differ from those for entering industrialized countries, as they were presented previously. This section looks at some strategic considerations that may be important due to the relative political and economic instability of LDCs in comparison with industrialized countries. Because a change in government or any number of other factors can change the "rules of the game" rapidly and significantly, the MNE manager should consider measures to protect against risk at every stage of a project in an LDC. Government policies enacted to improve the balance of payments could cut off exports from some foreign affiliate of the MNE to its local LDC affiliate, which might affect the MNE drastically by eliminating its perhaps substantial imports. Foreign direct investment is, of course, subject to many more possibilities of adverse policy or other environmental changes, ranging from nationalization to a national depression caused by a worldwide decline in the prices of primary goods. Before entering into business in a less developed country, the MNE manager needs to plan for such potential problems.

The Obsolescing Bargain

Before deciding what protection plan for the business should be carried out in an LDC, the MNE manager should consider the firm's bargaining position relative to that of the host government. The firm is in a much different position *before* investing or setting up its other business activity in that country than afterward, when assets have been deployed and are committed to a particular use. For example, before setting up an oil refinery, an oil company possesses several desirable characteristics from the viewpoint of the host government. The company will bring in money, machinery, people who can train local workers and managers, access to foreign oil customers, and so on. With such a favorable set of components, the FDI project generally looks very desirable to a host government, and it can often be used to obtain very favorable tax treatment and other incentives for the MNE. Once the refinery is in place, however, the bargaining advantage shifts somewhat to the host government. Now the company has physical assets present in the country and links to its other operations elsewhere. The government can now raise taxes and impose other costs on the company, which is to some extent captive in the country. The MNE's bargaining power has faded away to some degree, or obsolesced. The **obsolescing bargain** is the "contract" between company and government that includes the rules under which the affiliate operates; very often those rules become much less favorable to the company once it has committed its assets and the government has gained a stronger position.

Operating Strategies

Once the firm has chosen an entry strategy and protected itself as well as it can against the problem of the obsolescing bargain, it must adopt an **operating strategy.** One consideration will continue to be the maintenance of a strong bargaining position relative to the host government. This can be accomplished through maximizing the use of the firm's competitive advantages, such as proprietary technology and its international information and distribution networks and other links to affiliates in other countries. The more ties the firm maintains to inputs and markets in other countries, the less the host country in question can constrain the MNE without facing a reduction in the benefits it obtains from the MNE's local operations. A clear example is that of offshore assembly. An MNE's local television assembly plant in Taiwan is probably fairly safe from the vagaries of government policy shifts, since any adverse regulation could cause the firm to shift its assembly to Singapore, South Korea, or Hong Kong, and in addition the main production inputs usually come from the home country and the market to be served is usually a developed country or countries. Each of these aspects of the business of offshore assembly gives the firm bargaining strength relative to that of the host government even after the plant has been established.

As in developed countries, the firm's operating strategies in LDCs may focus on cost minimization, product differentiation, or market segmentation. In the less developed countries, there is often a much greater possibility of market segmentation through government protection. That is, in LDCs, where governments play a much larger role in operation of the economy, firms may gain protected market positions by obtaining government contracts or by receiving government protection against competitors in exchange for setting up a local affiliate. Thus, although competition still plays a large role in LDC business, government policies can create profitable market niches for firms that plan carefully and negotiate skillfully for them.

In dealing with the particular risks inherent in LDC operations, the firm has many options. As with other risks, the firm may eliminate or reduce these risks by avoiding LDCs, by insuring the project with some public or private insurer, or by hedging the exposed assets with local liabilities. In addition, the firm can diversify its international activities into other countries so that a particular LDC does not affect too much of its total operations.

The hedging strategies for both political and exchange risks have been discussed previously. The governments of many industrialized countries offer commercial and political risk insurance to exporters and direct investors doing business with LDCs. In addition to the common financial hedges to offset exposed local-currency assets, such as local borrowing, MNEs have employed a variety of other strategies for dealing with this risk. When assets must be kept in the local currency, firms have generally tried to place investments in assets that tend to keep pace with local inflation, such as real estate, government-backed securities with values tied to inflation or the U.S. dollar, and the local operation itself.

DEALING WITH LDC GOVERNMENTS

The government is a much more important participant in the economies of most LDCs than in the economies of industrialized countries. For that reason alone, MNE managers in LDCs need to be extremely sensitive to the issue of government/business relations. In addition, because most MNEs are headquartered outside LDCs, they are viewed as "foreign" in the LDCs where they do business. Thus, relations with the government (and the public) generally play a much more important role in LDC business than in IC business. **Foreignness** may be the most important issue in dealing with LDC host governments.

Other central issues that create tensions in the relations between MNEs and LDC host governments include:

- MNE financial policies, especially remittances of earnings that contribute to capital outflow.
- MNE employment practices that result in fewer host country employees than the government would like and MNE use of technology that is more capital intensive than the government would like.

- The size of MNEs relative to the economic size of host countries, which gives MNEs substantial economic power.
- The multinationality of MNEs, which enables the home country parent to make decisions on activities in the host country and to transfer people, money, and other resources into and out of the host country—decisions that the government of the host country is unable to control.

To succeed in dealing with LDC governments, MNE managers need to understand both sides of these issues and to take steps that reduce the tensions they cause. The bargaining model presented in Chapter 25 goes some way toward generating an understanding of this crucial relationship. A few specific issues are noted here.

Company *financial policies* often focus on minimizing company assets in LDCs with rapidly devaluing currencies and unstable economic conditions. Host governments, of course, do not want to see funds outflows of this type, which exacerbate the capital flight problem, so they regularly look for ways to constrain firms from transferring their earnings abroad. The MNE manager needs to find ways either to reduce outflows or to generate funds inflows (for example, through exports) that will reduce BOP pressure on the host government. This is often a very difficult task for the affiliate manager, since the MNE home office would prefer to see as much of earnings as possible remitted from high-risk, rapid-devaluation countries. It might be argued that the MNE would be best off if it reinvested its earnings in the host country as wisely as possible and remitted some funds on a regular basis. Local asset values can often be maintained against devaluation, and by not contributing to capital flight, the MNE would create goodwill for its continuing activities in that country. This is by no means an ultimate solution for the MNE, but it may enable the firm to operate in an LDC on a continuing basis, with better government relations than it would have otherwise.

The *employment practices* of MNEs tend to be criticized mainly because of the high unemployment in LDCs and the high visibility of MNEs. In fact, several studies show that MNEs tend to offer better compensation and training to their LDC employees than do local firms.[13] The "appropriateness" of the technology used in the LDC operations of MNEs can always be debated, but if that technology enables the firm to operate efficiently and competitively, then it can be viewed as contributing to the country's ability to maximize use of its available resources. In many cases, MNEs perhaps need to make public the number of people they employ, so that host governments and pressure groups will be forced to recognize their contributions on this score.

The *economic power* possessed by MNEs can appear quite overwhelming to an outside observer. The annual sales of many firms are larger than the annual GDPs of many countries. The amounts that firms spend to construct facilities surpass the investment capabilities of many governments. What must be recalled is that each government has the power to set the rules of the game for business in its jurisdiction. So if any firm exercises economic power in some fashion unacceptable to the host government, that government can easily intervene to constrain the firm. Nonetheless, firms do possess bargaining strengths relative to host governments, and a government that wants to keep a firm operating locally cannot raise restrictions indefinitely. The result is a recurring set of negotiations and bargaining between the two sides over how the benefits and costs of the MNEs' activities should be distributed between them.

Multinationality is the final focal point of tensions between MNEs and LDC governments. A firm with access to funds, people, markets, inputs, and so on, outside the host government's jurisdiction, has a clear advantage over that government. This advantage cannot be completely negated, though international codes of MNE conduct creating a multinational government policy structure toward MNEs have been debated (and some have been enacted). At present, however, MNEs still occupy a position of strength on the basis of their multinationality, since the codes of conduct have not been able to limit their practices very much.[14]

CONCLUSIONS

Much more attention to government/business relations is required in LDCs than in industrialized nations. A wealth of government-owned companies, strict limitations on company activities, and frequent rule changes make the path of the MNE difficult in LDCs. Given the size of the government sector in most LDCs and the active roles that most LDC governments play in business, MNE managers need to pay close attention to these governments both as regulators and as customers.

At present, international business in LDCs accounts for less than a third of total international business. Since LDCs have most of the world's population and a large portion of its natural resources, they constitute valuable target markets and sources of production inputs. Thus, despite the difficulties of underdeveloped economic infrastructures and often changing regulations, LDCs present many opportunities to MNEs.

The MNE manager can gain important insights into the treatment that the MNE is likely to receive in a particular LDC by studying that country's process of economic development. An LDC that follows the path of import-substituting growth is likely to impose trade barriers and protect local industry against foreign competition. An LDC that uses an export-promotion strategy is likely to foster a much more open business environment. These two broad approaches to development give only a macro perspective on the LDC. The examination of other aspects of economic development theory and policy as they apply to the LDC may offer additional useful insights into the environment there.

MNE managers in LDCs will always face the problem of foreignness. No matter how responsive to host government rules and preferences the MNE may be, it still represents foreign owners and decision makers. The MNE manager must be aware of the tension that this foreignness may engender and must be prepared to minimize it when possible.

Regardless of the strategy that it adopts to do business in a less developed country, the MNE needs to consider methods of protection against political risk, exchange risk, and commercial risk. Those methods, which have been discussed in other chapters, should form a part of the total strategy for ongoing business in an LDC. Since the firm's ability to gain an advantage in dealing with the host government declines once it has committed real resources in the host country (and thus it faces the problem of the obsolescing bargain), it requires both entry and operating strategies for risk protection.

QUESTIONS

1. Define "less developed country." Does Nigeria fit into your definition? Does Singapore? How about Portugal? Kuwait? What is an appropriate measure of economic development?

2. Describe the development strategies called export promotion and import substitution. Has either of these strategies demonstrated better results than the other in the past half-century? Explain.

3. Would it be possible to use the development strategy of Hong Kong in another country, such as Costa Rica? Why or why not?

4. Present a strategy that AT&T or L. M. Ericsson could use to compete in the Indian market for telecommunications. Use information from the chapter about rules on foreign business in India.

5. What risks does an MNE encounter if it agrees to accept a local partner and enter an LDC market with a joint-venture manufacturing plant? Assume that the company produces chemicals. How can the MNE deal with these risks?

6. Name four main concerns of LDC governments in their dealings with foreign multinational firms. What can the firms do to minimize tensions with the host government with regard to each of these concerns?

7. Explain how the "obsolescing bargain" operated in the case of any multinational oil company that was nationalized by a host government. What can a company do once nationalization has occurred?

8. Again considering the obsolescing bargain, what can a company do to maintain its bargaining power even after it has committed resources to a plant or other facility in an LDC host country?

9. Create a market entry strategy for a small textile manufacturing company from a developed country that wants to enter the Indonesian or Taiwanese market for synthetic fabrics. Make necessary (reasonable) assumptions, so that your answer covers the organizational form of the venture, the channel of distribution, the structure of decision making in the firm, financial concerns, and any other issues that you consider important.

10. Explain how offshore assembly could be a viable strategy for a U.S.-based machinery manufacturer that wishes to enter the Jamaican market.

REFERENCES

Cline, William. *International Debt and the Stability of the World Economy.* Washington, D.C.: Institute for International Economics, 1983.

Grosse, Robert. *Multinationals in Latin America.* London: Routledge, 1989.

Hagen, Everett. *The Economics of Development.* 4th ed. Homewood, Ill.: Richard D. Irwin, 1986.

Hofheinz, Roy, and Kent Calder. *The Eastasia Edge.* New York: Basic Books, 1984.

Kobrin, Steven. *Managing Political Risk Assessment.* Berkeley: University of California Press, 1982.

Samuels, Barbara. *Managing Risk in Developing Countries.* Princeton, N. J.: Princeton University Press, 1990.

World Bank. *World Development Report, 1990.* Washington, D.C.: World Bank, 1990.

NOTES

[1]Roy Hofheinz and Kent Calder, *The Eastasia Edge* (New York: Basic Books, 1984).

[2]U.S. Department of Commerce, *Survey of Current Business,* August 1971 and August 1990.

[3]See, for example, Everett Hagen, *The Economics of Development,* 3rd ed. (Homewood, Ill.: Richard D. Irwin, 1980), chap. 15; and I. M. D. Little, *Economic Development* (New York: Basic Books, 1982), chap. 6.

[4]See Steven Kobrin, *Managing Political Risk Assessment* (Berkeley: University of California Press, 1982), concerning empirical measures of political instability leading to loss outcomes for firms.

[5]See ibid. concerning expropriations in the international oil industry.

[6]For example, see Michael Nowak, "Black Markets in Foreign Exchange," *Finance & Development* (March 1985).

[7]Capital flight is considered to be a central cause of the continuing Latin American debt crisis. See, for example, Donald Lessard and John Williamson, *Capital Flight and Third World Debt* (Washington, D.C.: Institute for International Economics, 1987).

[8]See, for example, Michael Porter, *The Competitive Advantage of Nations* (New York: Free Press, 1990), chapters 3, 4.

[9]Business International Corporation, *Investing, Licensing, and Trading Conditions* (New York: Business International Corporation, January 1985), Brazil section, p. 7.

[10]Business International Corporation, *Investing, Licensing, and Trading Conditions* (New York: Business International Corporation, December 1984), Colombia section, p. 29. Only some specific products are subject to this countertrade requirement, although the list has been expanding since its initiation in 1984.

[11]Unemployment rates are taken from International Labour Office, *Yearbook of Labor Statistics* (Geneva: ILO, 1983).

[12]See, for example, Norman Gall, "How the Chicago Boys Fought 1000% Inflation," *Forbes,* March 31, 1980.

[13]See, for example, Jerry Ingles and Loretta Fairchild, "Evaluating the Impact of Foreign Investment," *Latin American Research Review* (1978); and Robert Grosse, "The Economic Impact of Foreign Direct Investment: A Case Study of Venezuela," in Grosse (1988).

[14]See Robert Grosse, "Codes of Conduct for Multinational Enterprises," *Journal of World Trade Law* (Sept./Oct. 1982).

Advanced Chemicals in Peru

One day in the summer of 1984, Robert London, general manager for Advanced Chemicals Corporation's Latin American Division, was debating his future at the company. The company had been growing rapidly and profitably in Latin America when he had accepted the offer to head the regional staff. Over the past three years, however, virtually every country in the region had suffered severe recessionary problems and a need to restrict the transfer of dollars overseas. This situation had made it impossible for London to demonstrate an aggressive, creative management style. His main function for most of the three years had been to serve as Advanced Chemicals' senior representative to each government in the region, pleading for the right to repatriate funds and to carry on his business without excessive new restrictions. Only in the past few months had any real hope appeared for an end to the prevailing crisis conditions.

Of the countries under London's control, Venezuela and Argentina were the largest markets, followed by Colombia and Peru. (Advanced Chemicals used a regional X product matrix for its international organization structure. Brazil and Mexico were each treated as a separate region, reporting directly to the home office.) At this time, the home office was negotiating a large joint-venture petrochemical plant with PDVSA in Venezuela, so London did not consider it opportune to pursue that market separately in his planning. The economic and political conditions in Argentina presented such a huge risk to major investment that he felt obliged not to spend time planning any large-scale venture there. In fact, London felt that of all the countries under his supervision, Peru probably offered the best combination of market potential and currently small Advanced Chemicals commitment, so that he could make a mark by creating a solid plan for business in that country.

Advanced Chemicals had at one time owned an agricultural chemicals plant in Lima and a paint plant in Trujillo. Neither of these investments had been very large, and both had been sold in the early 1970s, during the height of anti-American fervor in Peru and Chile. In 1963 Advanced Chemicals had established a pharmaceuticals formulating plant as a 50–50 joint venture with a Peruvian firm, and this operation had survived both the political problems of the early 70s and the debt crisis of the early 80s. According to the most recent internal records of Advanced Chemicals, the Peruvian venture had contributed $1.5 million to annual income and represented assets of about $4.2 million. For a $9 billion company, this operation was a drop in the bucket.

This case was written by Professor Robert Grosse for use in class discussion, 1984.

FIGURE 1

ADVANCED CHEMICALS Consolidated Income Statement, 1983 (in $ millions)				
Net sales		$9,257		
Area sales:			Industry segment sales:	
United States	$4,528		Industrial chemicals	$4,387
Europe	3,016		Plastics	1,764
Canada	583		Specialty chemicals	1,351
Latin America	467		Agricultural chemicals	1,280
Brazil	214		Industrial equipment	475
All other	449			
Cost of goods sold		7,698		
Selling and administrative costs		911		
Operating income		648		
Interest income		108		
Exchange gains (losses)		36		
Net income before taxes		792		
Taxes due		264		
Net income after taxes		528		
Earnings per common share		1.72		

Advanced Chemicals periodically received requests from Peruvian companies to form joint ventures with them for producing products ranging from cosmetics to polyethylene. In London's thinking, the goal of a country strategy should be to focus on a small number of products with good local market potential and a good fit in the company's global product plan. With this in mind, he began to put together a plan for Peru.

About the Company

In 1983, Advanced Chemicals was the third largest U.S. chemical company and the fifth largest chemical company in the world. Its annual sales were just over $9 billion, and its global assets were valued at about $15 billion. It owned 74 foreign subsidiaries in 26 countries, and it held a minority interest in 8 more foreign ventures. (Figures 1 and 2 present 1983 income statement and balance sheet data for Advanced Chemicals.) Latin American sales accounted for about 5 percent of the sales total, and assets in Latin America constituted about 3 percent of Advanced Chemicals' assets worldwide.

Advanced Chemicals' first Latin American business was a polyethylene plant built near Mexico City in 1951. This plant supplied a wide variety of plastic products to Mexico and other Latin American countries. The current value of the plant was over $100 million. In 1953, Advanced Chemicals undertook its first direct investment in Brazil, a plant to manufacture agricultural chemicals that it built near São Paulo. Within five years, it built two additional plants in Belo Horizonte, to produce plastic resins and specialty chemicals. After a period of slow growth in these subsidiaries, business boomed in the mid-1960s. Between 1962 and 1971, Advanced Chemicals established sales offices in 10 more Latin American countries and built new plants in Argentina, Venezuela, and Chile. Except for plastics and agricultural chemicals, the firm exported from the United

FIGURE 2

ADVANCED CHEMICALS
Consolidated Balance Sheet
December 31, 1983
(in $ millions)

Assets

Cash	$ 215
Marketable securities	508
Accounts/notes receivable	3,080
Inventories	3,455
Plant and equipment	7,537
Deferred charges	288
Total assets	$15,083

Liabilities

Notes payable	$ 957
Accounts payable	1,975
Taxes due	528
Long-term debt	3,909
Deferred taxes	895
Stockholders' equity	6,819
Total liabilities	$15,083

States virtually all of the products that it sold in Latin America. At this time, it had the second largest sales volume of any multinational chemicals company in that region.

Advanced Chemicals was organized on the basis of five product divisions and six regional divisions, as shown in the organization chart in Figure 3. Each of the divisions was run as a profit center, with inconsistencies negotiated away at the home office in Chicago. Marketing responsibility for all products in the Latin American region was assigned to the division headquarters (as with other regions), whereas production of the five main product lines was determined primarily at each of the product division headquarters. While home office negotiations for corporate resources were highly competitive among divisions, the Latin American group had always been in a weak position because of its relative insignificance in the company's total business. Nonetheless, success in that division had historically meant a step into the corporate executive committee for the person in charge.

The company had always maintained a large team of research and product development scientists, aiming primarily to generate new products for traditional industrial customers in the automotive, construction, agriculture, and health care industries. About 5.3 percent of its annual sales were devoted to the R&D budget worldwide. Products developed in the previous 10 years had generated over 80 percent of Advanced Chemicals' profits during its 60-year history. On the whole, the products that Advanced Chemicals sold in Latin America had already been sold successfully in the United States for several years and were fairly mature in the product life cycle.

Marketing in the Latin American region was budgeted at the regional office level, but advertising and other local marketing activities were initially established by each national subsidiary. In countries with no affiliates, marketing policy was set at the regional office. The marketing effort had traditionally

FIGURE 3

Organization of Advanced
Chemicals

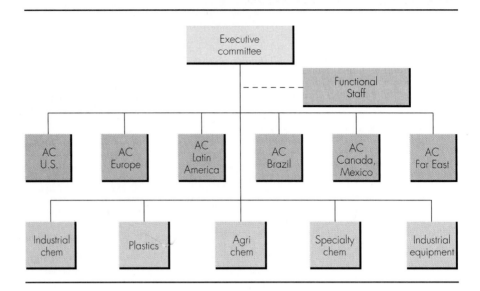

emphasized product quality and availability, though price had become a critical factor in the past five years. Marketing managers at the regional office spent their time mainly in offering advice to affiliate managers and in monitoring the sales of affiliates and distributors in the region. Except for the products produced locally and agricultural chemicals, there was no coordinated effort to promote other company products in the region.

About Peru

The Peruvian market for agricultural chemicals was dominated by foreign competitors, selling mainly fertilizers and pesticides. These products were usually not recent innovations, but rather products that had been used successfully in other countries for several years. Market share was highest for the two foreign firms that produced locally, though each of the eight main competitors had at least a 20 percent market share for one or more products.

The Peruvian market for plastics was also dominated by foreign multinational firms, though Petroperu (the state-owned oil company) was seeking to integrate downstream into this business. Again, the technology used in the products of interest was not new, and the main barriers to entry were the need for assured supply of feedstock, a distribution network for output, and basic capital costs.

Market segments existed for sales of other Advanced Chemicals products, but none of these segments appeared to be large enough to justify the planning and investment required for entry.

The following Appendix, an article from *Business Latin America*, provides some current information about the Peruvian economy and business conditions in general.

Business Outlook Peru[1]

Peru will be fighting its way out of a deep economic coma in 1984. Worse yet, it will try to mix a bitter dose of economy-stabilizing medicine with politicking for the presidential elections scheduled for 1985. Moreover, the global recovery will not boost Peruvian metals and minerals export prices until late in the year.

Also worrisome is the abrogation of a three-year Extended Fund Facility (EFF) with the IMF, which has stalled rescheduling negotiations with creditor banks for debt due in 1984 and frozen undisbursed monies from 1983 renegotiations. Even though the country will sign a one-year Fund standby agreement to replace the lost EFF, Peru will have a tough time arranging financing for a projected current-account deficit of close to $400 million.

Political situation. There is a 50/50 chance that the military will mount a preemptive coup if increased terrorism and broadened social upheaval further paralyze the government of Fernando Belaunde Terry. Heated campaign rhetoric pointing an accusing finger at the economic problems of the last few years could spark violent protest sufficient to goad the military into action.

Political and economic terrorism, emanating from the anarchic Sendero Luminoso, has spread into urban areas after being routed from the southern altiplano by a military sweep. Sendero will step up attacks on business operations, along with continued acts against utilities and military and police stations. MNC executives might be threatened by a rise in kidnapping. The undisciplined nature of recent military counterinsurgency efforts is a card in Sendero's favor; the armed forces risk spawning a broad-based rural guerrilla front should the present level of overkill in rural areas continue.

Barring a coup, politics will be heated and often bitter during the next year, as the contenders vie for power. The opposition center-left Alianza Popular Revolucionaria Americana (APRA) won a stunning victory in November's municipal elections, boosting the popularity of its leader, the youthful Alan Garcia, and giving the party a chance to win and take office for the first time in its history. While many think an APRA victory is assured, the most important question surrounds the party's choice of a coalition partner in Congress. The military would balk at a left-leaning bloc.

Belaunde's Accion Popular (AP) is reeling from its poor showing in last November's poll. In addition, internecine quarrels are debilitating the party and could leave it lifeless if the party does not find a unifying head for 1985.

The United Left (IU) placed Alfonso Barrantes as the Marxist mayor of Lima (where 42% of voters reside) and will run neck and neck with APRA through 1984. It is unlikely, though, that IU will figure into a coalition; the party will, however, be strong enough in Congress to influence policy. The other major party, the conservative Partido Popular Cristiano (PPC), will leave its partnership with AP in July to improve its chances for power.

Gross domestic product may show marginal growth but will be slow to recover from 1983's dramatic 13% decline. Growth will have to come from improved export prices, an upturn in the construction industry and agricultural production—socked by flood and drought last year. Some austerity in public spending will also cool recovery.

Industrial production will be flat—but a marked improvement on the 15% drop in output and market shakeout last year. Manufacturers will still cringe at the high cost of credit, but they will benefit from a rise in private consumption. Industry will finally get protection from cheap imports, which have hounded the sector since open competition began in 1981.

Textile manufacturers will increase production this year, benefiting from a countertrade deal with the USSR to cover arms imports. In addition, the sector will get a shot in the arm via higher levies on competing imports. However, a shortage of raw materials due to disease afflicting the cotton crop last year will mean higher imports; the resulting rise in costs could kill recovery.

The *chemical* industry will count on growth in agriculture to pull out of last year's doldrums. Those firms that can export will do well in 1984. *Pharmaceuticals* manufacturers will face more competition from generic imports as the government seeks to hold down costs of medicine subsidies. *Consumer goods* will benefit from a pickup in private consumption.

The *construction* industry, hammered last year by cutbacks in government contracts and foreign competition in ancillary industries, will rebuild thanks to protectionism and a rise in government-funded infrastructure and housing projects.

The *automotive* sector will no longer face unlimited competition from cheap imports. Local-content rules come on stream in 1984, and tariff hikes for finished imports will make locally produced cars more cost-competitive; nonetheless, sales will fall a further 20% unless purchasing power makes a dramatic comeback. Total 1983 sales were about 22,000 units (46% locally assembled), down 50% over end-1982.

Mineral production will remain steady—export volume rose an estimated 32% in 1983—but prices are the big question mark. Basic metals have not yet benefited from the global recovery. Shaky prices also mean a dearth of new investment and the shutdown of some government projects.

The 1984 government-spending program exonerates mining companies from a 5–10% export levy when prices fall below certain levels. Also, all export tax payments are credited against income tax.

Copper output will be up some 10% in 1984, after a 4% drop last year due to stagnant prices. Last year's output was 348,000 MT. *Silver,* on the other hand, could turn in a shining performance, with volume expected to increase 6% over last year, to 1.64 million fine kg, as prices rise steadily.

Iron ore output—3.5 million MT in 1983 (off some 7% from 1982)—will continue to drop this year owing to poor quality and lethargic markets. *Lead* production was up some 7% in 1983 and could rise by a similar amount this year—if prices go up. *Zinc* forecasts show a 5% price increase in 1984.

Petroleum output will be up some 4% this year. Flood-related disruptions knocked production down 11% to 174,000 bpd in 1983. Modest exports—around 30% of the total—are expected, maintained by a dampening local demand through dollar-pegged pump prices.

New investment prospects are getting tough competition from neighboring Ecuador, and Petroperu—the state oil company—will be pressing hard to discover new reserves. Proven reserve levels dropped to nearly 700 million bbl at end-1983, suggesting a need to import oil in the medium term.

Slightly over $200 million in new exploration investment is expected in 1984. Of that, Occidental Petroleum will invest around $100 million in jungle blocks; the firm will also upgrade existing wells and try to maintain current output at its old sites. Serpetro, Petroperu's technical subsidiary, may enter a $27 million joint venture with Hispanoil for seismic and drilling work. Belco plans to spend some $50 million on 32 new wildcats in 1984.

Agricultural production should rise 3% after last year's disastrous El Nino-induced weather wiped out most production for local consumption. The sector gets more emphasis and special credit facilities to upgrade existing enterprises in this year's budget. *Sugar* output will rise about 11% to around 500,000 MT, provided the weather holds, but an additional 16% will be imported to meet local demand. A high volume of other foodstuffs—rice, potatoes and consumable oils—will be imported.

The debt-laden *fishing* sector, once a major export earner, will be retooled away from fishmeal and into canning for local consumption as a result of severe 1983 losses. The disappearance of pilchard and anchovy resulting from the warm El Nino current wiped out the industry, and most fishing concerns will concentrate on meeting local consumption, with some exports of high-value shellfish products.

Investment. Public investment will be directed mainly at high-priority infrastructure rebuilding and new housing projects, with some upgrading of major hydroelectric and mining projects expected. Some S200 billion (S2,388:$1) in public bonds will be issued. Public investment equaled 7% of GDP last year, and it will be difficult for the government to prevent a widening of the budget deficit in an election year.

Private investment, normally heavily weighted to the petroleum sector, is another big question mark in 1984. Other private outlays will be in the form of reinvestment and will be contingent on perceived political risk and the cost of credit.

Labor costs will rise less than the rate of inflation, as high un- and under-employment—encompassing some 50% of the workforce—make job security a key concern. But the union movement will be highly politicized as workers flex their electoral power for the elections; union membership is expected to grow during the coming year. Labor will strike over the loss of purchasing power, as well as for political reasons. The APRA-affiliated CTP can be expected to do the party's bidding; rumors are rife that terrorists are infiltrating the communist labor confederation, CGTP. No changes are expected in the Labor Code or strike regulation law in this election year.

Prices will rise around 110% this year after a record 125% COL increase in 1983. Budget deficits in the range of 7–10% of GDP—mainly overruns in the bloated, inefficient state-company sector—were the main contributors, although the high cost of credit, currency devaluation, higher import costs, a strong dollar and gradual elimination of basic foodstuffs subsidies all fuel Peru's 70% structural inflation.

Credit availability will tighten and the effective cost of credit will increase—through up-front fees and daily interest charges. Dollar credit—now over 40% of the system's total—will remain expensive at about one to two percentage points above LIBOR. Dollar loans will get hit with an additional 0.25% levy on the total.

Imports and exports. Imports will drop another 6%—after a 23% fall in 1983—to around $2.5 billion, a response to higher costs and a move toward protectionism. Exports should rise more than 6% to $3.14 billion—after a 3.5% drop in 1983—as prices of metals and minerals begin to climb; full recovery in nontraditionals is still a ways off; oil exports remain stagnant. Peru's trade balance will be some $650 million in the black—on the heels of last year's $300 million surplus.

Exchange rate. The preannounced three-month exchange rate will be abandoned and minis reinstituted at or slightly above monthly inflation—with a possible maxidevaluation at the end of the first quarter. The sol fell nearly 130% last year, to S2,275:$1 at year-end, and is expected to drop to S4,800–5,000:$1 by end-1984.

Peru's *balance of payments* will continue to suffer from overborrowing by state companies and the high cost of credit. The country's loss of the IMF's EFF and its subsequent replacement with a one-year standby are making creditors edgy and reluctant to provide new loans. Foreign banks will lay out self-liquidating trade credit, but access to new monies needed for 1984—about $400 million—is jeopardized by uncertainty regarding the country's financial plans.

The current-account deficit could be as low as $400 million or as high as $1 billion in 1984, depending on whether new loans are forthcoming, undisbursed monies are released and the trade surplus increases by a healthy amount. It is highly likely, however, that a drawdown on reserves—$1 billion at end-1983—will be necessary in 1984.

NOTE

[1]Business International Corporation, *Business Latin America* (New York: Business International Corporation, February 1984), pp. 44–46.

Chapter

23

Eastern Europe and China

This chapter examines business conditions and opportunities for international firms that seek to do business in or with the formerly communist countries of Eastern Europe plus China. The key aspects of these countries for international business managers are presented and discussed. Most important, the role of private business in such countries is considered. Since many forms of international business are still restricted in these countries, emphasis is placed on those activities that are accessible to foreign firms. Methods for dealing with host country governments, which present huge political risks as they open their economies and societies, are presented. The main goals of the chapter are to:

1. Explain the characteristics of Eastern European countries that are important for international business managers.

2. Show what forms of international business are common and appropriate in these countries.

3. Consider entry and operating strategies for Western firms in this highly controlled environment.

4. Present an example of recent developments in Czechoslovakia, so that the international firm's manager will see the range of economic and political issues raised by the opening of this country to private-sector business.

INTRODUCTION

This chapter discusses the issue of doing business in Eastern European countries, which until 1989 operated as centrally planned economies. During the Cold War between the United States and the Soviet Union after World War II until the end of the 1980s, it was necessary to consider international business with the countries of the Soviet bloc as categorically different from that with noncommunist countries. Business transactions with partners in the Soviet bloc had to be considered form both business and political perspectives—that is, such dealings could be evaluated from the normal business view of profit/loss expectations; but they also had to be considered from the view of how such dealings affected the national interests of the home countries in the capitalist world. When capitalism and communism were vying for leadership in the world economy, the lead countries on each side routinely examined their economic interactions with the other side from a political viewpoint. That period of time was marked with numerous occasions on which business transactions were prohibited when one government or the other (usually the capitalist one) decided to impose political sanctions on the other.[1]

When Mikhail Gorbachev began his program of perestroika (economic opening) in the Soviet Union in 1985, the process of transition toward a market-based economic system in Eastern Europe began. In 1989, with the decisions of several Eastern European countries to form elected governments and to break away from the Soviet bloc—and the Soviet Union's decision not to interfere in this process—the "privatization" of the region began. The fall of the Berlin Wall, which separated East and West Germany, in November of 1989 symbolized the full-scale opening of Eastern Europe to elected governments and to market-based economies in which MNEs can play a much wider role than before.[2]

Because the Eastern European countries have just begun the process of capitalist development, the political risks involved in doing business there should not be underestimated. The large and fairly developed economies of this region appear quite attractive to firms from North America, Western Europe, and Asia— but the possibilities for changes in government policies toward business are huge. This issue must be confronted by any firm seeking to enter this large and potentially high-growth region.

This chapter is structured similarly to those on industrialized and less developed countries. The first section defines the countries of interest and typical forms of international business that occur there. The second section notes key characteristics of Eastern European countries plus China that affect the MNE. The third section discusses government policies toward foreign MNEs. The fourth section sketches entry and operating strategies for MNEs in Eastern Europe and China. Last, the example of Czechoslovakia is used as a basis for demonstrating some of the specific problems and opportunities experienced by MNEs seeking to do business in Eastern Europe today.

Definition of Eastern European Countries

The nations of concern in this chapter are the countries that formerly belonged to the Soviet bloc, plus the People's Republic of China. The definition of these countries is clear in this sense, though a lot of rhetoric has been produced on whether the countries should be called Central Europe or Eastern Europe. Since the Soviet Union indeed forms most of what could be labeled Eastern Europe, the former label makes sense. Since the Cold War terminology of East/West division is such an accepted part of our vocabulary, this chapter continues with the label "Eastern Europe" for discussing the Soviet bloc countries: USSR, Bulgaria, Czechoslovakia, Hungary, Poland, Romania, and Yugoslavia. The German Democratic Republic is *not* discussed other than in statistics, since it ceased to exist with the German reunification of 1990.

Selected countries in Eastern Europe plus China are listed in Table 23–1, along with some broad characteristics of their economies. While China alone comprises almost one fourth of world population, notice that it accounts for less than 5 percent of world GNP—China clearly is a less developed country. Also notice that the economies of the Eastern European countries have macroeconomic characteristics similar to those of their Western European neighbors, though with lower levels of per capita income, lower levels of international trade, and generally lower growth rates—these are clearly industrial countries.

During the period of the Cold War, business operated through government-owned and -managed companies, with decisions on pricing and production levels largely determined by the central planning organs, rather than by consumer demand.[3] Free enterprise remains substantially limited in these countries even today, since the government sector still owns most business, and the transition to greater private-sector participation is slow in its advance. However, this broad picture of communist countries fails to give an idea of the real possibilities that existed even before the fall of the Berlin Wall for noncommunist firms to carry out business with them. For that purpose, some evidence about the kinds of business that have taken place between MNEs and Eastern European countries in recent years will be useful.

Main Forms of International Business

Until 1990, very few examples existed of Eastern European countries allowing foreign firms to hold controlling ownership of business ventures within their borders. Prior to this time, and even today in terms of the bulk of ventures, most

TABLE 23–1

Economic Characteristics of the East European Countries and China

Country	GNP, 1989 ($ billions)	GNP per Capita, 1989 ($)	Real Growth 1989 Est. (%)	Inflation 1989 Est. (%)	Exports, 1988 ($ billions)
			Measure		
Bulgaria	51.2	5,710	−0.1	12	20.3
Czechoslovakia	123.2	7,878	1.0	1.5	24.5
East Germany	159.5	9,679	1.2	n.a.	30.7
Hungary	64.6	6,108	−1.3	18	19.1
Poland	172.4	4,565	−1.6	640	24.7*
Romania	79.8	3,445	−1.5	0*	11.5
Soviet Union	2,659.5	9,211	1.4	6	110.7
Yugoslavia	129.5	5,464	−1.0	2,700	13.1
China	350.0	320	11.2	19.5	59.4
European Economic Community†	4,059.7	12,514	3.5	3.7	1,055.4

*1987
†1988

Sources: International Monetary Fund, *Direction of Trade (1990 Yearbook)*; U.S. Central Intelligence Agency, *Handbook of Economic Statistics, 1989* (Washington, D.C.: CIA, 1989); *U.S. World Factbook 1990* (Washington, D.C.: CIA, 1990).

international business involving Eastern European countries is carried out through nonequity methods such as exports and imports, licensing agreements, management contracts, countertrade, and turnkey ventures, or through minority joint ventures.[4]

While historical data remain difficult to obtain about most business activities in Eastern Europe, export and import information is relatively accessible. Table 23–2 presents some of the main characteristics of *international trade* flows involving these countries. Until the end of the Cold War, most of the exports and imports in this region were shipped between Soviet bloc members; today trade has opened up very significantly with the rest of the world, though principally with Germany and other European Community members.

Much of the imports into Eastern Europe consists of manufactured goods, especially high-tech electronics, instruments, chemicals, and the like. Grain shipments from the United States and Canada also are an important part of such imports. Much of the exports from Eastern Europe consist of raw materials such as oil and natural gas (from the Soviet Union) and a variety of relatively low-tech, low-cost manufactures. In recent years exports of chemicals, food, textiles, and wood products from Eastern Europe to Western Europe have become very significant.

Other important categories of international business include **technology transfer agreements** in the form of licenses, turnkey ventures, and sales of process or product technologies. These are very common between East European purchasers and West European firms, but less so between U.S. firms and East European purchasers. Examples of these types of agreements are shown in Table 23–3. Generally, the agreements are between Eastern European purchasers and large, well-established Western (or Japanese) firms. The East European licensees tend to prefer dealing with sellers whose long-established track records for sales and service inspire confidence that they will remain accessible to meet future needs.

TABLE 23–2A

International Trade by Eastern European Countries and others, 1989 (in millions of U.S. dollars)

From	To: Czechoslovakia	GDR	Hungary	Poland	Romania	USSR	China	Yugoslavia	US	EEC
Czechoslovakia	—	n.a.	486	618	520	n.a.	469	446	86	2,580
GDR*	n.a.	—	591	499	906	n.a.	300	268	143	1,618
Hungary	593	607	—	229	186	2,890	115	359	290	2,448
Poland	785	577	289	—	175	3,269	352	339	357	4,051
Romania	528	863	144	150	—	4,340	380	142	353	2,510
USSR	n.a.	n.a.	2,219	2,625	3,515	—	1,768	2,040	713	14,957
China	374	326	83	374	265	1,699	—	25	3,988	4,720
Yugoslavia	404	311	285	433	118	2,699	60	—	697	5,234
United States	54	94	122	414	156	4,271	5,807	501	—	86,570
EEC	2,609	1,799	3,288	4,323	758	13,769	6,912	7,420	84,477	

*The German Democratic Republic formally reunited with the Federal Republic of Germany on October 5, 1990.
Source: International Monetary Fund, *Direction of Trade (1990 Yearbook).*

TABLE 23-2B

International Trade of Eastern European Countries and China by Industry, 1987 (in millions of U.S. dollars)

	USSR	Czechoslovakia	GDR	Hungary	Poland	China
Exports						
Machinery and equipment	16,721	14,231	14,755	6,355	15,530	3,220
Fuels, minerals, metals	56,098	3,018	5,133	2,022	3,555	8,595
Agricultural and forest products	6,372	1,448	2,090	4,279	1,259	5,850
Manufactured consumer goods	3,716	3,877	4,918	3,268	3,531	9,930
Imports						
Machinery and equipment	39,746	9,104	10,568	5,537	8,130	14,855
Fuels, minerals, metals	10,465	8,836	11,777	4,304	7,971	3,895
Agricultural and forest products	16,725	2,612	4,060	2,673	2,786	2,325
Manufactured consumer goods	13,680	1,391	1,767	1,892	2,147	10,700

Source: Central Intelligence Agency, *Handbook of Economic Statistics, 1989* (Washington, D.C.: CIA, 1989).

TABLE 23-3

Licensing Agreements between Western Companies and East European Countries plus China

Company	(Date)	Country	Product
Coca-Cola (United States)	(1988)	Czechoslovakia	Soft drink formulas
Cypress Semiconductor (United States)	(1990)	USSR	Circuit designs
Hitachi (Japan)	(1989)	China	Videotape recorders
Italmachiniplan (Italy)	(1988)	USSR	Leatherware
Marubeni Deutschland (Germany)	(1988)	USSR	Methaneite production
Mercedes-Benz (Germany)	(1988)	China	Trucks
Micropro (United States)	(1988)	Hungary	Wordstar technology
Necchi (Italy)	(1990)	USSR	Refrigerator compressors
Nokia Cables (Finland)	(1990)	USSR	Soviet cable technology
Occidental Petroleum (United States)	(1988)	China	Phosphoric acid production
Philips (Netherlands)	(1988)	China	Exchange boards
Philips (Netherlands)	(1988)	USSR	Semiconductor technology
Pierre Cardin (France)	(1988)	Hungary	Clothing manufacturing
Polaroid (United States)	(1988)	China	Cameras
Sani-Serv (United States)	(1988)	Poland	Fast food
Satic (Portugal)	(1988)	Hungary	Hungarian irrigation technology
Sifco (United States)	(1989)	China	Forging
Snecma (France)	(1989)	China	Jet engine technology
Snia Engineering (Italy)	(1990)	USSR	Paper for currency
Technip (France)	(1989)	China	Ammonia and urea complex
Toyota (Japan)	(1989)	China	Automobiles
Vestra Union (France)	(1988)	USSR	Clothing manufacturing
Vivat Holdings (Great Britain)	(1988)	Czechoslovakia	Jeans

Source: Paul Surovell (ed.) INTERFLO, 1988–1990.

Joint ventures are another category of international business that has been growing between East European partners and multinational firms from Western Europe, North America, and Japan. McDonald's restaurant in Moscow, which opened in 1990, is a good example of the new wave of foreign business entries that have begun to operate as foreign-owned (in this case 49 percent owned by McDonald's Corp.). While full or majority ownership still is not commonly permitted to foreign firms, joint ventures are proliferating in East Europe. A few examples of such ventures are listed in Table 23–4. Like the technology transfer agreements, these joint ventures tend to involve very large, experienced MNEs. Most of the joint ventures are very large, since the Eastern European governments have tended to prefer attracting a small number of foreign participants

TABLE 23–4

Joint Ventures between Western Companies and Eastern European Countries plus China

Company	Country	Name and Date of Joint Venture	Ownership (West/East)	Product
Agfa-Gevaert & Vienna Trade	Hungary	Asi (1990)	50/50	Market and service business equipment
Avibras Aerospacial (Brazil)	China	INSCOM (1989)	n.a.	Market communication satellite launching
Bouygues (France)	Bulgaria	Interstroy (1989)	n.a.	Commercial construction
Central Cooperative Bank (Austria)	Czechoslovakia	Gestin (1989)	n.a.	Tourism
Ciba Geigy	China	No name (1988)	n.a.	Pharmaceuticals
Fiat (Italy)	USSR	No name (1989)	30/70	Automobiles
GEC Plessey (Grt. Britain)	USSR	Comstar (1989)	n.a.	Telecommunications
Highmed System (Canada)	Hungary	Rolitron (1989)	n.a.	Dialysis equipment
Hyundai (South Korea)	USSR	No name (1990)	n.a.	Lumber production and ship repair
IKEA (Sweden)	Poland	No name (1989)	n.a.	Furniture
J. L. Forklift Tryk (Denmark)	Bulgaria	No name (1990)	50/50	Forklift trucks
Johnson & Johnson (U.S.)	China	No name (1988)	n.a.	Bandages
Kiser Research (U.S.)	Hungary	CompuDrug USA (1988)	n.a.	Computer software
Levi Strauss (U.S.)	Hungary	No name (1988)	50.6/49.4	Clothing
McDonald's (U.S.)	USSR	No name (1988)	49/51	Restaurants
Minolta (Austria)	USSR	Minolta Trading Ukraine (1990)	33/67	Service office equipment
Minolta Camera (Japan)	USSR	No name (1990)	n.a.	Copiers
Northern Telecom (Canada)	China	No name (1988)	n.a.	Communications equipment
Occidental Petroleum (U.S.)	China	No name (1988)	55/45	Coal plant
Pepsico & McCormick (U.S.)	China	No name (1988)	n.a.	Seasoning manufacturing
Philips (Netherlands)	Czechoslovakia	Avez (1989)	n.a.	VCRs
Rhone-Poulenc (France)	Hungary	Rhone Poulenc Agro Borsod (1990)	50/50	Plant production agent
Samsung (South Korea)	Hungary	No name (1988)	n.a.	Color TVs
Schwinn (U.S.)	Hungary	No name (1989)	51/49	Bicycles
Senetek (Denmark)	Czechoslovakia	Tessek (1989)	n.a.	Chemicals
Siemens (Germany)	Yugoslavia	No name (1989)	n.a.	Telecommunications
Siemens (Germany)	Poland	No name (1990)	49/51	Digital exchanges
U.S. West (U.S.)	Hungary	No name (1990)	49/51	Cellular telephones
Valmet Paper (Finland)	China	No name (1988)	n.a.	Machinery
Warner Lambert (U.S.)	China	No name (1989)	n.a.	Pharmaceutical capsules

Source: Paul Surovell (ed.) INTERFLO, 1988–1990.

that can generate large amounts of production of known quality. This situation is changing, as the countries open their economies to more foreign as well as domestic, private-sector business under more kinds of agreements.

General Electric Company carried out one of the major joint ventures in Eastern Europe during the early 1990s with its purchase of 50 percent of the Hungarian lighting manufacturer, Tungsram. This $U.S. 150 million investment gave GE a major foothold in the European market for light bulbs, which GE has not served through local production for several decades. General Electric is using the venture to serve both the domestic Hungarian market and the European market for light bulbs from Tungsram's 12 manufacturing plants, adding to GE's European lighting business. Although the means of payment of dividends from Hungary was not known, it is likely that payment in light bulbs that can be sold elsewhere in Europe would suit both GE's and Hungary's interests.[5]

KEY CHARACTERISTICS RELATING TO MNEs

Concept and Function of the Marketplace

As the Eastern European countries moved from communist economies to more market-oriented systems at the end of the 1980s and into the 1990s, the role of the marketplace in society began to be redefined. This process is still underway, and it remains to be seen just how large the market's role becomes in each country and how market forces are controlled through public policy. These countries still remain highly centralized, with most business carried out through state-owned enterprises and with highly bureaucratized policy controls on business.

Despite this broad reality, even during the Cold War East European countries did not completely ignore market signals. Market activities existed in each of the countries before the dramatic shift in governments in 1989. Especially in China and Yugoslavia, there were and continue to be industrial firms partially or totally owned by individuals rather than by the state. In the 1980s there were numerous examples of Chinese experiments in capitalism through small, individually owned companies as well as efforts by state-owned enterprises to operate in Hong Kong, a British colony that will revert to Chinese control in 1997. Even before the large-scale economic opening in the Soviet Union, farmers were given the opportunity to produce some crops for their own account, in addition to their main jobs in communes or cooperative farms.[6] These examples have mushroomed into many more and larger businesses, as the formerly communist nations build their market systems.

In order to buy from and sell to Western firms, the formerly communist countries have always had no choice but to function in the market system. While production within the Eastern European countries and China remains primarily state-owned even now, export sales to the West and import purchases from the West are conducted along more or less market-based lines. That is, exports must be sold through a marketing effort to find and contract with Western purchasers, and imports must be contracted and paid through market-based trade financing methods (although the specific financing methods include much more countertrade and forfaiting than are used in Western Europe, North America, or Japan). This means, essentially, that international business opportunities do exist for Western firms in the formerly communist countries even before domestic business opportunities open up through changed legislation and policy that permit development of internal market economies.

Social and Cultural Differences

Social and cultural differences unquestionably play a major role in business between Eastern European and outside partners, whether from Western Europe, North America, or Japan (the main sources of ventures in Eastern Europe today). Business practices in the formerly communist countries remain highly bureaucratized, since the managers of newly developing firms were largely trained in running state-owned enterprises. In addition, the government remains the largest business owner and operator in all of these countries for the near future.

In addition to the differences in business practices, the problems of language, social practices, and ethnic preferences must be faced in business with Eastern Europe and China. Overcoming the substantial hurdles involved in doing business in these countries requires both an ability to deal with the rapidly changing business systems and an ability to cope with language differences, consumers who formerly had little experience in market transactions, and ethnic groups who make a country such as the Soviet Union really a group of markets rather than one homogeneous one.

One study examined the factors that influence success in business negotiations with the Chinese.[7] The study found that knowledge of Chinese business practices was very important to success but that knowledge of Chinese social customs and language was relatively unimportant. The Chinese were apparently more interested in the characteristics of the product or service than in the supplier's ability to communicate well in Chinese or to "fit in" socially. (This finding may be biased, however, because only Western firms were polled, and not Chinese partners.) The conclusion to draw here is that social and cultural differences do matter, and in particular that the issues related to differences in business practices are most important.

GOVERNMENT POLICIES AND CONCERNS RELATED TO MNEs

Government participation in business is moving from state ownership of virtually all business to a more regulatory environment, as in the countries of Western Europe. China is obviously the exception, with a communist government still in power in the early 1990s. Excepting China then, the Eastern European countries are reducing the role of the state as owner of industrial enterprises and replacing that ownership with regulation. Market transactions are permitted and even encouraged, with the state retaining the role of overseer, promoter of selected sectors, and still part owner of many businesses. (The process of change after many decades of operating communist economies is not likely to be quick and easy; hence, foreign firms must not expect to find the opportunities for market access and "normal" (capitalist) business practices to be anything other than time-consuming and arduous.)

Perhaps the most important concern for MNEs seeking opportunities in Eastern Europe are the political risks involved. Because the transition from communist to more market-based economic systems is only recently underway, it is not possible to anticipate future shifts in policy toward business. Most of that policy is being defined at present. While Cold War problems such as the huge losses suffered by Caterpillar and General Electric in their contracts to supply the Soviet natural gas pipeline project (see box) may be gone, other problems will surely arise. The economic downturns suffered during the transition to market systems will undoubtedly result in government policy shifts, some of which may harm the interests of foreign MNEs.

IB
ILLUSTRATION

The Soviet Gas Pipeline Controls

The difficulty of choosing and implementing U.S. economic policy with respect to the Soviet Union is well illustrated by the restrictions placed in 1981–82 on the participation by U.S. companies in construction of a natural gas pipeline from the USSR to Western Europe.

After the Soviet invasion of Afghanistan in 1979, President Carter imposed a variety of restrictions on the dealings of U.S. firms with the Soviet Union. Beginning with the highly visible and politicized boycott of the 1980 Olympic Games in Moscow, the Carter administration sought to cut back on U.S. business with the USSR. Actually, few limitations other than denying the American athletes permission to participate in the Games were imposed at that time—despite public rhetoric to the contrary. Grain shipments and the sale of nonmilitary goods continued through 1980.

When President Reagan took office in 1981, he moved to use U.S. economic policy to put pressure on the Soviet Union. Following the crack-down on the Solidarity union in Poland by the Soviet-backed government in December of 1981, he imposed an embargo on U.S. goods shipped for the construction of a pipeline connecting Russian oil and gas suppliers with Western European markets. The embargo was lifted in November 1982. During the year of the embargo, such American firms as General Electric and Caterpillar lost contracts for shipment of industrial and construction equipment worth over $2 billion.

Initially, General Electric and other U.S. suppliers tried to switch the production of their equipment out of the United States into their European subsidiaries, to avoid the U.S. rules. By June 1982, the embargo was extended to cover the overseas affiliates of firms that operated in the United States. This policy led to a large number of lawsuits seeking to enjoin the U.S. government from extending its jurisdiction outside the country. Before the issue could be resolved in court, the sanctions were eliminated. By this time, however, GE and Caterpillar, among other U.S. firms, had lost very substantial business.

The political risk presented by conflict between the superpowers clearly placed U.S. firms at a disadvantage relative to European and Asian suppliers to Eastern European customers. It appears that additional business was lost to U.S. firms as a result of the pipeline incident, since bids for future projects have gone increasingly to non-U.S. suppliers. This claim is difficult to document, but the evidence seems to support it. Komatsu (Caterpillar's main competitor worldwide) received an additional $800 million of Soviet contracts in 1982 and 1983, while Caterpillar's Soviet business dropped off dramatically. Similarly, some of GE's European competitors gained major new contracts for Soviet sales, while GE's Soviet business declined for several years.* ■

*For more details on this situation, see David Yoffie and Sigfrid Bergenstein, "The Soviet Gas Pipeline," Harvard Business School case #9-384-007.

Growth Policies

As the Eastern European countries attempt to place their economies on a competitive basis with respect to Western European countries, the main kinds of international business that are actively pursued will likely be those that help to develop the industrial base in each country. With relatively low wages and other production costs, plus relatively low-tech manufacturing facilities in place, these countries can be expected to follow comparative advantage into export of fairly standardized goods and ones based on their abundant natural resources. In particular, as noted in Table 23–2B, Eastern European countries are exporting petroleum-based products (especially from the Soviet Union) and some manufactured goods, while importing electronic and other high-tech products plus grains (especially from the United States).

The specific growth plans established by each of the formerly communist countries are likely to vary substantially between countries. The Soviet Union is a large oil exporter, and so can count on significant foreign exchange earnings from that source. Czechoslovakia produces no oil, but has a relatively more modern industrial base; thus exports of manufactured goods are likely to be a mainstay of that country's trade balance. All of these countries face an inability to generate adequate foreign exchange to meet their demands for imported industrial machinery to build infrastructure and other import needs; paying for these imports will continue to be a major stumbling block to MNEs seeking to operate there.

ENTRY AND OPERATING STRATEGIES FOR MNEs

Entry Strategies

Unquestionably, the most difficult aspect of doing business in Eastern Europe and China today is gaining access to the market in the target country. Because of the time and money necessary to pursue this kind of business, small firms and firms with a need for short-term results face an extremely difficult situation. Business with Eastern European countries and China therefore tends to be the province of large, experienced MNEs that are willing to negotiate for protracted periods and to incur large precontract costs and that can then provide large volumes of sales or large-scale projects to their Eastern partners.

The range of **entry strategies** available depends greatly on the specific country and on the time when entry is sought. Access to the country's market is generally easier when the availability of foreign exchange reserves is less limited (just as in the rest of the world, but exacerbated here where there has been little history of borrowing from foreign private-sector banks). Foreign ownership remains limited de facto to minority joint ventures in most cases, though exceptions are beginning to appear, especially outside of the Soviet Union. In broad terms, the possible entry strategies do not include wholly owned ventures but virtually all other kinds of international business vehicle. The most frequent kind of entry remains importing; but numerous industrial cooperation agreements such as licenses, joint ventures, and countertrade arrangements are being used. Table 23–5 portrays the legal environment facing foreign investors in 1990.

The competitive advantages that appear most useful in doing business in Eastern Europe and China are proprietary technology, managerial experience in dealing with these countries, the ability to commit human and financial resources for several years before concluding a business agreement, and the availability of a multinational marketing network that can be used to sell

TABLE 23–5

Eastern Europe's Morning After: How the East Will Be Won Conditions for foreign investment in Eastern Europe

	Poland	USSR	Hungary	Yugoslavia	Bulgaria	Czechoslovakia	Romania
Ownership permitted foreign partner in joint venture	Min. 20% or investment of US$50,000	No limits	Min. 20%	No limits	No limits	Max. 49%	Max. 49%
Corporate tax rate	30%	30%	40%	23–30%	30%	50%	30%
Years of tax-exempt status	3–6	2–3	Up to 5	3	None	None	Up to 5
Average tax rate on foreign partner incomes	30%	20% (in Far East 3%)	10–20%	20%	10–30%	25%	10% when income is transferred abroad
Conditions for repatriating profits	No charge if company holds surplus of foreign currency	Transfer possible after taxation of dividend	Must transfer through central bank	No limits	Transfer possible after taxation of dividend	Transfer possible after taxation of dividend	Transfer possible after taxation of dividend
Number of joint ventures and foreign enterprises (Spring 1990)	1150	1200	1000	7900	35	50	Officially 8, actually 3 or 4
Foreign capital currently engaged (in millions)	$200	600	600	8550	15	25	20
Industries with highest foreign investment	Food, garment, lumber, trade, construction	Machine/tool, electrical, raw materials	Food and agriculture, chemical, machine/tool	Food and agriculture, trade, services	Chemicals, electronics	Machine/tool	Machine/tool, food and agriculture

Source: *Banking Gazette, Poland* as reproduced in *The WorldPaper* (Boston, Mass.: World Times, Inc.), October 1990.

countertraded products. These competitive advantages are mentioned frequently in discussions of existing ventures of MNEs in Eastern Europe and China, such as the licensing agreements and joint ventures listed above and the countertrade deals listed below.

Operating Strategies

Given that Western-owned facilities are the exception rather than the rule in Eastern European business, most of the **operating strategies** used by MNEs in their dealings with these countries relate to contractual ventures. That is, the ventures are export/import contracts or technology transfer agreements, for which the MNE must negotiate initial conditions and evaluate performance, but not actually manage a facility in Eastern Europe. Operating strategies in this context involve the collection of payments for exports or licensing fees. The joint ventures that do exist have tended to be managed to a significant extent by the East European partner up to now—but this relationship is changing as the economies continue to open and as the ventures adopt market-based strategies. A major concern for the MNE is the relationship with the East European partner, that is, getting a highly bureaucratic system to make decisions, getting the government to issue permissions to import, pay suppliers, and carry out other necessary parts of a project, and especially maintaining good relations in such a rapidly changing environment as the rules on business evolve.

Two major kinds of international firm are developing business in Eastern Europe and China. First, the traditional multinational enterprises such as Coca-Cola, American Express, General Motors, Marriott, and others are exploring direct investments to produce their traditional products and services to serve these newly accessible markets. General Motors, for example, contracted in 1990 to invest more than $U.S. 150 million in an engine manufacturing plant and a components plant in Hungary. Dow Chemical similarly has contracted to build a $U.S. 16 million plastics-making joint venture in Hungary, as well as to build a $U.S. 1 billion plant in the Soviet Union.[8]

Second, firms run by people with family ties to Poland, Hungary, China, etc., are pursuing both market-serving investments to build on their managerial expertise and knowledge of language and customs, as well as offshore production facilities to benefit from low-cost labor in those countries. These ventures have become quite frequent in China, where Hong Kong and Taiwan Chinese people have established offshore manufacturing plants and some local market-serving ventures. Such ethnic ventures are equally likely to develop in Eastern Europe, as those countries permit more direct investment in the 1990s.

Dealing with Political Risk

Political risk in East-West business arises from two important sources: the host government and the home government. The Soviet natural gas pipeline discussed above presents a clear example of the home-country risk involved in doing business with a country that subsequently becomes alienated from the MNE's home government. This phenomenon is not limited to communist countries; many MNEs have suffered from home-country policies aimed at the government of South Africa, the government of Iraq, and others through the years.

Host governments cause political risk in Eastern Europe simply because the policy regime is in such a state of change. Unless important policy changes can be predicted successfully, they will remain as a serious risk in this region.

In China, which remains a communist country, the risks are more pronounced, since both home and host governments could intervene in an MNE's Chinese business for political reasons or for economic reasons. The Tienanmen Square incident in 1989 demonstrated the kind of political event that could lead to Western government sanctions on China, as well as signaling a Chinese government position that could easily become anti-foreign in its business policy.

These political risks can be handled in various ways. First and most obviously, the firm can avoid the risks by avoiding business in these countries. Second, the firm can look for insurance companies to transfer the risk via insurance policies. (OPIC today offers some coverage of investments in Eastern Europe, and EXIMBANK likewise has some trade financing guarantees available for sales to these countries.) Third, firms can adapt their ventures to reduce the political risks through selling accounts receivable from Eastern Europe buyers to intermediaries such as banks, factoring companies, and forfaiting companies (on a nonrecourse basis). They also can look for local liabilities to offset local assets in the same country. Finally, the political risk can be diversified by having operations in other countries that diminish the impact of Eastern European business on the firm's total activities.

Countertrade and Other Efforts to Obtain Credit

Credit is a major concern of Eastern European countries. There is far more demand for Western products in Eastern Europe than the reverse. Because foreign exchange markets are in the process of opening, foreign currencies are generally scarce and expensive. China's yuan remains inconvertible at this time. In sum, access to acceptable means of payment will continue to be a problem in these countries in the near future.

One method that is used to avoid immediate payment in dollars or other hard currency is to finance imported purchases with bank credit or **supplier credit.** Another method is to force Western exporters to accept payment in products rather than money (i.e., *countertrade*). Both of these methods are widely used in East/West trade and other East/West business arrangements.

Some of the countertrade agreements that have been made over the years are quite colorful. Pepsi-Cola agreed to sell its soft drink in the Soviet Union and to receive payment in Stolichnaya vodka. Fiat set up an automotive plant also in the Soviet Union, and received payment for the plant in cars. The German manufacturer, Krupp, sold industrial machinery to Hungary in exchange for canned ham, steel wool, and several other products. Other, more prosaic and more recent ventures are listed in Table 23–6.

Bank financing for importers in Eastern Europe was fairly widely available for many years, due to the countries' histories of creditworthiness. During the international debt crisis of the early 1980s, several of the Eastern European countries were forced into rescheduling of their foreign bank loans, with Poland and Romania facing the most difficult situations, which have not yet been resolved. In the late 1980s, commercial bank lending to the region began to expand again. While acceptance financing for exporters to Eastern Europe is not commonly available, receivables can often be discounted through forfaiting companies, most of which are affiliated with large banks anyway. (*Forfaiting* is discussed in Chapter 19.)

TABLE 23–6

Selected Countertrade Deals between Eastern and Western Partners

Company	Country	Date	Products Involved
Agresco (Israel)	USSR	1990	Israeli fruits and vegetables for Soviet goods to be determined
Asahi Tsushin (Japan)	China	1989	Swap TV shows and movies between the two countries
Imar & Brital (Italy)	USSR	1988	Italian building for Soviet souvenirs
Israel Citrus (Israel)	Yugoslavia	1988	Israeli fruit for Yugoslav wood
Leyland Daf (Great Britain)	China	1988	British trucks for frozen prawns and human hair
Miju (South Korea)	USSR	1990	Korean shampoo for Soviet vodka and beef tallow
Nippon (Japan)	China	1989	Japanese switchboards for Chinese circuits
Philips (Netherlands)	Albania	1988	Dutch electronic components for Albanian cement and tobacco
Pig Improvement Co. (Great Britain)	Cuba	1988	British breeding pigs for Cuban sugar
Sov Nor Shipping (Norway)	USSR	1989	Soviet ships, US fast food, and Bermudan and Norwegian shipping
World Class Products (United States)	USSR	1989	Taiwan sewing machines for Soviet handicrafts through U.S. company

Source: Paul Surovell (ed.) INTERFLO, 1988–1990.

Western exporters frequently offer trade credit to their Eastern European buyers. Such terms are common, since sales tend to be large and competition from other Western firms is often substantial.

Even with all of these methods for dealing with financing problems, difficulties remain. The weak economies of this region (and China) make exporting difficult, and thus paying for imports remains a problem. Frequent hard-currency shortages put pressure on Western exporters to arrange complex countertrade transactions. In sum, financing is a key problem in business with Eastern Europe and China today.

AN EXAMPLE–DOING BUSINESS IN CZECHOSLOVAKIA

Czechoslovakia is the third largest East European country, after the Soviet Union and Poland. Its population was 15.6 million and its GDP in 1989 was $U.S. 123 billion. The country had been under communist rule since 1948. Beginning in 1987, the communist government began a process of economic reforms that reflected earlier attempts at liberalization that had been crushed by the Soviet Union in 1968. Following a visit by Soviet President Mikhail Gorbachev, who urged faster progress to open the economy, the process of political and economic change escalated, culminating in the rejection of communist one-party rule in November of 1989. Vaclav Havel, a noted playwright, was elected President in December 1989. In mid-1990 the first free elections since 1946 were held, confirming Havel's presidency.

During 1990, with the newly elected president and parliament, Czechoslovakia embarked on a pathbreaking and massive strategy to develop a market economy. The economic reform package adopted in 1990 established the legal basis for private enterprise, joint stock companies, open foreign trade, and a reduced role of the central planning apparatus. What does all of this mean to interested firms from the market-economy countries?

First and foremost, the Czech economy remains primarily centrally planned and limited in its accessibility to Western firms. Most companies in Czechoslovakia are government-owned, although a process is underway to privatize most of the major and many of the smaller industrial firms. When government ownership is sold to the private sector, first right to purchase shares is offered to Czechs. For the next several years, the character of the economy will still be dominated by state-owned firms—even though the extent of central planning is being reduced, and the state-owned firms should begin to operate on a more competitive basis.

Second, access to foreign exchange remains a problem. On January 1, 1991, the koruna became convertible within Czechoslovakia. However, the shortage of foreign currency has not disappeared, and thus access to official dollars, Deutsche marks, etc., is heavily restricted. Also, the official exchange rate used to buy foreign currency is far below (fewer dollars per koruna) the market rate (as evidenced in the black market). Together these two factors mean that profit remittance, purchase of imports into Czechoslovakia, and other foreign exchange demands will be significantly limited for at least the next few years. Countertrade and other creative financing methods will continue to be crucial parts of business strategy for operating in this country.

Historically, before 1948, Czechoslovakia's most extensive international business contacts have been with its neighbor, Germany. This linkage is likely to revive, as German companies take the lead in establishing joint ventures, industrial cooperation agreements, and other alliances with Czech firms and government agencies. Industries that are most developed in Czechoslovakia at present include: iron and steel, machinery and equipment, cement, glass, and motor vehicles. While this does not imply that only these industries are appropriate targets of foreign firms, they do constitute potential candidates for sourcing manufactured goods that will be sold elsewhere in Europe, benefitting from Czechoslovakia's current low wage setting.

One of the most frustrating obstacles facing Western businesspeople in Czechoslovakia is the state of flux in government there. Not only has the country moved from a one-party communist system in 1989, but the new parliamentary system is complicated by the demands for greater autonomy by state (provincial) governments, most importantly in Slovakia. Each level of government is designing new institutions and policy directions, such that firms cannot count on stable regulatory conditions. It can be expected that, despite the trend toward more open markets, as time goes by and as economic growth slows on occasion, more limitations will be placed "temporarily" on such things as access to foreign currency and perhaps the firm's ability to lay off workers. These uncertainties make it clear that foreign business will move with care into Czechoslovakia during the early 1990s.

The most common form of international business that involves Czechoslovakia is not surprising—exports and imports. The interesting feature of this trade is that a large percentage of it has some countertrade component. The most important sources of foreign exchange earnings are machinery and transport equipment, which together contribute more than half of all earnings. Recent import data show that machinery and transport equipment also constitute the largest categories of value imported. Czechoslovakia is also a net food importer. In 1988, 79 percent of Czechoslovak international trade was with other communist countries.

Although Czechoslovak law has been reformed to permit 100 percent foreign ownership in many businesses, interest by both foreign and Czech firms has been primarily in joint ventures. The joint venture law was revised extensively in 1990, resulting in important clarification of the avenues available to foreign firms. The law requires all joint ventures to be approved by the Ministry of Finance, which can thus delay the process of starting such a business significantly. Any imports of goods or inputs must be approved by the Ministry of Foreign Trade, which likewise can impose delays in the process of obtaining necessary production materials or in exporting output to foreign buyers. Foreign exchange earned from exports can be retained by the joint venture, except for 30 percent, which must be sold to the State Bank. While joint ventures can be formed in most industries, ventures with existing state-owned companies must first be offered to Czech investors before foreign investors are allowed to participate. These stipulations may change over time, but they indicate the complexity of regulation facing foreign firms in their efforts to establish business beachheads in Czechoslovakia.

One interesting example of the kinds of major projects that are developing between foreign investors and Czech partners is General Motors' joint venture agreement with Bratislavske Automobilove Zavody in Slovakia. GM has agreed to assemble Opel cars and transmissions in the new venture, which will sell primarily to the domestic market. This project increases GM's presence in East Europe, where the firm also assembles cars and engines in two other plants in Hungary and (formerly East) Germany.

CONCLUSIONS

Business in Eastern Europe and China will become increasingly important through the 1990s, as these countries become more a part of the industrial world and as their markets become more accessible to MNEs from Western Europe and elsewhere. Because of the drastic government policy changes consequent to the decision of most of these countries to pursue market-based economies, political risk related to the rules changes is a dominant concern in the years ahead. This fact, plus the highly bureaucratic regulatory environments that now exist, make these countries potential targets mostly for large, multinational firms that can forego profits on such ventures for several years of negotiations and during early start-up periods.

The main products that appear in trade with Eastern European countries are lower-tech manufactures and raw materials coming from Eastern Europe and higher-tech manufactures and some consumer goods going to Eastern Europe. Customers in Eastern Europe typically are government-owned firms for industrial goods, though final consumers are becoming accessible to MNEs for consumer goods.

QUESTIONS

1. Which are the main East European countries? What are the main differences between these countries and the rest of the world, as far as international business is concerned?

2. What is the most common form of East-West business? How does this compare with international business between other countries?

3. Explain how Western firms generally try to market their products and services to Eastern European customers. What are some of the most important difficulties involved?

4. What are the major types of products exported from the West to the East? What do the Eastern countries sell in return? Why do you suppose that East-West trade has emphasized these products, rather than more consumer goods and other services?

5. Why are there so few Eastern-bloc investments in Western countries, in contrast with the fairly substantial number of Western joint ventures, turnkey ventures, and licensing projects in Eastern countries?

6. Explain how a Western company that exports to an East European country can finance the accounts receivable from its customer, if the terms of the deal call for payment partly in money and partly in products, payable one year from the exporting date.

7. As part of your company's strategy for sourcing production in more than one country, you have been considering the possibility of producing electric motors in Hungary, for sales in Western Europe. You already have a plant in France, but the lower cost of production in Hungary would offer a valuable cost advantage in competing with other European firms. What are some of the key costs and benefits of such a strategy?

8. What competitive advantages would be most useful to an MNE in negotiating with an East European country to sell its industrial machinery to that country? Explain why each advantage is important.

9. Why are home countries of MNEs concerned with the East-West trade of these firms? What policies do the firms usually encounter as a result?

10. How can a firm deal with the political risk inherent in any venture in an East European country? (Assume that the venture is a partially owned factory in Yugoslavia.)

REFERENCES

Business International Corporation. *Business Eastern Europe.* New York: Business International, biweekly newsletter.

China Business Review.

Manufacturers Hanover. "Eastern Europe: Review and Outlook." New York: Manufacturers Hanover Trust Corporation, May 1990.

Surovell, Paul. *Interflo.* Maplewood, N.J. (monthly East-West business newsletter).

Tung, Rosalie. "U.S.-China Trade Negotiations: Practices, Procedures, and Outcomes," *Journal of International Business Studies,* Fall 1982.

U.S. Central Intelligence Agency. *Handbook of Economic Statistics, 1990.* Washington, D.C.: CIA, 1990.

NOTES

[1] Some relatively recent examples include the U.S. intervention in construction of the Soviet natural gas pipeline (discussed below), the U.S. boycott of the Moscow Olympics in 1980, and U.S. sanctions against China after the Tienanmen Square uprising in 1989.

[2] The Soviet Union formally decreed the end to its ban on private property on August 9, 1990. See, Elisabeth Rubinfien, "Soviet Union Declares End to Bar on Private Property," *The Wall Street Journal* (August 10, 1990). p. A8.

[3]See William Ebenstein and Edwin Fogelman, *Today's Isms,* 8th ed. (Englewood Cliffs, N.J.: Prentice Hall, 1980), chap. 1, for a clear discussion of how communist countries functioned during the Cold War period.

[4]Turnkey ventures usually involve continuing licensing agreements, so that the foreign partner remains linked to the project even after the keys have been turned over to the East European partner.

[5]See Amal Kumar Naj and Barry Newman, "GE to Buy 50% of Hungarian Lighting Firm," *The Wall Street Journal,* November 15, 1989, p. A2; and Jonathan Levine, "GE Carves Out a Road East," *Business Week,* July 30, 1990, pp. 32–33.

[6]N. P. Condee, "The Farmers' Markets," *Institute of Current World Affairs,* 1985.

[7]Rosalie Tung, "U.S.-China Trade Negotiations," *Journal of International Business Studies,* Fall 1982.

[8]Craig Forman, "U.S. Firms Plunk Down Cash in East Bloc," *The Wall Street Journal,* June 1, 1990, p. A12.

Case

Volkswagen heads East (or Skoda heads West)

Introduction

Competition in the global auto industry has become increasingly fierce among the dozen surviving major manufacturers in the early 1990s (see Chapter 24 for more details). With the dramatic successes of the Japanese leaders (Toyota, Nissan, and Honda), both the North American and European industries have become subject to intense rivalry among U.S., Japanese, and European automakers. Table 1 shows the positions of major competitors in Western Europe during 1990. These conditions have led to calls for protection in the European Community against outside producers, as well as responses by the European car companies looking to solidify their positions.

The increasing intensity of competition in Europe appears to be due to several factors. First and perhaps foremost, the Japanese firms expanded their local production aggressively in North America during the 1980s, and now they are looking to the European market as the last major target in the global industry where their positions are weak. The leading Japanese firms, with their high-quality and low-cost cars, produced growing profits and market shares during the late 1980s at the same time as their U.S. and European rivals (broadly speaking) have faced declining shares, low profits and/or losses, and generally difficult conditions. Second, the opening of Eastern Europe that began with Soviet President Gorbachev's policy of perestroika has led to aggressive strategies by several firms to build business in Eastern Europe. And third, the European Community's goal of achieving much greater economic integration by the end of 1992 has led Japanese and U.S. automakers to pursue more extensive local production in Europe. These firms want both to benefit from region-wide economies of scale that the reduced commercial barriers will allow and to avoid being excluded by whatever protectionism may occur against non-European firms after 1992.

One of the most active responses of the European firms has been to pursue business in Eastern Europe, in the countries of the former communist bloc. Of course, the most rapid expansion has been into the region that was formerly East Germany. There Volkswagen negotiated a joint production agreement with IFA Kombinat Personenkraftwagen to make Polos and Golfs (to replace the infamous two-stroke East German Trabant), Opel (part of General Motors) agreed to build a new assembly plant in Eisenach (to replace the East German Wartburg), BMW

This case was written by Prof. Robert Grosse and Prof. Vendulka Kubalkova as a basis for class discussion, 1991.

TABLE 1

Western Europe's Auto
Market in 1990 (Jan.–Oct.)

Company	Sales in $US Millions	Percent Change vs. Year Earlier	Market Share
Volkswagen	1,739	+1.9%	15.2%
Fiat	1,624	−4.9%	14.2%
Peugeot Citroen	1,483	+1.0%	13.0%
General Motors	1,344	+2.7%	11.7%
Ford	1,324	−3.7%	11.6%
Renault	1,117	−5.0%	9.8%
Mercedes-Benz	373	+2.8%	3.3%
Rover	344	−5.8%	3.0%
BMW	314	−5.4%	2.7%
Volvo	204	−10.3%	1.8%
Japanese	1,339	+6.1%	11.7%
Others	235	−5.0%	2.0%
Total	11,440	−0.9%	100.0%

Source: *The Economist* (December 15, 1990), p. 74.

invested in machine tools and parts manufacturing, and Ford established an extensive dealer network—all by the end of 1990.

In addition, the European majors have been pursuing investments and alliances in other East European countries, from Poland to Czechoslovakia. For example, Fiat has agreed to form joint ventures in Poland and the Soviet Union for auto production. Opel has agreed to assemble cars and components in Hungary and in the Soviet Union. Ford has agreed to produce auto parts in Hungary. More than a dozen major investment contracts had been signed by the automakers by the end of 1990.

This set of conditions provides the background to the decision of Czechoslovakia's Skoda auto works to sell part ownership to an outside automaker, so that Skoda could survive the opening of the Czechoslovak economy in the 1990s.

Skoda Automobile Company, Mlada Boleslav

Skoda has been the main automobile manufacturer in Czechoslovakia and in East Europe. It was spun off in 1945 from the Skoda Industrial Works, which had been established in 1859. Skoda Works, a top-caliber engineering company, competed on level terms with the finest German and American companies of the day. General Electric, Krupp, and Siemens were then its peers, not its superiors. Skoda cars were popular on European roads between the two world wars. Even under communism, Skoda was known as the most efficient auto producer in the Soviet bloc, though its plants and cars were not longer competitive in comparison with West European vehicles. The Soviet Union used a primitive form of protectionism when it simply ordered Skoda's management to completely halt the development of new cars and the modernization of production.

Skoda's three assembly plants were producing about 185,000 cars per year in 1989. Only one model, the Favorit, based on the eight-year-old design of the Italian Bertone, was in production at that time. The firm employed about 21,000 workers, of which 1,600 were Soviet-style gulag prisoners, and sold $US 588 million of cars in 1989. With output of 10 cars per worker per year, Skoda's productivity was at least three times lower than that of auto companies in the

West. The firm has been accumulating losses at a rate of 200 million Czech crowns per month since the opening of the economy.

The Czechoslovak government, as owner of Skoda, faced a daunting task when the country became independent of the Soviet Union in 1990. Because the cornerstone of reform was the establishment of a market-based economy, competitive firms would be necessary for the future. This implied that some of the main state-owned companies, that provided many jobs and very significant income, would likely have to be privatized in some form or other. The government realized the hopelessness of Skoda's entering directly into competition with well-established European rivals such as Volkswagen and Fiat, not to mention General Motors and Ford. Thus, it was decided to look for a Western partner that could provide up-to-date technology and market access outside of Czechoslovakia—in return for part ownership of Skoda that would allow the acquirer immediate access to the Czechoslovakian market and to existing distribution channels there.

The Czechoslovak government's main concern in selling Skoda to a foreign buyer was that production in Czechoslovakia would not be reduced or terminated, but contrarily that it would be expanded and that jobs would be guaranteed. Also, the government wanted to ensure that the Skoda name would be maintained as a Czechoslovakia-based automaker. These points imply that Skoda would remain a large employer in Czechoslovakia, and that it would continue to generate large income there. Since the local market will take several years to build up purchasing power relative to West European countries, it was expected that the foreign buyer of Skoda would export a significant amount of the locally-produced cars through its international dealership network. While the government wanted to maintain majority local ownership over Skoda, apparently this concern was not an overriding one.

The Competition between Volkswagen and Renault/Volvo

In 1990, with the assistance of Price Waterhouse, the Czechoslovak government formally opened a bidding process for foreign purchase of part ownership in Skoda. Twenty-four foreign automakers examined the Skoda offer. These included General Motors and Ford as well as the main Europe-based firms. Almost all of them withdrew from the process before submitting final bids, leaving Volkswagen and a team of France's Renault and Sweden's Volvo as the only potential buyers. Apparently the reasons for which most of the possible bidders withdrew were two: The truly daunting cost of upgrading (or simply replacing) Skoda's production facilities, and the expected limited market within Czechoslovakia for several years into the future.

Renault and Volvo, both in fairly weak financial conditions at the time, offered to invest about FF 14 billion (just under $US 3 billion) in Czechoslovakia over 10 years. They agreed reluctantly to maintain the Skoda name and to export cars into the European Community market.

The Renault/Volvo offer was dwarfed by Volkswagen's bid. VW agreed to invest DM 9.5 billion (about $US 6.5 billion) over 10 years, to guarantee jobs in Czechoslovakia, and to preserve Skoda as a separate division in Volkswagen (as had been done with the acquisition of Spain's SEAT in 1986). VW's stated intent was to place Skoda at the inexpensive end of its product line and to expand market share in that segment (along with sales from SEAT). Volkswagen planned to expand production in Czechoslovakia to double the current level of output by 1995.

The bidding was not as one-sided as it may appear, since VW had to overcome the Czechoslovak government's concern about selling Skoda to a German buyer. (German direct investors constituted about 70% of total Western foreign investment in Czechoslovakia by 1991.) Traditional Czechoslovak opposition to German firms had to be transcended in order to convince the government to accept the VW bid.

Skoda's trade union, concerned over proposed drastic layoffs by the Renault/Volvo consortium, demanded that Volkswagen be chosen as the partner, contending that it clearly offered better employment guarantees and fringe benefits. The Czech government denied this to be a factor in its final decision and stressed the generosity of the VW offer—which in financial terms was equal to 1/10 of total Czechoslovakian GNP! The Czech Prime minister, Peter Pithart, listed as the main reasons for choosing Volkswagen the proposed technology investments, impact on employment, willingness to respect the Skoda brand name, and VW's leading position in the European auto market. The Czechs, distrustful of socialist economic practices, apparently also disliked the fact that Renault was state-owned. In addition, Volkswagen agreed to maintain in production the existing Favorit (with a new engine) for consumption in the former East Germany and in Czechoslovakia as one of the cheapest cars available.

Implications for Volkswagen

Volkswagen has now committed itself to a huge capital investment in a politically unstable country with greatly limited purchasing power. In addition VW has agreed to preserve the jobs of the existing Skoda workers and to expand production (and presumably employment) during the 1990s. This commitment comes at the same time as the growth of competition in the European auto market and when VW has very limited market shares in North America and Japan.

In exchange for the costs of this agreement, Volkswagen received 31% ownership of Skoda in 1991 and an increasing share up to 70% ownership by 1995, as VW's capital investment increases. Tax treatment and other incentives are not publicly available at this time, but one might assume that some favorable treatment was offered by the government.

This strategy creates a huge risk for Volkswagen during the 1990s. If Skoda cannot be turned into a competitive international firm, VW will have used up precious resources at a time when the firm is already subject to serious competitive pressures in its traditional European domain.

Postscript

The Skoda joint venture and the acquisition of the East German Trabant's manufacturer are by no means the only VW initiatives in its quest to establish itself as the leader in the East European automobile industry. Since the Skoda bid, Volkswagen has also gained a majority stake in another Czechoslovakian automobile manufacturer for which it bid in competition with General Motors. The Slovak Bratislava Auto Works (BAZ) will become the second VW enterprise in Czechoslovakia and its 19th production facility in the world when the investment is completed. With an initial investment of $US 35 million in 1991, Volkswagen will acquire an 80% stake in BAZ. The remaining 20% will belong to the Czechoslovak government. From its Slovak BAZ plant Volkswagen will produce 3,000 Passats annually, increasing the production to 30,000 cars or more by 1993.

5

This commencement ceremony at the University of Miami
demonstrates the growing internationalization of business
schools.
Courtesy of University of Miami School of Business

A LOOK TO THE FUTURE

At the Chicago Mercantile Exchange, traders busily buy and sell in the futures markets.
Gregory Murphy/Journalism Services, Inc.

653

Chapter

24

Industry Profiles

This chapter contains extensive case studies of four major industries—the petroleum, automobiles, banking, and telecommunications industries—in which international competition is involved. Each section explores industry characteristics such as locations of production and consumption, recent history, and industry structure. In addition, individual firms and their competitive strategies are discussed. The main goals of the chapter are to:

1. Provide a clear picture of competition in the four industries in the early 1990s.

2. Illustrate the concepts developed throughout the book.

3. Show how both large and small firms participate in various activities within each industry.

4. Focus on the international aspects of each industry.

5. Offer a single framework of examination, so that all four industries can be compared and seen in a similar light.

INTRODUCTION

This chapter provides a view of four major industries that have figured prominently in international business in the 20th century: *petroleum, automobiles, banking,* and *telecommunications.* The purpose of the chapter is to explore the international aspects of these industries, from competition among multinational firms to international structure of production, looking at the various stages of production, from initial processing to consumer sales. More specifically, the purpose is to present basic information about the industries and then to examine the implications of current conditions and expected changes for international business managers.

The chapter offers an overview of the nature of competition in four extremely important international industries of the 1990s. While one cannot become an industry expert after reading these few pages, it is possible to gain from them a better understanding of the pressures facing firms in these industries and the relative positions of some of the largest firms. By selecting four distinctive types of industry (natural resource, high-tech, service, and smokestack), we are able to offer insights that have application to a wide variety of additional industries and firms.

Four Industries

The *petroleum* industry is arguably the single most important industry of the past 30 years. Oil is the most important energy source used in the 20th century, as well as being the base of the petrochemical industry. Oil is a relatively scarce natural resource, and supplies of oil are substantially located in less developed countries (especially the Middle Eastern countries). The cartel of less developed oil-producing countries shifted the balance of economic power somewhat away from the industrial nations and toward the oil-producing nations during the 1970s. And finally, in the present context, trade and direct investment in the oil business constitute a major portion of total international business. Beginning with the Arab oil embargo and the OPEC (Organization of Petroleum Exporting Countries) price hikes in 1973 and 1974, crude oil prices have gone from about $US 2 per barrel to almost $US 40 per barrel by 1980, and then back to around $US 20 per barrel by 1985, then again up to $US 30 in 1990.

After numerous nationalizations in LDCs during the mid-1970s, the petroleum industry has evolved from a fairly small number of vertically integrated MNEs (the "Seven Sisters" and a handful of others) to a multiplicity of firms and contractual arrangements. These changes have had an enormous impact on consumers, governments, and firms in other industries. Inflation in the industrialized countries rose from an average of around 6 percent per year in the early 1970s to well over 12 percent by 1980. (One reason for inflation was expansionary government monetary and fiscal policies in industrialized countries to mitigate the negative effects on employment and income caused by the huge transfers of financial wealth to the oil-exporting countries.) Worldwide recessions occurred in 1975–76 and 1980–83, after major hikes in oil prices. The ripples from these changes are still being felt today.

The *automotive* industry is a traditional "smokestack industry," that involves large-scale, capital-intensive production facilities with assembly lines, a heavily unionized work force, and fairly standardized (or at least mature) products, which emphasizes price competition in the final product market. Unlike the petroleum industry, this industry is not based on a single raw material but is a heavy user of a number of industrial inputs, among which are steel, glass, rubber, and oil. Competition in the production aspect of this industry remains the province of firms in industrial countries, with strong competitors in the United States, Europe, and Japan. However, the production of components, assemblies, and even full automobiles has been shifting more and more significantly to low-cost locations around the world. This is the youngest of the four industries, having first come into existence at the end of the 19th century.

Banking contrasts sharply with the petroleum and automotive industries. Banking is a service that requires few raw materials. The provision of domestic banking services is highly regulated in every country, though the eurocurrency market is relatively unrestricted in a few countries (primarily the industrialized nations). Banking has been closely tied to the oil industry, not only as a source of loans and deposits, but also as the major vehicle through which "recycling" of the money ("petrodollars") earned by OPEC countries in the 1970s took place. Both banking and the petroleum industry supply fairly standardized products. Competition in banking is often based on nonprice factors, such as service or regulatory conditions. Banking is by far the oldest of our four industries.

The *telecommunications* industry differs greatly from the other three. This industry has existed since the advent of the telegraph in the 1840s, and it has continually faced dramatic competitive shifts as new technology has been developed. From telegraph to telephone to television, the industry has repeatedly led technological advancement in the modern world. In the 1980s, the advances were related primarily to the integration of the computer industry with telecommunications. Building on the use of tiny transistors embodied in silicon chips, both computers and telecommunications switching equipment have become almost infinitely complex and at the same time relatively inexpensive and widely available to consumers during the past decade. The competition among firms in the telecommunications industry has changed rapidly with each new generation of computer technology—from memory increases to communications advances and improvements in processing speeds. During the past decade or so, the telecommunications industry has become characterized by the use of offshore assembly in Southeast Asia for the production of telephones, televisions, computer chips, and many other products. In the 1990s, telecommunications has generally been regarded as the epitome of the high-tech industries.

International Aspects

Our intent in this chapter is to highlight the international aspects of each of the four industries that are covered. The next four sections provide a look at the cross-country structures of each of these industries, at the history that has led to its current competitive environment, and at its major firms and some of their competitive strategies. Particular emphasis is placed on the ownership arrangements that pervade each industry—for example, banking in most countries is fragmented geographically and primarily locally owned, whereas telecommunications equipment is produced globally by a small number of multinational firms. A wide variety of contractual agreements arose in the petroleum industry as governments nationalized oil production, but these governments still need the MNEs for technical assistance, access to foreign markets, and other services. Automobile manufacture remains the province of a small number of MNEs, but marketing, service, and parts production all involve thousands of smaller competitors in many countries. Although the examples presented below focus on MNEs, an attempt is also made to demonstrate the involvement of smaller firms in each industry.

OIL

Sources of Production and Consumption

Most of the world's proved oil reserves are located in the Middle East, as shown in Figure 24–1. Saudi Arabia alone has proved reserves totaling about 255 billion barrels, in comparison with the 26 billion barrels of the United States and the 58 billion barrels of the Soviet Union.[1] The numbers in Figure 24–1 portray a major shift in oil reserves since World War II. Before that time, the United States was the largest oil-producing nation, supplying over half of the world's demand. (Most of this U.S. production went to serve U.S. consumption.) Major discoveries in the Middle East during the late 1940s catapulted Saudi Arabia ahead of all other oil producers. The Ghawar oil field alone had proved reserves of 60 billion barrels.

On the demand side, as may be expected, the industrialized countries account for most of the world's oil use. The United States leads the consuming nations, with annual consumption of about 6 billion barrels of oil out of a total world consumption of about 19 billion barrels per year.

Recent History

The oil industry has been dominated by U.S.-based firms plus Shell and BP during most of its existence. Since the founding of Standard Oil of New Jersey in 1882, that firm (the core of which became Exxon) has been the industry

FIGURE 24–1

World Distribution of Proved Oil Reserves (In billions of barrels as of January 1, 1990)

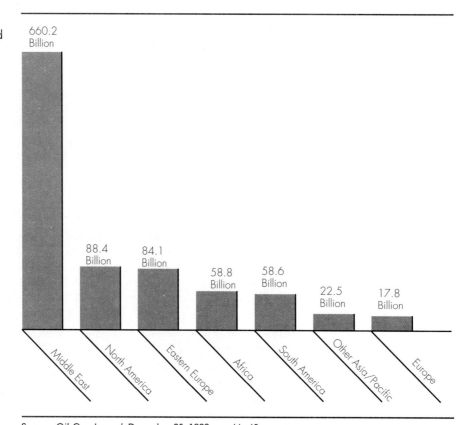

Source: *Oil-Gas Journal*, December 25, 1989, pp. 44–45.

leader. (In 1986, however, Royal Dutch Shell took over the position of industry leader, when the parent firm purchased the 49 percent of its U.S. subsidiary that was not already owned.) During the first half of the 20th century, a group of vertically integrated firms in the United States and Great Britain achieved substantial positions in all phases of the industry in the noncommunist world, from exploration to the operation of gasoline stations. These firms (Exxon, Mobil, Texaco, Socal, Shell, Gulf, and British Petroleum) were labeled the **Seven Sisters** because of the similarities in their size and strategies.[2] With the merger of Gulf into Socal (or Chevron) in 1985 and the increased importance of Amoco (Standard Oil of Indiana), plus the truly global nature of the oil business today, perhaps the leading oil industry firms should now be called the **"Major Multinationals."** (Table 24–1 below lists the largest oil multinationals and a few of their characteristics.)

Early Oil Producers The United States was the largest producer of oil during the first half of this century. As exploration in other countries grew during the

TABLE 24–1

Competitive Strengths of 12 Major Oil Companies

Company	Annual Sales, 1989 ($US millions)	Competitive Advantages
1. Exxon*	86.656	Worldwide distribution network, access to multiple sources of crude, proprietary technology, financial strength, and cash flow
2. Royal Dutch/Shell Group*	85.528	Similar to those of Exxon
3. Mobil*	50.976	
4. British Petroleum (including Sohio)*	49.484	
5. Texaco*	32.416	Marketing strength and ability, multiple sources of crude, proprietary technology
6. Chevron*	29.443	
7. Amoco*	24.214	
8. Aramco (Saudi Arabia)	n.a.	Inexpensive oil and built-up cash reserves, ability to produce lots or little oil and force the market to adjust, greatest crude reserves
9. Total Compagnie Française des Petroles	16.927	Government protection in France
10. Atlantic Richfield	15.905	
11. Petróleos Méxicanos	15.258	Inexpensive oil and built-up cash
12. Petróleos de Venezuela	13.677	Inexpensive oil and built-up cash
13. Kuwait Petroleum Corp.	11.796	Inexpensive oil and built-up cash

*Major Multinational.
Source: "The International 500," *Fortune*, July 30, 1990.

1940s, discoveries in the Middle East quickly led that region to surpass the United States as an oil producer. The companies involved in oil exploration and production in the Middle East were the Seven Sisters plus a few foreign competitors. Exploration in Algeria, Nigeria, Venezuela, Indonesia, and several other LDCs also led to expanded worldwide oil production, which reached about 18 million barrels per day in 1960.

Throughout this period, the multinational oil companies operated through **concessions** in oil-producing countries (i.e., agreements with governments to extract and sell oil in exchange for paying taxes, fees, and other charges) and controlled most of the oil being produced. The governments of the producing countries gained substantial revenues through fees and royalties on oil sales. Land was used by the oil companies under concession from host governments, and these governments were paid fixed per barrel royalties on the oil produced. It was not until the early 1950s that Middle Eastern countries began charging income tax (at a 50 percent rate) on sales of oil. Since the oil companies sold most of the oil to their own downstream affiliates for refining and subsequent processing, they were able to keep wellhead prices low, and thus to keep taxes to host governments low. In September 1960, five of the LDC host countries joined together to form **OPEC (Organization of Petroleum Exporting Countries)**, specifically to protect their interests in obtaining stable and higher returns on oil production. Since then, OPEC has expanded to 13 members, which control about two thirds of the world's oil supply. During the course of the 1960s, the OPEC countries chipped away at the oil companies' control of the oil industry, mainly by raising royalties and taxes.

By 1970, the power balance in the oil industry had shifted dramatically in favor of host governments. "Whereas oil had accounted for about 10 percent of the total energy consumed in Western Europe in 1950, its share was more than 55 percent by 1970. In Japan over the same period, oil's share rose from 9 percent to 33 percent. Imports accounted for virtually all the oil consumed in both areas."[3] Even the United States began to import a substantial quantity of oil from OPEC suppliers. Not only did global demand create a seller's market for petroleum, but supply conditions had shifted by 1970 to the point where OPEC provided about 60 percent of noncommunist output. And finally, through the education of increasing numbers of students from Saudi Arabia, Iraq, Venezuela, and other countries in the world's leading universities, a base of managerial skills was being developed to manage OPEC oil for the specific benefit of these countries rather than for the benefit of the oil companies. Each of these shifts pushed the obsolescing bargain farther in favor of the producing countries.

The Role of Arabian Gulf Oil   Looking back at this period, two events appear to have set the stage for the incredible upheavals of the 1970s. First, the Arab-Israeli War in 1967 led to the closing of the Suez Canal, through which much of the Arabian Gulf oil was transported to Europe. This event highlighted the growing dependence of the industrialized countries on Arabian Gulf oil, and it also focused attention on U.S. support for Israel, which created very serious tensions between the United States and the Arab countries. Second, a construction accident in 1970 caused the temporary shutdown of the Trans-Arabian Pipeline, requiring all Arabian Gulf oil to be shipped much farther away—around the Cape of Good Hope in South Africa—to reach European buyers. This event led to increased oil prices and a successful demand for higher taxes by OPEC members, thus reinforcing the oil-producing nations' awareness of their bargaining strength.

In 1971, the Arabian Gulf countries and Libya successfully forced negotiations with the oil companies to set oil prices through agreements between the governments and the companies and to raise taxes on the oil sold. These agreements, signed in Tehran (Iran) and Tripoli (Libya), marked the first time that producing countries had achieved dominant influence over crude oil pricing. Following this success, the members of OPEC began pressing for ownership of the oil production facilities. By the end of 1972, Saudi Arabia, Abu Dhabi, and Qatar had negotiated to buy 51 percent of the oil-producing facilities within their borders over a 10-year period.

The **nationalization** of oil companies and the control of pricing by OPEC members jumped ahead again in September 1973, when another Arab-Israeli war broke out, and the Arab countries unilaterally raised their oil prices and embargoed oil shipments to the United States and the Netherlands (because these two countries showed support for Israel in the war). Crude oil prices (at $US 2.70 per barrel in early October) were raised 35 percent on October 16, 1973, and 131 percent on January 1, 1974. The OPEC governments raised taxes on the oil companies to 85 percent of income and royalties to 20 percent of the list price of crude oil. Greater government ownership of oil companies operating within the OPEC nations was also demanded, and by the end of 1974 most of the OPEC nations had achieved 60 percent ownership.

Since 1974, the nationalization of oil companies within the OPEC nations has proceeded to complete local ownership in most cases. Crude oil prices are now set by OPEC governments without negotiations with the companies. After a few years of price increases that approximately kept pace with inflation, the Iranian crisis of 1978, which led to the overthrow of the shah's government, disrupted the supply of oil from that country. OPEC raised prices accordingly throughout 1979. By year-end, consumers' fears of a new oil shortage and OPEC's reaction to panic buying had enabled OPEC to increase oil prices 95 percent, to $US 26 per barrel. This second oil price shock was followed by two years of steadily increasing OPEC prices, which peaked at $US 34 per barrel in October 1981.

Oil consumers reacted to the continuing upward spiral of oil prices by trying to conserve energy in their existing activities, by switching to alternative energy sources, and by simply cutting down on energy-intensive activities. The effects of these reactions were slow to be felt, but by 1982 the fuel efficiency of U.S. automobiles had been raised to over twice the 1972 level (mileage of over 30 miles per gallon was common for new cars, compared to about 15 miles per gallon in the early 1970s), coal and nuclear power were replacing oil in many electric utilities, and both residential and commercial electric power use (per customer) had dropped noticeably. These reactions, as well as a worldwide recession and the emergence of major new oil supplies in the North Sea and North America, had created an oversupply of oil by the end of 1982.

By the mid-1980s, world oil sales had shifted away from the OPEC countries, which now sell only about 40 percent of the world total, to other suppliers such as Norway, Mexico, the United Kingdom, and Canada—countries that do not follow OPEC market-sharing practices. Also, sales of oil on the "spot" market, which, unlike OPEC sales, are not tied to long-term contracts, rose in the mid-

1980s to almost one third of total crude oil sales. Some OPEC (and other) producers have placed substantial amounts of their production into this market, and many oil companies make their purchases increasingly without long-term contracts (i.e., on the spot market). Finally, the OPEC countries themselves have been discounting their prices substantially during the 1980s oil glut, so that the posted price published by OPEC countries is no longer a good measure of actual sales prices. In fact, in late 1985, OPEC abandoned attempts to control its members' oil-pricing policies. The cartel has failed to maintain its monopoly control over oil supply—though only after more than a decade of successful operations that led to huge transfers of wealth from industrial countries to OPEC members.

Renewed efforts to fix crude oil prices succeeded to some extent in 1987, when OPEC agreed to a price of $US 18 per barrel. This agreement was achieved despite the all-out war between Iran and Iraq and the widespread use of discounts and other efforts of OPEC members to sell more than their production allocations in the cartel. Prices soared again when Iraq invaded and annexed Kuwait in 1990. The price of oil futures rose above $US 40 per barrel before the market settled back to prices in the $US 20–30 range. Price volatility now is a regular feature of the oil market, while consumption remains fairly stable.

Industry Structure

The ownership of companies producing *crude oil* shifted from almost exclusively, the Seven Sisters and other private firms during the first half of this century to almost exclusive host government ownership (in the LDCs) by 1980. Figure 24–2 bears out this point. Both exploration for new oil and downstream processing of crude oil, however, are still dominated by the oil companies. One would expect the OPEC governments to be interested in downstream production, and indeed in 1990 refining capacity within OPEC was about 6.2 million barrels per day, compared to worldwide refining capacity of about 74.0 million barrels per day. Unfortunately for the OPEC refineries, oil demand dropped sharply during the early 1980s and refining became an unprofitable or marginal venture in many cases. Several OPEC countries had begun to process farther downstream, into petrochemicals,[4] but petrochemical demand has stagnated in the past few years. While it appears that OPEC-based firms will supply substantial amounts of downstream products to world markets in the long run, their progress thus far has been curtailed by weak demand worldwide.

One can conclude that upstream oil production in LDCs has been very largely taken over by governments, in contrast with the production and distribution of all stages of oil-based products, which are largely owned and controlled by private companies—though even at the downstream stages many independent companies are major competitors along with the Major Multinationals. Figure 24–3 depicts the present structure of the petroleum industry, which is in marked contrast with that of the pre-1970 period when vertically integrated companies dominated the entire industry. Notice specifically that the *refining* stage of the industry is the only one that is still dominated by the Major Multinationals and that many independent firms exist in the stages of exploration, transportation of both crude and final products, and marketing. The Majors are vertically integrated through the industry, so that they can benefit from shifts in market conditions that favor firms in one stage or another. At various times in the history

FIGURE 24–2

International Oil Companies'
Equity Interest in Middle East
Crude Oil Production—
1965–1987

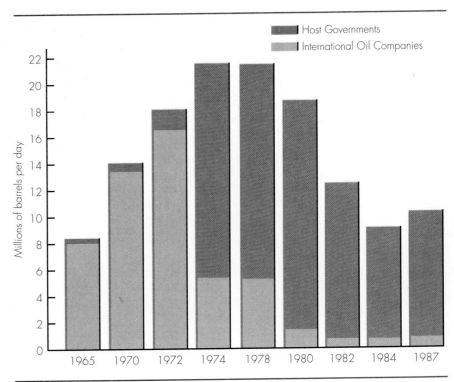

Sources: Exxon Corporation, *Middle East Oil*, p. 35. Data from *Annual Statistical Bulletin, 1987*,
Organization of the Petroleum Exporting Countries, and Exxon Corporation estimates.

of the industry, transportation of crude (when John D. Rockefeller built Standard
Oil), ownership of crude (when OPEC successfully raised prices in the 1970s),
and access to final markets (at times when demand conditions are weak) have
been the key to the competitiveness of large firms in the industry.

The number of major participants in the crude oil production and refining
stages has increased since government-owned companies from OPEC have entered these stages of the industry. In the LDCs, the vertically integrated private
companies such as the Major Multinationals have been forced to take small
minority ownership positions or to sell their technology and management services through contractual agreements. However, the very first stage in the industry, exploration, and the activities farthest downstream, such as the manufacture of petrochemical products, are generally dominated by the vertically
integrated private companies, which possess knowledge of markets and distribution channels plus proprietary production and exploration technology. The
obsolescing bargain (see Chapter 22) has enabled oil-producing LDCs to
wrest control of the raw material almost completely away from the MNEs, but
those parts of the petroleum industry that demand sophisticated technology or
access to marketing channels in other countries remain the province of the
MNEs.

One would expect OPEC oil firms to extend their activities throughout the
industry as they develop the necessary expertise and market access. The notable

FIGURE 24-3

A Sketch of the Global
Structure of the Petroleum
Industry, 1986

Company	Stage	Key Competitive Factors
Major Multinationals, hundreds of independent exploration companies, national oil companies	**Exploration**	Technology, funds, legal access to the area
Major Multinationals, Aramco, National Iranian Oil Company, Petroleos de Mexico, other national oil companies, and other private oil companies	**Crude oil production**	Access to oil, funds
Major Multinationals, Greek and other shipowners, independent pipeline owners	**Transportation of crude**	Access to ships and pipelines
Mostly the Major Multinationals; also national oil companies and some private ones	**Refining**	Supply of crude, funds, access to markets
Major Multinationals, independent truckers	**Transportation of final products**	Ships, trucks, access to markets
Dow, Du Pont, ICI, Monsanto, BASF, and thousands more, including the Major Multinationals	**Petrochemical production**	Access to refined oil products, technology, access to markets
Thousands of owners and franchisees in most countries	**Gasoline stations**	Access to gasoline, good location

lack of success of government-owned companies in international competitive markets to date, however, does not portend the emergence of new Exxons from among the OPEC countries. Even so, several of the state-owned firms, such as Petroleos de Venezuela, have expanded overseas into downstream businesses.

The *technical* structure of the petroleum industry is such that independent firms can compete in one or more stages of Figure 24–3 without full **vertical integration.** The refining stage, however, does require specialized equipment for handling different grades of crude oil—so each refinery is constructed to process a particular type of crude (e.g., Saudi Arabian light or Venezuelan heavy). A major advantage exists, therefore, for a firm that integrates *crude oil production* and *refining*. On the other hand, gasoline, fuel oil, and other distillates can be purchased from many different refineries without important differences in quality. Thus, gasoline station operators can do business without owning refineries or other upstream installations. Such independent operators are at a disadvantage, however, when the supply of gasoline is limited (as in 1974 and 1979). In such times, vertically integrated firms or firms with guaranteed (contractual) access to gasoline possess a major competitive advantage.

Numerous manufacturers compete at the petrochemical production stage of the industry without owning supplies of crude oil or distillates. In petrochemical production, the key competitive advantages are proprietary technology and market access, neither of which requires upstream ownership of supplies. This is not to deny that all of the Major Multinationals actively compete in petrochemicals and that some chemical firms have chosen to obtain guaranteed supplies of oil through upstream integration (e.g., Du Pont's purchase of Conoco in 1983).

Firms

Some of the major competitors in the global petroleum industry today are listed in Table 24–1. The table shows some important competitive advantages of the Major Multinationals and several of the national oil companies. Notice the clear contrasts between the government-owned firms, which possess large quantities of proved crude reserves (and money), and the privately owned Major Multinationals, which possess worldwide distribution systems, marketing knowledge, and proprietary technology. In the early 1990s, Exxon and Shell were the most powerful firms in the industry, though the other Majors had strong competitive advantages relative to all other firms and were dominant in particular market segments as well. Useful additional details on the competition among these firms can be found in a number of recent accounts of this key industry.[5]

AUTOMOBILES

Distribution of Activity Worldwide

The motor vehicle industry is the world's largest manufacturing industry. Its activities spread throughout the globe, with over 85 percent of production and a similar portion of consumption taking place in North America, Western Europe, and Japan. While substantial natural resources are used in the production of cars and trucks (and other motor vehicles), that production is still located primarily in the major industrial markets. Figure 24–4 shows the distribution of automobile production and consumption worldwide over the past half-century. Notice that although production in North America had fallen to about one fifth of the global total by 1982, consumption in that region still accounted for about one third of total world consumption. This implies, of course, that North America was the major net importer of automobiles in the world during the 1980s. Among the reasons for North America's position as an importer of automobiles are lower production costs and greater precision in production in Japan (and Europe), the easy access of foreign producers to the North American market, a continuing higher quality ranking of Japanese and German cars relative to their American competitors, and finally the huge size of the North American market relative to other markets around the world. These and other reasons for this situation are explored below.

Because automobiles are composed of fairly standardized components, there has been a tendency to place greater reliance on low-cost locations for the production of components and the assembly of automobiles. In the 1970s and 80s, Brazil, Mexico, and Korea in particular became important sources of supply of parts and assemblies to the auto industry. Brazil alone assembled almost a million autos (in addition to producing auto parts) in 1980, when about 27 million autos were produced worldwide. The increasing use of low-cost locations appears quite likely to continue into the 1990s.

FIGURE 24–4A

Global Automobile Production

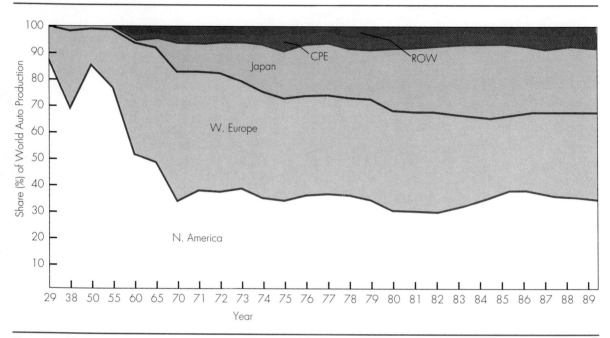

Share of world automobile production by region, 1929–89.

Source: Roos and Altshuler (1984), p. 20, and *Automotive News*, 1990 market data book issue.

Recent History

Historically, the automobile industry has been dominated by American firms, in particular by General Motors and Ford. This dominance began in the early 1900s, when Henry Ford's company brought standardized parts and mass production, plus the use of a continuous assembly line, into operation. Prior to 1900, for the first 20 years of the industry's existence, German and French manufacturers produced most of the automobiles in use. By 1923, Ford and General Motors (GM) together accounted for 91 percent of world auto production—and their combined share remained above two thirds of the world total until after World War II.[6]

Through strategies of foreign direct investment, Ford and GM obtained strong market positions in Europe and North America. During the 1930s, Ford set up manufacturing facilities in England, Germany, and France. GM chose acquisitions of existing European firms, buying Vauxhall in England and Opel in Germany in the late 1920s. (Both firms were denied permission to establish manufacturing in Italy, where they would have competed with state-owned Fiat.) Both Ford and GM also operated manufacturing facilities in Canada.

After World War II, competition from non-U.S. firms began to heat up. High tariffs on imported autos, support for state-owned manufacturers, and rapidly growing European economies led to a boom in European production by such companies as Renault, Volkswagen, and Fiat. (The Ford and GM affiliates in England and Germany also grew rapidly in this environment.) When the European Common Market was established in 1958, European producers were able to take advantage of economies of scale that resulted from serving the six-country market instead of the relatively small national markets. By 1973, the

FIGURE 24-4B

Global Automobile Consumption

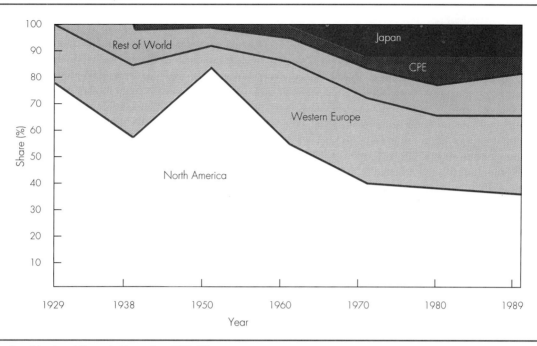

Share of world automobile market by region, 1929–89.
Source: Roos and Altshuler (1984), p. 23, and *Automotive News*, 1990 market data book issue.

European Community market was about the same size as the North American market, and European automakers were beginning to enter the U.S. small-car market very successfully.

At the beginning of the postwar period, auto production in Japan lagged far behind that in Europe and North America. Japanese auto production was less than 1 million vehicles per year until the late 1960s. By 1970, however, it had hit 3 million and Japanese auto exports to the United States had reached a market share of more than 4 percent. And by 1980, Japanese exports accounted for almost 23 percent of the U.S. auto market. Like the European autos, the Japanese autos were smaller than their U.S. counterparts and offered a low-cost alternative to U.S. buyers.

The success of Japanese cars in the U.S. market led to pressure from the domestic companies for protection. By 1981 **Voluntary Export Restraints (VERs)** were negotiated between Japan and the United States that limited the number of Japanese cars imported. (The limit was 4.2 million cars per year in 1990. See Chapter 9 for more discussion.) To avoid losses of market share, the Japanese auto firms made substantial investments in production facilities in the United States during the 1980s. By 1990, the Japanese "transplant" factories were producing over 2 million cars per year in the United States.

Industry Structure

In most countries, the automobile industry is dominated by models designed and produced elsewhere. That is, a small number of manufacturers in a handful of industrial countries make virtually all of the cars and trucks used in the world's almost 200 countries. (Six firms produce over two thirds of world auto output.) From a different perspective, the three major markets for autos are North America, the European Community, and Japan. All of the six largest auto firms manufacture vehicles in at least two of these areas in dozens of plants. In sum, the industry is highly concentrated among six firms: in descending order of size, General Motors, Ford, Toyota, Nissan, Renault, and Volkswagen. (Fiat and Peugeot-Citroen are not far behind Volkswagen in size, though they are far less multinational outside Europe than any of the six largest firms.) Table 24–2 depicts some features of the ten main competitors in the world auto industry.

As with the petroleum industry, the automobile industry includes thousands of additional firms that are involved in various stages of its operations, from the production of components to the final sale of cars and trucks to retail customers. What distinguishes the six (or eight) major multinational auto firms is their control of the *final assembly* stage of production. These final assemblers produce less than half of the total value added in the industry. The rest comes from suppliers, such as tire firms (e.g., Goodyear, Michelin, Bridgestone) and drive-train manufacturers (e.g., TRW, Borg-Warner, Dana); distributors, such as the thousands of independent new car dealers in the industrial countries; and financiers, such as the major commercial banks.

Among the six largest firms in the industry, General Motors and Ford are more vertically integrated than the others, while Toyota and Nissan are much less integrated than the others. Also, the Japanese firms have traditionally specialized in smaller, less-expensive cars and have achieved a much better quality record than their foreign competitors. These positioning strategies have brought the Japanese firms greater success during the past two decades, when customer preferences have favored more-differentiated and less-expensive vehicles. In

TABLE 24–2

Major Competitors in the International Automobile Industry

Firm	Home Country	Annual Sales, 1989 (in $ millions)	Competitive Advantages
General Motors	U.S.	$126,974	largest size and largest distribution network
Ford	U.S.	96,933	large size and diversification, innovative skills
Toyota	Japan	60,444	low-cost production, good labor relations, best financial situation, high-quality image
Daimler-Benz	Germany	40,616	reputation for very high quality
Fiat	Italy	36,741	government support
Chrysler	U.S.	36,156	relatively low costs and recent good image
Nissan	Japan	36,078	low-cost production, good labor relations, high-quality image
Volkswagen	Germany	34,746	government support
Renault	France	27,457	government support
Honda	Japan	26,484	good labor relations, high-quality image

Source: "The International 500," *Fortune*, July 30, 1990.

particular, the competitive edge of the Japanese firms has resulted from their ability to adapt models to changes in consumer tastes and to serve the low-cost end of the market with relatively high-quality products.

The Six Major Multinational Automotive Firms

The six largest multinational auto firms have somewhat different corporate strategies and structures. This section points out some characteristics of these firms that are relevant to global competition with their rivals. The firms are presented in declining order of size (i.e., annual sales).

General Motors has been the largest auto company in the world for most of the auto industry's history. In 1989, GM's annual sales were almost 50 percent larger than those of its nearest competitor. GM has traditionally made a wide variety of large autos that constitute over half of its total production, while filling out its product line with medium, compact, and subcompact vehicles. Among GM's main competitive advantages are its financial capacity to respond to problems and opportunities around the world with massive funds when needed, its highly diversified portfolio of production facilities in the industrial countries and in LDCs, and its base in the United States, the largest national market for motor vehicle sales. Recently, GM has also demonstrated a willingness to cooperate with foreign rivals in production and research (see NUMMI case in Chapter 12), thus benefiting from those firms' skills as well as its own.

Ford Motor Company has been the second largest manufacturer in the auto industry for most of its existence. Ford's product line is similar to that of GM, though Ford has only half of GM's worldwide volume. Historically, Ford has been somewhat more vertically integrated than any of the other major auto firms, with its own very large steelmaking operation and its greater in-house production of other inputs. Ford's major competitive advantages include its long and successful experience operating in foreign markets, its base in the United States, and its innovative capacity, as shown (for example) by its introduction of the compact Mustang model in 1965, its importing of the Fiesta model from Europe in the late 1970s, and its introduction of the Escort, the world's best-selling car in 1989.

Toyota is the larger of the giant Japanese auto producers, both of which have become multinational competitors only in the past two decades. Toyota's growth rate has far surpassed those of the American and European firms since 1970, and it has been one of the best examples of the "Japanese challenge" to world business in the 1980s and 1990s. That is, with its advances during this period in competition with the other major firms in many national markets, Toyota has demonstrated most of the attributes of successful Japanese MNEs. Its competitive advantages include far lower production costs and greater production efficiency than those of any of the non-Japanese firms, harmonious labor/management relations, excellent quality control, vehicles with relatively low gasoline consumption, a successful focus on smaller cars, and great financial stability (with zero long-term debt).

Fiat became the second largest European auto producer (after Daimler-Benz) by pursuing a strategy of diversification into all major automobile segments. Beyond the traditional, economical small to intermediate-sized Fiats, the firm now owns Alfa-Romeo (producer of high-performance, sporty cars), Lancia (large, classic luxury cars), and Ferrari (high-performance sports and race cars). With its protected domestic market, in which Fiat has a 60 percent market share, the company has expanded throughout Europe and into North America with overseas production and sales. Fiat's broad strategy emphasizes styling and high performance, especially in the acquired divisions.

Nissan, Japan's second largest auto maker, presents much the same success story as Toyota. The company became a major multinational competitor during the 1970s and 1980s, and its competitive advantages largely parallel those of Toyota. That is, Nissan benefits from low production costs, highly productive labor, and consistently high quality products. While Nissan rode the wave of Japanese auto success in the U.S. market by selling small, inexpensive models during the past two decades, its growth has been slower than that of either Toyota or Honda. Nissan's most recent strategic direction in the United States has been to position itself as the high-fashion, high-performance Japanese producer. The introduction of cars such as the Maxima (rated the most trouble-free car sold in the U.S.), the luxury model Infiniti, and another new-styled compact car for 1992, has established Nissan in this market position relative to its Japanese rivals.

Volkswagen is the most multinational of the European auto producers, with plants in the United States, Mexico, and Brazil. The Beetle, Volkswagen's initial entry into the American market (in the 1950s), was tremendously successful and led Volkswagen to dramatic growth through the 1960s. Since that time, the firm has not enjoyed such strides ahead of its rivals. Volkswagen became the first major foreign automaker to set up production in the United States, with its Westmoreland, Pennsylvania, plant, purchased in 1974. Although this venture was only moderately successful and was later sold, similar direct U.S. investments have been made by Volkswagen's major non-U.S. competitors. Volkswagen's major competitive advantages include its reputation for reliability (established by the Beetle), its protected base in Germany, and its focus on the small-car market segment.

This overview of six of the largest automakers is offered as a sketch of the competitive conditions in the automobile industry rather than as a precise definition of the capabilities or difficulties of these firms. It is intended to give some insights into the current and future shape of the industry around the world.

BANKING
Worldwide Distribution of Activities

The fundamental services rendered by banks are the lending of funds and the taking of deposits. The "raw materials" of the banking industry are deposits and other sources of funds, and the main "output" of the industry is credit in the form of loans and other instruments. In addition, banks offer many other financial services that generate income, such as issuing guarantees of performance on behalf of clients, serving as intermediaries for the purchase/sale of financial instruments other than deposits and loans, and making a market in such instruments as foreign exchange. Finally, banks provide nonfinancial services such as *information*—about market trends for various products, about economic and political conditions in various countries, about financial market conditions at home and abroad, and about other matters of interest to clients. In some countries, commercial banks participate directly in markets for stocks and bonds (i.e., in investment banking) and in markets for real estate, insurance, and other financial services. Our discussion will focus primarily on the two traditional banking functions: taking deposits and lending—and more specifically on these functions in the international context.

Every country has a domestic banking system that is regulated by a domestic monetary authority (typically a central bank) and involves participation by locally owned financial institutions. In this sense, banking activities are distributed across the globe—in capitalist and communist countries, in rich and poor countries. Many countries limit participation in domestic financial markets to locally owned institutions, with foreign banks allowed only to have representative offices or to operate only indirectly through relations with local banks. Such limitations exist in the formerly communist countries, and they are also fairly extensive in less developed countries. This means that much of international banking takes place through "correspondent banking relations," that is, through transactions in which a bank in one country deals at arm's length with its counterpart in another country. It also means that there are far fewer multinational banks than there are multinational industrial corporations.

In the industrialized countries and in a handful of LDCs (Panama, Hong Kong, Bahrain, the Bahamas, the Cayman Islands, and a few more), international banking transactions are relatively open to foreign-owned financial institutions and free of most limits (other than those intended to ensure prudent banking practices) on the lending and deposit-taking practices of participating banks. The eurocurrency markets flourish in this environment, as do dealings in foreign exchange and other internationally transferable financial instruments.

The international spread of bank affiliates outside their home countries is depicted in Table 24–3. Notice that the main centers of foreign bank activity are the main countries involved in eurocurrency transactions—the industrialized nations plus a handful of LDCs that offer legal incentives to attract foreign bank activity.

Recent History

In general, banking offices and services have followed industrial clients into new types of business and into new countries through the years. In the 18th and 19th centuries, this meant that British, French, Spanish, and Dutch banks established overseas networks of affiliates to support the business taking place within the colonial systems of their respective countries. Even today, the presence of British banks (e.g., Barclays and Lloyds) in former British colonies, of French banks (e.g. Crédit Lyonnais and Banque Nationale de Paris) in former French colonies, and so on, is greater than one might expect, considering the small markets of many of these nations and their distance from their former home countries.

In the first half of the 20th century, when Great Britain and the United States were the largest industrial powers, banks from these two countries extended their overseas activities as British and American multinational industrial firms spread their mines, factories, and offices throughout the world. By 1960, there were about 5,000 foreign branches and agencies of commercial banks headquartered in major industrialized countries (still dominated by the more than 4,000 affiliates of British banks in the British Commonwealth, mainly throughout Africa and Asia).[7] American banks in particular faced a regulatory structure that encouraged overseas expansion, since domestically all banks were limited to expansion within one state only, and then often only on a restricted basis. The "money center" banks from New York extended their activities aggressively into Europe and elsewhere during this time.

TABLE 24-3

Banks' Global Network of Overseas Branches, Affiliates, and Subsidiaries

Country of Origin	U.S.A.	U.K.	France	Germany	Switz.	Neth.	Argen.	Brazil	Mexico
U.S.A.		47	14	12	7	3	8	3	1
Japan	48	28	14	3	1	0	2	1	0
U.K.	21		3	3	3	3	1	1	0
Brazil	16	4	2	3	0	2	4		1
France	15	16		6	4	1	2	1	0
Germany	13	14	3		0	0	1	1	0
Canada	12	9	1	4	1	1	1	0	0
Italy	12	12	2	4	1	1	2	0	0
South Korea	11	6	1	1	0	1	0	0	0
Spain	11	7	10	2	0	1	0	3	0
Hong Kong	9	5	1	0	2	1	0	0	0
Australia	7	12	0	1	0	0	0	0	0
Venezuela	7	0	1	0	0	0	0	1	0
Mexico	6	4	0	0	0	0	0	0	
Switzerland	6	12	1	2		1	0	0	1
Netherlands	5	8	0	1	0		1	0	0
Bahrain	3	3	0	1	0	0	0	0	0
Argentina	2	1	1	0	0	0		2	0
Others	95	107	26	10	5	1	0	6	0
Total	299	295	80	53	24	16	22	19	3

Sources: U.S.A. data: *Institutional Investor,* September 1987; U.K. data: *The Banker,* November 1987; All other countries data: *The Bankers' Almanac and Yearbook,* 1987.

During the 1970s, international banking was struck by the dramatic shift in wealth between industrialized nations and OPEC developing nations that resulted from the two oil crises; the banking industry responded by recycling the "petrodollars" generated by this shift. As was seen in the section on the oil industry, this recycling led to a very large increase in lending to nontraditional borrowers, such as governments in less developed countries. It also led to the establishment of new multinational banks in the oil-exporting countries and to the creation of a financial center in the Middle East (in Bahrain).

The structure of international financial dealings with LDCs changed remarkably during the decade of the 70s. In the two preceding decades, most of the lending to governments in less developed countries had come from official sources, such as foreign government departments (e.g., the U.S. Treasury) and international agencies (e.g., the International Monetary Fund and the World Bank). During those decades, approximately two thirds of the loan financing provided to LDC governments had come from official sources, and the remaining third from commercial banks. By the late 1970s, financing of this kind had grown dramatically and had shifted toward the private sector, so that commercial banks now provided about two thirds of such financing (particularly to large LDCs such as Brazil and Mexico), and official agencies the remainder.[8]

TABLE 24–3

continued

						Host Area					
Vene.	Japan	Hong Kong	Bahrain	Egypt	Nigeria	South Africa	Bahamas	Cayman Islands	Panama	Singap.	Malasia
1	22	20	9	2	1	0	59	67	7	18	3
0		15	1	0	0	0	1	4	5	18	1
0	5	8	7	1	2	0	5	22	1	11	1
1	2	1	2	0	0	0	3	10	3	2	0
0	7	8	8	1	0	0	1	4	6	11	0
0	6	7	0	0	0	0	0	4	1	4	1
0	5	7	2	1	0	0	5	3	2	5	1
0	2	4	0	1	0	0	1	1	0	4	0
0	3	3	2	0	0	0	0	0	1	2	0
2	1	1	1	0	0	0	2	4	1	0	0
0	1		2	0	0	0	1	0	0	4	2
0	3	3	0	0	0	0	0	2	0	4	0
	0	0	0	0	0	0	0	0	3	0	0
0	0	0	0	0	0	0	2	3	0	0	0
0	2	2	2	0	0	0	6	5	3	3	0
0	3	3	0	0	0	0	0	1	1	3	1
0	0	0		0	0	0	0	1	1	1	0
0	0	0	0	0	0	0	0	1	3	0	0
0	14	29	16	10	1	1	6	24	5	31	6
4	76	111	52	16	4	1	92	156	43	121	16

Among the industrialized countries, competition among banks has developed in line with changes in the competitiveness of manufacturing firms. That is, as U.S. (and British) firms have lost market share to competitors in Europe and Japan, so too have U.S. (and British) banks faced increasing competition from German, Swiss, and Japanese banks in many countries. Also, as national governments have permitted more participation by foreign banks in their economies, the competition among banks has become much more international.

Industry Structure

The banking industry is structured somewhat differently in each country. In the United States, there are over 14,000 commercial banks. Federal law substantially limits an individual bank's activities in more than one state. Nonetheless, about 20 of the largest banks, with assets of over $U.S. 20 billion apiece, carry out almost half of the value of U.S. banking transactions. In Great Britain, where nationwide banking is permitted, a group of six very large banks (Barclays, National Westminster, Midland, Lloyds, Royal Bank of Scotland, and Bank of Scotland) dominate the domestic market and own most of the 14,000 bank branches throughout the country. Over 400 foreign banks participate in the international segments of the market. In Venezuela, seven local banks hold 60 percent of the banking deposits, and they control most of the international segment as well. Foreign banks are limited to ownership of 20 percent of the equity in a Venezuelan bank.[9] All in all, domestic banking activities are much less concentrated in the United States than in other countries, but international banking activities are fairly concentrated everywhere.

The *eurocurrency* market, the largest financial market in the world, is located mainly in the financial centers of the industrialized countries,[10] plus a handful of offshore sites such as Hong Kong, Panama, and Bahrain. The banks participating in this market at any location generally belong to the group of multinational banks noted in Table 24–4. (The eurocurrency market is discussed in some detail in Chapter 7.)

Participation by government-owned institutions is especially important in banking, since governments establish the rules of the game in each country and since they can pursue goals other than profit as part of their banking strategies. Typically, the largest and most important commercial banks in less developed countries are state owned, and this situation also exists in a few industrialized countries, such as Sweden and France. The major French banks, which are all government owned, provide an excellent example of such institutions, dominating the domestic market and competing actively in the euromarkets. The services offered by state-owned banks do not differ from those offered by their private sector competitors; in international banking the only noticeable difference between state-owned and private sector banks is that the state-owned banks serve some captive clients (namely, government agencies and companies).

Major Banking Competitors

The 50 most important commercial banks in the world are listed in Table 24–4 according to their rankings by assets. Notice that the dominance of U.S.-based banks has disappeared over the past decade and that there is a fairly even distribution of leading banks among the United States, Japan, Canada, Germany, France, Great Britain, and a few other European countries.

The particular competitive advantages possessed by the multinational banks listed in Table 24–4 are somewhat difficult to assess. If we use the number of foreign affiliates as a measure of experience in international business, then the British banks have a large advantage. If we consider the diversity of financial services offered, then the Japanese banks with ties to large trading companies are probably the most active outside the realms of deposit taking and lending. To some extent, the banks that can minimize their costs of providing financial services show the greatest profitability, since the cost of obtaining funds is fairly similar for all of the banks in question. In this case, it is the diverse group of banks that show the greatest returns on assets that possess a cost advantage. (Clearly, the multinational banks that have access to funds in a number of countries have a probable cost-of-funds advantage over local banks in any one market that offers limited borrowing sources.) The advantage of a well-known brand name is possessed by all of the banks listed; indeed, any bank with over $U.S. 40 billion in assets is generally considered trustworthy! A final competitive advantage worth noting is an existing customer base in one country that can be extended overseas as clients establish operations in other countries. Banks based in the United States, home of the largest number of multinational enterprises, should have an advantage in this regard, with their access to more clients in the domestic market.

An interesting aspect of competitive advantage in banking is the positioning of large multinational banks in competition with smaller local banks in national

TABLE 24–4

The World's Largest Commercial Banking Corporations, 1989

Bank	Shareholders' Equity ($ million)	Total Assets ($ billion)	Net Income ($ million)
1. Fuji Bank Group	11,041.0	365.6	1,399.1
2. Dai-Ichi Kangyo Bank	10,962.4	388.9	1,507.7
3. Caisse Nationale de Credit Agricole	10,901.9	242.0	829.3
4. Sumitomo Bank	10,736.9	377.2	1,583.0
5. Barclays	10,713.5	204.9	765.8
6. Mitsubishi Bank	10,181.9	352.9	1,315.7
7. Citicorp	10,076.0	230.6	498.0
8. National Westminster Bank	9,759.8	186.5	333.9
9. Sanwa Bank	9,335.9	350.2	1,228.7
10. Industrial Bank of Japan	9,251.6	268.5	633.5
11. Industrial and Commercial Bank of China	8,638.7	150.9	2,838.7
12. Deutsche Bank	8,599.5	202.3	789.2
13. Union Bank of Switzerland	8,149.9	113.9	583.4
14. Bank of China	7,682.3	103.3	1,071.6
15. Hong Kong and Shanghai Banking Corp.	7,483.3	133.0	702.5
16. Compagnie Financiere de Paribas	6,967.7	138.7	958.5
17. Credit Lyonnais	6,696.3	210.7	595.5
18. Japan Development Bank	6,297.9	64.9	321.6
19. Tokai Bank	6,152.4	225.8	491.6
20. Swiss Bank Corp.	6,152.3	105.1	484.7
21. Mitsui Bank	5,817.0	206.9	590.5
22. BankAmerica Corp.	5,534.0	97.2	1,103.0
23. Banco do Brasil	5,502.7	67.0	97.5
24. Long-Term Credit Bank of Japan	5,469.2	183.3	400.5
25. Dresdner Bank	5,415.8	147.0	382.9
26. Rabobank	5,336.5	90.0	468.8
27. Credit Suisse	5,158.8	88.9	507.6
28. Mitsubishi Trust & Banking	5,137.9	212.0	587.3
29. Bank of Tokyo	5,082.8	198.3	472.5
30. Banque Nationale de Paris	5,061.3	231.5	629.6
31. Monte dei Paschi de Siena	5,048.1	68.4	n.a.
32. Royal Bank of Canada	5,008.7	88.5	462.1
33. Chase Manhattan Corp.	4,998.0	106.4	−665.0
34. Westpac Banking Corp.	4,933.8	76.1	621.0
35. Sumitomo Trust & Banking	4,694.6	197.9	557.2
36. Banco Bilbao Vizcaya	4,693.4	69.8	916.7
37. Security Pacific Corp.	4,637.0	83.1	740.6
38. Midland Group	4,577.3	100.3	−327.5
39. JP Morgan	4,495.0	87.6	−1,275.0
40. Societe Generale	4,481.0	164.8	686.4
41. Lloyds Bank Group	4,474.5	92.4	−801.1
42. National Australia Bank	4,407.1	51.2	614.0
43. Taiyo Kobe Bank	4,377.2	174.5	405.4
44. Canadian Imperial Bank	4,178.7	78.5	386.1
45. C.D.R. delle Provincie Lombarde	4,078.3	66.4	512.0
46. Abbey National	3,939.9	59.7	290.6
47. Commerzbank	3,870.9	112.8	332.2
48. Toronto Dominion Bank	3,745.2	47.8	561.7
49. Chemical Banking Corp.	3,705.0	70.9	−482.2
50. Istituto Bancario San Paolo de Torino	3,683.4	108.7	511.6

Source: "The Euromoney 500," *Euromoney*, June 1990.

markets. Since such competition usually occurs for domestic banking activities, it will not be discussed here. However, a number of useful analyses of the subject are available in the literature.[11]

TELECOMMUNICA-TIONS

Telephone Service and Production Worldwide

In every country, telephone *service* is provided by a local company (typically owned by the government), regardless of the skills needed to operate the system or the source of the equipment used. The *production* of telephone equipment, on the other hand, is dominated by half a dozen firms worldwide. Because the provision of telephone service is viewed as a strategic issue in the national economy, this industry is influenced by political as well as economic factors. While historically companies such as ITT (International Telephone & Telegraph) operated telephone systems in some less developed countries, by 1985 the ownership of national telephone systems virtually everywhere except the United States had become the province of national governments or their chosen domestic companies.

Producing the high-tech equipment that is used to transmit and receive telephone and other telecommunication signals requires huge capital and technological resources. Therefore, the production side of telecommunications still remains in the hands of corporations—though often with strict contractual arrangements between these corporations and governments to disallow corporate activities perceived to be against the national interest.

The production of telecommunications equipment ranges from sophisticated manufacture of incredibly tiny integrated circuits to assembly of the telephone units used in homes and offices. While most of the really technology-intensive work is done in a few industrialized countries by very large MNEs, assembly of telephones and some components, such as silicon chips, is now done in a wide variety of countries, especially in the low-cost NICs of Southeast Asia (namely Taiwan, Singapore, Hong Kong, and South Korea). Because of the pervasive nationalism in the provision of telephone service, equipment standards have never become standardized and a wide variety of standards still exists among countries.[12]

Recent History

The recent history of the provision of telephone *service* largely follows the pattern of raw materials production around the world. That is, less developed countries declared the telephone service industry to be a "national resource," and in the 1960s and 70s such countries nationalized their telephone systems. Then in the late 1980s and early 1990s, several of these same countries and some industrial nations have moved to *privatize* their telephone service provision (for example, in the UK, Chile, Mexico, and the Philippines).

On the other hand, telephone *equipment production* has followed the spread of new technology, with competition among a few large firms supported by their national governments and with fewer than 10 major competitors dominating production worldwide since World War II. The most important technological changes during the past 40 years have been the development of satellite transmission, the use of optical fibers in telephone cables, and the introduction of silicon chips of increasingly tiny dimensions to replace vacuum tubes and then transistors for information storage and switching. As these changes occurred, the competitors in the industry remained mostly the same, but their competitive positions shifted, depending on the extent to which they took advantage of the new technological opportunities.

The most important recent events that have altered competition in the telecommunications industry have been the denationalizations of telephone companies in some less developed and industrialized countries, and the opening to competition of telephone equipment production. These events are discussed in more detail below.

Industry Structure

This discussion focuses on the production side of the telecommunications industry and on international telecommunication service. Domestic telecommunication service, which is either government owned or greatly government controlled in all countries, will not be discussed here.

The telecommunications industry is now in a state of rapid transition. Due to the "information revolution," microelectronics has become the focal point of the communications business. Tiny silicon chips that can store more than 1 million bits of information per chip are being widely produced, and 4 mega-bit chips are coming into large-scale production. Such chips are used in typewriters, telephones, computers, and even in the equipment that switches telephone calls from one location to another (that is, telephone exchanges). Manufacturers of telephones and other telecommunications equipment must act quickly to master the new technology and create products that utilize it. The companies that modernize their products rapidly will survive. Those that do not will be pushed out of the market.

Perhaps even more important than the technological factors that influence competition in the telecommunications industry are national technical standards. There are no universally accepted standards that would allow companies to standardize their products worldwide. In addition to technical differences in the provision of electricity (e.g., 120-volt power versus 220-volt power), there are government-imposed standards for telecommunications equipment that differ even among the closest European neighbors, let alone countries as far apart as Japan and the United States. Such standards favor domestic companies over their foreign competitors and lead to a fragmenting of competition internationally. This problem has been reduced significantly in Europe, through negotiation of common standards as part of the EC–1992 initiative.

Despite these problems, the providers of telecommunications equipment are mostly large, diversified MNEs. Although many components are produced by smaller firms in various industrialized countries and some LDCs, the bulk of telecommunications switching gear, satellites, and other equipment used internationally is made by fewer than a dozen firms worldwide. Each of these firms has a large share of its home country market and competes actively in dozens of other countries.

Firms

Telecommunications is an international industry. The telephone systems of virtually every country in the noncommunist world have been installed and supplied by a handful of companies. The most important are American Telephone & Telegraph (AT&T) based in the United States; Northern Telecom based in Canada; Siemens, based in West Germany; L. M. Ericsson (LME), based in Sweden; and Nippon Electric Corporation (NEC), based in Japan. Each of these companies has diversified into other industries, though telecommunications is a multibillion-dollar part of each company's annual sales. Table 24–5 presents some basic background information about these companies.

The strategies of the five companies diverge to some extent. Ericsson has focused most of its corporate resources on development of the so-called office of the future, in which data processing, telephone conversations, and word processing will all be operated through an electronic system. (IBM, which entered the telecommunications market from the data processing business, has also chosen to place substantial company resources into the development of an electronic office.) On the other hand, Siemens has been moving more cautiously in the telecommunications market, while also using its resources to support expansion in many other businesses, such as power-generating equipment and electrical machinery. The following paragraphs offer a brief commentary on the competitive strategies of the five companies.

Until January 1, 1984, *AT&T* operated the local and long-distance telephone systems in most parts of the United States. (A few areas were served by General Telephone & Electronics Corporation.) About 80 percent of AT&T's more than 1 million employees worked in operating telephone companies that provided service to firms and individual households. On January 1, 1984, AT&T divested all of its local telephone operating companies, retaining only long-distance and international service, plus telephone manufacturing, telecommunications research, and corporate headquarters. Because of its history as the highly regulated near-monopolist supplier of telephone services in the United States, AT&T is viewed as being at a great disadvantage in knowledge of how to market its products to potential customers. Currently, AT&T appears to be focusing on the creation of the "office of the future," based on the telecommunications technology that it has developed. It has entered the market for desktop computers with machines that uses its very advanced operating system, UNIX. It has been mounting an effort within the United States to provide full office automation to its numerous clients. For several years, it has offered satellite communications to private users as well as telephone companies. In general, AT&T is aiming to produce and market products and services across the full range of the telecommunications industry.

Northern Telecom has been the most internationally diversified of the telecommunications competitors, due largely to its relatively limited home market in Canada. The company has private branch exchange (PBX) manufacturing operations not only in North America, but widely spread through Europe (France, Ireland) and Asia (China). Telecom is largely focused on the telecommunications equipment manufacturing business, and is much less diversified across industries than its key international competitors. This firm has demonstrated its technological leadership and its ability to compete internationally by being the first (and by 1990 the only) non-Japanese supplier to Nippon Telephone and Telegraph, the Japanese telephone company. By positioning its recent PBX, the Meridian system, as an "open system," Northern Telecom has entered the "global" telecommunications market of the 1990s with a product that can meet local standards in most countries and has a greater number of data and voice lines than most other PBXs at the time.

L. M. Ericsson's approach to the office of the future is to coordinate the word processing, telephone, and data processing functions through switching equipment

TABLE 24–5

Five Telecommunications
Companies

AT&T

Founded in 1885
Headquarters in New York
Employs 304,200 people worldwide
1989 sales—$36.1 billion
Main business segments:
　Western Electric
　Communications information systems
　International
　Bell Labs
Major recent product:
　System 85 private branch exchange
Important competitive advantages:
　Best R&D (Bell Labs)
　Well positioned for "electronic office" because of long U.S. experience

---

Northern Telecom, Ltd.

Founded in 1914
Headquarters in Mississauga, Ontario
Employs 47,000 people worldwide
1989 sales—$6.1 billion
Main business segments:
　Telecommunications
　Cables
　Semiconductors
　Other
Major recent products:
　Meridian PBX
　Sonet (synchronous optical network)
Important competitive advantages:
　Reputation for high-quality products
　Experience in international competition

L. M. Ericsson

Founded in 1876
Headquarters in Stockholm
Employs 71,000 people worldwide
1989 sales—$6.5 billion
Main business segments:
　Public telecommunications $2.7 billion
　Information systems   1.5 billion
　Cable   1.0 billion
　Defense systems   0.5 billion
　All other   0.8 billion
Major recent products:
　AXE central switching unit
　MD 110 digital subscriber exchange
Important competitive advantages:
　Quality of products
　Experience in production of telephone exchanges

Nippon Electric Corporation

Founded in 1899
Headquarters in Tokyo
Employs 73,080 worldwide
1989 sales—$24.6 billion

TABLE 24–5

concluded

Main business segments:	
Communications	37%
Computers and industrial electronic systems	24%
Electronic devices	24%
Home electronics	10%
Major recent product:	
NEAX digital switching system	
Important competitive advantages:	
Reputation for high-quality products	
Major semiconductor producer	

Siemens

Founded in 1847
Headquarters in Munich
Employs 353,000 people worldwide
1989 sales—$36.8 billion

Main business segments:	
Telecommunications and security systems	$5.8 billion
Energy and automation	7.2 billion
Nuclear power	7.1 billion
PBX and data systems	5.8 billion
Medical equipment	3.0 billion
Electrical and automotive systems	2.4 billion

Major recent product:
EDX-C stored-program control switching system
(for telex)
Important competitive advantages:
"Systems manufacturer," focuses on selling complete systems
Manufactures own semiconductors
Reputation for high-quality products

such as the PABX that the firm already produces. This approach differs from that of IBM, which appears to be basing its office of the future on a central computer, with telephone switching and other functions coordinated through the computer. LME has gained expertise in office equipment through its acquisitions of Datasaab computer company and Facit typewriter company in 1981. Information systems became a major part of LME's business, with sales equal to those of its telecommunications division in the mid-1980s. As the second largest supplier of telecommunications equipment in markets other than the United States (behind CGE, the French firm), LME has a substantial experience advantage over AT&T, NEC, and Siemens. After failing to achieve a significant position in computers, Ericsson sold its data processing division in 1988 and refocused on telecommunications.

Nippon Electric Corporation has a far smaller overseas marketing network than the other four companies. Therefore, one aspect of its strategy is to expand the international part of its business, focusing especially on the United States. NEC relies on its image as a supplier of high-quality electronic products, though its after-sale service is viewed as poor by many critics. Much like AT&T, until recently NEC sold much of its equipment directly to the Japanese telephone company, a related firm. Since NEC began to look for outside customers, its approach has been weak in the marketing area. Its strengths lie in its ability to produce very reliable equipment and in its low costs due to the use of efficient Japanese and Asian labor. Its present strategy is to merge its activities in the computer and communications areas toward the emerging industry of information technology. NEC expects to lead this industry in technology development.

Siemens is the second most diversified of the five companies. Its products range from light bulbs to nuclear power plants, with about a third of its sales in telecommunications. Except for its telecommunications division, Siemens is quite similar to the U.S.-based General Electric Company. As the largest private sector company in Germany, Siemens plays a very important role in that country's economy. Its competitive advantages appear to lie in a reputation for reliable, well-designed products and for after-sale service. A major criticism of the company is that it moves very bureaucratically, reacting to competitors' advances rather than leading the market. In the telecommunications market, the ability to introduce products that use the latest technology has become more and more important during the past decade. Thus, Siemens will probably have to become more innovative to compete effectively in this market in the future. Through licensing and joint ventures with two California firms, it has entered the market for computer chips. This strategy is expected to help Siemens design state-of-the-art telecommunications products.

No one can know the future. It is not possible to forecast exactly which of the five companies will produce the best results in the 1990s. Nonetheless, based on the competitive advantages and the current strategies of the companies, it is possible to gain some useful insights into the likely direction of future competition.

CONCLUSIONS

Each of the four industries that have been examined in this chapter has been important internationally during the 1980s and into the 1990s. All four are linked through financial transactions and information networks, though no individual firms own businesses in all four. Each of these industries also involves competitors ranging from the largest multinational enterprises all the way down to the smallest local bank, gas station, or telephone vendor. While the discussion has focused on large firms that participate in several segments of the market, the activities of thousands of smaller firms play an important role in the total picture—especially when the large MNEs are excluded from market segments that are protected for local, typically smaller, competitors.

Despite the great importance of government regulation and participation in these industries, the dominant firms in the international parts of the industries are mostly private sector corporations. During the 20th century, government-owned enterprises have not gained the level of international diversification that their private counterparts have achieved. This fact does not deny the growing activities of such firms as Petrobras (based in Brazil), Crédit Lyonnais (based in France), or Nippon Telephone & Telegraph (based in Japan) in other countries. In the future, a much greater share of global business may very well be held by public sector corporations, depending on how firms, both public and private, respond to future competitive challenges. Many of the leading state-owned firms, such as British Petroleum and NTT, are being privatized to some degree, and this change is creating partially state-owned MNEs.

While only the telecommunications industry is necessarily based in the rapidly changing electronics field, the banking industry has clearly become more and more dependent on international communications and data processing, and the petroleum industry utilizes sophisticated electronic equipment for information processing, production machinery controls, and even exploration. Companies in the automobile industry are moving to "factories of the future," which feature extensive use of industrial robots. The nature of competition in each of these four industries is changing as such technological shifts occur and as government policies toward foreign private sector enterprises change.

QUESTIONS

1. Explain the importance of *technology* in the petroleum, automobile, banking, and telecommunications industries.
2. What firms are major competitors in the oil refining business in the United States, Europe, and the Middle East? What firms are major competitors in the gasoline sales business? Why is there a substantial difference between the two?
3. What are the key factors that determine the competitiveness of banks in domestic markets in (*a*) the United States and (*b*) Latin America?
4. What are the key factors that determine the competitiveness of banks in international financial markets in the United States and Europe?
5. Describe the competitive positions of AT&T, LME, and NEC in the production of global telecommunication equipment production. Which strategy do you think will work best in the next five years? Why?
6. The oil industry is based on a natural resource that governments have increasingly chosen to nationalize in the past two decades. Why does the telecommunications industry, which uses almost no natural resources, face similar government restrictions?
7. Do you expect to see more or fewer international banks in the next 10 years? Why?
8. Which countries are the main producers of crude petroleum? Which countries are the main consumers of oil-based products? What can multinational oil companies do to benefit from this situation?
9. How would you expect IBM's entry into the telecommunications industry to affect competition in that industry? What will be the probable impact of IBM's entry on the other firms mentioned in the text?
10. Describe a set of market segments in the petroleum, automobile, and telecommunications industries that would be appropriate ones for small firms to enter. Explain why each of these segments would be potentially viable for a small firm.

REFERENCES

Aliber, Robert. "International Banking: A Survey," *Journal of Money, Credit, and Banking,* November 1984, part 2.

American Petroleum Institute. *Oil & Gas Journal.* Various issues.

Anderson, Robert. *Fundamentals of the Petroleum Industry.* Norman: University of Oklahoma Press, 1984.

Crane, Dwight, and Samuel Hayes. "The Evolution of International Banking Competition and its Implications for Regulation," *Journal of Bank Research,* Spring 1983.

The Economist, "International Banking," (annual supplement in March issue).

Exxon Corporation. *Middle East Oil.* New York: Exxon, 1984.

Fortune, "The International 500," (annual August issue).

Odell, Peter. *Oil and World Power.* 8th ed. Middlesex, England: Penguin Books, 1986.

Roncaglia, Alessandro. *The International Oil Market.* Armonk, N.Y.: M. E. Sharpe, 1985.

Sampson, Anthony. *The Seven Sisters.* New York: Basic Books, 1979.

_____ . *The Money Lenders.* New York: Penguin Books, 1983.

Womack, James, Daniel Jones, and Daniel Roos. *The Machine that Changed the World.* New York: Rawson Associates, 1990.

World Motor Vehicle Data. Detroit: World Motor Vehicle Association, various editions.

NOTES

[1] *Oil & Gas Journal,* December 25, 1989.

[2] The firms competed actively against each other in many contexts, but not in pricing. The U.S. firms often have sought U.S. government support for their mutual interests.

[3] Exxon, *Middle East Oil,* p. 24.

[4] See *Oil & Gas Journal.*

[5] Anthony Sampson, *The Seven Sisters* (New York: Basic Books, 1979); Robert O. Anderson, *Fundamentals of the Petroleum Industry* (Norman: University of Oklahoma Press, 1984); and Peter Odell, *Oil and World Power.*

[6] *World Motor Vehicle Data.*

[7] Dwight Crane and Samuel Hayes, "The Evolution of International Banking Competition and Its Implications for Regulation," *Journal of Bank Research,* Spring 1983, p. 41.

[8] Data calculated from World Bank, *World Debt Tables* (various issues), and Bank for International Settlements, *Lending by Group of 10 Banks to Nonresident Borrowers* (various issues).

[9] Data on United States, Great Britain, and Venezuela are from Business International Corporation, *Investing, Licensing, and Trading Conditions* (New York: Business International Corporation, 1989 country issue for each country).

[10] Bank for International Settlements semiannual data on nonresident deposits in group of 10 commercial banks, June 1990.

[11] See, for example, R. Alton Gilbert, "Bank Market Structure and Competition," *Journal of Money, Credit, and Banking,* November 1984, pp. 617–45; also see Gerald Hanweck and Stephen Rhoades, "Dominant Firms, 'Deep Pockets,' and Local Market Competition in Banking," *Journal of Economics and Business,* 1984, pp. 391–402.

[12] See, for example, *Business Week,* March 31, 1986, pp. 68–70.

25

Multinational Enterprises and the World Order: A Look to the Future

This chapter attempts to project the key concerns of international business managers to the end of the century. It looks at government policies, internal company activities, the economic environment, and the political environment. It suggests changes that will take place in the kinds of business carried out by multinational enterprises. In general, it extrapolates into the future and interprets with respect to international firms some of the key technological, regulatory, and social trends that are already under way. The main goals of the chapter are to:

1. Demonstrate the importance of technological change in determining business patterns.

2. Discuss possible shifts in government policy toward MNEs.

3. Consider the likelihood of the MNE's survival.

4. Project likely shifts in competitive conditions in international industries.

5. Project likely shifts in relationships between managers and workers, between managers and company owners, and among managers within the MNE.

INTRODUCTION

This chapter looks to the future. What will be the key concerns of MNE managers in the year 2000? How will MNEs deal with home and host governments and societies as the number of MNEs grows and as national priorities shift? And what will be the major characteristics of international business a decade from now? The answers to these questions cannot be known for certain, but some of the broad outline of future conditions can be read from today's circumstances. Without speculating too extensively, we will give an outlook on some of the important issues that are likely to face managers in international business during the next 10 years.

The next section discusses a range of issues that will present major challenges to managers in international firms in the future. Then a perspective is offered on the sometimes rocky, sometimes smooth, but always important relations between international firms and governments. It is argued that as a reaction to competitive conditions and to external pressures, such as government demands on firms, companies will increasingly become **international contractors,** using contractual relationships rather than ownership in many international business situations. The fourth section examines key aspects of the structure and conduct of competition in global markets. This is followed by a look at important developments in internal company relations among workers, managers, and owners and, finally, some conclusions.

MAJOR MANAGERIAL CONSIDERATIONS FOR INTERNATIONAL FIRMS

Technology

Technology is arguably the most important input in the production of goods and services, since it determines the manner in which capital, workers, and other factors are utilized. Since it is not possible to know what inventions will be made in the future, it is likewise impossible to know what key innovations will transform the workplace.

In the industrialized countries, we have seen a continuing trend toward the production of such services as recreation, government, and computer programming during the past half-century. *Employment* in agriculture, fishing, and other sources of food products has been declining, while the *production* of food products has continued to grow (due to laborsaving advances in production technology). Similarly, employment in manufacturing has ceased to grow substantially, and has even been declining in some countries—again while output has continued to rise due to greater efficiency and more use of other production factors. The trend toward greater employment in the provision of services will probably continue in the industrialized countries, though not to the complete exclusion of manufacturing and the production of raw materials.

One important reason for continuing to manufacture in industrialized countries, despite the lower production costs that often exist in LDCs, is the importance of **spillover benefits** from manufacturing. When a firm produces automobiles in Detroit, that production leads to related production of tires, steel, glass, and so on to supply the automakers, which in turn leads to the development of new products and processes through the experiences of the various manufacturers. Such spillover benefits help maintain the technological advantages of the innovating countries—which would be lost if manufacturing were fully transferred to other countries.[1]

There are other important reasons for continuing to manufacture. For one, some products can be produced only where technical knowledge is available; these products include high-tech electronics, specialty chemicals, and aerospace vehicles. Another reason is that firms do not want to subject all of their manufacturing to "country risk" problems (which are particularly prevalent in LDCs), so they typically diversify production into both DCs and LDCs. Finally, some products are simply cheaper to produce and distribute in industrialized countries, which are the main markets. All of this implies that manufacturing will continue to be a very significant base of the economies of industrialized countries.[2]

An important aspect of technological development is its impact on the workplace. The clearest tendency in technological change is that such change generally leads to a reduced need for production inputs, or to changes in the amounts of certain inputs needed, or to greater satisfaction of consumer demands—in each instance raising the economic welfare of society. Based on this reasoning, we can expect future technological change in industrialized countries to reduce the amount of time required for work and to increase the amount of leisure time. Though the tendency is the same in less-developed countries, high levels of unemployment and highly skewed income distributions will continue to limit the benefits of technological change in such countries as compared with industrialized countries.

A specific change in workplace activity that has occurred recently and promises to continue into the future is office computerization. Microcomputers have revolutionized the performance of many business tasks—from typing to copying, to mailing, to financial forecasting—and this has led to greater decentralization of work. More people carry out office activities at home, with fewer trips and more telecommunication to the office. Since more and more people are employed in office-type activities, in manufacturing firms as well as service providers, and in government as well as the private sector, computer-related changes in the office environment are radically altering how people do their jobs. From the perspective of the MNE manager, those firms that carry out this transition most effectively will gain a competitive advantage over rivals.

Government/Business Relations

If we ignore the possibility of a war between major industrial powers, which could dramatically alter government/business relations, then changes in government policies are likely to be incremental during the next decade. That is, national governments recognize the benefits and costs of allowing MNEs to operate. Therefore, these governments will continue to impose policies that constrain MNEs from undertaking what they view as undesirable activities (e.g., massive destabilizing currency transfers, production switching to avoid labor disputes, pollution-causing production, electronic transfer of "sensitive" information across national borders), and they will continue to try to attract MNE activities that they view as desirable (e.g., local R&D, manufacturing, transfer of knowledge). This broad agreement that MNEs are "legitimate" actors in business was truly confirmed by the fall of the Berlin Wall and the Eastern European countries' efforts to attract MNEs there.

At the transnational level, intergovernmental agreements on policy toward MNEs remain very elusive. The attempts of several organizations to formulate codes of conduct and other transnational policies have been relatively unsuccessful. Aside from further agreements to share information about company activities and some standards on corporate behavior, such as nonintervention in government affairs, major transnational policies that would affect the investment or major operating decisions of MNEs appear unlikely.

The United Nations began an effort to create a **Code of Conduct on Transnational Corporations** soon after the call in 1972 for a **New International Economic Order** that would redistribute wealth to give the less developed countries a greater share. The aim of this code is to prescribe guidelines or rules whose observance will ensure that multinational firms more fully serve national goals in the countries where they operate. Issues such as technology transfer, international financial transfers, labor relations, and information flows, constitute the core of the proposed code. Although the United Nations members have been negotiating for more than 20 years, several major disagreements still block the final passage of the code. However, the United Nations members are fairly well agreed on the main provisions of the code, most of which are noted in the accompanying box.

At the multilateral level, other initiatives besides the UN Code of Conduct have taken front stage in the past several years. Certainly, the European Community's EC–1992 effort to advance regional integration through a wide-ranging set of common rules and policy harmonizations is creating a European policy environment that will become more and more uniform among the member countries. This will result in a much more important role for the European Community in dealing with MNEs—on antitrust, taxes, labor relations, and many other issues—and a situation in which those MNEs that operate without European affiliates may face less-favorable treatment than those operating from within the Community. Essentially a code of conduct will be produced through common, *multilateral* legislation in the EC that gives the European governments more leverage in dealing with the *multinational* firms.

A similar phenomenon is occurring in North America, with the establishment of the U.S.–Canada Free Trade Agreement and the negotiations for a U.S.–Mexico Free Trade accord, which presumably would include Canada as well. This trading bloc can be expected to harmonize more of its member countries' treatment of MNEs, primarily on trade issues, but potentially on other economic concerns too. The bold steps by Mexico to link itself more closely to the United States beginning in 1989 have generated a wholesale scramble by other Latin American countries to forge economic ties and potentially to move into a Western Hemisphere trade alliance. This possibility is greatly limited by the huge differences in the levels of economic development of the potential member countries, but the global wave of promarket policy that is underway could very well lead to a significant trade partnership in the Americas.

The regional groupings could include an Asian component, either if Japan is able to join other countries there to form a trading bloc, or if the Asian countries (perhaps plus Korea and Taiwan) industrialize rapidly enough and integrate their economies enough to create a major market there. Whether or not the Asian countries join North America and Europe as regional economic blocs, the blocs that do develop will offer greater opportunities for MNEs to realize scale economies within each region, along with greater challenges from the firms that are attracted to try to serve the huge regional markets.

The less developed countries generally moved toward more favorable regulation of MNEs in the 1980s compared with the two previous decades. They have turned away from the strategy of inward-looking development, characterized by heavy emphasis on import substitution, to a more outward-looking view, in which greater participation of foreign firms is permitted. As LDC government managers become more expert in dealing with MNEs, however, they are tending

**IB
ILLUSTRATION**

The United Nations Code of Conduct on Transnational Corporations*

In mid-1991, final agreement on this code still faced a number of hurdles. However, the overriding structure of the code was in place and was broadly accepted. Major sections of the code cover the following subjects:

Policy toward MNEs

1. *Observance of Domestic Laws in Host Countries.* Local subsidiaries, branches, and other affiliates of MNEs are to be subject to the national laws of the country in which they operate.

2. *Settlement of Disputes between MNEs and Countries.* The host government has the right to choose the court or other legal arbiter of disputes involving firms within its jurisdiction.

3. *Noninterference in Domestic Political Affairs.* MNEs should not engage in activities that undermine the host country's political, social, and constitutional systems.

4. *Respect for National Sovereignty.* MNEs must respect the national sovereignty of host countries and the right of host countries to exercise sovereignty over their natural resources and wealth.

Policy toward Governments

5. *Fair and Equitable Treatment.* MNEs should receive fair and equitable treatment from host governments.

6. *National Treatment.* Subject to needs for national security and other government policy goals, MNEs should receive treatment similar to that received by domestic enterprises in similar circumstances.

7. *Nationalization and Compensation.* States have the right to nationalize assets of MNEs, and compensation is to be paid according to applicable legal rules.

8. *Funds Transfers by MNEs.* MNEs are entitled to transfer all payments legally due. Transfers are subject to relevant legislation of the host country such as foreign exchange laws.

The bilateral assignment of responsibilities to companies and governments follows the structure of the OECD Code (1976) and is intended to create a stable business environment conducive to foreign direct investment and other company activities that stimulate economic development. ∎

*See, for example, United Nations Center on Transnational Corporations, *CTC Reporter*, Spring 1990, which discusses the code effort from several perspectives.

to follow the industrial countries in demanding more from these firms. (Since 1985, for example, the Brazilian government has demanded that all micro- and mini-computers sold in the country be locally manufactured.[3]) Nevertheless, the broad sweep of openness is quite clear from Latin America to Asia and in between.

Very important exceptions to the basic trend are firms in raw materials industries whose ownership LDC governments took or kept in the 1960s and 1970s. These governments show every sign that they will continue to own and control such state-owned firms without private sector participation. On the other hand a strong trend toward **privatization** clearly is underway in other industries, from manufacturing to public services. As a result, opportunities are growing for MNEs to enter directly in formerly restricted industries and to work with raw materials industries via licensing, management contracts, and other creative "strategic alliances" with the state-owned firms.

The phenomenon of *privatization* has become a very important signal worldwide of governments' willingness to permit a greater role to the private sector in economic development. From the sale to the public of British Airways to the sale of the Argentine telephone company to foreign investors, all the way to the denationalization of many industries in the Eastern European countries, the number and value of privatizations in the past decade is truly awesome. This process is continuing today, and portends increasing MNE/host government *ownership* links, as state-owned firms are partially sold to MNEs, and then the public-private joint ventures make their way forward.

Company/Society Relations

While market-oriented government policy has become more widely accepted in recent years, so also has the demand for greater corporate responsiveness to national concerns such as pollution control, fair labor relations practices, and so on. International firms undoubtedly will face growing demands for accountability for their actions worldwide. Union Carbide's need to meet claims due to the industrial accident in 1984, when its joint venture plant in Bhopal, India, leaked deadly gas that killed more than 2,000 people,[4] is one striking example in which corporate responsibility was essentially forced on the firm—and such demands can be expected to increase in the future. The joint venture itself, a limited liability company, had far too few assets to settle those claims, and the parent company stepped in to meet the costs.

Despite popular movements that favor smaller firms (promoted, for example, by E. F. Schumacher's *Small is Beautiful*) and a less-bureaucratic society, large MNEs with competitive advantages, including scale economies and international information transfer, play an increasing role in business worldwide. This is not to say that all business is becoming more concentrated, but rather that more firms are becoming multinational. In the United States, the rate of growth of small firms is far greater than that of large MNEs—but so also is the rate of failure of the small firms.[5] On balance, one may conclude that small local firms and large MNEs will continue to coexist, without any trend toward either smaller or larger average firm size.

Industry Structure

The 1980s witnessed a dramatic rise in very large corporate mergers in the industrialized countries. From Bridgestone's purchase of Firestone, to CGE's purchase of ITT's telecommunications operations in Europe, to Hoechst's purchase of Celanese Corporation, these "megamergers" have become almost commonplace. At the other end of the size spectrum, thousands of tiny firms have become multinational in the same industries in which the megamergers have occurred. And even the largest firms have either chosen or been forced to contract out some of their activities, rather than internalizing, again adding to the number of competitors. Industry structure is perhaps becoming more change-able, though not any more or any less concentrated on average.

One result of the mergers and acquisitions that have been taking place is that newly formed competitors often shake up previous industry structures. When a chemical company buys an oil company, the vertical linkages involved affect competitive conditions in both the oil and the chemical industry. The chemical company (e.g., Du Pont) obtains a guaranteed source of supply of raw material at a relatively low price, and the oil company (e.g., Conoco) gains a customer for a substantial part of its output. This kind of competitive positioning is sure to continue, resulting in major realignments of firms in each industry. (Note that such realignments are due to the acquisition strategies of firms, rather than to technological changes, which are another factor tending to remake industry structures.)

Perhaps the most striking shift in international industry structure that has developed in the past few years is the use of *strategic alliances*. These cooper-ative agreements between firms that often are competitors in other contexts are remaking industry structures in numerous ways. First, as in the auto industry, direct competitors such as Toyota and General Motors have formed joint ven-tures to produce cars together, to benefit from the management skills of one partner (Toyota) and the market access of the other (General Motors). Literally dozens of additional ventures have been formed, involving all of the major competitors in this global industry. Chrysler, which owns 12 percent of Mitsu-bishi, jointly produces cars with Mitsubishi in Illinois; Renault and Volvo each own 45 percent of the other's truck and bus producing subsidiaries; a full listing of these auto industry alliances would take more than this entire page. While certainly all of the cooperative ventures will not last, the key question is whether they contribute to industry stability or disintegration. Thus far, market shares have varied significantly, but the major players in the industry have not.

In other industries such as computers, alliances for the purpose of develop-ing new products such as memory chips or new technologies such as risc-based logic chips and superconductors have sprouted up in the United States and Europe. These ventures often group half a dozen or more competitors that pool funds for research on the new products, hoping to take away knowledge that will enable each to survive in this very capital-intensive business. Thus far, these ventures have been highly unstable (e.g., U.S. Memories, which was dis-banded in 1989), leaving the competitors mostly to develop their technologies separately.

The strategic alliances have the potential to remake industry structures as they redefine the boundaries of competitiveness and cooperation. At present there is no clear picture of what kinds of alliances in which industries can survive for long periods of time; this picture may become more focused as we move through the 1990s.

Company Internal Relations

One of the most intractable problems of industrial society has always been the **alienation** of workers from their jobs.[6] When jobs consist of carrying out a few functions within a large, impersonal assembly line or a complicated production process, such alienation is commonplace. Over time, industrial psychologists and other investigators have developed ways to reduce the severity of this problem. One way is to move workers into different kinds of work during the day, to maintain mental alertness. Another is to involve workers in company decision making, whether through worker representation on plant councils or boards of corporate supervision (as in Germany's codetermination), or through quality circles, or through the Japanese "ringi" system of consultative decision making. The goal of all these techniques is to create a more productive, more satisfied work force. As the problem of alienation has become more widely recognized, solutions are being more extensively implemented.

The problem is far from solved, as demonstrated by the occurrence of strikes and demonstrations from time to time in all of the industrialized countries. However, as manufacturing and raw materials production become more mechanized and as more workers function in office environments rather than in factories or fields, the severity of the problem is reduced to some degree. The future human relations problems of companies will tend to relate to fair treatment and participation in decision making. As noted above, many methods of increasing participation have been tried, and more are being developed all the time. One key source of future competitive advantages will be the skill to manage human relations within the firm so that employees are motivated and productive and the human capital investment they embody is challenged and tapped.

Relations between Developed and Less Developed Countries

The political environment plays a part in the MNEs' future, not only through dealings with individual host and home countries, but also through broader political relations among blocs of countries. The powerful blocs of North America and Europe (plus Japan) will play a continued dominant role in dealing with MNEs. If less developed countries become more integrated into the international market system, then substantially greater MNE activity will develop in those countries.

Because the LDCs each face different levels of economic development, different resources, different political goals, and so on, no grouping of such countries appears likely to confront the MNEs in the future. Barring the emergence of successful interest groups such as OPEC in the 1970s, the LDCs will probably continue to cooperate with industrialized countries, seeking financial aid and other assistance and not opposing the basic market economy that is used. This does not mean to say that relations between the two groups of countries will proceed smoothly in the future, but rather that the disputes between them will probably not lead to fragmentation of the international economic system. In fact, what appears more likely is the integration of countries such as those in Latin America with the North American industrial nations—and the integration of the "newly-industrializing" nations of Eastern Europe with the European Community—and possibly some of the Asian countries with Japan.

SURVIVAL OF THE MNE?

Concerns and Bargaining Strengths

Previous chapters have discussed the relative bargaining positions of MNEs and governments in industrialized, less developed, and formerly-communist nations. Drawing from those discussions, a list of significant factors that should determine bargaining positions in the future is shown in Table 25–1. As long as a country can supply raw materials used in production or offer a market significant enough to attract MNE business, that country will possess a bargaining capability vis-à-vis MNEs that enables it to channel their activities in return for allowing them access to the materials or market. On the other side of the coin,

TABLE 25–1

Bargaining Chips of MNEs and Governments

Governments	Companies
Control over access to raw materials	Control over technology
Control over market access	Control over international transmission of information
Setting the rules of the game (e.g., the role of private enterprise, the operation of state-owned firms)	Production-switching capability
	Access to export markets
Setting specific rules on MNEs—taxes, permissions, etc.	Flexibility to change strategy and activities limited only by preferences of owners
The obsolescing bargain	Economies of scale and scope
	Control over financial resources

as long as an MNE has some proprietary capability that governments see as desirable, such as product technology or distribution channels into foreign markets, plus the ability to move to another country if a government is not sufficiently cooperative, that MNE will possess a bargaining capability relative to the governments. (MNEs are limited in their choice of strategies by their owners' preferences for management of the firm, while governments are limited by their constituents' preferences, as expressed through either a voting process or some more authoritarian method of control.)

The relationships between MNEs and governments will continue to operate as bargaining situations—favoring one or the other as political, technological, competitive, and other conditions change. The obsolescing bargain will continue to characterize business/government negotiations, requiring company managers to plan their entry and operating strategies to recognize the "hostage" effect of placing fixed assets in any government's jurisdiction (including that of the home country). While governments are discovering new methods of obtaining benefits from MNE activities all the time, there is no tendency to eliminate MNEs as actors in international business, since many of their bargaining advantages remain proprietary and highly "appropriate" (i.e., capable of being protected by the firms).[7]

The New MNE—The International Contractor

From the bargaining situations described above, and due to increased competition from other firms, MNEs are experiencing more and more pressure to externalize their activities. Whether it be the demand of a host government to take on a local partner on the enticement of a joint research project with a rival firm to reduce R&D costs, pressures are mounting toward increased contractual arrangements between firms. Simultaneously, the previous reliance on wholly owned affiliates, especially preferred by U.S.-based firms, has shifted toward a greater willingness to utilize nontraditional methods such as joint ventures, licensing or service contracting, turnkey ventures, and combinations of these, as managers realize the relative profitability and strategic viability of such arrangements.

As additional small firms become multinational (by establishing affiliates in three or more countries), the tendency is again to externalize some activities, especially when the firm's resources or skills do not permit it to go beyond its core activities. What we are seeing, in essence, is that even small firms are looking at multiple countries as their markets—rather than being constrained by national borders in their strategy making. Then, as corporate expansion occurs, and given low costs of international transportation and easy communication, they seek new markets or products in different countries. Just as small domestic firms often contract out for parts of their business, so too do the new small multinationals, which face similar constraints on their activities.

In sum, large MNEs are utilizing more externalized contracting due to regulatory constraints and both small and large firms are using externalized contracting due to their internal economic and managerial constraints. Both of these trends foreshadow the rise of the **international contractor (INC),** as discussed in Chapter 2. The INC is defined as a firm that carries out business activities in at least two countries, but without necessarily owning affiliates in both. The INC operates from a home office that controls the use of its key competitive advantages, such as proprietary production technology and its international information network. The home office also decides when to utilize the INC's competitive advantages through internalized operations such as local and foreign subsidiaries and when to sell knowledge or some other intermediate goods to potential customers. The INC is still a multinational firm, in the sense that it possesses multinational operations; its difference from the MNE lies solely in its lack of dependence on *ownership* of affiliates as the main vehicle for using its competitive advantages in different national environments. (The MNE, in fact, is a subset of the INC.)

The international contractor, like the MNE, may be a small or a large firm. The INC is in principle more open to nontraditional means of doing business around the world. For example, when Citibank discovered that its data processing skills were in demand by clients and competitors around the world, it chose to sell more than just its banking services. Now Citibank sells dozens of services to outside clients—access to a global computerized information network, technical support to clients that want to use the system, the software for record-keeping in such banking activities as customer deposit and loan accounts, technical support for use of that software, and so on. Rather than internalizing these services completely, Citibank has chosen to contract out for their use and expand its sales into markets that the bank itself cannot enter and into services that it previously limited to internal use.

Many other examples of international contractors exist. General Electric Company, the U.S.-based diversified electrical products manufacturer, has added a trading company to its portfolio of businesses. The trading company seeks outlets for GE products in most countries of the world and tries to dispose of products that it has received in payment from customers unable to pay in hard currency. GE has even used the trading company to sell the products of other firms in international markets, functioning somewhat like the Japanese Sogo Shosha as a middleman between a producer and the ultimate purchaser.

Conflicts between MNEs and Governments

The management of conflicts with home and host governments is already a crucial MNE task, and that task will become even more important in the future. Gladwin and Walter (1980), for example, found evidence of 650 such conflicts involving a sample of only five multinational firms during the period 1969–78.

Behrman and Grosse (1990) examine in detail the areas of potential and actual conflict between MNEs and governments—areas ranging from transfer pricing to interference in domestic political affairs, from employment practices to technology transfer.

Behrman and Grosse have developed a framework that offers useful insights into the key strategic considerations. This framework is shown in Figure 25–1. They reason that corporate strategy for managing a conflict (or cooperation) situation with a government should be based on an evaluation of: (1) the bargaining resources held by the government and the company; (2) the stakes that each party has in the situation; and (3) the goal congruence or similarity of interests between government and company in the particular situation. All three dimensions contribute to the MNE's bargaining power relative to the government, and strategy to deal with the government should be based on an accurate assessment of the firm's bargaining strengths and weaknesses.

For example, a firm that finds itself in position M will have a very favorable opportunity to receive desired treatment by the government, since all three bargaining dimensions favor the firm. This kind of situation occurs when, for

FIGURE 25–1

The Bargaining Relationship between MNE and Host Government

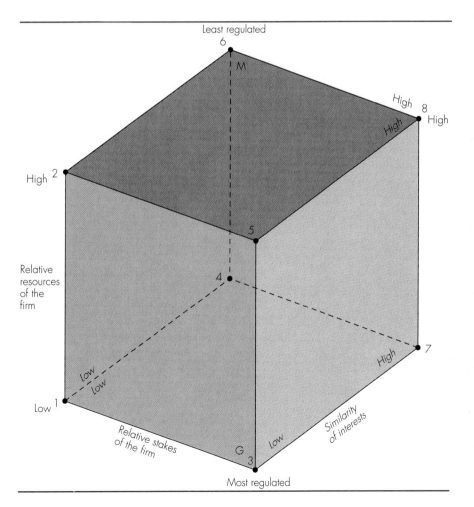

example, a high-tech firm seeks to do offshore assembly in an LDC. The firm offers employment and technology transfer, plus exports from the country; the firm has other alternative locations to carry out the offshore assembly; and the country is (typically) interested in attracting this kind of business. Contrast this example with point G, where the government is likely to have a much stronger bargaining position than the firm. This situation can be illustrated by a country with a large market dealing with a low-tech, relatively small MNE—for example the Brazilian government negotiating with U.S. consumer products firms. In this context, the government has a relatively large bargaining resource, namely control over access to the desirable market. The government has little at stake in the situation, since other consumer products from various industrial and less developed countries presumably offer similar products to those available from our example firm. And finally, the firm is assumed to be interested in serving the local market rather than exporting, so the government will probably not improve its balance of payments from this firm's activities. In sum, a strong bargaining position results for the government when the firm does not offer major help in pursuing national goals, when the firm has more at stake, and when the goals of each actor are rather divergent. Any situation of government/company bargaining can be analyzed in this framework, leading to a better understanding of the firm's options in seeking favorable treatment.

COMPETITIVE CONDITIONS

The structure and intensity of competition in market-based economies is subject to major changes when technological advances take place, when mergers or divestitures occur, when governments alter the rules of the game, and when other unanticipated events occur (e.g., the OPEC cartel's successful oil price hikes in 1973 and 1979, the breakups of AT&T in 1984 and NTT (Nippon Telephone & Telegraph) in 1985, the Latin American debt crisis of the 1980s and the fall of the Berlin Wall in 1989). This section comments on the kinds of competitive impacts that can be expected from each type of major change in conditions.

Changes in Technology

Technological innovations undoubtedly will continue to cause drastic upheavals in industry structure. Each new type of transportation vehicle has either replaced its predecessor or created a separate market for a new kind of transportation service. Each advance in communications technology has resulted in new firms and new interrelations in the communications industry. Even innovations in such low-tech areas as restaurants (e.g., the fast-food restaurant chains and the diversification of single-food providers) and recreation (e.g., the shift to high-tech running shoes) have greatly reshuffled industry structures. International restaurant chains were almost unknown 25 years ago, but McDonald's and Burger King now span much of the world. One or two brands captured most of the athletic shoe market in the 1950s and 60s, but now dozens of competitors make exotic and often quite expensive running shoes (e.g., Etonic, New Balance, and Nike, in addition to the longer-established Adidas, Pumas, and Keds).

What these technological shifts portend are major industry restructurings, many of which cannot be foreseen. On the other hand, some likely focal points of such restructurings *can* be recognized. For example, the future competition in computers, telecommunications, and transportation vehicles will surely differ tremendously from that of today; the expected change is readily anticipated.

However, it is difficult to judge which of the existing firms will survive and how the new industries will be structured.

Mergers, Acquisitions, and Divestitures

A second major cause of industry restructuring is company growth or decline via the purchase or sale of parts of the business. As has been noted repeatedly, vertical integration is often accomplished through acquisition of upstream or downstream firms. Similarly, reduction in firm size is often carried out through divestiture of divisions or subsidiaries. Each time an acquisition or divestment occurs, the competition in the industries involved changes to some degree. When the players are large (e.g., Nabisco and R. J. Reynolds, Du Pont and Conoco, General Motors and Electronic Data Systems on the expansion side and on the contraction side, ITT's sale of Continental Baking and even its telecommunications division, Pan American Airlines sale of its Pacific routes, and International Harvester's sale of its farm equipment business), the impact on the industries is substantial. When the players are small, the impacts are less extensive, but the industries are affected nonetheless. And, of course, today's small firms may evolve into tomorrow's major competitors through acquisition strategies.

Government-Owned Firms

Among the less developed countries, the euphoria of the 1960s and early 1970s, when many LDCs viewed government-owned firms as the answer to foreign-owned multinationals, has ended. State-owned companies do not automatically use more "appropriate" technology or possess the competitive advantages of MNEs. (Specifically, they have neither the multinational information networks nor the access to foreign markets of MNEs.) Based on this reasoning and on the relatively scanty economic success of state-owned firms during the past two decades, such firms are not growing noticeably in number or importance. This is not to imply that state-owned companies will disappear from the competition, but rather that their limitations are being recognized and that LDCs are in many cases finding a place for MNE participation in the same industries.

Among industrialized countries, the economic costs of operating state-owned firms has led to many privatizations in the 1980s. Conrail (in the United States), NTT (in Japan), British Telecom (in the United Kingdom), the chemical giant Montedison (in Italy), and many other government firms have been partially or totally sold to private sector buyers. The implication of all this is mainly that future competition will not be dominated by state-owned firms, but rather by MNEs and local firms that can develop sustainable competitive advantages, such as those resulting in economic efficiency. The less developed and formerly communist countries are now part of this trend as well.

LDCs versus Industrialized Countries

The differences between conditions in the developed, industrialized countries and conditions in the less developed countries should not be underemphasized. The changes in competitive conditions discussed above are likely to be accompanied by much more upheaval in the LDCs than in the industrialized countries. For example, even though state-owned companies are seen to be relatively inefficient in competition with private sector firms, many LDCs will (for "political" reasons) continue to bear the economic costs of operating some of them. Also, the changes in technology and in company size that will reshape industrial markets will not necessarily pass on to the LDCs in the same manner. The main result of the telecommunications revolution will probably be their use of different suppliers of communications and data processing equipment—since almost all of the competing firms are from industrialized countries. By the same token, the major mergers and divestitures that will redefine industry structures in global industries will in most cases probably only replace one foreign supplier with another in LDCs. On the other hand, domestic firms in such LDCs as the newly industrializing countries may become competitive in world markets—as appears to be happening in South Korea, Singapore, Hong Kong, Taiwan, and Brazil, and as has already happened in Japan.

COMPANY INTERNAL CONDITIONS

A look to the future of international business should focus not only on external, environmental conditions but also on internal (labor and personnel) issues related to the international firm. This section considers these latter issues and the relationship between owners and managers.

Labor/Management Relations

As industries become more mature, especially extractive and manufacturing industries, their labor requirements tend to decline. Greater efficiency in production often leads to reduced need for factors of production, particularly labor but also capital and other inputs. This tendency does not portend declining overall employment, because it is offset by growing employment in new industries and perhaps by shifts to more employment in the service sector, as discussed previously. Given the declining labor requirements of maturing and standardized industries, the political and collective bargaining power of unions in those industries (as such unions are now constituted) is bound to decline too.

These unions will disappear completely or will be replaced in importance by new unions in the new industries or by some alternative form of labor/management relations. That is, the United Auto Workers, the United Steel Workers, the textile unions, and several other unions will continue to decline in membership and in importance. (It is not unthinkable that the International Ladies' Garment Workers' Union (ILGWU) will not exist a decade or two from now.) These unions will be replaced by other (perhaps new) organizations of workers in, for example, electronics manufacture and biotechnology production and by worker groups in the service sector (many of which already exist). The trend away from employment in manufacturing will not eliminate conflicts between labor and management; however, those conflicts will be altered from shop floor concerns to office problems.

Current trends toward worker participation in management and/or ownership of firms in the industrialized countries may succeed in reducing the conflict between workers and managers to a very low level. Efforts to achieve Japanese-style worker productivity and commitment to the firm are likely to continue as long as the Japanese model appears to yield superior results. Apart from the Japanese model, the "excellent" firms recognized by Peters and Waterman (in *In Search of Excellence*) demonstrate the kind of focus on maintaining a satisfying, stimulating work environment that seems to succeed in many countries. Thus, it is conceivable that labor/management relations will generally improve because of the widespread recognition of the value of such improvement.

Personnel Relations

One thing that becomes more and more clear in large MNEs is that the future international contractor will employ people of many nationalities and many ethnic groups—because the corporation obtains benefits from employing locals in some countries and because the benefits of the geocentric approach to management fosters global recruitment of personnel. The competitive advantage gained from hiring the best people available, regardless of nationality, is evident in the large, successful MNEs even today.

Dow Chemical Corporation, for example, has in recent years named as head of its Latin American headquarters a North American, a Latin American, a Greek, and then a Frenchman. Each of these executives has had experience in senior positions in the company elsewhere in the world (e.g., in the European headquarters and the Asian headquarters and at corporate headquarters in Michigan), and each has continued to move up the corporate ladder. The personnel strategy of Dow Chemical is to hire the most qualified people available in the locations where they are needed and then to move these people—regardless of nationality—to new posts as their skills and the firm's needs dictate.

Management/Owner Relations

Large industrial corporations today are generally owned by large numbers of shareholders, none of whom control large percentages of the total stock of the firm. The separation of management from ownership is a fundamental characteristic of free-market development in the 20th century. This basic separation will probably continue, though more and more ways are being discovered to channel managers' efforts to serve owners' interests. (The popularity of leveraged buyouts in the late 1980s appears to be due to the ability of outside investors to locate firms in which a divergence has arisen between company capabilities, based on owners' interests, and the market value produced by managers' actions and reflected in share prices.)

Some interesting variations on this theme occur in the state-owned companies, in which management is often government appointed and the sole shareholder is the government itself. This relationship between owner and manager is quite different from the one that exists in the large private firms, and it leads to different corporate goals and strategies.

Small firms may have closely held shares that belong to the managers themselves. In such firms, there is no separation of owner from manager, and the managers presumably always make decisions that are in the owners' interest. This eliminates the problem of suboptimal performance (and the pursuit of personal goals rather than corporate ones), which can plague large, widely held firms.

CONCLUSIONS

The future is unknowable. Hopefully, the above discussion has offered some idea of the kinds of environment, external and internal, in which the international firm will operate during the next decade.

Probably the most visible characteristic of multinational enterprises 10 years from now will be the much larger number of such firms. As transportation and communication become even cheaper in the future, more and more firms will view their markets as multicountry regions—or even the whole world. The names of some of the largest firms will change, and many new products will emerge, but the overriding feature will be the global nature of competition.

In this context, the *international contractor* will become the model for successful competitors. That is, firms that can adapt their ownership structures and strategies to accommodate differences in national rules, conditions, and preferences will prevail. No longer will ownership of subsidiaries be the basic building block of growth; control over business activities in different locations will also be achieved through such means as management contracts, supply agreements, and joint ventures. Flexibility in dealing with government negotiations, supplier-customer relations, internal human resource management, and business rivalries will become an even more important competitive advantage than it is now.

In government negotiations, the international contractor will face much more rigorous bargaining, in which it will have to demonstrate the social benefits of its operations to receive continuing government approbation of its activities. Governments in less developed countries as well as in industrialized nations have become aware of their strengths in bargaining, and they will assert those strengths in dealing with INCs.

In supplier-customer relations, the INC will find many more "foreign" suppliers of goods and services in every country. Hence, the need for a competitive strategy based on some sustainable advantage (such as low cost, differentiated product, or government protection) will become increasingly important.

Internal human resource management within the INC will become a greater concern as competition increases and as firms seek such competitive advantages as higher worker productivity and labor peace with management. Many Japanese firms are perceived as having an advantage in human resource management today; in the future, firms in other countries (Korea and Singapore, for example, but also possibly the United States and Germany) will attain a similar advantage, and that advantage will become more indicative of good management than of cultural background.

Business rivalries will not become more severe in all industries in the future, but it is most likely that they will become more international. That is, firms from many countries will compete in multiple national markets, resulting in greater multinationality of competition. As always, the more competitive firms will tend to drive out the less competitive, and barriers to market entry and exit will preclude huge numbers of firms from competing in many key sectors—but the competitors that do participate in each market will come from more countries.

Managers will continue to need the technical tools that they acquire in business schools and the practical experience that they acquire in the business world. Seeing the environment clearly and defining and carrying out competitive strategies effectively will continue to be the keys to successful management in international business.

QUESTIONS

1. What is the international contractor? How does it compare with the multinational enterprise?
2. What important bargaining strengths of INCs will enable them to negotiate successfully with governments in the future?

3. What important bargaining strengths of national governments will enable them to negotiate successfully with INCs in the future?

4. How will changes in technology affect the business environment of the 1990s? Specifically, how will new telecommunications technology affect competition in the computer industry in the next decade?

5. How will the INC be able to justify its legitimacy in the eyes of host governments? That is, what social benefit generated by INC activities makes it valuable to host governments?

6. What role will government-owned firms play in the competition of the 1990s? In what industries will such firms be prevalent?

7. List and explain major conflict areas between INCs and national governments that will cause tensions and perhaps crises between the two. How can managers deal with these conflict areas?

8. What characteristics of small INCs will enable them to compete internationally in particular products or market segments during the 1990s?

9. What kinds of international business activity can be expected to occur in less developed countries during the 1990s?

10. What industry or business would you choose to be in when the year 2000 arrives? What are the international business aspects of that industry or business? How will you try to compete with rival firms?

REFERENCES

Behrman, Jack N., and Robert Grosse. *International Business and Governments.* Columbia, S.C.: University of South Carolina Press, 1990.

Boddewyn, Jean J. "Political Aspects of MNE Theory." *Journal of International Business Studies,* Fall 1988.

Gladwin, Thomas, and Ingo Walter. *Multinationals under Fire.* New York: John Wiley & Sons, 1980.

Ohmae, Kenichi. "The Global Logic of Strategic Alliances." *Harvard Business Review,* March–April 1989.

————. *Triad Power.* New York: Free Press, 1985.

OECD. "Declaration of OECD Member Governments on International Investment and Multinational Enterprises." Paris: OECD, 1976.

Perlmutter, Howard, and David Heenan. "Thinking Ahead." *Harvard Business Review,* March–April 1986.

Porter, Michael. *The Competitive Advantage of Nations.* New York: Free Press, 1990.

Root, Franklin. "Some Trends in the World Economy and Their Implications for International Business." *Journal of International Business Studies,* Winter 1984.

NOTES

[1] See Porter (1990) chapter 4 for a compelling argument about the dynamic competitiveness produced for core and supplier firms that benefit from these spillovers.

[2]This conflicts with the view presented by Norman Jonas in "The Hollow Corporation," *Business Week* (March 3, 1986), which argued that major U.S. firms are becoming "hollow corporations," doing their manufacturing abroad or contracting it out to foreign suppliers.

[3]Brazil's restriction on computer imports has been cited extensively (e.g., in Business International Corporation's *Business Latin America.*) The rules have evolved over time, so for current limits it is best to obtain current documentation directly from the Brazilian government or through a Brazilian embassy.

[4]See Paul Shrivastava, *Bhopal: Anatomy of a Crisis* (Cambridge, Mass.: Ballinger, 1987).

[5]See monthly data in "General Business Indicators," in the *Survey of Current Business.*

[6]P. J. D. Drenth, H. Thierry, P. J. Willems, and C. J. de Wolff, *Handbook of Work and Organizational Psychology* (New York: John Wiley & Sons, 1984).

[7]This bargaining process is analyzed in detail in Behrman and Grosse (1990).

Glossary

A

Absolute Advantage or Absolute Cost Advantage   The production cost advantage that one country may have over another when one (or both) of two products is cheaper to produce in the first country.

Accounting System   A numerically based method for keeping track of assets, how assets are funded, sales, expenses, and so on.

Accounts Receivable Management   The strategy used by some MNEs to adjust their A/R to reduce exchange risk and to optimally time funds transfers.

Airway Bill   A document analogous to the bill of lading but used for air transport.

Alienation   The problem in industrial societies that some workers become dissatisfied with their jobs due to boredom, lack of stimulation, and impersonality.

Andean Pact   A regional integration group formed in 1967 that today includes Bolivia, Colombia, Ecuador, Peru, and Venezuela.

Antitrust   The concern of governments that a firm or firms may gain excessive market power and act to monopolize markets and potentially harm consumer interests. Antitrust policy, often called competition policy, is used by governments to deal with this issue.

Appropriability   The nature of a technology that enables the innovator to protect it from use by competitors and to obtain economic rents from it.

Appropriate Technology   Technology that is suitable for the distribution of factors of production in the country where it is used. In countries where labor is relatively abundant, for example, appropriate technology would be relatively labor-intensive.

Association of Southeast Asian Nations (ASEAN)   A regional integration group formed in 1967 that includes Indonesia, Malaysia, the Philippines, Singapore, and Thailand.

Automatic Adjustment Mechanism   The economic response that occurs when a BOP imbalance arises. When a trade deficit exists under flexible exchange rates, a currency devaluation usually occurs to stimulate exports and reduce imports. Under fixed exchange rates, domestic inflation is expected to be lower than foreign inflation, leading to relatively lower domestic prices and again increased exports and reduced imports.

B

Back-to-Back Letter of Credit   A form of pretrade financing in which the exporter uses the importer's letter of credit as a basis for seeking credit from a bank, which in turn backs its letter of credit to the exporter with the demonstrated likelihood of ability to repay that the importer's L/C represents.

Balance of Payments (BOP)   The financial record of all transactions between residents of one country and the rest of the world for some given time period.

Balance of Payments Accounting   A double-entry bookkeeping system that is used to record transactions that appear in the balance of payments.

Balance of Payments Adjustment   The automatic response of an economy to an imbalance in a country's international transactions. If a trade deficit occurs, it usually leads to a currency devaluation and/or reduction of domestic prices relative to prices in other countries.

Balance Sheet Hedging   The MNE strategy of using financial hedges (such as forward contracts) to avoid translation risk that would potentially adversely affect the firm's balance sheet.

Bank Draft   The means of payment for an export/import transaction. The draft may be a *sight draft,* i.e., payable when received, or a *time draft,* payable at the time specified on the document itself.

Banker's Acceptance   A form of posttrade credit for the exporter, in which the exporter sells the account receivable to a bank at a discount in exchange for immediate payment.

Bargaining Unit   All employees in a group that are covered by the same labor contract.

Basic Balance   A balance of payments that measures all of the current account items plus the country's net exports of long-term capital during some time period.

Bill of Lading   A shipping document that is used as evidence of a contract for shipping merchandise and as a claim of ownership of the goods.

Board of Supervision   A group of employee-elected and shareholder-elected representatives that has major control over management decisions and that appoints the top managers. Usually found in Germany, Benelux, and Northern Europe.

Branch   An office or extension of the parent company in a foreign country that is not incorporated in the foreign country.

Brand or Trade Name   A name, often protected by a trademark, used by a firm for its product(s). The name may, over time, come to connote high quality, good service, or some other favorable attribute that attracts purchasers away from similar products made by other firms.

Broadline Global Competition   The competitive strategy that implies production of a wide range of products in one or more industries with sales in many countries.

Brokers' Market   The market for exchange of financial instruments between any two parties using an intermediary (broker) similar to an auctioneer to unite buyers and sellers. The foreign exchange brokers' market in the United States makes up a large part of the trades that involve two banks as buyer and seller.

Business Unionism   A union philosophy stressing maximizing economic returns to union members rather than social or societal reforms to advantage working classes.

Buy-Back Agreement   A form of countertrade in which the initial export sale is for a capital good that is used to produce products which are subsequently used as payment by the importer.

C

Call Option   An option contract that entitles the purchaser to *buy* a fixed amount of foreign exchange at a fixed price in the future.

Capital Controls   Limits on access to foreign exchange. These controls limit not only capital outflows but also imports, which cannot be paid for if capital controls disallow the payments.

Capital Flight   The export of financial resources by residents of a country, typically in response to a situation of economic or political crisis.

Caribbean Basin Initiative (CBI)   A U.S. government policy begun in 1983 that attempts to stimulate private-sector business in the Caribbean and Central America through tariff reductions and other incentives.

Caribbean Common Market (Caricom)   A regional integration group formed in 1973 that includes former British colonies in the Eastern Caribbean.

Cartel   A group of producers of a product that attempts to monopolize the product and fix prices and quantities to maximize their gains. OPEC is the most successful cartel of countries in history.

Certificate of Origin   A shipping document that states the country of origin of the merchandise.

Code of Conduct on Transnational Corporations   An intergovernmental agreement sponsored by the United Nations that is intended to spell out rules of good corporate behavior for MNEs in host and home countries. The Code still was not approved within the United Nations by the end of 1987.

Combined Transport Document   A document analogous to the bill of lading but used for shipping when there is more than one form of transport involved.

Commercial Invoice   The exporter's bill of sale that describes precisely the merchandise and terms of sale.

Common Market   A customs union which additionally allows freedom of movement of capital and labor (i.e., factors of production) between member countries.

Competitive Advantage   Any characteristic possessed by a firm that enables it to achieve lower costs, higher revenues, or lower risk than its competitors.

Competitors   Rival firms. Companies based domestically or overseas that compete against the firm in question in a given market.

Concession   A legal agreement between a host country and a firm in which the country gives the firm the right to explore for, extract, and sell oil in exchange for specified taxes, fees, and other charges.

Consignment   A legal form of sale in which the recipient of a producer's goods takes possession of the goods but does not own them. Payment is made for sale to customers when the goods are sold rather than upon shipment from the producer to the consignee.

Consolidated Report   A financial report such as an income statement or balance sheet that presents an international firm's total (global) including overseas subsidiaries, licenses, and other activities.

Consolidated Statement   An accounting statement showing the combined operations of parent and subsidiaries.

Consolidation   The process of preparing a consolidated statement whereby line-by-line summations of parent and subsidiary accounts are ultimately presented.

Contingent Liability   A contractual commitment that requires the issuer to deliver whatever instrument is specified (for example, foreign exchange) if the buyer chooses to exercise it.

Continuous R&D   A strategy under which the firm develops new technology incrementally, based on extensions of its existing technology. This can be contrasted with R&D in new areas where the firm is not already active.

Control   Monitoring operations, taking decisions to conform to plans and, when necessary, taking decisions to change plans or behaviors to eliminate variations from plans in any organization.

Controlled Foreign Corporation   A foreign corporation 50 percent or more owned by U.S. shareholders, that is, U.S. citizens or corporations holding at least 10 percent of the common stock each.

Conversion Loss   Receipt of lower revenues than expected because the exchange rate has changed and the foreign-currency receivable was originally worth more of the home-country currency than was ultimately received. Conversion losses may also arise from an increase in foreign currency payables and are realized losses.

Copyright   A legal contract under which a government agrees to protect the originator of a literary, musical, dramatic, or other work from unauthorized use by outsiders.

Cost Method   A method used in preparing a parent company's non-consolidated accounting reports that treats income at the affiliate's level as being received by the parent only when the affiliate's dividends are actually received by the parent.

Cost Minimization   An operating strategy under which the firm or SBU attempts to compete based on low prices and low costs.

Council for Mutual Economic Assistance (CMEA or Comecon)   The regional integration group led by the Soviet Union and comprised primarily of Eastern European countries, though also including Vietnam, Cuba, and Mongolia. This group is also called the Soviet Bloc.

Counterpurchase   A form of countertrade in which the initial export sale is paid for by later shipments of goods by the importer.

Countertrade   A means of posttrade financing that involves payment in goods rather than money for an export sale. Barter of one product for another is the simplest form of countertrade.

Currency Diversification   The strategy of reducing the impact of unexpected currency fluctuations by undertaking activities in a variety (portfolio) of different currencies.

Currency Inconvertibility   The situation that arises when a firm is unable to gain access to foreign exchange in the normal market(s) of a country. This is generally the case in communist countries and often occurs in LDCs when economic crises arise.

Current Account Balance   A balance of payments that measures a country's exports of goods and services, minus its imports of goods and services, plus its net receipts of unilateral transfers during some time period.

Customs Union   A regional economic integration group that uses both unrestricted trade between member countries *and* a common policy toward trade with outside countries.

D

De Facto Protectionism   Non-tariff forms of protection used by countries to restrict imports. The United States uses "voluntary" quotas on Japanese autos and has tried to "jawbone" other countries to reduce their exports to the United States and to increase their imports of U.S. goods.

Debt/Equity Ratio   The capital structure of a firm. The average debt/equity ratio differs from country to country.

Delivered Cost   The cost of producing and shipping a product to the target market. This includes total production cost, cost of insurance and freight, tariff cost, and any other cost involved in getting the product to the market.

Demand Patterns   Measures of the characteristics of goods and services purchasec by consumers in different countries. Demand patterns tend to be similar in countries at the same stage of economic development.

Differentiation Advantage   A competitive advantage obtained by a firm that is able to successfully convey the quality or cost differences of its products or services compared to those of rival firms.

Diffusion   The spread of new technology throughout the market.

Disinvestment   Divestiture. Disinvestment occurs when a firm sells or otherwise disposes of a foreign direct investment.

Diversification   Entry into a different business activity outside of the firm's traditional business. This may be a different product, stage of the production process, or country.

Documentary Collection   A means of paying for an export/import transaction that uses only a draft and other informational documents, but *not* a letter of credit.

Documentary Draft   A sight or time draft that is accompanied by instructions and other documents but no L/C.

Double Taxation   Taxation of the earnings of a multinational firm by two countries. This occurs when a foreign subsidiary pays tax in the host country, and then the same profits are taxed (usually with a credit or deduction) by the home country of the parent firm.

Dual Economy   The economy in a less developed country in which some of the firms and households (for example, in cities) participate in the market sector with links to other countries. The other part of the economy is isolated from the international economy (on the periphery) and often operates at a subsistence level (for example, in rural areas).

Dumping   Selling at an unfairly low price in an import market. The U.S. Government has defined dumping as selling below the cost of production or selling below the price in the firm's domestic market.

E

Eclectic View   Dunning's theory of international business that explains MNE activities based on their ownership advantages, their use of internalization, and on locational factors.

Economic Integration   Expansion of commercial and financial ties among nations. It is expected that greater economic integration of the world will lead to more efficient production and greater output, thus potentially making all countries better off.

Economic Risk   The foreign exchange risk that future cash flows of the firm will be unexpectedly affected by future changes in exchange rates.

Embargo   A quota with maximum imports of zero units. That is, a total disallowance of imports of the product being embargoed (or on all imports from the country being embargoed).

Enterprise Union   A union comprised of employees at a single company. Typical to Japan.

Entry Strategy   A method used by an MNE for entering a foreign market. These include exports, direct investment, licensing, franchising, turn-key ventures, and other contractual forms.

Equity Method   A method used in preparing a parent company's nonconsolidated accounting reports that treats income at the foreign entity's level as being received by the parent (for reporting purposes) when it is earned by the foreign entity.

Eurobond   A bond denominated in any currency other than that of the country where it is issued.

Eurobond Market   The market for bonds denominated in any currency other than the local one in any country. Most eurobonds are dollar-denominated bonds issued outside of the United States.

Eurocurrency Market (or Eurodollar Market)   The market for short-term foreign-currency-denominated instruments such as bank deposits in any country. The bulk of the eurocurrency market involves dollar-denominated bank deposits outside of the United States.

Eurodollar   A U.S. dollar-denominated bank deposit located outside of the United States. Most eurodollars are time deposits or certificates of deposit.

Euromarkets   Markets for short- or long-term financial instruments in any country in which the instruments are denominated in currencies other than the local one.

European Community (EC, or Common Market)   The association of Western European countries formed in 1957 that has eliminated most tariffs among members, established a common external tariff, harmonized some fiscal and monetary policies, and broadly attempts to increase economic integration among the member countries.

European Currency Unit (ECU)   A composite currency similar to the SDR, whose value is based on a weighted average of the currencies of the European Community. Although it is only an accounting convention (i.e., an ECU bill does not exist), the

ECU is being used increasingly to denominate international bond issues and other large international financial transactions.

European Monetary System (EMS) A mini-IMF organized by the members of the European Community. The EMS observes exchange rate fluctuations between member-country currencies and makes loans to member governments, primarily to serve the goal of balance of payments stability.

Exchange Controls Government-imposed limits on use of foreign exchange, generally used to restrict outflows of funds from a country. They include limited access to foreign currency at the Central Bank, and multiple exchange rates for different users, among other methods.

Exchange Rate The price of one currency in terms of another.

Exchange Risk The possibility that a firm will not be able to adjust its prices and costs to exactly offset exchange rate changes. Not only must exchange rates be able to vary, but the variations must not be fully anticipated.

Exchange Risk Adaptation The strategy of adjusting the firm's activities to reduce the potential impact of unexpected exchange rate changes. This may be done through financial hedging or other adjustments in the foreign currency activities of the firm.

Exchange Risk Avoidance The strategy of avoiding dealings in currencies that are viewed as having high exchange risk, and/or charging higher prices when exchange risk appears to be higher.

Exchange Risk Transfer The strategy of eliminating or reducing exchange risk by contracting with insurance providers to cover possible exchange rate-induced losses.

Exercise Price The price at which an option may be used to buy/sell foreign exchange.

Eximbank The Export-Import Bank of the United States, the main U.S. Government agency responsible for assisting U.S. exporters via loans and loan guarantees.

Export/Import Transaction The basic activity of international trade.

Export Promotion A strategy for economic development that focuses on increasing a country's exports to generate foreign exchange and stimulate domestic production. This is an outward-looking development model.

Expropriation The forced takeover of a company's assets by the host government without compensation (or with inadequate compensation).

Externalization The opposite of internalization. A market or production process is externalized when the firm stops carrying out the activity itself and contracts with an outside firm or agent to do it.

Extractive FDI Direct investment used by the MNE to obtain raw materials such as oil, copper, or other metals, agricultural products, etc.

F

Factoring Selling an account receivable at a discount to an intermediary company called a factor. The exporter receives immediate (discounted) payment, and the factor receives eventual payment from the importer.

Fair Value The portion of a firm's activities that can be determined to be carried out in a given jurisdiction. The fair value is crucial to efforts by governments to tax MNE activities.

Financial Accounting Disclosure The presentation of the consolidated statements, showing both income and balance sheet accounts.

Financial Transfers Methods used by MNEs to move funds internationally, such as profit remittances, fee payments, payments for intracompany shipments, and loans.

Flexible Multi-Item Factory A factory that is usually labor intensive and thus capable of producing several different products without large capital costs.

Follow-the-Leader Strategy   The strategy of oligopolistic reaction. It implies that the follower waits to see how an industry leader operates (e.g., in introducing new technology), and then pursues a copycat strategy in areas that appear profitable.

Foreign-Base Company   A *controlled foreign corporation* that derives a substantial portion of its income from investments, sales, services, or shipping.

Foreign Corrupt Practices Act   A U.S. law that prohibits certain kinds of bribes and questionable payments, requires internal accounting control procedures regarding such payments, and the imprisonment of company officials guilty of evading these requirements.

Foreign Currency Option   An option contract that gives the holder the right but not the obligation to exercise it to purchase a given amount of foreign currency at a fixed price during a fixed time period. Contract specifications are similar to those of futures contracts, except that the option requires a premium payment to purchase (and it does not have to be exercised).

Foreign Direct Investment   The extension of controlling ownership by a firm from one country over a firm in another country through new investment or acquisition.

Foreign Exchange   A financial instrument that carries out payment from one currency to another. Common instruments of foreign exchange include bank drafts, wire transfers, forward and futures contracts, and cash.

Foreign Exchange Market   The market(s) in which financial instruments denominated in one currency are traded for instruments denominated in other currencies. Typically, a country's main foreign exchange market is carried out through the commercial banking system.

Foreign Investment Controls   Government-imposed limits on the ability of firms to undertake foreign direct investment. These typically restrict FDI *inflows*, though they have been used to try to limit the outflow of FDI as well.

Foreign Sales Corporation   A legal entity through which a firm can channel exports and derive special income tax benefits.

Foreign Sales Corporation (FSC) Act   A U.S. Government law that replaces the Domestic International Sales Corporation (DISC) legislation. The FSC is a foreign company that exports for a U.S. firm, which may show its export profits in the FSC and avoid U.S. taxation on a percentage of the earnings until they are remitted to the parent U.S. firm.

Foreign Sourcing   Producing or purchasing products or production inputs from a foreign location, typically to lower costs. Many electronics firms source their memory chips in their own plants or through contracts with local firms in Taiwan or Singapore to lower the costs.

Foreignness   The characteristics of a firm or person that cause it to be viewed as different from domestic firms or people. Foreignness is often associated with foreign ownership, foreign styles, and different languages.

Forfaiting   A means of posttrade financing analogous to factoring. Forfaiting is used primarily for large capital goods exports to Eastern European countries.

Forward Foreign Exchange Market (Forward Market)   The contractual form used by commercial banks to offer their clients the opportunity to fix an exchange rate for future delivery of one currency for another.

Franc Area   The group of former French colonies that continue to use the French franc as an acceptable currency and/or tie their currency values to the franc.

Free-Trade Area   A regional economic integration group that implements policy for unrestricted trade between member countries, but leaves each country free to set its own policy with outside countries.

Functional Currency   The "home country" currency of the parent or the subsidiary which is used in preparing and presenting accounting reports at the operations level.

Futures Foreign Exchange Contract (Futures Contract)   A legal contract similar to a forward contract, except that it is traded on a securities exchange and has fixed specifications such as maturity date, contract size, and trading limitations during the contract's life.

G–H

Gain-Sharing Agreement   An agreement between management and labor (typically in the United Kingdom) to share economic gains, usually because of new equipment being installed.

GATT   The General Agreement on Tariffs and Trade, the world's main intergovernmental organization that seeks to reduce barriers to international trade. GATT currently has 90 member governments.

Global Focus   A generic competitive strategy in which the international firm sells in one market segment in multiple countries.

Global International   An organization of trade unions from countries around the world.

Government Relations   That part of a firm's activity that involves dealing with home and host governments.

Grossed-Up Dividend   The dividend received by the parent, plus the withholding tax on the dividend plus the amount of income taxes paid by the subsidiary on the income that generated the dividend.

Home Country   The country in which the MNE is headquartered, and usually where most of the shareholders live.

Horizontal Integration   Entry by a firm into a similar business activity in a new location. Restaurant chains, for example, are horizontally integrated providers of food service.

Host Country   Any other country, except the home country, where the MNE does business.

I–K

Import Substitution   A strategy for economic development that focuses on creating domestic industries to replace imported products and services. This is an inward-looking development model.

Industrial Espionage   The effort by an outsider to illegally obtain protected technology from its originator.

Industrial International   An affiliate of a *global international* representing workers' interests within a specific industry.

Industrial Relations   Employer-employee relationships where employees are treated as groups rather than individuals.

Industrial Relations Staff   The company's management group concerned with labor-management affairs.

Industrial Relations System   An overall perspective on how the interests of workers, managements, and societies come together in determining employment terms and conditions.

Industrialized Countries (ICs)   Nations whose economies are dominated by industrial production rather than agriculture or raw materials, whose per capita incomes are high relative to the rest of the world, and who use market economies.

Information Disclosure   Provision of data about company activities to governments in countries where the firm operates.

Information Transfer   The transmission of information from one country to another within an MNE. This issue is important in government relations, since some types of information being transferred are considered sensitive by the governments.

Infrastructure Basic economic underpinning of a business system such as roads, accessible electric power, telephone service, and other utilities, that are important to a firm that wants to operate locally.

Innovation A technology change that is successfully introduced into the marketplace, that is, a new product.

Insurance Certificate A shipping document that demonstrates insurance coverage for the merchandise, naming the exporter and the insuror.

Interbank Market The market for exchange of financial instruments between commercial banks. Most foreign exchange in the United States is traded in the interbank market.

Interest Parity The condition that investment in a domestic financial instrument or hedged investment in a foreign-currency instrument of similar risk, maturity, and other characteristics yields the same return.

Internalization Extension of ownership by a firm to cover new markets, new sources of materials, and new stages of the production process. Internalization is the business strategy counterpart to the economics terms *vertical integration* and *horizontal integration.*

International Contractor A firm that does international business; that is, a firm involved in exports, direct investment, international licensing, or any other form of business that crosses national boundaries.

International Distribution The shipment of products or services between countries. This is a source of potential competitive advantage for multinational as opposed to domestic firms.

International Diversification An ability that exists for MNEs to reduce the firm's risk by operating facilities in more than one country, thus lowering the risk of problems in any one country.

International Fisher Effect The condition that an interest rate differential on similar instruments between two countries is eliminated by an offsetting exchange rate change between their currencies.

International Labor Office A United Nations affiliate with representation from employers, unions, and governments concerned about employment terms and conditions.

International Monetary Fund (IMF) The organization of 146 national governments that seeks to maintain balance of payments stability in the international financial system. The IMF observes exchange rate regimes and fluctuations (but does not set rates), lends funds to member governments to help in balance of payments crises, and performs other functions toward achieving international financial stability.

International Transaction A purchase or sale that involves a seller and a buyer in different countries.

International Union A union with regionals or locals in more than one country.

Intertemporal (or Interest) Arbitrage Exchange arbitrage that involves buying foreign exchange in the spot market, investing in a foreign currency asset, and converting back to the initial currency through a forward contract. This is done when interest parity does not hold.

Invention The creation of new knowledge that may have application to business or industry.

Inventory Management The strategy used by some MNEs to reduce inventories by pooling different affiliates' stocks and to reduce political and/or exchange risk by holding inventories in less risky countries.

Keiretsu Networks of large numbers of suppliers, intermediaries, and other related firms that have formed industrial power centers in Japan after World War II.

L

Labor Agreement   Same as the *labor contract*.

Labor Contract   The terms and conditions of employment as negotiated between management and a union.

Leontief Paradox   The surprising finding by Wassily Leontief that the United States in 1947 had a higher capital/labor ratio in production of import-competing products than in exports. That is, U.S. exports are relatively more labor-intensive, and imports more capital-intensive, despite the relatively greater availability of capital in the U.S. than in other countries.

Less Developed Country (LDC)   A country in the third world. The LDCs are countries primarily in Africa, Asia, and Latin America with relatively low per capita incomes and relatively high dependence on primary materials industries.

Letter of Credit (L/C)   A contract between an importer and its bank that transfers liability for paying the exporter from the importer to the importer's bank.

LIBOR   The London interbank offered rate. This interest rate is a daily average of those quoted by major banks in London to accept deposits of at least $US 1 million from other banks or high-quality clients.

Lockout   Management not allowing a group of employees to work.

Long-Term National Financial Markets   Capital markets in different countries, that is, markets for long-term financial instruments such as stocks and bonds in different countries.

Low Cost Unit Factory   The production location with lowest costs, either because of low wages or large capital investment (and production scale economies).

M

Macrorisk   The political risk that exists for all firms (or all foreign firms) in a particular country.

Major Multinationals   The world's largest oil companies. They include: Royal Dutch Shell, EXXON, Mobil, British Petroleum, Texaco, Chevron (Socal), and Amoco.

Make-Versus-Buy Decision   The choice for a firm either to produce a product or input for itself or buy it from an outside supplier. By producing them within the firm, internalization of those inputs' production takes place.

Management Information System   The accumulation and presentation of data and information pertinent to the effective management of the multinational enterprise.

Management Technology   The knowledge used to operate a business, that is, the managerial skills that enable a firm to compete by using its resources efficiently.

Market Allocation   The strategy used by MNEs to restrict activities of each affiliate to specified markets, to avoid competition among these units.

Market Sector   That part of a dual economy that is marked-based and is connected to international business with the industrial countries.

Market Segmentation   An operating strategy under which the firm or SBU attempts to compete based on defining and pursuing a niche or segment of the total market, such as the highest quality segment, or the smallest size segment, and so on.

Market-Serving FDI   Direct investment used by the MNE to produce and sell its products or services in the host country.

Maturing Product   A product which is produced by several firms, whose technology is no longer monopolized by the innovating firm, and which faces increasing price elasticity of demand.

Microrisk   The political risk that exists for a particular firm or industry in a given country.

MITI   The Japanese government agency; the Ministry of Trade and Industry.

Monopoly Power   The economic strength that MNEs possess relative to other firms and relative to governments because of their size, their availability of information, and their multinationality.

Most-Favored-Nation   A principle in international trade regulation that is used by members of GATT. If a trade barrier is reduced between any two members of GATT, that same benefit is automatically extended to all other GATT members under the most-favored-nation principle.

Multilateral Netting   The strategy used by some MNEs to reduce international funds flows between affiliates by canceling redundant cash flows and transferring only the net amounts necessary.

Multinational Marketing   Selling the product in several different country markets.

Multinational Sourcing   A capability that exists for MNEs to find or set up production sources in more than one nation, thus enabling the firm to lower its costs relative to firms that produce or buy in only one country.

Multinationality   The essence of the MNE. By operating simultaneously in several countries, the MNE is able to transfer information about prices and demand conditions, move funds and products to safer or otherwise preferable locations, and generally escape the limitations imposed by the environment in a single country.

N

National Focus   The competitive strategy that implies adaptation of products to each national market in which the firm operates.

Nationalization   The forced takeover of a company's assets by the host government *with* compensation. Sometimes this is achieved by requiring sale of controlling ownership to local investors, still leaving the MNE with some partial ownership.

New International Economic Order   An idea created in the United Nations in the early 1970s that intended to develop mechanisms for redistribution of income between rich and poor countries. The effort was essentially dropped after the oil crisis of 1973–74, though the concept remains in discussion.

National Money Markets   The short-term financial markets in individual countries. These include markets for instruments such as treasury bills and short-term bank deposits as well as commercial paper, banker's acceptances, and other instruments that mature in less than one year.

Newly Industrializing Country (NIC)   Among the LDCs, one of the rapidly-growing countries that have proceeded farthest along the road to industrialization. NICs include South Korea, Hong Kong, Taiwan, Singapore, and Brazil.

Nontariff Barriers (NTBs)   Government-imposed restrictions on imports other than tariffs which also limit imports. They include licensing requirements, prior deposits, bureaucratic delays, and many more restrictions.

O

Obsolescing Bargain   The situation that exists *after* an MNE commits its capital and human resources to an investment project in a host country. The MNE's bargaining position relative to the host government diminishes (obsolesces), since it has important resources at risk in the host country. Over time, the government typically gains even greater ability to force the firm to follow its desired goals as the firm becomes more integrated into the local economy.

Official Settlements Balance   The "bottom line" balance of payments when all private sector transactions have been accounted for and all that remain are official exchanges between central banks (and the IMF). This balance measures the country's new inflows of official holdings of foreign exchange, SDRs, gold, and the country's borrowing position at the IMF.

Offshore Assembly The overseas production of goods whose inputs are fabricated in one country, typically done to reduce labor costs. That is, basic materials are made in one country, they are shipped abroad for assembly or processing, and then the final products are shipped to the target market for sale.

Offshore Production Either offshore sourcing or offshore assembly.

Operating Strategy The day-to-day method of doing business that an MNE must tailor to conditions in each host country. Operating strategy is dependent on the degree and kind of government regulation, competitive conditions, and other factors.

Opportunity Cost The potential gain foregone in any business activity that is given up by hedging against the risk of loss on that activity. The opportunity cost of a forward contract is the lost foreign exchange earnings that would have occurred if the contract were not used and the exchange rate had changed favorably to the firm. For a country the opportunity cost of using resources in one activity is the cost of foregoing the next best alternative use of those resources.

Orderly Marketing Agreement An intergovernmental agreement to limit imports of a product(s). These agreements are usually made when imports are visibly hurting the domestic industry and the importing country cannot demonstrate that the importing firms are dumping or otherwise operating illegally.

Organization of Petroleum Exporting Countries (OPEC) The multinational cartel of oil producing countries that successfully raised the price of oil by over 400 percent in 1973–74 and again by over 200 percent in 1979.

Organization for Economic Cooperation and Development An intergovernmental organization that has as members the industrialized countries (the first world). The OEC is concerned with economic and social issues.

Overall Objectives The broad goals of a firm at the highest level. This could also be called the mission of the firm.

P–R

Patent A legal contract under which a government agrees to protect a possessor of proprietary technology from use of the technology by unauthorized outside users.

Pattern Bargaining An industry-wide bargaining strategy characterized by a contract settlement with one company that establishes a basis for other firms in the industry to follow.

Periphery That segment of a country's population that is least advantaged economically. Also, the periphery countries of the world are the LDCs.

Personnel Evaluation Measurement of performance of company employees done for the purpose of salary determination, job assignment, and other uses.

Political Union A type of economic integration that calls for full political integration between countries, that is, creation of a single political jurisdiction (country).

Portfolio Investment The purchase of financial instruments such as stocks, bonds, bank deposits, and so forth, by an investor; in our context the investor would be from one country and the investment in another country.

Posttrade Financing Credit extended to the exporter or importer after shipment but before this firm receives its payment for the goods.

Pretrade Financing Credit extended to an exporter to enable that firm to produce the goods that will be exported. This is a form of working capital financing.

Product Differentiation An operating strategy under which the firm or SBU attempts to compete based on non-price factors such as quality, service, and other product characteristics.

Product Technology The knowledge used to produce any product, that is, the information that specifies the product's characteristics and uses.

Production Allocation Assigning production that is needed globally to various subsidiaries.

Production Smoothing Allocating production to various subsidiaries with the intention of maintaining relatively steady output levels at all locations.

Proprietary Technology Knowledge about how to make a product (or service), how to operate a production process, or how to run a business, that one firm possesses and that other firms do not. The innovating firm is able to protect this technology for itself, either through legal means (e.g., patent or trademark) or by secrecy.

Protected Niche The competitive strategy that implies obtaining government protection for the firm's activities in the countries where it operates.

Public Good A product that can be used repeatedly without being used up. Technology is a public good, because using it does not deplete it.

Purchasing Power Parity The condition that an inflation differential between any two countries is eliminated by an offsetting change in the exchange rate between their currencies.

Put Option An option contract that entitles the purchaser to *sell* a fixed amount of foreign exchange at a fixed price in the future.

Quota A quantity restriction on imports. The number of Japenese cars imported into the United States has been limited by a "voluntary" quota during much of the 1980s.

Regional Economic Integration Expansion of commercial and financial ties among countries in a regional group, leaving the rest of the world outside of the group. Five forms of regional economic integration have been identified during the post-World War II period, ranging from free trade areas to full economic and political unions.

Regional International An organization of trade unions from a specific region of the world, for example, Western Europe.

Reporting Currency The parent company's currency used in preparing and presenting accounting reports at the parent level.

S

Scale Economies in Advertising The condition where the incremental costs of each unit of advertising expenditure are declining, for example, where fixed costs of advertising copy preparation can be allocated to an increasingly large total market as additional ads are placed in different markets.

Scale Economies in Distribution Cost reductions achieved by shipping large quantities of products, thus lowering the unit shipping costs relative to competitors that ship lower quantities.

Scale Economies in Financing Cost reductions gained by borrowing large quantities of funds at lower interest and other cost than charged to borrowers of smaller quantities.

Scale Economies in Production Cost reductions achieved by a large size production facility. When large-scale output is achieved, low unit costs result (relative to competitors operating smaller-scale facilities).

Scale Economies in Purchasing Cost reductions gained by buying large quantities of inputs at lower unit costs than those paid by buyers of smaller quantities.

Seasonal Factory A factory that can handle large variations in employment and capacity usage over the year, for example, at Christmas time.

Sequential Entry Strategy   An MNE strategy that implies market entry through a relatively inexpensive step such as exports or licensing, and a buildup of commitment into joint venture ownership and/or full subsidiary ownership.

Seven Sisters (or the Major Multinationals)   The world's largest oil companies. In the late 1980s they included: Royal Dutch Shell, EXXON, Mobil, British Petroleum, Texaco, Chevron (Socal), and Amoco.

Shunto   The "spring wage offensive" in Japan characterized by coordinated collective bargaining by *enterprise unions* seeking wage increases that mainly pertain to cost-of-living and industry productivity concerns.

Sight Draft   A means of payment for an export contract in which the draft (essentially a check) is payable upon delivery to the exporter. The draft is often used in conjunction with a letter of credit.

Skunk Works   A think-tank environment used by some MNEs to encourage researchers to pursue new projects in small teams without excessive bureaucracy from the mainstream business of the firm.

Social Benefit/Cost Ratio   The sum of all social benefits generated by a potential project divided by the sum of all social costs generated by the project. If the ratio is greater than one, the project should be undertaken, from the host country's perspective.

Sogo Shosha   The Japanese trading companies, such as Mitsubishi Shoji and Mitsui Bussan.

Sourcing FDI   Direct investment used by the MNE to produce its products or inputs overseas for eventual sale back in the home country (or in other countries).

Sovereignty   Control over the national economy.

Special Drawing Right (SDR)   The official currency of the IMF. The SDR is a composite currency based on the weighted values of the dollar, yen, mark, French franc, and the British pound. New SDRs are issued infrequently by the IMF, and this currency is used as the unit of account for transactions with the IMF.

Specialized International   A component of an intergovernmental agency which represents workers' interests and views within that agency.

Spillover Benefits   Positive externalities. To a country, spillover benefits accrue when a business activity is undertaken and it has positive impact beyond the success of the venture itself (such as additional employment, improved balance of payments, etc.). To a company, spillover benefits accrue when an activity is undertaken that has a positive impact on the rest of the firm's business in addition to the activity's own success.

Standardized Product   A product that is produced by many firms, whose technology is well known, and which faces very price-sensitive demand. Commodities are generally standardized products.

Sterling Area   The group of former members of the British Commonwealth that continue to use the British pound as an acceptable currency and/or tie their currency values to the pound.

Stewards' Council   An elected group of worker representatives, not a union, to negotiate with management on labor agreements and the solving of workers' problems. The Stewards' Council is more commonly found in the United Kingdom.

Strategic Alliance   A cooperative agreement between two or more firms. Such alliances range from joint ventures with mutual part-ownership of a venture to cross-licensing, joint marketing, joint research, and other types of contractual arrangements.

Strike   A group of employees' refusal to work.

Subpart F Income   Income received from a *foreign-based* company.

Subsidiary   A foreign corporation whose stock is more than 50 percent owned by the parent company and is therefore controlled by the parent company.

Subsidy   As refers to international trade, a subsidy is some cost-reducing privilege offered by the government to domestic firms to stimulate their competitiveness so that they may be more successful against imports.

T

Tariff   A tax placed on imports that thereby raises the price and restricts the quantity of imports.

Technology Advantage   A competitive advantage gained from creation or obtaining of proprietary technology.

Technology Intensity   The amount of technology used relative to capital and labor in production of a product or service.

Technology Intensive   Depending more on research and development (i.e. technology) than other firms in the same or other industries. A technology intensive firm is generally one that spends more on research and development or has more scientific and technical staff than other firms in a given context.

Technology Transfer   The passage of product or process technology, or management skills, from one firm to another, or between affiliates of a multinational firm.

Three-Way (or Triangular) Arbitrage   Exchange arbitrage among three currencies which involves beginning in one currency, passing through each of the other two, and ending in the initial currency.

Time Draft   A means of payment for an import/export transaction. The time draft is payable after delivery at the time stated on the draft. It is often accompanied by a letter of credit guaranteeing the payment.

Trade Adjustment Assistance (TAA)   A U.S. government policy that offers aid to workers laid off because of competition from imported goods. This mechanism attempts to alleviate the burden on people who are hurt by the operation of comparative advantage in international trade, which leads to contraction of some domestic industries and expansion of others.

Trade Balance   Comparison of the value of merchandise exports minus the value of merchandise imports for a given country for a given time period. A surplus trade balance implies exports greater than imports; a trade deficit implies imports greater than exports.

Trade Creation   Generation of new exports between members of an economic integration group, due to lowering of trade barriers between them.

Trade Diversion   Replacement of exports from non-members of an economic integration group because of increased internal trade among the members.

Trade Financing   Credit extended to an importer by the exporter, or a commercial bank or some other intermediary, that enables the importer to pay for the merchandise, presumably until it is sold and the importer receives funds to pay.

Trademark   A legal contract under which a government agrees to protect the originator of the distinctive mark, word, design, or picture, from unauthorized use by outsiders.

Trading-with-the-Enemy Act   A U.S. government law that forbids U.S. firms from doing business with countries that are from time to time listed as enemies; for example, North Korea, Cuba, and Vietnam.

Traditional Sector   The poorer part of a dual economy that is based on traditional agriculture, hunting, or fishing, and is weakly connected to the market sector.

Transaction Efficiencies   The gains of economic welfare generated by operation of MNEs because they are (sometimes) more efficient than smaller, uninational firms.

Transaction Risk   The possibility that a foreign currency-denominated transaction will be worth less (or more) than expected in local currency when the transaction is completed in the future.

Transfer Price   The price for products, components, and so forth, traded among units within the same multinational enterprise.

Translation Loss   An accounting loss reflected in adjustments to accounting statements at the end of an accounting period to record changes in home-country currency values caused by changes in foreign currency based receivables, payables, or other assets or liabilities.

Translation Risk   The possibility that a firm's balance sheet entries will be changed in domestic currency due to changes in exchange rates that affect foreign-currency accounts.

Trigger Price Mechanism   A system used by the United States during 1978–82 to limit imports of steel products. The trigger price was the estimated cost of producing each steel product in Japan, the world's low-cost producer of most steel products. Firms attempting to import at prices below the trigger prices faced penalties for dumping in the U.S. market.

U–V

Unbundling   A strategy of governments to try to force MNEs into sharing more of their benefits with the local country; for example, through shared ownership, required technology transfer, local content requirements, and so forth.

Universal MIS   A management information system that is common to all operations, whether at the parent or subsidiary levels.

Value-Added Tax   A tax applied on the value added by each manufacturer or distributor during the production and marketing of a product.

Vertical Integration   Entry of a firm into a different stage of production in its own industry. The auto company, Ford, not only produces cars, but it is vertically integrated into steel production.

Voluntarism   A tradition among British workers that their interests in unions is a fundamental right, and that they will respect each individual's right to work or not work to secure benefits from management.

Voluntary Quota   An orderly marketing agreement under which the exporting country agrees to limit exports to some predetermined level or some percentage of the importing country's market.

W–Z

Weighted-Average Cost of Capital   The firm's cost of funds, measured as the cost of each source of funds weighted for that source's part in total funding.

Weighted-Average Exchange Rate   The exchange rate used in translating income and expense accounts at the end of an accounting period. It takes into account the relative movement of exchange rates during the period and adjusts the consolidated statement to reflect some weighted mean rate.

Works Council   An elected group of employee representatives that have legal rights to certain company information and to co-determine with management certain issues, especially those pertaining to safety. The Works Council is more commonly found in continental Europe.

Zaibatsu   The pre-World War II Japanese holding companies that controlled major industrial empires.

Index

NAME INDEX

SUBJECT INDEX